CONSTITUTIONAL CHOICES

CONSTITUTIONAL CHOICES

Laurence H. Tribe

Harvard University Press
Cambridge, Massachusetts, and London, England

Printed in the United States of America

10 9 8 7 6 5 4

This book is printed on acid-free paper, and its binding materials have
been chosen for strength and durability.

Library of Congress Cataloging in Publication Data

Tribe, Laurence H.
  Constitutional choices.

  Bibliography: p.
  Includes indexes.
  1. United States—Constitutional law—Interpretation
and construction. I. Title.
KF4550.T786 1985   342.73   84-19235
ISBN 0-674-16538-1 (alk. paper) (cloth)   347.302
ISBN 0-674-16539-X (paper)

For Kerry and Mark
May they choose well

PREFACE

Constitutional choices must be made; to all of us belongs the challenge of making them wisely. We make them at many levels and in many ways. Judges must make them whenever choosing among alternative interpretations of the Constitution. Presidents and governors make them whenever choosing among judicial nominees of differing constitutional perspectives. Legislators must make such choices in confirming or rejecting these nominees, in voting for or against measures challenged as constitutionally infirm, and in proposing or disposing of possible constitutional amendments. As lawyers or as scholars, all of us must make constitutional choices in the cases and causes we argue, in the constitutional viewpoints and principles we espouse or reject, and in the stands we take upon learning of the decisions made by others. Such choices must be made as well by government bureaucrats charged with implementing the law, by writers who describe contemporary society, by historians who construct and reconstruct our past, by voters when they decide who will exercise the power to appoint our judges, and by all of us as we challenge or defend prevailing practices in the Constitution's name—whether as victims of those practices, as perpetrators of what others call injustice, or as those who think of themselves as neutral observers.

The Constitution is in part the sum of all these choices. But it is also more than that. It *must* be more if it is to be a source either of critique or of legitimation. Thus, just as the constitutional choices we make are channeled and constrained by who we are and by what we have lived through, so too they are constrained and channeled by a constitutional text and structure and history, by constitutional language and constitutional tradition, opening some paths and foreclosing others. To ignore or defy those constraints is to pretend to a power that is not ours to wield. But to pretend that those constraints leave us no freedom, or must lead us all to the same conclusions, is to disclaim a responsibility that is inescapably our own.

I write in part out of a conviction that constitutional choices, whatever else their character, must be made and assessed as fundamental choices of principle, not as instrumental calculations of utility or as pseudo-scientific calibrations of social cost against social benefit —calculations and calibrations whose essence is to deny the decision maker's personal responsibility for choosing. The point deserves particular emphasis at a time when the Supreme Court, long our nation's principal expositor of the Constitution, is coming increasingly to resemble a judicial Office of Management and Budget, straining constitutional discourse through a managerial sieve in which the "costs" (usually tangible and visible) are supposedly "balanced" against the "benefits" (usually ephemeral and diffuse) of treating constitutional premises seriously,[1] and in which proposed constitutional rulings are examined less within a judicious framework of first principles than within a bureaucratic framework that asks only what each possible decision would add to, or subtract from, the decision maker's latest step.[2]

My reply to this grim metamorphosis of constitutional argument into a deferential adjunct of executive administration is not to propose an alternative method: the very idea of "method," with its illusory suggestion of the precise and the systematic, is mostly an outgrowth of technocratic thought and practice and is thus the antithesis of humane struggle with those commitments and visions that are the stuff of genuine constitutionalism. My reply to the trend I see in the Supreme Court's work is therefore not to propound any competing formula, but to proceed instead in a spirit that questions all formulas as devices for concealing the constitutional choices that we must make— and that we cannot responsibly pretend to "derive" by any neutral technique.

This book is about our making of such constitutional choices. It does not offer a theory of choice; rather, it is an experiment in choosing. By describing and analyzing, by advocating and criticizing, a range of constitutional choices across a spectrum of constitutional contexts, I hope to enrich our understanding of what the Constitution is and what it might be. This book seeks to achieve that goal by collecting a series of essays in constitutional law. The studies are meant to be largely self-contained, but loosely connected; the whole will, I hope, add up to more than the sum of its several parts.

Although the sixteen essays fall naturally into three groups of chapters ("The Nature of the Enterprise," "The Separation and Division of Powers," and "The Structure of Substantive Rights"), the basic problems the essays address cut across the boundaries separating the essays into those three categories. In particular, the dangerous allure of proceduralism (chapters 1, 2, 3, 5, and 8), the paralyzing seduction of neutrality (chapters 1, 2, 13, and 15), and the morally anesthetizing imagery of the natural (chapters 4, 14, 15, and 16) are subjects not confined within a particular section.

Likewise, the hidden (and sometimes not-so-hidden) tilt of various constitutional doctrines toward the perpetuation of unjust hierarchies of race, gender, and class (chapters 5, 8, 12, 13, 14, 15, and 16) is the subject of part II almost as much as of part III. And the potential of various forms of constitutional argument to deflect judicial responsibility for crucial substantive choices onto external circumstances or remote actors unites many of the essays in all three parts of this collection (chapters 1, 2, 4, 5, 6, 10, 11, 15, and 16).

These essays touch both on enduring constitutional themes and on such contemporary matters as the Equal Rights Amendment (in chapters 3 and 15), a Human Life Amendment or Statute (in chapters 3 and 5), a Balanced Budget Amendment (in chapter 3), the War Powers Resolution (in chapter 6), regional banking (in chapter 10) and arbitrage bonds (in chapter 11), the contract rights of public bondholders and private pension beneficiaries (in chapter 12), and the implications of new medical technology for the abortion controversy (in chapter 15). Some of the essays in each part of this volume were inspired by problems I encountered in preparing congressional testimony (chapters 3, 4, 5, and 15), in consulting with particular clients (chapters 10 and 11), or in working on specific cases (chapters 3, 10, and 16). Most were inspired to some degree by puzzles I encountered in the course of teaching and reflecting on the evolution of constitutional law generally.

Living with the Constitution as an advocate and participant in various controversies—and so thinking about possible strategies of constitutional litigation and argument—has enriched my sense of what questions are worth asking, how questions that courts might wish to evade might be recast to make them less avoidable, and what might count as decent answers.

Much of what constitutional scholars write these days either focuses so closely on constitutional doctrine, or looks to matters so distant from doctrine, as to bear no real resemblance to *doing* constitutional law—to constructing constitutional arguments and counterarguments or exploring the premises and prospects of alternative constitutional approaches in concrete settings. Such constitutional *problem solving*, I recognize, is in less academic vogue nowadays than is discussion of constitutional *voice*: what it means for judges to expound the Constitution, how the vulnerability of judges relates to their authority, why their pronouncements succeed or fail in winning respect. Although such issues recur in the essays that follow, the core of my concern is the making of constitutional law itself—its tensions and tendencies; its puzzles and the patterns they make; its limits as a form of activity; in a word, its horizons.

Making those horizons more clearly visible, more amenable to understanding and critique, is my central aim. If I succeed in evaporating a cloud here or a layer of mist there and, thus, in displaying more lucidly a broader span of the constitutional horizon and its curvature, this volume will have achieved most of what I hoped to accomplish by writing it.

The treatise I published in 1978, *American Constitutional Law*, represented a more global effort; it was an attempt to roll the constitutional universe into a ball and show it as a unified whole. Although I do not at all regret that effort, and am in fact at work on a second edition that I hope will improve as well as update the first within a few years, time and events have replaced many of my certitudes with doubts, leaving me quite happy to defer a revised synthesis a while longer.

Publishing these essays in the meantime, rather than reducing and polishing them into pieces of that more comprehensive later work, has been a liberation for me. I would not wish to squirrel the essays away until they can be folded into a larger study, one in which they fit elegantly but no longer reflect my freshest thoughts on the issues they seek to treat. I would rather publish them now—rough edges only partly trimmed and links only tentatively forged—in the season of their completion.

Four of the essays in this collection and parts of two others have been published elsewhere in a slightly different form. Chapter 2 appeared as "The Puzzling Persistence of Process-Based Constitutional

Theories," 80 *Yale L.J.* 1063 (1980). Chapter 3 appeared in part as "A *Constitution* We Are Amending: In Defense of a Restrained Judicial Role," 97 *Harv. L. Rev.* 433 (1983). I first expressed some of the ideas in that essay in a lecture at the University of Washington Law School in October 1979 and developed others in an unpublished essay written jointly with William Fisher, J.D., Harvard Law School, 1982. I thank the students and faculty at the University of Washington, my new colleague Professor William Fisher, and David A. Sklansky, J.D., Harvard Law School, 1984, for helpful discussion of some of these ideas.

Chapter 4 consists substantially of the text of the Harris Lecture delivered on March 21, 1983, at the Indiana University Law School in Bloomington, published as "Toward a Syntax of the Unsaid: Construing the Sounds of Congressional and Constitutional Silence," 57 *Indiana L.J.* 515 (1982). For that essay I owe much to Professor Kathleen Sullivan, J.D., Harvard Law School, 1981 (then my student, now my colleague); John M. Bredehoft, J.D., Harvard Law School, 1983; William C. Foutz, Jr., J.D., Harvard Law School, 1983; and James A. Kirkland, J.D., Harvard Law School, 1984. Chapter 5 expands on my testimony before the Subcommittee on Courts, Civil Liberties, and the Administration of Justice of the House Judiciary Committee, June 3, 1981, which was read into the Congressional Record by Senator Gary Hart of Colorado (127 Cong. Rec. S.6780 [daily ed. June 23, 1981]) and was published as "Jurisdictional Gerrymandering: Zoning Disfavored Rights Out of the Federal Courts," 16 *Harv. C.R.-C.L. L. Rev.* 129 (1981).

Chapter 6 appeared as "The Legislative Veto Decision: A Law By Any Other Name?" 21 *Harvard Journal on Legislation* 1 (1984). For research assistance on earlier versions of this analysis I am indebted to Brian Koukoutchos, J.D., Harvard Law School, 1983, and Thomas Rollins, J.D., Harvard Law School, 1982. Chapter 14 appeared in part as "Perspectives on Bakke: Equal Protection, Procedural Fairness, or Structural Justice?" 92 *Harv. L. Rev.* 864 (1979).

I gratefully acknowledge the imaginative and tireless assistance of several excellent students at Harvard Law School: on Chapter 7, William A. Hunter, J.D. '84, and Brian Koukoutchos, J.D. '83; on Chapter 8, William A. Hunter and David A. Super, J.D. '83; on Chapter 9, Brian Koukoutchos; on Chapter 10, Joan I. Greco, J.D. '84; on Chapter 11, William A. Hunter; on Chapter 12, David A. Sklansky, J.D. '84; on Chapter 13, David A. Hoffman, J.D. '84, and James G. Pope,

J.D. '83; on Chapter 14, Brian Koukoutchos; on Chapter 15, Joan I. Greco; and on Chapter 15, William A. Hunter and Brian Koukoutchos.

For overall assistance in bringing these essays together as a book, I am deeply indebted to the persistent and insightful help of William A. Hunter, now a member of the Vermont State Senate. Will's perceptiveness and patience should stand him in good stead as he moves along what I am confident will be a progressive political trajectory.

For helping me to recognize that there really is a book here and not simply a series of related essays, I thank my wife, Carolyn, and my friend Robert Shrum. And finally, for the intellectual ferment and challenge that made this book possible, I thank my colleagues and students at Harvard Law School.

CONTENTS

PART III
THE STRUCTURE OF SUBSTANTIVE RIGHTS

CONSTITUTIONAL
CHOICES

I

THE NATURE OF
THE ENTERPRISE

CHAPTER ONE

THE FUTILE SEARCH
FOR LEGITIMACY

Saying anything at all about how constitutional choices in general might be validated as "legitimate" even if controversial seems nearly pointless these days; that is not this book's agenda. When it comes to legitimacy, all has been said already, and what has been said is all so deeply riddled with problems that it seems hardly worth restating, much less refuting or refining.

Who could disagree that constitutional decisions—choices among competing constitutional arguments and meanings—ought to, and necessarily do, represent something less whimsical and personal than the unconstrained "will of the judges"?[1] Yet who could believe that constitutional decisions and choices might reflect anything as external and eternal, impersonal and inexorable, as the "will of the law"?[2] For starters, anyone who claimed to *know* what the "will of the law" was on such troubling matters as the reflection of biological differences in legal categories or the relationship among children, parents, religious authorities, and political communities or the imposition of uniform federal standards on state and local government structures would properly be suspected of megalomania. And anyone who claims to know what the "will of the law" is on such even more perplexing matters as the relations among representative government, majority rule, minority status, and individual rights in our political system is likely to invite only polite chatter followed by prolonged inattention.

Yet I do not mean to play the cynic or the legal nihilist. I am neither. In truth, just as I am not writing for those who feel confident that canons of appropriate constitutional construction may be convincingly derived from some neutral source, so I am also not writing for those

3

who have convinced themselves that "anything goes" as long as it helps end what they see as injustice; that constitutional law is only a legitimating mask for what those in power can get away with; or that it is only a tame language in which those who might otherwise foment violent revolution can couch their demands in forms the regime might accept without losing face.

No one who is persuaded that the categories of constitutional discourse, or of law generally, are readily rendered determinate and certain—and no one who believes that those categories are inherently empty, infinitely malleable, and ultimately corrupt—need read any further. For all the writing and work I do ventures repeated acts of faith that more is at stake than that; that constitutional interpretation is a practice alive with choice but laden with content; and that this practice has both boundaries and moral significance not wholly reducible to, although never independent of, the ends for which it is deployed.

The customary gambit in attaching such moral significance to the enterprise of construing and enforcing the Constitution is to propound normative criteria for how that enterprise may legitimately be conducted—criteria of fidelity to constitutional text, to some sort of contemporary or historical consensus about meaning and purpose, to the preservation of some version of representative government thought to be implicit in the Constitution, to the defense of rights perceived as implicit in some distinctly American vision, or to any of a number of other suggested ideals. Those who struggle to ground anything as complex as judicial review in any such more deeply secure foundation seem to me destined to leave us, and themselves, unsatisfied—caught in an infinite regress in which each reply (say, "Because that is what the framers intended") begets but deeper questions about why the reply should count as an answer at all (as in, "Why should their mere intentions matter?").

So this is not a book proposing still more such criteria or even discussing previously advanced criteria of this sort in any great detail. Nor is this a book purporting to describe the forces of politics and culture that in fact *do* tend to constrain the constitutional enterprise as conducted by the various institutions that play a role in its evolution. Whatever light these essays cast on issues of that sort will at best be indirect—a light derived from one observer's efforts not to make constitutional law seem worth doing but simply to illuminate the choices involved in actually doing it.

I would be less than candid if I did not admit at this point that my reasons for proceeding in this way include one that is fairly personal: it's what I think I can do best. But I am also moved, I genuinely believe, by a sense of the ultimate futility of the quest for an Archimedean point outside ourselves from which the legitimacy of some form of judicial review or constitutional exegesis may be affirmed.

Even if we could settle on firm constitutional postulates, we would remain inescapably subjective in the application of those postulates to particular problems and issues. For, at *every* level of constitutional discourse—from controversy about which forms of argument (if any) "trump" others (does evidence of framers' intent trump inference from constitutional structure?), to controversy over the existence and nature of the overall mission (if any) of the Constitution (is it to enhance democracy or secure dignity? is it to encourage reform or preserve continuity?), to dispute over the meaning of particular constitutional phrases (what is an "unreasonable search or seizure" or "cruel and unusual punishment"?)—there is no escape from the need to make commitments to significant premises. And these may be premises that others do not share and that no one can claim to have "discovered" in a privileged place external to the disputants themselves and insulated from who they are and what groups they belong to.

Anyone who insists, for instance, that "fidelity to text" must be the core commitment of a constitutionalist must confront the indeterminacy of text and must justify giving to one or another vision of language such binding force over our lives. And anyone who argues that the only values courts may properly impose without fairly direct (how direct?) textual support are those of improved political representation[3] must make a choice no less "subjective" and contestable than one who insists upon the protection of personal dignity or the fulfillment of American ideals[4] as the only suitable lodestars for the mission of extratextual review.

That all of these supposedly distinct visions are collapsible into one another[5] vividly illustrates the subjectivity of the task of selecting and applying them. Worse, all of these visions presuppose a readily understood method or metric for measuring the relative distance between various proposed values or norms and whatever is supposed to count as the noncontroversial core of constitutional claims—the document's text, say, or the plain intent of the framers. Norms that are not close enough to this core, and only such norms, need meet the special demands such theories posit: for each theory, there exists a set of substantive claims about constitutional meaning that the theory ranks as sufficiently close to the Constitution's core (perhaps its "literal" language or its framers' "demonstrable" intent) to require no special derivation from the theory's preferred source of noninterpretivist reasoning (a source such as enhancing democracy or divining our national aspirations).

But is any such measure of relative distance from the core—or even of secure location within the core—really imaginable? Compare, for example, the claim that the First Amendment protects pornography with the claim that the First, Ninth, and Fourteenth Amendments protect sexual intimacy. Advocates of the pornography claim may say that even a portrayal of sex that degrades and subjugates women is surely "speech" and is thus entitled to the First Amendment's protection in terms of norms fairly inferable "from the Constitution itself." Advocates of the sexual intimacy claim may say that physically expressing sexual feeling to another is no less a form of communication—and may indeed be less coercive, and thus more purely "speech"-like—than depicting sex to a distant audience may be. Which group is advancing notions more remote from, say, the Constitution's text and thus bears the heavier burden of justifying judicial imposition of its "values"? Is the recent invalidation of the legislative veto in the name of Article I, Section 7[6] more or less an instance of extratextual adjudication than was, for example, the invalidation of the federal ban on labor union officeholding by Communists in the name of the Bill of Attainder Clause[7] or the identification of knowing or reckless falsehood as a First Amendment prerequisite of liability for defaming a public official?[8]

For me, such questions seem basically unanswerable; theories that offer or presuppose answers to them—*any* answers—seem not worth pursuing with passion or even worth criticizing in great detail. In declining to join the recently renewed rush toward theories that purport to answer such questions and to provide foundational criteria that will render judicial review legitimate within—and only within—determinate boundaries, I by no means suggest that the legitimacy of judicial review (or, for that matter, of majority rule *without* judicial review) is ever unproblematic. On the contrary, it is largely because I believe that all exercises of power by some over others—even with what passes for the latter's consent—are *and must remain* deeply problematic that I find all legitimating theories not simply amusing in their pretensions but, in the end, as dangerous as they are unconvincing.[9]

One danger such theories pose is that, by contrasting whatever they hope to render legitimate (for example, nontextual judicial review or judicial review in "human rights" cases) with what they seek to portray as needing no special legitimation (for example, judicial review in terms of the text itself or majoritarian democracy or "self-government"), they encourage us all to forget that *no* exercise of power, in any society the planet has ever seen, is genuinely unproblematic.[10] A second danger is that, having developed their legitimating rationales for certain exercises of judicial power, or of power deployed by "democratically" elected representatives, such theories tend to silence debate and to still doubt just when debate and doubt seem to me most needed, making such excruciatingly hard cases as the Supreme Court's abortion decision of 1973[11] seem easy—easily wrong for some theorists[12] or easily right for others,[13] but *easy* nonetheless. Yet it is exactly when cases that trouble others *seem* easy from a given point of view that we should most deeply question how that point of view enables some to filter out so much to which we all ought to remain sensitive—how it enables some to feel (or at least to sound) smug even when others remain in such turmoil.

This is not to advocate permanent skepticism or indecision or to urge a halt to confident and even deeply committed advocacy of constitutional positions. It *is* to say that, *in matters of power, the end of doubt and distrust is the beginning of tyranny*. Thus, judges who come to believe that some part of the coercive force they wield is, thank heaven, legitimate after all and, thus, need no longer be a source of personal anguish[14] are to be feared almost as much as are those judges who happily proceed without any theoretical worries at all, and are far more to be feared than are those who worry but whose worries are unabated by any neat legitimating formula.

Scholars and commentators wield a kind of power, too—not the direct coercive force wielded by courts and the police, but a power to affect belief and thus, to some degree, to shape social reality. Like judges, those who study and write about the work of courts—and those who read such writings—may be lulled into a false repose by theories that purport to legitimate the scholar's proper enterprise as one of "merely" objective and unbiased description of text or history, or one of dispassionate and careful observation of doctrine or theory. Such repose is false because *all* social description and observation are bound up in the describer's and observer's point of view. Substantive perspective, reflecting the observer's past and context, is inescapable;

its influence on perception and description is pervasive. The corollary is not that full and honest reporting is impossible or dispensable but only that it is attainable at best in approximation—when the viewpoints and values that inform and shape it are perceived as deeply and exposed as starkly as the author finds possible, and when alternative perspectives are set forth with as much fairness and force as the author can muster.

That life is finite and filled with other tasks means, of course, that no debate can go on forever, that many debates must end *as if* some result had been reached, and that *all* debates must proceed with the help of at least *some* premises shared by every participant. But to say this is not to deny that contingency pervades all, and that even shared premises must remain contestable. Thus, whenever I suggest in these essays, for want of space or of humility, that one or another decision seems to me "plainly right" or "plainly wrong," or that some proposal or position is "clearly" consistent (or inconsistent) with the Constitution, I hope my words will be understood as shorthand not for a conclusion I offer as indisputably "correct" but solely for a conviction I put forward as powerfully held—a conviction with which I mean never to end debate but always to advance it.[15]

CHAPTER TWO

THE POINTLESS
FLIGHT FROM SUBSTANCE

In deciding constitutional cases, the Supreme Court has often invoked a vision of how politics should work, justifying judicial intervention as a response to supposed gaps between that vision and political reality. Legislation or other governmental action is of constitutional concern, the Court suggests, when it seems to obstruct political representation and accountability—by blocking speech or voting, for example—or when it reveals the existence of past or present obstructions—by distributing the law's benefits and burdens in ways that show a particular group to have been denied fair representation.[1] By invalidating legislative or administrative acts of this sort, the Court can reason, it avoids controversial judgments about substantive issues left open by the Constitution's text and history and safeguards the representative character of the political process.

It is easy to see why courts would be attracted to this way of describing the content and role of constitutional law. Such a substance-denying account permits courts to perceive and portray themselves as servants of democracy even as they strike down the actions of supposedly democratic governments.[2] But other constitutional theorists, unencumbered by the judiciary's rhetorical needs, also find the idea of perfecting process, and process alone, to be powerfully magnetic.[3] In the most recent and lucid argument for a process-perfecting view of constitutional law, John Ely's *Democracy and Distrust*, the vision is boldly stated:

> [C]ontrary to the standard characterization of the Constitution as "an enduring but evolving statement of general values," . . . in fact the selection and accommodation of substantive values is left almost entirely to the political process and instead the document is overwhelmingly con-

9

cerned, on the one hand, with procedural fairness in the resolution of individual disputes (process writ small), and on the other, with what might capaciously be designated process writ large—with ensuring broad participation in the processes and distributions of government.[4]

Yet it is not difficult to show that the constitutional theme of perfecting the processes of governmental decision is radically indeterminate and fundamentally incomplete. The process theme by itself determines almost nothing unless its presuppositions are specified, and its content supplemented, by a full theory of substantive rights and values—the very sort of theory the process-perfecters are at such pains to avoid. If that proposition, which this essay seeks to elaborate, is correct, it leaves us with a puzzle: why do thoughtful judges and scholars continue to put forth process-perfecting theories as though such theories could banish divisive controversies over substantive values from the realm of constitutional discourse by relegating those controversies to the unruly world of power?

THE CONSTITUTION'S OPENLY
SUBSTANTIVE COMMITMENTS

One difficulty that immediately confronts process theories is the stubbornly substantive character of so many of the Constitution's most crucial commitments: commitments defining the values that we as a society, acting politically, must respect. Plainly, the First Amendment's guarantee of religious liberty and its prohibition of religious establishment are substantive in this sense.[5] So, too, is the Thirteenth Amendment, in its abolition of slavery and repudiation of the Constitution's earlier, ostensibly procedural, protections of that institution.[6]

In many of its parts, the Constitution also evinces a substantive commitment to the institution of private property and to the contractual expectations that surround it. The Just Compensation Clause of the Fifth Amendment is an obvious example.[7] The Contracts Clause of Article I, Section 10 is another.[8] The old substantive due process, which is obviously an important part of our constitutional history and thus significant for our understanding of what the Constitution is about, also served to protect the transactions and expectations to which the institution of private property gives rise.[9] A number of critics have charged that the old substantive due process is inconsistent with the language of the Due Process Clause itself.[10] But the words that follow "due process" are "of law," and the word "law" seems to have been the textual point of departure for substantive due process.[11] Whatever our views of the substantive due process heyday, most of us would readily concede that the framers of the 1787 Constitution adopted a federal system of government organization in order to, among other goals, help secure the institution of private property.[12] When Madison, in his theory of faction, suggested that shifting the legislative responsibility for certain problems from the state to the national level could help assure that majorities would not trample minority rights,[13] the problems he had in mind were largely economic;[14] the minority rights the federal system would protect were, for the most part, rights of property and contract.[15]

Religious freedom, antislavery, private property—much of our constitutional history can be written by reference to just these social institutions and substantive values. That the Constitution has long addressed such matters, and often with beneficial effect, ought to surprise no one. What is puzzling is that anyone can say, in the face of this reality, that the Constitution is or should be predominantly concerned with *process* and *not* substance.

But our constitutional reality poses even deeper problems for process theorists. Even the Constitution's most procedural prescriptions cannot be adequately understood, much less applied, in the absence of a developed theory of fundamental rights that are secured to persons against the state—a theory whose derivation demands precisely the kinds of controversial substantive choices that the process proponents are so anxious to leave to the electorate and its representatives.

THE SUBSTANTIVE ROOTS OF PROCEDURAL NORMS

Much of the Constitution does indeed appear to address matters of procedure. Sometimes the subject is *adjudicative* process—the process due to individuals who become defendants in criminal or civil litigation or targets of administrative actions. Elsewhere, the Constitution focuses on *representative* process—including the process that governs the election of Congress,[16] of the President,[17] or of state representative bodies.[18] That the *subject* in all these cases is procedure, however, is not to say that the *meaning* and *purpose* of the Constitution's prescriptions on each such subject are themselves merely procedural. There is no reason to suppose that "constitutive" rules—rules defining the basic structure of political and legal relations—can or should be essentially neutral on matters of substantive value.

The very dichotomy just drawn—between adjudicative and representative process—would prove incoherent without a substantive theory. How do we decide which *form* of participation the complaining individual may claim: the right to be heard as a litigant, or the right to be counted as a voter? The question whether individuals may insist on being heard by rulemakers, for whom they have already (directly or indirectly) voted, has bedeviled administrative law since the turn of the century.[19] How the government chooses to deal with individuals—as individuals or en masse—cannot be dispositive. For, at least sometimes, government action that purports to deal with groups is unconstitutional precisely because it does *not* deal with individuals as such: the conclusive presumption decisions[20] and the mandatory death penalty cases,[21] however opaque they might otherwise be, establish this much, as does Justice Powell's opinion in *Regents of the University of California v. Bakke.*[22] Conversely, in at least some circumstances, there is no constitutional infirmity in relying only on representative, or even directly democratic, processes to deal with individuated grievances: individual zoning variances may be made the subject of local referendum;[23] and unions, as delegatees of federal power,[24] may bind members of bargaining units to the terms of wage bargains or, indeed, of individual grievance negotiations, even though the unions do not act as representatives of individuals *as individuals.*[25]

The question of whether adjudicative or representative process is required in a given context simply cannot be analyzed in terms of how fairly and accurately various participatory processes reflect the interests and inputs of those governed by them. Deciding what *kind* of participation the Constitution demands requires analysis not only of the efficacy of alternative processes but also of the character and importance of the interest at stake—its role in the life of the individual as an individual. That analysis, in turn, requires a theory of values and rights as plainly substantive as, and seemingly of a piece with, the theories of values and rights that underlie the Constitution's provisions addressing religion, slavery, and property.

Once one has decided whether the Constitution requires adjudicative or representative process in a particular setting, one must again rely on substantive values in elaborating the requirements of either procedural form. Consider first the problem of adjudicative process. Certainly the Fifth Amendment's Self-incrimination and Double

Jeopardy Clauses embody concerns for protecting individual dignity in the criminal process.[26] A substantive concern for individual privacy necessarily underpins the Fourth Amendment.[27] Other superficially procedural provisions of the Constitution, such as the rights to counsel, confrontation, bail, and jury trial, echo similar themes; they function, often at some cost to the efficiency and accuracy of fact-finding,[28] to prevent the government from treating individuals in the criminal process as though they were objects.[29]

Even outside the criminal context, elaborating rights of adjudicative process requires recourse to a substantive theory. Procedural due process rights are not simply means of protecting whatever entitlements happen to be conferred by legislation or administrative regulation. Otherwise, the drafters of an entitlement could frame it in the procedural terms of their choice, and the constitutional guarantee would be reduced to a right to receive whatever process the drafters had defined as due.[30] But that view has been repeatedly rejected by the Supreme Court, which has never fully embraced a purely positivist theory of procedural due process.[31] The only alternative theories, however, are ones that posit a right to individual dignity, or some similarly substantive norm, as the base on which conceptions of procedural fairness are constructed.[32]

If process is constitutionally valued, therefore, it must be valued not only as a means to some independent end, but for its intrinsic characteristics: being heard is part of what it means to be a person.[33] Process itself, therefore, becomes substantive. There is a curious irony here. One who holds that constitutional law should aim chiefly to perfect process is apparently unable to treat process as *itself* valuable. For, to see why process would itself be intrinsically valuable is to see why the Constitution is inevitably substantive. Instead, the perfecter of process must treat process as ultimately instrumental, as but a means to other ends, and thus must regard as secondary what he would at the same time celebrate as primary.[34]

The process theorist is similarly confounded by questions about the right to vote—the quintessential procedural right in the realm of politics. Voting-rights issues commonly take one of two forms. One set of issues concerns *who* votes. Is the electorate to include racial minorities, women, District of Columbia residents, eighteen-year-olds?[35] Is it to include only property owners, only property owners and parents, only residents, only citizens?[36] What of the disenfranchisement of children?[37] Who votes, it turns out, is a profoundly substantive question.[38] For *who* participates—who counts—in the electoral process is a question that must precede any inquiry into the fairness of the process itself. The issue goes not to fairness procedurally, but to our sense of who constitutes a political community, and of which relations in society must be horizontal rather than vertical, fraternal rather than hierarchical. And if *any* question is plainly substantive, that question is fundamentally so.[39]

The second set of issues concerns how voting power is to be allocated among those who are included within an electoral constituency. Sometimes, in this context, the Supreme Court looks to whether the election is one that chooses representatives or one that resolves a one-shot issue,[40] or whether voters are voting as individuals or as, say, property owners.[41] But generally, the Court has enforced the famous rule announced in the reapportionment cases: one person, one vote.[42] The obvious substantive underpinnings of this rule—its role as an expression of the equal respect in which we as a society aspire to hold each individual[43]—the theorists of perfecting process must ignore. They can defend the rule only hesitantly, claiming, for example, that it is merely a matter of administrative convenience.[44] Again we observe the irony already revealed in the adjudicative process cases: because embracing process for its own sake means embracing process as substance—as an expression of the value in which we would hold individuals—theorists who would defend constitutional law as ultimately reducible to the quest for perfection of process cannot themselves treat process as primary.[45] Again the puzzle deepens: as the next section will show, theorists of perfecting process not only are undercut by their inability affirmatively to advocate process as such, but their negative critique of obstructed process is stunted as well.

THE QUANDARY OF WHOM TO PROTECT

For those who would fill the gaps left by the Constitution's ambiguities and silences with representation-reinforcing principles, perhaps the core "process value" is the value of protecting certain minorities from perennial defeat in the political arena. The theme was anticipated by John Marshall;[46] it assumed a central role for Harlan Fiske Stone;[47] it signally motivated Earl Warren;[48] and it has been elaborated by numerous scholars,[49] most powerfully in the work of John Ely.[50] The idea seems as simple as it sounds reasonable: governmental action that burdens groups effectively excluded from the political process is constitutionally suspect. In its most sophisticated form, the resulting judicial scrutiny is seen as a way of invalidating governmental classifications and distributions that turn out to have been motivated either by prejudiced hostility or by self-serving stereotypes.[51]

It all sounds pretty good—until we ask how we are supposed to distinguish such "prejudice" from principled, if "wrong," disapproval. Which groups are to count as "discrete and insular minorities"? Which are instead to be deemed appropriate losers in the ongoing struggle for political acceptance and ascendancy?

To begin with, of course, the theory must clearly distinguish itself from its *reductio ad absurdum*: "whichever group happens to lose the political struggle or fails to command the attention of the legislature . . . is—by that fact alone—a discrete and insular minority."[52] How about focusing on immutability, discreteness, insularity? For the process theorist, all such features might seem helpful in suggesting why a legislature would regard some groups as "different" and thus fall prey to cruel or self-servingly careless stereotyping. Or such features may signal why other groups would fail to interact with a group considered "different," or to engage in the usual protective logrolling.

But features like immutability are neither sufficient[53] nor necessary.[54] For in looking at social attitudes toward groups, one cannot simply play Linnaeus and engage in taxonomy. One cannot speak of "groups" as though society were objectively subdivided along lines that are just there to be discerned.[55] Instead, people *draw* lines, attribute differences, as a way of ordering social existence—of deciding who may occupy what place, play what role, engage in what activity. Thus, in order to justify the role of chattel that blacks initially played in our society, we may have differentiated that role by describing it in terms of the most obvious distinguishing feature of the people who played it, thus equating race and role.[56] This equation, and thus the "group," survived the Civil War and the Thirteenth Amendment. It did so not simply by reason of confusion or inertia, but because the role that society allowed blacks remained partly unchanged; thus, the need to justify the role by differentiating it, by seeing not the role but the group—"inferior" blacks capable of nothing better anyway—persisted.[57]

The temptation to think of groups as simply given is exacerbated by the complex interaction between social attitudes and those identified as group members. Individuals who find themselves so identified may indeed see themselves as group members; because they approve of the options that society leaves them and want to protect those options, they identify the options with themselves, the differentiated "group."[58] Alternatively, assertion of group status may be a form of internal exile, a way of repudiating the limited possibilities for action that the larger social structure would allow, a choice of "exit" rather than "voice."[59]

This way of thinking about groups, I believe, captures not only much of the dynamics of race, but also much of the social significance of religion, alienage, gender, sexual preference, legitimacy, wealth—traits we as a society commonly use in separating out groups.[60] Views about the "differentness" of groups generally, therefore, may reflect an interacting set of judgments about activities or options or roles, expressed sometimes harmoniously and sometimes dialectically by *both* "we" and "they."[61] If so, the conclusion that a legislative classification reveals prejudicial stereotypes must, at bottom, spring from *a disagreement with the judgments that lie behind the stereotype*: judgments about the propriety of the options left to individuals or the burdens imposed on them.

Consider several illustrations. Burglars are subject to widespread hostility: indeed, the activity that defines the group is everywhere legislatively prohibited. Are burglars therefore a "suspect class"? Of course not. Suspect status is unthinkable—but only because of the substantive value we attach to personal security and the importance for us of the system of private property and its rules of transfer, which the burglary prohibition preserves.[62] If we speak of burglars as a class, we do so as a way of giving form to our view that burglary *is* a "different" activity, different not so much because burglars visibly define a group as because we disapprove of the activity, deny it any claim to protection as a right.

Homosexuals, too, are subject to widespread hostility; legislation penalizing homosexuals and homosexual practices is common.[63] Homosexuals often do not identify themselves by sexual preference when acting politically, and generally do not "come out of the closet" to refute the traditional stereotypes.[64] But even if they did, legislation might be unaltered. Coming out of the closet could dispel ignorance, but it may not alter belief. Legislators may see homosexuals as "different" not out of ignorance, but on principle—on the basis of a morality that treats certain sexual practices as repugnant to a particular view of humanity and, thus, regards people who engage in those practices as "other."[65] Such legislation can be rejected only on the basis of a principle that is equally substantive: a view of what it means to be a person and to have a sexual identity.[66] Process and prejudice thus seem profoundly beside the point. Any constitutional distinction between laws burdening homosexuals and laws burdening exhibitionists, between laws burdening Catholics and laws burdening pickpockets, must depend on a substantive theory of which groups are exercising fundamental rights and which are not.[67]

Indeed, even laws putting blacks and women "in their place"— banning racial intermarriage, say, or excluding women from combat— are likely to reflect neither simple hostility nor self-serving blindness but *a substantive vision of proper conduct*—a vision that no amount of attention to flaws in the political process could condemn or correct. Accordingly, the idea of blacks or women as properly segregated beings can be rejected *only* by finding a constitutional basis for concluding that, in our society, such hierarchical visions are substantively out of bounds, at least as a justification for government action.[68] And such a finding would in turn entail a theory of unenumerated substantive rights, rights at best *suggested* by constitutional text and history, rights whose necessarily controversial elaboration the process theorists seek to eschew.[69]

The crux of any determination that a law unjustly discriminates against a group—blacks or women or even men[70]—is not that the law emerges from a flawed process or that the burden it imposes affects an independently fundamental right,[71] but that the law is part of a pattern that denies those subject to it a meaningful opportunity to realize their humanity. Necessarily, such an approach must look beyond process to identify and proclaim fundamental substantive rights—including *substantive rights to participate* on equal terms in the evolution of law and policy. Whatever difficulties this may entail, it seems plain that important aspects of constitutional law, including the determination of which groups deserve special protection, can be given significant content in no other way. Thus, it is puzzling indeed that purely process-based approaches—designed to deny the need for, and legitimacy of, any such substantive theory—should nonetheless continue to find such articulate proponents and persist in attracting such perceptive adherents.

THE CLOSED CIRCLE OF POLITICAL OPENNESS

If protecting minorities requires a theory of substantive rights, might another value, that of "political openness"—of clearing the channels for change through speech and voting—be salvaged as a unifying theme for the process-minded?[72] First Amendment theorists such as Alexander Meiklejohn have pursued this general line, with varying degrees of success.[73] But there are at least three fundamental difficulties with any effort to reduce substantive rights to mere mechanisms for channel-clearing. The first problem is the inherently incomplete nature of channel-clearing as an aim. Why *should* politics be open to equal participation by all? Does that norm itself not presuppose some substantive vision of human rights? Why would a vision rich enough to support a reasonably complete theory of political openness not also suffice to generate a theory of which substantive claims individuals may make against the majority?

The second problem is the absence of any plausible stopping point for channel-clearing theories. If the system must be open to change through peaceful persuasion, how do we distinguish between example and advocacy or between demonstration and assertion as forms of persuasion? If we do not draw some such distinction, life-style choices that seek to convince by demonstration—communal living arrangements or homosexual marriage, for example—are entitled to constitutionally protected status. Surely that is not what process theorists have in mind! Efforts to draw the necessary distinctions, however, are inevitably unsatisfactory. To accord special protection to advocacy alone is to censor those messages that can be conveyed only be example. Moreover, dichotomies such as speech and conduct, expression and action, or persuasion and instruction, do not in truth separate.[74]

If the acts of individuals may be demonstrations, and hence forms of persuasion, may not the same be said of the acts of government?[75] The actions of government define expectations, confer legitimacy, establish a status quo, and thus necessarily shape the nature and distribution of interests and attitudes in society itself. The state shapes society almost as much as society shapes the state: this is the third problem that any channel-clearing theory must confront—but cannot surmount without losing its "procedural" status.

Government subsidies to "major" political parties, for example, or the failure of state governments to provide funds to compensate school districts lacking "rich" property tax bases, are government actions that affirm some aspects of the status quo as desirable, and others as inevitable. Such government actions are at present constitutional,[76] as are governmental decisions that inculcate the young with the standard public virtues and defeat the self-defining, value-forming, and power-amassing efforts of all but the more standard social groupings.[77] Unable to support a challenge to such exercises of power, a truly procedural channel-clearing theory seems doomed to irrelevance, for without such challenge government may well be able to shape the "will" of the governed in the image of those who govern,[78] reducing consent and representation to all but empty ideals.

This should not seem too surprising: that domination can appear in the guise of democracy is hardly a novel observation in the late twentieth century. The puzzle is that the failure of substance-denying theories even to speak to this danger should be so readily and persistently excused or overlooked.

A BROADER ROLE FOR CONSTITUTIONAL THEORY

One final and closely related puzzle—a puzzle that may follow from the very aspiration to purge constitutional discourse of inevitably controversial claims about substantive rights and values—is the willingness of so many to embrace substance-denying theories in the face of the virtually total incapacity of such theories to inform the *content* of public discussion, debate, and decision. One can perhaps understand the appeal to judges of a theory purporting to instruct them that they are to construe the Constitution so as to reinforce representation—that is, fill in the blanks so as to perfect democracy as an unexamined "given." But what can be the appeal of such a theory to an elected representative—especially one who regards the Constitution as addressed to *all* who govern,[79] and who accordingly wonders whether some of the "interests" of his constituents ought, as a constitutional matter, to be resisted rather than represented?[80] And what can be the appeal of such a theory to a citizen who regards the Constitution as addressed to the people at large, and who, accordingly, asks which of his preferences—for dominating women, perhaps, or for denigrating the working class—the citizen ought to suppress or even change?

Perhaps the impoverished relevance of the Constitution for everyone *except* judges under a process-based and substance-denying theory is to be offset in some way by the theory's supposed ability to improve constitutional argument, analysis, and adjudication in the judicial branch. But are we really to believe that the way judges decide cases will be powerfully and beneficially affected by theories linking the judiciary's constitutional role to the supposed failures of political process? Might not the care and humility that we are entitled to expect of judges instead be *undermined* if judges were indeed persuaded that much judicial activism is simply a corollary of democracy?

Most process-based theorists and their followers evidently have seen little point in analyzing what the general acceptance of their views would be likely to do to the actual course of constitutional argument and decision. The views they espouse apparently strike chords so responsive, accord with beliefs so deep, that inquiry into probable effects—like close attention to counter-examples and logical gaps— seems beside the point. But if this is so, then we are left with a final puzzle: what does it say about our situation, and about the prospect for constitutional theory, that views so deeply problematic continue to exert so powerful a grip upon our thought?

CHAPTER THREE

THE FALSE EQUATION OF PROCEDURALISM WITH PASSIVITY: A CONSTITUTION WE ARE AMENDING— AND CONSTRUING

Attempting to escape substance,[1] like seeking legitimacy in other controversy-denying strategies,[2] is more likely in the end to relax the inhibitions of a dangerously ambitious judiciary than to restrain the imperial tendencies of a wisely cautious judicial branch: to say that one is merely the voice of the framers' intentions or of a contemporary consensus, or the perfecter of popular mechanisms for choice devised by others, is to lose touch with the need for continuing self-doubt in the exercise of adjudicatory power.[3]

In fact, there is a vicious circle here. If anyone were to succeed in persuading people generally that the enterprise of constitutional exegesis could safely and legitimately be left to process-perfecting and representation-reinforcing judicial experts, and that the enterprise itself had no substantive content beyond that of exposing and repairing essentially technical obstacles to fair participation and adequate representation, then there would be little for anyone but a judge (or a student and critic of judicial behavior) to discuss, much less do, with respect to constitutional matters. Constitutional concerns would all be reducible to issues in how best to adjust the machinery of representative government to assure that it truly represents those who wish to be represented. Indeed, if the Constitution's open phrases and partial clues are not to be construed to achieve more substantive aims than that, then this rule of construction is presumably a command directed not solely to judges but to *all* whom the Constitution binds.[4] And, if that is so, then exhortations that judges pay heed to the constitutional deliberations of the other branches are calls to empty and ultimately circular dialogue, as each participant listens in vain for *something* of substance in the musings of the other.

The upshot of substance-denying constitutional aspirations is thus not only the paradoxical liberation of the judiciary to pursue substance mindlessly without openly acknowledging what it is doing, but the equally paradoxical paralysis of the citizenry and its elected representatives in what should be the shared enterprise of constitutional discourse. Thus, those who claim that overly active judges will sap the political strength and vision of the people and their chosen officials may well be correct, but in a surprising sense. They are likely to be correct *not* because people need to be left free to compromise basic rights if they are to get on with the challenges of effective governance—an argument I find impossible to square with a constitutional commitment to human rights as constraints on all public policy—but because people need to be drawn into, not excluded from, the task of construing what is, after all, *their* Constitution. And the form of "judicial activism" that is best calculated to exclude all but the "experts" from that task is the form that—in the name of constraining activist judges—proclaims its mission, and that of proper constitutional argument generally, to be neutrally procedural and thus remote from deep and divisive issues of substance.

Among the most illuminating arenas in which this perhaps unexpected paradox is currently being played out is that of amending the Constitution—an activity successfully completed only twenty-six times since 1787 and one to which increasingly frequent resort seems likely in the modern era. The supposition that debates over what the Constitution *means* are different in kind from debates over what it should be *made to say*—with the former belonging solely to the judges and academics and the latter belonging exclusively to everyone else— could readily lead, in the amendment context, to an unwisely intrusive role by judges in construing and policing the constitutional process by which the text of the Constitution itself is changed.

To understand how this might be so, we would do well to begin with basics. Despite the contention by four justices in *Coleman v. Miller*[5] that Congress enjoys "sole and complete control over the amending process, subject to no judicial review,"[6] complete judicial abstention from questions of amendment procedure has never been a realistic option. Could anyone really believe, for example, that a court would feel bound to treat the Equal Rights Amendment (ERA) as part of the Constitution if Congress determined that the thirty-five states that had ratified the amendment as of July 1, 1982, constituted the three-fourths of fifty required by Article V? Or suppose that Congress, reasoning that the Seventeenth Amendment's transformation of senators into direct representatives of state electorates effectively modified Article V, resolved to permit the senators of states that had neither ratified nor rejected the ERA to vote as the functional equivalents of state legislatures. Could anyone believe that a court would—or should—respect such a decision?

But to recognize a role for the federal judiciary in policing the outer boundaries of the amendment process—in determining, that is, what limits Article V sets on the freedom of Congress, of state legislatures, and of other governmental institutions in carrying out their responsibilities within the process—is not to say *where* federal courts should set those limits. In other words, the affirmation that Article V, no less than any other part of the Constitution, is entrusted to the courts for construction tells us nothing about what construction courts should adopt.[7]

In particular, such an affirmation leaves open perhaps the most pressing question of Article V jurisprudence: whether the Supreme Court should develop its *own* comprehensive standards for determining the circumstances, if any, under which a state's ratification of a proposed amendment may be rescinded or a congressionally set deadline for ratification altered, or whether the Court should instead treat such matters as largely—although not exclusively—within Congress' discretion.[8] Should Article V be read to mean, for example, that Congress is to play *no* role, either at the time an amendment is proposed or at the time it is promulgated, in deciding how a particular sequence of ratifications and rescissions is to be cumulated—that the "score" is to be kept in accord with counting rules made strictly by judges? For some, only such an absence of judicial deference to Congress could prevent the "amendment process . . . [from] becom[ing] a wonderland of uncertainty."[9] I disagree. Even if rules made by judges could, without undue sacrifice of flexibility, be made more certain and predictable in their application than congressional discretion could be,[10] added certainty in the application of Article V is an insufficient virtue to warrant the enormous vices that exclusive judicial control would entail.

Among those vices is the danger, warned against most recently by Justice Powell in *Goldwater v. Carter*,[11] of having the Supreme Court closely "oversee the very constitutional process used to reverse [its] decisions."[12] One recent commentator trivializes the objection by noting that only a few amendments have been designed literally to overturn Supreme Court decisions,[13] and by observing that the abuses at which amendments take aim are attributable at least as frequently to other branches as to the Court.[14] What this argument disregards is that, at least when *Congress* proposes an amendment to the states (as it has proposed all the amendments thus far adopted), the suggestion of a change in the Constitution's text almost inevitably reflects a deep national dissatisfaction with the way constitutional law—elaborated in our system principally, although (one hopes) not exclusively, by the courts—has theretofore resolved a matter.[15] The resort to amendment—to constitutional *politics* as opposed to constitutional *law*—should be taken as a sign that the legal system has come to a point of discontinuity, a point at which something less radical than revolution but distinctly more radical than ordinary legal evolution is called for.[16] To say that at such a moment in history we should necessarily conduct our legal business as usual, seeking certainty and harmony rather than tolerating discord, is to miss the very essence of the event at hand.

I do not suggest that the "legitimacy" of the system would crumble if, for example, the federal judiciary were to rebuff as invalidly ratified a human life amendment[17] that had been narrowly rescinded by a ratifying state at the very moment the thirty-eighth state added its yes vote, or that had received its final ratification during a congressionally decreed extension of the time initially set for ratification. I am uncomfortable with the entire notion of "legitimacy,"[18] and later in this volume I express my doubts about the similar thesis that only Congress' plenary power over the jurisdiction of federal courts makes review of legislation by those courts acceptable in a democratic republic.[19] I *do* urge that the Supreme Court would act unwisely were it to hold—when all concede[20] that text, history, and policy leave the issue in equipoise—that the Court rather than Congress ought to decide such matters as whether the circumstances surrounding particular legislative rescissions should lead us to view the rescissions as mere symbolic gestures[21] when the result of so viewing them would go to the very roots of the legal system that the Court itself had helped to construct and maintain and that the nation seemed inclined to change.

This position should not be confused with the view that "constitutional" criteria for resolving such issues could not be crafted without significant deference to Congress. They *could* be; the question is whether they *should* be.

The problems posed by broad judicial review of amendment procedure can perhaps best be understood by considering a closely related issue: judicial supervision of amendment substance. Both because of its intrinsic interest and because of the light it may shed on procedural matters, the judiciary's potential role in the substantive arena merits more attention than it has so far received. Consider the question of how well or badly a human life amendment, a balanced budget amendment, or a gun control amendment would "fit" within the Constitution. Although the Supreme Court has never asserted authority to invalidate amendments because of poor fit,[22] judicial abstention in this area is required not, as one might at first suppose, by a complete lack of constitutional criteria for adjudication, but by other considerations entirely. The Constitution does provide guidance of a sort—not decisive, but suggestive—for assessing the appropriateness of proposed amendments. Far from being a mere assortment of unconnected rules and standards, the Constitution can surely be understood as unified, although not rendered wholly coherent,[23] by certain underlying political ideals: representative republicanism,[24] federalism,[25] separation of powers,[26] equality before the law,[27] individual autonomy,[28] and procedural fairness.[29] We may choose to reject some or all of these ideals, to override them, or to recast them, but as long as we retain some commitment to the Constitution—as long as we are amending it instead of discarding it—we cannot simply ignore its fundamental norms.[30] An amendment prohibiting atheists from holding federal office, for example, would clash with the current Constitution's paramount concern for freedom of conscience[31] no less than a statute to the same effect would run counter to the current Establishment Clause.[32]

Of course, there can be disagreement about whether a proposed amendment does break radically from fundamental values that run— and should continue to run—through the Constitution, and about whether any such break is warranted in light of still more fundamental values. Proponents of an amendment authorizing states to ban abortions, for example, argue that the amendment would reinforce the Constitution's concern for fairness and its overriding respect for the sanctity of human life,[33] whereas opponents suggest that such an amendment would offend the fundamental constitutional values of privacy, individual autonomy, and equality.[34] Not only is the list of fundamental constitutional norms open to debate, but the very identity of "the Constitution"—the body of textual and historical materials

from which the norms are to be extracted and by which their application is to be guided—is itself a matter that cannot be objectively de-
duced or passively discerned in a viewpoint-free way.[35]

But disagreements over an amendment's "fit" within the substantive framework of constitutional law, like disagreements over what
that framework includes, indicate not that the appropriateness of the
amendment is not a "constitutional" question, but only that no single
"answer" is readily available. All constitutional interpretation contains such elements of indeterminacy: the Constitution cannot itself
dictate, in a manner that frees its users of responsibility for choice,
how it is to be approached.[36]

Despite this unavoidable dependence on perspective, on point of
view, "the Constitution"—wherever we draw its boundaries and however we read its contents—is not simply a mirror, nor is it an empty
vessel whose users may pour into it whatever they will. The Constitution tells us *something*, and what it says—although necessarily read
through lenses we ourselves bring to the task—must be the touchstone
for evaluating the substantive appropriateness of any proposed
amendment.[37]

In addition to such substantive criteria of amendment appropriateness as the Constitution's specific provisions may suggest, the structure and character of the document as a whole impose certain functional constraints. The Constitution serves both as a blueprint for
government operations and as an authoritative statement of the nation's most important and enduring values. Highly specific and controversial substantive restrictions—amendments banning intoxicating
liquors,[38] federal budget deficits,[39] or handguns, for example—seem
out of place in the document regardless of the desirability of the substantive policies they codify.[40] As the history of Prohibition illustrates,
enacting such measures through constitutional amendment rather
than by statute[41] renders them dangerously resistant to modification.
As importantly, such amendments trivialize the Constitution and diminish its educative and expressive force as part of our political and legal culture. The value of the Constitution as an evolving repository of
the nation's core political ideals and as a record of the nation's deepest
ideological battles depends significantly on the limitation of its substantive content to what all (or nearly all) perceive to be fundamen-
tals;[42] a document cluttered with regulatory specifics could command
no such respect.[43]

Yet these criteria of amendment appropriateness surely must not be elaborated or enforced by courts—not because they fail to reflect principle as opposed to mere policy or prudence, and not because courts are less adept than Congress at detecting the "consensus" that some observers believe an amendment should reflect,[44] but because allowing the judiciary to pass on the merits of constitutional amendments would unequivocally subordinate the amendment process to the legal system it is intended to override and would thus gravely threaten the integrity of the entire structure.[45] Such criteria must therefore be applied by Congress (or by a constitutional convention) when it considers whether to propose an amendment, and by state legislatures (or state conventions) when they vote on ratification. The merit of a suggested constitutional amendment is thus a true "political question"—a matter that the Constitution addresses, but that it nevertheless commits[46] to judicially unreviewable resolution by the political branches of government.[47]

Questions concerning the *process* of constitutional amendment are, of course, somewhat different—but only somewhat. Because of the interest in predictability of amendment procedure, and because judicial review of procedural questions would allow courts to control the content of amendments only indirectly and only in part, courts may properly be less hesitant to adjudicate procedural challenges to proposed amendments and ratification processes than to pass on the substantive suitability of those amendments. Still, many of the concerns motivating judicial abstention from substantive review of constitutional amendments counsel substantial, albeit less than total, deference when courts are faced with challenges to ratification procedures approved by Congress.[48] In both types of cases, judicial supervision would significantly undercut the independence of Article V from normal legal processes and erode its special role in the constitutional scheme. And in both types of cases, the Supreme Court would frequently be asked to pass on the legitimacy of actions taken to correct perceived flaws in its own jurisprudence—a task with uncomfortable implications for the integrity of the judicial enterprise.

It is true that even such nondeferential judicial review of the ratification process would leave Congress with one mechanism for insisting on its own views: Congress would still be able to write procedural rules directly into a proposed amendment's *text*. Once an amendment is ratified by three-fourths of the states, any procedural provisions in its text are insulated from judicial review, even when the ultimate result is to nullify an amendment that courts would properly deem valid and binding absent the procedural conditions in its text.[49]

But as the exclusive means of giving Congress power to force its procedural views on the courts when it feels it must, this approach is unpromising. It would create a troublesome one-way ratchet: it would allow Congress unreviewably to *impede* the amendment process under Article V (for example, by expressly allowing rescissions and disallowing extensions) but would prevent Congress from *facilitating* the amendment process (for example, by expressly disallowing rescissions and allowing extensions) in any manner that nondeferential judicial review might fail to approve. That result can hardly be a satisfactory solution to a problem the essence of which is to find a way to protect the amendment process from obstruction by the very tribunals whose interpretation of the Constitution an amendment may be designed to overturn. Solving *that* problem plainly demands a posture of judicial deference to congressional provisions that facilitate ratification no less than to provisions that impede ratification. And this posture in turn demands judicial deference to procedural provisions that Congress writes into the *resolutions* by which it proposes amendments for ratification no less than to procedural provisions that Congress inserts into the *texts* of the proposed amendments themselves.

In each case, courts should ask themselves how seriously an adjudication on the merits of a challenge to some aspect of an amendment's ratification or rejection would threaten the unique role of the amendment process—an inquiry that should lead courts to broad deference on procedural as well as substantive aspects of amendment ratification.

In short, remembering that it is an *amendment* to the Constitution we are considering may be almost as important as remembering that it is a *Constitution* we are, in the end, amending and construing—and remembering that, because *neither* process may be emptied of substance or subjectivity, *both* must engage the judiciary in a more candid and collaborative way than the pretense of proceduralism permits.

CHAPTER FOUR

CONSTRUING THE SOUNDS OF CONGRESSIONAL AND CONSTITUTIONAL SILENCE

The temptation to leave my thoughts about silence unspoken has been considerable; as Calvin Coolidge once observed, "I have noticed that nothing I never said ever did me any harm."[1] But the invitation to deliver the Harris Lecture provided an irresistible opportunity to venture certain speculations, tentative though they were, on the elusive and vital topics of congressional and constitutional silence. A decade ago, Reed Dickerson of the Indiana law faculty perceptively addressed a related set of issues in his classic work on statutory interpretation.[2] And four years ago, the Indiana University Press published an elaborate meditation on the nature of silence by Bernard Dauenhauer.[3] As Dauenhauer observed, silence surely is "a rich and complex phenomenon."[4] At times, indeed, silence can be genuinely eloquent—as when the accused stand mute before their tormentors in Arthur Miller's play *The Crucible*,[5] or when civil rights protesters conduct a voiceless vigil in a segregated public library, searing the community's conscience with what the Supreme Court called their "silent and reproachful presence."[6]

The arts of silence and inaction are no strangers to lawmakers. Vermonters recall a tale about Reid Lefevre, one of the giants—literally and figuratively—of the Vermont legislature in the 1960s. Lefevre, nicknamed "King Reid" partly because of his size and partly because of his role in running a traveling small-town circus in the legislative off-season, had a winning argument against docking state legislators' pay for days when they were away from the capitol. "As I look around this chamber," King Reid would say, "it occurs to me that many of our members make their greatest contribution to the legislative process on days when they aren't here."[7]

However right King Reid may have been as a matter of fact, there has been a longstanding resistance, as a matter of law, to the idea that legislative inaction or silence, filtered through a judicial stethoscope, can be made to sound out changes in the law's lyrics—altering the prevailing patterns of rights, powers, or privileges that collectively constitute the message of our laws. I wish to explore first, the nature and sources of that resistance; second, the reasons for the failure of that resistance as reflected in the persistent willingness to hear legal music in the sounds of silence; and, finally, an approach that I believe better reflects both the objections to hearing sounds in legal silence and the necessity of doing just that from time to time—both with respect to the silences of Congress and with respect to what Justice Jackson once called "[the] great silences of the Constitution."[8]

THE RESISTANCE

With the demise of the notion that legislators merely "discover" and "declare" eternal legal truths—and that courts merely apply legal principles that emanate from the "brooding omnipresence" of a background of common law[9]—it would naturally be thought crucial to ground each law's moral force largely in the positive process by which the law came to be. And, under any view of law that thus traces the legitimacy of legislation in significant part to what may be called "due process of lawmaking"[10]—and that regards "legislative determination [as] provid[ing] all the process that is due" when government is "*creat-[ing]* substantive [law]"[11]—legislative omissions necessarily offer no substitute for duly enacted provisions. For insofar as a law's claim to obedience hinges on that law's *promulgation* pursuant to agreed-upon processes for the making of laws, it becomes decisive that those processes do not include *failing* to enact a legal measure.

Under any such approach, it seems axiomatic that the *words* of a statute—and *not* the legislators' intent as such—must be the crucial elements both in the statute's legal force and in its proper interpretation.[12] As Justice Jackson put the matter in his concurrence in *Schwegmann Brothers v. Calvert Distillers Corp.*,[13] since "it is only the words of the bill" that the House and Senate pass and that the President endorses, and since all other materials are outside the enactment process proper and are only haphazardly available to the general public, it seems difficult to justify even giving legal effect to "legislative history."[14]

Thus, as Jackson wrote in another concurrence two years later, the Supreme Court must proceed "by analysis of the *statute* instead of by *psychoanalysis* of Congress."[15] "Never having been a Congressman," Justice Jackson said, he would feel hopelessly "handicapped in that weird endeavor."[16]

If legislative intent is of problematic relevance, legislative inaction—*whatever* intent it might signal—is a fortiori a forbidden source of law. Justice Rutledge, concurring in *Cleveland v. United States*,[17] had no doubt that, "in view of the specific . . . constitutional procedures required for the enactment of legislation," an "action *or nonaction* not taken in accordance with the prescribed procedures," should be given no "legislative effect."[18] For him the "vast differences between legislating by *doing nothing* and legislating by positive enactment" weighed heavily against giving legislative effect to the former.[19] As Justice Frankfurter had written for the Court six years earlier, in *Helvering v. Hallock*,[20] the Court "walk[s] on quicksand when [it tries] to find in the *absence* of . . . legislation a controlling legal principle."[21]

Nor is this resistance to imputing meaning to congressional silence mere post-*Lochner* era mimicry of a classically English and European insistence on just "reading" the enacted law. For the resistance has American roots reaching at least as far back as the landmark case of *Murdock v. Memphis*.[22] Section 25 of the Judiciary Act of 1789 had conferred on the Supreme Court appellate jurisdiction over certain state judgments but expressly excepted those supported by independent state grounds. The 1867 Act of Congress amending the Judiciary Act reenacted Section 25 but omitted the sentence containing that express exception. At issue in *Murdock* was whether Congress' omission to reenact the exception should be treated as de facto enactment of the *opposite* principle—namely, that the Court could exercise jurisdiction over state decisions resting on nonfederal grounds. The Court held that the omission by Congress should not be so treated, noting that it was impossible to tell why various members of Congress had chosen not to reenact the express exception,[23] and stressing that, had Congress intended to do an about-face on such an important subject, it could—and hence should—have said as much "in positive terms; . . . [in] plain, unmistakable language."[24]

If the resistance to according legislative effect to anything short of express enactments thus has old roots, so do the seeds of its failure, for it has long seemed plain that certain kinds of congressional silence simply cannot be ignored. In *Murdock* itself, for instance, although the

Court refused to treat the omission of the last sentence of Section 25 as an *enactment*, it did treat that omission as a *repeal* by implication.[25] How else, after all, could the omission have been viewed? I turn, then, to the failure of the resistance.

THE FAILURE

That the battle to resist giving any effect at all to legislative silence was destined to be a losing one is perhaps best illustrated by the opinions of five justices—including Frankfurter and Jackson—in the 1952 *Steel Seizure* case.[26] That case arose from a major wage dispute between the steel companies and their employees in late 1951, during the Korean War. The union announced a strike to begin April 9, 1952, on the eve of which President Truman told his Secretary of Commerce, Charles Sawyer, that he was going to give him the "dirtiest job" he had ever given anyone—namely, supervising a national takeover of the steel mills.[27]

Truman had considered and rejected five other options: (1) doing nothing and letting the steel mills close, which would interrupt the flow of materials to United States troops in Korea; (2) invoking Section 18 of the Selective Service Act of 1948, which applied only to seizures of plants failing to fill certain defense orders; (3) invoking the condemnation provisions of section 201(b) of the Defense Production Act of 1950, which were slow, cumbersome, and costly; (4) invoking the "cooling-off" provisions of the Taft-Hartley Act of 1947, which risked antagonizing labor and causing wildcat strikes; and (5) trying, with the help of federal contract money, to pressure the steel companies into acceding to the union's wage demands, which risked accelerating inflation and disrupting Congress' price stabilization program.

When Truman instead took the course of having Secretary Sawyer order the steel mills to keep operating—but under the United States flag, prepared to take all future orders from the President—he triggered a now legendary struggle. Fourteen impeachment resolutions were introduced in Congress,[28] and when the steel companies sought an injunction against the Secretary of Commerce in *Youngstown Sheet & Tube Co. v. Sawyer*, the solicitor general refused even to let Sawyer see the government's brief.[29] On June 2, 1952, the Supreme Court held the President's steel seizure an unconstitutional arrogation of legislative authority.[30]

Justice Black's opinion for the majority reasoned that

> the use of the seizure technique to solve labor disputes in order to pre-
> vent work stoppages was not only *unauthorized* by any congressional
> enactment; prior to this controversy, Congress had *refused to adopt* that
> method of settling labor disputes. When the Taft-Hartley Act was un-
> der consideration in 1947, Congress *rejected an amendment* which would
> have authorized such governmental seizures in cases of emergency.[31]

Since "the Constitution is [not] silent" about "who shall make
laws,"[32] Congress' *omission* left the President powerless to act as he did.
Despite what he had said twelve years earlier in *Hallock*, Justice Frankfurter stressed in his concurring opinion that "Congress chose not to
lodge this power in the President."[33] True, Congress could have *forbidden* presidential exercise of the seizure power—something Chief Justice
Vinson, joined by Justices Reed and Minton, stressed that Congress
had *not* done.[34] But to do so explicitly, Justice Frankfurter reasoned,
"would be not merely infelicitous draftsmanship but almost offensive
gaucherie."[35] Justices Burton[36] and Clark[37] evidently agreed—as did
Justice Jackson, who, despite his pronouncements both a year earlier
(in *Schwegmann Brothers*) and a year later (in *United States v. Public Utilities Commission*), found Truman's seizure "incompatible with the . . .
implied will of Congress."[38]

Thus, a decisive majority of five justices treated Congress' silence
as speech—its *nonenactment of authorizing legislation* as a legally binding
expression of *intent to forbid* the seizure at issue.[39] Judges who, *in principle*, resist giving legal effect to Congress' silence thus come out differently when they hear a "negative pregnant" in that silence—and, perhaps, when the public acceptability of their intended holding is
bolstered by the illusion that the power they wield traces to *Congress'*
will rather than to *their own*.

Fostering that illusion is an especially easy temptation in adjudicating "constitutional common law"[40]—those areas of law in which the
Supreme Court imposes on state and local government, or on the federal executive, but a tentative vision of the Constitution's commands—a vision that Congress is left free to override and replace with
its own. In such cases, reading in the "silence of Congress" an indication of *its* "will" represents an attempt by judges to disclaim responsibility for altering the legal landscape by passing the buck to Congress—and thus is, as Clarence Shenton wrote, "an especially palpable
attempt to make it appear that the power exercised by the Supreme

Court proceeds from Congress."[41] Worse still, Congress itself may well conspire in this buck-passing—for, having said nothing, its members are free in turn to point right back to the courts when called upon to defend what the courts claim that Congress has, by its silence, brought to pass.

Such Alphonse-and-Gaston constructions of congressional silence have been frequent in adjudication of one of the Constitution's own most conspicuous silences—the "dormant" Commerce Clause. The *words* of the Commerce Clause say only that "Congress shall have power . . . to regulate Commerce . . . among the several states."[42] But courts have long heard in the very silence those words delimit an implied negative against unduly burdensome or discriminatory state or local interferences with free trade across state lines—even in areas where Congress has not expressly legislated preemptively. In deciding whether to uphold state regulations under this implied limitation, judges have purported to "hear" in congressional silence both tacit veto and tacit consent. In *Leisy v. Hardin*,[43] for example, Justice Fuller wrote for the majority that Congress' silence with respect to an area of interstate commerce—that is, its nonenactment of any law either regulating that area or allowing the states to do so—"indicates its will that such commerce shall be free and untrammelled."[44] The dissenters to that ruling, on the other hand, read in Congress' long "silence and inaction" in the face of judicially sustained state restrictions[45] precisely the opposite will—namely, congressional "inten[t] that the law should remain" as it had been.[46]

Such judicial discovery of ambivalent meanings in Congress' silence was captured with lovely irony by Thomas Reed Powell in a 1938 essay.

[C]ongress has a wonderful power that only judges and lawyers know about. Congress has a power to keep silent. Congress can regulate interstate commerce just by not doing anything about it. Of course when congress keeps silent, it takes an expert to know what it means. But the judges are experts. They say that congress by keeping silent sometimes means that it is keeping silent and sometimes means that it is speaking. If congress keeps silent about the interstate commerce that is not national in character and that may just as well be regulated by the states, then congress is silently silent, and the states may regulate. But if congress keeps silent about the kind of commerce that is national in character and ought to be regulated only by congress, then congress is silently vocal and says that the commerce must be free from state regulation.[47]

Yet *not* to attribute such different meanings to congressional silence risked either imposing an unjustifiably inflexible unitary regime on the states, or leaving the states free to strangle the national economy while Congress slept or attended to other concerns.[48]

Whether inspired by a desire to avoid such doctrinal dead ends, by a wish to disclaim responsibility, or by a realistic appreciation for the necessary indeterminacy of any enacted text, the persistent judicial focus on what Congress might have *wanted*, as revealed by its words *or* its silences, represents a seemingly decisive defeat for the longstanding resistance to giving legislative effect to anything short of positive enactments. As Justice Holmes wrote over half a century ago, "[a] word is not a crystal, transparent and unchanged, it is the skin of a living thought and may vary greatly in color and content according to the circumstances and time in which it is used."[49] From seeing that words—including the words appearing in statutes and constitutions—communicate only in cultural, social, and political context, it has been only a short (if misguided) step to treating what those words say and what they omit as merely *signs* of the ideas and desires that inspired their use—as windows into the thoughts of the time in which they emerged.

Such treatment obviously inverts the positive-enactment view by describing the *words* of a statute—or the gaps in those words—as only "the best evidence of what Congress *wanted*,"[50] making what Congress wanted the very object of our search rather than merely the frame for our understanding of what Congress *said*.[51] In its most extreme form, such treatment subsumes statutes within the common law model, viewing legislative enactments as mere pieces of a legal puzzle—pieces judges may feel free to rearrange as they "discern" that what lawmakers once assumed or wanted has since grown obsolete.[52]

Resistance to giving weight to silence in the understanding of legislative or constitutional messages thus gives way before two overriding temptations: the judicial—indeed, universally human—temptation to pass responsibility on to others by saying one is *describing* their will when one is, in truth, *prescribing* what is to be; and the temptation to look not just to text but to *context*, of which silence—the very *boundary* of speech—is necessarily a part. Indeed, to decree that we must ignore legal silences altogether is no more plausible than to command that we ignore the uncovered parts of a canvas or the pauses in a sonata. As Susan Sontag reminds us, "[t]o look at something which is 'empty' is still to be looking, still to be seeing something—if only the ghosts of one's own expectations . . . Silence remains, inescapably, a form of speech . . . and an element in a dialogue."[53]

THE RESOLUTION

We must therefore reformulate and reduce to more plausible dimensions the resistance to silence as a source of law if the failure of that resistance is to be replaced with even a modest success. Without a more explicit grammar of how silences may and may not operate in the interpretation of law—a syntax of the unsaid—we may *say* that law cannot be made by silence, but the echo will return: "Oh yes it can; just watch!"

In such a grammar, I believe that silences can properly have only two sorts of significance: (a) a significance as *operative legal facts* that is derived not from the internal states of mind that various silences may be thought to manifest, but from external constitutional norms;[54] and (b) a significance as parts of the historical *context* of actual enactments.[55]

Silences as Operative Legal Facts

The search for external criteria to give operative legal effect to congressional silence can profitably begin by revisiting *Youngstown Sheet & Tube Co. v. Sawyer* (the *Steel Seizure* case).[56] Justice Douglas' concurrence in that case rested on an analysis of Congress' silence quite different from that of the justices in the majority who treated Congress' silence as an indication of its *will* that the President be barred from unilaterally seizing national industries.[57] Justice Douglas reasoned:

> The power of the Federal Government to condemn property is well established . . . But there is a duty to pay for all property taken by the Government. The command of the Fifth Amendment is that no "private property be taken for public use, without just compensation." That constitutional requirement has an important bearing on the present case.
>
> The President has no power to raise revenues. That power is in the Congress by Article I, Section 8 of the Constitution. The President might seize and the Congress by subsequent action might ratify the sei-

zure. *But until and unless Congress acted, no condemnation would be lawful.* The branch of government that has the power to *pay compensation* for a seizure is *the only one able to authorize a seizure or make lawful one that the President has effected.* That seems to me to be the necessary result of the condemnation provision in the Fifth Amendment. It squares with the theory of checks and balances expounded by Mr. Justice Black in the opinion of the Court in which I join.[58]

Justice Douglas' theory of *executive*-legislative relations perhaps "squares" with Justice Black's, but the theory of *judicial*-legislative relations Douglas here propounds does not: for Justice Douglas, Congress' silence bars the challenged action by President Truman *not* because it signals a *desire* by Congress that Truman act otherwise, but because the *underlying constitutional rule*, as Douglas would have the Supreme Court announce it, makes the sort of thing Truman did *void absent explicit prior consent by Congress.* In Justice Douglas' view, the executive must not be free to confront Congress with a fait accompli—a situation in which Congress is duty-bound to raise revenues for compensation payments that it might have chosen *not* to raise. In light of that constitutional rule, Congress' silence is a *fact* operating to bar unilateral executive seizure, *not* mere *evidence* that Congress did not want to authorize such seizures, or that it wanted to forbid them.

I would agree with the view I take to be at least implicit in Justice Douglas' opinion—namely, that the guide to the meaning of certain congressional silences is the Constitution itself. Where constitutional clauses—in the *Steel Seizure* case, the Just Compensation Clause read in juxtaposition with the Revenue Raising Clause—require the *consent* of Congress, Congress' *silence* has legal significance as a controlling operative fact.[59] The several clauses providing that only the consent of Congress, or of the Senate, can authorize certain steps—such as a state's entry into an interstate compact[60] or the President's making of a treaty or appointment of a Supreme Court justice[61]—provide paradigmatic examples. Although the Court has at times purported to discern congressional consent under such clauses where such "consent" was at best *implicit*,[62] I would read those clauses to render any congressional silence (or major ambiguity) in these areas a bar to the corresponding state or executive action. And the doctrines developed under the "dormant" Commerce Clause[63] can similarly be recast as constitutional rules that determine when Congress' clear and affirmative authorization is needed for state or local interference in the national market—

and thus when Congress' silence (or ambiguity) must be read not as an acquiescence in, but as a bar to, such interference.

Under this approach to congressional silence, courts cannot properly avoid the necessary first step of articulating and defining the relevant constitutional norm that determines what effect silence as such is to have.[64] In the *Iran Hostage* case,[65] the Court wrongly sidestepped that articulation when it purported to hear a different sound than the *Steel Seizure* Court had heard in a similar congressional silence decades earlier.

Dames & Moore, a private contractor, claimed that Iran's Atomic Energy Organization owed it some $3.5 million for services performed. In December 1979 the contractor sued Iran, the Atomic Energy Organization of Iran, and several Iranian banks in a United States District Court to recover the money. To secure whatever judgment might ultimately be forthcoming, the district court attached some of the bank's property.[66]

The President's Hostage Settlement Agreement[67] nullified all such attachments—all such attempts to tie the assets down—and suspended the underlying claims, relegating them to an Iran-United States claims tribunal in exchange for release of all our hostages the next day. This was not a moment for fainthearted jurists to express misgivings, and few observers could have been genuinely surprised when the Supreme Court unanimously upheld the President's action.[68]

The attachments, according to the Supreme Court, were not really "property" because they had all been executed pursuant to a conditional license issued by the President shortly after the hostages were taken in November 1979. The President had frozen the assets and had said, in effect, that, until further notice, certain attachments were going to be allowed. So the interest anyone subsequently acquired in those attachments was itself subject to what one might call defeasance by the fulfillment of a condition subsequent.[69]

The problem of *preexisting claims* was harder. The suspension of a preexisting claim looked very much like a taking of property. And if it was a taking of property, there would presumably have to be some form of just compensation if, ultimately, there were not enough funds or not a fair enough process in the international claims tribunal to make the claims reasonably whole. As to that risk, the Court said it was premature to worry—because, if and when compensation would be due, there would be time enough for companies like Dames &

Moore to sue the United States in the Court of Claims and collect their money.[70]

But that would present Congress with the very sort of fait accompli that the *Steel Seizure* precedent, in the Douglas version endorsed here, rules out absent explicit prior authorization by Congress: only the branch that *holds the purse strings* may constitutionally trigger action that could *drain the purse.* Congressional silence would thus be a bar to such action.

In *Dames & Moore v. Regan,* however, the Court treated Congress' silence as *non*-silence. Unlike those members of the *Steel Seizure* majority who viewed Congress' failure to enact *explicit* authorization of executive seizure as signalling its intent to forbid such actions, the Court in *Dames* found implicit congressional authorization of executive suspension of claims in three not-quite-applicable pieces of legislation[71]—plus, perhaps, the national mood of celebration. Although the Court recognized the absence of actual congressional authorization, it found Congress had "indicat[ed] acceptance of a broad scope for executive action in circumstances such as those presented in this case."[72]

Purporting to "hear" a different intent in congressional silence in the *Iran Hostage* case than in the *Steel Seizure* case amounted to an attempt to disclaim direct judicial responsibility for the result. The Court might instead have upheld President Carter's action by itself taking responsibility for articulating a different underlying *constitutional* rule that, unlike the one deemed to control the *Steel Seizure* case, left the President free in such circumstances to seize the property at issue first and go to Congress for approval later. Had the Court taken this first step, it would have been required to distinguish the *Steel Seizure* case by explaining why, in its view, the congressional silence in the two cases had *not* a different *sound,* but rather a different *significance* in light of what the Court took to be the governing constitutional norm. Alternatively, if painfully, the Court might have held that the governing norms rendered President Carter's action no more valid, even if more popular, than President Truman's had been. In either event, the outcome would flow from the Court's own reading of the Constitution: the buck would stop with the justices themselves.

Once the Court has defined and defended a constitutional norm that would say no to certain actions unless Congress has actually *legislated* a yes, there must be a heavy burden on anyone seeking to find a yes in Congress' silence on the matter. Only if convinced that due process of lawmaking under the structure created by Article I *permits* Congress to "say" yes without enacting it—a burden I doubt could be met often, if ever—could one properly find actual authorization in silence or, indeed, even in ambivalent speech.

The Supreme Court in effect found such a burden unmet in *Kent v. Dulles*,[73] in which the Court held that the Secretary of State was not authorized to deny passports on the basis of Communist party affiliation. Although claiming not to reach the "question of constitutionality,"[74] the Court in fact held that the sort of liberty the Secretary claimed authority to restrict could not be abridged without at least a clearly enabling exercise of Congress' "law-making functions"[75]—and that such authority could *not* be "*silently* granted by Congress."[76]

In contrast, the Court skirted the burden of showing that such "structural due process" would permit silent lawmaking in *Haig v. Agee*,[77] in which the Court read in Congress' silence implicit approval of executive power to withhold or revoke passports on similarly troublesome grounds. The Court in *Agee* attempted to transform *Kent* from a determination about constitutional authority to a mere effort at mindreading in the face of congressional silence.[78] But *Kent* made sense *only* as a constitutional ruling about the operative significance of the absence of any expressly applicable authorizing statute, *not* as a ruling about Congress' state of mind—for Congress there had actually passed a law that specifically barred passports for Communists; that law simply *had not* "*yet become effective.*"[79]

Finally, it should be noted that Congress may, if engaged in an otherwise valid exercise of its lawmaking power, *itself* confer operative legal significance on future congressional inaction. "Sunset" provisions and one-house vetoes provide two such techniques for fixing in advance norms—here, legislative rather than constitutional—for ascribing meaning to congressional silence. Sunset provisions do so by creating situations in which *inaction* by a future Congress will lead a law to *lapse* when it would otherwise have survived. And the one-house veto technique does so by making the fact of *joint inaction* by both houses for a specified period the *condition precedent* for an agency's action under its delegated authority to become final.[80] Once authority has been delegated in this special way, such inaction by Congress functions *not* as a "sign" of unenacted "intent," but rather as an operative fact giving final effect to an otherwise incomplete exercise of delegated power.

Silence as Historical Context

What Congress has legislated necessarily takes its meaning in part from the context in which Congress chose the words it did, and Congress' silence or inaction may—and sometimes must—be treated as *part* of that context for purposes of faithfully construing contemporaneous and subsequent enactments. Contextual silences that may well be relevant to statutory construction include: (1) Congress' silence respecting extant *decisional law* that had construed the very statutory language Congress has chosen to reenact—a silence which, coupled with reenactment, may be read to imply adoption of that law;[81] and (2) Congress' prior or contemporaneous rejection of proposed *amending language* or other legislation that would have enacted the very interpretation of a statute that a litigant later claims a statute *did* enact.[82]

When and how far to treat such silences as part of the context of any given statute pose questions no different in kind from those presented whenever the historical setting in which a legislature spoke must be described; those questions cannot be answered by recourse to separation-of-powers limits. For, in regarding such silences as contextual, the Court is neither giving legal force to *inaction itself* nor "find[ing] in congressional *silence alone* the adoption of a controlling rule of law."[83] Thus, judicial protest that giving such factors *any* weight involves judicial legislation[84] seems to cry wolf.

Not *all* silences may legitimately be read as part of statutory context, however. In particular, justifying an interpretation of a prior enactment by pointing to what a *subsequent* Congress did *not* enact seems incompatible with our constitutional structure. Although silence contemporary with, or antecedent to, the legislative speech one is construing adheres to and delimits that speech[85]—thus furnishing potentially relevant context—a *later* silence shares no such boundary with that speech. A recent District of Columbia Circuit Court opinion upholding the authority of the Secretary of Labor to fire members of the Department of Labor Review Board at will[86] is guilty of confusing these two kinds of silence: the circuit court read such authority into a 1972 Act of Congress based partly on proposed protection for board members that Congress considered but did not adopt earlier in 1972[87]—which is fine—but *also* partly on proposed protection that Congress declined to adopt *in 1981*[88]—which is unacceptable. And the Supreme Court, despite its own repeated warnings that uses of *post*-enactment history can be dangerous,[89] keeps making just such uses.[90]

In my view, then, our tasks in formulating a syntax for legislative silence are twofold: first, to articulate constitutional rules that give legislative silence or inaction operative legal effect independent of any state of mind that might be thought to lurk behind and thus to explain that silence; and second, to propound practices and principles of statutory construction, consistent with those constitutional rules, that treat prior and contemporary (but not subsequent) silence or inaction as part of the context for construing legislative enactments. No other ways of plumbing such silence appear to me compatible with our constitutional structure of lawmaking and its implicit safeguards for political accountability.

Of course, nothing in the Constitution *says* any of this in so many words. Not even Article I, Section 7, expressly *states* that *only* duly enacted bills may have the force of law, any more than the commerce clause expressly *says* that certain state or local intrusions into the national market are void (while others are valid) when Congress fails to speak. In a sense, then, it is *constitutional* silence, as a necessary part of the constitutional structure,[91] to which we ascribe significance whenever we elaborate norms for construing what Congress has not said.

CONSTITUTIONAL SILENCE

In deciding *how* to give meaning to what Justice Jackson called the "great silences" of the Constitution,[92] the issue is typically how to construe not constitutional silence *alone*, but rather the juxtaposition of constitutional statement in one realm with the *absence* of statement in an adjacent field. Although they have not previously, to my knowledge, been so viewed, two of the Constitution's most enigmatic but crucial provisions—included as the capstones of the Bill of Rights—specifically address how certain constitutional silences, or juxtapositions of silence with statement, are to be read. The Tenth Amendment provides: "The powers not delegated to the United States by the Constitution, nor prohibited by it to the States, are reserved to the States respectively, or to the people."[93]

This amendment, in addressing the powers "*not* delegated," is best understood as an instruction on how to read the Constitution's silences with respect to national governmental authority: on that subject, we are told, "silence" means "prohibition."

But just as statutory amendments may be read against the background context of what they displaced,[94] so constitutional amendments may, and perhaps must, be read against such a context as well.[95] The Tenth Amendment, read in light of its own omission of the language that had been used in the Articles of Confederation—which reserved to the states all national powers "not *expressly* delegated"—appears a less than complete prohibition. The result of *that* reading, indeed, is *McCulloch v. Maryland*[96]—which held that, notwithstanding the absence of *express* constitutional delegation to Congress of power to create a national bank, such a power was *implicitly* delegated by the Constitution, within the meaning of the Tenth Amendment, through the entire edifice of national powers read in conjunction with the Necessary and Proper Clause. In the same tradition, *United States v. Nixon*[97] found in the Constitution's silence respecting executive privilege[98] no prohibition against judicial inference of such a privilege from unenumerated principles with constitutional underpinnings.[99]

In illuminating contrast to the Tenth Amendment, the Ninth Amendment provides: "The enumeration in the Constitution, of certain rights, shall not be construed to deny or disparage others retained by the people."[100] Unlike the Tenth Amendment's direction as to the Constitution's silences bearing on national powers, the Ninth Amendment's instruction is that *rights-related* silences do *not* mean prohibition: they "*shall not* be [so] construed."[101] Silence here is *not* the fence it is under the Tenth Amendment, but an invitation to identify unenumerated rights.[102] Again, the background context helps explain this instruction about silence: Madison introduced the Ninth Amendment as a specific response to the arguments of Hamilton and others that those rights not enumerated in the Bill of Rights would otherwise be given up to the government.[103]

Here, as elsewhere, the rule of construction we articulate in attributing specific meaning to the ninth or any other amendment or constitutional provision will necessarily be both *indeterminate* and *incomplete*. It will be *indeterminate* in that we have had to make choices (as to the role of history, for example) not *themselves* fully specified by the Constitution in deciding *how to construe* the constitutional rule in question. And it will be *incomplete* in that we have emerged with instructions that cannot themselves be *applied* without making still further choices (choices regarding *which* unenumerated rights to recognize, for instance) that the Constitution itself may *constrain* but does not *dictate* in any conclusive way.

Throughout this process, it is crucial that we resist the temptation to treat *either* text *or* silence as mere *evidence* of unenacted *ideas* or *desires* on the part of others: whatever the sources and limits of its moral force, the Constitution—ratified under the processes specified in Articles V and VII—surely does *not* bind us directly to the unmediated "*intentions*" of its framers or ratifiers, any more than we can be bound by the unlegislated "*intentions*" of congressmen.[104]

It is also crucial to observe that the Constitution itself expressly suggests rules of construction such as those of the Ninth and Tenth Amendments—rules that are indeterminate and incomplete but nonetheless powerful—almost exclusively with respect to *omissions* and *silences*, rather than with respect to *statements* as such. At a few points—as with the presidential oath of office in Article II, Section 1, Clause 8—the Constitution specifies by rule the legal significance to be given the official utterance of certain words. Almost always, though, no such specification is provided. For with respect to *words*—whether as included in the Constitution or as enacted by Congress—any adequate rule of construction must, of necessity, reach outside the system in order to incorporate by reference something akin to a community of shared understandings, without which such words could convey no reasonably fixed meaning. But with respect to *silences*—omissions of words in the Constitution or in congressional enactments—reference to such external pointers seems inherently unavailing: as potential carriers of ideas that a speaker may share with an audience, silences resist convincing translation even with the generous aid of all available cultural and social cues to meaning.

Yet silences enjoy a compensating feature: their potential *determinacy*. On any given occasion and with respect to any given subject, after all, there are *many* ways to speak, and much that may be *said*, but only *one* way to *be silent*.[105] The potentially infinite regress of rules of construction—and of *meta*-rules for construing *those* rules[106]—can thus come to a rapid halt when (and perhaps only when) we deal with *silence*—provided we *accept responsibility* for stating explicit rules that specify the legal effects we will deem such silences to have, independent of the shared (or unshared) understandings or intentions those silences might be conjectured to reflect.

Having accepted such responsibility—not by ascribing it passively to what we say the framers or others may have intended or supposed, but by admitting that we are actively proclaiming through the Constitution's language the principles for which *we* believe it stands—not under its compulsion but for reasons we are prepared to defend in the Constitution's terms as best we can—we will have gone as far as legal discourse allows. Beyond that point, we must seek what solace we can from Wittgenstein's reprieve: "Whereof one cannot speak, thereof one must be silent."[107]

II

THE SEPARATION AND DIVISION OF POWERS

CHAPTER FIVE

SILENCING THE ORACLE: CARVING DISFAVORED RIGHTS OUT OF THE JURISDICTION OF FEDERAL COURTS

This essay discusses the recurring barrage of proposals in the early 1980s to curtail the jurisdiction of the federal courts: at least eighteen such proposals were pending in the House of Representatives in June of 1981.[1] Those unfamiliar with the tenor of those never-enacted but often-threatened measures might well conclude that lawyers and legalism had for a time taken over Capitol Hill altogether or perhaps that the nation as a whole had developed an unaccountable fascination with matters that, in more robust times, would have seemed too technical and arcane to be of general concern.

In truth, of course, no interest in the arcana of jurisdiction as such lay behind the proposed bills; their proponents, without exception, fastened on "jurisdiction [only] as a means to an end,"[2] the end being nothing less than the de facto reversal—by means far less burdensome than those required for a constitutional amendment[3]—of several highly controversial Supreme Court rulings dealing with such matters as abortion, school prayer, and busing.

Many will believe, as I do, that these issues are far too complex, their rights and wrongs far too ambiguous, to admit of indignant certitude and unhesitating moral outrage—in either direction. To all who share this view, the potential suitability of the underlying controversies for current resolution through constitutional amendment may seem problematic. Especially if the amendment process is deemed an inappropriate means of inducing and cementing change where, as with abortion, there seems at most a prospect for barely achieving (and not necessarily long retaining) the supermajorities specified by Article V,[4] the notion of a right-to-life amendment to overturn decisions such as *Roe v. Wade*[5] may seem misguided even to someone who regards those decisions as wrong.[6] Whatever one's view on this broad issue, proponents of legislative solutions short of amendments may persuasively urge the folly of too lightly turning to the amendment option—and the corresponding wisdom of choosing legislative reversal of misguided precedents whenever that option is open. But accepting all of that for the sake of argument, it simply does not follow that legislation to restrict the jurisdiction of the Supreme Court, of lower federal courts, or of both, is a defensible response to the rulings that inspired the bills before the House in 1981.

At stake in any such response—particularly if it becomes a more or less common reaction to constitutional rulings that seriously displease a popular majority that finds itself not quite able to overturn them by amendment—is nothing less than the survival of a distinctly American institution, that of review of legislative and executive action by an independent judiciary entrusted to enforce the Constitution. In South Africa, by contrast, section 59(2) of the 1961 Constitution expressly provides that, with very few exceptions, "[n]o court of law shall be competent to enquire into or to pronounce upon the validity of any Act passed upon by Parliament," and some observers point to this exclusion of judicial review as an important part of the reason that South Africa's "Parliament has been able to ride roughshod over individual liberty."[7]

Needless to say, this is not South Africa. But how much of the difference between us might be traced to an independent judiciary? That, no one knows. It has been suggested, though, that the constant presence of an independent judiciary lends an otherwise unavailable legitimacy to Congress, whose enactments might, in the absence of potential review, more readily be mocked as naked expressions of political power. The Supreme Court's very silence, its failure to strike down most of what Congress enacts, thus serves as a tacit sign that *politics has been contained by principle.*

For those who favor judicially unchecked congressional power to define federal court jurisdiction, the argument at this point takes a curious twist. Perhaps Congress shines in the reflected glory of the Court's independence, they say, but it is no less true that the Court—indeed, the federal judiciary as a whole—shines in the reflected glory of Congress' electoral mandate—and does so only because a popularly elected Congress, armed with what such advocates allege to be plenary control over the jurisdiction of all federal courts, lends an otherwise unavailable legitimacy to these unelected tribunals by consenting, through its voluntary inaction, to whatever jurisdiction such courts are able to exercise.[8] Congress' silence, in a word, serves as a second tacit sign, a sign that *principle has been embraced by politics.* Eliminate Congress' plenary control over the jurisdiction of the federal judiciary, we are told, and the embrace is broken, the judiciary's legitimacy shaken, the entire structure jeopardized.[9]

But surely the proponents of that view have pushed their point too far. For one thing, the argument just summarized would imply that *no* congressional control of jurisdiction could safely be struck down; but I have yet to meet the advocate of sweeping congressional power who would not concede at least that an Act of Congress denying federal jurisdiction where blacks sue whites or where Catholics sue Protestants would be, and ought to be, held flatly unconstitutional. Beyond that, whatever one might believe about the legitimating effect on the judiciary of a congressionally wielded, if mythical, Sword of Damocles that hangs, but does not fall, over every federal judge's head, it is another matter entirely to suggest that the legitimacy of *either* branch would be enhanced were the sword indeed to fall and the Supreme Court to take the blow lying down. How much legitimacy could Congress possibly derive from the approval of a Court so supine? Can the puppet master truly bask in the approval of a mere puppet? And how much democracy could possibly rub off on the Court from a Congress that, merely by couching its laws in jurisdictional terms, could rewrite virtually all the rules at will and unreviewably decree what "democracy" really means? On the contrary, if a mythical Sword of Damocles is to work at all, it must continue to be held high— and never truly tested by being allowed to drop as it would if the bills under consideration in the early 1980s were to pass.

There is a suggestive parallel in the case of Richard Nixon, who sought to show his allegiance to principle, and thereby to shore up his faltering legitimacy, by visibly binding his fate to the work of an "independent" special prosecutor, who derived a considerable part of *his* legitimacy, in turn, from being ultimately answerable to an elected President. So far so good. But the moment the sword fell, and the President asserted his authority by selectively withholding evidence that the prosecutor sought to use, the spell was broken and the President, unprotected even by his electoral mandate, ended up falling on the sword himself—so exposed had his ploy left him to judicial defeat.[10] Congress would repeat Mr. Nixon's mistake were it to forget that the awesome power some think it has so long held in reserve over the

Court could, if unleashed, turn against Congress itself. True, the Court's own role in causing such a turnabout would be more difficult than in the *Nixon* case, since the Court would on this occasion find itself arrayed against both of the other branches and would, to make matters even worse, be attempting to maintain its own power.[11] But, at all events, if the constitutional infirmities in the proposed enactments are indeed as glaring and extreme as I believe they are, then the Court can hardly shrink from so holding—and the legitimating efficacy of Congress' supposed jurisdiction-checking power becomes questionable indeed.

In the first instance, of course, Congress itself must assess the constitutionality of those enactments; its oath to uphold the Constitution requires no less. But under our system it has become axiomatic that the authoritative constitutional verdict will be that of a court—ultimately the Supreme Court—when a case posing the issue is properly presented.[12] One might take the view that no such case could *be* properly presented because jurisdiction-restricting laws just lift things out of the judicial system all by themselves. To take that view, though, would be to cede literally boundless power to Congress—and to forget the way a federal court, almost of necessity, operates.

A litigant before such a court urges dismissal of the case, or denial of a remedy, on the basis of a statute limiting or eliminating jurisdiction; the court then looks at the statute—it has jurisdiction, everyone seems to agree, to do at least that.[13] And when the court looks, it necessarily sees not only the statute but, standing behind it, the Constitution: that is what the supremacy of the Constitution has come to mean.[14] So the court must decide whether the statute is valid in light of whatever the Constitution seems to say on the subject. Much of what the Constitution has to say will not be terribly explicit—but that's nothing new. "The tacit postulates" of the constitutional plan, Justice Rehnquist and Chief Justice Burger reminded us in 1979, "are as much engrained in the fabric of the document as its express provisions."[15]

As Congress and the courts assess proposed congressional controls over federal jurisdiction, the relevant "express provisions" and "tacit postulates" they encounter will fall into two categories. First, there will be *internal limits* set by the nature and sources of the power Congress is exercising when it attempts to define the jurisdiction of a federal court. What Congress seeks to do in the name of such power may simply be outside the authority granted. Second, there will be *ex-*

ternal limits set by the constitutional terrain Congress has chosen (or happened) to traverse. Depending upon how the authority granted to Congress is deployed, its use may conflict with a right or prohibition that constrains *all* federal legislation, however amply "authorized."

INTERNAL LIMITS

The Substantive Role That the Constitution Assigns to the Supreme Court

Unlike the "inferior courts"—which exist only insofar "as the Congress may from time to time ordain and establish" them under Article III[16]—the Supreme Court owes its being to the Constitution itself: "The Judicial Power of the United States," Article III proclaims, "shall be vested in one supreme Court"; "shall extend" to the categories of cases and controversies enumerated in Section 2 of Article III; shall "origina[te]" in that Court, as a forum for initial trial, "[i]n all Cases affecting Ambassadors, other public Ministers and Consuls, and those in which a State shall be Party"; and shall, in all other cases within Article III, fall within an "appellate Jurisdiction, both as to Law and Fact, with such Exceptions, and under such Regulations as the Congress shall make."

While Congress may do nothing to restrict or expand the Supreme Court's original jurisdiction,[17] the Exceptions and Regulations Clause has generally been thought to contain few if any internal limitations governing congressional control over the Court's appellate jurisdiction.[18] Yet the text at least suggests that a total abolition of appellate jurisdiction would be impermissible; in particular, the reference to exceptions and regulations indicates that something substantial is to remain after Congress' subtractions have been performed. Moreover, vague though the standard may be, a strong argument may be made that exceptions and regulations in this context are void to the degree that they leave the Supreme Court incapable of fulfilling its "essential role . . . in the constitutional plan"[19]—the role of vindicating the supremacy of federal over state law (and of the Constitution over other sources of federal law) and the uniformity of such federal law as exists.[20]

Because all but two[21] of the bills pending in the House in 1981 sought to carve out of the Court's appellate jurisdiction a range of questions encompassing major constitutional issues and to simultaneously extract those questions or controversies from the inferior federal courts,[22] the upshot would be *no* judicial forum capable of assuring either the supremacy *or* the uniformity of entire bodies of federal law, a result that must be condemned as unconstitutional if the Court's basic role is believed to be constitutionally assured.[23]

Article III's Implicit Concept of "the Judicial Power"

The power envisioned in Article III is the power to "decide . . . [cases] conformably to the law, [including] the constitution . . . This is of the very essence of judicial duty."[24] This implies, in turn, that Congress cannot blind an Article III court to a relevant constitutional issue or provision—or, indeed, to any relevant proposition of federal law— nor can Congress replace what the court sees in the legal landscape before it with a picture more to Congress' liking.[25] Most important, Article III courts cannot be forced to "close their eyes on the constitution, and see only [Congress'] law."[26]

Yet just such a requirement would be imposed by H.R. 2365 (Evans), which purports to strip all federal courts of jurisdiction over questions going to the validity of statutes that discriminate by gender in military registration, induction, training, or service. Whatever its other vices,[27] the fatal flaw in H.R. 2365 viewed from the perspective of Article III is that it leaves federal courts in the impossible position of having to decide cases in which such statutes as the Military Selective Service Act are relevant—cases in which such statutes may indeed be the only sources of authority for the action those courts are being asked to take[28]—but to do so while "clos[ing] their eyes on [at least part of] the constitution." This an Article III court cannot do: authorized to decide a case, it must decide the case constitutionally—or not at all.[29]

Beyond this internal requirement of completeness, Article III imposes a further requirement of efficacy. For Article III courts are charged to resolve only actual cases or controversies, as opposed to offering mere "opinions in the nature of [legal] advice."[30] To "constitute a proper 'controversy,' " an "asserti[on] [of] a right [must be] susceptible of judicial enforcement."[31] It follows that Congress may not so truncate the jurisdiction of an Article III court as to empower it to "decide" a legal controversy while denying it any means to effectuate its decision, whether by issuing an appropriate command or by rendering a judgment that in itself alters the concrete legal relationship of the parties and the options open to them.[32] Congress' broad authority to regulate the panoply of available remedies, in other words, stops short of the power to reduce an Article III court to a disarmed, disembodied oracle of the law lacking all capacity to give tangible meaning to its decisions.[33]

Thus, for example, H.R. 73 (Ashbrook) and H.R. 900 (Hyde), both of which would deprive all lower Article III courts of authority to issue any restraining order or injunction in any case arising out of a state law restricting abortions or abortion funding, seems inconsistent with the efficacy requirement of Article III.[34] For what is a federal court to *do* under these provisions if a woman proves, in a suit properly filed under the Civil Rights Act of 1871 (now 42 U.S.C. § 1983), that she has been subjected to arrest, to repeated interrogation, and to threats of prosecution by defendant state and local officers solely because she has made attempts to arrange for an abortion in the exercise of her rights under *Roe v. Wade?*[35] Suppose she shows further that her efforts to obtain preventive relief from the state courts have been and are likely to remain unavailing[36]—perhaps because those courts have (mistakenly) supposed that Congress, by "defining" fetuses as persons,[37] could overturn *Roe v. Wade* without a constitutional amendment.[38] If the court concludes, as I believe it should, that the woman is entitled to prevail, that court can hardly be satisfied merely to mail her a congratulatory postcard. Yet H.R. 73 and other similar bills[39] leave the court with nothing more effectual to offer. It follows that the court should hold the remedy-withdrawing provision of H.R. 73 invalid: "[For] Congress . . . to confer . . . jurisdiction and at the same time nullify entirely the effects of its exercise are not matters heretofore thought, when squarely faced, within its authority."[40]

Similarly, H.R. 1079 (Hinson) and H.R. 1180 (Ashbrook) purport to strip all Article III courts of jurisdiction to "require the attendance at a particular school of any student because of race, color, creed, or sex," even if such courts determine that no other decree could give effect to their constitutional determinations. Such a restriction violates the requirement that decisions made by Article III tribunals not be doomed to futility from the start.[41]

The same may be said of H.R. 114 (Bennett), which seeks to strip all lower federal courts of jurisdiction directly or indirectly to "modify" any state court order that could have been or could still be reviewed by the state's highest judicial body. No matter that the order may be directly relevant to a case properly before a federal court, that the court may have found both the order and the state's avenues for its modification constitutionally defective, and that only a decision by the federal court operating directly upon that order could vindicate a claim of right inseparable from the case as a whole—even so, says H.R. 114, the order is inviolate. Article III does not permit such evisceration of a federal judicial tribunal.

EXTERNAL LIMITS: THE SUBSTANTIVE RESTRAINTS IMPOSED BY THE CONSTITUTION

The Supreme Court has observed that "[t]he Constitution is filled with provisions that grant Congress or the States specific power to legislate in certain areas; these granted powers are *always* subject to the limitation that they may not be exercised in a way that violates other specific provisions of the Constitution."[42]

Nothing in the text, history, or structure of the Constitution remotely suggests that Congress' power over Article III jurisdiction should differ in this respect—that invocation of such power should magically give Congress a free ride through the rest of the document. If such magic were available, Congress could "sanction the achievement . . . of any impairment of . . . rights whatever so long as it was cloaked in the garb of the realignment of [jurisdiction]."[43] Federal damage actions could be made available to whites only; injunctions against censorship could be limited to those who publish from a federally approved list. The possibilities are endless. The framers cannot lightly be charged with having left open a clear path to such total obliteration of the constitutional enterprise.

Fortunately, such precedent as exists acquits the framers of so gross a blunder. The Supreme Court in *United States v. Klein*[44] struck down an attempt by Congress to withhold the Court's jurisdiction where the congressional act in question, in the Court's view, abridged the President's power under Article II, Section 2, to grant reprieves and pardons for federal offenses. And in the one relevant, full-dress federal appellate consideration of the question since *Klein*, the Second Circuit Court of Appeals concluded[45]

> that the exercise by Congress of its control over jurisdiction is subject to compliance with at least the requirements of the Fifth Amendment.

That is to say, while Congress has the undoubted power to give, withhold, and restrict the jurisdiction of courts other than the Supreme Court, it must not so exercise that power as to deprive any person of life, liberty or property without due process of law, or to take private property without just compensation.

Unhappily, the proposition that these external limits do not simply evaporate the moment jurisdiction-curtailing power is invoked—however obvious and even undeniable in theory—fares considerably less well in practice. Many who initially concede the point proceed to talk as though it had little or no bite—beyond condemning rules that entirely close a federal court's doors for all purposes to members of a racial minority, perhaps, or to all who have ever exercised a specific constitutional right.[46] As we shall see, though, subtler but no less effective devices for manipulating jurisdiction can abridge independently secured rights in ways that may be shown to be unconstitutional under well-settled principles.

Impermissible Burdens on Constitutional Rights

The Supreme Court recognized decades ago that constitutional rights would be unacceptably jeopardized not only if laws could be enacted directly forbidding or penalizing their exercise, but also if laws could be enacted making their exercise the occasion for withholding or withdrawing benefits or privileges that would otherwise have been available.[47] It is immaterial that the benefits might have been abolished altogether; the point is that, having been provided generally, such benefits may not be withdrawn simply because the designated rights have been, or are being, exercised.[48] Nor is it decisive that the benefits are withdrawn only briefly and narrowly; the Constitution forbids their withdrawal whenever it may cause significant hardship.[49] Finally, there need be no showing that the rule withdrawing the benefit is in fact designed to discourage or to penalize exercise of the right. To the extent the withdrawal *has* any such purpose, it is *per se* unconstitutional.[50] But it bears emphasis that *intent to deter or penalize exercise of a right need not be shown;*[51] even inadvertent burdens on such exercise are unconstitutional unless the rule causing them is proven necessary to the attainment of a compelling objective—one unrelated to the prevention of the right's exercise, and one with respect to which the burdens in question are neither over- nor under-inclusive.[52]

The Removal of Government Protection

The kind and degree of protection various rights are to receive—the combination of executive and judicial enforcement authority to be conferred—is left largely to the political judgment of the responsible legislature.[53] Although respectable arguments might be made that, in modern circumstances, "the right of every individual to claim the protection of the laws, whenever he receives an injury,"[54] entails a congressional obligation to "ordain and establish" lower federal courts in sufficient numbers and with sufficient powers to protect constitutional rights against hostile state and local action,[55] that is by no means the conventional view, and I will not assume it here. Even so, however, access to any form of judicial relief at least shares with the franchise the characteristic that, if it is to be provided at all, it must be provided evenhandedly; it "cannot be granted to some litigants and capriciously or arbitrarily denied to others without violating the Equal Protection Clause"[56] or its equivalent under the Fifth Amendment.[57]

But far more than asymmetry or inequality is at stake when Congress effectively protects some rights while handing only a paper shield to the rights it disfavors. That a state may not structure its programs of benefits so as to deter or penalize the exercise of protected rights without compelling justification[58] is the rule even though it may be exceedingly difficult in particular cases to decide whether a program really does have such a forbidden effect or structure.[59] But when Congress decides to withdraw federal protection *as such* from some rights and not others, that withdrawal directly invites hostile state and private action against those who exercise the rights thereby abandoned.[60] The distinction between skewed incentives and any such invitation comes down to the difference, for example, between (1) temporarily withholding a benefit from migrants who arrive in a new state (whether such a rule really deters or penalizes is a question requiring subtle choices and comparisons), and (2) announcing to the receiving state that those who maraud against newcomers will not be prosecuted. That sort of announcement does not just tip the scale against the exercise of a right; it virtually offers a bounty to those who would subject the right to attack.

Consider, for example, the legal machinery enacted shortly after the Civil War to supplement all available state remedies with both criminal[61] and civil[62] federal mechanisms to defend Fourteenth Amendment rights from assault under color of state or local law. Withdrawing any significant part of such federal protection from a list of disfavored rights would have to be regarded, on its face, as encouraging hostile action toward such rights by state and local officials—rather like declaring "open season" on the rights thereby blacklisted.[63] If even a mere "omission to protect" may at times amount to "denying . . . equal protection,"[64] then this sort of targeted abandonment must be both such a denial and a severe impingement upon the rights thus placed beyond the shield of federal protection. With respect to some rights, *post hoc* remedies, through actions for money damages, might be both necessary and sufficient for meaningful protection;[65] with respect to other rights, the only meaningful relief might be an injunction before the fact.[66] Unless Congress is merely replacing one remedial structure with another that is as protective of the constitutional right at stake,[67] withdrawing a basic civil or criminal line of defense from such a right is tantamount to authorizing its deprivation. Courts would have to scrutinize such authorizations strictly—and would probably invalidate them.[68]

This is not to say that Congress is necessarily compelled to provide federal protection for Fourteenth Amendment rights. If Congress were to withdraw the federal shield altogether or nearly so, repealing large segments of the corpus of civil or criminal law[69] that Congress had previously erected upon Section 8 of Article I and Section 5 of the Fourteenth Amendment, it seems unlikely that the resulting jeopardy to any given right would be as great as in the case where specific rights were singled out for special sacrifice. At least the task of finding a well-fitting justification (other than the forbidden one of stamping out disfavored rights) would be eased if so broad a change were to be enacted. Thus wholesale repeal, even under strict scrutiny, would not necessarily be invalidated. It is *selective* repeal that sends a clear signal to hostile state and local officials[70] and makes far more difficult the task of finding a neutral, close-fitting justification. And in the search for such a justification, it does not matter whether Congress has proceeded by exercising control over the executive branch, over the judicial branch, or over both; the external limits on Congress' treatment of rights are the same in each case.

It is irrelevant that Congress' power to create "exceptions" to the Supreme Court's appellate jurisdiction is spelled out in so many words, while its power to create gaps in federal criminal or civil protection is

but an inescapable inference from the breadth of the authority conferred on Congress by Article I, Section 8, and by the Fourteenth
Amendment, Section 5. Such specificity does not even show that
Congress' affirmative authority to fashion exception-riddled protection is greater in the sphere of federal court jurisdiction than in any
other. And it certainly does not show that Congress' authority to take
these steps *in a way that threatens independent rights* is somehow enhanced when the vehicle Congress employs is that of carving up federal judicial power in particular. In short, the vice of slicing disfavored
rights out of a significant federal shield of protection, executive or judicial or both, is *not* that the power of Congress to construct such a
shield encompasses no power to enact exclusions. *The vice is that the
power to construct, coupled with the power to exclude, together confer no license to destroy.*

In another context, Justice Rutledge put it this way: "No logic but
one which nullifies the historic foundations of the [Fourteenth]
Amendment . . . could support [its] emasculation . . . [through the]
hack work [of] cutting out some of the great rights the Amendment se-
cures but leaving in others."[71]

The 1981 Proposals.

The work of which Justice Rutledge spoke was done with a dull
(but conspicuously single-edged) knife in designing the several jurisdictional provisions for abortion—H.R. 73 (Ashbrook), H.R. 867
(Crane), H.R. 900, section 2 (Hyde), and H.R. 3225 (Mazzoli). All but
H.R. 867 leave the Supreme Court's jurisdiction intact but deprive
lower federal courts of jurisdiction to award preventive relief—not in
all abortion-related controversies, but only where preventive relief is
sought in a case involving any state law or municipal ordinance that
prohibits or restricts abortions or the provision of public funding or other assistance for abortions. So not only are Article III courts told that,
if they rule for the woman, they can provide no timely relief;[72] the
courts and all interested parties are also told that, although the woman can obtain no relief, a representative of the fetus, invoking the
state's duty of equal protection to the unborn as a "person,"[73] can invoke these courts' injunctive jurisdiction to halt state aid for abortion
clinics or for poor women seeking abortions—and presumably also to
end the practice, invidiously discriminatory if fetuses are to be deemed
"persons," of letting people kill them with impunity.[74]

The net result is that these bills not only proclaim, to hostile local and state agents, that women seeking to assert their rights under *Roe v. Wade* are fair game—and thus effectively invite suppression of their rights—but also seek to enlist the aid of federal courts in *pressuring* states and municipalities to *accept* the invitation—much of this, evidently, in the name of states' rights! One can only describe this entire set-up as a joint state-federal antiabortion venture, one whose sole effects—I will leave it to others to supply "neutral" motives—would be to undermine *Roe v. Wade*, and then to go even further by pushing state laws toward a uniform national position banning as homicide everything from morning-after pills, to IUDs, to abortions that are needed to prevent severe, permanent injuries to thirteen-year-old girls who have been incestuously raped. As in *Klein*[75] and *Battaglia*,[76] any court could see the substance through the tissue-thin jurisdictional veneer of such measures and would strike the provisions down as long as *Roe v. Wade* was still on the books.[77]

It is edifying to observe what happens to legal efforts of this type when their proponents try to broaden the focus—in response, I would guess, to fears that nothing so targeted toward, and tilted against, a specific right could pass for an honest piece of jurisdictional handiwork, and that nothing could more blatantly "withhold . . . jurisdiction [only] as a means to an end."[78] What happens, it seems, is that somebody digs a constitutional crater so wide that one wonders whether anybody is really reading these bills with any care. To be specific, H.R. 867 (Crane) would cut out of all federal courts all cases arising out of any state or local law "which relates to abortion." I suppose this means that no federal court could hear a challenge to a state law requiring "defective" fetuses to be aborted whenever three doctors insist—if H.R. 867 were the law. Or how about a challenge to religious and political discrimination in chronic disease benefits under a state statute which, as it happens, "relates to abortion" because that is one of the things the statute also covers? It looks like H.R. 867 would have to kick that one out of all federal courts, too. Would such results be avoidable through proof that they were not intended? I doubt it: jurisdictional statutes are the last to be read in a woolly-headed, "spirit-of-the author" sort of way; jurisdiction is supposed to be clear-cut, mechanical, yes-or-no—not the occasion for a separate lawsuit or for a session with tea leaves.

Although the sweep of H.R. 867 may help a bit in the search for a neutral, well-fitting justification, one suspects that such a justification will be as shallow as it is neutral when viewed in light of the bill's bizarre inroads on federal jurisdiction as a whole. So the broader question posed is: to what extent can jurisdictional excisions be saved by the strategy of embedding them in major excavations? The next section points toward an answer.

Facially "Neutral" Jurisdictional Withdrawals: The Role of Impact and Intent

In *Hunter v. Erickson*,[79] a city charter amendment prevented the city council from "implementing any ordinance dealing with racial, religious, or ancestral discrimination in housing without the approval of the majority of the [city's] voters."[80] On its face, the amendment drew no distinctions among racial and religious groups, subjecting "Negroes and whites, Jews and Catholics . . . to the same requirements if there is housing discrimination against them which they wish to end."[81] Yet, despite this appearance of neutrality, in which "the law on its face treats Negro and white, Jew and gentile in an identical manner,"[82] the Supreme Court had no hesitation in recognizing "the reality . . . that the law's *impact* falls on the minority."[83] Why did impact alone suffice to trigger strict (hence, fatal) scrutiny even here, in a case about racial minorities? It may just have been the year: the heyday of the intent requirement[84] still lay a half-decade ahead. But I think the reason was in part the right at stake: this was not just a raw deal for minorities in housing or in some other sector—it was an obstacle to fair access to the levers of change and vindication; at stake was the right to invoke legal and governmental process in one's favor.[85] As we saw earlier,[86] one need not show *intent* to deter or penalize exercise of a right so long as one can show that a law's *effect* is to withhold ordinary levels of protection with respect to that right. In *Hunter*, that was the law's precise effect—and its fatal defect.

With this in mind, it should not be too difficult to unlock whatever mystery the "voluntary prayer" proposals[87] might still contain. With minor variations, all of them purport to strip all federal courts of jurisdiction over all cases arising out of any state or local law or rule which "relates to voluntary prayer" in public schools and buildings. Of course, a public school regulation providing a five-minute prayer every morning at the start of school, excusing only those children whose parents have personally asked for exemption, and proclaiming the entire package to be "voluntary," would "relate to" voluntary prayer. So would a rule saying that Protestants and Catholics can pray in empty public buildings at night, but not Jews. So would a law forbidding prisoners to pray—voluntarily—in jail. All these cases are beyond the reach of any federal court, if any of the proposed bills are enacted.

All of them, taken at their broad face value, appear to violate Article III in their impact on the Supreme Court,[88] and almost certainly violate the First Amendment's religion clauses as a whole—since they remove altogether the federal shield around all rights involved with prayer, by anybody's definition a central religious expression and experience. In the absence of a really convincing reason to pick this category in particular for a total transplant to the state judiciary—a convincing reason that does not relate to loosening the hold of the First Amendment in this area, but nonetheless snugly fits the category chosen—I would have to say these laws are doomed to collapse.

But even if their breadth would prop them up were we to look no further, we must still ask whether the *impact* of these laws would fall with special force on some narrower right—or, alternatively, whether these laws are *intended* to achieve a narrower and less defensible goal. I would guess that everyone knows what these laws are for and how they are likeliest to be invoked: freeing public schools to hold official but "voluntary" prayer sessions, in violation of decisions like *Abington School District v. Schempp*[89] and *Engel v. Vitale*.[90] Four of the bills come right out and say so in their preambles;[91] they are offered as measures to limit federal jurisdiction "to enter any judgment, decree, or order, denying or restricting as unconstitutional, voluntary prayer in any public school." I would imagine neither impact nor intent would confound too many judges here—the bills would be held void under both the First Amendment's Establishment Clause and the Due Process Clause of the Fifth Amendment.

For reasons too similar to warrant extended analysis, the surface neutrality of the bans on race-specific pupil assignments in H.R. 1079 and 1180, both discussed above under "Article III's Implicit Concept of 'the Judicial Power,'" would probably yield to an assessment of the *Hunter v. Erickson* form and would then be struck down under the Fifth Amendment. But H.R. 869 (Crane) is worth pausing over, at least briefly. It goes much further than the others: it would remove from all federal courts all jurisdiction over any case arising out of any state law or rule "which *relates to* assigning or requiring any public school student to attend a particular school because of his race, creed, color, or sex."[92] Back in the 1950s there was a rule "relating" to that very subject in Topeka, Kansas—a rule which required black and white children to attend separate (but, of course,"equal") schools because of their race. As everyone knows, that rule was struck down in *Brown v. Board of Education*.[93] But H.R. 869, if enacted and upheld, would have deprived the Supreme Court and all lower federal courts of jurisdiction in *Brown*—and in most of the school segregation decisions since 1954. So, for the reasons already developed with respect to H.R. 72 on school prayer, I believe H.R. 869, in addition to violating Article III, would violate the Due Process Clause of the Fifth Amendment.

In all of these cases, I believe an analysis of the text, structure, and impact of the jurisdictional provision suffices to require its invalidation, with forbidden *intent* furnishing useful but not indispensable clues. But if others think the analysis flawed without the introduction of intent, they would have to confront the issue to be considered next.

CONGRESS' RESPONSIBILITY

Congress' duty to comply with the Constitution's mandates derives not solely from the risk that courts may otherwise strike down Congress' enactments, but from the oath in Article VI binding every member of Congress "to support this Constitution." Whatever a court might say as to some of the measures analyzed in this chapter,[94] the members of Congress surely can have no doubt that all jurisdictional restrictions of the sort that were pending before them in 1981 are designed, obviously and transparently, to circumvent constitutional rulings of the Supreme Court by a method markedly less onerous than the amendment procedure set forth in Article V. Doubtless aware of this forbidden aim, Congress should regard itself as duty-bound to reject the pending measures—whatever its predictions as to how a court might rule on each of them.

Especially pernicious would be a congressional decision to limit jurisdiction in the hope that federal judges, frightened by Congress' jurisdictional assault and fearful of even more serious attacks to follow, would either be cowed into (erroneously) upholding unconstitutional limits on their own jurisdiction or pressured into (hypocritically) reversing the decisions—on such issues as abortion, busing, prayer, and the like—that provoked the public's dissatisfaction and its spasms of legislative rebuke to the courts. It is to be hoped that Congress will never permit any such calculus to corrupt its decisions in this area.

Congress could, of course, decide to enact jurisdictional limitations it believed unconstitutional, fully expecting that the Supreme Court or another federal court would promptly strike the limitations down. Such a decision too would be completely irresponsible. In taking it, Congress would presumably be motivated by a wish to curry favor with some constituents while passing the buck for constitutional enforcement to the federal judiciary—which could then be dramatically denounced, in feigned surprise and with calculated political effect, for undemocratic elitism, judicial imperialism, and arrogant hyperactivity. But whatever Congress' motive for enacting legislation that it knows (or ought to know) is unconstitutional, and whatever the eventual reaction of the federal courts, the cost of such cynical manipulation of our most fundamental and unifying body of law—the cost in reduced credibility for already wounded institutions and in diminished power for already weakened sources of normative guidance—is bound to be far too high to make the gambit worthwhile.

THE DELICATE TASK OF ADJUSTING
CONSTITUTIONAL PRINCIPLE WITHIN
THE FEDERAL STRUCTURE

Even if doing so would be entirely constitutional, redrawing the boundaries of federal court jurisdiction along deliberately outcome-determinative lines should be done only with the greatest caution and the clearest possible showing of need and efficacy. Even on the most optimistic of assumptions, state courts—recognizing themselves to be bound by the Constitution and constrained to follow the Supreme Court's authoritative decisions construing it—would simply replicate the very rulings that had inspired Congress' jurisdictional restructuring, thereby freezing the law until fact patterns clearly beyond the Supreme Court's precedents come along to melt the ice and replace it with a churning chaos—of fifty states moving in fifty different directions in their understanding and extension of the governing constitutional norms. That would, in turn, destroy the uniformity that is so crucial on matters supposedly governed not by fifty distinct bodies of state law but by a single constitutional rule. Unless such diversity is secretly sought—even in dealing with the one document that, above all others, binds the nation into a legal whole—as a way of revising constitutional rulings that some dislike but cannot muster enough support to overturn by amending the Constitution itself, its virtue is difficult to fathom.

After all, the Supreme Court has found it intolerable for federal constitutional restraints even on matters as localized as police interrogation to vary from state to state.[95] Is it not even less tolerable for a person's ability to vindicate a right under the First Amendment's Religion Clauses, or under the Fifth Amendment's Due Process Clause, to vary with geography? If there is any question on which ours must be not fifty laboratories but truly "one nation, indivisible," that question is the fundamental meaning of the genuinely constitutive features of our polity—the provisions that make ours an open society aspiring to equal justice under law.

It is true, of course, that the specific requirements of equal justice under law, and the correct construction of the several constitutional provisions that combine to express those requirements, are not self-evidently (or, often, even incontrovertibly) etched into the Constitution. And it is true that some people's convictions about what the Constitution demands in such matters, and what it places beyond the reach of ordinary majorities, will necessarily seem deeply misguided to others. It is inevitable, therefore, that much of what *any* group of judges—or of lawmakers—would have to say to us about these issues (including what they would have to say about the existence of consensus or conflict on such issues, and about the constitutional significance of such consensus or conflict as may exist) would seem wrong, would make some of us wish we had not asked the question (or at least had not heard the answer). And it is probably inevitable too that, whenever this happens, a lot of us—lacking enough votes, under our own rules, to *rewrite the message* (or to redraw the boundary within which the decoding of the message will be entrusted to judges)—would be tempted to *silence the medium*.[96]

It's an old story. Remember the kings in children's fables who used to cut out the tongues of messengers who bore bad tidings or put out the eyes of oracles who saw things the kings wanted to deny? That kind of reaction is understandable—too understandable, I think, to be dismissed with the derision or contempt it sometimes occasions. But however understandable, the reaction is also dangerous and flatly un-constitutional—too plainly unconstitutional to be even arguably le-gitimate, and in any event much too dangerous to be worth trying. If we permit ourselves shortcuts of this sort—preferring legislatively de-creed silence or linguistic legerdemain[97] to the hard substantive strug-gle that amendment battles are properly all about—the Constitution's soaring guarantees will soon ring hollow indeed, sounding "only a promise to the ear to be broken to the hope, a teasing illusion like a munificent bequest in a pauper's will."[98]

CHAPTER SIX

ENTRUSTING NON-LEGISLATIVE POWER TO CONGRESS

THE JUDICIARY'S RENEWED ASSERTION OF STRUCTURAL CHECKS ON CONGRESSIONAL INNOVATION

At least since 1976, the Supreme Court has been anything but receptive to Congress' more innovative assertions of authority. Three major decisions, especially the legislative veto case, *INS v. Chadha*,[1] have undermined Congress' assertions of control on separation of powers and/or federalism grounds. The first two of those decisions—*Buckley v. Valeo*,[2] dealing with the Appointments Clause, and *National League of Cities v. Usery*,[3] dealing with state sovereignty—appear thus far to have been signposts to nowhere in particular.

Buckley v. Valeo, to be sure, triggered renewed caution within the Justice Department and in Congress lest proposed statutes confer on officials appointed by Congress rather than the federal executive in accord with Article II, Section 2, Clause 2, "significant authority pursuant to the laws of the United States."[4] But *Buckley* has had no acknowledged judicial offspring. Indeed, the case seems to have been essentially ignored in *Chadha*, the one recent decision that may be partially understood as an application of *Buckley's* teaching about who may exercise authority pursuant to federal statutes. *Buckley* appears in *Chadha* only as a vague symbol that separation-of-powers concerns are to be taken seriously.[5]

Unlike *Buckley*, *National League of Cities* has been noted in an impressive array of Supreme Court opinions. But all such subsequent decisions have thus far distinguished, rather than followed, *National League of Cities* itself.[6] Indeed, on at least one important occasion when *National League of Cities* seemed directly pertinent, the Court overlooked that precedent altogether.[7]

Of course, it is too early to say whether *Chadha*, the third in the trio of cases imposing new structural limits on Congress, will similarly prove to be less a fount of legal development than one more episodic judicial outburst against the pragmatic accommodations of our times.[8] But it seems plain even now that no clear unifying vision—and surely no vision the framers of the Constitution would have recognized as theirs—emerges from the *Chadha* opinion. Although the opinion refers broadly to the framers' wisdom in not "permitting arbitrary government acts to go unchecked,"[9] it seemingly countenances both an executive apparatus and a federal bureaucracy more autonomous and unaccountable in wielding their power than Congress itself could ever have become by using the legislative veto device.

What emerges from *Buckley, National League of Cities*, and *Chadha* taken as a group is less a coherent picture of checks and balances than a sense of judicial frustration and desire—a frustration with governmental structures that have long since outgrown the framers' dreams, and a desire to reclaim—for the judiciary as the "least dangerous"[10] branch, or for the states as the most modest—some measure of the power that, under the exigencies of modernity, Congress has sought to centralize along the banks of the Potomac.

THE LEGISLATIVE VETO DECISION: ITS UNSPOKEN PREMISES

The separation-of-powers ideal—variously decried as vaguely foolish[11] or praised as truly fundamental[12]—remains a central theme for the Supreme Court. When striking down the legislative veto in *INS v. Chadha*, the Court described "[t]he provisions of Art. I [as] integral parts of the constitutional design for the separation of powers."[13]

The intense controversy surrounding the legislative veto is as old as the device itself. Since 1932 Congress has passed a wide range of legislative veto procedures allowing it, or one of its houses or committees, to review and revoke the actions of various federal agencies and departments.[14] Some two hundred statutes containing half again as many legislative veto provisions have been enacted—more than half of them since 1970.[15] The President's power to reorganize the executive branch, to impound appropriated funds temporarily, to introduce

American armed forces into foreign conflicts, to provide nuclear fuel and technology to other nations, and to sell sophisticated weaponry abroad are all statutorily constrained by the purported authority of one or both houses of Congress to exercise what may loosely be called a legislative veto.[16]

The legislative veto has become steadily more important since its conception in the waning days of Herbert Hoover's administration.[17] The veto offered lawmakers a way to delegate vast power to the executive branch or to independent agencies while retaining the authority to cancel particular exercises of such power—and to do so without having to pass new legislation or to repeal existing laws. Whatever the practical virtues or vices of the veto,[18] its popularity as a means of controlling agency action and executive discretion has been enhanced by two other apparent advantages. First, the veto afforded Congress a visible means of stemming the tide of executive regulation of American life and industry. Such regulation is at the lowest ebb of its popularity since the beginning of the modern regulatory period.[19] Second, the veto appealed to many who resist deregulation but espouse increased democratic control over those regulations which remain.[20] Yet, though the legislative veto appeared to stand at the confluence of the desires to curtail regulation, restrain the executive, and assert the prerogatives of popular control, it also stood at the intersection of a number of doctrines that cast grave doubt on its constitutional validity.

The constitutionality of the legislative veto was tested not on the battlefield of so crucial an executive prerogative as the power to wage war, but in a skirmish over the authority to suspend the deportation of a small class of aliens. Congress, weary of handling such matters through cumbersome special immigration bills, delegated to the Department of Justice's Immigration and Naturalization Service (INS) limited discretion to suspend deportations, subject to a legislative veto within a specified period by either the Senate or the House of Representatives.[21] Jagdish Rai Chadha, born in Kenya of Indian parents, had come to the United States under a student visa with a British passport. In order to suspend deportation when his visa expired, Chadha applied for permanent resident status under section 244(a)(1) of the Immigration and Nationality Act.[22] That provision permits an alien who has been a continuous resident of the United States for seven years, who is of good moral character, and whose deportation would cause him to suffer extreme hardship, to become a permanent resident.[23] Kenya refused to take Chadha back on the ground that he was a British, not a Kenyan, citizen, and the United Kingdom told Chadha that he would not be allowed to immigrate for at least a year.[24] Since Chadha was literally a man without a country, the immigration judge, acting on behalf of the attorney general, granted Chadha's request and suspended his deportation.[25]

A year and a half later, Representative Eilberg (D-Pa.), chairman of the Subcommittee on Immigration, Citizenship, and International Law of the House Judiciary Committee, introduced a resolution striking Chadha and five others from a list of 340 resident aliens to whom the INS had decided to accord permanent resident status.[26] The House of Representatives approved the resolution, thus vetoing the suspension of those six deportations. That House action allowed the suspensions of the deportations of the other 334 aliens to become final, thereby permitting those aliens to remain in the United States. The resolution was adopted without debate or recorded vote.[27] The INS judge agreed with Chadha that the legislative veto provision in section 244(c)(2) was unconstitutional but decided that he had no authority to rule on that question. He therefore ordered Chadha deported.[28] Following the affirmance of his deportation order by the INS, Chadha filed a petition for review in the United States Court of Appeals for the Ninth Circuit. That court upheld Chadha's constitutional challenge to the legislative veto.[29] After plenary consideration of the case, the Supreme Court held it over to the following Term for reargument. In 1983 the Court affirmed the appellate judgment.[30]

The demise of the legislative veto was not without its harbingers. Eleven Presidents have gone on record at one time or another to challenge the constitutionality of at least some forms of congressional veto.[31] At least five Presidents have vetoed legislation containing congressional veto provisions on the express ground that they considered such provisions unconstitutional.[32] Others have declined to do so but have raised specific objections to the veto provisions.[33] It is therefore understandable that the Justice Department has occasionally conceded the unconstitutionality of a legislative veto provision in open court, even while representing the federal government.[34]

Much, although far from all, of the controversy over the legislative veto was resolved when the Supreme Court held in *INS v. Chadha* that the one-house legislative veto provision in section 244(c)(2) was unconstitutional.[35] In an opinion by Chief Justice Burger,[36] the Court held that *all* action by Congress that is "legislative" in "character"[37] must be taken in accord with the "single, finely wrought and exhaustively considered, procedure"[38] set out in the "explicit and unambiguous provisions" of Article I.[39] Those provisions expressly mandate both *bicamerality* (passage by a majority of both houses)[40] and *presentment* to the President for possible veto (with a requirement of two-thirds of each house to override),[41] not simply when Congress *purports* to be legislating but whenever it takes action that must be *regarded* as "legislative."[42] Otherwise, the separation of powers—which the Court saw as more than "an abstract generalization"[43]—could be betrayed by congressional lawmaking masquerading as something else. Given the "hydraulic pressure inherent within each of the separate Branches to exceed the outer limits of its power,"[44] the Court must police all such attempts by Congress to circumvent the bicamerality and presentment checks on its authority. A law by any other name is still a law.

According to a majority of the Court, the House veto of Chadha's status as a permanent resident alien *had* to be viewed as "an exercise of legislative power."[45] Thus, since it was neither approved by both houses nor presented to the President for signature or veto—two independently fatal flaws—the House's action was doubly unconstitutional.[46]

That "a law is a law is a law" is hard to refute. But that statement sheds little light on *why* the veto at issue in *Chadha* was so "law-like" an action that it "had" to be deemed legislative. Certainly the Court's careful enumeration of the "four provisions in the Constitution, explicit and unambiguous, by which one house *may* act alone with the unreviewable force of law, not subject to the President's veto"[47] is of no help in deciding which of the actions that a house might seek to take *pursuant to a statutory delegation of power* are inherently "legislative" in nature.[48]

The Court's only direct attempt at defining this set of inherently legislative actions is also not particularly illuminating. The Chief Justice explained that the veto of Chadha's suspension of deportation was "essentially legislative" because it "had the purpose and effect of altering the legal rights, duties and relations of persons . . . outside the legislative branch."[49] Absent the veto, after all, Chadha would remain in the United States. Therefore, "Congress has *acted* and its action has altered Chadha's status."[50] Moreover, "[w]ithout the challenged [veto] provision in § 244(c)(2), this [change of status] could have been achieved, if at all, only by legislation requiring deportation."[51] In a sense, all of this may be so.[52] But the same observations could apply with equal validity to nearly *all* exercises of delegated authority.

Nearly all such actions alter legal rights, duties, and relations, thereby changing the legal status of persons outside the legislative branch in ways that, *without* the challenged delegation, could have been achieved, if at all, only by legislation.

Both through rulemaking and through case-by-case dispositions, exercises of delegated authority change legal rights and privileges no less than do full-fledged laws. Unlike such laws, however, these actions need meet neither the bicamerality requirement nor the presentment requirement. Indeed, as Justice White stressed in his thoughtful dissent,[53] we live in a sprawling administrative state in which "legislative" power, in the exact sense employed by the *Chadha* majority, is *routinely* exercised by the federal executive branch, by the headless "fourth branch of the government,"[54] and even by private individuals and groups.[55] These exercises of power all occur without any of the structural checks the *Chadha* Court held indispensable when similar power is wielded by legislators pursuant to otherwise indistinguishable statutory delegations of authority to Congress or to one of its parts. Yet the absence of those checks is evidently deemed immaterial in these many cases.

In other words, it is only when power is delegated to Congress (or to part of that body) that the Court insists on squeezing such power into one of the three classic pigeonholes envisioned by the framers, labeling that power "executive," "judicial," or "legislative." The Court therefore appears to suppose that, although members of the executive or judicial branches (or of hybrid entities difficult to classify as either) need not be seen as acting purely in their executive or judicial capacities when they act pursuant to a statutory delegation from Congress, members of the *legislative* branch must be seen as acting purely in their *lawmaking* role even when they are simply discharging duties delegated to them by statute. It is as though the mere fact of statutory delegation obviates the need for formal classification of the power delegated when the recipient of such power is *outside* the legislative branch, while the fact of delegation somehow becomes altogether irrelevant in assessing an exercise of delegated power by part of the legislative branch itself.

The only imaginable justification for what Justice White called "this odd result"[56] lies in a principle never expressly articulated by the majority: "that the legislature can delegate authority to others *but not to itself*"[57]—that the *only* sort of authority Congress or any of its parts may exercise, whether pursuant to statutory delegation or otherwise, is that of *making laws*. Although the *Chadha* majority never says this in so many words, it seems to recognize that the decision's pivotal rationale is indeed to be found in this unspoken premise. In a relatively cryptic footnote, the majority admits that agencies and executive officers commonly wield "quasi-legislative" power[58] without the safeguards of bicamerality and presentment. The Court proceeds to distinguish such exercises of power solely on the ground that those who wield it are executive officers—that is, officers whose appointment is by the Chief Executive or his subordinates and whose conduct is always subject to judicial review for compliance with duly enacted statutory standards.[59]

Such judicial review is, admittedly, unavailable to ensure that legislative vetoes are wielded only in the circumstances, and for the reasons, contemplated by the underlying statute. For, even if all veto-delegating statutes were to specify the conditions under which legislative vetoes could be invoked—something most such statutes certainly do not attempt[60]—the Speech or Debate Clause[61] would presumably prevent any court from holding a member of the House or Senate accountable for that member's vote on a veto resolution.[62]

The same insulation from judicial review may also exist, however, even with respect to exercises of delegated authority by officers *outside* Congress. Even the *Chadha* majority conceded that Article III limits on the federal judiciary would ordinarily prevent federal courts from reviewing exercises of executive or administrative discretion *favorable* to the private parties whom Congress seeks to regulate: witness the attorney general's suspension of deportation of Chadha himself.[63] Thus, even where the available criteria for judicial review might create more than an illusory predicate for holding the agents of delegated power within statutory bounds in the context of a properly justiciable case or controversy,[64] the case-or-controversy requirement itself refutes the notion that the exercise of congressionally delegated authority by agents outside Congress "is *always* subject to check by the terms of the legislation that authorized it."[65]

Thus the *only* functional objection peculiarly applicable to the exercise of statutorily delegated power by all or part of Congress itself—as opposed to such exercise of delegated power by an agent or agency *external* to Congress—must be the proposition that entrusting members of Congress with such power ipso facto confers upon federal lawmakers the mantle of "officers" of the United States government, in violation of the Appointments Clause[66] and of the Incompatibility

Clause.[67] It is noteworthy that the *Chadha* majority not only failed to mention but also seems not to have envisioned[68] any such rationale for its holding. Instead the Court insisted that invocation of the legislative veto at issue in the case before it *had* to be regarded as an exercise of *legislative* authority[69]—a "characterization [under which] the practice does not, even on the surface, constitute an infringement of executive . . . prerogative."[70]

One must, nonetheless, ask whether this rationale that "Congressmen cannot be officers" could be put forward to declare the veto unconstitutional. Its key premise would, of course, have to be that the delegation of legislative veto authority to Congress (or to part of that body) automatically makes the members of Congress who are entrusted with such veto power into "officers of the United States." The objection would then have to be made that these officers were not appointed by the executive branch in the manner required by Article II, Section 2, Clause 2.[71] To add the final blow, it would be stressed that the very membership of these officers in Congress violates the Incompatibility Clause of Article I, Section 6, Clause 2.[72]

The argument is a tidy one—but it confronts at least one major problem. Neither is there, nor could there be, any general principle that anyone to whom a federal statute delegates a significant decision-making role on which the rights or duties of persons outside Congress may depend becomes, by virtue of such delegation, an "Officer of the United States" within the meaning of the Appointments Clause and the Incompatibility Clause. If such a principle existed, then Congress could not "confer upon the *States*"—which are surely not United States "Officers"—"an ability to restrict the flow of interstate commerce that they would not otherwise enjoy."[73] And the private individuals and groups to whom decision-making roles were delegated in *Currin v. Wallace*[74] and *United States v. Rock Royal Co-Operative*,[75] for example, would have been United States officers whose failure to be appointed in accord with Article II would have constituted fatal constitutional flaws in the statutory schemes upheld in those two landmark decisions.

What made the members of the Federal Election Commission (FEC) United States "officers" in *Buckley v. Valeo* was the significant executive responsibility those FEC members exercised under the Federal Election Campaign Act of 1971.[76] The responsibility exercised by the House and Senate under the reservation of legislative veto authority struck down in *Chadha* seems profoundly different. Whether viewed as the *unicameral rejection* of an action taken by the attorney general in those instances where a veto is cast by one house or viewed as the *bicameral acceptance* of a legislative proposal made by the attorney general in those instances where neither house vetoes the attorney general's suspension of deportation,[77] what Congress does in cases like *Chadha* hardly seems to involve congressional interference with the "execution" of any enacted law. Indeed, it bears repeating here that the *Chadha* majority itself was at pains to insist that the power at issue in the veto is "legislative" in nature.[78]

Whatever classification scheme one may adopt for other purposes, the core concern of the Appointments and Incompatibility Clauses hardly seems to be activated by legislative vetoes of the sort involved in *Chadha*. That concern, which is tied closely to the Constitution's rejection of parliamentary government, is to ensure that federal executive power is located under the ultimate direction of a single President chosen by and responsive to a national electorate. Such power is not to be dispersed among a series of ministries selected from the national legislature, each headed by a congressman answerable only to a local constituency.[79]

Giving Congress a legislative veto over certain intrinsically executive functions, such as the initiation of criminal prosecutions,[80] or entrusting a legislative veto to a congressional committee or committee head, might significantly implicate this antiparliamentary concern. But treating *all* legislative vetoes[81]—or even all vetoes in situations analogous to that in *Chadha*—as a threat to the Constitution's choice of a presidential over a parliamentary system seems altogether implausible, particularly in an era when presidential politics may be no less sectional than congressional politics often is.

Apart from this antiparliamentary rationale, Chadha might be deemed defensible on an entirely different ground in those special contexts where Congress or one of its houses uses a legislative veto either to decide the legal fate of an identifiable individual or to pass upon the conformity of generic rules or regulations to the underlying statute. In such cases, the task Congress has delegated to itself is arguably too "adjudicative" in character to be performed by anything but a court. Perhaps sensing the difficulty of reconciling this argument with the longstanding judicial approval of agency action "construing" Congress' laws in both generic and individual settings,[82] Justice Powell, whose concurring opinion was the only one to voice this particular view, endorsed it only as applied to action by a legislative body adversely affecting the legal status of a specific person. Such action, he opined, offends "not only . . . [the Constitution's] general allocation of power, but also . . . the Bill of Attainder Clause," which concretely embodies "the Framers' concern that trial by a legislature lacks the safeguards necessary to prevent the abuse of power."[83]

The most striking thing about any such rationale for the *Chadha* result—either in the broader form represented by a ban on delegating adjudicative tasks to bodies other than courts, or in the narrower form espoused by Justice Powell—is that this rationale would *divorce the Chadha decision entirely from objections to the legislative veto as such.* For if exercise of the legislative veto is objectionable because it usurps the functions of an Article III court by "construing" preexisting law in a manner binding on the federal judiciary, that objection seemingly remains even if such usurpation is engaged in by both houses acting with the signature of the President.[84] And, even more clearly, if exercise of the legislative veto is objectionable because it amounts to trial by legislature, that objection persists even if bicameral action and presentment to the President are assured. Chadha's claim under the Bill of Attainder Clause would not have been weakened in the least had his exile from this country been legislatively decreed by the House and Senate acting through an ordinary bill designating Chadha and his five covictims for deportation notwithstanding the attorney general's favorable ruling—a bill solemnly passed with the political safeguards of bicamerality and duly signed by the President in full conformity with the Presentment Clause.[85]

Thus, to whatever extent it is the usurpation-of-judicial-function theme of *Chadha*, or its bill-of-attainder flavor, that may commend its factual outcome to some observers, the Court's legal holding seems even harder to defend than the invalidation of "an entire class of statutes based on . . . a somewhat atypical and more-readily indictable exemplar of the class."[86] For in truth, the *Chadha* decision—if viewed through a usurpation-of-adjudication lens or a bill-of-attainder lens—is not an exemplar of "the class" of legislative vetoes *at all.*

Chadha thus seems remarkable particularly because it is so *transparently* perplexing. The gaps in the Court's argument are almost too obvious, leaving one with the strange feeling that comes from confronting an edifice in which the flaws seem too conspicuous to be accidental, rather like approaching a building with windows but no door.

Surely the architect knew that the omission would strike others as a
defect in design. But if the architect knew, then are we perhaps over-
looking something?

Two speculations suggest themselves. The first is that *Chadha* represents a return to a form of constitutional exegesis that simply proclaims intelligible essences more than it purports to explain or to justify philosophical or practical premises. "The legislative veto simply *is* a
perversion of the Constitution's design," the *Chadha* Court seems to
announce; "those who cannot 'see' it that way are just out of touch."
"In essence," the Court may be saying, "the role the framers envisioned
for Congress is the only role Congress may be assigned to play—while
entities the framers never dreamed of may be assigned such hybrid
roles as Congress chooses to concoct." The second possibility is that
Chadha represents only a transition to a more thoroughgoing repudiation of the constitutional upheaval that led to the approval, beginning in the mid-1930s, of the modern administrative state. Even if
Chadha makes little sense against a backdrop of nearly limitless judicial tolerance for delegations of lawmaking authority to federal agencies and commissions, the decision would at least be of a piece with a
significant judicial tightening of the limits within which Congress may
entrust *anyone* with lawmaking power.[87]

In the end, for those who find neither of these speculations a satisfying enough answer, *Chadha* must remain something of a mystery.
Neither the near unanimity with which the Court decided *Chadha*,
nor the breathtaking sweep of the Court's holding, are easily explained by anything in the Constitution's text, history, or structure;
by the force of the Court's own logic; or by the thrust of any analysis
thus far advanced, at least to my knowledge, in the decision's defense.
That *Chadha* realigns power in America in an extraordinary exercise
of what some like to call "judicial activism" is clear enough. *Why* the
Court has chosen to take this step remains unclear.

ALLOWABLE METHODS OF EX POST CONGRESSIONAL
RESTRAINT ON EXECUTIVE AND AGENCY ACTION
AFTER *CHADHA*

Just how much and in what precise ways the *Chadha* decision realigns
governmental power also remains to be seen. That the ruling, purely
as a matter of arithmetic, "[struck] down in one fell swoop provisions

in more laws enacted by Congress than the Court has cumulatively invalidated in its history,"[88] seems indisputable. But how "monumental [a] change [will result] in the way government does business"[89] will surely depend (a) on how many devices *analogous* to legislative vetoes are actually felled by *Chadha's* ax; and (b) on how many of the provisions rendered inoperative by *Chadha* must be deemed *inseverable* from, and thus fatal to, the entire delegations of authority to which those provisions are attached.

So far as *Chadha's* reach into analogous areas is concerned, even the most cursory analysis uncovers many legislative methods for containing, after the fact, the power delegated to agencies, commissions, or the executive branch that simply do not implicate the holding of *Chadha* at all. Thus, even the broadest reading of *Chadha* contains nothing that would prevent Congress from enacting "report and wait" provisions. The Federal Rules of Evidence and of Civil Procedure are already governed by such provisions—mandating that rule changes shall not take effect as law until after the legislative session in which they have been reported to Congress by the attorney general.[90] Such laws give Congress a greater opportunity to pass otherwise valid legislation denying legal effect to those executive, agency, or court actions with which it disagrees. Similarly, a law declaring that no administrative agency rule would take effect until affirmatively approved by a joint resolution of Congress and presented to the President,[91] though perhaps unwise, would nevertheless be constitutional. Nothing in *Chadha*, and nothing in the Constitution, prevents Congress from reducing the regulatory agencies to the status of advisory study commissions.[92] Refinements of this type of continuous legislative scrutiny are also possible. For example, a rule that all proposed regulations, or all regulations of a certain description, are automatically to be introduced as congressional resolutions and brought to a floor vote in both houses within a fixed time, subject to delay beyond that time only pursuant to a majority vote in both chambers, would be less cumbersome than requiring the regulatory state to grind to a halt while proposed regulations wandered endlessly from one committee to another. The constitutional validity of such a scheme follows quite plainly from the Constitution's reservation to each house of the prerogative to determine its own rules of operation.[93]

May Congress specify by statute the circumstances in which approval by *both* houses—in the form of a further statute, a step such as an explicit declaration of war, or a concurrent resolution expressly approving a presidential request—must be obtained by the Chief Executive in order for a particular exercise of presidential power (such as an arms sale, an impoundment of funds beyond a stated time or amount, or various troop deployments abroad) to occur or to continue? Provided the contested presidential action is not altogether beyond Congess' constitutional power to constrain,[94] the answer to this question does not depend on *Chadha*—for such congressional specification and delegation of power circumvents neither presentment nor bicamerality.[95] The answer depends, rather, upon the extent to which Congress may, within limits, *define the boundary* between (a) the zone in which the executive *may* act absent statutory *prohibition*,[96] and (b) the zone in which the executive may *not* act absent statutory *authorization*.[97] That Congress may indeed specify such a boundary, within a fairly wide band whose outer limits are defined by the federal judiciary, seems an inescapable corollary of Congress' broad Article I powers and of its undoubted authority, by creating rights based on federal statute (for example, rights of property), to add to the circumstances in which executive action (for example, action seizing property) would be unlawful absent further statutory authorization.

Having declined to forbid a contested presidential action by statute, and having declined to condition that action on specific congressional approval, may Congress nonetheless specify by statute that such presidential actions may not occur, or must cease, if either house so demands within a stated time—or if Congress so directs by a concurrent resolution not subject to presidential veto? *Chadha* strongly suggests not. Even if the presidential action subjected to legislative veto represents an exercise of authority inherent in the executive office (albeit limitable by Congress) rather than a discharge of authority traceable entirely to a delegation by Congress, it is the delegation *to* Congress, or to one of its houses, of a continuing role in the implementation of extant laws that *Chadha* forbids.[98]

The upshot of this analysis is that, after *Chadha* as before, "[t]he Constitution provides Congress with abundant means to oversee and control [both] its administrative creatures"[99] and the semiautonomous executive branch. Justice White may be correct in concluding that "the alternatives [to the legislative veto] to which Congress must now turn are not entirely satisfactory"[100] and that the Court had insufficient warrant for constraining Congress as it did in *Chadha*. But that constraint, while considerable, is far from total.

LEGISLATIVE VETO PROVISIONS: AN OCCASION TO RETHINK THE PROBLEM OF SEVERABILITY

What follows for a law as a whole and for actions taken under its authority when a legislative veto mechanism included in the law is held unconstitutional? An analysis of that question may shed useful light on the general problem of severability and on the nature of judicial review itself.

Legislative veto provisions that simply purport to constrain exercises of inherent executive authority—such as section 5(c) of the War Powers Resolution[101]—if struck down under *Chadha*, leave in place whatever residuum of authority the Constitution itself entrusts to the executive over the matter at hand absent a valid statutory limitation by Congress. No real problem of severability is posed in this circumstance.[102]

In contrast, striking down a legislative veto provision that is attached to an exercise of authority wholly dependent on an underlying delegation by Congress typically does pose a genuine severability problem. Congress might have chosen to withhold the delegated authority altogether, rather than see it survive shorn of the veto that Congress had insisted on retaining for itself or for one of its houses or committees. Once the veto provision is held void and thus unenforceable, it may always be argued that a court cannot permit the delegated authority to be exercised even in cases where *no* veto occurs (and, a fortiori, in cases where there has been a veto). Therefore, the court must strike down the entire law.[103] Indeed, the question of who bears the burden of persuasion in determining Congress' intent may even be irrelevant. It may not matter whether, as the *Chadha* majority held, the presence of a boiler-plate severability clause (of the sort most laws contain) raises a presumption that Congress would have enacted the law even without its veto provision;[104] or, as Justice Rehnquist argued in dissent, Congress should be strongly (although not conclusively) presumed to have made an all-or-nothing choice.[105] For clearly, whatever Congress *would have done* if the veto device had been unavailable to it at the time of the underlying law's enactment, the fact is that Congress *has not enacted* the law in a veto-free form.

When a severability clause is regarded as an instruction to judges that they ought to act *as if* Congress has enacted a veto-free law (or, indeed, any other law severed from a portion subsequently held to be unconstitutional), the clause seems nothing more than an invitation for courts to disregard the absence of any actual enactment of the severed law in accord with Article I's strictures. The constitutional safeguards of bicamerality and presentment are thereby abandoned, and a new law is created by judicial fiat.[106] Given the President's inability to exercise an "item veto," it is particularly striking that the law at issue was enacted, and presented to the President for veto or signature, *as a single entity* and *not* as two distinct pieces of legislation. It seems especially odd for these concerns to be overlooked in *Chadha*—the very decision that held the legislative veto device void precisely because of its failure to meet the bicamerality and presentment requirements.

On the other hand, the option of *refusing* to sever the invalid provision so as to leave the underlying law in effect once its unconstitutional veto provision has been held void and rendered inoperative poses separation-of-powers problems of its own. After all, striking down a provision "fully operative as a law"[107] simply because Congress passed that provision only on a mistaken guess about how courts would treat *another* provision seems akin to invalidating one otherwise perfectly sound statute solely because those who voted for it wrongly supposed that another, closely related statute would be upheld. Moreover, if a severability clause is read as a legislative mandate that the two provisions should be regarded as two distinct laws, the President's failure to veto the entire measure, or its passage over his veto, may be treated as satisfying the presentment requirement as to each provision separately regarded.

If the debate is conducted in these terms, the antiseverability position seems the winner by a wide margin. This position avoids the apparent trap of judicial legislation. Moreover, the antiseverability viewpoint requires a court to invalidate the entire law *not* because of Congress' mistaken assumption as to the invalid part but because of Congress' failure to *enact* the remainder, and to present it to the President, as a separate piece of legislation.

There is another ground, however, on which the survival of nearly all laws infected by invalid legislative veto devices may be supported— a ground available even for laws containing no severability clause at all. At least where no legislative veto has been exercised in the case before the reviewing court,[108] it may be argued with considerable force that a litigant who is subjected only to an exercise of the underlying authority delegated by Congress has *no standing to invoke the rights of the third parties* who would be injured were the legislative veto to be used to their disadvantage.[109] Unless a law is void because of some defect in the process by which it was enacted, only very special considerations—such as the avoidance of an intolerable chill of First Amendment rights—would warrant facial attack by *all* litigants who are subject to a law where the constitutional defect in that law is salient in only a few of the law's applications.[110]

Even in the absence of a severability clause, the consequence of holding a law's legislative veto device unconstitutional is not, after all, to *excise* that device,[111] leaving behind a truncated law that Congress never passed. Rather, the consequence is only to hold that the law Congress *did* pass is unconstitutional *as applied to cases in which the law's veto provision is invoked*. When the veto has *not* been used, the law may well be constitutionally inoffensive. Any suggestion that enforcing the law when no veto occurs entails treating the mere inaction of the House and Senate as legislation[112] betrays a basic misunderstanding of the objections to congressional legislation through silence.[113]

These observations leave open the question of remedy in a case in which the legislative veto *has* been cast—as it had been in *Chadha* itself. Once the invalidity of the immigration law as applied against Chadha is conceded, permitting *him* to invoke the deportation-suspension action taken by the attorney general on his behalf, pursuant to Congress' underlying delegation of authority in that immigration law, may seem to give him the benefit of a law that Congress simply did not pass in the veto-free form that he seeks to have applied to him.[114]

Despite the analytic appeal of the resulting argument against Chadha—and indeed against giving *any* litigant the benefit of an agency adjudication or rule which has been subjected to a legislative veto that a court later decides to invalidate—it seems most unpalatable to conclude that the very invalidity of the veto device has the de facto effect of vetoing, albeit judicially, any agency action that has actually been subjected to it! Since a court could not *enjoin* future uses of the veto,[115] the upshot would be to render the *Chadha* holding binding only to the degree Congress might choose to obey it—a result that is hard to swallow, even for those who think *Chadha* was wrongly decided.

To escape this nasty conclusion, one need only accept a somewhat more modest view of precisely what a federal court does when it strikes down a veto provision in a case like *Chadha*, or indeed invalidates any provision of any law. Rather than conceiving of the court as enforcing the law "minus" its invalidated provision—a law the legislature never enacted—perhaps one should simply understand the court as resolving the controversy before it in terms of the *entire* body of law applicable to that controversy, the entire Act of Congress (*not* the Act "minus" any offending portion) *plus the Constitution*.[116]

So conceived, the Court's holding in *Chadha* is that, because of the bicamerality and presentment requirements of Article I, the only way to give constitutional effect to Congress' enactment in the case at bar—that is, the only way to give effect to the Constitution while enforcing, to the degree possible and to the extent consistent with its meaning, the statute Congress enacted—is to treat Congress' specific action in exercising a "legislative veto" against Chadha as incapable of abridging whatever rights Chadha otherwise enjoys under the law that Congress passed. That Congress might not have conferred such rights upon Chadha had it anticipated this outcome is interesting but immaterial to this perspective. Invalidation of the entire law would result only if one could show that the meaning of the entire law Congress enacted was so thoroughly and radically compromised by the invalidation of the law's veto device that, as a matter of ordinary statutory construction, the stump that remains after the veto branch has been cut off ought to be given no legal effect at all.

This approach to severability regards courts not as choosing how much or how little of a law to "strike down" but as resolving controversies in a manner that rejects only such claims based upon a given law as are themselves deemed incompatible with the Constitution. Such a perspective avoids the several paradoxes to which the more heavily intent-based approaches to severability—the approaches ordinarily employed by the Supreme Court[117]—give rise. In particular, the approach urged here avoids both the puzzle of how a court can ever choose to enforce a law "severed" into a form that was never duly enacted and the converse puzzle of how a court that views itself as powerless to enforce a law "minus" a severed veto can ever effectuate its holding that the veto's exercise should be disregarded.

Under the view urged here, a law's total invalidity would follow from a holding that the law's application in a given case, or in a given class of cases, is unconstitutional only when the entire law's very invocation is held to be inconsistent with the Constitution. Such an inconsistency could be found when the law is not duly enacted, is vague in all applications, is facially overbroad under the First Amendment, or deals with a matter beyond the enacting jurisdiction's authority. Under the approach here proposed, inseverability would *never* follow from the mere prospect that the legislature might not have enacted the law at all if it had known that the offending aspects or applications of that law would not survive.

Of course, if Congress were actually to *enact*, as part of a law, an explicit *non*severability clause—directing that no part of the law should survive if a certain portion, or a certain set of applications of the law, were invalidated—then an adjudication of unconstitutionality would necessarily doom the law in its entirety, simply as a matter of statutory interpretation. Similarly, if a fair reading of a law is that it cannot have been meant to apply *at all* once certain parts or applications had been excised, then ordinary canons of interpretation would leave the law a nullity once such partial invalidity had been decreed.[118] But these quite rare instances of total nullification would be far more exceptional under the view proposed here than they are apt to be under the much looser approach to inseverability that has characterized adjudication in the past.

The ambitiousness of the Supreme Court's wide-ranging holding in *Chadha* presents more than a puzzle in divining the Court's aims; it presents, as well, a challenge in confining the dislocation caused by the Court's ruling. The Court's own lack of restraint in destroying "an important if not indispensable political invention"[119] need not, and should not, inspire a similar abandon on the part of those who must be guided by the Court's work.

CHAPTER SEVEN

ENTRUSTING FEDERAL JUDICIAL POWER TO HYBRID TRIBUNALS

The framers designed a system of separate, partially distinct, and interdependent powers as a barrier to the tyranny that experience taught them could result should the legislative, executive, and judicial functions ever accumulate in the same hands. The Constitution accordingly contains a system of checks and balances between and among the branches as a "self-executing safeguard against the encroachment or aggrandizement of one branch at the expense of the other."[1]

The Supreme Court's vigilance in protecting against perceived threats of interbranch encroachment has on occasion led to a triumph of constitutional formalism over political flexibility. Political inventions, "important if not indispensable"[2] to an activist government, and hardly threatening to the containment of tyranny, have been sacrificed on the altar of fidelity to strained readings of the Constitution; such inventions have been the victims of typically unacknowledged judicial choices.

The independence of the federal judiciary is at least as important a constitutional value today as it was when Hamilton articulated the need for it in *Federalist* 78 and 79: "[A]s liberty can have nothing to fear from the judiciary alone, but would have everything to fear from its union with either of the other departments; . . . [permanence in office] may therefore be justly regarded as an indispensable ingredient in its constitution, and, in great measure, as the citadel of the public justice and the public security."[3] Next to life tenure, Hamilton argued, "nothing can contribute more to the independence of judges than a fixed provision for their support . . . [A] power over a man's subsistence amounts to a power over his will."[4] But fidelity to the principle of judicial independence no more dictated the formalistic outcome of

Northern Pipeline Construction Co. v. Marathon Pipe Line Co.[5] than fidelity to the principle of separation of legislative and executive powers required the formalistic decision in *INS v. Chadha.*[6]

In *Marathon*, discussed in detail below, the Supreme Court held that the Bankruptcy Reform Act of 1978[7] was unconstitutional because it conferred Article III judicial power upon bankruptcy court judges who lacked life tenure and protection against salary diminution. But *Marathon* was no more about bankruptcy[8] than *Chadha* was about immigration; both cases were, instead, about the conflict between formalism and flexibility. The triumph of formalism represents a defeat for political and institutional innovation of the sort that may well be essential to the functioning of an ambitious government.[9]

JUDICIAL INDEPENDENCE AND LEGISLATIVE POWER

Article III, Section 1, declares that "the judicial Power of the United States, shall be vested in one supreme Court, and in such inferior Courts as the Congress may from time to time ordain and establish." It further provides, as institutional safeguards of judicial independence, that the judges of all such courts shall have life tenure during good behavior and be immune from reductions in salary.

Despite this relatively unambiguous language, "it has long been settled that Article III does not express the full authority of Congress to create courts, and that other Articles invest Congress with powers in the exertion of which it may create inferior courts."[10] The Supreme Court has had a difficult time offering a lasting answer to the question of how far Congress may go in creating tribunals to resolve questions falling within the subject matter jurisdiction of Article III courts, but unencumbered by the tenure and salary limitations of Article III. In a series of cases spanning more than a century and a half, the Court has upheld the constitutionality of several such hybrid tribunals while fervently endorsing the principle of judicial independence. The Court's quest for a principled distinction between Article III adjudicative power and all other kinds of dispute-resolving authority, like Diogenes' search for an honest man, has taken many roads. The Court has enjoyed little more success than Diogenes.

In *American Insurance Co. v. Canter*,[11] the Court through Chief Justice John Marshall held that, "[a]lthough admiralty jurisdiction can be exercised in the states, in those courts only which are established in pursuance of the third article of the constitution," Congress could provide for the exercise of that power in the Florida territory by courts unprotected by Article III tenure requirements. These were not courts whose jurisdiction came from the judicial power of Article III, but "legislative Courts, created in virtue of the general right of sovereignty which exists in the government, or in virtue of that clause which enables Congress to make all needful rules and regulations, respecting the territory belonging to the United States."[12] The Court reasoned that in legislating for the territories, "Congress exercises the combined powers of the general, and of a state government."[13] When exercising the powers that are similar to those of a state government in creating a court, Congress is no more bound by the structural safeguards of Article III than is a state government engaged in the same enterprise.[14]

Whatever the arguments for giving Congress unfettered discretion[15] in creating tribunals in geographic areas where it exercises such "combined powers," they provide no basis for creating federal tribunals operating in the states and created under the general powers of Congress enumerated in Article I, Section 8. Yet, in the cases subsequent to *Canter*, the Court has found several different ways of upholding the delegation of adjudicative authority to non–Article III courts.

In *Murray's Lessee v. Hoboken Land and Improvement Co.*,[16] a unanimous Court upheld the power of Congress to devise a summary proceeding—conducted by executive officers—to collect a debt due the government from one of its customs agents. The Court rejected the plaintiff's argument that the subject matter of the controversy was "judicial"—and therefore subject to the structural requirements of Article III—because the act of 1820 authorizing the summary proceedings by executive officers also provided for judicial review of the officers' actions. The argument incorrectly "assumes that the entire subject-matter is or is not, in every mode of presentation, a judicial controversy, essentially and in its own nature, aside from the will of congress to permit it to be so; and it leaves out of view the fact that the United States is a party."[17]

The question of the customs agent's liability was certainly within the subject-matter jurisdiction of the federal judiciary as a controversy "to which the United States shall be a Party."[18] However, since the United States could claim sovereign immunity, no suit on the subject could be entertained in an Article III court unless the United States consented. "Though they might have withheld their consent, we think that, by granting it, nothing which may not be a subject of judicial cognizance is brought before the courts."[19]

The choice of tribunal then was one that Congress could make. "[T]here are matters, involving public rights, which may be presented in such form that the judicial power is capable of acting on them, and which are susceptible of judicial determination, but which congress may or may not bring within the cognizance of the courts of the United States, as it may deem proper."[20] These "public rights" matters, which Congress may assign to a non–Article III court—or to any other form of tribunal consistent with due process[21]—do not include "any matter which, from its nature, is the subject of a suit at the common law, or in equity, or admiralty."[22] Those matters are so inherently judicial that they may not be purloined from Article III tribunals.[23]

Even if, as Justice White was to charge in *Marathon*, "*Murray's Lessee* implicitly undermined Chief Justice Marshall's suggestion that there is a difference in kind between the work of Art. I and Art. III courts,"[24] that suggestion was resurrected in *Ex Parte Bakelite Corp.*,[25] where the Court denounced as "fallacious" any argument that "assumes that whether a court is of one class or the other depends on the intention of Congress, whereas the true test lies in the power under which the court was created and in the jurisdiction conferred."[26] The Court in *Bakelite* considered a request for a writ of prohibition to restrain the Court of Customs Appeals from reviewing findings of the Tariff Commission. The argument was that, since such tariff matters must ultimately be decided by the President, they are clearly not "cases or controversies" and, thus, are outside the jurisdiction of an Article III court. Writing for a unanimous Court, Justice Van Devanter found that the Court of Customs Appeals was a legislative court—even though its judges enjoyed life tenure and it was called "a United States court"—because the matters brought before it "include nothing which inherently or necessarily requires judicial determination, but only matters the determination of which may be, and at times has been, committed exclusively to executive officers."[27] Justice Van Devanter listed a number of legislative courts, such as the Court of Claims, which exercise jurisdiction over "nothing which inherently or necessarily requires judicial determination [but only] matters which are susceptible of legislative or executive determination."[28]

A scant three years later, however, the Court approached the matter rather differently when, in *Crowell v. Benson*,[29] it held that "there is no requirement that, in order to maintain the essential attributes of the judicial power, all determinations of fact in constitutional courts shall be made by judges."[30] The *Crowell* Court rejected a challenge to the constitutionality of a provision of the Longshoremen's and Harbor Workers' Compensation Act which "contemplates, as to questions of fact . . . the findings of the deputy commissioner, supported by evidence and within the scope of his authority, shall be final."[31] The Court upheld the exercise of this adjudicative power by a non–Article III officer over charges that it violated the Due Process Clause of the Fifth Amendment as well as the provisions of Article III regarding the exercise of the judicial power of the United States. The Court reached this conclusion even though the case was "one of private right, that is, of the liability of one individual to another under the law as defined."[32] The scheme was deemed consistent with Article III because it still reserved to an Article III court "full authority . . . to deal with matters of law" and, thus, provided "for the appropriate exercise of the judicial function in this class of cases."[33] In addition, the Court held that "determinations of fact [that] are fundamental or 'jurisdictional' " are also subject to de novo review in an Article III court. In his famous *Crowell* dissent, Justice Brandeis argued that there was no basis for a contention that denial of a right to a trial de novo on jurisdictional facts "is in any manner subversive of the independence of the federal judicial power."[34] He suggested that any limits on Congress' power to assign determination of controversies to administrative bodies or legislative courts came from the Due Process Clause and not from Article III.[35]

Whatever coherence the Court had brought to this confused area of constitutional law was lost the very next year when "Justice Sutherland's opinion in *Williams v. United States*[36] introduced intellectual chaos."[37] In *Williams* and a companion case, *O'Donoghue v. United States*,[38] the Court decided that the Court of Claims was a legislative court while the Court of Appeals and the Supreme Court of the District of Columbia were constitutional courts.

The cases arose as challenges to the application of the Legislative Appropriation Act of 1932,[39] which attempted to reduce the salaries of judges "except judges whose compensation may not, under the Constitution, be diminished during their continuance in office."[40] The comptroller general of the United States determined that judges of the courts of the District of Columbia and of the Court of Claims were subject to the pay reduction because the courts were legislative and not constitutional.[41] In *O'Donoghue*, the Court found that—notwithstanding a contrary dictum in *Bakelite* and other cases—the District of Columbia courts were Article III courts. Justice Sutherland's analysis was rigorously literal: if a federal tribunal exercises power over cases such as those enumerated in Article III, Section 2, then it is "*ipso facto*" an Article III court. "The fact that Congress, under another and plenary grant of power, has conferred upon these courts jurisdiction over non-federal causes of action . . . does not affect the question."[42] If the judicial power conferred on a court extends to the cases enumerated in Article III, then the court *is* an Article III court, whether or not the Constitution allows Congress to impose duties on that same court which it could not constitutionally impose on federal courts in the states.[43]

In *Williams*, the companion case, the Court embraced a rigorous theory of the separation of powers: "a power definitely assigned by the *Constitution* to one department can neither be surrendered nor delegated by that department, nor vested by *statute* in another department or agency."[44] However, in the same opinion the Court mangled literalism by holding that, while Article III explicitly states that the federal *judicial* power "shall extend . . . to Controversies to which the United States shall be a Party,"[45] the Court of Claims is nevertheless a *legislative* rather than a judicial court because the constitutional text must be "construed . . . as though it read 'controversies to which the United States shall be a party *plaintiff* or *petitioner*.' "[46]

This literalism, which at least possessed some virtues of clarity and ease of application, seemed to go the way of the dodo and the great auk in the decisions which followed *Williams* and *O'Donoghue*. In *Glidden Co. v. Zdanok*,[47] Justice Harlan, writing for a three-member plurality,[48] repudiated the strict dichotomy between Article III authority and non–Article III power and reversed *Bakelite* and *Williams* in holding that both the Court of Customs and Patent Appeals and the Court of Claims are Article III courts after all.[49] Justice Harlan abandoned the time-honored quest for a principled distinction between constitutional and other courts. He explained that the Supreme Court's past sanctions of legislative and administrative tribunals which exercised Article III authority were justified in each case by a "confluence of practical considerations."[50] This ad hoc, pragmatic approach was reaffirmed a decade later in *Palmore v. United States*,[51] where the Court noted that "the requirements of Article III, which are applicable where laws of national applicability and affairs of national concern are at stake, must in proper circumstances give way to accommodate plenary grants of power to Congress to legislate with respect to specialized areas having particularized needs and warranting distinctive treatment."[52]

Since his "practical" approach made it impossible to distinguish Article III from Article I courts consistently on the basis of the work they do, Justice Harlan proposed a new test: "whether a tribunal is to be recognized as one created under Article III depends basically upon whether its establishing legislation complies with the limitations of that article; whether, in other words . . . its judges . . . are allowed the independence there expressly or impliedly made requisite."[53] This is tantamount to saying that Article III courts are those staffed by Article III judges; Article I courts are those without such judges. "A hundred and fifty years of constitutional history, in other words, had led to a simple tautology."[54] But like its jurisprudential ancestors, Glidden's resolution was not destined to endure.

THE MARATHON DECISION

When presented with a challenge to the constitutionality of the Bankruptcy Reform Act of 1978 in Northern Pipeline Construction Co. v. Marathon Pipe Line Co.,[55] the Supreme Court found itself to be of two minds. The plurality, led by Justice Brennan,[56] attempted to impose order on the confused and confusing constitutional history of Article III by cramming exceptions to Article III into three pigeonholes and invalidating any that did not fit. Justice White wrote for the three dissenters,[57] who surveyed the precedents and found them to be little more than "landmarks on a judicial 'darkling plain' where ignorant armies have clashed by night."[58] He concluded that, in the last century and a half, we have strayed too far from Article III's clear and simple scheme to turn back now and that the only practical solution is to read Article III "as expressing one value that must be balanced against competing constitutional values and legislative responsibilities."[59]

The plurality opinion took as its touchstone the "inexorable command" of Article III, Section 1, that the judicial power of the United States may be exercised only by judges having both life tenure and irreducible salaries.[60] By retreating to the Constitution's text and even the Declaration of Independence[61] for pristine proclamations of judicial independence which had long since been sullied,[62] the plurality overlooked the confusion that has reigned in this field since Chief Justice Marshall's problematic opinion in *Canter*. Justice Brennan refused to acknowledge that any significant erosion of the tenure and salary protections had occurred since the "late colonial period,"[63] and insisted that all of the cases in which the Court has sanctioned exceptions to Article III belong to three narrow categories of "exceptional" grants of power to the executive and legislative branches.[64] The non–Article III courts of the territories[65] and the District of Columbia[66] are authorized by the "extraordinary control" over these geographical areas given Congress by Article IV, Section 3, Clause 2, and Article I, Section 8, Clause 17, respectively.[67] And the establishment by Congress and the executive of courts-martial[68] is authorized by the special military powers conferred by Article I, Section 8, Clauses 13 and 14, and Article II, Section 2, Clause 1.[69] Finally, the legislative courts and administrative agencies that adjudicate matters involving public rather than private rights[70] are created pursuant to the "exceptional power[] bestowed upon Congress by . . . historical consensus."[71]

The plurality argued that, since the bankruptcy courts "do not lie exclusively outside the States of the Federal Union," nor "bear any resemblance to courts-martial," they do not fit into either of the first two pigeonholes.[72] And, since the substantive legal right at issue in the *Marathon* case was not the "restructuring of debtor-creditor relations" under the federal Bankruptcy Clause[73]—which the plurality said is arguably a matter of "public" rights but, rather, Northern's *state*-created right to sue Marathon for breaches of contract and warranty in order to augment its estate, the public rights exception provides no haven either.[74] Therefore, Justice Brennan concluded, the exercise of jurisdiction over Northern's contract claims by the "adjunct" bankruptcy court violated Article III.[75]

The dissent argued that the principles underlying the three categories of exceptions to Article III complement each other; "together they cover virtually the whole domain of possible areas of adjudication."[76] A major problem is that, because the *Marathon* plurality adduced no unifying principle for its three exceptions, there is no reason to assume that its laundry list of acceptable non–Article III courts is exhaustive—that the list may not sprout additions on command.

The plurality sought to link its three pigeonholes into a single unit by arguing that exceptions to Article III's "inexorable command" are recognized by the Court in the three situations it identified only because of "certain exceptional powers bestowed upon Congress by the

Constitution or by historical consensus."[77] Justice Brennan admitted that these extraordinary grants are nowhere to be found in the constitutional text, but insisted that they are "firmly established in our historical understanding of the constitutional structure."[78] But the plurality's "historical consensus" is little more than a grudging acceptance of precedents too ingrained in our governmental apparatus to be exorcised at this late date, and its "unifying principle" is but an adamant refusal to tolerate still more exceptions to Article III. The plurality simply put its foot down and cried, "Enough!" If the bankruptcy courts will not fit comfortably into the plurality's procrustean bed, then they must be dismissed.

The dissent would instead create another exception because it could not see how the Constitution's delegations of legislative power over the military and the District of Columbia are any more "extraordinary" than any of the *other* grants of power in Article I, Section 8.[79]

Although refreshingly straightforward and highly practical, the dissent's readiness to reduce Article III, Section 1, to the status of just another factor in a balancing test seems disturbing enough to account for the plurality's reaction.[80] The plurality recoiled from any such radical move because it could identify no limiting principle which would prevent Congress from supplanting "the independent Art. III Judiciary through a 'wholesale assignment of federal judicial business to legislative courts.' "[81]

The Court's decision in *Marathon* reveals that it takes the independence of the federal judiciary very seriously indeed. If the only function of the "least dangerous branch" were to expound the Constitution and thereby keep the other two branches in check, then perhaps Article III would be satisfied so long as there were ultimately some appeal to an Article III court on constitutional issues. But the Constitution's prescription of life tenure and irreducible salaries for the judges "*both* of the supreme and inferior Courts"[82] suggests that the framers also saw the independence thereby achieved as essential to the quality of even more routine federal judicial decision making.[83]

This requires a reevaluation of Justice Brandeis' view of Article III in his dissenting opinion in *Crowell v. Benson*: "If there be any controversy to which the judicial power extends that may not be subjected to the conclusive determination of administrative bodies or federal legislative courts, it is not because of any prohibition against the diminution of the jurisdiction of the federal district courts as such, but because, under certain circumstances, the constitutional requirement of due process is a requirement of judicial process."[84] Although that view has been endorsed by several scholars,[85] and even though the *Marathon* plurality's emphasis on the need for independent and impartial judges could be motivated by due process concerns, Justice Brandeis' suggestion does not fully explain the *Marathon* decision. It surely cannot be a due process requirement that state law contract actions, such as Northern's claim against Marathon, be tried before a judge with lifetime tenure and a guaranteed salary, because the vast majority of such claims have always been tried in state courts presided over by judges elected for a term of years whose compensation is at the whim of the state legislature. Furthermore, if Congress had declined to create lower federal courts at all, or had declined to bestow upon them exclusive[86] bankruptcy jurisdiction, even federally created claims would be tried by those same state-court judges. The reason that Congress may not itself establish an Article I court wherever it could have chosen to rely on the state courts, and the reason it may not confer on Article I courts jurisdiction over rights it has not created, must be that, regardless of how the *states* may choose to intermingle *their* legislative and judicial branches, the Constitution demands that the essential attributes of the *federal judicial power* be lodged *only* in Article III judges.[87]

In accord with this renewed emphasis on the separation of powers as an independent rationale for an independent federal judiciary, the plurality in *Marathon* drew a sharp distinction between rights created by Congress and those created by the Constitution.[88] This distinction—in a sense, simply the old public-private rights dichotomy dressed in new robes—delineates the area in which the separation of powers rationale operates. Since the Constitution's checks and balances are designed principally to guard against "encroachment or aggrandizement" by Congress at the expense of the other branches,[89] the separation of powers doctrine is implicated least in those situations where Congress is providing for the adjudication of rights it has itself created: "Congress . . . clearly has the discretion, in defining that right, to create presumptions, or assign burdens of proof, or prescribe remedies; it may also provide that persons seeking to vindicate that right must do so before particularized tribunals created to perform the specialized adjudicative tasks related to that right."[90] When the right in question is *not* a creature of federal statute, however, invasions of the sphere traditionally reserved to the judiciary cannot be justified as incidental to Congress' power to define rights that it has brought into being.

The Supreme Court acknowledged this difference between constitutionally recognized and congressionally created rights as early as its decision in *Ng Fung Ho v. White*, [91] on which *Crowell* had relied. In *Ng Fung Ho*, the Court drew a distinction between jurisdiction to deport a known alien, which could be conferred on an executive agency, and jurisdiction to deport someone who claimed to be a United States citizen, which could be lodged only in the Article III judiciary.[92] Congress may create a special tribunal to conduct deportation proceedings in regard to aliens because it has plenary authority over immigration; but if the person involved can make a colorable claim to being a citizen of this country, then only an Article III court may authoritatively decide the question of citizenship. For to deport someone who claims to be a citizen may be to deprive that person of "liberty" guaranteed by the Constitution itself. The Court's theory seems to have been that, if a constitutional right is potentially involved, Article III's requirements of federal judicial independence must be met at *every* level of federal adjudication, and not only on appeal—where the reviewing court is restricted to considerations of law. To accept a regime that required only some degree of appellate review by an independent judge " 'would be to . . . establish a government of bureaucratic character alien to our system, wherever fundamental rights depend . . . upon the facts, and finality as to facts becomes in effect finality in law.' "[93]

The distinction between constitutional and federal statutory rights, while perhaps appealing, is problematic as applied by the plurality in *Marathon* because that case did not appear to involve any constitutional right; respondent Marathon objected to the bankruptcy court's assertion of jurisdiction over Northern's damages claim for breach of contract—a creation of state common law.[94] The plurality lumped constitutional and state-law rights together because they are both "independent of and antecedent to the reorganization petition that conferred jurisdiction upon the Bankruptcy Court."[95] Since the plurality conceded that a discharge in bankruptcy "may well be a 'public right,' "[96] it appears to follow that Congress might, as an incidental exercise of its power to make "uniform Laws on the subject of Bankruptcies,"[97] assign the restructuring of debtor-creditor relationships to a special non–Article III tribunal. All of the analysis in the plurality opinion beyond its invalidation of bankruptcy court jurisdiction over antecedent state-law claims therefore seems to be pure dictum.[98]

This is not to say, however, that the *Marathon* decision is wholly without import for Congress' power to assign adjudication of federal statutory matters to legislative courts. The plurality's off-hand concession that discharge in bankruptcy "may well be a 'public right' " is by no means beyond debate. The Constitution grants Congress supreme authority to legislate with respect to bankruptcy in order that there might be nationally "uniform Laws" on the subject, as the text of Article I indicates.[99] A discharge in bankruptcy is not necessarily a "public right" simply because it is a creature of federal law. Bankruptcies involve private disputes between debtors and creditors; they are not matters "which arise between the Government and persons subject to its authority in connection with the performance of the constitutional functions of the executive and legislative departments."[100]

In *Atlas Roofing Co., Inc. v. Occupational Safety and Health Review Comm'n*,[101] the Supreme Court distinguished the power to route adjudication of statutorily created public rights to Article I tribunals from the power similarly to dispose of private rights found in state statutory or common law. The Court in this case found the Occupational Safety and Health Act of 1970 (OSHA)[102] constitutionally sound because the only matters it sent to an administrative agency were adjudications of its newly imposed federal statutory duty to maintain safe working conditions; existing state statutory and common law remedies for the actual injury of workers were still to be tried only in state courts or in Article III federal courts.[103] The Court made it clear in *Atlas Roofing* that Congress possesses this adjudicative flexibility *only* in cases where " 'public rights' are being litigated—e.g., cases in which the Government sues in its sovereign capacity to enforce public rights created by statutes within the power of Congress to enact."[104] The approval of administrative fact-finding and enforcement in public rights cases does not at all implicate "[w]holly private tort, contract, and property cases, as well as a vast range of other cases."[105] Since a proceeding in bankruptcy is initiated by the petition of a debtor or of creditors and does not involve the government as an enforcing party "in its sovereign capacity," it is hard to see how a discharge in bankruptcy *could* be a "public right."

Even if rights do not always sort themselves neatly into these two categories, and even if the distinction between public and private rights constitutes some sort of spectrum, some rights clearly fall at the private end. Even if the restructuring of debtor-creditor relations under the bankruptcy laws were held to be a matter of public right, for example, such constitutional rights as freedom of expression and equal protection of the laws, which adhere to individual citizens, would not even *arguably* be "public" for this purpose. The Article I grant of authority to Congress to write uniform bankruptcy laws, like the power to regulate interstate and foreign commerce, contains no guidance as to the content or purpose of any resulting federal legislation. Congress is free to enact and repeal such bankruptcy and commerce laws as it wishes. But the substantive principles enshrined in the Bill of Rights and the Thirteenth, Fourteenth, and Fifteenth Amendments exist independent of any enforcing legislation; they are the creations not of Congress but of the Constitution.[106] Therefore, for example, Congress probably could not, as an incidental exercise of its power to enforce the Civil War Amendments, channel private lawsuits under the Civil Rights and Voting Rights Acts to an administrative agency or a legislative court. Congress has broad discretion to decide what sort of tribunal will adjudicate government civil enforcement actions of public rights, but federal *constitutional* rights—at least to the extent that their enforcement is entrusted to federal rather than state forums—are protected by Article III's guarantee of an independent judiciary.

The practical significance of this distinction between congressionally created and constitutional rights is marred in two respects. *First*, that a right is constitutional in origin, and therefore the proper province of the Article III judiciary, does not necessarily mean that it will receive significantly greater protection than will a congressionally created right. Thus, although the Fifth Amendment right against self-incrimination was at stake in *United States v. Raddatz*, the Supreme Court there held that a suppression hearing may be presided over by a federal magistrate unprotected by Article III's tenure and salary provisions so long as the final determination on admissibility of the defendant's statements is made by the district court judge.[107] If the magistrate's ruling is not self-executing, there is no constitutional infirmity.

This test is dangerously formal in application. The magistrate's ruling on the voluntariness, and hence the admissibility, of Raddatz' statements was technically not self-executing because the Federal Magistrates Act[108] requires the district court to make a "*de novo* determination" of the portions of the magistrate's report to which objection is made. But the Supreme Court held that a "*de novo* determination" was not the same thing as a "*de novo* hearing,"[109] and concluded that because the magistrate was acting as an adjunct to the district court, and therefore more closely under the court's control than an administrative agency, judicial review need not be as thorough and the district court was under no obligation to hear the evidence and witnesses itself before approving the magistrate's decision.[110] Yet the suppression hearing in *Raddatz* turned wholly on the credibility of the witnesses; it was a classic swearing contest.[111] The majority, through Chief Justice Burger,[112] explicitly assumed it unlikely that a judge would ever *reject* a magistrate's proposed findings on credibility without hearing the witnesses and expressed doubt that to do so would be acceptable,[113] but held it perfectly all right for the judge to *accept* the magistrate's conclusions. This means that the protection of independent judicial scrutiny is more assumed than real, for unless the district judge guesses blindly, the federal court will accept the magistrate's decision on credibility as presumptively correct and the magistrate's determination effectively becomes the *final* determination.[114]

The second problem with using the distinction between constitutional and public rights to divide Article III from Article I courts is that the extent of Congress' control over even its legislatively created rights is unresolved. The plurality in *Marathon* would only say that, when Congress creates a substantive right, it "may have something to say about the proper manner of adjudicating that right."[115] That Delphic pronouncement is of little help. Nor, since *Marathon* was decided on the ground that an Article I bankruptcy court could not assert jurisdiction over state-law claims, does the case provide any implicit holding as to Congress' power to create adjuncts or agencies to adjudicate federal statutory rights.[116]

Nevertheless, Justice White repeatedly argued in his dissent that, if any constitutional significance were attributed to the self-executing nature of bankruptcy court orders, most of the government's administrative apparatus would be thrown into doubt.[117] He is certainly correct that the plurality's comparison between contemporary bankruptcy court practice and the administrative practice described in *Crowell v. Benson*[118] is less than instructive in light of the fact that administrative law had undergone a major metamorphosis since 1932.[119] The ultimate fact-finder in most administrative proceedings today is a commission that has not heard the witnesses testify[120] and that is under no obligation to defer to the findings of the hearing officer.[121] *Crowell's* requirement of de novo review of "jurisdictional facts" has fallen into desuetude, as the *Marathon* plurality admits.[122] Moreover, modern courts, unlike those in the forty-year-old administrative practice which the plurality reviews, usually defer to an agency's interpretation of the statute it is enforcing as well as to its factual findings.[123]

However, a closer reading of the plurality opinion negates such dire predictions of adverse impact on modern administrative practice. Although its rhetoric was broad, the *Marathon* plurality applied its "self-executing" test only when private or constitutional rights were at stake. Therefore, the clear statements elsewhere in *Marathon*[124] and in *Atlas Roofing*[125] that Congress may provide for the litigation of public rights in administrative tribunals are likely to remain fully operative. Furthermore, although it has often been supposed that judicial review of agency determinations of questions of law is constitutionally required,[126] the plurality in *Marathon* arguably took a step *back* from this position by noting that the precedents merely "suggest" that such review by an Article III court is mandatory.[127]

If nothing else, the result in *Marathon*, as well as the plurality's sweeping language and its remark that even public rights "presumptively" belong in Article III courts,[128] indicate that the Supreme Court is choosing to give formal separation of powers concepts renewed life in this area—without much heed for practical consequences.[129] Perhaps the Court's willingness to parse congressional allocations of jurisdiction suggests that the Article III requirement of an *independent* judiciary is once more an independent shield for constitutional and other private rights. But, given the formality of the Court's inquiry in *Raddatz*, Article III may be less a sturdy shield than a matador's swirling cape.

CHAPTER EIGHT

CHOKE HOLDS, CHURCH SUBSIDIES, AND NUCLEAR MELTDOWNS: PROBLEMS OF STANDING?

There is a venerable tradition in American constitutional jurisprudence of courts seizing substantive power in the name of renouncing authority. The tradition is as old as *Marbury v. Madison*,[1] but can be put to far less noble uses. Among the tradition's most pernicious manifestations is the purported denial of Article III authority to adjudicate those claims which the Court's substantive doctrines would require it reluctantly to *accept* on the merits, coupled with selective receptivity to those claims the Court is anxious to reach in order to *reject* them on the merits. This essay on contemporary developments in the law of standing explores two examples of the former and one of the latter. Although it is tempting to try to sweep the cases together and make doctrinal generalizations about standing, this essay does so only in a tangential way, since the cases I will explore have far more to do with the underlying substantive claims than with the law of justiciability. Nonetheless, the Court's opinions *are* phrased in general terms, and it is worth thinking about what our law of standing would look like if these problematic precedents were taken seriously and followed consistently.

"Standing" is that aspect of the law of justiciability that is concerned with identifying which parties may raise legal arguments or claims.[2] As applied in the federal courts,[3] the core of standing is the requirement of "injury in fact" to the claimant, which generally—although not inevitably—is conceived as an application of Article III's "case or controversy" requirement.[4] "Injury in fact" may be ascertained by the courts or recognized, in substantive or procedural terms,[5] by an Act of Congress.[6] In addition, or as a corollary to the "injury in fact" requirement, the Supreme Court has generally required some showing that the challenged action "caused" or contributed to the litigant's injury.[7] This standard is sometimes stated in reverse, as a demand that the litigant show that his or her injury might be alleviated by relief against the challenged action.[8]

Beyond this, the law of standing has detoured to address a variety of special situations and problems. For a brief period, it appeared that the Court, as a prudential matter,[9] would compel all litigants to show a "logical nexus between the status [or interest] asserted and the claim sought to be adjudicated."[10] The Court has developed a complex theory of "taxpayer standing" as a partial exception to its general insistence upon having "Hohfeldian" litigants.[11] And the Court has regulated both those challenges based upon injuries done to claimants by third parties[12] and those raising the claims of third parties.[13]

Recent Supreme Court decisions, however, have displayed an increased willingness on the Court's part to allow its view of the merits— and the favor or disfavor with which it views particular kinds of challenges—to dictate its conclusions as to whether standing requirements have been met. The result has been the creation of special, largely unprincipled, exceptions to the basically liberal rules of standing to keep out cases of a kind the Court does not want to have to deal with.[14] At the same time, the converse has been true: the Court has gone out of its way to consider the merits of particular cases that it wanted to decide even where the claimants' standing was at best tenuous under the standards of the formal rules.[15]

The existence of these trends, the tension between them, the Court's failure to hew to any line with much consistency, and the relative paucity of articulated justifications that has always plagued standing doctrine, make a satisfactory theory of standing especially elusive.

CITY OF LOS ANGELES v. LYONS

At a little after 2 A.M. on the morning of October 6, 1976, Adolph Lyons, a twenty-four-year-old black man,[16] was driving in the City of Los Angeles when he was pulled over to the curb by two police officers who had spotted a burned-out taillight on his car. According to the uncontradicted evidence in the record before the Court,[17] the officers greeted Lyons with drawn revolvers, ordered him to face his car, spread his legs, clasp his hands to his head, and submit to a "pat-down search."[18] He complied with each demand. When he lowered his hands after the search, an officer "slammed them onto his head," apparently hurting him with the ring of the keys he was holding.[19] He complained of the pain, and "[w]ithin five to ten seconds, the officer began to choke Lyons by applying a forearm against his throat. As Lyons struggled for air, the officer handcuffed him, but continued to apply the choke hold until he blacked out. When Lyons regained consciousness, he was lying face down on the ground, choking, gasping for air, and spitting up blood and dirt. He had urinated and defecated. He was issued a traffic citation and released."[20] Lyon's larynx was damaged,[21] but he might have considered himself lucky: since 1975, at least sixteen other people subjected to choke holds, twelve of them black males, have been killed.[22]

Lyons sued in federal district court for damages against the individual police officers and for declaratory and injunctive relief against the city's further use of choke holds "except in situations where the proposed victim of said control reasonably appears to be threatening the immediate use of deadly force."[23] He based his claims on the First, Fourth, Eighth, and Fourteenth Amendments to the United States Constitution. Lyons offered substantial evidence showing the extreme medical dangers of choke holds and the city's extensive training in, and promotion of, their use.[24] After a series of procedural twists, the district court granted a preliminary injunction and the Court of Appeals affirmed.[25] Successive stays by the Court of Appeals and by the Supreme Court prevented the injunction from taking effect. In May 1982 the city suspended use of the choke hold in most circumstances, but the Supreme Court, at the city's urging, rejected Lyons' argument that the case had become moot.[26]

Instead, the Court held that Lyons had no standing to seek the injunction in the first place. It discarded or disregarded without comment "[t]he fundamental aspect of standing . . . that it focuses on the *party* seeking to get his complaint before a federal court and not on the *issues* he wants to have adjudicated,"[27] or on "the precise nature of the relief sought."[28] Writing for a five-to-four majority,[29] Justice White held that "Lyons has failed to demonstrate a case or controversy with the City that would justify the equitable relief sought."[30] The Court conceded Lyons' standing to sue for damages,[31] but it found Lyons' allegations fell "far short of the allegations" necessary for standing to seek an injunction. It demanded that Lyons show, apparently to a certainty, that he would again be choked without provocation or that the city had ordered or authorized that he be.[32] This bears stark contrast to the convoluted chains of contingencies the Court has been willing to follow in commercial cases,[33] and the Court gave no indication why this level of certainty was necessary. It did, however, note that the assertions it insisted upon would be "unbelievable" and "incredible."[34] Apparently, then, the only allegations sufficient to support standing are those that will assure the Court of an alternative means of dismissing the case: failing to prove the allegations made.[35] Despite the Fourth Amendment's explicit protection of private parties from the "chilling" of their personal liberties,[36] the Court brushed aside Lyons' fears of future chokings as irrelevant to the standing inquiry.[37]

The Court also sought to justify its action on traditional equitable theories urging restraint.[38] Managerial concerns have led the Court to decline massive structural intervention into the operations of a local criminal justice system, a police force, and the Ohio National Guard in *O'Shea v. Littleton*,[39] *Rizzo v. Goode*,[40] and *Gilligan v. Morgan*.[41] Although acknowledging the structural difference between *Lyons* and these cases,[42] the Court found it irrelevant to jurisdictional questions of standing,[43] yet it repeatedly relied upon the cautions against supplanting local authority that the far more interventionist remedies of those cases engendered.[44] It misconstrued, quite inexplicably, the Court of Appeals' holding that Lyons had a live controversy while he was being choked[45] and that "normal rules of equity" hold a case not "moot merely because the complained of conduct has ceased."[46] Mechanically repeating its earlier holding that the case was not moot, the Court in effect held that, since the earlier choking had stopped, the case was not live unless it could be shown that it would recur.[47] The Supreme Court's rejection of the Court of Appeals' finding that the dispute was "capable of repetition yet evading review" was still more remarkable: it held that Lyons' damages remedy meant that his injury would not "evade review."[48] Presumably, if Lyons were later strangled to death, his survivors' damage action would, in the Court's view, adequately redress any constitutional violation.[49] Lest anyone mistake its point, the Court went on to hold that the damage action was "an adequate remedy at law"[50] negating one of the prerequisites to invoking equitable jurisdiction.[51]

The Court declined "the invitation to slight the preconditions for equitable relief" out of its "recognition of the need for a proper balance between state and federal authority."[52] The brutality of the police action notwithstanding, the opinion concluded that a federal court is not the proper forum for the litigation of these constitutional issues. The Court's paramount concern was with preserving the "special delicacy of the adjustment . . . between federal equitable power and State administration of its own law"[53]—even when the effect of such deference to state authority was the rather indelicate treatment of Adolph Lyons' body and constitutional rights.

Before assessing what the Court's holding in *Lyons* would mean if taken seriously as a precedent, we turn to a second exhibit: the Court's avoidance of a ruling on the merits of a challenge to a federal subsidy to a church.

VALLEY FORGE CHRISTIAN COLLEGE v. AMERICANS UNITED FOR SEPARATION OF CHURCH AND STATE

When Americans United for the Separation of Church and State (Americans United) learned in September 1976 that the Department of Health, Education, and Welfare (HEW) had a month earlier given a 77-acre tract of land with an Army hospital on it to the Valley Forge Christian College, they decided to make a federal case out of it. The college, whose faculty members are required to be "baptized in the Holy Spirit and living consistent Christian lives" and whose administrators must all be affiliated with the Assemblies of God,[54] said it planned to use the property to expand its program of " 'systematic training . . . to men and women for Christian service as either ministers or laymen.' "[55] Although HEW appraised the land alone at $577,500, it transferred the entire property without charge after applying a 100 percent "public benefit allowance."[56]

Americans United sought a federal district court declaration that the transfer was null and void and an order compelling the return of the property to the United States. The group claimed standing as taxpayers under the doctrine of *Flast v. Cohen*.[57] In *Flast*, the Court had held that, even though citizens generally have no right to bring suits seeking the enforcement of laws against others who may have violated them,[58] taxpayers have standing to challenge congressional exercises of the taxing and spending power allegedly in violation of the Establishment Clause. The *Flast* Court found the Establishment Clause had been intended as a specific limitation on the power to tax and spend in that one of the prime evils against which its proponents sought to guard was taxation to support favored religions or religion in general.[59]

In *Valley Forge*, the Court sought to avoid *Flast* by pointing to all available factual distinctions between the two cases without regard to whether anything of consequence turned on those distinctions. The earlier case did not control, the Court held, because in *Flast* the transfer was made under Article I, Section 8's *spending* power whereas Valley Forge Christian College received its land under the *disposition of property clause* of Article IV, Section 3, Clause 2.[60] The Court also held that taxpayer standing extended only to actions of Congress itself, not to actions of administrative agencies authorized by Congress.[61]

As Professor Choper has said, "those are certainly accurate distinctions. Indeed, this case was called *Valley Forge* and the other was called *Flast v. Cohen.* [T]hat is an accurate distinction as well. But . . . the Court's distinctions in respect to *Flast* are quite formalistic and ephemeral."[62] The distinction between the "spending" and "property" clauses is at best a nearly meaningless artifact of accounting practice, separating current expenses and depreciation from capital expenditures. The Court in evaluating the legitimacy of congressional enactments long ago stopped examining legislation with respect only to the specific clause under which Congress may have thought it was acting: legislation is upheld based on the actual legitimacy of its means and ends pursuant to the totality of the grant of, and limits on, legislative power.[63] Indeed, under *McCulloch v. Maryland*'s view of the Necessary and Proper Clause,[64] both "spending" and "disposition of property" could probably be accomplished under either clause. In the context of a taxpayer's challenge, the distinction makes particularly little sense: before land, buildings, or cash could be spent or disposed of, they had to be acquired, almost invariably with federal tax dollars.[65]

By recognizing taxpayer standing to challenge acts of Congress but not congressionally authorized acts of administrative agencies like HEW, the Court turned the usual hierarchy of presumptions of legitimacy on its head. Anonymous civil servants in HEW—at best, the appointed Secretary—now receive more protection for their actions than the elected and politically accountable Congress does for its. The choice to classify the transfer as one by HEW rather than by Congress also seems almost totally whimsical. Congress may not be able to execute either spending or property transfers on its own, but neither may executive officials make disbursements without congressional authorization. If a statutory challenge was crucial, the plaintiffs in *Valley*

Forge could have challenged the Federal Property and Administrative Services Act of 1949, under which HEW had made the transfer. The Act could have been attacked either for granting HEW discretion to make dispositions in aid of religion or for exceeding the bounds of permissible delegations by not limiting administrative discretion in ways that would foreclose such transfers.[66]

Flast was an action against the Secretary of Health, Education, and Welfare and others "to enjoin the allegedly unconstitutional expenditure of public funds" under an authorizing statute.[67] The plaintiffs there "disclaim[ed] any intent to challenge as unconstitutional" the Act in its entirety;[68] they merely contended that the specific expenditures of funds to aid parochial schools were either ultra vires "or, in the alternative, that if [the defendant's] actions are deemed within the authority and intent of the Act, the Act is to that extent unconstitutional and void."[69] The *Flast* Court did not distinguish between the plaintiffs' statutory and constitutional claims when it held they had standing, properly noting that "[t]he fundamental aspect of standing is that it focuses on the party seeking to get his complaint before the federal court and not on the issues he wishes to have adjudicated."[70] But there was some indication that HEW's actions in *Valley Forge* were also ultra vires.[71]

The challenge by Americans United to the underlying statute went precisely as far as, but no farther than, that advanced by the *Flast* plaintiffs.[72] The Court's efforts to distinguish between the two cases on the basis of the agency whose action is "the source of [the] complaint"[73] seems disingenuous as well as irrational. This approach appears particularly perverse in view of the concern animating part of the *Flast* majority about attempts to evade by subterfuge the Establishment Clause and the Court's decisions prohibiting public aid to religious schools.[74] A license to fund religion merely by invoking the "property" clause—and perhaps giving in-kind aid or setting aside the funds a year in advance so that they become "property"—is almost more than the architects of these "numerous" and "notorious . . . subterfuges" could have imagined.[75]

The mood changes from one of resistance to receptivity, however, as we shift from an unwelcome attack on church subsidies to an attack the Court seemed eager to entertain and to rebuff on the merits: an attack on Congress' plan for encouraging nuclear power plant construction.

DUKE POWER CO. v. CAROLINA ENVIRONMENTAL STUDY GROUP

Two organizations and forty individuals living near the McGuire and Catawba nuclear power plants under construction by Duke Power Company brought an action in federal district court in 1973 to try to stop construction of the facilities. The complaint alleged that licenses to build the plants should not have been granted and that the Price-Anderson Act, limiting the liability of the power company in the event of a nuclear accident, was unconstitutional. In the lower courts, the issuance of the licenses was upheld, but the plaintiffs prevailed in the challenge to the Act.[76] In marked contrast to *Lyons* and *Valley Forge*, the Supreme Court seemed to go out of its way to find that there was no problem with plaintiffs' standing when the case of *Duke Power Co. v. Carolina Environmental Study Group, Inc.*,[77] reached it on direct appeal—despite the fact that plaintiffs' standing could have foundered on the perennially troublesome "causation" corollary to the requirement of "injury in fact."

Congress had passed the Price-Anderson Act in 1957 in response to requests from the nuclear power industry. Private power companies contended that they would be forced to forego nuclear development if their liability in the event of a major nuclear accident were not some-how limited by federal statute.[78] The Act fixed a $560 million ceiling on liability for nuclear accidents resulting from the operation of federally licensed nuclear power plants. Since Congress had enacted this limit on liability because it was persuaded that private industry would not otherwise participate in developing nuclear power, plaintiffs argued that invalidation of the Act, and the subsequent reimposition of the risk of liability on the industry itself, would force Duke Power to halt construction on its plants.

The District Court held the Price-Anderson Act violative of due process because it failed to assure nuclear accident victims adequate compensation; the Supreme Court reversed the judgment on the merits.[79] The Supreme Court read the complaint as alleging that the Price-Anderson Act deprived plaintiffs of their property without due process of law in violation of the Fifth Amendment—principally by arbitrarily limiting the plaintiffs' state-law right to recover full compensation for tort injuries in the event of nuclear catastrophe. Of course, plaintiffs could be unjustly deprived of their property according to this theory *only if* an accident occurred causing damages in excess of the statutory ceiling. The record indicated the probability of an accident of that magnitude to be slight, although theoretically calculable.[80] In addition, plaintiffs' injuries would go uncompensated *only if* Congress did not enact extraordinary relief provisions to cover the amount of claims in excess of the statutory ceiling. But Congress had made an express commitment to consider just that course of action.[81] And adding to the string of contingencies, plaintiffs' remedies at state law were limited as a practical matter by the financial resources of the utilities and manufacturers of reactor components; the record raised grave doubts that private industry could pay a judgment approaching the $560 million limit.[82] Thus, the injuries, consisting of any uncompensated losses plaintiffs would suffer in the event of a nuclear disaster, were extraordinarily speculative; the Court has often denied the justiciability of claims that presented mere possibilities of future injuries, indefinite both in degree and in nature.[83] It was no surprise therefore that the Court in *Duke Power* chose to put both the ripeness of the controversy and plaintiffs' standing to litigate it on a different basis, focusing upon the immediate adverse effects on the plaintiffs once the plants began operation. "[W]e need not determine whether all the putative injuries . . ., particularly those based on the possibility of nuclear accident and the present apprehension generated by this future uncertainty, are sufficiently concrete to satisfy constitutional requirements. It is enough that several of the 'immediate' adverse effects were found to harm appellees."[84]

The Court found "injury in fact" to plaintiffs in two of the allegations in the complaint: first, the environmental and aesthetic consequences of thermal pollution on two lakes used for recreational purposes, and second, the possible health and genetic consequences of emissions of nonnatural radiation into the environment.[85] The Court acknowledged that the more difficult question was whether "the exercise of the Court's remedial powers would redress the claimed injuries"—that is, whether there was a "but for" causal link between the Price-Anderson Act and the construction of the plants.[86] The lower court had found a "substantial likelihood" that such a link existed, a finding the Supreme Court was "bound to accept" since it did not find it "clearly erroneous."[87] The majority rejected the position that, as a matter of law, an injury could not be traced to a challenged action, for purposes of Article III jurisdiction over the challenge, whenever the prospect of effective relief would depend upon the choices of a third party.[88]

The Court similarly upheld the plaintiffs' standing over objections that their injuries lacked sufficient "nexus" with the rights invoked. The plaintiffs' environmental and health injuries that satisfied the "injury in fact" requirement were not within the ambit of the Fifth Amendment property rights that the Price-Anderson Act allegedly infringed; plaintiffs could claim at most a Fifth Amendment right to just compensation if one of the plants melted down or exploded, not a right to prevent the plants from causing any injury in the course of normal operation. If the Court had insisted on subject matter nexus between the injuries claimed and the rights invoked, plaintiffs would have been out of court.[89] This result was avoided by the Court's novel holding that the nexus requirement is applicable only in cases involving questions of taxpayer standing[90] and in cases implicating the rights of third parties.[91] The Court reasoned that any prudential considerations which the nexus requirement might be thought to serve—whether they be concerns about the proper role of the judiciary in a democratic society or about the interests of third parties—ordinarily are served adequately by the constitutional demand for an injury in fact that will be prevented or redressed by the relief requested.[92] At least outside the special context of taxpayer suits, "nexus" is simply an unnecessary and hence unwarranted extension beyond the Article III "cases or controversies" requirement.[93]

By clearing away potential hurdles to plaintiffs' standing that it might have found insurmountable in a case whose merits it was less eager to reach, the Supreme Court went on to find—not surprisingly—that the Price-Anderson Act violated neither the due process nor the equal protection components of the Fifth Amendment.[94]

A BRIEF RESTATEMENT OF THE LAW OF STANDING

Over the years, the Supreme Court has relaxed substantially many of the formal rules of standing and has jettisoned altogether some of their more anomalous doctrinal quirks. The Court has nonetheless continued to insist that "to satisfy Article III, the plaintiff must show that he personally has suffered some actual or threatened injury as a result of the putatively illegal conduct of the defendant."[95] It has clearly indicated, however, that this "injury in fact" is "the sole requirement for standing to sue under . . . Article III"[96] and that "the courts . . . lack the authority to create prudential barriers to standing" where Congress has granted parties standing in circumstances falling within Article III's "case" or "controversy" concept.[97] Even this limitation means less than it might appear to mean: "[T]he actual or threatened injury required by Art. III may exist solely by virtue of statutes creating legal rights, the invasion of which creates standing."[98] Therefore, an appropriately defined statutory right may confer standing upon virtually anyone who can allege[99] any kind of injury going beyond the purely ideological.[100] The Court has explicitly distinguished the constitutional requirement of "injury in fact" from its preferences for cases that may vindicate "individual rights," for cases brought by the "best suited" litigant, and for cases involving injuries "peculiar to [the litigant] or to a distinct group of which [the litigant] is a part."[101]

Beyond cases where standing is statutorily conferred,[102] the Court's application of the "injury in fact" standard has been varied and somewhat arbitrary. This should hardly be surprising given the extremely nebulous character of that requirement.[103] Once again, it becomes necessary to review the kinds of alleged injuries the Court has or has not found sufficient.[104] As discussed above, the Court has continued to insist that no one has a cognizable interest in how the criminal justice system operates against others, but it has not carried this principle over to prevent challenges to tax benefits given third parties, at least where the challenge could possibly improve the litigant's own tax position,[105] and has remained receptive to litigants alleging environmental,[106] aesthetic,[107] or social interests.[108]

The Court generally has recognized alleged future injuries. Stating that "[o]ne does not have to await the consummation of threatened injury to obtain preventive relief,"[109] the Court allowed nursing home residents to sue to prevent threatened transfers to other facilities.[110] The Court has allowed officeholders to challenge prohibitions and penalties on their running for other state offices without actually defying those limits.[111] And a union intending "conduct arguably affected with a constitutional interest"[112] and showing a "credible threat of prosecution" for that conduct was allowed to attack regulations on labor representation elections, consumer publicity, and boycotts.[113] But, as we have seen in *Lyons*, the Court was not willing to extend to injuries to be inflicted by the police[114] the principle that "past wrongs are evidence bearing on whether there is real and immediate threat of repeated injury."[115]

The *Lyons* result appears similarly anomalous since the Court has implicitly recognized that "problems capable of repetition, yet evading review"[116] are exceptions to traditional standing principles just as they are exceptions to mootness doctrine.[117] In *City of Revere v. Massachusetts General Hospital*,[118] for example, the Court allowed a hospital to raise a prisoner's due process and Eighth Amendment rights to state-funded medical treatment even though he had long since recovered from his injuries.[119] No showing was made that the prisoner personally was likely to be involved again in a similar incident. But if the Court had failed to rule on the claim, future prisoners might be deprived of the alleged right without having adequate opportunity for review by the Supreme Court.[120] Similarly, in *Reeves, Inc. v. Stake*,[121] the Court entertained a challenge to South Dakota's selling priority for in-state consumers of cement produced at its plant despite the fact that, at the time, all interested purchasers could receive as much cement as they wanted. The Court reasoned that, because the priority had been effective against interstate buyers in the past, and because economic conditions could make it a barrier in some future years, the buyers had suffered sufficient threatened injury.[122] This result presumably was influenced by the seasonal nature of the cement industry: periods of scarcity might last only one or two seasons, preventing Supreme Court review while they were still current.

Although standing remains a federal question insofar as it involves cases in the federal courts,[123] the Court has recognized an increasing number of situations where the operation of state law may confer standing valid even for federal purposes. A party to state proceedings asserting interests that would not by themselves suffice for standing in federal court may nonetheless be able to invoke the Supreme Court's appellate jurisdiction if the state court judgment would preclude relitigation in federal court of interests that are federally cognizable.[124] Although the Court in *Valley Forge* narrowly limited the federal taxpayer standing rule of *Flast v. Cohen*[125] to "congressional exercises of the power to tax and spend conferred by Art. I, § 8,"[126] the Court in *Marsh v. Chambers* accepted the standing of a state taxpayer and legislator to challenge the employment of a Presbyterian minister to open legislative sessions with a prayer.[127] Since the Establishment Clause was not originally applicable to the states,[128] the Court could hardly make much of whether the act was one of Congress[129] or whether the power to hire the chaplain and hold the prayer services was a power upon whose exercise "the Establishment Clause . . . operates as a specific constitutional limit."[130] The grant of standing would therefore seem to rest upon a view that the proper functioning of state governments is a far more palpable right of a state's citizenry than the legitimacy of the federal government is of American citizens generally.[131] Finally, the Court held in *City of Revere* that, to invoke prudential considerations for refusing to review a state court judgment because of deficiencies in the prevailing parties' standing would "serve no functional purpose": the respondents or appellees would be allowed to keep the very judgment the doctrine of standing would seek to deny them, and the petitioner or appellant would derive no benefit from the objection.[132] The *Revere* Court implicitly rejected the option of vacating the state court judgment and ordering the complaint dismissed, an extremely intrusive procedure to impose upon the state courts.[133]

The Court has also taken some steps toward recognizing a partial doctrine of "standing-by-necessity." The Court has long accepted a justiciability-by-necessity exception to the mootness doctrine for repeated and short-lived injuries.[134] In *United States Parole Commission v. Geraghty* it reiterated this view while noting that "mootness" and "standing" are really but two ways of looking at the same problem.[135] That *some* party must be able to challenge an alleged constitutional violation, at least where the subject has not been committed to the discretion of a coordinate branch, is implicit in decisions limiting standing "to those litigants best suited to assert a particular claim."[136] In *Duke Power Co. v. Carolina Environmental Study Group*, the Court emphasized that its prudential limitations on standing were focused primarily upon the assertion of third-party rights[137]—cases, of course, where the third parties will generally be able to assert their own rights. Granting standing to the third party would thus be unnecessary if some sound prudential reason justified a denial.[138]

Where the third parties for some reason cannot or are unlikely to assert their own rights, the Court has made an exception to its prudential rules and granted standing.[139] And in *Davis v. Passman*,[140] to vindicate the Court's role as final interpreter of the Constitution, as announced in *Marbury v. Madison*,[141] the Court has recognized a presumption in favor of the judicial enforceability of constitutional rights.[142] "At least in the absence of a textually demonstrable constitutional commitment of an issue to a coordinate political department, we presume that justiciable constitutional rights are to be enforced through the courts. And, unless such rights are to become merely precatory, the class of those litigants who allege that their own constitu-

tional rights have been violated, and who at the same time have no effective means other than the judiciary to enforce these rights, must be
able to invoke the existing jurisdiction of the courts for the protection
of their justiciable constitutional rights."[143] It seems unlikely that the
Court will proceed in the near future to articulate formally a general
theory of "standing-by-necessity." Nonetheless, if *Marbury* is to remain
the cornerstone of federal constitutional jurisprudence,[144] the Court
will be compelled to move in this direction, at least within the limits
specified in *Geraghty* and *Davis*.[145]

Two of those limits are "a textually demonstrable constitutional
commitment of an issue to a coordinate political department" and the
absence of any discernible injury to anyone.[146] And, in *Valley Forge
Christian College v. Americans United for Separation of Church and State,
Inc.*,[147] as we have seen, the Court made emphatically clear its unwillingness to extend the doctrine of taxpayer standing to fill in these
gaps.[148]

However, in another example of general liberalization of standing
rules, the Court has repeatedly reaffirmed the principle that a party attacking a statute as unconstitutionally discriminatory has standing to
challenge it as unconstitutionally underinclusive, even if the remedy
may be to extend the statute's burdens to exempt classes rather than to
unburden the plaintiff, or to eliminate a discriminatory benefit altogether rather than extend it to the plaintiff.[149] Even though the plaintiff's relief is entirely out of the Court's hands,[150] and even though one
would, in fact, expect a class of persons already singled out for discriminatory treatment to receive few gratuities from the state,[151] the
Court has allowed such challenges to these statutes because they
would otherwise be immune to review.

More broadly, the Court has definitively adopted "a relaxed
form"[152] of the causation requirement. In *Duke Power*, the Court noted that "our recent cases have required no more than a showing that
there is a 'substantial likelihood' that the relief requested will redress
the injury claimed."[153] This requirement may be met by showing only
"a 'fairly traceable' causal connection between the claimed injury and
the challenged conduct."[154] Just as the "injury in fact" may be procedurally generated,[155] so too the redress expected may be only an improvement in the party's procedural situation.[156]

A party may also be estopped to deny its opponent's standing if it
has proceeded as though the challenged action or rule of law was relevant to the opponent's legal status.[157] Although normally the parties

may not stipulate to the courts' jurisdiction, the adverse party may concede or admit facts showing or suggesting causation.[158] Claimants may show a sufficient causal link even if their fates will remain subject to their opponents' discretion if a favorable decision will entitle the claimants to fuller or more favorable consideration.[159] Indeed, the Court has been willing to follow very complex and attenuated chains of discretionary and factual uncertainties to find some scintilla of evidence that a favorable decision might potentially lead to a benefit for the plaintiff.[160] The Court repeatedly has refused to speculate about intervening circumstances or choices third parties might make that would deprive plaintiffs of any redress for their injuries even upon prevailing with their claims.[161]

One significant exception to this liberal trend in assessing causation issues has been the Court's application of the harmless error rule in reviewing criminal convictions. There, the Court has held "that it is the duty of a reviewing court to consider the trial record as a whole and to ignore errors that are harmless, including most constitutional violations."[162] The Court requires defendant-appellants with clear injuries in fact—criminal convictions—to show a causal link between acknowledged violations of their rights and those injuries by convincing the Court that, absent the abuses, it is not "clear beyond a reasonable doubt that the jury would have returned a verdict of guilty."[163] Although "beyond a reasonable doubt" is the correct constitutional standard of proof,[164] the trial judge or reviewing court is not the correct constitutional fact-finder.[165] In other cases, the Court has decided questions of standing on the basis of the claimants' allegations alone and thereby avoided depriving parties of their rights to trials and, where applicable, jury determinations of disputed facts.[166] When judges, especially judges who did not hear the evidence, examine the record, draw inferences, and resolve conflicts in testimony and questions of credibility to determine if a constitutional violation caused the defendants' convictions,[167] the defendants automatically lose at least one constitutional right, the right to a jury's evaluation of the permissible arguments and evidence pertaining to the defendants' guilt or innocence.[168] Moreover, in some cases an even heavier burden of showing that constitutional wrongs caused convictions, articulated variously as "more substantial indications of . . . likelihood" or a "reasonable possibility," has been imposed upon defendant-appellants.[169] These cases provide a pointed reminder that "[t]he causation requirement is . . . highly manipulable; its isolation by the Supreme Court as a separate element of the injury in fact requirement poses a serious risk that, in the guise of causality analysis, federal courts will engage in an unprincipled effort to screen from their dockets claims they substantively disfavor."[170]

As we saw above in the discussion of *Duke Power*, the Court has dispensed altogether with the troublesome "nexus requirement" except in the special context of taxpayer suits.[171] Similarly, the Court has liberally treated the closely related issues of surrogate and third-party standing.[172] *Duke Power*[173] stands for the proposition that, once litigants show *any* injury in fact to themselves, they may raise any objections they have to the challenged conduct.[174] The main limitation on surrogate standing now seems to be adequacy of representation.[175] Groups may assert the rights of their members[176] and individuals may assert the rights of groups to which they belong.[177] Claimants may also raise claims based upon the rights of those likely to have substantially similar interests in the future with respect to the challenged action.[178] Although groups may not sue merely to "vindicate bystander interests in the rule of law,"[179] they do have standing if they assert that the challenged action interferes with their *activities* on behalf of an ideological principle, as opposed to the attainment of that goal as such.[180] Similarly, litigants with claims based on the First Amendment may often assert the interests of other persons whose expression or receipt of expression might be curtailed by a decision adverse to the litigant.[181] And a state "may act as the representative of its citizens . . . where the injury alleged affects the general population of a State in a substantial way."[182] Finally, the claim of a right to act as representative of others is *itself* a cognizable interest, in effect allowing litigants to pursue third parties' substantive claims when the litigants themselves have none currently.[183] Once again, however, far stricter rules of standing have been imposed on criminal defendants to prevent their asserting third-party rights.[184]

THE DOCTRINAL IMPLICATIONS OF LYONS

A survey of the cases where standing would necessarily have been denied under the *Lyons* approach demonstrates the extreme and unprecedented nature of the Court's rejection of completed harm as constituting an "injury in fact" and of its demand for certainty of future injuries before a party may seek injunctive relief. Most or all ballot access cases[185] seeking prospective relief would have to be dismissed after the election at issue was held since no one could ever prove with certainty that the candidates indeed would seek access in a future election,[186] would meet all legitimate access requirements,[187] and would be denied access for illegitimate reasons.[188] Yet *Clements v. Fashing*,[189] decided only a term before and nowhere cited in *Lyons*, allows standing to obtain declaratory and injunctive relief on a far less substantial showing.[190]

Voting rights cases would probably suffer a similar fate.[191] Questions about state and national political conventions would disappear once the closing gavel came down.[192] Abortion cases,[193] particularly given the inherent vagaries of human reproduction, would have to be filed and litigated during the subject pregnancy—indeed during the trimester of the alleged deprivation of rights[194]—apart from suits for damages.[195] And most durational residency requirement cases[196] would dissolve once the plaintiff had completed the specified period, especially since the plaintiff would be hard-pressed to "make a reasonable showing that he will again be subjected to the alleged illegality."[197]

Perhaps the most startling example of a case whose grant of standing would be overruled if *Lyons* were to be accepted at face value as a standing case is *Regents of the University of California v. Bakke*.[198] Although the case was not originally brought in a federal court, the Supreme Court's jurisdiction to review the California Supreme Court's judgment depended upon precisely the same kind of standing analysis.[199] Allan Bakke unsuccessfully applied for admission to the University of California at Davis Medical School's entering classes in both 1973 and 1974.[200] Following his rejections, he, like Adolph Lyons, filed an individual action for mandatory, injunctive, and declaratory relief against the Davis "Special Admissions Program."[201] He sought an order compelling his admittance to a later class of the Medical School but apparently never demanded that he be allowed to join either of the classes to which he had been denied entry.[202] One of those classes presumably completed its studies a few months after certiorari was granted; the other graduated shortly before the Court announced its judgment.[203] Unlike Lyons, Bakke sought no damages for his alleged prior wrongful rejections.[204]

Since Bakke, like Lyons, did not and probably could not claim redress that would have undone the alleged wrong committed against him, his claim was for future, preventive relief only: he sought an order forbidding Davis to again deny him admission to later entering classes for the allegedly unconstitutional reasons that caused his prior rejections. Similarly, Lyons sought protection against future allegedly unconstitutional chokings. If Bakke's continuing lack of a medical education resulting from the consummated acts of the past supplied him standing to demand admission to a future class, then surely Lyons' continuing throat injury and continuing fear of police chokings gave him standing to have the police prevented from choking him again. If a finding of constitutional violations in the past admissions decisions freed Bakke from having to show that he would in the future suffer a wrongful denial of his rights—or estopped Davis from questioning whether he would—then a simple showing that Lyons had been wrongfully choked in the past should entitle him to the same presumption of recurrence that Bakke enjoyed. Fluctuations in the quality of applicant pools,[205] different evaluations of Bakke's own qualifications,[206] and Bakke's ever-advancing age[207] might well have prevented his admission to the 1978 entering class without regard to the Special Admissions Program. By contrast, there was no indication that any factors that led to Lyons' strangling materially changed.[208]

Bakke, suing as a white person subject to discrimination, could hardly have made the allegations the *Lyons* rule required: "not only that he would have another encounter with" the Davis Admissions Office "but also . . . the incredible assertion" either (1) that the Admissions Office "*always*" rejects any white applicant, whether or not he has superior qualifications, or (2) that the regents of University of California "ordered or authorized" the Admissions Office "to act in such a manner."[209] Even if Bakke did make these allegations, he still would be denied standing since his assertions would certainly be "belied by the record made on the application for . . . injunction."[210]

Bakke's claim also is considerably weaker than Lyons' on the equitable principles on which the Court relied. Denial of a medical education starting in a particular year at a particular institution hardly seems as "irreparable" an injury as loss of life, serious bodily injury, or even a continuing fear of venturing where one might encounter the police.[211] Nor would "the injury that" Bakke "allegedly suffered in" 1973 and 1974 "go unrecompensed; for that injury he has an adequate remedy at law."[212] Damages would far more adequately make up for Bakke's alleged lost income than would a survivors' action compensate Lyons for his life, or a tort claim for damage to his voice and larynx.[213] Bakke's remedy was far more intrusive upon the state institution in his case than the injunction Lyons sought would have been for the Los

Angeles Police Department. Bakke sought wholly to bypass the admissions process and replace the Medical School's professional evaluation with the courts' judgment that he should be admitted to the entering class of 1978. He never had to show either that the Medical School would not have admitted him to the class of 1978 without judicial intervention[214] or that he would be admitted to that class if the Special Admissions Program was discontinued.[215] Lyons, on the other hand, was explicitly prepared to leave the decision on applying choke holds to the police and even allowed for "reasonable" errors abridging constitutional rights:[216] the standard the police were to apply was that people would not be choked "except in situations where the proposed victim of said control reasonably appears to be threatening the immediate use of deadly force."[217] The "reasonably appears" standard fully responded to the exigencies of rushed police decision making on the streets; beyond that, the issues Lyons asked the Court to decide were merely ones of police policy little different in kind from procedures specifying how and when to conduct searches, arrests, lineups, and interrogations—all questions on which the Court has been willing to constrain police administrators.[218] Surely these questions were far more clearly within judicial competence[219] than sifting two to three dozen applications for each vacancy at a medical school.[220]

The point, of course, is that the *Lyons* rule effectively bars challenges to arbitrary, individuated abuses by requiring "incredible" and "unbelievable" assertions that the alleged arbitrary abuse is precisely what it is not: absolutely uniform across a broad, clearly and currently definable class.[221] Yet if that assertion is somehow made and proved, the plaintiff risks being thrown out of court as "no more entitled to an injunction than any other citizen" for an injury shared in common.[222] If some classes of possible victims, such as the members of a particular racial group, may anticipate that they will, for that reason, be denied some right while other, less starkly definable groups, like those in the criminal justice cases,[223] may not anticipate obviously predictable actions against them, then the Court has in effect imported into all cases alleging arbitrary, occasional deprivations of constitutional rights the requirement that a "suspect classification" be shown.[224]

Alternatively, the Court—by imposing "strict in theory, fatal in fact"[225] standing requirements on plaintiffs alleging pretrial abuses of criminal justice rights, while allowing, for example, those claiming violations of rights to reproductive choice[226] liberal standing to prevent those violations[227]—is creating a hierarchy of constitutional rights for purposes of standing analysis.[228] Yet only one Term before, in *Valley Forge*, the Court explicitly renounced the existence of any such hierarchy.[229] In some cases, a state's past abusive acts work a forfeiture of its control of the decisions involved;[230] in others, where different substantive rights are involved, the state nonetheless is made beneficiary of an irrebuttable presumption of legitimacy through recognition of "the special delicacy of the adjustment to be preserved between federal equitable power and State administration of its own law."[231] Contrary to what should be true of rules under, or inspired by, Article III, the standing principles expounded in *Lyons* are not the least bit uniform across kinds of causes of action.[232] And because of their great artificiality and abstraction, the constraining rules imposed in one case may not be so intuitively obvious in their application to another that the Court needs even to raise them where it chooses, for whatever reason, to reach the merits.[233]

Despite the clarity and growing simplicity of the standing doctrine, its basic structure remains impressionistic and highly discretionary. It remains a brooding omnipresence with the potential to descend upon and annihilate otherwise indisputable claims for the protection of individual rights.[234] In *Lyons*, the Court used a finding of insufficient standing to extend the principles of extreme judicial deference to the judgment of military authorities initially developed in such cases as *Hirabayashi v. United States*[235] and *Korematsu v. United States*[236] to the actions of the police on the streets of American cities.[237]

Lyons must therefore be understood as a decision of substantive law, despite the Court's formal reliance on the doctrines of standing and despite the procedural mess in which the case reached the Court.[238] Accordingly, it should be analyzed and criticized as such.[239] The case represents a further extension and reification of the Court's general, sweeping respect and deference for men in uniform[240] that has overridden a wide range of substantive law claims.[241] The Court seems to be treating the issues Lyons raised as ones constitutionally committed to the discretion of the police[242] and thus immune from judicial review,[243] except insofar as an after-the-fact damages action may be available.[244] The Court's general trend toward exempting police conduct from judicial scrutiny prior to, or in the absence of, a criminal trial[245] certainly deserves a more principled and straightforward explanation than the Court has thus far offered.[246] Its suggestions that the answer is in recourse to the state courts have become increasingly muted and unconvincing.[247] Its pat urgings of appeals to the "local authorities"[248] are as politically unrealistic as always where applied to deprivations of the rights of a few discrete individuals within a large polity,[249] especially in view of the Court's own contemporaneous decisions limiting the channels of social debate.[250] Its claims of police necessity[251] ring more and more hollow with each additional decision expanding police freedom of operation, not uncommonly at the expense of some important constitutional right.[252] So, too, do its oft-repeated assurances of judicial vigilance against police abuses.[253] These cases in general, and *Lyons* in particular, offer sad proof of the consequences for principled, rational discourse when a sufficient majority of a decision-making body sets its collective mind, for whatever reason, on a particular result.[254]

Similarly, in *Valley Forge*, the Court used standing to avoid a decision on the merits.[255] Its holding represented in part an aversion to citizen actions for "waste" against the federal government. The Court seemed irked that the plaintiffs had "learned of the conveyance through a news release"[256] and that none of the individual plaintiffs were residents of the state where the property was located.[257] In an era when many federal agencies frequently face accusations of waste and mismanagement of public resources, the Court may have been apprehensive about letting these accusations be aired in federal court.[258] If spending programs seemed more appropriate targets for litigation to the Court, it may be because the Court believes they tend to be fewer,[259] larger,[260] and more purposeful[261] than property disposition arrangements.[262] However dubious these assumptions may be in the abstract, once something as important as a practical immunity from judicial review is made to ride on the distinction between "spending" and "property disposition," the lines can be expected to blur altogether.[263]

It seems odd to be discussing important substantive issues concerning police behavior and religious subsidies—as well as nuclear meltdowns—in a section denominated "standing." It is far more odd—and dangerous—to watch the Supreme Court deciding those substantive issues behind a facade of "standing" analysis. The Supreme Court's trend toward more liberal general standing rules—often developed in cases like *Duke Power* when the Court wants to reach the merits—is to be welcomed.[264] But our relief that the Court has removed or reduced the burdens that many hypertechnical rules of standing place on general litigants should be tempered by a recognition that the Court's new bifurcated standing analysis is proving "fatal in fact"[265] to large and important classes of claimants and, through them, ultimately to certain vital, though currently disfavored, constitutional rights.[266] These latter cases are stark testimony to the "trend of resolving cases at the 'threshold' while obscuring the nature of the underlying rights and interests at stake."[267]

CHAPTER NINE

THE ERRANT TRAJECTORY OF STATE SOVEREIGNTY

Prior to the mid-1970s, "states' rights" were more rhetoric than reality. It was always understood that under the Tenth Amendment those powers not delegated to the national government were reserved to the states and to the people.[1] "States' rights" were the things left over after the content of national power was determined. Throughout the history of the Supreme Court, the content of national power waxed and waned. But there was never any serious doubt that, if something was within the affirmative power of the national government, it was without the reserved authority of the several states. In that sense, states' rights never functioned the way that individual rights did. Individual rights operated as trump cards over exercises of congressional power that were affirmatively authorized by the Constitution. But states' rights were not an override; they were a residue.

In *National League of Cities v. Usury*,[2] for the first time in our history, the Supreme Court expressly sculpted out of the amorphous clay of states' rights a true override—a veto on otherwise authorized congressional legislation. From the start, there has been a great deal of controversy about the meaning—and the wisdom—of *National League of Cities*, where the Court struck down a garden-variety federal wage-and-hours regulation as applied to state and municipal employees.[3] And subsequent decisions rendered by the Supreme Court suggest that the confusion and discord spawned by *National League of Cities* have not been limited to commentators and lower courts, but have been shared by the justices themselves. At first, the Court applied the new Tenth Amendment[4] trump straightforwardly, reaching predictable and unanimous decisions in *Hodel v. Virginia Surface Mining & Reclamation Ass'n.*[5] and *United Transportation Union v. Long Island R.R.*

121

Co.[6] But in three later cases—*FERC v. Mississippi*,[7] *Community Communications Co. v. City of Boulder*[8] and *EEOC v. Wyoming*,[9]—narrow majorities of the Court handed down problematic decisions rendering the future of the trump highly uncertain. Although the most basic message of *National League of Cities*—that some things the Constitution affirmatively authorizes the national government to do to individuals and entities it nonetheless prohibits Congress or the executive from doing to the states—probably remains valid, the location and contours of these islands of state sovereignty have become something of a growing mystery.

In *Hodel v. Virginia Surface Mining & Reclamation Assn.*,[10] the Supreme Court voted unanimously [11] to uphold against a Tenth Amendment attack the Surface Mining Control and Reclamation Act of 1977.[12] The Act sets detailed requirements for strip-mining, including rules for restoring strip-mined lands to their original contours. The Act offered the states the option of either formulating their own programs in conformity with minimum federal standards or defaulting to a program of regulation to be financed and administered by the Department of the Interior.

In a straightforward opinion, Justice Marshall laid the challenged provisions of the statute next to a three-part test derived from *National League of Cities*.[13] In order to succeed, a claim that commerce power legislation is invalid under the Tenth Amendment as interpreted in *National League of Cities* must establish that the challenged law regulates the "States as States," addresses matters that are "indisputably 'attribute[s] of state sovereignty,'" and directly impairs the ability of the states "to structure integral operations in areas of traditional governmental functions."[14] The Court's inquiry was brief because the challenged provisions of the Surface Mining Act governed "only the activities of coal mine operators who are private individuals and businesses,"[15] and thereby failed to satisfy the first part of the test. Since the states were still free to promulgate whatever regulations they wished so long as they were not inconsistent with minimum federal guidelines, *Hodel* was a preeemption case, pure and simple. The Court declared that the Tenth Amendment in no way "limits congressional power to pre-empt or displace state regulation of private activities affecting interstate commerce."[16] The only limitation is that the means selected be "reasonably related" to the regulatory purpose.[17]

The oral argument in *Hodel* revealed at least several justices groping for ways to translate into doctrine their intuitive sense that Congress had finally reached matters of purely local concern, in an area—land use—traditionally reserved to the states, with legislative findings of links to interstate commerce that were transparent fabrications. Yet because of the fairly clear line drawn in *National League of Cities* between the plenary power of Congress to substitute national for state policy in any sphere of private life subject to the dual jurisdiction of national and state governments, and the limited power of Congress to interfere with the structuring by the states of traditional state government functions, it would have made no sense for the Court to backpedal and announce that certain subjects—such as land use—are so intrinsically local that Congress may not regulate them even when their cumulative impact affects interstate commerce. As Justice Jackson is said to have put the matter, "if interstate commerce feels the *pinch*, it matters not how local is the *squeeze*." Because it could find no judicially enforceable limit on this side of the dividing line, the Court unanimously confirmed that the only islands of state sovereignty are those that rose from the sea with *National League of Cities*.[18] In short, in *Hodel*, the Supreme Court took doctrine seriously.

One of the problems with *National League of Cities* is that it left unclear *which* state and local government functions are so "traditional" that Congress may not under the Commerce Clause impinge on their performance by the states.[19] In *United Transportation Union v. Long Island R.R. Co.*,[20] the Court began to delineate the perimeter which circumscribes the states' "traditional functions."

The state of New York sought to avoid the application of the Railway Labor Act[21] to a dispute between the state-owned Long Island Railroad and the unions. The case thus presented a classic *National League of Cities* question: given that the Commerce Clause undeniably empowers Congress to regulate the labor relations of the nation's railroad companies, does the application of such legislation to a railway owned and operated by a state violate the Constitution's vision of federalism as celebrated in the Tenth Amendment?[22] The Court, speaking through the Chief Justice, engaged in a routine application of the tripartite test as set out in *Hodel* and focused exclusively on part three, the requirement that the "States' compliance with federal law would directly impair their ability 'to structure integral operations in areas of traditional functions'" if the law is to be struck down.[23] Although that determination might ordinarily be a difficult one, in this case the Court did not have to write on a clean slate because in *National League of Cities* itself the Court had explicitly exempted from its holding several cases involving federal regulation of state-run railways.[24] That specific exception, plus the long history of federal regulation of railroads, made *Long Island R.R.* an easy case.

The Chief Justice, however, went further to explain that the holding was not based merely on *National League of Cities* dicta or on a purely retrospective view of which state functions are "traditional." Even while reciting at length the history of private railroads and their federal regulation, the Court claimed that "traditional function" was not meant to be an historical hammerlock on protected state activity but merely a requirement that a reviewing court inquire into whether federal regulation would "hamper the state government's ability to fulfill its role in the Union and endanger its 'separate and independent existence.'"[25] Those phrases by themselves are opaque vessels which provide little if any guidance.

The distinguishing principle must be that, whereas such activities as law enforcement and fire protection can effectively be administered on a state or local basis, Congress, as the unanimous Court emphasized in *Long Island R.R.*, must have the authority to regulate railway labor disputes throughout the country if our national network of railroads is to function efficiently.[26] Yet the Court in its dicta appeared to be reaching for a broader rule that the states may not be allowed, "by acquiring functions previously performed by the private sector, to erode federal authority in areas *traditionally* subject to federal statutory regulation."[27] This reading of the opinion is buttressed by the Chief Justice's quotation of his concurring opinion in *Lafayette v. Louisiana Power & Light Co.*,[28] where he wrote: "It should be evident, I would think, that the running of a business enterprise is not an integral operation in the area of traditional governmental functions."[29] The Court also stressed that New York knew full well when it acquired the railroad that it did so subject to a long-standing and comprehensive scheme of federal regulation; indeed, both the state and the unions operated in accord with and made use of the procedures of the Railway Labor Act for thirteen years after the acquisition.[30] In a sense New York had notice that it acquired the railroad subject to the RLA; by operating under that federal law for thirteen years without claiming any impairment of its sovereignty, New York became estopped from objecting to the RLA. Although this point would appear to be irrelevant to the Commerce Clause analysis, the fact that the Court spent several paragraphs at the close of the opinion making it suggests that the Court's obvious, albeit disclaimed, reliance on history may well cut both ways. That is, just as an area traditionally occupied by private enterprise which historically has been the province of federal regulation cannot be immunized by *National League of Cities* simply because a state takes on the role of proprietor, so a function that has not historically been federally regulated may be presumptively immune from federal interference even when a state takes it over. For example, a state that decides to begin the provision of funeral home and burial services can perhaps claim protection from future federal interference under the Commerce Clause since there was no history of regulation to give the state notice.[31]

The self-disciplined devotion to doctrine that characterized both *Hodel* and *Long Island R.R.* is all the more anomolous because of its absence from the next major states' rights decision. In *Federal Energy Regulatory Commission v. Mississippi*,[32] the Supreme Court effectively abandoned the approach it had taken to Tenth Amendment cases since *National League of Cities.* The three-part test for claims challenging Commerce Clause legislation, which had been fundamental to the Court's analysis in both *Hodel*[33] and *Long Island R.R.*,[34] was relegated to a footnote by the majority opinion in *FERC v. Mississippi.*[35]

The dispute in *FERC* involved a challenge by the state of Mississippi to certain provisions of the Public Utility Regulatory Policies Act of 1978 (PURPA)[36] on the grounds that they were an invasion of state sovereignty and hence a violation of the Tenth Amendment.[37] The majority and the dissent agreed that the part of PURPA requiring the FERC to prepare and promulgate in consultation with the state public utility commissions (PUCs) a series of rules exempting certain electrical generating facilities from state laws was a straightforward example of preemption and therefore no problem.[38] Similarly, there was agreement that requiring the state PUCs to "implement" these federal regulations was constitutional because, given the interpretation of the rules in this case, all they required was that the Mississippi Public Service Commission exercise its already existing jurisdiction over a few disputes analogous to the kind it already routinely handled.[39]

The Court divided sharply over the remaining PURPA provisions.[40] These required the state PUCs, as a condition to their further regulatory activity in this area, to "consider" a set of FERC proposals. The statute describes in great detail the procedures which the state authorities must follow when evaluating these proposals, but does not compel the states actually to adopt them.[41] In stark contrast to the passing attention given the three-part *National League of Cities* test by the majority, Justice O'Connor made it the backbone of her dissent and concluded that Titles I and III of PURPA offend all three of the criteria as they were laid out in *Hodel*.[42]

First, Titles I and III direct their commands solely to the states, telling their PUCs which proposed standards to consider and in what manner.[43] Second, they "address attribute[s] of state sovereignty" by commandeering the agenda of a state agency and telling it how to structure its policy-making process.[44] Finally, the dissent argued that by taxing the limited resources of state agencies concerned with utility regulation, a traditional state function, PURPA directly impairs the ability of the states to "structure integral operations in areas of traditional governmental functions."[45] The majority agreed by implication with Justice O'Connor's analysis with respect to the first and second points, but disagreed on the third.[46]

The majority, in an opinion by Justice Blackmun, disagreed with Justice O'Connor even though it "acknowledge[d] that 'the authority to make . . . fundamental . . . decisions' is perhaps the quintessential attribute of sovereignty."[47] The Court went so far as to conclude that "the ability of a state . . . administrative body—which makes decisions and sets policy for the State as a whole—to consider and promulgate regulations of its choosing must be central to a State's role in the federal system,"[48] yet deprived the Mississippi Public Service Commission of that very freedom of operation. This wholly unprecedented step[49] was treated lightly by the majority and justified by brief reference to three cases. The majority considered *Fry v. United States*[50] analogous because, in applying a national wage-price freeze to state employees, the federal government in *Fry* was directing state decision makers to *refrain* from taking the action of raising pay.[51] Surely telling a state that it temporarily may not increase its financial burden is distinguishable from ordering it to take up federally dictated business in a federally dictated way. *National League of Cities* itself distinguished *Fry* as a minimally intrusive[52] step, which "displaced no state choices as to how governmental operations should be structured, nor . . . force[d] the States to remake such choices themselves."[53] Justice Rehnquist emphasized, moreover, that the imposition of the wage freeze was only temporary and was necessitated by a national emergency requiring national action.[54]

Justice Blackmun then made a brief excursion into Indian law [55] to cite *Washington v. Fishing Vessel Association*[56] for the proposition that "federal law [can] impose an affirmative obligation upon state officials to prepare administrative regulations."[57] The Court in that case held no such thing. The power of the federal court in *Fishing Vessel Ass'n.* derived from the fact that various state fishing regulations were in direct contravention of a federal Indian treaty[58] and that, as parties to the litigation, the state fish and game agencies could be ordered to comply with the district court's ruling.[59] The *Fishing Vessel Ass'n.* Court expressed its doubt that state agencies "may be ordered actually to promulgate regulations having effect as a matter of state law," and therefore directed that, should the state authorities be unwilling or unable to comply, the district court should take over supervision of the state fisheries and issue its own detailed remedial orders.[60]

Finally, the majority cited *Testa v. Katt*[61]—a case holding that state courts must entertain federal claims which parallel the state claims such courts would entertain—as an indication that the federal government has some power to enlist a branch of state government to further federal ends.[62] Yet the state courts in *Testa v. Katt*, unlike the PUCs in FERC, did not have the power to set their own agendas.[63] Furthermore, as Justice Powell pointed out in his dissent, *Testa* took the state courts as it found them—it did not alter their internal procedures as PURPA does—and it limited its holding to cases where the state court already had adequate jurisdiction "under established local law" to hear the federal action.[64]

The majority in FERC is presumably encouraged in its cavalier treatment of these cases by its belief that its holding does not represent a significant intrusion into state sovereignty for the simple reason that, while PURPA requires state PUCs to *consider* certain federal proposals, it does not *compel* their *adoption*.[65] In fact, if a state is willing to forego regulation of utilities altogether, it need not even consider the suggested federal standards. The majority likens this exercise of conditional preemption to the legislative scheme in *Hodel*, where the states could continue to regulate strip-mining so long as their laws and rules were consistent with minimum federal standards.[66] The problem with that comparison is that the Court in *Hodel* indicated that requiring such affirmative acts on the part of the states could very well transgress the principles of the Tenth Amendment as expounded in *National League of Cities*. On the very same page from which the majority in FERC takes its quotations, Justice Marshall wrote for the unanimous Court in *Hodel* that the legislation challenged there was constitutionally acceptable because the states were "not compelled to enforce the steep-slope standards, to expend any state funds, or *to participate in the federal regulatory program in any manner whatsoever.*"[67]

The majority's argument is that, so long as any and all state action in a given area is preemptible by reason of congressional Commerce Clause power, Congress may predicate permission for future state activity on any terms it wishes; the apparently greater power to preempt includes the supposedly lesser power to dictate conditions on which a state may act. This argument may be acceptable insofar as it merely requires that state regulations of private conduct comply with federal regulations of the same conduct, as in *Hodel*. But in *FERC* the majority stretches the argument beyond reason by implying that the power to require affirmative action of the states and the power to coerce structural changes in the state regulatory apparatus are also "lesser" included powers of preemption. The majority seems to assume that, so long as the *end* defined by complete federal preemption is constitutionally permissible, it matters not which *means* Congress uses to approach the limits of federal power. Yet surely Justice O'Connor is correct that "[t]he Constitution permits Congress to govern only through certain channels. If the Tenth Amendment principles articulated in *National League of Cities* . . . and *Hodel* . . . foreclose PURPA's approach, it is no answer to argue that Congress could have reached the same destination by a different route."[68]

In support of its argument, the majority draws an analogy to the federal spending power, saying that conditions can be attached to federal handouts to the states so as to dictate to them on subjects that are not properly of federal concern, citing *Oklahoma v. Civil Service Commission*.[69] The Court argues that the same power to condition exists under the Commerce Clause, and that Congress may "'resort to all means for the exercise of a granted power which are appropriate and plainly adapted to the permitted end.'"[70] Yet the majority fundamentally misconstrues the holding in *Civil Service Comm'n.* by saying that, because the "end" there was the disbursement of federal funds, Congress could parcel out its money on any terms it wished. That argument proves far too much. The *method* in *Civil Service Comm'n.* was disbursement of funds; the *end* was better public service in the administration of "funds for national needs," as the opinion in that case explicitly states.[71] The majority in *FERC* misses the crucial point that the end must in itself be constitutionally permissible. So although Congress may condition grants-in-aid to the states so as to enhance the quality of administration of funds for the national highways, it may not predicate the grant of food stamp appropriations on a state's agreement to move its capital to a federally designated location,[72] or offer a state the choice between paying state and local employees a designated wage and firing them and closing down operation of the basic services they perform.[73] The spending power does not allow wholesale federal interference in inappropriate and unrelated areas in the form of bribery.[74]

Moreover, analogies to the spending power do not advance the majority's argument for an expansive reading of coercive power under the Commerce Clause because the Court in *National League of Cities* explicitly distinguished the spending power, along with Section Five of the Fourteenth Amendment, as sources of congressional authority that might support intrusions into state operations that would be impermissible if grounded on the Commerce Clause.[75]

The *FERC* majority's reasoning that Congress may dictate any terms it pleases so long as it could preempt state activities altogether simply cannot be taken literally. As Justice Powell points out in his dissent, under this "threat of preemption" reasoning, Congress could reduce the states to mere "federal provinces."[76] That such a result would run afoul of the notions of state sovereignty delineated in *National League of Cities* is suggested by the similarity of the language used by the Chief Justice just one week after that landmark decision, when he wrote that its purpose was to "arrest the downgrading of States to a role comparable to the departments of France, governed entirely out of the national capital."[77]

More specifically, so long as *National League of Cities* is law, a broad reading of *FERC* cannot be sustained because the expansive preemption principle it announces would completely eviscerate the Court's holding in *National League of Cities* itself. The majority in that case specifically conceded that the legislation at issue, the Fair Labor Standards Act (FLSA), was "undoubtedly within the scope of the Commerce Clause."[78] According to a broad reading of *FERC*, this means that—since the areas subject to the FLSA were preemptible—Congress had the authority to dictate wages and work conditions to the states as a condition of their continued employment of personnel to provide traditional services with respect to the areas at issue: in effect, the states could continue to patrol the public highways and clean up the public hospitals (rather than having these tasks federally preempted) only on the condition that they pay public employees in these areas according to a federal schedule. Yet that is exactly what *National League of Cities* held Congress could not require. A broad reading of *FERC* would thus blow a hole in *National League of Cities* large enough to throw Mississippi and the other forty-nine states through, but the Court explicitly denied that it was overruling or even undervaluing the earlier case.[79]

The *FERC* majority limited its holding by saying that it does "not purport to authorize the imposition of general affirmative obligations on the states."[80] Nor did the majority feel it was necessary to make "a definitive choice between competing views of federal power to compel state regulatory activity."[81] All the Court held, then, is that Congress can condition a state's exercise of *some* of its regulatory power over private entities in a preemptible area on the state's *consideration* of a few federal proposals. It does not follow, for example, that Congress could require a state to adopt a policy of indifference to the hazards of nuclear waste disposal as a condition of regulating electrical utilities. The majority itself saw its holding as a narrow one, because it simply did not consider PURPA's requirements to be a significant intrusion upon state sovereignty.[82] A narrow reading of the Court's opinion is further necessitated by the majority's concession that the ability of a state administrative body "to consider and promulgate regulations of its choosing must be central to a State's role in the federal system."[83] If *FERC* is thus severely limited to its facts, its narrow holding presumably would not allow Congress under the Commerce Clause to compel states to *adopt* federal proposals, to consider *only* federal proposals, or even to conscript a *significant* portion of a state's regulatory apparatus in the manner in which PURPA drafts state utility commissions into the federal bureaucracy.[84]

Justice O'Connor is probably correct in her judgment that the novelty of PURPA's scheme may have obscured the majority's vision.[85] The nature of the congressional coercion in *FERC* is different from that in *Hodel*, the case that the majority finds so instructive. In *Hodel*, Congress said to the states, "Do it our way, or *we* will do it ourselves." In *FERC*, Congress told them, "Do it our way, or else *no one* will do it," thereby offering the states a choice between compliance and creation of a regulatory vacuum from which their citizens would suffer.[86] It might be answered that PURPA does not really offer the states such a

Hobson's choice, because they can continue regulating if they just take a little time to look at a few federal proposals. But this is precisely PUR-PA's vice: independent of the substantive policy result, it tells the states how to go about their governmental business. It assaults the structure of state decision making by telling the states exactly *how* to decide, by prescribing such things as hearing procedures and reporting requirements and by dictating the scope of public involvement in the regulatory process.[87] The majority argued that, by involving the state utility commissions and thereby vindicating the value of local participation in government,[88] PURPA preserves and furthers federalism more than would a scheme of outright federal preemption.[89] Yet the latter simply tells the states to get out of the way; the former compels the states to do the federal government's bidding.[90]

It may be virtually impossible to halt the erosion of state sovereignty caused by preemptive federal legislation, because the Supremacy Clause is essential to our federal system of government; national cohesion and national policy coherence demand it. But we surely can avoid insulting the states by ordering them about like so many federal bureaucratic lackeys when the federal constitutional rights of individuals are not at stake. It is just this sort of condescension that *National League of Cities* ostensibly addressed and seemingly proscribed. It is one thing for the Constitution to dictate the way of the world to the states and quite another for Congress to do so. The Commerce Clause, after all, empowers Congress to regulate commerce, not to regulate the states.

Even if the inroads PURPA makes on state regulatory autonomy do not appear significant, their ultimate cumulative effect should be of concern. FERC, as Justice Powell notes, could well be a fateful first step. No one expects Congress to obliterate the states in one fell swoop. "If there is any danger, it lies in the tyranny of small decisions—in the prospect that Congress will nibble away at state sovereignty, bit by bit, until someday essentially nothing is left but a gutted shell."[91]

Nor should we be dissuaded from that objection because the affront that FERC works on the states may seem to be merely symbolic. The Tenth Amendment may certainly be invoked even when there is no real danger that Congress is literally on the verge of emasculating state government. After all, in *National League of Cities* itself no claim seriously could have been made that the imposition of wage-and-hour regulations on the states would threaten their meaningful existence.[92]

What is required, and what is lacking in the majority opinion in
FERC, is a "sensitivity to the legitimate interests of both State and National Governments."[93]

The majority in FERC v. Mississippi accused Justice O'Connor of
expounding an "almost mystical" view of state sovereignty.[94] That
criticism seems overly harsh in light of the fact that the Court has
been unable to provide a satisfying picture of the new federalism since
its inception in National League of Cities. The formulations of Tenth
Amendment principles in that case were so Delphic in their ambiguity
that observers could draw no real conclusions as to the decision's
meaning; they could make at best the most tentative suggestions.[95]

Attempts to gain a grasp of the Court's conception of federalism
are especially frustrated by cases in which the Court, apparently unaware that it is doing so at all, renders decisions having enormous implications for Tenth Amendment doctrine. In Community Communications Co. v. City of Boulder,[96] the Court faced the question of whether
the state action exemption from Sherman Act liability announced in
Parker v. Brown[97] applies to municipalities which exercise self-government under a home-rule provision in the state constitution. The Colorado Constitution "vests" in "the people" of every town with a population of two thousand or more "the full right of self-government in both
local and municipal matters."[98] With respect to those matters, the City
Charter and ordinances made pursuant thereto "supersede" the laws
of the state.[99]

In 1979, Community Communications, which had been the sole
operator of cable television services in Boulder for fifteen years under a
nonexclusive city license, informed the Boulder City Council that it
planned to take advantage of the expansion in service made possible
by new technology. Afraid that Community Communications might
thereby gain an insurmountable advantage over would-be competitors who were finally willing to enter the market, the City Council
enacted an ordinance prohibiting the established company from expanding operations for three months.[100] When Community Communications sought an injunction restraining the ordinance on the
grounds that it violated the Sherman Act, Boulder claimed that its ordinances were exempt from antitrust scrutiny under the doctrine of
Parker v. Brown. Justice Brennan, writing for the five-member majority,[101] concluded that even assuming the moratorium was within the
power delegated to Boulder by the Home Rule Amendment,[102] "[it

could not] be exempt from antitrust scrutiny unless it constitute[d] the action of the State of Colorado itself in its sovereign capacity, or unless it constitute[d] municipal action in furtherance or implementation of clearly articulated and affirmatively expressed state policy."[103] The Court ruled that a policy of neutrality toward local ordinances is not enough to protect local governments from the Sherman Act, and the Home Rule Amendment is by definition a neutral delegation: the state legislature is without power to legislate regarding home-rule municipalities in areas preempted by local enactments, so it cannot "affirmatively express" a *state* policy.[104]

The rationale for the Court's holding in *Boulder* that federalism is not implicated when a local ordinance is preempted by a federal statute is that ours is a dual system of government—a sovereign nation of many sovereign states—which has no place for sovereign cities.[105] Only the sovereign states are immune from Congress' antitrust laws, and they can cloak their political subdivisions with that aegis of sovereignty only by enacting an explicit anticompetitive policy at the state level. The majority contends that its holding renders a state "'no less able to allocate governmental power between itself and its political subdivisions. It means only that when the State itself has not directed or authorized an anticompetitive practice, the State's subdivisions in exercising their delegated power must obey the antitrust laws.'"[106] Yet by telling the states that they may delegate their powers but not their limited sovereign immunity from the Commerce Clause, the Court forces the states to bear the burden of regulating for their municipalities and prevents them from allowing local governments to experiment and profit from their different experiences.

Such direct interference with the relationship a state chooses to establish with its political subdivisions flies in the face of long-standing Supreme Court precedents, which the *Boulder* majority overlooked. As Justice Moody wrote in *Hunter v. Pittsburgh*,[107] "The number, nature and duration of the powers conferred upon these [municipal] corporations and the territory over which they shall be exercised rests in the absolute discretion of the State . . . The State, therefore, at its pleasure may modify or withdraw all such powers . . . repeal the charter and destroy the corporation . . . In all these respects the State is supreme, and its legislative body, conforming its action to the state constitution, may do as it will, unrestrained by any provision of the Constitution of the United States."[108]

Even more perplexing is the *Boulder* Court's unacknowledged assault on the principles of federalism celebrated in the Tenth Amendment. The majority ruled that principles of federalism prevent the Sherman Act, at least absent a clear contrary choice by Congress, from preempting state policy which supplants competition with regulation, but that the laws of the states' political subdivisions are not similarly protected. As Justice Rehnquist noted in his dissent, the Court had never before set different standards for determining the preemptive effects of federal statutes on state and local laws.[109] Moreover, *National League of Cities v. Usery* explicitly held that, if principles of federalism place a state beyond the reach of a particular exercise of congressional Commerce Clause authority, then the state's political subdivisions are equally immunized.[110] Certainly the text of the Tenth Amendment itself provides no basis for the distinction between state and local government made in *Boulder*. It reserves the same sphere of residual powers to the "States respectively, or to the people." And the Colorado Home Rule Amendment explicitly "vests" the "power of self-government" in those same "people."[111]

National League of Cities was not cited by any of the opinions in *Boulder*[112] let alone questioned, and its Tenth Amendment challenge to Commerce Clause legislation on behalf of both states and localities was expressly affirmed a few months after the *Boulder* decision in *FERC v. Mississippi*.[113] However, the implicit structure of the proposition underlying the Court's thinking in *Boulder* is strikingly parallel to the explicit reasoning of *FERC*. Just as PURPA allows states to follow any substantive policy they wish so long as they use federally prescribed methods to consider and choose that policy, so the Sherman Act as interpreted by the Supreme Court in *Boulder* allows the states to supplant congressionally legislated promarket policies with anticompetitive practices so long as the substantive decision to do so is made at the state, not the local level. In each case Congress is indifferent to the substantive outcome but, because it could preempt the entire area, it may insist that the state adopt a particular decision-making procedure or a particular decision-making hierarchy.

Given the decisions in *FERC* and *Boulder*, it should have come as no surprise when the Court voted five-to-four[114] in *Equal Employment Opportunity Commission (EEOC) v. Wyoming*[115] to deny a Tenth Amendment challenge to a federal regulation very much like the law struck down in *National League of Cities*. In 1974 Congress extended the Age Discrimination in Employment Act (ADEA) to state and local governments. A game warden who had been employed by Wyoming was involuntarily retired at age fifty-five pursuant to state law. He sought relief from the Federal EEOC, which brought a suit against the state. The district court dismissed the suit on the ground that the application of the ADEA to Wyoming, like the application of the Fair Labor Standards Act to the states in *National League of Cities*, impermissibly interfered with the state's ability to structure relations with its employees.[116]

The Court applied the familiar *Hodel* test and concluded that the Tenth Amendment did not immunize Wyoming from the extension of the ADEA. The majority agreed that the ADEA regulated the states as states,[117] but did not reach the question whether the ADEA addressed indisputable attributes of state sovereignty.[118] The case turned on the Court's conclusion that the ADEA did not directly impair Wyoming's ability to structure integral operations in areas of traditional governmental functions. It was simply a matter of degree, and Justice Brennan, writing for the Court, observed that the ADEA worked a less severe intrusion than did the FLSA in *National League of Cities*.[119] The critical point for the Court was that Wyoming—like Mississippi in the FERC case—was free to pursue its goals so long as it observed a few federal procedural requirements along the way. The state could fulfill the goal of assuring the physical fitness of its employees by conducting individualized fitness examinations or by demonstrating that the ages set out in its mandatory retirement policy constituted bona fide occupational qualifications (BFOQs) for particular positions.[120] Therefore, Justice Brennan stressed, the ADEA did not completely override Wyoming's "discretion to achieve its goals *in the way it thinks best*," but merely tested the state's methods against a "reasonable federal standard."[121]

It may be no great imposition to require the state to jump through a hoop like a BFOQ test, but if that statutory test has an high threshold,[122] then a "reasonable federal standard" becomes more a wall than a mere hurdle. It is not immediately clear why allowing a state to retire its employees whenever it wishes only so long as it meets a "reasonable federal standard" is less intrusive than allowing a state to pay its employees whatever it wishes only so long as it meets a reasonable federal minimum wage. Yet the latter is exactly the kind of imposition which the Court found impermissibly onerous in *National League of Cities*.

EEOC can be distinguished only by the fact that the ADEA contained escape hatches that Wyoming made no attempt to use, whereas there was no way to avoid paying the higher wages dictated by the FLSA.

The *EEOC* majority conducted an "essentially legal, rather than factual"[123] inquiry into the practical impact of the ADEA and concluded that there would not be any significant impairment of the state's operations. The ADEA allowed the state to restructure its pension and insurance programs to provide relatively lower benefits for older employees; the increased costs of higher wages for senior employees would be offset by savings on those workers' pensions.[124] Finally, unlike *National League of Cities*, where it appeared likely that applying the FLSA to the states would hamper their capacity to provide basic services to their citizens,[125] Wyoming made no claim that its mandatory retirement policy served any broader social or economic policies,[126] and those suggested by the dissenters were highly speculative.[127] The Court added that, even if some broader purpose for the law could be imagined, it might not be sufficiently significant to outweigh a well-defined federal interest under the fourth and final prong of *Hodel*, the balancing test that Justice Blackmun first set out in his concurring opinion in *National League of Cities*.[128]

The thrust of these cases seems to be to reduce *National League of Cities* to the status of a curiosity or a cry in the wilderness. Yet however bleak the future might appear for the New Federalism, one ought to await a more direct and less ambiguous signal before concluding that the Supreme Court is jettisoning a major constitutional doctrine. The dissents in both *FERC*[129] and *Boulder*[130] suggest that the members of the majorities know not what they do.[131] The Court may have lost its way among the dense thickets of doctrinal rubrics to such a degree that it is no longer able to see the federal forest.

The confusion in the case law probably results from the Court's own uncertainty: it could not say exactly what the constitutional infirmity with the legislation in *National League of Cities* was,[132] nor did it know exactly where it was going, but the Court was certain that allowing Congress to tell states and cities how much to pay their firemen and janitors simply did not sit well with the judicial stomach. The Court's reaction was instinctive—more visceral than cerebral. The same queasiness about federal encroachment was evinced in *Hodel*, but the Court swallowed hard and approved it because the legislation there regulated only private entities. With its unanimous holding in *Long Island R.R.*, the Supreme Court told us that the states as states are protected from federal control only when the activities in question are the historical province of state or local government and when there is no overriding federal need for nationally uniform regulation. *FERC v. Mississippi* and *EEOC v. Wyoming* are the odd men out, because modest extrapolation from the previous cases would have argued strongly for different results. In the last analysis, the majorities in *FERC* and *EEOC*—or Justice Blackmun, at least—simply may have regarded the facts as less troublesome than those in *National League of Cities*. The emphasis in both majority opinions on the insignificance of merely requiring the states to jump through a few federal hoops before they get to their destinations may well mean that the balancing approach which Justice Blackmun first applied in his concurrence in *National League of Cities* now commands a majority. But the fact that there has been only one vote to overrule *National League of Cities*[133] suggests that, even if the Supreme Court has never used that case as authority to strike down congressional legislation, it may yet find an appropriate case in which to do so.

The flood waters may be rising, but state sovereignty still thrives on a few islands in the stream of commerce. The result in *EEOC v. Wyoming* could have been changed by a single vote, and in an era characterized by increasing conservatism and widespread concern for states' rights—and with the prospect of more like-minded appointments to the Supreme Court—it would be unwise to bury *National League of Cities* just yet.[134] Such an obituary could well turn out, like the early reports of Mark Twain's death, to be greatly exaggerated indeed.

CHAPTER TEN

CONGRESSIONAL ACTION AS CONTEXT RATHER THAN MESSAGE: THE CASE OF INTERSTATE BANK MERGERS

Whatever constitutional limits state sovereignty might impose on the authority of *Congress* to wield its commerce power over the states, it is quite a different matter to decide how federal *judicial* supervision of state actions affecting such commerce should be shaped by concededly valid exercises of Congress' commerce power that bear on, but that *neither expressly authorize nor specifically forbid*, the state actions at issue. When Congress has spoken in an area of concern to state and nation alike, but has not spoken precisely to the point, what are courts—and the state officials whose actions courts will review—to make of the sheer *fact* of Congress' specific intervention? Should that fact be treated as a clue to what Congress *might* have said or thought about the state action in controversy had its attention been focused on that action? Should Congress' action instead be entirely *ignored* once one concludes that the federal legislation Congress enacted is not directly controlling? Or is there some intermediate, and perhaps more legally candid and politically responsible, way in which the judicial choices that define the options open to state regulators ought to reflect, without purporting to be mandated by the hidden intentions behind, the choices Congress *did* make?

That question is potentially posed by an intricate dispute raging in the early 1980s in the field of regional banking. Under the Douglas Amendment of the federal Bank Holding Company Act of 1956 (BHCA),[1] a bank holding company may not acquire a bank located in another state unless expressly authorized to do so by a statute of the target bank's state. Nineteen states have enacted statutes allowing some forms of acquisition of banks within the state by out-of-state bank holding companies.[2] For example, Connecticut,[3] Massachusetts,[4] and Rhode Island[5] have passed laws allowing out-of-state bank holding companies from *other New England states*, and *only* from those states, to acquire in-state banks. All three New England statutes also have reciprocity requirements.[6]

Three intriguing questions are raised by the Douglas Amendment and banking plans such as those enacted by the New England states. First, does the amendment authorize at least some state actions that would otherwise be condemned under Commerce Clause scrutiny? Second, is state authorization for regional—but not unlimited inter-state—banking among the state actions that are thus authorized? Third, if regional banking laws are not sufficiently authorized by Congress in the Douglas Amendment, how should the New England state laws be evaluated under the Commerce Clause?

This essay suggests that, even if the Douglas Amendment were held not to *authorize* regional banking statutes, the amendment would nonetheless act as an *operative legal fact* that decisively alters proper Commerce Clause analysis of a regional banking plan; it is the con-gressional action of shaping the relevant legal context, rather than ex-pressing Congress' view of the issue at hand, that the banking ques-tion most significantly illuminates.[7]

Given the existence of the Douglas Amendment, a state's decision for regional banking eliminates the home state's federally authorized competitive edge over outside states, while creating a competitive edge for some of those outside states over others.[8] I will suggest in the analy-sis that follows that this sort of trade-off is not one with which the Commerce Clause should be especially concerned. But before that ar-gument can be developed, the Douglas Amendment and the New England statutes must be considered in more detail.

The Douglas Amendment was one aspect of the compromise be-tween the House of Representatives' version of the Bank Holding Company Act of 1956[9] and a version reported out of the Senate Com-mittee on Banking and Currency. The House version of the BHCA contained an absolute prohibition on interstate banking; the Senate Committee version subjected interstate banking to Federal Reserve Board approval, but contained no other restrictions. The Douglas Amendment to the BHCA is brief and seemingly clear enough:

> [N]o application shall be approved [by the Federal Reserve Board of Governors] under this section which will permit any bank holding company or any subsidiary thereof to acquire, directly or indirectly,

any voting shares of, interest in, or all or substantially all of the assets of any additional bank located outside of the State in which the operations of such bank holding company's banking subsidiaries are principally conducted . . . unless the acquisition of such shares or assets of a State bank by an out-of-State bank holding company is specifically authorized by the statute laws of the State in which such bank is located, by language to that effect and not merely by implication.[10]

In short, a bank holding company may not acquire a bank located in another state unless explicitly permitted to do so by statute in the target bank's state.

The legislative history, although meager,[11] does reveal that the immediately Balkanizing effect of the amendment was well understood by its framers. For, at the time the amendment was passed, no state had enacted specific statutory authorization of interstate bank mergers;[12] thus, absent further state action, all interstate bank mergers were flatly prohibited by Congress.

The situation created by Congress prompted a variety of responses among those states willing to lift the barrier to interstate bank mergers. As of early 1984, nineteen states have enacted legislation lifting that barrier to one degree or another, all but two of them in a way that discriminates among states. Only Alaska[13] and Maine[14] permit unlimited entry by out-of-state banks. New York conditions merger authorization on the existence of reciprocal legislation in the acquiring bank's state.[15] Three other states condition authorization on the presence within the state of banks already operated by the acquiring bank.[16] Five more limit merger authorization to the establishment of special-purpose banks by entrants meeting certain financial eligibility requirements and prohibit subsidiaries of out-of-state bank holding companies from competing with local banks for customers.[17] Two states authorize out-of-state banks to acquire only "failing [in-state] banks."[18]

Finally, six states have enacted regional reciprocal legislation. Utah allows entry by out-of-state bank holding companies located in any of several western states.[19] Georgia and Kentucky do the same thing with regard to a group of southeastern states.[20] Connecticut, Massachusetts, and Rhode Island [21] condition merger authorization on two major requirements. First, the acquiring bank holding company must have its principal place of business in a New England state; second, that state must have reciprocal legislation authorizing acquisitions by bank holding companies from the target state.[22]

THE DOUGLAS AMENDMENT AND CONGRESSIONAL AUTHORIZATION OF STATE ACTION AFFECTING COMMERCE

The Commerce Clause is an affirmative grant of power to Congress; only the "negative implications" of the clause restrict state power to burden interstate commerce. Thus, Congress may authorize state actions burdening commerce which would be struck down under Commerce Clause scrutiny in the absence of the federal legislation at issue. Courts have said that they require an explicit congressional statement of such authorization in order to exempt state action from Commerce Clause scrutiny.[23] However, the words of the McCarran-Ferguson Act, often considered the archetype of congressional authorization, undercut the rigidity of the "explicitness" requirement in that the language there used ("silence on the part of the Congress shall not be construed to impose any barrier to the regulation or taxation of [the insurance] business by the several States")[24] is by no means a straightforward *grant* of power to the states to regulate the insurance business in a way otherwise prohibited by the Commerce Clause. Nonetheless, in *Prudential Insurance Co. vs. Benjamin*,[25] the Act was held to have congressionally ratified a South Carolina tax on out-of-state insurance companies doing business within that state, even though the tax was not matched by any comparable tax on in-state insurance companies and therefore discriminated on its face against interstate commerce in a manner that obviously would not have survived judicial scrutiny in the absence of such congressional action.

The Douglas Amendment may lack words quite as suggestive as those of the McCarran-Ferguson Act; yet, like that Act, the amendment manifests an undeniable intention by Congress to authorize at least *some* barriers to interstate bank mergers which, if independently established by a state absent the amendment, would indisputably violate the Commerce Clause. Any suggestion that, despite the Douglas Amendment, *all* state-imposed or state-tolerated burdens on interstate commerce are just as vulnerable as they would be had Congress done nothing would run up against insuperable difficulties. Such a suggestion would entail a view that, even with the amendment, states must be open to out-of-state bank acquisitions to the same degree they are open to in-state acquisitions. A state that simply mirrors the effect of the Douglas Amendment by passing a statute prohibiting acquisition of in-state banks by all out-of-state bank holding companies would, under this logic, violate the Commerce Clause if any intrastate acquisitions were simultaneously allowed. Yet this assertion is surely paradoxical, for we would be left with a state statute identical in effect to a federal statute (and indeed redundant given the federal statute) found unconstitutional for lack of congressional authorization. Thus, although Congress may not have anticipated a state statute prohibiting all interstate mergers while permitting intrastate combinations (because the Douglas Amendment makes such a statute unnecessary), the amendment must be understood to authorize just such a statute.

Since the House proposed, and the Congress rejected, a version of the BHCA in 1956 that would have prohibited *all* interstate acquisitions, authorization of state mechanisms for selectively allowing *less* than all interstate acquisitions also seems almost as compelled by logic and congressional expression as is the complete barrier to interstate banking absent state action to the contrary. If congressional authorization were limited to complete prohibition of interstate banking by the states, a breach in the barrier by a state law—an allowance of *one* interstate bank acquisition, for example—would seem to require the state to allow *all* interstate acquisitions. This is a reading of the amendment suggested neither by its language nor by legislative history, and one decisively rejected by the United States Court of Appeals for the District of Columbia Circuit.[26] The Douglas Amendment should therefore be read to authorize a state selectively to allow some out-of-state holding companies to acquire banks inside the state without elimination of all state control over interstate banking.

Yet, even if a state is authorized to keep out all or some out-of-state bank holding companies, or to allow in, for example, only small out-of-state banks, it does not automatically follow that it has been authorized by Congress to allow entry only by companies headquartered in a limited number of specified states. Although authorization of a complete barrier to interstate acquisitions and of a partial lifting of the barrier based on jurisdictionally neutral financial characteristics seem compelled if the amendment is to make any sense at all, partial liftings based on a holding company's home state arguably were not contemplated by the Douglas Amendment and may not be entailed by its logic.[27] At first glance, such partial liftings might suggest the type of state discrimination least tolerated under the Commerce Clause.[28]

But authorization of the regional limitation as such may not be necessary. Partial state liftings of the barrier to interstate mergers, *against the background of the Douglas Amendment*, do not unduly burden interstate commerce if it is the case that, given the Douglas Amendment, such state actions involve no *added* burdens of the sort the Commerce Clause should presumptively be deemed to forbid.

In other words, even if a court were to reject the view that the Douglas Amendment actually authorized the action taken by a state that discriminates among other states, it should nonetheless find that that state's action does not impermissibly burden interstate commerce. This conclusion involves viewing the Douglas Amendment as congressional action which alters the legal environment in which Commerce Clause analysis of regional banking limitations must be conducted.

COMMERCE CLAUSE IMPLICATIONS OF REGIONAL BANKING IN LIGHT OF THE DOUGLAS AMENDMENT

This analysis is most easily understood, with no loss of generality, if three states—Connecticut, Massachusetts, and New York, for example—are used to illustrate the situation. It is clear that a complete barrier to interstate bank mergers has been authorized by Congress in the Douglas Amendment. Thus, Connecticut may pass a statute favoring Connecticut bank holding companies over bank holding companies of Massachusetts and of New York in the market for Connecticut banks, and Massachusetts may pass a statute similarly favoring Massachusetts bank holding companies over those of Connecticut and New York in the market for Massachusetts banks. Connecticut's regional banking plan, in contrast, *eliminates* the authorized favoritism for Connecticut bank holding companies over Massachusetts bank holding companies; the two groups compete equally for the acquisition of Connecticut banks. Because the barrier against New York bank holding companies is maintained, however, the Connecticut plan *creates* a favoritism for Massachusetts bank holding companies over New York bank holding companies in the market for Connecticut banks.[29]

The difference between the Connecticut system and that set up by Congress is, of course, a net *increase* in interstate commerce: some acquisitions previously forbidden *by federal law* are now permitted, and no acquisitions previously allowed are now prevented.[30] Yet the laws also set up two previously nonexistent competitive disadvantages for banks from New York: *first*, a clear competitive disadvantage vis-à-vis Massachusetts banks in the market for the acquisition of Connecticut banks; and *second*, a conceivable competitive disadvantage vis-à-vis the newly strengthened banks of Connecticut. In the absence of the Douglas Amendment, such effects on interstate competition deliberately created by state-imposed burdens would be constitutionally impermissible.[31] But *given* the Douglas Amendment, the state has imposed *no* burdens. Rather, it has *removed* preexisting burdens imposed by the federal government. The significance of each of these changes— the increase in commerce and the new competitive disadvantages for New York—will be discussed in turn.

Increase in Commerce

The Supreme Court has recognized a "market participation" exception to Commerce Clause scrutiny of state actions.[32] Although the increase in commerce created by Connecticut's regional banking plan obviously does not fit literally and squarely under that market participation exception, an examination of the actual cases in which the exception has been developed suggests that the *logic* underlying the exception is manifestly broader than the "market participation" label at first indicates. The exception's logic indeed mandates that the increase in commerce created by the regional banking plan must count significantly toward the plan's constitutionality.

In 1976 the Supreme Court first carved out an exception to Commerce Clause scrutiny for action a state takes as a participant in, rather than a regulator of, the market. In *Hughes v. Alexandria Scrap Corp.*[33] the Court placed within this exception a state's action as purchaser of abandoned auto hulks; in *Reeves Inc. v. Stake*[34] the Court found a state's action as a seller of state-produced cement similarly exempt from Commerce Clause scrutiny; and in *White v. Massachusetts Council of Construction Employers*[35] the Court expanded the exception to authorize government as contractor to impose a requirement of preferential treatment for city residents on those who undertake city-funded construction.[36]

The uneasy fit between the exempted state actions and their characterization as "market participation" rather than regulation is notable. In *Hughes* and *Reeves*, Maryland and South Dakota respectively did not enter a presumably unmanipulable market with the profit-maximizing goals implied in the phrase "market participation." Instead, the states intended their entrances to affect the flow of commerce so as to enhance *public* values—improvement of the environment[37] or increased supply of a needed product[38]—at the expense of the state as a "business." Market participation and market regulation are not mutually exclusive; indeed *Hughes* and *Reeves* are examples of market participation as a *form* of market regulation. The fact that, when the state participates in the market, its primary goal is rarely profit-maximization undercuts one of the Court's rationales for the participant exception: that the state as business is "burdened with the same restrictions imposed on private market participants."[39] Many of the restrictions on private market participants control behavior through the profit-maximization goal; when the state can continue indefinitely to operate as a "losing proposition," many legal as well as economic pressures lose their usual force.

In *White* one may assume that Boston entered the construction business not primarily to affect that market but to fulfill certain city needs at acceptable cost. Yet the particular policy in question—requiring at least half the work force on city-funded construction projects to reside in the city—is not comparable to any usual private market participant goal. Once again, the state or city uses its position as market participant to regulate for the enhancement of public values.

Indeed, in *Reeves* the Court supported its decision with sovereignty considerations that hardly fit the image of the state as a simple "market participant": Commerce Clause scrutiny would interfere with the state's role as a "'guardian and trustee for its people'";[40] it would hamper the state's "ability to structure relations exclusively with its own citizens";[41] and it would diminish the value of the states as social and economic laboratories.[42]

If the image of the state as a simple market participant is an inappropriate limiting principle for *Hughes*, *Reeves*, and *White*, what saves the state actions in those cases from Commerce Clause scrutiny? The sense of fairness in allowing a community to retain the public benefits created by its own public investment may be a better justification for the "market participant" immunity in these three cases than is the market participant rationale itself.[43] The broader theme that underlies each case seems to be *creation* of commerce:[44] whatever the state's ultimate goal, the state is approaching that goal by channeling its resources into commerce rather than by placing restrictions on commerce already in existence.[45]

When a barrier to commerce is imposed from *outside* the state, it may be treated as no different from other "natural" obstacles to particular types of transactions.[46] In *Hughes* the lack of buyers of processed auto hulks offering a profitable price was an obstacle blocking the processing of a significant number of abandoned cars. Maryland lessened the obstacle to some degree by buying hulks. In *Reeves* lack of supply blocked purchases of cement by state residents; the state lessened the obstacle by providing additional supply. Similarly, Congress imposed a barrier blocking all interstate bank mergers; Connecticut, Rhode Island, and Massachusetts have each cut a hole in the barrier.

Whatever its theoretical underpinnings, the market participant exception indicates that it is the *mode* and *result* of state discrimination, rather than the simple *fact* of discrimination, on which Commerce Clause analysis—or even applicability—will turn. In this light, a Commerce Clause analysis of the New England regional banking plan that places independent significance on discrimination, apart from the effects of the entire plan on the *net* level of commerce, is inadequate.[47]

The principle that necessarily underlies the market participant–market regulator distinction is that, when the state is *creating* commerce that would not otherwise exist, it has greater freedom to *shape* that commerce than when it is merely *intruding* into a previously existing private market. Of course, if a state legalizes, in part or in whole, an activity the state *itself* has previously forbidden, it may not regulate the transactions in the newly "created" market in a way that it would otherwise not have been permitted to do under the Commerce Clause.[48] But when the state creates the market in the first place by removing a barrier *put in place by exogenous forces*, it should be able to enjoy largely unfettered freedom in creating the contours of that market.

Competitive Disadvantages Imposed on New York

In one sense, there is nothing "new" or unauthorized about the competitive disadvantage of New York vis-à-vis Massachusetts under the Connecticut plan. Congress clearly authorized favoritism for Massachusetts bank holding companies over New York bank holding companies, *when that favoritism is established by Massachusetts.* What *was* arguably unauthorized was not the discrimination between Massachusetts and New York, but merely the establishment of that discrimination *by Connecticut.* Should this shift in the *source* of the discrimination be deemed of special Commerce Clause concern? It is strongly arguable that it should not. For, in order to make the shift,

Connecticut must eliminate a congressionally authorized (and *more* politically suspect) *home-state favoritism*—favoritism for Connecticut's *own* bank holding companies over those of Massachusetts—so as to establish a (*less* suspect) *other-state favoritism*—favoritism for Massachusetts bank holding companies over those of New York.

State action which favors home-state over out-of-state commerce is subject to strict Commerce Clause scrutiny because residents of one state are not represented as voters in other states; accordingly, it is feared that each state will engage in economic protectionism at the expense of unrepresented outsiders. When state action favors intrastate commerce, the costs and benefits of that state action cannot be assumed to have been fairly weighed, because those bearing the costs are not represented by those imposing them and reaping the gains.[49] But when such economic protectionism is both endorsed by Congress, as in the Douglas Amendment, *and* in no way enhanced or increased but instead *reduced* by a state's action, the basic rationale for strict Commerce Clause scrutiny is absent. So long as Connecticut cuts down its *own* competitive edge in the market for Connecticut banks while it imposes a competitive disadvantage only vis-à-vis Massachusetts banks, there is no apparent reason to fear that parochial self-interest, and the nonrepresentation of outsiders in Connecticut's legislature, have unacceptably distorted the political balance of costs and benefits that Connecticut struck.[50]

There might, finally, be an argument that, by enacting the reciprocal legislation, Connecticut has acted to advance its *own* narrow interests by giving *its* banks a market in Massachusetts while protecting them from competition against New York bank holding companies. However, Connecticut is able to create this sort of home-state advantage only by giving up an even greater home-state favoritism that it had enjoyed previously by the grace of Congress.

Surely it is not a violation of the Commerce Clause for a state to gain one home-state advantage by giving up another that has been even more favorable to it in the past, one that Congress had authorized. For example, there is no Commerce Clause violation when a state cuts its corporate income tax in an attempt to attract outside industry, since the costs of the move are borne by the same people who reap the benefits. Only when the costs may be externalized, and the benefits internalized, does the Commerce Clause clearly disapprove of self-interested moves on the part of a state.

THE DOUGLAS AMENDMENT AS AN "OPERATIVE FACT" IN COMMERCE CLAUSE ANALYSIS

The fact that the Douglas Amendment *may* be held not to "authorize" a regional banking scheme as such does *not* allow a Commerce Clause analysis to proceed *as if the Amendment did not exist.* The amendment does exist, and it both imposed and implicitly authorized each state to enact a complete barrier to interstate banking. An analysis which proceeded as if the amendment did *not* exist would find a regional scheme like that of the New England states an explicit barrier to commerce not because it lets banks from *some* states *in,* but because it keeps banks from all *other* states *out.* Yet at least *part* of the "keeping out" *has* been authorized by Congress. Thus, when one evaluates the impact on commerce of the regional system insofar as it may be *un*authorized, what is at stake is the *marginal difference* between the complete ban on interstate banking authorized by Congress and the partial ban chosen by the states that have decided to lift the congressional ban in part. If a court focused on more than the marginal difference, it would condemn a scheme like Connecticut's even for burdens authorized and indeed imposed by Congress, but would perversely be required to leave Congress' barrier untouched while striking down Connecticut's partial lifting of the barrier.

This comprehension of the range of effects attributable to congressional action is necessary to evaluate intelligently the Commerce Clause significance of the Douglas Amendment and of state regional banking plans promulgated in its wake. Between authorization and irrelevance, congressional action can decisively alter the environment in which Commerce Clause analysis must be played out: it can alter that environment in a manner that justifies—and indeed requires—different *judicial* choices as to the validity of challenged state actions, even when it does not enable courts to *attribute* those choices to the intent of Congress. Here, as elsewhere, courts cannot properly escape accountability for making constitutional choices—even when the Constitution's structure *links* those choices to laws enacted by Congress.

CHAPTER ELEVEN

GUAM'S VANISHING BONDS: A VIGNETTE IN TAXATION WITHOUT LEGISLATION

When the Guam Economic Development Authority (GEDA)[1] decided in the fall of 1983 that it wanted to raise revenue for territorial economic development by floating what are referred to in the trade as "arbitrage bonds," it is doubtful that its members expected the project to raise constitutional questions involving such fundamental issues as the separation of powers and recalling such famed precedents as that of President Truman's seizure of the steel mills during the Korean War.

But the proposed bonds, although perfectly legal under statutory schemes enacted by the Congress, generated intense opposition from the executive branch, specifically the United States Department of the Treasury. Perhaps because time was short, and the need was perceived as urgent, Treasury officials decided to do a little lawmaking of their own in December 1983. Never mind that the lawmaking function is clearly assigned to Congress under the Constitution: as Anthony Lewis argued in a contemporaneous column detailing other executive branch abuses, "[t]he imperial Presidency is on the rise again."[2]

Although, as I will discuss below, the executive action involving Guam arguably violated both the letter and the spirit of the Constitution, it may well be that a federal court, in response to any legal challenge to that action, would hold the controversy a nonjusticiable one. Nonetheless, all members of the executive and of Congress are sworn to uphold the Constitution as part of their oaths of office; behavior that transgresses constitutional norms is as great a threat to our system when it is immune to judicial review as when it can be successfully challenged in court. Indeed, the American system requires that the oath to uphold the Constitution exercise a particularly powerful constraint on political behavior when unenforceable by judicial action.[3]

GUAM AND THE "ARBITRAGE LOOPHOLE"

Arbitrage bonds have been thorns in the side of the United States Treasury Department ever since smart investment bankers conceived them some years ago as a way for borrowers, lenders, and brokers all to make money at the Treasury's expense.[4] These bonds are devices whereby state or territorial governments borrow money for further investment in the money market, usually by purchasing long-term Treasury bonds.[5] Since the lenders (bondholders) do not have to pay tax on the interest they receive from the borrowing governments, they are willing to accept a relatively low interest rate. Since the borrowing governments do not have to pay tax on the considerably higher interest they receive from investing the proceeds in the money market, the "spread" between tax-exempt and taxable interest rates is available to any government that can amass a suitable amount of capital. The result is a right to draw money almost at will from the federal treasury. The benefits are divided between the borrowing governments, the lenders (who tend to be wealthy individuals and large institutions), and the brokers and lawyers who put such deals together. Everyone prospers from this form of federal largesse—except the federal government itself and, of course, those whose taxes the federal government collects. Since the Treasury is understandably sensitive about issuing blank checks, making arbitrage bonds taxable has been a long-time Treasury objective.[6]

As long ago as 1969, the Treasury persuaded Congress to close the arbitrage loophole as far as state and local governments were concerned.[7] The Treasury argument carried the day in Congress because, federal tax officials argued, tax-exempt bonds were an inefficient form of subsidy,[8] and because limiting the power to float arbitrage bonds would not interfere with any unique state function, as might be the case if the United States tried to tax the interest paid on state bonds for such public purposes as highway construction.[9]

In 1983, as the Reagan administration faced mounting federal deficits,[10] the Treasury went to Congress to seek legislation plugging loopholes in the statutes governing the issuance of tax-exempt bonds.[11] The Committee on Ways and Means was receptive to Treasury's request, and on October 19, 1983, reported favorably H.R. 4170, encompassing many of the executive's proposals, including one that made territories and the District of Columbia subject to all the same restrictions on tax-exempt bonds as were states and municipalities.[12]

Although the bill contained a number of retroactive effective dates,[13] this provision was slated to take effect on the general effective date of the bill, January 1, 1984. If the Congress went along with the Committee on Ways and Means, territories would no longer be able to float arbitrage bonds as of January 1, 1984. Congress did not act on the proposed legislation before adjourning for its Christmas recess on November 18, 1983.

In President Reagan's first three years in office, his administration had grown increasingly stingy in its appropriations to the territories.[14] Therefore, it was not unforseeable that there would be a last-minute rush by the territories to take advantage of the "window" left open in the congressional committee's bill in order to write themselves checks from the federal till. Puerto Rico got in under the deadline with ease, with a $450 million bond issue completed December 5, 1983.[15] The GEDA was not far behind, with a bond issue scheduled for completion in the last week of 1983.[16] Even as Guam was preparing its issue, the Virgin Islands was at work on another, and Puerto Rico had plans for two more, totaling more than $600 million.[17]

But as Christmas neared, with Congress out of session and with the Guam bonds in the final process of being issued, the federal money mandarins, including Treasury Secretary (and former Merrill Lynch Chairman) Donald Regan, saw an opportunity to strike a blow for the United States Treasury[18] by derailing Guam's bond deal—even though it was legitimately within the window that had been left open in the Ways and Means Committee bill. On December 20, 1983, the Treasury made a formal public announcement disclosing that it would ask Congress to give the 1983 tax reform an effective date of December 21, just early enough so the reform would apply specifically to the Guam issue.[19] Knowing that such a threat would prove fatal to the marketability of the bonds, the territory and its underwriters quickly sought to change the Treasury's mind.[20]

Two distinct constitutional issues were raised by the Treasury's action. The first involved the retroactive nature of the tax that the Treasury proposed, which was troubling for several reasons. If the proposed legislation were enacted after the bonds had been issued, it would sharply reduce the value of the bondholders' property by reducing the value of the income stream represented by the interest payments. It would put the Guam bonds in a different legal posture from the essentially identical bonds issued by Puerto Rico only two weeks before. And it would represent, in effect, a reduction of the dollar benefit the federal government (through its territory) had promised to those from whom it had borrowed money (the bondholders).

A second and independent objection to the Treasury's action was that the circumstances of the announcement meant that the issue would in all likelihood be forever moot: the *announcement itself* would mean the end of the deal, allowing the executive to accomplish by fiat what the Congress *might* not even have the constitutional authority to do—and might at all events have chosen *not* to do.

THE RULE OF RETROACTIVE ENACTMENT

The general rule is that economic legislation may be enacted retroactively.[21] In *Welch v. Henry*,[22] the Supreme Court upheld a Wisconsin tax on dividends against a challenge that its retroactive imposition, on dividends earned prior to enactment, infringed due process:"Taxation is neither a penalty imposed on the taxpayer, nor a liability which he assumes by contract. It is but a way of apportioning the cost of government among those who in some measure are privileged to enjoy its benefits and must bear its burdens. Since no citizen bears immunity from its burdens, its retroactive imposition does not infringe due process."[23] But the special facts of the Guam case might have made that general rule inapplicable.

First, the Supreme Court has held that there is a difference between the retroactive taxation of *income received* during a previous time period and the retroactive imposition of a new tax on a *transaction completed* during a previous period. In *Untermyer v. Anderson*,[24] for example, the Supreme Court struck down the imposition of a new gift tax on a gift completed two weeks prior to the enactment of the tax, relying on the earlier case of *Blodget v. Holden*,[25] which had held that it was "wholly unreasonable that one who, in entire good faith and without the slightest premonition of such consequence, made absolute disposition of his property by gifts should thereafter be required to pay a charge for so doing."[26]

Given all that is known about the GEDA bond issue at which the proposed law would transparently have been targeted, it would be fairly easy to calculate with considerable precision the dollar amount by which the Guam bonds would be reduced in value through the retroactive removal of their tax-exempt status and the subsequent exposure to income taxation of the interest payments to the bondholders. The legislative removal of such tax-exempt status in the special circumstances of this case would therefore be the *functional* if not the *formal* equivalent of imposing a transfer tax on the bond sale in the amount by which the economic value of the bonds was reduced. If the proposed tax on the interest paid on the bonds was viewed not as a new tax on the income, as in form it would be, but instead as a tax on the transaction, the controlling constitutional precedent would seem to be *Untermyer* rather than *Welch*, and the Constitution might then be construed to forbid the retroactive imposition of the tax in question.[27]

Second, a court might look with special disfavor on a federal attempt retroactively to tax interest received on money loaned to a "subsidiary" of the federal government itself—here, the territory of Guam. Such a law would arguably constitute an abrogation of the obligation the government owed to those who had lent it money by buying the bonds. Unlike a change in the federal tax treatment of *state* or *municipal* bond income, this change in the treatment of *territorial* bond income would amount to a unilateral modification by the federal government of a contract made in good faith with that government. Prohibiting such modification in the name of the Constitution would no doubt be problematic, especially when one keeps in mind the great latitude courts have accorded governments that withdraw statutory benefits on which people have come to rely.[28] Such a prohibition might well follow, however, from a powerful strand of doctrine in American constitutional jurisprudence.[29] The Supreme Court has grown very suspicious indeed of retroactive measures by any level of government that abrogate that government's statutory commitments to individuals who have extended credit to an entity of that same government on the strength of those commitments. The need for judicial oversight of statutory changes affecting the obligation of contracts is thought to be heightened when government's "self-interest is at stake"[30]—as it is whenever a federal promise, such as a promise of tax-exempt status for territorial bonds, induces individuals or institutions to lend money to the United States, or to any of its governmental alter egos or subsidiaries, including federal territories.[31]

Third, the fact that Puerto Rico had completed a nearly identical bond offering only a short period of time prior to the planned Guam issue raised the possibility of a claim under the Uniformity Clause.[32] Although this aspect of the proposed legislation might not ultimately have proven constitutionally fatal,[33] it would certainly have stimulated discussion in Congress.[34] By its unilateral action, the Treasury foreclosed any such debate about the fairness of the line-drawing between Puerto Rico and Guam and deprived the residents of Guam of any protection which might have been offered them—by Congress, if not by the courts—under the Uniformity Clause.

UNILATERAL ANNOUNCEMENT—AND THE SEPARATION OF POWERS

A question in some ways more basic than, and certainly antecedent to, all of these was whether the action of the executive in formally announcing its opposition to the bond issue and its intention to seek retroactive legislation removing the bonds' tax-exempt status was *itself* a violation of constitutional norms—not of retroactive taxation, but of separation of powers.

Of course the Treasury could make strong arguments about the utility of its position. As Congress had confirmed by its actions in 1969 and 1983, there were solid political and economic arguments against the institution of arbitrage bonds. If the Treasury did nothing, Guam's bonds would no doubt issue, exposing the government to millions of dollars of lost revenue over the life of the bonds. Although the Treasury could always say nothing while the bonds were being issued and sold and wait to propose retroactive legislation later—after the bonds were already issued—there would certainly be political and perhaps constitutional objections to depriving investors of the tax exemption they had thereby been led legitimately to expect.

By nonetheless relying on Congress to make the decision retroactively, the Treasury would at least be assuming the risk that Congress might choose not to press its constitutional power to the outer limits. For Congress might well refrain—as it has often done in the past to avoid the real or apparent constitutional problems posed by retroactivity—from making its tax measures as retroactive as the Constitution might permit. In contrast, making the formal announcement December 20 was calculated to leave nothing to chance: by derailing the bond deal before it was consummated, the Treasury was able to avoid the uncertainty both of the legislative process and of judicial review, undoubtedly a "plus" for tax policy—but a distinct "minus" for values of government under law.

Generally, of course, the announcement of executive intentions is far from unconstitutional. Not only is it axiomatic that the executive proposes and the legislature disposes, but the Constitution itself provides the framework for executive proposals to the legislature: "[The President] shall from time to time give to the Congress Information of the State of the Union, and recommend to their Consideration such Measures as he shall judge necessary and expedient."[35]

But the announcement about the Guam bonds in December of 1983 was no ordinary executive recommendation. Had Congress been in session, and had different circumstances surrounded the bonds, there might have been a political argument that the retroactive taxation of territorial arbitrage obligations would constitute taxation without representation, since Guam lacks voting representation in Congress.[36] But whatever *political* concern there might be for the fact that this constituted taxation without representation in the legislative process, the circumstances of the Treasury announcement raised the *constitutional* concern that it was taxation *without any legislation at all*.

The effect of the executive proposal was not measured by its impact on a skeptical political body, but by its impact on a hypersensitive investment community. Whether or not the executive might ultimately have been able to convince Congress of the wisdom, and Congress and the courts of the constitutionality, of its proposed retroactive enactment, the timing of the Treasury announcement foreclosed the issue entirely. For Congress was not in fact in session; by the time it was back in business, the January 1, 1984, cutoff date in the Ways and Means Committee bill would have come and gone. Unless Congress were then to take the affirmative (and most unlikely) step of accepting the committee bill in general but amending it to open a new and highly specific window for the "grandfathered" issuance by Guam, within some specified period shortly after enactment, of tax-free arbitrage bonds exactly corresponding to those whose sale had been halted by the Treasury at the eleventh hour, there would be no later opportunity for the GEDA to issue the tax-exempt bonds killed by the executive's action. Investors would thus have to buy the bonds in December 1983 with the Treasury cloud over them—or not buy the bonds at all. At a time when federal deficits were as high as they have ever been in history,[37] and with long-term interest rates at a two-year peak,[38] the bond market was a buyers' market; no buyer was going to go for the pig in a poke represented by bonds that the Treasury had targeted for loss of tax-exempt status within months of the time they were issued.[39]

Because the bonds were arbitrage bonds, they were especially sensitive to the Treasury announcement. Had they been general obligation bonds, which the territory might have floated in order to build an infrastructure improvement such as a highway or a hospital, the market might have compensated for the risk of the loss of tax exemption by driving the price of the bonds down, thereby raising the effective interest rate. However, since these bonds were feasible for the territory to float *only* because of the spread between tax-exempt and taxable interest rates, the possibility of loss of tax exemption made them virtually unmarketable.[40] This was a case where the power to tax would clearly be the power to destroy,[41] and where even the power formally to *propose* the tax—especially while the Congress was not sitting[42]—was no less destructive.

There are other contexts in which a unilateral executive announcement may spell the end of a proposed financial transaction without raising constitutional problems of the sort raised by the Treasury's action here. When the Federal Trade Commission or the Department of Justice announces that it wants more information about a proposed merger or acquisition, or that it is planning to seek an injunction against such a transaction, the effect in the financial market may be to pass a death sentence on the transaction. But *those* executive announcements, unlike this one, are made pursuant to a constitutional scheme of enacted legislation, a body of laws that charge those executive agencies with the responsibility for monitoring just such combinations and seeking judicial relief when they believe there is a threat of an antitrust violation.[43] Other bodies of enacted legislation may authorize the executive—or even private actors—to make announcements which will have the direct and intended effect of delaying or destroying proposed market transactions.[44]

There is, of course, no underlying statutory basis for executive announcements proposing the introduction of legislation with an effective date retroactive to the date of such announcements, although the practice is common in tax legislation.[45] Retroactive effective dates are proposed in order to prevent last-minute changes in position which will frustrate the purpose of the legislation. Similarly, when the President wants to encourage some activity to be undertaken as soon as possible, he may announce that his proposal to Congress will include a retroactive effective date so that people will not refrain from acting until Congress has finally enacted the proposed measure.

Partial legislative action, and announcements by prominent congressmen, can have similar legislative effects. Indeed, the reporting of H.R. 4170 by the Ways and Means Committee on October 19, 1983, had the undoubted effect of *stimulating* the market for tax-exempt arbitrage bonds issued prior to January 1, 1984. Had the chairman of the Ways and Means Committee made a statement similar to the Treasury's on December 20, *that* news might have had an effect similar to that of the announcement of the Treasury's intentions. Although the chairman's announcement would not have raised separation of powers issues, it would have clashed with the constitutional norm of bicameralism and of equality *within* the legislative branch.[46]

When Congress is in session, announcements by the executive or by powerful congressional figures—or partial legislative action—may be countered with sharp responses by other political actors who do not agree. In the face of such debate, it will be less likely that persons outside government will assume that the announced proposals will in fact be enacted without modification than it was for the prospective investors in the Guam arbitrage bonds to assume that the Treasury would get its wish.[47] The situation at the time the Treasury made its announcement was significantly different: Congress was in recess until some time in January 1984—after the cutoff date proposed in the Ways and Means Committee bill.[48] Although some announcements may be part of the constitutional scheme, this one was not. For its aim was *not* genuinely to *recommend* legislation, but to *change behavior* so that no legislation would be necessary.

The difficulty in drawing lines around what is permissible executive or legislative "speech,"[49] and the problems that would be encountered in trying to hold a member of the House or Senate, for example, accountable for such an announcement of pending legislation under the Speech or Debate Clause,[50] suggest that this is not an easy area in which to construct constitutional rules of much precision—nor an area into which many courts would be eager to stray. But the fact that a court might predictably be reluctant to venture into the political thicket created by these political acts which have essentially legislative effects simply means that controversies arising over these forms of behavior may well be nonjusticiable.[51] Inasmuch as both congressmen and members of the executive branch are individually sworn to uphold the Constitution whether or *not* courts hold their feet to the fire, they should obviously seek to conform their behavior to the Constitution's text and structure, its controlling premises and postulates, even in the absence of potential judicial review.

The Constitution is "[e]xplicit and unambiguous" in its prescription and description of the respective functions of the Congress and of the executive in the legislative process.[52] "The principle of separation of powers was not simply an abstract generalization in the minds of the Framers: it was woven into the documents that they drafted in Philadelphia in the summer of 1787."[53] The Supreme Court quoted this passage in *INS v. Chadha* to emphasize that the validity of a political practice or invention—in that case, the legislative veto—is not to be tested by how "efficient, convenient, and useful" it is "in facilitating the functions of government," but by its fidelity to these constitutional provisions.[54] The Court's *Chadha* opinion makes clear that it will not uphold governmental shortcuts—no matter how convenient, efficient, or widespread—if they are deemed to conflict with a literal reading of the legislative provisions of Article I.[55]

Although the outcome in *Chadha* may not have been as clearly dictated by Article I as the Court believed,[56] the unilateral executive action affecting Guam—unlike the legislative veto condemned in *Chadha*—was taken pursuant to no statute duly enacted by Congress.[57] And, however appealing the arguments justifying the Treasury's action on grounds of efficiency and convenience may seem, they hardly answer the objections to this form of reasoning long ago set forth by the Supreme Court in the *Steel Seizure* case.[58] Justice Black, in his opinion for the Court, and Justices Jackson and Douglas, in their separate concurring opinions, there rejected arguments in defense of President Truman's unilateral seizure of the steel industry strikingly similar to those the Treasury would have to make here and did so in a context where the threat to the nation's security was far greater than any the Treasury faced in December 1983.

As Justice Black wrote for the Court, "[t]he Constitution limits [the Executive's] functions in the lawmaking process to the recommending of laws he thinks wise and the vetoing of laws he thinks bad."[59] No matter what the reasons might be for a particular policy, and no matter what evidence might be offered that similar exercises of executive power had taken place in the past, Justice Black concluded that "[t]he Founders of this Nation entrusted the lawmaking power to the Congress alone in both good and bad times. It would do no good to recall the historical events, the fears of power and the hopes for freedom that lay behind their choice. Such a review would but confirm our holding that this seizure order cannot stand."[60]

In his separate concurrence, Justice Jackson similarly concluded that, however persuasive the arguments might be for declaring the existence of inherent executive powers to meet emergencies, their existence "is something the forefathers omitted." Hypothesizing that "they suspected that emergency powers would tend to kindle emergencies," Justice Jackson concluded that the only way to preserve free government was to ensure "that the Executive be under the law, and that the law be made by parliamentary deliberations."[61]

Justice Douglas acknowledged that executive power has the outward appearance of efficiency in contrast to legislative power: "There must be delay while the ponderous machinery of committees, hearings, and debates is put into motion. That takes time; and while the Congress slowly moves into action, the emergency may take its toll in wages, consumer goods, war production, the standard of living of the people, and perhaps even lives."[62] But, Justice Douglas replied, quoting from Justice Brandeis' dissent in *Myers v. United States*, "'[t]he doctrine of the separation of powers was adopted by the Convention of 1787, not to promote efficiency but to preclude the exercise of arbitrary power. The purpose was, not to avoid friction, but, by means of the inevitable friction incident to the distribution of the governmental powers among the three departments, to save the people from autocracy.' "[63]

Justice Douglas based part of his conclusion that President Truman's action in the *Steel Seizure* case was unconstitutional on the fact that the President's action constituted a taking, which required compensation under the Fifth Amendment. Since only Congress has the power to raise revenues, an unauthorized action by the President that will commit government resources offends the constitutional system because it forces the Congress later to raise the revenues needed to pay the compensation.[64] Justice Douglas assumed that the steel companies would have no problem collecting if they brought suit under the Fifth Amendment. His objection was that the action of the executive essentially *forced Congress' hand*, since it would have no choice but to appropriate the money for the taking at a later date.[65] Similarly, in the context of the Guam bonds, the fact that Congress could later provide the foundation for the executive action at issue cannot answer the constitutional objection raised by that unilateral executive action. For Congress could repair the harm done by the Treasury *only* by opening a new window of the sort described above—an action that is the functional equivalent of appropriating money that Congress might never have chosen to appropriate.

The Constitution describes with some specificity the procedure for enacting legislation. That process, requiring the concurrence of both houses of Congress, followed by presentation to the President for his signature, is—as Justice Douglas in *Steel Seizure* and the Court in *Chadha* observed—a slow and often cumbersome one. But it is the system that the Constitution commands: efforts to improve its workings must fit within the parameters set by the Constitution.[66]

The constitutional values underlying the provisions of Article I, which prescribe a deliberately cumbersome legislative process, are not those of fair notice but are the more structural values of circumscribing power to assure both its political accountability and its deployment in accord with preexisting legal constraints designed to assure full deliberation.[67]

The concern that, although proposals are being discussed in Congress, potentially affected individuals may rearrange their affairs so as to immunize themselves from the legislative changes under discussion encourages Congress to enact legislation which is retroactive to the date it was first announced. But this practice, however venerable, seems constitutionally problematic for two reasons. To the extent it unfairly surprises those affected by the changes, it violates norms of due process, which have their counterpart in criminal law in the prohibition of ex post facto laws. And to the extent such legislation gives a de facto legislative power to the legislator or executive proposing the legislation (as in this case), it violates the structural norms of Article I.

As Justice Douglas concluded in his *Steel Seizure* concurrence: "We pay a price for our system of checks and balances, for the distribution among the three branches of government. It is a price that today may seem exorbitant to many. Today a kindly President uses the seizure power to effect a wage increase and keep the steel furnaces in production. Yet tomorrow another President might use the same power to prevent a wage increase, to curb trade-unionists, to regiment labor as oppressively as industry thinks it has been regimented by this seizure."[68]

The tax code may be a perfect example of the price we pay for a system of checks and balances. It may be an inefficient and inequitable way of raising revenue. Efforts to reform the tax code may stagnate as "emergencies mount and the Nation suffers for lack of harmonious, reciprocal action between the White House and Capitol Hill."[69] But the Constitution makes abundantly clear, in one of the few areas where nearly all the constitutional choices have truly been made *for* us, that the power to *execute* laws does not include the power to *make* them—even when the laws may be very good ones indeed.

III

THE STRUCTURE
OF SUBSTANTIVE
RIGHTS

CHAPTER TWELVE

COMPENSATION, CONTRACT, AND CAPITAL: PRESERVING THE DISTRIBUTION OF WEALTH

There is no doubt that a constitution might well define and defend "property" and "contract" along lines that center upon vital aspects of human personality and community—and in ways that protect both as the roots simultaneously of autonomy and interdependence. But no constitutional doctrine of property or contract that relies principally on requirements of public purpose and monetary compensation to justify and limit governmental impairments is likely to embody in any meaningful way such intangible and inherently noncompensable values as these.

Manifestly, whatever personal dispossession, political disenfranchisement, or religious desecration might be worked by a state assault upon an individual's or group's property claims or contractual rights will be constrained hardly at all by constitutional principles whose operational core is a cost-internalization norm that the public must pay a fair market price for what it confiscates, coupled with a largely irrelevant ban on confiscations that serve purely private ends.[1] Doctrines of this sort are far better calculated to protect a very different value—that of immunizing from majoritarian rearrangement extant distributions of wealth and economic power, almost as though such patterns and distributions of capital reflected something decreed and indeed sanctified by nature rather than something chosen by the polity.

The tilt against redistribution is anything but concealed in these doctrines. On the contrary, that tilt has long been among our law's proudest boasts. Thus, in a memorable dictum in 1798, Justice Chase grandly announced the Supreme Court's unequivocal condemnation of any law attempting to "take property from A and give it to B."[2] Al-

165

though the Constitution has been understood more ambiguously on this subject in the intervening two centuries, it remains the official line that legislative authority—whether to take, to tax, or to regulate—may not be deployed solely to redistribute wealth in the private interest of the beneficiaries of such state action.[3] And although this distributional conservatism has in part been simply a matter of judicial disposition, the Constitution itself dictates some degree of respect for settled economic arrangements by banning legislation that impairs contractual arrangements[4] or takes property without just compensation.[5]

The persistent appeal of these two textual girders, which enabled them to survive the collapse of the elaborate edifice of economic liberty that the Supreme Court built around them, is illustrated by recent Supreme Court decisions enthusiastically invoking both their letter and their spirit. Although neither of these girders imposes substantive limits beyond those of due process on the public purposes for which, with just compensation, private contracts may be undone or private property interests transferred, the upshot of the anti-impairment and just compensation requirements—especially as they have been applied and amplified by the Supreme Court—is to prevent much redistributive or otherwise "unsettling" economic regulation for which the public is unable or unwilling to pay, or for which such payment would conflict with the redistributive rationale itself, thereby creating a built-in tilt in favor of significant aspects of the economic status quo.

THE CONSERVATIVE DOCTRINE OF JUST COMPENSATION: PREVENTING THE ENDS BY UNDERCUTTING THE MEANS

The constitutional requirement that no property be taken without just compensation may be more important for what it renders pointless than for what it directly prohibits. Imagine a federal statute directing eminent domain proceedings to be filed against all family investment portfolios worth over five million dollars and devoting the interest earned on the taken securities to inner-city vocational training programs. The law would probably be constitutional: Congress has ample affirmative power under the Commerce Clause, and the purpose served by the takings—the funding of programs designed to increase employment—would clearly qualify as public.[6] The catch is that the government would have to *pay* for the securities—rendering the takings useless as a means of financing the training programs. The just compensation requirement thus prevents—by making futile—the use of the eminent domain power as a direct source of redistributable revenue. As an immediate consequence, the government is blocked from using takings solely as a means of directly redistributing wealth.[7]

To some extent, the constraint is only on the *form* of legislative action, not on the substance. Since the burial of *Lochner v. New York*,[8] the Supreme Court has tacitly recognized at least some forms of economic redistribution as legitimate, if not quite respectable, uses of the government's *regulatory* power. The state may, for example, place a regulatory floor on individuals' financial well-being,[9] and it may put a ceiling of sorts on economic inequality by regulating bargaining relationships.[10] And, in the wake of the Sixteenth Amendment,[11] the use of the *tax* power to redistribute wealth—at least indirectly—has never been seriously challenged.[12] The legislature may thus accomplish much redistribution without having to pay compensation simply by substituting a different statutory form—regulation or taxation—for explicit use of the eminent domain power.

But the just compensation requirement cannot always be so easily evaded; there are limits to the kinds of circumvention the Court will condone. Particularly difficult to accomplish are highly focused transfers of wealth—what may be termed "spot redistributions." Taxes, necessarily applied across the board,[13] are poorly suited to effect such microtransfers. Finely tuned exercises of the police power can transfer wealth with considerable precision, but the Court has repeatedly struck down regulation that it thought amounted to uncompensated taking. In *Pennsylvania Coal Co. v. Mahon*,[14] for example, the Court invalidated a state statute that overrode private contractual arrangements by forbidding anthracite coal mining that threatened the integrity of overlying dwellings, except where the owner of the coal also owned the surface rights. Writing for the Court, Justice Holmes acknowledged that "property may be regulated to a certain extent," but declared that "if regulation goes too far it will be recognized as a taking."[15] Predictably, the difficulty of determining how far is "too far" has plagued the Court for the last six decades. Government regulation—by definition—involves the adjustment of private rights for public benefit; to require compensation whenever the law curtailed the potential for economic exploitation "would effectively compel the government to regulate by purchase."[16]

Unable to articulate clear criteria for when regulation becomes an uncompensated "taking," the Court has resorted to ad hoc examination of the particular circumstances of each case, giving special attention to the extent of monetary injury and disruption of settled economic expectations caused by the challenged regulation—in effect, the law's redistributive impact.

The Court's approach to alleged regulatory "takings" was well illustrated by its decision in *Penn Central Transportation Co. v. New York*.[17] The Court there allowed New York City, as part of a plan to preserve the historic and aesthetic value of Grand Central Station, to prevent the construction of a fifty-three-story building atop the station. The Court found that the city's regulatory action would result in long-term economic gain for the city as a whole, thus significantly benefitting those "expropriated" as well: landmarks attract people to New York and create business for Penn Central, the owner of the station, along with the rest of the city.[18] Penn Central could not complain of being the only, or even an especially frequent, victim of historic preservation orders,[19] nor even of suffering very greatly in this particular instance: the diminution of property value was limited by the facts that (1) the law did not in any way interfere with Penn Central's primary use of the land as a railroad terminal containing office space and concessions, (2) not all development of the air space above Grand Central was categorically prohibited, and (3) the city gave Penn Central valuable "transferable development rights" which could be used on its other parcels of land nearby.[20] Whatever injury Penn Central could be said to have suffered after these circumstances were taken into account, the Court was willing to allow to go uncompensated.

The upshot is that, when faced with a regulation that not only (1) advances some public interest, but also (2) falls short of wholly destroying any traditional element of basic property rights, (3) leaves much of the commercial value of the property untouched, and (4) includes at least some reciprocity of benefit, the Supreme Court is unlikely to find a compensable taking. Thus, for example, *Agins v. City of Tiburon*[21] upheld open-land zoning that significantly limited the economic value of some residential acquisitions but was enacted in the interest of coherent land development and environmental policy. The zoning plan was unanimously held not to be a compensable taking. No conventional property rights were wholly destroyed, much of the value was left, and the owners could expect in the long run[22] to gain as much as they would lose.[23] In *Agins*, as in *Penn Central*, the Court thus sustained the challenged regulation only after satisfying itself that the law posed no significant threat to the existing distribution of capital.

COMMON SENSE AND COMMON LAW AS LIMITS ON POSITIVIST NOTIONS OF PROPERTY

"Spot redistributions" of the sort struck down in *Pennsylvania Coal Co. v. Mahon*[24] are not the only means by which legislatures can use regulation to circumvent the just compensation requirement and the antiredistribution principle underlying that requirement. The demise of *Lochner*[25] coincided with growing judicial acceptance of positivist approaches to property and contract rights: property and contract, the Supreme Court has recognized, are for the most part what the state says they are.[26] By redefining property rights, the legislature therefore can—at least in theory—alter traditional patterns of wealth distribution in quite radical ways. The Supreme Court, however, has sharply limited such definitional reform by tempering its positivism with a strong dose of judicial intuition about the nature of property and contract.

Indeed, much of the Court's jurisprudence of takings is built upon supposedly commonsense views of what the "taking" notion is all about.[27] The average justice of the Supreme Court, like the average person in the street, apparently believes that he (or she) knows a taking when he (or she) sees one. The Court seems at times to find the constitutional test transparent, and its duty simple: "to lay the article of the Constitution which is invoked beside the statute which is challenged and to decide whether the latter squares with the former."[28] What this mechanical notion of judicial review obscures is the fact that the Constitution does not provide its own template for identifying "property," much less "takings," and the Court's decisions in recent years suggest that it is sanctifying the common law—and conventional patterns of capital distribution—in the guise of drawing on common sense.[29]

One such case—not particularly controversial but revealing all the same—is *Webb's Fabulous Pharmacies, Inc. v. Beckwith*,[30] in which the Court unanimously struck down Florida's attempt to define as public property the interest earned on a private fund that had been deposited with a state court in the course of an interpleader proceeding. Webb's was in dire financial straits, and another pharmacy chain, Eckerd's, agreed to purchase its assets. In compliance with state law, Eckerd's tendered the purchase price to a state court and interpleaded Webb's and some two hundred of its creditors. The clerk of the court deposited the purchase fund in an interest-bearing account and deducted a statutorily determined sum as a fee for services rendered.[31] The fund was ultimately paid to a court-appointed receiver, but the clerk retained nearly $100,000 in interest pursuant to a state statutory command that "[i]nterest accruing from moneys deposited shall be deemed income of the office of the clerk."[32]

The Supreme Court unanimously disagreed, invoking the "usual and general rule" that the interest follows the principal.[33] The interest was not retained as a fee, for a statutory fee had already been deducted.[34] The interest therefore belonged to the creditors of Webb's as an "incident of ownership" of the principal.[35] The Florida Supreme Court had held that, since there was no statutory or other state-law requirement that funds deposited in the court's registry be invested, and since the very statute that directed investment also declared that the interest earned thereby was public property, the state took only what it itself had created.[36] The Supreme Court conceded that, since the Constitution itself creates no property rights, property is essentially what the state says it is,[37] yet rejected the state court's "bitter-with-the-sweet" argument nonetheless.[38] Substituting its own Lockean notion of property for the only applicable positive law, the Court declared that "a State, by *ipse dixit*, may not transform private property into public property without compensation."[39] Some sticks simply may not be purloined by the state from a property owner's Hohfeldian bundle. Just as the ownership of a chicken farm includes the right to a tranquil sky overhead, regardless of positive law to the contrary,[40] so the bundle of property rights in a fund temporarily deposited with a court includes the right to the interest that it earns, no matter how the state legislature or courts may have chosen to characterize the fund.

The principle at the heart of *Webb's*—that intuitive notions of private property place limits on the positivist power of the state to redefine property rights—also guided the Court's decision in *Fuentes v. Shevin*,[41] a case that in some respects differed strikingly from *Webb's*. *Fuentes* concerned the constitutionality of state statutes authorizing summary seizure by state agents of a person's possessions—without prior notice or hearing—upon the ex parte application of any self-proclaimed creditor who claimed a right to the property and posted a security bond. The laws were challenged by purchasers of household goods that had been summarily seized when the sellers charged defaults on installment payments.

The purchasers lacked full title—they had signed conditional sales contracts providing for forfeiture in case of default—and the sellers' allegations put even the partial title of the buyers in dispute. Moreover, the deprivation, at least in theory, might have been only temporary—the statutes allowed the purchasers to recover possession of their goods by posting their own security bond. Nevertheless, the Court held the seizures unconstitutional. Writing for the Court, Justice Stewart declared that, regardless of any more lenient preexisting positive law, only in "extraordinary situations" may a state seize a person's property without first providing an opportunity for the person to be heard.[42] Just as the common law of commerce made interest an unseverable incident of principal, so the "common law" of chattels made the right to a predeprivation hearing a normal incident of chattel ownership, largely immune from even *prospective* legislative tampering.[43]

Despite its proconsumer flavor, *Fuentes*, like *Webb's*, is thus a fundamentally conservative decision.[44] In each case the Court elevated its intuitive notion of what constitutes ownership to a constitutional limit on positive law. By refusing to allow state legislatures to redefine property rights too radically, the Court powerfully reinforced the protection of existing patterns of capital distribution provided by the ban on "spot redistributions."

CONFINING PROTECTION TO THE CONCRETE AND THE CONVENTIONAL

Takings law serves to conserve capital distributions as much by what it does *not* protect as by what it does. For although the Supreme Court has effectively enshrined traditional property rights that seem to it obvious, rendering them practically impervious to the vicissitudes of positive law, the Court has been reluctant to grant *any* degree of constitutional protection to less conventional property claims. Not every stick in a bundle of property rights has been deemed entitled to the staunch judicial protection displayed in *Webb's* and *Fuentes*; some sticks have seemed far more problematic. If a particular property interest is highly speculative or evanescent, it is harder for a court to judge whether what one is given in exchange for its expropriation is sufficient compensation. The Supreme Court's practice in cases involving such nontraditional property claims has generally been to find that there has been no taking at all.

In *Duke Power v. Carolina Environmental Study Group*,[45] the property alleged to have been "taken" was intangible in the extreme. The respondents there challenged the federal Price-Anderson Act, which limited to $560 million the right to recover for injuries caused by an accident at a nuclear power plant. The case presented interesting questions of standing and ripeness[46] that the Court resolved in favor of the respondents, in all likelihood because it seemed important to reach the merits.[47] And, on the merits, the Court found no taking where respondents lost a right to an uncertain recovery, in the "exceedingly remote" event of a nuclear accident, from utility companies with private insurers—and gained instead a guarantee of compensation that, although limited, would be awarded regardless of fault and distributed equally among claimants, avoiding a "race to the courthouse."[48]

The Court also rejected the respondents' claim to a right under the Due Process Clause to be free of nuclear power or to "take advantage of the state of uncertainty which inhibited the private development of nuclear power."[49] The argument was that private insurance companies would not have insured nuclear power plants for any amount approaching the estimated liability for a major nuclear mishap, and without such insurance private utility companies would probably not have built the reactors. The Price-Anderson Act was therefore a deliberate decision to expose some people to the risk of nuclear meltdowns and other catastrophes because Congress thought nuclear power development was in the public interest. Thus, for government to deny full compensation to the potential victims would surely sacrifice the few to the many or even, if one thinks the primary beneficiaries of nuclear power plants are the utility companies that lobbied for the Price-Anderson Act,[50] to a different, more influential, few.

An apparently minor point in the majority opinion would now seem to be crucial. The Court repeatedly emphasized the fact that Congress had expressly committed itself to take whatever further emergency action would be necessary to aid victims of a nuclear accident should the insurance fund prove insufficient.[51] This guarantee thus becomes pivotal in the holding that the victims of a future accident were not deprived of property. Yet the constitutionality of the Price-Anderson Act cannot possibly turn on a congressional promise to "make everything all right" in the event of a nuclear disaster, for such a pledge would not be binding on a subsequent Congress. Citizens have no more of a vested property interest in statutorily promised government benefits than they do in any rule of the common law,[52] and the congressional pledge of *future* legislative appropriations in the Price-Anderson Act is obviously even less dependable than are the more traditional entitlement programs. No future victim could possibly enforce that pledge in court.

Thus *Duke Power* can only be understood as a judgment by the Court that the "property" of which plaintiffs claimed to have been deprived simply did not look like anything the court was prepared to *call* property; it was far too problematic. The China Syndrome and other nuclear accidents were considered unlikely in the extreme. Full recovery in the event of disaster would be highly uncertain given state tort law and the limited financial resources of the utilities and their insurers. And, even if full recovery for an accident were achieved, the worst-case, Nagasaki scenarios were so horrific as to make *any* damage award inadequate. In exchange for this extremely contingent and evanescent "property" interest, the plaintiffs received strict-liability recovery out of an established fund as well as the benefits of nuclear power which Congress found so compelling. The Supreme Court decided that the deal was fair enough; there was no taking.

The Court came to a similar conclusion in the Iranian claims case, *Dames & Moore v. Regan.*[53] In response to the seizure of the American embassy and the taking of hostages in Iran, President Carter, pursuant to his authority under the International Emergency Economic Powers Act (IEEPA), froze all Iranian assets within the jurisdiction of the United States. Prejudgment attachments against such assets were conditionally authorized, but the President barred entry of any final decree. As part of the agreement that ended the hostage crisis, the President revoked the conditional licenses to attach, nullified the attachments, and ordered that all Iranian assets be transferred to the Federal Reserve Bank of New York for return to Iran. Creditors with enforceable contract rights lost the ability to satisfy their claims against Iran out of the previously frozen assets. Their only recourse was to arbitration in a special international claims tribunal, which possessed a limited capacity to satisfy the enormous claims of creditors, because it held only $1 billion dollars and a pledge—of obviously dubious value—of future payments by Iran. Thus, the settlement sacrificed the financial interests of a narrow class of American creditors and forced them to bear the entire economic burden of obtaining the release of the hostages.

The Supreme Court took a narrow view of the takings issue and answered only the formal question of whether the government had destroyed the creditors' property interests (liens) by nullifying the attachments of Iranian assets obtained pursuant to the President's conditional licenses.[54] The Court, in an opinion by Justice Rehnquist, held that, because the "petitioner's attachments [were] 'revocable,' 'contingent,' and 'in every sense subordinate to the President's power under the IEEPA,' . . . petitioner did not acquire any 'property' interest in its attachments of the sort that would support a constitutional claim for compensation."[55] The IEEPA made it clear that businesses conducting trade with foreign countries should not rely on the availability of foreign-owned assets in the United States, because in times of trouble those assets would become bargaining chips in a game of diplomatic poker.[56] And, without access to unconditional attachments, creditors had unenforceable and essentially worthless claims. The settlement, then, deprived creditors only of the right to sue the Ayatollah, who was unlikely—to put it mildly—to pay his debts to the financial minions of "The Great Satan." Balanced against the loss of this problematic right of action was the provision of a crack at the $1 billion fund held by the international claims tribunal, and the opportunity to sue the federal government under the Tucker Act on the grounds that the suspension of claims against Iran may constitute a taking.[57] Given the uncertainties of foreign policy and the evanescent character of foreign assets, Iran's creditors got about what they should have expected—so the Court held that there was no taking.

THE FETISH OF PHYSICAL INVASION: TRIUMPH OF FORM OVER FUNCTION

Although the Supreme Court's sense that certain traditional property rights should inhere in ownership, regardless of the dictates of positive law, typically reinforces the capital-preservation logic of the just compensation requirement, the implications of the two occasionally diverge, and they tend to do so sharply in cases concerning state laws that allow third parties to trespass physically upon private property. The power to exclude others from one's property is close to the intuitive core of many people's conception of what it means to *own* property, but the monetary harm from trespass is often minimal. Predictably, the Supreme Court has been less than consistent in its approach to laws authorizing physical intrusion. In two recent cases, the Court has applied its usual ad hoc approach, paying close attention to the degree of actual economic disruption. In a third case, however, the Court abandoned this approach in favor of a per se requirement of compensation for all permanent, physical invasions of even the most trivial variety.

PruneYard Shopping Center v. Robins[58] involved the right of a privately owned shopping center to resist the use of its property as a public forum. The PruneYard consisted of 21 acres, 10 restaurants, and more than 65 shops, which were visited by 25,000 people every day.[59] To resist use of the area by students seeking signatures on a petition, no plausible privacy claim could be made, nor a claim of protecting any right of intimate association. However, the owner of the shopping center had a general rule, neutral as to subject matter, prohibiting public expression other than the business-related variety. Unlike the ancient Greek *agora*, the PruneYard saw itself solely as a marketplace of goods, not a marketplace of ideas. Thus, when high school students tried to set up a booth to solicit signatures for a petition opposing a United Nations resolution, they were summarily ordered off the premises.

The California Supreme Court, however, interpreted the state constitution's free speech clause as entitling the students to set up their booth in the PruneYard—perhaps subject to reasonable time, place, and manner regulations—despite the fact that the shopping center was private property.[60] The PruneYard argued that California, by inviting third persons onto its property to conduct their petition drive, was taking its property without just compensation.

In a unanimous opinion by Justice Rehnquist, the Supreme Court disagreed. The Court conceded that the right to exclude others from one's property has long been held to be a fundamental element of one's bundle of property rights.[61] But the owner had *not* chosen to exclude people from the PruneYard—indeed, its purpose was to attract people there to spend money—and the Court could find no indication in the record that permitting free expression would significantly impair the value of the PruneYard *as* a shopping center, especially since the owner could impose reasonable time, place, and manner restrictions to limit the disruption of commercial activity. In these circumstances the

Court refused to view the fact that appellant's property had been "physically invaded" as determinative.[62]

A huge shopping center open to the general public understandably did not appear to the Court to be the kind of *traditional* "property" from which one has a federal constitutional right not only to exclude the public but also to extend invitations conditional upon what one's visitors have to say while on the premises. As a consequence, the positivist argument that California possesses a "residual authority that enables it to define 'property' in the first instance"[63] carried far more weight in *Prune Yard* than it did in *Webb's Fabulous Pharmacies*, where the Court held, just as unanimously, that interest follows the principal no matter what the state's law may say to the contrary.[64]

The Court's decision in *Prune Yard* was consistent with the approach it had taken to government-authorized trespass in *Kaiser Aetna v. United States*,[65] although in the earlier case the Court found the authorization to be a taking requiring compensation. In 1961 as part of its subdivision development of an area on Oahu and with the prior approval of the Army Corps of Engineers, Kaiser Aetna spent millions of dollars to convert a landlocked, 2-foot-deep fish pond into a navigable body of water connected to the Pacific Ocean by an 8-foot-deep channel.[66] A private marina-style community accommodating some 22,000 residents was constructed around the pond; about 1,700 of the residents paid fees for the maintenance of the marina.[67]

In 1972 a dispute arose between Kaiser Aetna and the Corps of Engineers over public access to the pond—which was by then a "navigable water" in fact even if still "fast land" under Hawaiian law. Did the government effect a taking by saying to the general public, "Come on in, the water's fine"? True, there had been no expropriation as such. But the government was regulating the property by imposing a navigational servitude that effectively invited actual physical invasion by third parties.[68] Unlike the Prune Yard, the pond was the sort of private property for which excluding the public was a critical stick in the bundle.[69] The government-invited gatecrashers would enjoy without charge a marina that residents paid annual fees to maintain. The Court, here also in an opinion by Justice Rehnquist, repeatedly stressed that Kaiser Aetna had spent millions of dollars developing a marina community on the assumption that it would stay private and not become a public aquatic park.[70] The majority held that, although the consent of the Corps of Engineers to Kaiser Aetna's development plans could not estop the United States from now placing the pond under a navigational servitude, it *could* engender investment-backed expectations rising to the status of property rights for which the government must pay when it effectively nationalizes them.[71]

In *Loretto v. Teleprompter Manhattan CATV Corp.*,[72] however, the Court departed strikingly from the approach it had taken in *PruneYard* and *Kaiser Aetna*. Prior to 1973 cable television (CATV) companies like Teleprompter had given landlords 5 percent of their gross revenues from users living in the landlord's property in exchange for the landlord's authorization of the necessary CATV installations. In order to facilitate tenant access to the important educational and community benefits of CATV, New York passed a law requiring all landlords to allow installation of CATV cables in exchange for a $1 fee.[73] The landlord was not to bear the costs of installation, however, and not only could demand that installation conform to reasonable conditions necessary to protect the appearance and safety of the premises, but was entitled to indemnification by the CATV company for any damage resulting from installation, operation, or removal of the CATV facilities.[74]

When a disgruntled landlord seeking a larger profit sued Teleprompter for trespass, the Supreme Court abandoned its now-familiar ad hoc approach in favor of a per se rule: a permanent physical occupation authorized by government is a taking without regard to any public interests it may serve.[75] The majority opinion treats a few feet of 1/2-inch cable and a couple of small metal boxes—the totality of the offending installation—as having effectively destroyed the landlord's use of his roof space.[76] We are told that to allow a "stranger" to "invade" and "exercise complete dominion" over the landlord's property is "literally to add insult to injury."[77] The majority even takes the dissent to task for underestimating the size of the CATV installation, which actually displaced more than 1 1/2 cubic feet![78]

This obsession with permanent physical invasions of even the most de minimis variety borders on fetishism. The majority apparently finds merely *temporary* uncompensated limitations on the right to exclude, such as that in *PruneYard*, to be less constitutionally offensive even though the economic deprivation of those incursions far exceeds that worked by CATV installations.[79] New York can force Penn Central not to build a multimillion dollar, fifty-three-story office building above Grand Central Station, but it cannot force Jean Loretto to abide a couple of 1 1/2-foot high boxes and some 1/2-inch cable above her apartment building.[80]

The final oddity of the *Teleprompter* decision is that the majority concedes that its analysis turns upon the fact that the CATV company, rather than the landlord, *owns* the offending installation. For the Court claims that its holding does not affect the state's power to require landlords to *provide* such things as mailboxes, smoke alarms, and utility connections. The reason is that, although the expense in those situations is imposed directly on the landlord, and her dominion over her property is certainly impaired, *she owns the installation*, albeit unwillingly.[81] This distinction is of critical importance to the majority because ownership would permit the landlord, not the CATV company, to decide how the cables were to be stapled to the roof and hence to control the aesthetic impact of the installation. But even this meager distinction collapses, since the majority admits that New York's laws give the landlord authority to prescribe reasonable conditions to protect the appearance of the premises and the right to demand indemnification for any damage. The *only* burden remaining on the landlord is the inconvenience of initiating minor repairs. Although the majority is correct that such a burden is "cognizable,"[82] it hardly amounts to cleaning out the Augean stables and is, in any event, a lame excuse for abandoning an apparently workable balancing test in favor of a talisman-like invocation of "permanent physical invasions."

A comparison of *Teleprompter* and *Penn Central* at least suggests that the Supreme Court's taking cases conceal no crude capitalist agenda: in *Penn Central* an expensive real estate development project by a corporate giant lost out to the cause of historic preservation; in *Teleprompter*, the needs of important, new information technology gave way to the formal property rights of small urban landlords. Evidently, the Court sees itself, or at least wishes to depict itself, as protecting property neutrally—as the *Constitution*, not capitalism, dictates. Yet the Court's "Constitution" is anything but inevitable: it is increasingly the Constitution as *Lochner*-style common law. The rooftop space invaded by the law struck down in *Teleprompter* certainly looks more like *traditional* property than does the volume of air above Grand Central Station that was protected by the law upheld in *Penn Central*. One suspects that there would be a closer fit between the Court's sense of property and the demands of fairness and efficiency in postindustrial society were the Court's imagination less captivated by common law anachronisms resembling those the Court dutifully enforced from the 1890s to 1937. By saying, "We know a taking of property when we see it, and this physical occupation by third parties, however insignificant, is it," the Court perpetuates the myth that the Just Compensation Clause is a template that judges may simply lay atop the facts so as to detect a taking if any rough pieces are seen to protrude beyond the edges. Critical analysis would be fostered by a more candid concession of the choices the Court necessarily makes when it follows common law habits as though it were merely doing arithmetic.[83]

WITH A LITTLE HELP FOR OUR FRIENDS: THE CONTRACT RIGHTS OF THOSE WITH UNCOMMON CLOUT

If recent twists and turns in Compensation Clause doctrine have occasionally obscured the doctrine's deep bias against economic redistribution, a similar bias has been starkly apparent in the modern resurrection of the Contract Clause. Originally intended as a bar against debtor relief legislation,[84] the Contract Clause from the start has served largely to protect the settled economic expectations of the wealthy. And just as the Supreme Court has struck down statutory redefinitions of property rights that, making an end run around the Compensation Clause, threatened traditional patterns of capital distribution, so it has refused, over time, to allow legislatures to define contract rights so as to write the Contract Clause out of the Constitution. Indeed, during the past decade the Court has given the clause new bite, using it to create a sharp division between the constitutional rights of those with sufficient clout to exact contractual concessions individually and directly from the government, and the rights of those whose only economic protection derives from politically secured statutory entitlements. The former may hold the government to its word absent compensation[85] or compelling necessity; the latter may insist only that any decision to cut off their benefits have a minimally rational basis and be carried out with a modicum of regularity.

The Contract Clause remained largely dormant during the *Lochner* era—the Due Process Clause and other constitutional provisions did most of the needed work—and was nearly interred altogether in *Home Building & Loan Ass'n v. Blaisdell*,[86] in which the Supreme Court upheld a Minnesota mortgage moratorium that allowed state courts retroactively to extend the period of redemption from foreclosure sales. The Court noted that the impairment of mortgage contracts was limited to the duration of the economic emergency declared by the state legislature, but the crux of its opinion was that one of the "rules" which may be read into every contract at its inception is the rule that all *other* rules are subject to change whenever the legislature reasonably decides that such change is essential to economic health. This reservation of corrective power was considered an essential "postulate of the legal order."[87]

The Court's holdings in *Blaisdell* and *Ogden v. Saunders*[88] that every private contract is subject to the positive law that predates its formation obviously have the potential to eviscerate the clause. But any such reading is discouraged by subsequent cases, for the Contract Clause was invoked successfully several times in the decade after *Blaisdell*, with the Court finding even some purely remedial changes too "oppressive and unnecessary" to pass constitutional muster.[89] The degree to which contracts were impaired was an important factor in evaluating challenged statutes. Yet although the courts continued to recognize the rule, first announced in *Pennsylvania Coal v. Mahon*[90], that the Just Compensation Clause put a limit on government regulation of property, the parallel shield of the Contract Clause gradually fell into disuse. The Supreme Court seemed to adopt the view that contract rights had no special constitutional status, and that statutes impairing contractual obligations would generally be upheld on a rationality test if they arguably promoted the economic welfare of the general public.[91]

The protective shield of the Contract Clause lay practically forgotten[92] for three decades until the Court dusted it off and put it to use in *United States Trust Co. of New York v. New Jersey* in 1977.[93] In a four-to-three decision,[94] the Supreme Court there held that the Contract Clause rendered void the retroactive 1974 repeal of a 1962 bi-state statutory covenant that limited the ability of the Port Authority of New York and New Jersey to subsidize rail passenger transportation from revenues and reserves pledged as security for consolidated bonds issued by the Port Authority. The 1962 convenant had been adopted "with full knowledge" of the concerns that ultimately led to its repudiation; any subsequent changes were found to be "of degree and not of kind."[95] Moreover, the "purpose of the covenant was to invoke the constitutional protection of the Contract Clause as security against repeal."[96] If New York and New Jersey could do what they tried to do in 1974, "the Contract Clause would provide no protection at all."[97]

The major modern expansion of the Contract Clause came the following year in *Allied Structural Steel v. Spannaus*.[98] The Court there struck down a Minnesota statute designed to protect certain workers' expectations of receiving pensions. The law provided that when a company employing at least one hundred workers—of whom at least one was a Minnesota resident—terminated a pension plan or closed a facility in Minnesota, "pension rights" would vest for all employees of ten years or more.

Allied Steel had a pension plan whereby an employee's rights vested at a time determined by one of several formulae, depending on age at retirement, but generally after much longer than ten years of working for the company. Allied expressly reserved the unilateral right to terminate the plan at any time and then to distribute among its employees whatever assets were in the pension fund.[99] Although the company's contributions to the pension fund were irrevocable once made, the pension plan did not obligate the company to make specific contributions or impose any sanctions on it if it failed to fund the plan adequately. The employee, then, had a right to a pension only if he or she met the various criteria and "if the company remained in business *and elected* to continue the pension plan in essentially its existing form."[100]

Justice Stewart, writing for the majority,[101] found that the law worked "a severe, permanent and immediate change"[102] in the expectations of the parties by "nullif[ying] express terms of the company's contractual obligations and impos[ing] a completely unexpected liability in potentially disabling amounts."[103] In a sense, the statute did not impair Allied Steel's obligations, as the dissent pointed out, but increased them.[104] But to argue that the Contract Clause was therefore not implicated at all seems too wooden: after all, the same argument could be made of a law retroactively doubling the rents tenants had agreed to pay landlords for residential dwellings.

The Court, although avoiding the words "strict scrutiny," seems to have applied just such an exacting standard of review to the Minnesota law by invoking the "compelling state interest" and "necessary means" tests.[105] The Court also stressed that the legislation in question was retroactive, and in an area not previously regulated by the state, so that the company would not have expected the rules on pension plans to change.[106] Thus, a decision by Allied Steel to close a plant or terminate a pension plan would have consequences it would not have had prior to the law's enactment: the company would be required to meet obligations it had not foreseen.

The first problem with this reasoning is that, although Minnesota had not previously regulated pension plans, it had long regulated workers' compensation, of which pension benefits are but a subset.[107] Second, the statute added obligations to employment contracts only if a pension plan was terminated or a plant was closed after the effective date of the law.[108] This sort of retroactivity—where obligations are added to preexisting contracts by virtue of postenactment conduct—does not seem distinguishable from applying minimum wage, maximum hours, and health and safety regulations to a company that previously bought, for instance, a bakery in reliance on there being no such laws. In both cases the company's future business plans may be significantly influenced by these *prospectively applied*, unforeseen laws. Yet, in the latter case, such laws are almost routinely upheld. In *Usery v. Turner Elkhorn Mining Co.*, [109] mine operators never expected to be held financially liable for employee disabilities resulting from black lung disease, especially since the mine workers may have contracted the ailment before its cause was understood and prophylactic measures were known.[110] Nevertheless, the Supreme Court upheld a statute imposing such onerous responsibility after only minimal review.[111]

The *Spannaus* decision could thus represent a back-door return to the jurisprudence of *Lochner*, especially given the Court's exacting economic scrutiny and its use of highly ambiguous tests. As Justice Brennan noted in dissent, "[t]he necessary consequence of the extreme malleability of these rather vague criteria is to vest judges with broad subjective discretion to protect property interests that happen to appeal to them."[112]

The Court has made it clear that its manipulable born-again Contract Clause analysis will not be deployed to uphold all claims alleging unconstitutional impairment of contracts. In *Energy Reserves Group (ERG) v. Kansas Power & Light Co. (KPL)*,[113] the Court unanimously rejected a challenge to a state natural gas regulation.[114] ERG and KPL had contracted for the sale of natural gas and had included within their agreements provisions for redetermining the purchase price in accord with any change in the comprehensive laws that might set a new price ceiling. In the wake of the deregulation of natural gas by the federal government, Congress empowered the state legislatures to engage in further regulation of the intrastate natural gas market. In response to that invitation, Kansas promptly imposed price controls on intrastate gas.[115] When ERG sought to redetermine the purchase price in accord with the governmental escalator clause of its contract with KPL, the utility refused on the ground that the new Kansas gas legislation prohibited the activation of such price redetermination clauses.[116]

The Court applied the analysis it had used in *United States Trust Co.* and *Spannaus* to hold that there was no violation of the Contract Clause. The Kansas gas regulations were not special-interest legislation of the kind struck down in *Spannaus*, because they affected the entire natural gas industry and were not aimed at merely one or two firms.[117] Moreover, the Kansas law was an attempt to deal with the "important social problem" of protecting consumers from rapidly rising gas prices caused by federal deregulation, while the pension legislation in *Spannaus* was tailored to affect the retirement benefits of only a small fraction of industrial workers.[118] The Court was willing to defer to the legislative determination of the public interest in *Energy Reserves Group* since, unlike the situation in *United States Trust Co.*, the state itself was not a party to any of the contracts affected by the new laws.[119]

The Court further distinguished *Spannaus* on the ground that the businesses there could not have foreseen disruption of their pension agreements since the state had never directly regulated pension plans, whereas Kansas had regulated sales of natural gas for seventy-five years.[120] All contracts for the purchase of natural gas in Kansas were explicitly geared to extensive state and federal regulation, and depriving ERG of windfall profits on its gas could not be said to disrupt its expectations, since no one in the industry could have anticipated federal deregulation.[121]

Similarly, the Court in *Exxon Corp. v. Eagerton*[122] unanimously sustained against Contract Clause challenge a state statute increasing the severance tax on oil and gas production and forbidding producers from passing on the increase to their customers. Noting that the pass-through prohibition served a broad social purpose and applied to all oil and gas producers—not just to those with preexisting, contrary sales agreements—the Court concluded that the contractual impairment caused by the statute was fully constitutional because it was merely "incidental to its main effect" of protecting consumers.[123]

Notwithstanding decisions such as *Energy Reserves Group* and *Exxon*, the reborn Contract Clause provides a considerable degree of security to those who have something tangible (like money) to offer that enables them to conclude contracts directly with the government, especially in comparison to the paltry protection the Court's reading of the Contract Clause provides to those whose minimal economic clout forces them to rely on statutory rather than contractual concessions. Just how ephemeral statutory concessions can be was made clear in *Railroad Retirement Board v. Fritz*,[124] which upheld Congress' ill-informed divestment of statutorily scheduled retirement benefits for a whole class of railroad employees. The Railroad Retirement Act of 1974 phased out "dual benefits"—railroad pensions *plus* social security—both prospectively and, to a degree, retrospectively: the Act cancelled benefits to which many workers had been entitled by statute as of their retirement from railroad work. What marked the statute—superficially a garden-variety effort at cutting costs by eliminating "double-dipping" into the national treasury—as unique was the curious pattern of deprivation the statute wove. The retirees who lost money were not those with fewer years of service to their credit but those who had retired longer ago. Specifically, retirees who had left the railroad industry prior to 1974 lost their "vested" benefits unless they had worked on the railroad at least twenty-five years; retirees who quit in 1974 or later retained these benefits even if they had worked barely ten years.[125] Thus, those who had the bad luck of having severed their connections with the railroad before 1974 took it in the neck, while employees with no more seniority, but who were lucky enough to have worked on the railroad for one day after January 1, 1974, smiled all the way to the bank.

By a seven-to-two vote,[126] the Supreme Court held that the law did not constitute a denial of equal protection under the Fifth Amendment. The majority, speaking through Justice Rehnquist, applied minimal scrutiny and asked only for "some reasonable basis" for the legislative formula, which it then proceeded to supply by what Justice Brennan in dissent aptly called tautology.[127] The Court assumed purpose from result by concluding that, because the Act divested some retirees but not others, Congress must have intended to do just that.[128] Justice Rehnquist's circular argument comes surprisingly close to saying that Congress may indeed "take from A to give to B." Justice Stevens concurred in the judgment but was unwilling to accept the majority's merely "conceivable" or "plausible" rationales for the unequal treatment meted out by the Railroad Retirement Act.[129] Instead, he called for the justices to put their imaginations to work to find a principle that, even if not the one Congress had in mind, would provide a reasonable and impartial lawmaker with a basis upon which to distinguish among the classes of retirees. He concluded that since Congress' mission was to cut costly "windfall benefits" and since it arguably had a "duty . . . to eliminate no more vested benefits than necessary to achieve its fiscal purpose," the choice of currency of railroad service—as a kind of antiseniority basis on which to distinguish among retirees—was "impartial."[130]

Justice Brennan's reply to both the majority and concurring opinions was an admonition to consider reality. He examined the legislative history of the act and agreed with the express findings—never repudiated—of the district court that Fritz and his fellows were shortchanged by a Congress that *had no idea* that it was depriving any of these retirees of an earned and promised benefit. The highly complex legislation had been drafted by "representatives of railroad management and labor, whose self-serving interest in bringing about this result destroy[ed] any basis for attaching weight to their statements."[131] The group of dispossessed retirees was not represented on the panel that wrote the law or in the hearings on the law before Congress.[132] When the Act's proponents told the congressional committee that no retirees were being frozen out, there was no one there to contradict them. Thus, there was every reason to believe that this law was a craftily engineered accident, not a deliberate legislative approximation of a dividing line nor a well-informed policy decision by Congress to gore one person's ox in order to get a little more for someone else. In fact, this is precisely the sort of "circumstantial evidence"[133] that convinced the *Spannaus* Court that what it had before it was impermissible special-interest legislation: the selective divestiture of the pension benefits of a particular class of retirees certainly had a suspiciously "narrow focus," and the desire to save the contents of the pension fund coffers for the benefit of a class of currently employed railroad workers hardly seemed to address an "important social problem."[134]

Justice Rehnquist's retort was that the real facts and real reasons behind the Act were constitutionally irrelevant, and that Congress' alleged ignorance of what it was doing was no excuse: unfortunate, improvident, or even semiconscious legislation is a fact of life, and the injured citizen is remitted to the democratic process for relief.[135] Justice Brennan was not satisfied here with mere political protection—yet he had argued in his dissent in *United States Trust Co. v. New Jersey* that constitutional limits on state power to play fast and loose with bond obligations were unnecessary because government conduct would be "adequately policed by the political processes and the bond marketplace itself."[136] The difference, of course, is that the victimized bond-holder whom the Contract Clause protected in *U.S. Trust Co.* was a powerful financial institution with $300 million in Port Authority holdings,[137] while the victims in *Fritz*—for whom the Constitution was not invoked—were retired blue-collar workers. The voting booth and the petition are apparently sufficient protection for the interests of the hoi polloi, but not for the interests of the coupon-clipping financial elite.[138]

The most alarming prospect of the decision in *Fritz* is that all nine justices took for granted the unavailability of any claim that Congress had taken property in violation of the Fifth Amendment. Fritz and his cohorts were scheduled to receive certain retirement benefits. They had spent years expecting and planning on that income. Their expectation was written into the statute—and then suddenly repealed. The Court split over the issue of whether the criterion which cut Fritz off was a rational one, but what about the fact that something that a class of workers had banked on was almost literally taken out of their pockets? On *that* issue, the Court, *without a single dissenting voice*, held that there was no taking of property, "since railroad benefits, like social security benefits, are not contractual and may be altered or even eliminated at any time."[139] Those who invest their money in government bonds are entitled to judicial process and constitutional guarantees, but for those who invest their time and toil in exchange for promised government pension benefits, "the legislative determination provides all the process that is due."[140]

The net effect of prevailing principles of property and contract is to build in a strong tilt in favor of those with sufficient economic clout to win bilateral contract protection vis-à-vis the government, while providing virtually no protection for those whose only power lies in concerted political action. First, what they manage to win can be *legislatively revoked* with virtually no judicial review—as Gerhard Fritz has learned; second, their legislative gains may even be *judicially canceled* if the laws add obligations to those that the other side has assumed by contract—as the former employees of Allied Structural Steel now know. Relaxing the level of judicial scrutiny under the Contract Clause would reduce this disparity to some degree but would still leave the least powerful groups in our economy largely defenseless against the sort of economic warfare conducted by the railroad management and recent retirees in *Fritz*.

Recognizing our constitutional law's built-in bias against redistribution of wealth should initiate rather than close off inquiry. The worst conclusion a reader could draw from the preceding discussion is that we have no choice other than scrupulously respecting existing patterns of capital distribution: "The Constitution says not to redistribute, and that's that." Like all parts of the Constitution, Compensation Clause and Contract Clause doctrine are human creations, constantly in the process of being re-created. Little is inevitable about any of it. The rules are often changed not only by altering the terms of the Constitution, but also by bringing to the document different hopes and concerns. Among the most important lessons of the Burger Court's dramatic resuscitation of the Contract Clause is that, even unamended, the Constitution is, to a substantial although importantly bounded degree, what all of us make of it.

Alleviation of the substantive tilt discussed in this chapter need not require a diminution of the protections currently provided to entrenched wealth, although some such diminution might well be sensible. What is most wrong with our law's treatment of property and contract is not what that treatment excessively *protects* but what it largely *ignores*: the need for economic and emotional security among the vast majority of Americans who lack the financial clout necessary to secure it themselves in a marketplace increasingly dominated by large corporations and unions and various appendages of the government. Their security depends on interests less conventional than fee simple titles or premiums earned on principal. And the Constitution offers ample material out of which doctrines could be fashioned to protect those interests.[141]

CHAPTER THIRTEEN

SPEECH AS POWER: OF SWASTIKAS, SPENDING, AND THE MASK OF "NEUTRAL PRINCIPLES"

Although the First Amendment may indeed be "the Constitution's most majestic guarantee,"[1] the protection of free speech has by no means been a universal or eternal feature of American constitutional law. Throughout the course of history, devotion to the First Amendment has waxed and waned with the political tides. Even in periods when the protection of free speech has enjoyed the greatest support, the First Amendment rights of those in positions of power and wealth have generally found greater favor than the First Amendment rights of those less well situated. In short, the constitutional axiom of free expression has been only slightly more immune to the pressures of politics, culture, and the marketplace than any other aspect of our laws.[2]

This essay explores some of the present, and past, configurations of First Amendment protection, with an eye to what has been called the "central meaning" of the First Amendment—equality.[3] Each section of the essay looks for that meaning, or lack of it, in a particular facet of First Amendment jurisprudence. The first section places the principle of free speech in the context of its checkered history, in which periods of greater protection have alternated with periods characterized by a less solicitous approach.

The balance of the essay examines more recent developments along a variety of axes that mark the complex interrelationship between free speech and political, social, and economic equality. The second section, for example, looks at the contemporary political arena in light of a harsh reality: that is, that speech, as it now comes to us, is usually anything *but* "free." Section three focuses on the courts' use of a rather formalistic speech-conduct distinction to limit the availability of First Amendment protection for labor unions, while simultaneously finding the same mix of speech and conduct to merit protection in the context of a civil rights struggle. The fourth section considers another formalistic distinction—right versus privilege—as a doctrinal tool for cutting off the free speech rights of those who rely on the government as an employer, provider of benefits, or property owner. In the fifth section, the Supreme Court's increasing protection of "commercial speech" is analyzed (1) in terms of the Court's apparent preference for allocational efficiency over distributional equity, and (2) as an example of the Court's propensity to divide First Amendment principles into separate doctrinal categories, each with its own distinctive principles.

The various approaches suggested in this essay may appear to map out discrete avenues into the jurisprudence of the First Amendment. Yet they share at least one common feature in that each avenue purports to find its way by reference to purely "neutral" principles—for example, that the First Amendment protects speech rather than conduct, or the right to express ideas rather than the right to propose commercial transactions. These seemingly neutral principles, however, when applied in the decision of particular cases, tilt decidedly in the direction of existing concentrations of wealth and influence. Thus, the essay concludes with a brief consideration of the Nazis' proposed march in Skokie, Illinois, and asks whether the conventional justification for defending the Nazis' right to march—based on the "neutral principles" of the First Amendment—provides a wholly adequate explanation for that defense. It may well be that, in the end, our commitment to the First Amendment requires us to guarantee a forum for Nazis and others whose thought we hate. What is not so clear is how much we can count on similar protection when it is our *own* thought that *others* hate, and whether the commitment to untrammeled expression is compelled by a devotion to assertedly neutral principles or whether instead a more substantive, egalitarian principle should lie at the core of First Amendment argument and decision.

THE FIRST AMENDMENT IN CONTEXT: HISTORY

In the popular view of the First Amendment, free speech and expression are among the most broadly enjoyed and universally enforced principles of our Constitution—part of the political bedrock on which the republic was built. It has become commonplace to view the courts, wielding the shield of the First Amendment, as fairly consistent defenders of freedom of speech and expression.[4] Those who take this view have left the impression that the nation's courts did not encounter important First Amendment issues until World War I.[5] But this assumption simply cannot withstand scrutiny.[6] For example, in the struggle over the Sedition Act of 1798,[7] the country's first major free speech fight, the lower federal courts—then bastions of the Federalist Party—were only too anxious to convict members of the rival Democratic Party of the crime of uttering "false, scandalous, and malicious" criticisms of the federal government.[8] Popular pressure, organized by Thomas Jefferson and James Madison, forced the effective repeal of the Act before the issue reached the Supreme Court.[9]

Moreover, it is simply not true that the Court faced no important free speech decisions until World War I. The Court was in fact confronted with substantial First Amendment issues in the late 1800s and early 1900s, but responded by repeatedly declining to protect free speech.[10] During this period, for example, the Court upheld a libel conviction against a newspaper for statements critical of the President and the Secretary of War,[11] affirmed a court order enjoining a union from stating that a company was on its "We don't patronize" list,[12] upheld a city ordinance that barred use of a city park for public addresses unless the mayor's permission had been obtained in advance,[13] and approved an Ohio law that required that films be approved by a board of censors before being shown to the public.[14] In only one prewar case did the Court rule for a free speech claimant on First Amendment grounds.[15]

When change finally came, it was in the context of a major political upheaval. The election of Franklin Roosevelt to the presidency in 1932, upsurges in the labor movement in 1933 and 1936, and Roosevelt's "court-packing" scheme, all had their impact.[16] Whether or not the Court's increasingly protective stance was directly "caused" by popular pressure, the political developments of the New Deal era clearly hastened and deepened the Court's commitment to the protection of free speech.[17] Communists, union activists, and Jehovah's Witnesses boldly exercised their rights of expression and, when forbidden or penalized by government, pushed their cases to the Supreme Court.[18]

It was not long before the Court's new-found sensitivity to free speech issues was put to the test. In March 1946 Winston Churchill delivered his famous "iron curtain" speech at Fulton, Missouri. Within a few years, the Cold War was in full swing. Congress and state legislatures began churning out antisubversive legislation. The story of the Supreme Court's collapses in the face of the "Red scare" has often been told.[19] Suffice it to say that the Court, confronted by an aroused popular movement, chose conformity over the continued assertion of First Amendment values.[20] The Red scare was the most visible aspect of a general shift toward more conservative politics. Perhaps the most important legislative manifestation of this shift was the Taft-Hartley Act of 1947, which cut back many of the gains made by labor in the 1930s.[21] Newspapers and radios trumpeted the dangers of growing union power. Coincidentally with the declining popularity of unions, the Court gradually gutted the protection for labor picketing which it had established in the landmark 1940 case of *Thornhill v. Alabama.*[22]

The Court's next burst of First Amendment activism coincided with the rise of the civil rights movement in the late 1950s and early 1960s. In the words of Harry Kalven, the "Negro revolution" carried out an "almost military assault on the Constitution via the strategy of systematic litigation."[23] In pathbreaking cases involving state attempts to control the National Association for the Advancement of Colored People (NAACP), the Court for the first time explicitly recognized a right of association (as distinct from assembly),[24] and applied it to strike down such repressive devices as membership disclosure requirements,[25] loyalty affidavits,[26] and McCarthy-like legislative investigations.[27] The Court also found that the First Amendment protected such expressive activities of the civil rights movement as picketing[28] and sit-ins.[29] Just as the Court of the 1930s and 1940s had found it necessary to overrule or dodge the precedents of the pre–World War I period, the Court of the 1960s had to circumvent the obstacles to protection that it had erected during the Red scare.[30] The relationship between civil rights activism and changing First Amendment doctrine was by no means a mechanical one. Indeed, the Court had committed itself to intervene in Southern race relations even before the rise of the civil rights movement.[31] But the advance in First Amendment protection sprang from the commitment and the choices it represented,[32] not from eternal principles or adherence to precedent, which in truth functioned more as an obstacle than as a source of protection.

Over the past decade, the Supreme Court has been moving toward a new configuration of First Amendment values. This motion cannot be described simply as protective or nonprotective, interventionist or noninterventionist. The Court has expanded protection in some areas—striking down limitations on spending and contributing money,[33] asserting the First Amendment rights of corporations,[34] protecting commercial advertising,[35] and exempting boycott activity by a civil rights organization from economic regulation and tort law [36]— while simultaneously cutting back in other areas—further withdrawing protection from labor picketing,[37] sharply curtailing the free speech rights of government employees,[38] and excluding privately owned public areas from First Amendment scrutiny.[39]

It is important to see these developments not as deviations from timeless principles, but as part of the normal functioning of constitutional adjudication. This is not to say that the Constitution is an empty vessel to be filled with the values of a particular historical period. It is, rather, to suggest that the Constitution exists in intimate relationship with society as a whole and that the constitutional doctrines and choices of any particular period are outcomes of a complex interplay among text, history, and social forces. Whether one's purpose is critical or supportive, arguments grounded in social and historical context may in the long run prove more effective, and would surely be more honest, than outraged assertions of "ancient liberties."[40]

POLITICAL EQUALITY AND THE FIRST AMENDMENT

One area in which the Supreme Court has shown considerable sensitivity to social and historical context in recent years is that of voting rights. This sensitivity has not been matched, however, by a corresponding concern about inequalities of access to the political forums in which public issues are debated.

The Court has been willing to correct imbalances of power created by devices designed to disenfranchise blacks and other minority groups—such as malapportioned voting districts,[41] poll taxes,[42] and gerrymandering.[43] In doing so, the Court has no doubt been motivated by a growing awareness of political equality as a legitimating foundation for our form of government. Although individuals might not always win in the political process, it is possible to accept the outcome if one has an equal voice in the process.[44] It is thus not surprising that the Court has applied its most exacting equal protection scrutiny to enforce the principle of "one person, one vote."[45]

Yet in a society confronted with as many complex issues as ours, equality in voting is not enough. Overwhelming evidence indicates that gross inequalities of voice result in disproportionate influence over voters and legislators.[46] Hence the need to go beyond the principle of one person, one vote to embrace the ideal of one person, one *voice*. The Court's strongest statement of this ideal came in *Police Department of the City of Chicago v. Mosley*.[47] There, the Court struck down an ordinance that exempted labor picketing from a general ban on picketing near schools, and stated: "[t]here is an 'equality of status in the field of ideas,' and government must afford all points of view an equal opportunity to be heard."[48]

The ideal of equality under the First Amendment embodies both a negative and a positive aspect. The negative ideal of equality equates the maximum protection of individual liberty with the generality of the rule in question.[49] This ideal is clearly expressed, for example, in opinions limiting official discretion to pick and choose among speakers,[50] and in cases striking down restrictions that apply only to a narrow class of speakers.[51] Because the negative ideal treats equality merely as a means to the end of more liberty, it is vulnerable to the criticism that rigorous enforcement of the principle could encourage government to correct flaws of inequality not by eliminating selective restrictions but by extending them to everyone, thus suppressing more speech rather than less.[52] Moreover, this ideal can conflict with efforts to implement a more substantive conception of equality. Consider, for example, the Supreme Court's use of the ideal of generality to strike down legislation aimed at rectifying the impact of inequalities of wealth on the political process.[53]

The affirmative ideal of equality provides a firmer foundation for an egalitarian interpretation of the First Amendment. Seen through the lens of this ideal, equality is essential to the Constitution's protection of free speech and association.[54] The central place of equality is most apparent with regard to the First Amendment's function as a guarantor of self-government. Unlike some other liberties, the right to express oneself on matters of public concern has value largely in relation to the rights enjoyed by others. Although such liberties as the right to own property or to control conception may be useful in themselves, the right to vote, for example, is valuable only to the extent that it enables one to influence the political process.[55]

Equality is not a self-defining term, however.[56] What is egalitarian from one perspective may be grossly discriminatory from another. It should come as no surprise, for example, that the so-called "*Lochner* period" of constitutional law, which is now commonly viewed as a paradigm of antiegalitarian judicial intervention,[57] was justified at the time with reference to an egalitarian ideal.[58] A more recent example is provided by the campaign expenditure limitations passed by Congress in the wake of the Watergate investigations. Congress enacted these restrictions in part to reduce what it saw as the disproportionate influence of moneyed interests on the political process.[59] In the view of the Court, however, the ideal of equality is best served by prohibiting the government from enhancing the relative voice of some at the expense of others,[60] even if those whose activities are regulated by the legislation currently hold a massive advantage.

Discriminatory restrictions come in two general varieties: those which explicitly discriminate among types of speech or speakers; and those which are facially neutral, but fall unequally on different groups. Facially discriminatory restrictions may classify speech according to such criteria (from the most to the least problematic) as the viewpoint expressed, the identity of the speaker, and the subject matter of the expression. The Court has stated—and, for the most part, enforced—broad prohibitions against all three forms of such discrimination.[61]

With regard to facially neutral restrictions, I have suggested elsewhere that an approach based primarily on analysis of legislative motive would ferret out facially neutral restrictions that were actually motivated by viewpoint discrimination.[62] Such an approach, however, may not be sufficient to bar restrictions that are neither explicitly nor deliberately directed at the content of speech or the identity of a speaker but that nevertheless fall more heavily on some groups than on others.[63] If the groups that are differentially treated tend to express different views, the First Amendment concern for minimizing censorship is implicated. This problem is unavoidable with respect to restrictions that affect groups with different levels of wealth. As James Madison observed, "[t]he most common and durable source of factions has been the various and unequal distribution of property."[64] Even where there is no apparent divergence of views, the principle of one person, one voice is implicated because, to the extent that the voice of some groups is enhanced, the voice of others is muted.[65]

Consider two examples. In the first, a municipal ordinance places a $250 ceiling on individual contributions to referendum campaign organizations. In the second, a federal regulation prohibits the placement of "mailable matter" in mailboxes used to receive U.S. mail. As long as individuals are viewed in the abstract, both restrictions appear to be consistent with the principle of equality. The municipal ordinance in the first example leaves every individual equally free to contribute up to $250 or to employ some other means of propagating his message. The federal regulation in the second example leaves every individual equally free to buy stamps or to employ some other method of communication. However, when these individuals are viewed against the background of their actual conditions of life, it becomes apparent that both restrictions fall more heavily on some than on others. The $250 limit on contributions imposes no burden at all on people who do not have that kind of money to spend on political contributions anyway. Its impact falls solely on the relatively wealthy. Moreover, it is of little interest to wealthy individuals that they retain the right to canvass or pass out flyers. The wealthy tend to be a small group in society, and therefore tend to rely less on personal canvassing than on direct mail or newspaper ads to reach all of the residents of a city. Thus the ordinance, by restricting the favored means of expression of the rich, gives the poor a relatively greater voice than they had previously.

Like the $250 limit, the mailbox ban loses its egalitarian appearance once the affected individuals are placed in their social context. The regulation imposes no burden whatever on people who enjoy sufficient wealth to make paying for stamps preferable to hand delivery. Its impact falls solely on people who rely on volunteer labor to save costs.[66] The fact that they retain the right to buy stamps is small comfort given the obvious financial advantage held by wealthy people. Thus the regulation, by restricting the favored means of communication of less wealthy people, augments the voice of the rich.

The Court has had occasion to confront both of these situations. In *Citizens Against Rent Control v. City of Berkeley*,[67] the Court struck down the $250 contribution limit, in part on the assertedly egalitarian ground that"'[t]he First Amendment's protection against governmental abridgment of free expression cannot properly be made to depend on a person's financial ability to engage in public discussion.'"[68] But in *United States Postal Service v. Greenburgh Civic Associations*,[69] decided only six months earlier, the Court upheld the mailbox regulation without even mentioning the problem of discrimination based on financial status. Only Justice Marshall, dissenting, raised the issue.[70]

The response of the Court may be described, without exaggeration, as schizophrenic. At times, it seems that the Court wants to freeze channels of communication as they were at the moment it began to enforce the First Amendment.[71] At other times, however, it has shown a concern for the changed methods and increased costs of communication. A comparison of *Greenburgh* and *Berkeley* will serve to illustrate the contrast. In *Greenburgh*, Justice Rehnquist, speaking for the Court, quoted Justice Holmes's aphorism that "a page of history is worth a volume of logic," and launched into a history of the U.S. Postal Service from colonial times to the present.[72] From this history, he drew the conclusion that the Postal Service had always had the power to control access to mailboxes and held (this time making a leap of "logic" rather than "history") that it must also have the power to do so today. The opinion does not analyze the actual methods of communication available to the civic associations. The fact that they could not afford postage was of no concern to the Court because "appellees do not challenge the imposition of a fee for the services provided by the Postal Service."[73] Although in *Greenburgh* payment of postage fees was considered a viable alternative to door-to-door distribution, in *Berkeley* the Court did not consider door-to-door distribution as an alternative to direct mail. Instead, it asumed that there is a financial "cost of reaching the public" and assessed the burden on free speech imposed by the contribution limit in light of the cost of newspaper advertisements and direct mail.

The Court's rulings could also be described as schizophrenic in their approach to the associational rights of the parties in *Berkeley* and *Greenburgh*. In *Berkeley*, for example, the Court noted that the city ordinance did not (and, the Court opined, could not validly) attempt to limit *expenditures* of over $250 by separate individuals in support of ballot questions; it followed, the Court said, that the First Amendment protected the right of those individuals who wished to spend more than $250 to join forces—a right that would have been frustrated by the ordinance's limit on contributions. That right, according to the *Berkeley* majority, derived from the First Amendment's guarantee of associational freedom *and* "individual and collective rights of expression."[74] In *Greenburgh*, however, the Court did not see either the associational freedom or the collective rights of expression of the plaintiff civic associations as infringed by the postal statute. One explanation for this lack of concern might be that the only activity the associations in *Greenburgh* were prevented from undertaking together was the communication of their views by way of circulars hand-delivered to their neighbors' mailboxes. Yet in *Berkeley* the challenged ordinance would have left those who wished to pool individual contributions of more than $250 free to undertake any sort of political activity except spending more than a certain amount of their money together on a ballot question campaign.

Greenburgh and *Berkeley* could arguably be distinguished as involving different areas of law. *Greenburgh* concerns the doctrine of public forums, an area of law where tradition has always been important.[75] *Berkeley* involved contribution limitations, an area where the Court has been sensitive to requirements of effective communication under modern conditions.[76] But there does not appear to be any constitutionally cognizable reason why tradition should control in the public forum area, where it is used to justify the erosion of protection for inexpensive means of communication involving personal effort, while sensitivity to modern conditions prevails in the expenditure area, where it helps to insure a high degree of protection for those who pay surrogates to propagate their messages.[77] The decision to draw a bright line between the law of the public forum and the law of campaign regulation is, intentionally or not, a decision to favor methods of communication employed by the rich over those employed by the poor.

The Court's increasingly deferential approach to existing concentrations of wealth and power seems particularly inappropriate in light of rapid social and technological changes that have increasingly shifted the channels of public communication into private control. When the Court began to enforce the First Amendment in the 1920s and 1930s,[78] most people frequented public forums such as sidewalks, streets, and parks, through which they walked en route to work, shop, or play. Groups could reach a large proportion of the community by leafletting, picketing, or demonstrating in such locations. Radio was only beginning to rise as a major means of communication, and television was unknown.[79] The decline of traditional public forums such as parks and streets has been accompanied by the rise of privately owned shopping centers as key locations for reaching the public; inexpensive methods of communication such as leafletting, picketing, and soapbox orating have given way to expensive media such as electronic broadcasting, newspaper advertising, and direct mail.[80]

With the rise of the shopping center and the growth of suburban industrial belts, increasing numbers of people drive to their daily destinations. Shopping centers and large workplaces are often surrounded by privately owned parking lots, making leafletting difficult if not impossible.[81] Residential areas are more dispersed, again making canvassing and leafletting difficult. People have come increasingly to rely on television and radio for information. Newspapers, still a viable means of communication, are increasingly concentrated in the hands of a few large chains.[82] In short, more and more of the most important forums and means of communication are coming under the control of fewer and fewer private owners.

These changes in access to and control over the forms of public communication have eaten away at the average citizen's rights of expression and, thus, at the prospects for realizing free speech values. Inasmuch as those values are essential to the character of our constitutional order, it is not exaggerating to say that that order could be seriously threatened by a continued failure of the Court to take account of background institutions of power and the costs of participation in public dialogue.

PURITY AND OBSCURITY: THE SPEECH-CONDUCT DISTINCTION

When background relationships of power come to the foreground—as they do, for example, in labor picketing cases—courts often resort to formalism to conceal what might be viewed as a frank preference for one set of interests over another, or at least as a substantive choice of one constitutional vision over another. The speech-conduct distinction performs exactly this function in cases where expressive activity (typically, union activity) involves elements that could be characterized either as "speech" or as "conduct." By resolving these cases through categorization rather than analysis of the function that the expressive activity performs in each setting, courts have ignored the inequalities of access to communications media that prevail as much in the economic as in the political arena.

The Supreme Court's attempt to distinguish between speech and nonspeech elements of expression has reflected a recognition that words can be direct instruments of harm independent of the ideas they express. Revealing troop movements during wartime,[83] exposing undercover intelligence operatives,[84] and shouting "Boo!" at a cardiac patient,[85] are generally beyond the pale of First Amendment protection.

The distinction between speech and conduct has its roots in the pre–World War I period. At that time, it served as one of the Court's doctrinal weapons for removing virtually all protection from speech.[86] In *Gompers v. Bucks Stove & Range Co.*, [87] the leading case, a union was

enjoined from publishing or otherwise communicating the information that the plaintiff company was on its "unfair" and "do not patronize" lists. The Court unanimously rejected Gompers' argument that
the injunction constituted a prior restraint on speech, reasoning that
it barred only "verbal acts," not speech.[88] Exactly how these "verbal
acts" differed from the verbal acts that accompany other speech was
left unclear.[89] But the Court could not have been trapped in an inconsistency anyway, since it had rarely protected any "speech" at all.

Thus, right from the start, the trouble with the expression-action
or speech-conduct distinction was apparent: by itself it has no determinative content. It is impossible to imagine speech unaccompanied
by a "verbal act"—except, perhaps, speech of the extrasensory variety.[90] The idea that the word "speech" carries determinative content is
characteristic of the formalistic reasoning of the *Lochner* period. Somehow the justices were supposed to determine, scientifically and objectively, whether a particular expressive activity constituted "speech."[91]
There would be no equivocating over values. The hard choices—for
example, whether or not to protect a union's right to call a company
unfair—could thus be made without a forthright evaluation of the free
speech and property interests involved. Today, when "balancing" is accepted, though not necessarily approved,[92] as a mode of legal reasoning, courts have less need for such formalistic devices. Nevertheless,
the distinction lingers on.[93]

I have suggested elsewhere that the distinction is relatively harmless insofar as it functions mainly as a surrogate for a two-track analysis, in which "speech" substitutes for communicative impact, which
may not be regulated outside of narrow, specified exceptions, while
"conduct" stands in for noncommunicative impact, which may be regulated subject to a balancing test.[94] Indeed, a number of the opinions
employing the distinction could be reinterpreted as applications of
this two-track model.[95] But it must be noted that the doctrine has
been applied to shut off expressive activity only in cases involving inexpensive methods of communication, like picketing and demonstrating, which rely on the active participation and physical presence of
people to attract attention and convey the message.[96] The expenditure
of money, on the other hand, has been treated as pure speech.[97] The
principal "pure" alternatives to "mixed speech and conduct"—publication, electronic media, and direct mail—are expensive and lack the
emotional impact of personal interaction. The idea that speech by
large numbers of actively participating people should be given less pro-

tection than a barrage of published or broadcast material paid for by a single individual has an obvious, perverse impact on the prospects for realizing the ideal of one person, one voice. Thus, the speech-conduct distinction may well be a mask for discrimination against the methods of communications favored by the relatively powerless groups in society.

In a significant number of labor cases, the speech-conduct distinction has been employed to justify restrictions directed specifically at the communicative impact of expressive activity.[98] Indeed, the Court has recently added a new wrinkle to the distinction—the "signal" doctrine.[99] As articulated by Justice Stevens in his concurring opinion in *NLRB v. Retail Store Employees Union* (Safeco), the doctrine mandates a lowered level of protection for expression "that calls for an automatic response to a signal, rather than a reasoned response to an idea."[100] Though generally mentioned in the same breath as coercion, the idea of a signal by itself does not carry any implication of physical or economic coercion.[101] The idea appears to be, rather, that by triggering deeply held sentiments, picketing bypasses viewers' faculties of reason and, thus, in a sense brainwashes them into compliance with the boycott.[102]

Yet this aspect of labor picketing is common to other kinds of picketing, to most effective political communication, and to virtually all advertising—political or commercial—carried in the electronic media. Thus, the speech-conduct distinction, with or without the "signal" wrinkle, adds nothing to the underlying logic of the cases but does provide another superficially neutral facade to cover the Court's consistent denial of protection to labor picketing.[103] As a sorry relic of the pre–World War I period, it should be consigned to oblivion along with its comrades in arms, the "dangerous tendency"[104] and "constructive-intent"[105] doctrines.

The recent 7-1-0 decision in *NAACP v. Claiborne Hardware*[106] gives cause for hope that the Court may indeed be ready to reassess the speech-conduct distinction, at least as a trigger for minimal scrutiny. There, the NAACP called a boycott of white businesses in Claiborne County, Mississippi. The boycotters demanded reforms such as the desegregation of public facilities, improved city services in black neighborhoods, and the hiring of blacks as policemen, welfare workers, and store clerks.[107] Boycott supporters wearing black hats as symbols of boycott discipline picketed local businesses. They also marched, threatened violators with "social ostracism," and publically announced the names of boycott violators.[108] The issue before the Court was whether Mississippi could constitutionally punish these activities under its tort law, secondary boycott statute, or antitrust law. In what is perhaps the most powerful and far-reaching affirmation of First Amendment protection in recent years, the Court held all of the boycotters' peaceful activities protected. Justice Stevens, who originally announced the "signal" doctrine, did not even mention it in his lengthy and thorough opinion for the Court. Instead, he upheld the value of effective political advocacy, whether by means of communicating facts or by advocating action.[109] Neither the damage to neutral businesses nor the coercive aspects of the picketing could outweigh the value of the boycotters' expression. Justice Stevens concluded that, in order to punish violent activities associated with a protected boycott, the state would have to meet a heavy burden of connecting each violent incident with a particular individual's action, a burden not met in *Claiborne*.[110]

If there is a major weakness in the *Claiborne* opinion, it is the Court's reliance upon the "political" character of the boycott to justify protection.[111] As the Court has recognized in other contexts, the distinction between political and other types of expression is often difficult to draw.[112] Nevertheless, the Court drew such a line in *International Longshoremen's Association (ILA) v. Allied International*,[113] decided less than three months before *Claiborne*.

There, a union was enjoined from refusing to unload ships with cargoes from the Soviet Union—a refusal called for by the union in protest against the Soviet invasion of Afghanistan. The Court unanimously upheld the injunction, rejecting the union's First Amendment argument in a single short paragraph.[114] The contrast between *ILA* and *Claiborne* illustrates the utter manipulability of the political-economic distinction and the Court's hostility—perhaps unconscious but quite unmistakable—to the First Amendment rights of labor unions.[115]

Despite the flaws of the political-economic distinction in general, the analysis in *Claiborne* is in many ways a model of sensitivity to First Amendment concerns. In striking contrast to the terse and wooden treatment accorded First Amendment issues in the labor picketing cases, the Court carefully considered the political and social context of the NAACP boycott, recognizing, among other things, that the business and political power structures of Claiborne County were closely intertwined,[116] and that the boycotters were withholding their patronage "to challenge a political and economic system that had denied them the basic rights of dignity and equality that this country had fought a war to secure."[117] Such a "massive and prolonged effort to change the social, political, and economic structure of a local environment" could not lose protection solely because of a few "reptiles hidden in the weeds."[118]

The Court's approach in *ILA*, on the other hand, is a model of obfuscation and First Amendment insensitivity. For one thing, the Court failed to articulate a principled basis for distinguishing the ILA's boycott activities from those of the NAACP. One possible basis for the distinction might be the apparent symmetry, in the labor context, of regulating the use, by both labor *and* management, of "speech plus." Yet in most cases this symmetry is an illusion, for it is generally labor, not management, that must resort to the low-cost, demonstrative techniques of marching and picketing to communicate its views.

Moreover, the Court's reliance on congressional supervision of labor matters seems increasingly less appropriate. In theory, of course, employers and employees are supposed to get evenhanded treatment in the legal administrative framework within which labor disputes— including those involving free speech—are handled. In reality, however, workers have found themselves at a substantial disadvantage.[119] When unions speak out on political matters, for example, they must (upon request) refund to dissenting members the prorated cost of such activity.[120] Corporations do not have this problem; corporations may speak out on political subjects in spite of shareholder dissent.[121] Corporations also speak with a far louder voice, heavily outspending labor on the dissemination of their views.[122] Indeed, the proof of this imbalance of power can be seen in the results: "the failure of labor to pass any legislation affecting the basic structure of private sector bargaining since 1935," and the decline in the rate of union representation of American workers from 35 percent in the 1940s to barely 20 percent in 1980.[123]

The Court's apparent unwillingness to give unions the full measure of First Amendment protection cannot be justified by the argument that unions pursue narrowly economic goals. In the first place, this is simply not true of all unions, many of which, like the longshoremen's union in *ILA*, are willing to "hit the bricks" on issues other than wages and benefits. In the second place, to the extent that unions have forsaken broader issues, their current orientation has been shaped to a large degree by the Supreme Court itself—for example, in the Court's highly restrictive subject-of-bargaining doctrine.[124]

The opportunity to speak, whether through words or conduct, provides workers with one of their only effective counters to the dominant position held by employers. To allow the NLRA to operate as an exception to the First Amendment—rather than the other way around—leaves the labor movement with little constitutional or statutory protection for the type of activity that the Court found so worthy of protection in *Claiborne*.

THE PRIVATE SIDE OF GOVERNMENT POWER: THE RIGHT-PRIVILEGE DISTINCTION

In the same way that the seemingly neutral speech-conduct distinction masks the imbalance of power between employer and employee, the distinction between a citizen's "rights" and "privileges" often masks a preference for the interests of government over those of the individuals who are governed. Where the government's role resembles that of a private economic actor—as, for example, when government acts as employer,[125] property-owner,[126] or philanthropist[127]—the Court has used the "right-privilege" doctrine to give government a wider latitude to restrict speech.

The distinction between government as lawmaker or law enforcer, and government as property-owning entity, is an old one.[128] In this context, the thrust of the distinction is a doctrine that governmental restriction of speech violates a speaker's First Amendment rights only when accomplished by the deprivation of something to which he or she is independently entitled, such as private property or personal liberty.[129]

Since no one has a *right* to hold a public job,[130] or to receive government benefits,[131] or to enter government property,[132] government can grant or withhold these "privileges" at will. The potential effect of this right-privilege doctrine on the exercise of free speech rights can only be staggering: if strictly applied, it would strip nearly sixteen million government employees[133] of constitutional protection of speech, permit government to grant or withhold a vast array of vital public benefits according to the political views of the recipients, and leave would-be speakers with a right to speak, but nowhere to exercise that right.

Not too long ago, however, it appeared that the right-privilege doctrine was down, if not altogether out, in the First Amendment arena. The doctrine of "unconstitutional conditions" barred the government from conditioning the receipt of public jobs or other government benefits on the sacrifice of a constitutional right.[134] In *Pickering v. Board of Education*,[135] for example, the Court held that government employees, with the exception of high-ranking "policy-makers," could not be disciplined or discharged for constitutionally protected speech unless their expressive activities demonstrably impeded effective job performance or interfered with government operations.[136] And the doctrine of the public forum established the right of individuals to conduct expressive activities in "traditional" public forums such as parks and sidewalks and barred the government from discriminating on the basis of content in permitting expressive activities in "semi-public" forums such as schools and libraries, and even in government institutions not performing speech-related functions at all, such as military bases and prisons.[137]

Since then, the Court has cut back sharply on protection against the use of governmental power to restrict speech. In a series of recent cases, government—when acting in its "private" capacity[138]—has been given freedom to restrict not only the time, place, and manner of speech,[139] but also its content.[140] The results and reasoning in this series of cases suggest that the right-privilege distinction may have been interred a bit too soon.[141]

The first indication of a revival came in the little-noticed case of *Babbit v. United Farm Workers*,[142] which involved a challenge to Arizona's agricultural collective bargaining system. Under this system, an employer was compelled to recognize a union selected by its employees according to specified election procedures. The United Farm Workers Union argued that these procedures, which excluded a "substantial number" of its constituency from the election process,[143] violated farm workers' rights of association. The Court rejected this argument in a terse statement. Noting that Arizona was not obligated to provide any procedure for facilitating union recognition, the Court concluded: "That it has undertaken to do so in an assertedly niggardly fashion, . . . presents as a general matter no First Amendment problems."[144]

The next case was *United States Postal Service v. Council of Greenburgh Civic Associations*, where a postal service statute prohibiting the deposit of unstamped "mailable matter" in letter boxes was upheld against a challenge by civic associations that delivered their notices by hand in order to avoid postage costs: the Court, in an opinion by Justice Rehnquist, divided all public property into two categories, traditional public forums such as parks and streets and nonpublic forums. Assigning the mailbox to the second category, the Court ruled that the regulation need only be "reasonable" and "content-neutral" to pass constitutional muster.[145] Yet, as Justice Brennan pointed out in his concurring opinion, it was not only rather surprising to classify the mail delivery system—"a vital national medium of expression"—as a nonpublic forum, but it was unnecessary as well.[146] Given the other ways in which unstamped mailable matter might be delivered (under doors and the like), the government had quite plausibly urged the Court to find the challenged postal statute to be a reasonable "time, place, and manner" restriction on the civic associations' exercise of their First Amendment rights, a position with which Justice Brennan found himself in agreement. Under Justice Brennan's view, the mail system was clearly a public forum, but access to it could be regulated in a manner consistent with the First Amendment if the restriction was content-neutral, advanced a significant governmental interest, and allowed ample alternative channels for communication.[147]

The majority, however, took a more restrictive approach. Although the *Greenburgh* Court did not explicitly mention the right-privilege distinction, the result was consistent with the notion that, where the public does not have a right to enter, the government, should it choose to grant a privilege of entry, may impose restrictions subject only to minimum due process restraints.[148]

The five-to-four decision in *Perry Education Association v. Perry Local Educators' Association*[149] both affirmed and limited the approach announced in *Greenburgh*. Perry involved government acting both as property owner and as employer. The case arose when a school board granted one teachers' union the use of the teacher mailbox system to distribute its notices, while denying that privilege to another union. The favored union had won status as exclusive bargaining representative for the teachers by defeating the other in an election. The Court upheld the selective access policy as a "reasonable" restriction not intended merely to suppress the minority union's viewpoint. Justice

White's opinion for the Court[150] divides public property into three categories. First, in traditional public forums, such as streets and sidewalks, where the public has a right of access, the government may not impose content restrictions without a showing that they are "necessary to serve a compelling state interest and . . . narrowly drawn to achieve that end."[151] Second, on "public property which the state has opened for use by the public as a place for expressive activity," the government is not required to admit the public at all but, so long as it chooses to do so, it is bound by the same standards concerning restrictions on content or on the time, place, and manner of expression as apply in a traditional public forum.[152]

Third and last, on property which is not, either "by tradition or designation," a forum for public communication, the government may freely adopt restrictions provided they are "reasonable" and not merely an effort to suppress the speaker's viewpoint.[153] This three-way categorization of public property affirms *Greenburgh's* creation of a zone of governmental property interests within which the right-privilege approach prevails, but excludes from that zone not only traditional public forums, as did *Greenburgh*, but also other property which has been designated for public communication.[154]

The doctrinal structure articulated in *Perry* is, perhaps, more defensible than the test applied to determine the classification of particular property. The school mailbox system had been opened up to outside organizations such as the YMCA, Cub Scouts, and parochial schools. The Court nevertheless located the system in the third category, reasoning that "this type of selective access does not transform government property into a public forum."[155] This line of reasoning, standing alone, would seem to repudiate the very existence of the second category. For government could circumvent the prohibition on selective access in designated forums simply by designating them as open only to certain types of groups. But the Court attempted to shore up the decision by noting that, even assuming that selective access had created a limited forum, that forum would be open only to organizations which, like the Girl Scouts, seek to communicate on matters of interest to students, and not to organizations which, like the plantiff union, are "concerned with terms and conditions of teacher employment."

Apart from the problematic endorsement of discrimination based on the subject matter of speech,[156] this line of reasoning ignores the fact that the minority union alleged discrimination *among* organizations concerned with the terms and conditions of teacher employment. The Court found a rational basis for that differential treatment in the "status" of the majority union as collective bargaining agent. However, as noted by the dissenters, the board's policy was both over-inclusive, because it permitted the majority union to use the mail system for purposes unrelated to its special status, and underinclusive, because outside organizations with no special status were allowed to use the system.[157] The Court's acceptance of this loose fit contrasts sharply with the approach taken in *City of Madison v. Wisconsin Employment Relations Commission*, where the Court recognized that discrimination in favor of an exclusive bargaining representative can constitute viewpoint discrimination.[158]

In short, the Court indulged in a shell game, first throwing out a circular definition of the limited public forum, then trying to break the circle by noting the acceptability of subject-matter restrictions, and, finally, proceeding to apply minimal scrutiny to alleged viewpoint discrimination. It is hard not to agree with the dissenters that the Court avoided a rigorous analysis of the viewpoint discrimination issue by focusing on the public forum analysis. Thus, in effect, the decision extends the permissive attitude of the Court toward subject-matter distinctions in nonpublic forums[159] to cover viewpoint discrimination. Because the classification of the mailbox system as a nonpublic forum is grounded in circular reasoning,[160] *Perry* only obscures the distinction between a "limited public forum" and a nonpublic forum.

At bottom, *Perry* may be less a public forum case than a case indicating the Court's deference to the government's interests as an employer. This apparent deference was also evident in *Connick v. Myers*,[161] in which the Court upheld, five to four, the discharge of an assistant district attorney for circulating a questionnaire to her coworkers. The offending document asked employees for their opinions on such topics as job transfer policy, office morale, and pressure to work on political campaigns.[162] Harry Connick, the district attorney, objected especially to two questions, including the one concerning political pressure, "which he felt would be damaging if discovered by the press."[163] Justice White, writing for the majority, concluded that a public employee's First Amendment right to free expression at work is limited to "speech on matters of public concern," a category that did not include an "employee grievance" such as Ms. Myers questionnaire.[164] Hence, the state was justified in discharging Myers even though there was no demonstrable impairment of her ability to perform her duties.[165]

Connick resurrects the right-privilege doctrine for "private" speech by government employees. By hinging protection on the distinction between public and private speech, the Court has embarked on a difficult definitional course. The stated test, which includes the "content, form, and context" of the expression,[166] provides little guidance. As Justice Brennan pointed out in dissent, the Court significantly narrowed the concept of a public issue in holding that criticism of governmental officials is not necessarily of public concern,[167] but provided no clear alternative formulation. The mere fact that expression constitutes an employee grievance surely cannot be decisive, since the Court found that pressure upon employees to work on political campaigns was of public concern. Nor can the absence of partisan political concerns be determinative, since an employee grievance criticizing hiring and personnel management policies is of public concern if based upon a claim of racial discrimination.[168] What is clear is that, at least until the precise reach of *Connick* is determined, public employees, who often possess unique information,[169] will be discouraged from adding their voices to the debate on government performance.[170]

The revival of the right-privilege doctrine in the areas of public property and government employment was partly extended to government "largesse" in *Regan v. Taxation with Representation*.[171] Taxation with Representation (TWR) was a nonprofit organization that sought—through litigation and lobbying—changes in government tax policies. Because of TWR's lobbying activities, the Internal Revenue Service denied TWR's application for a tax classification that would have permitted it to receive deductible contributions. TWR challenged the IRS action as an unconstitutional discrimination, noting that veterans' organizations, which also engage in substantial lobbying activity, may nonetheless receive tax-deductible contributions for such lobbying under a separate provision of the Tax Code.[172]

In an opinion joined by all nine justices, the Court upheld the differential treatment. Justice Rehnquist, writing for the Court, noted that tax deductions are subsidies and, thus, that the decision not to permit TWR to receive tax-deductible contributions was a decision not to subsidize its lobbying activities. Selectivity in granting such "largesse"[173] is not subject to strict scrutiny; the government need only advance a "rational basis" to prevail.[174] The Court easily found a rational basis in Congress' desire to compensate veterans for their service to the country.[175]

Neither the opinion of the Court nor the concurrence by Justice Blackmun found it problematic that the veterans were rewarded with an amplified voice in the political process. But, under any meaningful kind of scrutiny, the Court would have asked why Congress chose this particular form of "compensation." And it is difficult to imagine a reason not grounded in a desire to increase the influence of the veterans' groups in the legislature, to the relative detriment of other groups. Although a variety of arguments could be advanced to support the constitutionality of such an objective,[176] all political subsidies based expressly upon speaker identity should be subjected to a meaningful level of scrutiny.[177]

Greenburgh, Perry, Connick, and *Regan* together represent a dangerous trend. In each the Court cuts off its constitutional analysis before assessing the particular interests involved.[178] Each appears to be grounded in deference to the government's need for flexibility in its proprietary roles. Yet it would seem that, were the government's interests as property owner, employer, or philanthropist really so compelling, those interests could stand up to at least some meaningful scrutiny. The only affirmative reason given by the Court for withdrawing protection is administrative efficiency.[179] Yet to accept administrative efficiency as an interest sufficient to justify minimal scrutiny of government action that penalizes criticism of government officials (as in *Connick*), that discriminates among competing organizations in granting access to government-controlled communications facilities (as in *Perry* and *Greenburgh*), or that subsidizes political influence by a particular interest group (as in *Regan*) represents a qualitative shift away from vigorous enforcement of the First Amendment's ban on viewpoint discrimination.[180]

The reemergence of the right-privilege distinction, though surprising given its apparent rejection in the 1960s, should not be exaggerated. The Court has stopped far short of a general revival. In *Regan*, for example, TWR had challenged the conditioning of all eligibility for deductible contributions on its refraining from lobbying activity. But, as Justice Rehnquist pointed out, TWR did not sacrifice anything affirmative by engaging in lobbying, because it could have obtained contribution deductibility for its *non*lobbying activities simply by setting up a second, wholly controlled subsidiary to carry them out.[181] The concurring justices warned that a restriction that did affirmatively penalize nonlobbying activities would pose a different constitutional question.[182]

The impact of *Connick* and *Perry* also remains to be seen. *Connick* leaves a substantial gray area of quasi-public speech which may or may not turn out to be protected. Similarly, the circular reasoning in *Perry* provides little clue as to the definition of a nonpublic forum. Thus, much terrain remains to be fought over, and the Court's decisions in such cases as *Thomas v. Review Board*[183] and *Widmar v. Vincent*[184] indicate that it is sensitive to the issue. Moreover, the most glaring cases, *Perry* and *Connick*, merely continue the general trend toward removing protection from all labor speech.[185] And even in that sphere, the retreat from protection is not yet a rout. Nonpolicymaking government employees continue to be protected from discharges based on party affiliation or on "public" expression.[186]

COMMERCIAL SPEECH IN THE MARKETPLACE OF IDEAS

Although labor unions have received less than ample protection for picketing, which the Court has characterized as "speech plus," commercial speech has won increasing First Amendment protection. In part, this development seems to reflect the greater wealth of corporations which, because they can afford impersonal, mass-media dissemination of their views, do not need any "plus" to get their message across. In addition, however, the Court's increased protection of commercial speech reflects what might be described as a *Lochner*-like hostility to regulation of the "marketplace" of ideas.

Justice Oliver Wendell Holmes introduced the phrase "marketplace of ideas" into the vocabulary of the First Amendment in 1919.[187] Despite the power of this metaphor, the Supreme Court did not extend First Amendment protection to the patois of the commercial marketplace until more than a half century after Justice Holmes first spoke of the rigor of market competition as the best test of the "ultimate good." In a "casual, almost offhand"[188] three-page opinion in *Valentine v. Chrestensen*,[189] a unanimous Court declined to protect speech which did nothing more than propose a commercial transaction.[190] The reasoning of *Valentine* has not, as Douglas later put it, "survived reflection."[191] In *Bigelow v. Virginia*,[192] the Court reversed the convic-

tion of a newspaper editor who had transgressed Virginia law by publishing an advertisement for a New York abortion referral service. The
Court made a valiant effort to distinguish *Valentine* on the ground
that the ad in *Bigelow* did more than simply propose a commercial
transaction since it indirectly communicated news about the existence
of abortion services and women's support organizations in New York,
and since the activity described in the ad pertained to the "constitutional interests of the general public."[193] A Court willing to go to such
lengths to protect commercial advertising might find meritorious information of public interest in a toothpaste ad.[194]

The Court expressly repudiated the *Valentine* doctrine one year
later in *Virginia Board of Pharmacy v. Virginia Citizens Consumer Council*,[195] and held that commercial speech is entitled to constitutional
protection, albeit less than that owing to some other forms of expression.[196] Such differential constitutional scrutiny is predicated on a
"'commonsense' distinction between speech proposing a commercial
transaction, which occurs in an area traditionally subject to government regulation, and other varieties of speech,"[197] such as political expression, which lie at the core of the First Amendment. Since commercial speech is animated solely by the profit motive, the Court
considers it a hardier breed of expression; profit is an antifreeze enabling such speech to resist, for example, the chill from state regulation intended to promote truth in advertising.[198]

For a doctrine in its infancy, commercial speech has demonstrated
remarkable vigor. In two companion cases in 1980—*Consolidated Edison v. Public Service Commission*[199] and *Central Hudson Gas & Electric v.
Public Service Commission*[200]—the Court revealed the implications of its
newfound solicitude for corporate speakers and commercial speech. In
Con Ed the Court, by a vote of seven-to-two,[201] struck down a utility
commission ban on the inclusion, in electricity bills mailed by public
utilities, of inserts promoting the utilities' position on controversial
public policy issues such as the use of nuclear power. Con Ed had
placed an insert advocating the use of nuclear energy in its monthly
bills to ratepayers. An environmental group in effect asked for equal
time, petitioning the Public Service Commission to compel Con Ed to
include inserts bearing opposing views in future bills.[202] Instead, the
commission declined to force utility ratepayers to subsidize *anyone's*
message about public issues, and prohibited utilities from using billing
inserts to "discuss political matters" or to "express 'their opinions or
viewpoints on controversial issues of public policy.'"[203] Such a ban,

Justice Powell wrote for a majority, was a clear content restriction which struck "at the heart of the freedom to speak."[204]

The suppression of Con Ed's bill inserts could not be justified simply by the fact that the speaker in question was a corporate rather than a natural person.[205] The Court also brushed aside the state's argument that its ban on bill inserts did not take sides or silence a particular point of view on an issue but instead simply excised an entire topic. The Court concluded that designating the subjects about which particular speakers could speak to particular audiences was a form of content censorship and was thus presumptively unconstitutional.[206]

The Public Service Commission had also argued that, because the limited space in a billing envelope is like the finite electromagnetic spectrum in *Red Lion Broadcasting Co. v. FCC*,[207] the state may regulate the use of that scarce resource to keep a monopoly from bombarding the public exclusively with its point of view. Justice Powell replied that this would at most be an argument for compelling Con Ed to insert competing messages in its billing envelopes, which New York was free to do,[208] even though the Public Service Commission had already abjured this alternative.[209] Yet there clearly are practical limits to the amount of material that can be inserted in a billing envelope. Thus, even if the Public Service Commission had required the insertion of competing messages, some messages would inevitably have had to be excluded. It is equally clear, as the majority pointed out,[210] that the capacity of the mail service is not finite in the same way that broadcast frequencies are.[211] But the reason that environmentalists and other groups wished to have their messages included with the utility's was not simply to get their message across on the same wavelength. The *cost* of sending their messages separately to Con Ed's customers— which these groups are of course free to do—may be prohibitive.

That way of putting it shows immediately what the problem is: there is an economic barrier. Opposition groups obviously must buy stamps and envelopes if they wish to make use of the postal system to reach utility ratepayers.[212] Therefore, the management and shareholders of the public utility get a sweet deal. They get to stuff the billing envelopes with their message at no extra cost to themselves, which is after all why they use a bill insert rather than a separate mailing. By allowing Con Ed's insert to take a free ride on a fixed resource over which the state has given the utility a monopoly, the Court indirectly forces ratepayers to subsidize the dissemination of a view with which they may not agree.

The majority dismissed this argument in a footnote, observing that nothing prevents the Public Service Commission from allocating all the marginal costs of the bill inserts to the shareholders of the utility.[213] However, as Justice Blackmun rightly pointed out in dissent,[214] it is the *fixed* costs that are at stake here, not the marginal costs. The fact that the bill insert does not cost the utility users anything *extra* does not really meet the objection that part of their money is being used to propagate a message with which they disagree.

Indeed, Justice Blackmun went further to argue that there was no possible allocation of costs that would not result in utility ratepayers subsidizing the cost of the utility's political messages. For unless the utility were required to pay for *all* the fixed costs of the mailings—such as postage, envelopes, and the costs of creating and maintaining the mailing list—the utility would still be getting a partial free ride. Yet requiring the utility to pay all such costs would be equivalent to the flat ban on political inserts that the majority had struck down.

In the companion case, *Central Hudson*, the Court ruled that New York could not completely ban utility advertising that promotes the use of electricity.[215] Unlike the messages on the bill inserts in *Con Ed*, the promotional advertising at issue here "related solely to the economic interests of the speaker and its audience."[216] It encouraged utility customers to buy more electricity from Central Hudson, and therefore arguably constituted the purest form of commercial speech. Justice Powell, once again writing for the Court, formulated a four-part analysis for determining whether a particular regulation of commercial speech is consistent with the First Amendment.[217] First, the speech must concern lawful activity and not be misleading. Second, the state interest advanced by the restriction must be "substantial." Third, the regulation must directly advance that state interest. Fourth, there must be a close fit between means and end, with no less restrictive alternative available.

There had been no allegations of deceptive advertising, and the use of electrical power is certainly legal; the first prong of the test was thus met. Justice Powell also accepted "without reservation the argument that [energy] conservation . . . is an imperative national goal" and agreed that the states have a "duty . . . to take appropriate action to further this goal."[218] Clearly, a ban on promotional advertising would decrease demand for electricity, which is precisely why Central Hudson took the trouble to challenge it.[219] The Court was not convinced, however, that the commission's ban on promotional advertising would not also suppress some information about energy-saving electrical devices or services which would cause a net decrease in total energy use, and therefore concluded that the ban was impermissibly broad.[220]

Justice Rehnquist, the sole dissenter, argued that there is ultimately no constitutional value served by closely controlling a state regulation of this sort while rubber-stamping—under a toothless form of minimum rationality review—a regulation that would, for example, force up the price of electricity or directly control its consumption and thereby achieve a result that, to everyone but eight members of the Court and a few dozen law professors, would look just like what the Public Service Commission had done in *Central Hudson*.[221] To Justice Rehnquist, the only difference between an undoubtedly permissible form of economic regulation and the commission's regulation of commercial speech is that one operates on the marketplace of ideas.[222] A sharp distinction between those two marketplaces cannot, in Justice Rehnquist's view, be long maintained. Just as experience has taught us that the "invisible hand" often fouls things up elsewhere in the economic market, so there can be serious market imperfections rooted in the information-exchange that underpins economic decisions,[223] especially if certain vendors have a monopoly advantage.

The majority's only response to this potent argument was a dictum suggesting that the state's conservation interest—though an insufficient rationale for a total ban—would justify restrictions on the format and content of utility advertising, and perhaps even a system of prior approval of advertising campaigns.[224] Indeed, the majority essentially acceded to Justice Rehnquist's view by positing that a narrower ban—one that did not forbid information about energy-saving devices—would have been upheld despite its silencing of truthful messages.[225]

Taken together, *Con Ed* and *Central Hudson* suggest that the Court is tacitly acting on a distinction between allocational and distributional imperfections in the market. Welfare economists distinguish between government intervention designed to improve allocational efficiency, which is concerned with the *total quantum* of satisfaction purchased, and that designed to alter the *pattern* of distribution and enjoyment by individuals and groups in society. During the *Lochner* era,[226] the Supreme Court looked favorably upon allocational remedies while lashing out at programs designed to redress unequal distributions of economic power. The Court repeatedly struck down economic legislation that had a redistributive aim or impact—usually laws favoring workers or consumers at the expense of business interests—while upholding legislation that was perceived as enhancing "the general welfare"—often by shoring up the "freedom of contract."[227]

The Court's analysis in Con Ed[228] is reminiscent of the Lochner Court's preference for allocational efficiency over distributional equity. The utility commission had argued that the insertion of materials concerning controversial issues of public policy in billing envelopes constituted a forced subsidy by utility ratepayers to the Con Ed monopoly for the propagation of its views, and that the utility's shareholders, not its customers, should bear the cost. The shareholders, after all, had both a voice and a vote in the formulation of the utility's policy, whereas the ratepayers were not even consulted. It is one thing to have one's money used to pay for group expression from which one dissents, and it is quite another to be compelled to subsidize the furtherance of views espoused by a wholly unaffiliated—and even opposing—party.[229] The Court was satisfied, however, that the commission could exclude the cost of the inserts themselves from the utility's rate base, thus insuring that the consumers would suffer no additional charge.[230]

In contrast, both the majority[231] and the dissent[232] in Central Hudson stated that allocational imperfections could justify state intervention in the marketplace of ideas where public energy policy is debated. A utility company receives increased income when it successfully promotes use of electricity by its ratepayers, and it can ultimately pass on to those same customers any increased costs that result from subsequent shortages in fuel caused by that accelerated consumption. Therefore, the wider economic costs of the utility media campaign for increased electrical use remain largely external to the utility's balance sheet. Surely, if the state may compel a utility to internalize those ultimate costs now by taking the increased operating costs out of profits—rather than passing them on to consumers in the form of higher rates—and may thereby encourage decreased energy use by the utility, the state may also encourage conservation by gagging that speaker who has a vested interest in profligate energy use from which the rest of the community will ultimately suffer.[233] The majority found no difficulty in holding that a flat ban on promotional advertising would be acceptable if it was not more extensive than necessary.[234] This promotion of the *total* public good is allocative intervention, not redistribution.

The majority in *Central Hudson*, however, saw the Public Service Commission's overbroad rule as suppressing the flow of information available to the public.[235] Furthermore, the suppression of Central Hudson's promotional advertising could be seen as an attempt to stifle speech by rich, powerful monopolies in order that weaker voices, such as those of individual citizens, conservation groups, or even the state government itself, might enjoy a better chance of being heard. And that sort of redistribution of opportunities for free expression is strictly taboo.

In any "market," the viability of the distinction between distribution and allocation is dubious.[236] Yet the Court continues to honor it implicitly. In *Citizens Against Rent Control v. Berkeley*,[237] where the Court struck down a $250 limit on contributions to committees supporting or opposing ballot measures, Chief Justice Burger, writing for the Court, vigorously attacked the validity of distributional regulation of speech and emphasized the importance of maximizing the total volume of ideas and information in the marketplace: "[T]he concept that government may restrict the speech of some elements of our society in order to enhance the relative voice of others is wholly foreign to the First Amendment, which was designed 'to secure the "widest possible dissemination of information from diverse and antagonistic sources,"' and to assure unfettered interchange of ideas for the bringing about of political and social changes desired by the people.'"[238]

This approach has been most rigorously applied in cases involving limitations on the expenditure of money.[239] Even where a state has advanced an ostensibly nondistributional purpose for financial restrictions, the Court, consistent with the *Lochner* approach to the economic marketplace,[240] has demanded a close correspondence between legislative means and ends. In *Berkeley*, for example, the means-ends fit that the Court demanded was so tight[241] that the case might be said to stand for the proposition that, regardless of the legislative *purpose*, an enactment which has the *effect* of mitigating the impact of financial inequality on opportunities for speech is unconstitutional interference with the "natural" advantage enjoyed by the wealthy. The government may not rob Peter of his megaphone in order that Paul might be heard above the din.

In *Metromedia, Inc. v. San Diego*, the Court approved a regulation of commercial speech that reduced the overall amount of billboard advertising but that left certain distributional inequities in place.[242] A San Diego ordinance banned all off-site commercial billboards and all but a very select category of noncommercial billboards without regard to where they were located. The upshot of the ban was that if you owned property, you could put up a sign to advertise your own goods or services, but not anyone else's; and nobody could put up a sign to convey a noncommercial message, unless it fell within certain narrow, content-based exceptions.[243] The plurality[244] considered the law's effect on commercial and noncommercial billboards separately, and upheld it as to the former while ruling it unconstitutional as to the latter. In the process of attempting to keep its doctrinal categories distinct, the Court managed to undermine the protection of both kinds of expression.

Prior to *Metromedia*, the disparity between commercial and noncommercial speech was not so marked, and the Court required persuasive justifications for government-imposed restrictions.[245] Yet in *Metromedia*, it took little, if any, evidence to convince the Court that the government's interests in beautifying the city and reducing motorist distractions were directly advanced by limiting commercial billboards,[246] and the Court overlooked the requirement that a complete ban be the least restrictive means to the desired end.[247] Furthermore, despite a professed commitment to a "particularized inquiry" into the competing interests and a "precise appraisal" of the impact on communication,[248] the plurality concluded that adequate alternate channels of communication remained available to billboard advertisers,[249] even though the parties in *Metromedia* stipulated that no alternatives existed for many billboard speakers.[250] The plurality seemed more concerned with the fact that San Diego gave more protection to commercial than noncommercial speech by prohibiting all but a few noncommercial billboards, while allowing businesses freely to advertise their goods and services on their own property.[251] This peevish insistence that states follow the Court's own hierarchy of values even beyond the First Amendment minima not only smacks of federal judicial imperialism,[252] but also suggests that the Court's propensity for doctrinal categorization may have degenerated into a reflex.

In allowing the distinction between on-site and off-site billboards to stand, the Court showed a surprising deference to the city's decision to limit commercial billboard access to those businesses that owned, or could afford, their own premises. The Court appeared unconcerned about the perverse distributive effects such an ordinance might have in "freezing out" less affluent business people.[253]

In *Metromedia*, as in *Berkeley*, the Court has thus failed to see the distributive effect of state regulation of speech as posing any constitutional difficulty. Similarly, recent decisions protecting commercial speech—notably, *Con Ed* and *Central Hudson*—show that proposing commercial transactions will receive more constitutional protection than urging abstinence from them. Indeed, commercial advertisers can recast their sales pitches in ideological terms[254] to circumvent an ordinance which—in accord with the *Metromedia* plurality's hierarchy—disfavors commercial speech. Those decisions, when paired with the Court's refusal to consider many forms of labor speech to be within the scope of the First Amendment,[255] indicate an unbalanced approach to the marketplace and the actors in it that is reminiscent of the *Lochner* era.

The distinction between commercial and noncommercial speech—like the speech-conduct distinction—also exemplifies a propensity for pigeonholing as a method for deciding First Amendment questions. Such a method masks the essentially political nature of the underlying issues by pretending to cabin judicial discretion within the limits established by the category itself.

This fragmentation of the First Amendment into a grab bag of rubrics under which different types of speech receive different degrees of protection[256] coincides with the Court's practice of treating each medium of communication as "a law unto itself."[257] Treating handbills differently from theatrical productions may accord with some people's notions of common sense, but it can lead to ridiculous conclusions. In *Metromedia*, for example, the Court solemnly stated, "We deal here with the law of billboards."[258]

Perhaps even more ominous was the cavalier way the plurality carved up commercial speech into separate subcompartments and then accepted differential treatment of on-site billboards without justification. This sort of pigeonholing endangers the pigeon.[259] If one parses First Amendment doctrine too fine, one may soon discover that little protection for expression remains. Ultimately, perhaps, the best we can hope for is a doctrine whole enough to nurture healthy suspicion of laws that unduly stifle voices seeking to be heard, with particular sensitivity to the effect of government regulation on less powerful speakers.[260]

NEUTRAL PRINCIPLES AND THE NAZI MARCH IN SKOKIE

In 1978, a planned march by a group of neo-Nazis through the streets of Skokie, Illinois, raised in a most painful form the question of whether the First Amendment's protection is truly universal.[261] The group had chosen Skokie for its display of swastikas and military uniforms because a high proportion of the town's seventy thousand inhabitants are Jews, many of whom had personally experienced the horrors of Nazi concentration camps.[262] The town passed various ordinances designed to bar the proposed march, which, in the town's view, would have inflicted direct psychic trauma on those residents who were Holocaust survivors.[263]

The Court of Appeals for the Seventh Circuit rejected Skokie's justification for the ordinances, holding that speech which inflicts such "psychic trauma" is "indistinguishable in principle from speech that 'invite[s] dispute . . . [or] induces a condition of unrest, . . . or even stirs people to anger.'"[264] The court concluded that the shock effect of the words could only be "attributed to the content of the ideas expressed,"[265] and held that, under the First Amendment, the state can no more restrict a Nazi rally in Skokie than it can prohibit a civil rights march in Birmingham.[266]

The ultimate outcome of *Skokie* raises fundamental questions about how we envision freedom of expression. *Skokie* would appear to represent a triumph of neutral principles. If we allow people to march in favor of peace, brotherhood, and equal rights, then we must allow others to parade in front of Holocaust victims to advocate hatred and genocide. It may be true that adherence to the First Amendment entails a willingness to be outraged. Yet our devotion to free speech is not rendered suspect if we react to *Skokie* with mixed feelings. Voltaire's grandiose pledge to defend to the death another's right to say that with which the philosophe could never agree is in many respects admirable. But a commitment to protect evenhandedly the expression of all sentiments can degenerate from an abiding faith in the First Amendment to an obsession with the "alluring abstractions" of neutral principles.[267] Before one martyrs oneself in the name of free speech on behalf of those who would make atrocity a virtue, one should at least pause to reflect upon the fact that martyrdom has always been stronger proof of the intensity than of the correctness of a belief.

It may simply be naive to chalk up *Skokie*[268] as the price we pay for the privilege of expressing ourselves on topics that concern us. Although our protection of the Nazis serves to buttress a neutral principle that condemns all content-based restraints on speech, it is hardly assured that such protection in the *Skokie* case will broadly enhance the right of free expression for others. The reality of First Amendment jurisprudence has never been—nor is it now—consistent application of that charter's blanket guarantees. Instead, constitutional protection for free speech emerges as a patchwork quilt of exceptions. And, as shown by its recent decisions involving First Amendment issues, the Supreme Court has been all too willing to endorse doctrinal rubrics that protect the speech of corporations[269] but not workers,[270] or that zealously guard the preferred expressive methods of the wealthy[271] while tolerating restrictions on those means of communication on which the less fortunate must rely.[272]

In the face of such inconsistent application of the First Amendment's guarantees, making a virtue of consistently applying an assertedly neutral principle in *Skokie*—even if that decision was in some sense "correct"—may be cause for little assurance or self-congratulation. At the very least, we should not be lulled into the belief that, if we but embrace neutrality for those who would exterminate some among us, its shield will automatically be available to protect us when it is *we* who cry for help. There are *choices* to be made. As its history has shown, the First Amendment is hardly self-executing. Thus, the painful dilemma of *Skokie* might be turned to good use by providing occasions for reexamination of principles and precedents under which free expression has *not*, in truth, been available to all.

CHAPTER FOURTEEN

DISMANTLING THE HOUSE THAT RACISM BUILT: ASSESSING "AFFIRMATIVE ACTION"

It has long been recognized that the Constitution is not "color-blind."[1] Indeed, to eliminate the persistent effects of racial prejudice and oppression, courts must often take race explicitly into account both in assessing constitutional violations and in formulating adequate remedies[2]—including remedies under which individuals who are innocent of wrongdoing must be denied opportunities because of their race in order that other individuals, equally innocent, be given opportunities from which their race would otherwise have effectively excluded them. In matters of race, at least, the threat of invidious prejudice and oppression comes from private as well as public sources, and the government must sometimes take the side of the oppressed. Therefore, the Thirteenth, Fourteenth, and Fifteenth Amendments have committed the nation to the affirmative task of eradicating racial discrimination and subjugation.

THE *BAKKE* DECISION

The Supreme Court, in *Regents of the University of California v. Bakke,*[3] divided the affirmative action dispute down the middle by ruling, five to four, that state educational institutions need not be color-blind in confronting the realities of race with "a properly devised admissions program,"[4] while striking down, in another five-to-four split, the particular admissions program before it—a program that set aside a specific number of places for which only disadvantaged minorities could compete.[5] The Court thus upheld the kind of affirmative action plan used by most American colleges and universities, and disallowed only the unusually mechanical—some would say unusually candid, others would say unusually impolitic—approach taken by the Medical School of the University of California at Davis.

As a matter of politics—or, more politely, of judicial statecraft—the decision may well have been ideal. The headlines could cry, "Bakke Wins Admission," while the lawyers and admissions officers would quietly read the subtitle: "affirmative action upheld." It is difficult to say whether a less ambiguous victory for race-conscious remedies would have invited backlash more than it would have emboldened reform. But it seems at least plausible that the surest path to equal justice in this troubled area is the twisted path the Court marked out—that, in this case, a straight line would not have been the shortest distance between two still-distant points.

My purpose is not to sort out the political ramifications of the decision, nor even to add my ink to the flood that is bound to be spent divining what each opinion meant or predicting where the Court will ultimately go in this field. My purpose is the more limited one of extracting several distinct themes from the *Bakke* decision and its progeny, and speculating on their independent significance for the future.

Bakke and Equal Protection

It would be foolhardy to attempt to derive too much meaning from *Bakke's* message in the area of equal protection. Only Justice Powell held the Davis quota violative of equal protection.[6] Indeed, only Justice Powell was prepared to subject state educational programs disadvantaging whites to the same degree of judicial scrutiny as programs disadvantaging blacks.[7] Justices Brennan, Marshall, and Blackmun applied only intermediate scrutiny, essentially to assure that the program under review did not in fact stigmatize and stereotype nonwhites or specially burden any other minorities.[8] And, although Justice White joined Part III-A of the Powell opinion requiring the strictest scrutiny,[9] he also joined the Brennan opinion in full[10] and was accordingly treated by Justice Powell as requiring less than fully strict scrutiny.[11]

To adopt Justice Powell's position on strict scrutiny would require a substantial, and a largely inexplicable, restructuring of contemporary equal protection law and theory. Under the usual theory, a predominantly white public body could choose to confer a comparative advantage on underprivileged members of racial minorities while comparatively disadvantaging all white applicants; on review, a court would have to assure itself that this was indeed the purpose and effect of the choice in question, and that the choice did not conceal any discrimination against a racial or other minority. But once having been so assured, the judiciary would lack the usual reasons to subject the choice to the sort of scrutiny that makes sense when prejudice against insular minorities seems to be present and when the political process accordingly seems unworthy of deference.[12] Since only Justice Powell embraced strict scrutiny despite the absence of any reason to suspect the existence of such prejudice, the decision should not be viewed as signaling a radical departure in the direction of broadened equal protection review.

Quite apart from this methodological point, the decision reflects considerations difficult to fit within traditional equal protection analysis. Justice Powell made plain that he would have found an affirmative action program valid even under the strictest scrutiny if it employed race in a more subtle manner—putting a thumb on the scale in favor of minorities "on an individualized, case-by-case basis."[13] What if such an approach produced results just like those of the Davis quota system? Justice Powell's reply was that "good faith would be presumed in the absence of a showing to the contrary."[14] What, then, was the bad faith in the Davis program? Why, its "facial intent to discriminate."[15] But to reason this way is to use the notion of discrimination in a most slippery manner. If it is not "discriminatory" in some invidious or otherwise forbidden sense to prefer minorities on a case-by-case basis, why is it "discriminatory" to do so more mechanically and in gross? There may be no satisfactory answer, but if there is, the mistake may be searching for it in the realm of equal protection.

Bakke and Procedural Fairness

"The denial to respondent of [his] right to individualized consideration without regard to his race," Justice Powell wrote, "is the principal evil of petitioner's special admissions program."[16] Seeming to express an aversion not simply to classifications based on race but to mass process as such, these words may betoken Justice Powell's recognition of an individual's right to be treated by the government as a unique and not a fungible being—a right that would retain vitality even in contexts that do not involve classifications based on race.[17]

Interpreting Justice Powell's position in this way would help to explain his distinction between permissible and impermissible race-conscious admissions programs. Justice Powell does not object to the granting of racial preferences by a university under any program that "treats each applicant as an individual in the admissions process,"[18] and that "does not insulate the individual from comparison with all other candidates for the available seats."[19] What seems at bottom to offend Justice Powell is the notion of a system whereby some individuals "are never afforded the chance to compete" for a state-provided benefit because they do not belong to a preferred group,[20] a system under which the bare fact of membership in a nonpreferred group "foreclose[s an individual] from all consideration."[21] But "[s]o long as the university proceeds on an individualized, case-by-case basis, there is no warrant for judicial interference in the academic process."[22]

To be sure, Justice Powell mixes the value of individualized treatment with the inherent odium of racial classification. For example, he seems more willing to accept quite mechanical gender-based classifications, although these also undeniably condition an individual's access to government benefits on the basis of group identity, on the ground that "the perception of racial classifications as inherently odious stems from a lengthy and tragic history that gender-based classifications do not share."[23] Moreover, he distinguishes hiring preferences for Indians essentially on the ground that such preferences are "not racial at all."[24] But Justice Powell's special aversion to mass treatment of individuals on the basis of race should not be permitted to obscure the decisive role played by his objection to mass process as such: nothing else stands between the individualized consideration of race he would deem permissible and the wholesale consideration of race he deems violative of the Fourteenth Amendment. In condemning "the pliable notion of 'stigma' [as] the crucial element in analyzing racial classifications,"[25] Justice Powell wrote:

All state-imposed classifications that rearrange burdens and benefits on the basis of race are likely to be viewed with deep resentment by the individuals burdened. The denial to innocent persons of equal rights and opportunities may outrage those so deprived and therefore may be perceived as invidious. These individuals are likely to find little comfort in the notion that the deprivation they are asked to endure is merely the price of membership in the dominant majority and that its imposition is inspired by the supposedly benign purpose of aiding others. One should not lightly dismiss the inherent unfairness of, and the perception of mistreatment that accompanies, a system of allocating benefits and privileges on the basis of skin color and ethnic origin.[26]

Moreover, Justice Powell cited "fairness to the individual" as the ultimate value imperiled by the classifications he would invalidate:

There also are strong policy reasons that correspond to the constitutional distinction between petitioner's preference program and one that assures a measure of competition among all applicants. Petitioner's program will be viewed as inherently unfair by the public generally as well as by applicants for admission to state universities. *Fairness in individual competition for opportunities, especially those provided by the State, is a widely cherished American ethic. Indeed, in a broader sense, an underlying assumption of the rule of law is the worthiness of a system of justice based on fairness to the individual.*[27]

It may well be that Justice Powell's failure to extend this perception to classifications overtly based on gender or on other traits beyond race weakens the force of his distinction between an individualized and a group-based admissions process. Justice Powell may also attach too much significance to what others perceive as a cosmetic difference between setting aside a fixed number of places for minorities in the admissions process and putting a thumb on the scale each time[28]—with a pressure that, as Justice Powell himself admits, "may vary . . .depending upon the 'mix' both of the student body and the applicants for the incoming class."[29] When the matter at hand is the allocation of scarce resources among too many applicants—whether medical school seats or public jobs or government contracts—perhaps the difference between making individualized comparisons (with a case-by-case preference for minorities) and clearly setting aside a number of places for minorities is too narrow a basis on which to ground a constitutional distinction—at least when the magnitude of the case-by-case preference is itself permitted to turn on the numerical "mix" admissions officers have already achieved.

But even if Justice Brennan and those who joined him are right in their view that the processes in question are truly indistinguishable,[30] what matters most is that all five of these justices focused not only on *results* but also on *process*—not only on the statistical impact of the university's program on Bakke's chances, but also on whether Bakke and his fellow applicants were being accorded fair treatment—which, in this case, all five of the justices equated with *individualized* treatment. Justices Brennan, White, Marshall, and Blackmun specifically noted that "Davis consider[ed] *on an individual basis* each [minority] applicant's personal history to determine whether he or she ha[d] likely been disadvantaged by racial discrimination."[31] More significantly, the four justices together insisted that the "excluded white applicant . . .receives no more or less 'individualized consideration' under [their] approach than under [Justice Powell's]."[32] Whether they were right or wrong, they at least did not choose to dispute directly Justice Powell's conclusion that properly individualized consideration, as an aspect of fair treatment, is mandated by the Fourteenth Amendment. Eventually, that conclusion may be more significant than any particular view of *Bakke* itself. For in a constitutional world concerned only with the naked outcomes of government choice, a concern for individualized consideration, or indeed for any substantive or structural dimension of fair process apart from its likely impact on results, would be misplaced. It is only if ours is *not* such a world—if process has substantive constitutional significance even when the end results are indistinguishable—that the vote cast by Justice Powell and the approach seemingly accepted by Justices Brennan, White, Marshall, and Blackmun are fully comprehensible.[33]

In another much less celebrated case decided the same Term as *Bakke*, the full Court appears to have recognized the constitutional significance of fair process as such—entirely apart from the instrumental role such process might play in assuring more accurate outcomes.[34] In *Carey v. Piphus*,[35] with Justice Powell delivering the opinion,[36] the Court ruled without dissent that a student's distress at being denied fair process was *itself* compensable in an action against school officials under the civil rights statutes,[37] even if the granting of fair process would not have prevented the student from being suspended. Since the student might have been suspended even after a fair hearing and might thus have missed the time from school in any event, it was inappropriate, on the facts of the case, to include in the damage award the value of time missed from school.[38] Also, because "there may well be those who suffer no distress over the procedural irregularities,"[39] such distress must be demonstrated as a factual matter if substantial damages are to be recovered. But given such a showing, distress alone would be appropriately compensable even if the substantive deprivation proves to have been justified.[40] Moreover,

[b]ecause the right to procedural due process is"absolute" in the sense that it does not depend upon the merits of a claimant's substantive assertions, and because of the importance to organized society that procedural due process be observed, . . . the denial of procedural due process should be actionable for nominal damages [even] without proof of actual injury.[41]

As the Court stated, "a purpose of procedural due process is to convey to the individual a feeling that the government has dealt with him fairly, as well as to minimize the risk of mistaken deprivations of protected interests."[42] In *Piphus*, then, as in *Bakke*, fair process was thought to have *intrinsic* and not merely *instrumental* constitutional significance.[43] And the most enduring significance of the Court's willingness to take the claims of individualization as seriously as it did in *Bakke* and *Piphus* may well be the support thereby added to the view that the Constitution protects fair process for more than merely instrumental reasons.

But, despite language in *Bakke* and *Piphus*, the intrinsic substantive value of individualized, and otherwise procedurally fair, government treatment has not generally been recognized by the Court.[44] Despite its historic basis[45] and intuitive appeal, the thesis that procedural fairness reflects the intrinsic value of assuring fair treatment as an individual and not simply the instrumental value of assuring correct outcomes has rarely been articulated by the Court and has often been overlooked.[46] In recent years, the Court has most frequently treated due process as simply a tool for minimizing substantively "unfair and mistaken deprivations"[47] of independently protected rights, entitlements, or interests. And, as the Court's decisions have made plain, once due process is confined to the role of assuring accuracy, the result—particularly when the stakes involve such government benefits as jobs or welfare—is to deprive the judiciary of any convincing basis on which to question the trade-offs arrived at by the political branches.[48] It is only if procedural fairness in general, and individualized process in particular, matter *apart* from their statistical impact on outcomes that the constitutional guarantee of fair process gives courts a trenchant doctrinal basis for criticizing certain political compromises as procedurally unfair to the persons injured by them.

But to accept the argument that fair procedures serve values beyond mere accuracy only begins the inquiry into when a given process is called for to protect those values. In particular, whenever it is claimed that the Fourteenth Amendment, either as a matter of equal protection or as a matter of due process,[49] mandates individualized procedure, one must ask at least three questions. First, one must ask how difficult it would be to serve the government's legitimate interests and to protect both privacy and evenhandedness while following the individualized procedure supposedly required. Second, one must assess the degree to which the individualized procedure would truly advance the cause of respecting personal dignity and individuality more than it would risk the dangers of excessive discretion and arbitrary or unduly ad hominem government action. Finally, one must evaluate the extent to which the responsiveness and accountability of the institutions and rules in question would be enhanced rather than compromised by implementing policy through individualized application of open-ended standards rather than through wholesale application of more mechanical rules.[50]

The last of these questions in particular might have posed difficulty for Justice Powell in *Bakke*. For it was at least plausibly asserted that the main impact of his vote, and of the Court's resulting invalidation of the Davis program, was to invite universities to do covertly what they could no longer do openly.[51] From a perspective that stresses political accountability and responsiveness, that risk can hardly seem an insignificant one. Paradoxically, however, it was just such a perspective that explains the final difference between Justice Powell and those of his brethren who voted to uphold the Davis program in its entirety. To understand that difference, it is necessary to view *Bakke* through yet another lens.

Bakke and Structural Justice

I have elsewhere developed the idea that judicial review is quite properly beginning to focus on a category of concerns poised midway between the conventional notions of procedural and substantive due process.[52] Within this category, the question is neither simply whether the *substance* of a government rule or policy accords with constitutional norms, nor simply whether the *application* of a given rule or policy to a particular case is *procedurally* acceptable, but whether the "*structures through which policies are both formed and applied, and formed in the very process of being applied*,"[53] are consistent with due process of law.[54]

The leading modern application of this principle is *Hampton v. Mow Sun Wong*,[55] finding inconsistent with due process certain federal civil service regulations excluding all aliens from employment. There it proved decisive for the Court that the broad employment disability challenged by aliens had been promulgated by an agency to which neither Congress nor the President had openly and clearly entrusted the sorts of foreign policy concerns that alone might have furnished persuasive justification for the rule. The agency was not found to have acted beyond its statutory mandate; that it might promulgate precisely the regulation challenged was sufficiently contemplated by Congress to rule out any holding that the choice was beyond the agency's statutory authority.[56] Nor was the statutory mandate itself deemed too broad to comply with constitutional prohibitions against standardless delegation by the legislature. Yet the political and bureaucratic structure through which the rule was formulated was such that the burdens the rule imposed were unwarranted as a matter of due process.

For Justice Powell, the Davis quota that resulted in Bakke's exclusion was subject to a similar infirmity.[57] To be sure, it was adopted in an exercise of the plenary authority over the University of California vested by the state constitution in the regents.[58] Yet just as the Civil Service Commission in *Hampton* could not exercise its plenary authority to inflict a significant deprivation on aliens for reasons having nothing to do with the concerns openly delegated to the commission, so too the regents could not exercise their plenary authority to inflict a significant deprivation on white applicants for reasons having nothing to do with the concerns openly delegated to the regents. Justice Powell thought the educational and academic mission explicitly delegated to the regents permitted them to seek a racially and ethnically diverse student body, although not by what he perceived as needlessly blunt means.[59] But the goal of identifying and rectifying past racial discrimination—which alone *might* have justified for Justice Powell the extreme measures Davis took—was not one properly within the ambit of the regents' consideration:

> We have never approved a classification that aids persons perceived as members of relatively victimized groups at the expense of other innocent individuals in the absence of judicial, legislative, or administrative findings of constitutional or statutory violations . . . After such findings have been made, the governmental interest in preferring members of the injured groups at the expense of others is substantial, since the legal rights of the victims must be vindicated. In such a case, the extent of the injury and the consequent remedy will have been judicially, legislatively, or administratively defined. Also, the remedial action usually remains subject to continuing oversight to assure that it will work the

least harm possible to other innocent persons competing for the benefit . . .

Petitioner does not purport to have made, and is in no position to
make, such findings. Its broad mission is education, not the formulation of any legislative policy or the adjudication of particular claims of
illegality . . . [I]solated segments of our vast governmental structures
are not competent to make those decisions, at least in the absence of
legislative mandates and legislatively determined criteria. Cf. *Hampton
v. Mow Sun Wong* . . . Before relying upon these sorts of findings in establishing a racial classification, a governmental body must have the
authority and capability to establish, in the record, that the classification is responsive to identified discrimination . . . Lacking this capability, petitioner has not carried its burden of justification on this issue.[60]

The only response of Justices Brennan, White, Marshall, and
Blackmun was that "the manner in which a State chooses to delegate
governmental functions is for it to decide."[61] Yet it was Justice Brennan, dissenting from the Court's initial validation of standardless
death penalty sentencing, who reminded us that the manner in which
such functions are delegated may be decisive in assessing the validity
of their exercise.[62] And it was Justice Brennan, writing for the majority
in *Florida Lime & Avocado Growers, Inc. v. Paul*,[63] who treated as relevant to the nationally preemptive effect of certain federal regulations
the fact that they had been drafted by a narrow group of Florida avocado growers and handlers rather than by lawmakers or officers with a
nationwide constituency and a broad policymaking mandate. Finally,
it was Justice Blackmun, writing for the majority in *Nyquist v. Mauclet*,[64] who invalidated a state law discriminating against certain resident aliens on the ground that the law's purpose—encouraging naturalization—was a permissible one only for the federal government, and
not for a state, to pursue.[65] Thus, the four justices who were prepared
to uphold the Davis program in its entirety seem to have given insufficient weight to the structural considerations adduced by Justice
Powell.

But, just as in the case of Justice Powell's invocation of individualized fairness, it is unclear that his structural concerns truly justified his
decision to invalidate the Davis program. It may be, as Justices Brennan, White, Marshall, and Blackmun stressed, that the ultimate result
of Justice Powell's position was simply to prefer an "approach [that]
does not . . . make public the extent of the [racial or ethnic] preference and the precise workings of the system" over a "program [that]

employs a specific, openly stated number,"[66] rather than to assure that the basic policy choice be made at a higher or different political level. Moreover, regulations of the Department of Health, Education, and Welfare expressly authorized all agencies receiving federal funds to "take affirmative action to overcome the effects of conditions which resulted in limiting participation by persons of a particular race, color, or national origin [e]ven in the absence of . . . prior discrimination" by the recipient.[67] And California officials had accepted federal aid for Davis well aware of that provision. Thus, the regents acted pursuant to far clearer authorization than the Civil Service Commission could invoke in *Hampton*. And, futher distinguishing *Bakke* from *Hampton*, the antialien rule struck down in the latter case both (1) had its "impact on an identifiable class of persons who, entirely apart from the rule itself, are already subject to disadvantages not shared by the remainder of the community,"[68] and (2) operated to deprive "a discrete class of persons of an interest in liberty on a wholesale basis."[69] White persons like Bakke, on the other hand, were neither subject to peculiar disadvantages apart from the rule challenged nor deprived of as significant an "interest in liberty." Finally, it is at least arguable that the factual predicate of past racial discrimination is too obvious to dispute and that achieving racial justice represents part of *every* government body's responsibility—and is in that respect distinguishable from more specialized missions like the conduct of American foreign policy. For all these reasons, one might well question how Justice Powell applied structural review in *Bakke*.

Yet, from a broader perspective, the individualized admissions process to which Justice Powell's pivotal vote in *Bakke* might lead seems not only "more acceptable to the public"[70] than a fifth vote for the Brennan wing would in all likelihood have been; it is surely also more reflective of a deep national aversion to explicit quotas to benefit racial minorities, and more responsive to a sense that, if such quotas are to be imposed at all, they should be imposed in a more deliberate and cautious manner and by a more broadly accountable body than was the case in *Bakke*. At the same time, had the Court ruled that an applicant's race cannot be considered at all when deciding whether to admit him or her to a federally funded program, it seems most unlikely that Congress would have found the resurrection of affirmative action politically possible; the costs of expressly inviting race-consciousness may have become intolerably high for any institution more politically exposed than the Court. Indeed, even for that tribunal, any more wholehearted embrace of race-conscious remedies than Justice Powell's might not have seemed possible. And perhaps that timidity will, as Justice Marshall prophesied in dissent,[71] return to haunt the nation for decades to come. But whatever else its legacy, at least *Bakke's* contribution to heightened awareness of process and structure as independently significant substantive dimensions of constitutional validity ought to be universally welcomed.

THE STATUTORY ISSUES IN *BAKKE* AND *WEBER*

Despite the temptation to reach the constitutional issue, one must take seriously the argument of Justice Stevens, joined by the Chief Justice and Justices Stewart and Rehnquist, that the constitutional question should not have been reached at all because the language of Title VI of the Civil Rights Act was clear: "No person . . . shall, on the ground of race, color, or national origin, be excluded from, be denied the benefits of, or be subjected to discrimination under any program or activity receiving Federal financial assistance."[72] That Alan Bakke was, "on the ground of race," "excluded from" a "program" of the University of California at Davis Medical School, and that it was a "program receiving Federal financial assistance," were undeniable facts, although it is true that Bakke's exclusion did not result from race *alone*: only his credentials and other nonracial admissions factors kept him from being admitted to one of the unreserved spaces that composed the majority of the entering medical school class.

There are only two apparent escapes from Justice Stevens' logic. The first is Justice White's: there is no private cause of action under Title VI.[73] Four justices rejected that argument because it was raised too late,[74] but it seems substantively misguided as well. Whatever the reasons to oppose funding cutoffs through private suits, Bakke was not trying to cut off federal assistance to Davis; there seems little reason to prohibit him from invoking a valid and applicable federal law to compel a recipient of such funds to comply with the law's terms.

The second, more satisfactory argument—that of Justices Powell, Brennan, Marshall, and Blackmun—is that the statute must be interpreted in light of the legislative intent, which clearly was *not* to prevent affirmative action for minorities. To be sure, legislative intent may be irrelevant when the statutory language is sufficiently clear.[75] But here the legislative history showed not only that Congress did not foresee in 1964 that whites might claim to be victims of racial discrimination when attempts were made to remedy past prejudice against minorities,[76] but also that Congress, in amending the Civil Rights Act in 1972, specifically refused to outlaw affirmative action for minorities.[77] The Court thus does not need to search the comments or motives of individual legislators to conclude that Congress did not mean to ban affirmative action in enacting Title VI. Still, the apparent clarity of the language poses a formidable obstacle not overcome by anything in the *Bakke* opinions upholding affirmative action.

A similar issue of the meaning of civil rights legislation was encountered in *United Steelworkers v. Weber*,[78] where the Court upheld against a statutory challenge a private affirmative action plan negotiated by an employer and a labor union that reserved 50 percent of the openings in craft-training programs for black workers until the percentage of black craft workers was commensurate with their representation in the local labor force. The Court, in an opinion by Justice Brennan,[79] ruled that §§703 (a) and (d) of Title VII did not condemn all private, voluntary, race-conscious affirmative action plans.[80] The crux of the Court's argument was that Title VII was meant to end racism and its vestiges, not to hinder racial progress. Since §703 (j) says that the Act does not "require" affirmative action for de facto racial imbalances, it seems clear that the Act still *permits* such action, for if Congress had wanted to outlaw all affirmative action, it would have said that Title VII does *not allow* it, let alone not *require* it.[81]

Even if one believes that Justice Rehnquist nonetheless makes the better argument at the level of statutory interpretation that Title VII should be construed as having been designed to forbid benign as well as invidious uses of race in the private employment sector,[82] there is a constitutional argument for *not* reading the statute that way which was overlooked by the *Weber* majority. The equal protection element of the Fifth Amendment's Due Process Clause may *forbid* Congress from passing a law barring all private agreements to redress racial discrimination.

In *Hunter v. Erickson*,[83] the Court struck down a law requiring the electorate to approve provisions addressing racial discrimination in housing since the impact of the law would be to hinder minorities seeking open housing. Despite its superficial symmetry, the city charter amendment struck down in *Hunter* was really meant, and would manifestly operate, to frustrate legal efforts to redress racial discrimination, because the Constitution and other federal laws already independently forbade laws which would *invite* racial discrimination in housing. Therefore, amending the process to inhibit race-conscious housing laws was only *apparently* evenhanded; it actually selected out racially remedial measures and put obstacles in their path, and their path alone.

Justice Rehnquist in *Weber* would have read Title VII as prohibiting the use of all race-conscious employment practices, regardless of purpose or impact. Yet, just like the law in *Hunter*, such an interpretation of Title VII would have only a superficial neutrality, since federal law already forbade *invidious* racial discrimination in private economic intercourse.[84] Therefore, Justice Rehnquist's reading of Title VII as barring the remedial use of race in private agreements would add the same sort of obstacles to minority efforts in seeking equality which the Court denounced as a violation of equal protection in *Hunter v. Erickson*.

Moreover, a congressional decision to prohibit labor unions and management from negotiating agreements to alleviate the effects of past discrimination—while allowing those same parties to negotiate wages, hours, benefits, pensions, dress codes, seniority plans, working conditions, and day care centers—would be highly suspect in itself. Permitting Congress to establish a labor law regime in which the parties can negotiate agreements on just about everything *except* affirmative action would be like allowing Missouri to maintain a property law system wherein the state courts would set aside all sorts of restraints on alienation *except* those convenants which perpetuated segregated neighborhoods—something the Court refused to allow in *Shelley v. Kraemer*.[85]

THE *FULLILOVE* DECISION

In *Fullilove v. Klutznick*,[86] the Court confronted a mandatory minority quota analogous to the one condemned in *Bakke*. This time, there was no way of avoiding the constitutional issue. The six-to-three decision[87] firmly established the legitimacy of affirmative action by upholding a provision of a federal public works employment program that set aside 10 percent of its total funds for procuring goods or services from minority business enterprises (MBEs). Chief Justice Burger, in his opinion announcing the judgment of the Court,[88] concluded that Congress had the power to regulate the practices of prime contractors on federally funded projects in this way under either the spending power or the commerce power because there was a "rational basis for Congress to conclude that the subcontracting practices of prime contractors could perpetuate the prevailing impaired access by minority businesses" even if those prime contractors could not be "shown responsible for any violation of antidiscrimination laws.[89] The Chief Justice repudiated the contention that Congress must act in a wholly "color-blind" manner,[90] and held not only that "innocent parties" may constitutionally be required to "shar[e] the burden" of affirmative action designed to "cure the effects of prior discrimination,"[91] but also that Congress was free to impose such a burden on the "assumption that in the past some nonminority businesses have reaped competitive benefit over the years" from the free ride resulting from "the virtual exclusion of minority firms from these contracting opportunities."[92]

The holding in *Fullilove* at first appears to be a closely confined one. The Chief Justice stressed that the affirmative action program at issue was modest. He characterized it as a temporary "pilot project,"[93] and further observed that the "burden" it imposed on nonminority businesses was "relatively light."[94] In addition, Congress had not discriminated against any disadvantaged group by excluding it from the program.[95] Most important to the Chief Justice was his conclusion that the administrative scheme established by Congress was highly flexible.[96] Unlike the rigid allocation of sixteen places in the medical school class in the Davis minority admissions program, the 10 percent set-aside in *Fullilove* was subject to several exemptions and could be waived by the Secretary of Commerce. There were, according to Chief Justice Burger, procedures for challenging and excluding from participation those MBEs whose competitive position could be shown not to have been adversely affected by past discrimination.[97] Yet, for all of the detailed attention that the Chief Justice devoted to the administrative guidelines, they simply do not support the reading he gave them. The concept of "unjust participation" on which he relied so heavily[98] is nowhere defined in the guidelines, which provide no means for assessing whether an MBE has indeed been the victim of discrimination, but only a procedure for challenging the participation of businesses that are not really minority-owned.[99]

The Chief Justice also repeatedly stressed that Congress had "abundant evidence" of discrimination with which to justify the MBE set-aside.[100] Yet all the evidence to which he referred came from past hearings on other legislation;[101] none of it was actually mentioned during the brief discussion on the floor of Congress.[102] The minority set-aside was offered as a floor amendment,[103] and no specific hearings on the set-aside were ever held: its consideration by Congress was "perfunctory."[104]

The Court's emphasis on the presence of both "abundant evidence" and administrative escape hatches make *Fullilove* appear to be a narrow decision. Yet, the fact that the evidence was relatively meager and largely derivative and that the administrative guidelines were less flexible than some members of the Court would have liked to believe suggests that *Fullilove*'s limiting factors may in fact be loopholes. One proposition about which there can no longer be any doubt is that some forms of meaningful affirmative action are clearly constitutional. Race-conscious remedies are now an accepted part of Fifth and Fourteenth Amendment jurisprudence.

Taken together, *Bakke*, *Weber*, and *Fullilove* suggest the disturbing conclusion that the current Court seems more willing to uphold quantitative race-specific remedies when the result disrupts "only" the prospective expectations of blue-collar tradesmen than when the result affects opportunities in elitist institutions such as medical schools—institutions in which "meritocracy" supposedly still thrives.

To be sure, the Supreme Court's rejection, in *Firefighters Local Union No. 1784 v. Stotts*,[105] of a district court order enjoining the layoff, under a last-hired first-fired seniority system, of black workers hired in Memphis under a consent decree entered in a Title VII case challenging the city's pattern of hiring firemen (where the decree had no provision about layoffs) might be understood as expressing commendable sympathy for the plight of innocent white workers and thus broadening the Court's sphere of concern from its elitist core. But, despite its broad dicta,[106] that decision dealt only with the narrow question of a court's power to issue an order governing layoffs when the consent decree on which the lawsuit was based dealt only with hiring.[107]

In any event, if one were to read the Memphis decision as giving worker seniority entrenched status either under Title VII—or, more broadly, as a matter of Fifth or Fourteenth Amendment law—the upshot would be more cause for lamentation than celebration. For no principled line seems possible between remedial power to restrict the future economic opportunities of innocent whites in order to place innocent blacks where they would have been in the hiring line but for discrimination, and remedial power to reclaim the entrenched economic gains of the blameless to the same end. Although remedies going this far might well involve a taking of property for a public purpose and thus require just compensation,[108] holding that such remedies are impermissible would be tantamount to the subordination of racial justice to whatever pattern of economic distribution our discriminatory past happens to have produced.

CHAPTER FIFTEEN

REORIENTING THE MIRROR OF JUSTICE: GENDER, ECONOMICS, AND THE ILLUSION OF THE "NATURAL"

When the Supreme Court rejects a claim under the Bill of Rights or the Fourteenth Amendment, Court-watchers generally divide into three camps. There are those who agree with the decision as a defensible or even wise elaboration of constitutional principles, those who denounce it as but another misfortune, and those who lament the decision but insist that even the dark cloud it represents has its silver lining. All three sets of responses are natural, but each tends to stress the short-term meaning of what the Court does at the expense of understanding what pattern the Court's rulings are most likely to make in the long run—a pattern far more likely to be revealed in the tacit assumptions and unquestioned premises that inform each justice's vision of American society than in how the justices have voted in any particular case.

The Court's struggles with questions of sexual equality vividly demonstrate the power of unarticulated, and therefore usually unchallenged, assumptions to warp constitutional analysis. The Court has had little difficulty perceiving the invalidity of statutes that on their face subordinate women as such—such as the Louisiana law struck down in *Kirchberg v. Feenstra*[1] which gave a husband the right, without his wife's consent, to dispose of property jointly owned with his wife. Yet, even the simple requirement that the state not use gross generalizations—whether based on statistics or mythology—to place sexually differentiated burdens on individuals has often been ignored where the discrimination in question was only the outermost manifestation of deep and extensive systems of sexual subjugation.

A telling example is provided by *Parham v. Hughes*,[2] in which the Court upheld a Georgia law that denied the father, but not the mother, of a child born out of wedlock the right to sue for the child's wrongful death unless the father had made use of the state procedure to legitimate the child. The plurality[3] found that fathers and mothers of illegitimate children were not "similarly situated"[4] because under Georgia law only the father could, by voluntary unilateral action, legitimate a child born out of wedlock. The plurality simply refused to evaluate this underlying invidious discrimination, by which Georgia defined legitimate children as those and only those whom the *father* acknowledged. Forced to choose among eliminating multiple layers of discrimination, striking down one layer while allowing the inequality created by the other layers to remain, or allowing the surface layer of discrimination to be justified by the layers beneath it, the Court took the judicially conservative but morally bankrupt third course.

Perhaps the most powerful unspoken assumptions are in play when the state regulates according to, or seeks to justify discrimination by reference to, physical characteristics that are indeed unique to one sex.[5] Because the Court has not developed a consistent approach to such state action, it has at times blithely ignored sex-specific physical differences that make the "similar" treatment of men and women invidious discrimination and has at other times focused on physical differences irrelevant to the issue at hand in order to uphold discriminatory laws. Thus, in *Geduldig v. Aiello*,[6] the Court upheld against an equal protection challenge a California public employees' insurance scheme that excluded coverage of pregnancy—while providing benefits for male-only procedures such as circumcision and prostatectomy and voluntary operations such as cosmetic surgery and sterilization. The Court found the scheme rational, demanding no further justification inasmuch as the plan discriminated not on the basis of gender but between pregnant and nonpregnant persons, the latter group comprising both males and females.[7] After the Court attempted to import its *Geduldig* reasoning into Title VII jurisprudence,[8] Congress responded with the Pregnancy Discrimination Act of 1978,[9] an amendment to Title VII clearly repudiating the "pregnant persons" fantasy.[10]

The recent case of *Michael M. v. Superior Court*[11] illustrates both the significance of the Court's underlying perception of the discrimination at issue and a dubious reference to sex-specific differences to excuse discrimination. In *Michael M.*, the Court sustained a seventeen-year-old boy's conviction for engaging in sexual intercourse with a sixteen-year-old girl, in violation of California's statutory rape law, under which she would not typically be prosecuted for engaging in the same conduct with him.[12] The law in question made it a crime for males of any age to engage in sexual intercourse with females under eighteen (other than their wives); it did not similarly criminalize non-marital sex between females over eighteen and males under eighteen.

As might be expected, the justices considered the issue to be the fairness of punishing Michael M. under a law that subjected him to prosecution solely on the basis of his gender. Justice Rehnquist, writing for a plurality, concluded that the law legitimately serves to deter unwed teenage pregnancy, a goal in terms of which the claimed discrimination against Michael M. was, he reasoned, no discrimination at all. Since "the risk of pregnancy itself constitutes a substantial deterrence to young females," whereas "[n]o similar natural sanctions deter males," the plurality opinion concluded that the gender-based statutory rape law "serves to roughly 'equalize' the deterrents on the sexes."[13] Moreover, extending criminal liability to the female was viewed as likely to deter her not from engaging in the offense, but from reporting it.[14]

The dissenting justices could not accept any such justification for Michael M.'s disparate treatment. Concluding that the actual purpose of the law was not to deter unwed teenage pregnancy but to protect the chastity of young women under nineteenth-century standards of moral virtue, the dissenters seemed to find particularly indefensible the notion of punishing Michael M. under a statute that discriminates between males and females on the basis of such outmoded sexual stereotypes.[15]

What seems most striking about Michael M. is not that five justices held that the law at issue did not violate the male defendant's right to equal protection, but that all of the justices appeared to view the case in terms of the reasonableness of the "discrimination" against males, focusing on the accuracy with which "natural" differences between males and females could support the challenged distinction in legal treatment.

But Michael M. could have been considered through another lens altogether, one through which none of the justices seems to have looked. For the law there at issue criminalized all sex acts involving unwed, underage females, but not all sex acts involving unwed, underage males. If the justices had focused on this discrimination against Michael M.'s female partner (who could have been prosecuted for aiding and abetting[16]) rather than on the discrimination against Michael M., their view of the case, if not the case's outcome, might have been radically different. In deciding whether such discrimination against young women is justified by concerns about extramarital teenage pregnancies, the Court could no longer invoke the supposed naturalness of immunizing the sex partner on whom the state relies for reporting the offense, and the Court could no longer focus solely on the fairness of the penalty structure vis-à-vis males—a group hardly "in need of the special solicitude of the courts," as Justice Rehnquist drily observed for the *Michael* M. plurality.[17]

Attention would shift, instead, to discrimination against women and would identify their persisting legal disabilities as parts of a subtle mosaic of oppression that is not genuinely framed by human nature, even though it is typically "justified" by invoking precisely such considerations. In *Dothard v. Rawlinson*,[18] for instance, an employee's very womanhood was made the justification for removing her from an employment situation (in a prison) where men were thought likely to harass or attack her sexually instead of ordering that measures be taken to stop the harassment itself. That "the sexes are not similarly situated"[19] in such cases as *Michael* M. and *Dothard* would not, to anyone less mesmerized by the ideal of law as a mirror of nature, be thought to *justify* a gender discrimination as noninvidious; it would instead raise the question whether such discrimination formed part of the law's systemic support for male supremacy.

Why the justices did not consider *Michael* M. through this lens—demanding justification for the law's more severe restrictions on premarital sex involving underage females than on premarital sex involving underage males—must be a matter of speculation. Perhaps for the nine men then on the bench, and for the boy in the dock, it seemed more natural to focus on the fairness of punishing him but not his partner. Did the impulse to focus on this facet of the case signal some lingering grudge against Eve? Did the Court's concentration on the male's harsh treatment under the California law express the sense that, for his female partner, pregnancy would be "punishment" enough? Did it reflect an unwillingness to confront the systemic character of the oppression of women in American society, and an inclination to treat any given discrimination, so far as possible, as an isolated and aberrant event?

The image of justice mirrored by *Michael* M. is one in which pervasive inequalities in the distribution of power and status are overlooked—one in which the evils to be extirpated are seen to lie in the law's occasional and irrational deviations from the "natural" rather than in the omnipresent realities that the legal order simultaneously reflects and re-creates with relentless rationality.

Thus, in the different but related setting of *economic* injustice, if the right to a hearing before repossession of one's personal belongings, for example, had been glimpsed through the alternative lens described here, that right might be more firmly rooted in notions of economic inequality and exploitation—and the enforcement of that right might involve more thorough-going changes in the lot of the dispossessed. Instead, the dispossessed now have a formal procedural right to hearings nearly useless for those without the funds and sophistication to enforce that right—those for whom the right is supposed to matter.[20] Indeed, the right itself all but vanishes when a state's abdication to creditors becomes complete and when creditors are invited by law to seize and sell, without a whisper of official involvement, the items for which such creditors claim not to have been paid. This practice was held by the Court in *Flagg Brothers, Inc. v. Brooks*[21] to be immune from constitutional scrutiny in a civil rights suit brought in federal district court, essentially on the ground that this is what creditors would "naturally" tend to do in the economic jungle: authorizing creditors to do what they would do anyway, the *Flagg* Court reasoned, mirrors economic reality accurately enough to free the state from any responsibility at all[22]—and thus to render inapplicable the protections afforded by the Fourteenth Amendment.[23]

An attractive vision of a unified doctrine recognizing various economic injustices as denials of equal protection of the laws is suggested by Michael Walzer's *Spheres of Justice*.[24] Walzer argues that the principle of equality under the law is offended not so much by the fact that there *are* rich and poor, as by the wide-ranging legal and social significance that the law gives to this disparity in material wealth. The problem is *not* that X has more money than Y, but that the law allows X's superior position in the material sphere to translate into a superior position in all other spheres as well. To put everything—health care, education, political power, personal autonomy, access to judicial relief—effectively on a cash basis is to create and perpetuate a world in which "all good things come to those who have the one best thing."[25] Such a regime provides not the equal protection of the laws, but the unequal hazard of the auction hall.[26]

The Court's refusal to subject classifications based on wealth to meaningful equal protection scrutiny may reflect a failure to perceive that money, the current dominant good, is converted into other social goods not by a natural process but by a sort of legal alchemy.[27] There was a time when the law overtly denied blacks equal protection by un-erringly translating skin color into status as master or slave. Today, this sort of unwarranted attribution of legal significance to "natural" differences is more subtle, but no less invidious.[28] The state makes women and men unequal before the law by automatically translating biology into social destiny, thereby denying women power over both their bodies and their futures.

The Court's willingness to uphold laws whose apparent injustice is thought simply to reflect the world's own cruelty—to women, to the poor, or to both—seems most vivid in a case like Harris v. McCrae,[29] which upheld a ban not on abortions as such but on federally funded abortions for those otherwise unable to pay for them. Having won abortion rights in the name of abstract personal privacy,[30] women were poorly situated to demand public funds for the exercise of such rights.[31] In the original Supreme Court decision upholding the right to choose, abortion was not perceived as involving the intensely pub-lic question of the subordination of women to men through the ex-ploitation of pregnancy, or the equally public question of the subordi-nation of the poor to the rich through the instrument of coerced childbirth for those unable to afford medical procedures placed by the state on an ability-to-pay basis.

If abortion had instead been regarded in this light, even equating developing fetuses with new-born infants would not end the inquiry. For although current law nowhere forces men to sacrifice their bodies and restructure their lives even in those tragic situations (of needed or-gan transplants, for example) where nothing less will permit their chil-dren to survive, those who would outlaw abortion (or who would re-fuse to fund it) would rely upon economic and physiological circumstances—the supposed dictates of the natural—to conscript women (at least poor women) as involuntary incubators and thus to usurp a control over sexual activity and its consequences that men (and perhaps wealthy women) take for granted. To one who regards this outcome as unjust, a right to end pregnancy might be seen more plausibly as a matter of resisting sexual and economic domination than as a matter of shielding from public control "private" transactions between patients and physicians. And, if this were seen to be the na-ture of the right at issue, then even the state's use of selective funding to encourage the birth of unwanted children might resemble a program to foster involuntary servitude more closely than an exercise of government's prerogative to set its own priorities.[32]

Any such reoriented vision of a woman's right to terminate her pregnancy[33] would have to confront the perception that prohibiting an abortion (and, a fortiori, merely refusing to fund it) does not compel a woman to take any *positive action* (such as donating one's blood or kidneys) but at most forces her to *refrain* from taking a life. Yet an abortion law that "evenhandedly" forces neither men nor women to donate their bodies to their unborn children, like a vagrancy law that forbids rich and poor alike to beg in the streets or sleep under the bridges of Paris, will seem nondiscriminatory only from a perspective that regards it as automatically just for "natural" distinctions to be reflected in legal categories,[34] and only from a perspective that views legal omissions—such as the omission to address the reality that women who engage in sex, unlike men who do so, risk pregnancy—as invariably needing no special justification.

If one were instead to recognize, as the Supreme Court sometimes has, that "the grossest discrimination *can* lie in treating things that are different as though they were exactly alike,"[35] then it might be possible to discern an invidious discrimination against women, or at least a constitutionally problematic subordination of women, in the law's very indifference to the biological reality that sometimes requires them, but never requires their male counterparts, to resort to abortion procedures if they are to avoid pregnancy and childbearing.

Suppose, for the sake of illustration, that women were enabled, by some simple medical procedure they might elect at puberty, to "redesign" their bodies so that they would thenceforth automatically miscarry within days of any pregnancy unless they took some suitable drug shortly after conception to prevent such miscarriage. A law compelling women to take this antimiscarriage drug after sexual intercourse (in order to save the lives of whatever unborn children they might be carrying) would be gender-specific on its face and would compel positive bodily sacrifices rather than seeming only to bar affirmative acts inflicting harm on the unborn. In a legal system that leaves men free to resist all comparably significant coerced bodily sacrifices to save their children's lives, such a law would accordingly be more difficult to sustain than would an antiabortion law or a refusal to fund abortions.

Yet does it not seem an arbitrary punishment of women for the mere fact of their physiological difference—for the role "nature" has assigned them in the reproductive cycle—to treat restrictions on abortion more tolerantly than we would treat forced ingestion of the hypothesized drug? The perspective proposed by this essay—and by this book as a whole—would regard any such incorporation of the "natural" into the "legal" as a deliberate *choice*, one by no means inevitable or inexorable, and one in need of constitutional justification in light of the way in which such naturalism retards full equality for half the human race.[36]

CHAPTER SIXTEEN

REFOCUSING THE "STATE ACTION" INQUIRY: SEPARATING STATE ACTS FROM STATE ACTORS

With the exception of the Thirteenth Amendment,[1] the Constitution does not directly concern itself with private actors; its self-executing guarantees of individual rights protect individuals only from conduct by the state. That is, the Constitution controls the deployment of governmental power and defines the rules for how such power may be structured and applied. The Constitution, therefore, is not a body of rules about ordinary private actions, but a collection of rules about the rules and uses of law: in a word, *metalaw.*

In the *Civil Rights Cases* of 1883,[2] classically treated as the first major articulation of this principle, the Supreme Court delineated "the essential dichotomy set forth in [the Fourteenth] Amendment between deprivation by the State, subject to scrutiny under its provisions, and private conduct, 'however discriminatory or wrongful' against which the Fourteenth Amendment offers no shield."[3] But particularly where ostensibly "private" power is the primary source of the coercion and violence that oppressed individuals and groups experience, it is hard to accept with equanimity a rigid legal distinction betweeen state and society. The pervasive *system* of racial apartheid[4] which existed in the South for a century after the Civil War, for example, thrived only because of the "resonance of society and politics . . . the close fit between private terror, public discrimination, and political exclusion."[5] So too, where it is the state's persistent *inaction* in the face of patterns of deprivation for which state and society seem to many to bear collective responsibility, the premise that only indentifiable state "action" may be called to constitutional account is deeply troubling. Indeed, that premise all too readily suggests, although it cannot logically or legally support, the conclusion that, as a substantive constitutional matter, the state owes no *affirmative* duties to its people. Thus, in a suit under 42 U.S.C. §1983 alleging a breach of constitutional duty by state officials in recklessly releasing a dangerous, mentally ill killer who proceeded to murder a woman on whose behalf plaintiff sued, the Seventh Circuit, evidently drawing strength from "state action" precedents, cavalierly opined that

> there is no constitutional right to be protected by the state against being murdered by criminals or madmen. It is monstrous if the state fails to protect its residents against such predators but it does not violate the due process clause of the Fourteenth Amendment or, we suppose, any other provision of the Constitution. The Constitution is a charter of negative liberties; it tells the state to let people alone; it does not require the federal government or the state to provide services, even so elementary a service as maintaining law and order. Discrimination in providing protection against private violence could of course violate the equal protection clause of the Fourteenth Amendment. But that is not alleged here. All that is alleged is a failure to protect Miss Bowers and others like her from a dangerous madman, and as the State of Illinois has no federal constitutional duty to provide such protection its failure to do so is not actionable under section 1983.[6]

That the state indeed had no such "duty" may or may not be so; but—given the circuit court's own recognition "that the line between action and inaction, between inflicting and failing to prevent the infliction of harm,"[7] is less than wholly clear—the absence of the alleged duty certainly does not follow from the principle that the Constitution addresses only the states. To the degree that the state "action" doctrine subliminally suggests otherwise, it is a subterfuge for substantive choices the framers did not necessarily make one way or the other.

For these reasons among others, it has become commonplace to attack both the philosophical presuppositions of state action theory—its grounding in an often dubious and hardly neutral dichotomy between state and society, public and private—and the actual generation of state action doctrine.[8] The Supreme Court itself has long recognized the intractable nature of the problems posed: "to fashion and apply a precise formula for recognition of state responsibility under the Equal Protection Clause is an 'impossible task' . . . Only by sifting facts and weighing circumstances can the nonobvious involvement of the State in private conduct be attributed its true significance."[9] As one commentator has observed, "This differs from Justice Stewart's famous 'I know it when I see it' standard for judging obscenity[10] mainly in the comparative precision of the latter."[11]

Despite the sweep of this assault, my purpose in this chapter is a modest one: not to offer any resolution of the deep difficulties of the distinction between the public and the private, but to pave the way for discussion of those difficulties by eliminating what seem to me largely collateral and avoidable confusions about what the prevailing doctrine in this area *is*. That doctrine is, in my view, considerably more consistent and less muddled than many have long supposed; my aim here is simply to develop the structure of that doctrine—less to defend it than to lay bare its essential logic, the better to expose it to such defense or attack as it may properly invite. The conventional wisdom on this subject—that the "doctrine" of state action is too deeply incoherent and internally conflicted to be taken seriously—seems to me flatly wrong and, if anything, obstructive of serious critical efforts. Indeed, it is my conclusion that the Supreme Court's state action cases display a surprisingly coherent pattern once one gets past their often neuralgic prose and views the cases through a suitably sequenced combination of two different lenses.

The first is a close-up lens that focuses on the actual participants in a controversy and examines the Constitution's application to the individuals and organizations who act as the state's agents. These "state actors" are the physical, three-dimensional manifestations of government authority. The second is a telephoto lens that looks beyond the human figures on the stage to examine the substantive law that provides the picture's background. This lens focuses on the Constitution's application to the state as an abstract construct, a legal order, a system of rules—the state *qua* state.

Most of the confusion and supposed incoherence of the Supreme Court's state-action analysis reflects (1) the attempted use of the *first* lens when only the second can properly identify the level at which the state might arguably have violated the Constitution in a given case, or (2) the attempted use of the *second* lens when only the first is made relevant by the procedural posture in which a particular lawsuit has posed an issue for judicial resolution.

STATE ACTORS: ABUSE OF THE AEGIS OF
GOVERNMENTAL AUTHORITY

At the outset one might ask how the first lens alone is *ever* capable of identifying state responsibility for an alleged injury—that is, why a Constitution that addresses the *states* should have any application at all to the individuals or other subsovereign entities who do the states' bidding. Thus, when a state's laws plainly forbid what the state actor has done, the *state itself* might readily argue that it is not involved or is not to blame. But the Supreme Court has long held that the state's accountability for the conduct of its officials and employees cannot be allowed to evaporate simply because the actor, being less than the state itself, has violated one of the state's own laws. In *Home Tel. & Tel. Co. v. Los Angeles*,[12] the Court held that, so long as the "officer or other representative of a State in the exercise of the authority with which he is clothed misuses the power possessed to do a wrong forbidden by the [Fourteenth] Amendment, inquiry concerning whether the State has authorized the wrong is irrelevant."[13] Thus the Constitution addresses, in effect, not only the states as juridical entities, "but also . . . every person whether natural or juridical who is the repository of state power."[14]

The clearest statement that the Court takes this principle seriously remains the case of *Screws v. United States*.[15] The Court there upheld the conviction under the criminal federal civil rights statute[16] of police officers who had beaten a black man to death after arresting him and knocking him unconscious. Even though murder was a felony, the Court concluded that, since the homicide was committed by the officers in the course of their official duties while they were clothed with the authority of the state, they had acted under "color" of law: "It is clear that under 'color' of law means under 'pretense' of law."[17]

CLOSE-FOCUS LENS: LOOKING FOR A NEXUS

The first lens becomes crucial whenever no act of the state qua state may successfully be blamed, at least in the particular lawsuit, for the injury alleged. In that event, the first lens looks at the nexus *between* the state and the person or entity whose choice or action *might* be so blamed. Generally, the closer the tie, the stronger the case for finding state action. However, it is important to realize that not even those persons who are on the state payroll are necessarily *always* state actors. In *Polk County v. Dodson*,[18] the Supreme Court held that a state-paid public defender was acting not as a state *agent* but as an *adversary* of the state in the context of the lawsuit that brought the matter to the Court.[19] Once Martha Shephard had been assigned Richard Dodson's case, she was acting on *his* behalf as *his* defense lawyer—"a private function, traditionally filled by retained counsel, for which state office and authority are not needed."[20] So when Shephard declined to prosecute Dodson's appeal on the ground that it was frivolous, the decision was attributable to her rather than to the state. She was not exercising power "possessed by virtue of state law and made possible only because the wrongdoer is clothed with the authority of state law,"[21] because private attorneys also have a professional duty not to clog the courts with frivolous appeals.[22]

This is not to say that a public defender is *never* a state actor. The Court noted that a public defender acts under color of law when he fires subordinates on the basis of their political party affiliation,[23] or extorts payment from a client's friends or relatives.[24] The Court left open the question whether a public defender would act under color of state law while engaged in other administrative and investigative functions.[25]

At the other end of the spectrum, the Court held in *Lugar v. Edmondson Oil Co.* that even a wholly private individual may be considered a state actor and held liable under §1983, if he acts in conjunction with, or obtains significant aid from, state officers acting in their official capacity in the seizure of disputed property pursuant to a state attachment procedure that violates the Due Process Clause.[26] Since the only action by the state in that case was the issuance of a writ of attachment by the court clerk and the formal, legal sequestration of the disputed property by the sheriff,[27] *Lugar* would appear to make private citizens potentially liable under §1983—subject to various "good faith" defenses that may well be available—whenever they are unfortunate enough to invoke a defective state law that requires even minimal involvement by state officials.[28]

In *Lugar* the plaintiff sued only the private oil company that attached his property and did not seek to hold the Commonwealth of Virginia responsible in any way. In *Burton v. Wilmington Parking Authority*,[29] the plaintiff sued *both* the private actor *and* the state entity in an effort to hold them both responsible for the refusal of the Eagle Coffee Shop—which was located in a city-owned parking garage—to serve him because he was black. The Court ruled that, if the nexus between a private entity and a public authority is tight enough to characterize their activities as a joint venture, then the state may be held responsible for at least some offensive acts by the private entity.[30] *Burton's* symbiosis analysis remains the high-water mark in a tide of state action doctrine that has since been almost constantly at ebb. The only recent application of this kind of joint enterprise notion was its curious use in *Little v. Streater*.[31] In that case a unanimous Court held that Connecticut was obligated to pay for blood-grouping tests requested by the indigent defendant in a paternity suit because of the state's "considerable and manifest" involvement in the suit.[32] Chief Justice Burger wrote that state action "undeniably pervaded [the] case": the plaintiff mother was compelled by Connecticut's welfare laws to bring suit against the father of her illegitimate child—if she wished to remain on welfare; the state attorney general was a party to the action and had the power to disapprove any settlement of the case; plaintiff's lawyer was paid by the state; and any support payments awarded by the court were to be paid directly to the state.[33]

Any hopes that *Streater* had resurrected the *Burton* symbiosis analysis were dashed when the Court subsequently refused to find state action in two cases where the state had insinuated itself into the operations of private organizations. Both the nursing homes involved in *Blum v. Yaretsky*[34] and the special school involved in *Rendell-Baker v. Kohn*[35] received the vast bulk of their funding from the government[36] and were heavily regulated by the state as well.[37] Yet in neither case did the Court find governmental responsibility for the conduct of the institutions in question. The best explanation for this seeming retrenchment by the Court may not be wholly doctrinal. First, unlike *Burton*, neither *Yaretsky* nor *Rendell-Baker* involved issues of racial discrimination, and the Court has usually been more willing to find state action when race was involved.[38] Second, the contemporary state action requirement has been tightened by the Court's concern about the expansion of the Constitution and the federal judiciary into what it regards as state and private bailiwicks. Third, both *Yaretsky* and *Rendell-Baker* involved arguably public functions which the states had contracted out to private enterprise, and the Court seemed hesitant to expand the Constitution's application to a pervasive practice.[39] Finally, and most important, the Court placed great emphasis on a careful examination of the role of the state in the *specific decisions* complained of in each case.

In *Blum v. Yaretsky*, Justice Rehnquist[40] wrote for the Court that "[f]aithful adherence to the 'state action' requirement of the Fourteenth Amendment requires careful attention to the gravamen of the plaintiff's complaint."[41] Several Medicaid patients had challenged their involuntary transfer or discharge from their nursing homes. Justice Rehnquist concluded that the decision to discharge or reassign a particular patient was a medical judgment about the patient's health needs made by a private physician,[42] to which the state merely *reacted* by lowering or terminating Medicaid benefits accordingly.[43]

In his opinion for the Court in *Rendell-Baker v. Kohn*,[44] Chief Justice Burger could not see how extensive regulation and almost exclusive funding by Massachusetts implicated that state in the decision of the director of the New Perspectives School to fire one of its teachers for opposing school policy. Although the New Perspectives School was under contract to fulfill several cities' statutory obligations to provide special schooling for troubled students and was extensively regulated by the state in that capacity,[45] there was hardly any regulation of personnel matters.[46] And even if state funds accounted for 99 percent of the school's operating budget,[47] the Chief Justice concluded that this in no way affected the relationship between the school and its faculty.[48] Director Kohn's decision to fire Rendell-Baker for siding with students in a school policy battle, however much it might stifle free speech, simply did not constitute action under color of state law.[49]

The Court in each of these cases found it significant—as it had in the public defender case—that the plaintiffs had not challenged any particular rules of the state as such. No state rules dealing with personnel discipline or dismissal existed in *Rendell-Baker*,[50] and the particular state rules about adjusting Medicaid benefits were not being directly challenged in *Yaretsky.*[51] This emphasis is consistent with the Court's refusal to find state action in *Moose Lodge v. Irvis*,[52] on the ground that the Pennsylvania liquor licensing policies that affected Moose Lodge were not connected with the specific Moose practice of excluding blacks.[53] Similarly, had the prison inmate who lost his hobby materials in *Parratt v. Taylor*[54] alleged, in his federal §1983 complaint against prison officials, a defect in the prison's *system* for delivering mail, for processing requests for lost items, or for responding to complaints after the fact—rather than alleging only random negligence on the part of an anonymous clerk—the outcome might well have been different.[55]

Despite the Court's unwillingness to impose constitutional limits on "private" (and sometimes even "public") actors who perform legally mandated state functions, there is a limit on the degree to which a state may avoid its constitutional duties by contracting out services and responsibilities. Although Yaretsky[56] and Rendell-Baker[57] make it clear that the "symbiosis" doctrine is the epitome of manipulability,[58] state efforts to evade the strictures of the Constitution by "sham arrangement[s] which attempt to disguise provision of public services as acts of private parties" ostensibly remain beyond the pale.[59] It is nevertheless unfortunate that more members of the Court do not perceive the wisdom of Justice Brennan's observation in Blum v. Yaretsky:

> In an era of active government intervention to remedy social ills, the true character of the State's involvement in, and coercive influence over, the activities of private parties, often through complex and opaque regulatory frameworks, may not always be apparent. But if the task that the Fourteenth Amendment assigns to the courts is thus rendered more burdensome, the courts' obligation to perform that task faithfully . . . is rendered more, not less, important.[60]

TELEPHOTO LENS: BRINGING THE BACKGROUND LEGAL ORDER INTO VIEW

As the Court suggested in Blum v. Yaretsky[61] and Rendell-Baker v. Kohn,[62] if particular state rules had themselves been properly challenged, a different kind of state action would have been at issue. The judicial lens would then have looked past the players and focused on the law itself: the state qua state.[63] Critics[64] have argued that the Court should have recognized that the legal rules themselves were the targets of the lawsuits brought in such cases as Flagg Brothers v. Brooks,[65] Moose Lodge No. 107 v. Irvis,[66] and Jackson v. Metropolitan Edison Co.[67] But such an argument oversimplifies those cases, for in each instance the legal rule involved remained in the background, never having been brought directly into focus in a procedural posture that would make this second state-action lens directly relevant to the controversy at hand.

In its decision in Flagg Brothers, the Court continued to elaborate on the conventional if largely empty categories of state action.[68] Ms. Brooks and her family had been evicted from their apartment, and the city marshall had arranged for the storage of their possessions in Flagg

Brothers' warehouse. Although Ms. Brooks from the start found the price for moving and storing her household goods exorbitant, she nevertheless authorized their storage. She had no practical alternative.[69] After a series of disputes over the amount of the charges being claimed by Flagg Brothers, Ms. Brooks was told to pay up or her furniture would be sold. She brought a Section 1983 suit in federal court against Flagg Brothers, claiming the right to some opportunity to be heard, prior to the sale of her belongings, on the amount owed.

The provisions of the New York Uniform Commercial Code (UCC) authorizing a warehouseman to sell goods entrusted to him in order to enforce his lien on such goods were never directly implicated in the case. The Supreme Court apparently assumed that, if the sale of the property were conducted by state officials without ever providing the owner of the goods with a hearing, that sale would violate the Due Process Clause. But the Court held that a private warehouseman's proposed sale of bailed goods to recover unpaid storage charges, even pursuant to the New York UCC self-help provision, was not an action attributable to the state. Justice Rehnquist began his state action inquiry for the *Flagg Brothers* majority by focusing not on the governmental *rules* implicated by the particular right asserted by Ms. Brooks, but on whether public or private *actors* were responsible for her injury. There had been no trace of overt official involvement—and this was sufficient[70] to distinguish the case from *Sniadach v. Family Finance Corp.*[71] and *Fuentes v. Shevin.*[72] In *Sniadach*, the statute had required the clerk of the court to issue the summons at the request of the creditor's lawyer;[73] in *Fuentes*, a clerk again was required to make out a writ of replevin upon the creditor's demand, and the sheriff then seized the property pursuant to the writ.[74] But the significance Justice Rehnquist attributed to the absence of overt official involvement made due process review turn on whether the legislative scheme happened to require the private party to enlist the participation of some minor functionaries, exercising merely ministerial powers. Since what was wrong in *Fuentes* and *Sniadach* was that the state was not reserving *enough* control over the coercive use of force, it would be perverse for the Court to conclude that the scheme in *Flagg Brothers* was *less* constitutionally infirm because the state withdrew even its rubber stamp and allowed deprivation of property to happen purely in the private sphere.[75]

It should be stressed that counsel for Ms. Brooks chose to argue that the sale by the warehouseman itself became a state act because of what the state's laws had done.[76] The Court's restrictive "public function" doctrine[77] doomed that approach from the beginning.[78] The mere fact that an actor *might* or *could* invoke the state law as a *defense* if and when sued in state court, for example, does not mean that the law is implicated in the federal suit against that action.[79] In a sense, the UCC self-help provision in *Flagg Brothers* was *never directly implicated* in Ms. Brooks's Section 1983 suit: the mere *existence* of that UCC provision did not convert the private creditor's act, which was all the plaintiff had actually challenged, into an act of the state of New York.

Justice Rehnquist made a telling observation in a footnote to his opinion for the Court: "There is no reason . . . to believe that the [plaintiff] could not . . . seek resort to the New York Courts . . . to . . . prevent the [challenged] surrender of [her] property."[80] Had Ms. Brooks *sought* such injunctive relief against Flagg Brothers and been denied it by a state court *on the ground that the state UCC provision barred the relief sought*, that ruling by the courts of New York would *itself* have constituted challengeable state action.

There are two principal ways of bringing such state laws or rules into issue in a federal court for substantive review of their constitutionality. The first is to bring the state rules into focus by suing, in either state *or* federal court, the state officials who possess the power, by virtue of the state rules at issue, to put "private" actors in a position to inflict injury—for example, by delegating governmental or monopoly power to private entities. In *Moose Lodge No. 107 v. Irvis*,[81] the Court held that a state-licensed private club's racial discrimination in serving liquor was not rendered subject to the Equal Protection Clause simply by virtue of the government's limitation of the availability of liquor licenses. But if the plaintiff had sued the members of the Pennsylvania liquor control board rather than the Moose, he could have directly charged the board members with suborning racism and aggravating its impact by handing out the privilege of a scarce liquor license without regard to the licensee's racist practices.[82] Similarly, in *Jackson v. Metropolitan Edison Co.*,[83] the plaintiff probably should have sued not Met Ed but the members of the public utility commission that gave Met Ed a monopoly and thus put it in a position to cut plaintiff off from *all* electrical power without providing due process in the termination proceeding.

What amounts to this very approach has often been used to obtain rulings on the constitutionality of challenged laws. Women challenged the Hyde abortion funding amendment by suing the Secretary of Health and Human Services who administered the law. The Hyde Amendment provided that a woman could not obtain Medicaid reimbursement for even a medically necessary abortion, although she would be reimbursed if she decided to have the child. The Supreme Court held in *Harris v. McRae*[84] that, even though federal law thus encouraged women to have children rather than abortions and encouraged doctors to give women child care services rather than abortion services, the federal government committed no wrong by skewing the woman's decision-making process. Although the merits of that judgment are debatable,[85] it is critical to note that no member of the Court hesitated to rule on the constitutional validity of the Hyde Amendment. The Court did *not* say Congress was not responsible because the clinics and hospitals that now refused to perform abortions were not state actors. Had the suit instead been brought against a physician who refused to perform a nonsubsidized abortion, the Court would no doubt have replied that the mere existence of a federal law that puts a doctor in a position to refuse services, and even makes it more likely that he will in fact do so, does not make him an agent of the government in such refusal.

The same method resulted in a ruling that a state campaign disclosure law was unconstitutional as applied in *Brown v. Socialist Workers '74 Campaign Committee*.[86] The Socialist Workers party sued the Ohio Secretary of State, charging that, by requiring the party to disclose its contributors and the recipients of its campaign disbursements, Ohio put both public and private actors in a position to subject members and supporters of the controversial organization to threats, harassment, and reprisals. The Court held that the First Amendment prohibited the state from facilitating such oppression.[87]

A final example is provided by *Larkin v. Grendel's Den*.[88] There a restaurant challenged a Massachusetts law that delegated to churches and synagogues the absolute, unreviewable power to veto any liquor license application within a 500-foot radius of the house of divine worship. Had the Section 1983 suit been brought against the Holy Cross Armenian Catholic Parish Church in federal court to challenge the church's invocation of its veto as violative of the Due Process or Establishment Clauses, the Supreme Court would no doubt have refused to consider the church to be a state agent acting under color of law. But by naming the Cambridge Licensing Commission and the members of the state Alcoholic Beverage Control Board as defendants in its Section 1983 suit, Grendel's Den was able to obtain from the Court a ruling on the constitutional merits of the law that gave churches the veto authority at issue.[89]

The second way to obtain a federal adjudication of the constitutional merits of a state law is to sue the primary injurer—even if a private party—in state court and seek review in the United States Supreme Court if and when the state court invokes the disputed state law to deny relief. To the degree that doctrines of official immunity necessitate suing only private actors, it becomes crucial to note the distinction the Supreme Court has drawn between private action that is *compelled* by the state and that which is merely *authorized or encouraged* by the state.[90] If the state law *mandates* a challenged private action, as in the case of a state rule that compels a liquor licensee to comply with its own racially restrictive constitution and bylaws,[91] then one may be able to obtain substantive consideration of the law in either a state *or* a federal court.[92] But if the state law merely *allows* the private actor to inflict injury—for instance, by cutting off one's electrical service[93] or selling one's stored furniture[94] without affording a hearing—but does not *mandate* that he do so, filing a state court suit is the necessary first step, since a federal court is likely to hold that the state is not implicated by its mere acquiescence in private behavior.[95] So long as the party injured or threatened with injury by a permissive state rule sues the private injurer in state court, and that tribunal then denies relief on the basis of the state rule, *that* invocation of the rule by the state court itself becomes "state action" reviewable on the merits by the Supreme Court.

The first clear indication that this was a viable approach came in Justice Stewart's concurring opinion in *Burton v. Wilmington Parking Authority.*[96] Although the majority of the Court held the coffee shop a state actor on its novel symbiosis analysis, Justice Stewart took the more direct approach of concluding that Delaware itself could be held accountable for Burton's ejection from the Eagle Coffee Shop inasmuch as the Delaware Supreme Court had upheld Eagle's "right" to deny Burton service because he was black by interpreting a state law as affirmatively authorizing racial discrimination.[97] Burton sued both the Eagle Coffee Shop and its landlord, the city of Wilmington, in state court. When the state supreme court denied him relief *by invoking a permissive state law* that it read to authorize acts of racism, Justice Stewart concluded that that judicial act was unconstitutional state action.

Similarly, had Ms. Brooks sued Flagg Brothers in a New York court to block its sale of her furniture, and had she then challenged, in an appeal to the Supreme Court, the New York court's invocation of the UCC self-help provision to deny her relief, the Supreme Court would have had to reach the merits of her claim since that state court deployment of the UCC would certainly have constituted "state action."[98]

Perhaps the strongest direct authority for the efficacy of this approach is the little-noted case of *Martinez v. California*.[99] There, a fifteen-year-old girl was murdered by a parolee. Her parents sued the California parole board, in the state's own courts, under 42 U.S.C. §1983.[100] The state court upheld a demurrer to the complaint on the basis of a California statute that conferred absolute immunity on parole boards for injuries caused by parolees.[101]

The Supreme Court unanimously held that the parolee's homicide was not itself action under color of law for purposes of Section 1983. Had the Court stopped there, *Martinez* would have looked like any number of decisions which, taken together, suggest that those individuals who are placed by the state in a position to do harm, and whose harmful conduct may even be encouraged by the state, are nonetheless *not* state actors under the Fourteenth Amendment. Yet the Court also unanimously held that for the California courts to refuse all relief, under Section 1983 or otherwise, on the grounds that the defendants were absolutely immune from liability for damages for actions of parolees, was to put at issue the state's immunity law: California may not be responsible for the acts of paroled killers, but it *is* responsible for its rules of tort immunity. Once those rules, or any others, are properly called into question in a case that reaches the Supreme Court, their validity must be ruled upon.[102] Thus, the *Martinez* Court held the immunity rules substantively valid but expressed no doubt that state action was indeed involved.

The same approach can be relied upon to obtain Supreme Court review on the merits at the behest of a defendant in state proceedings. In *Marsh v. Alabama*,[103] the Supreme Court reversed the state trespass conviction of a Jehovah's Witness who had distributed religious literature in a "company town" and been arrested by Alabama police at the behest of the town's corporate owners. The decision struck down the state's property laws to the extent they denied the protection of the First Amendment to the residents of company towns and those who wished to communicate with them. In *New York Times v. Sullivan*,[104] the Court did not hesitate to treat Alabama's common law of libel as state action and subject it to First Amendment scrutiny. A unanimous

Court did the same two decades later with respect to Mississippi tort law when it held, in *NAACP v. Claiborne Hardware Co.*,[105] that the state violated the First Amendment when it held individuals and organizations liable for damages for engaging in a peaceful economic boycott on public issues. In each case the state court invoked a state law that visited harm upon the defendants, who successfully challenged the constitutionality of that state action in the Supreme Court.

SHELLEY V. KRAEMER REVISITED

It is instructive to apply this dual-lens analysis to the most problematic and controversial of the state action cases: *Shelley v. Kraemer*.[106] The Court there held that Missouri's courts violated the Equal Protection Clause when they granted injunctive relief to litigants seeking to enforce privately negotiated, racially restrictive covenants.[107] The conventional wisdom has long viewed *Shelley* as unprincipled; critics charge that, by finding state action in mere enforcement by state courts of private contracts, the Court reduced the Fourteenth Amendment's state action requirement to a meaningless formality.[108] This approach gets off on the wrong foot by emphasizing the search for a "state actor," and thereby confuses the threshold issue of whether state courts are arms of the state with the substantive inquiry into whether those courts have transgressed the Fourteenth Amendment. The problem is not seeing that state courts are state actors—that, surely, is obvious. The problem is perceiving how the Missouri courts could violate the Constitution by "merely" enforcing a private system that citizens had imposed on themselves.

Shelley has typically been misread as holding that court-facilitated injury to black home-buyers from the state's neutral rule of enforcing all contracts without regard to racially harmful effects is sufficient to trigger strict scrutiny under the Equal Protection Clause,[109] and therefore that the Fourteenth Amendment requires the states to outlaw all private acts of racism whenever, as almost always, the individual might ultimately seek the security of judicial enforcement.[110] If *Shelley v. Kraemer* ever held anything so bold, it certainly does no longer, for in *Washington v. Davis*[111] and its progeny the Court declared that disparate adverse impact on a racial minority is not sufficient to make a facially neutral law or body of rules unconstitutional or even suspect.

For example, the state itself has committed no wrong if it enforces neutral trespass laws at the behest of a bigoted homeowner.[112]

A more fruitful mode of inquiry is to examine the property laws that the Missouri courts enforced in *Shelley* to determine whether they were, in fact, facially "neutral." Like other states, Missouri treats most restraints on the alienability of real estate as judicially unenforceable: to enforce any such restraint, a state court must first find that the *substance* of the restraining covenant is reasonable and consistent with public policy.[113] Therefore, the issue is not whether *any* judicial enforcement of racially invidious private arrangements constitutes racially invidious state action, but whether a state may *choose* automatically to enforce restrictive covenants that discriminate against blacks *while generally regarding alienability restraints as anathema.* The real "state action" in *Shelley* was Missouri's facially discriminatory body of common and statutory law—the quintessence of a racist state policy. The state court's refusal to invalidate the racist covenant before it was simply the overt state act necessary to bring the state's legal order to the bar of the United States Supreme Court.

This lesson of *Shelley* has not always been fully comprehended. The Court's selective amnesia on this subject may be best illustrated by the Court's consideration in 1982 of two cases in which states retreated on the extent to which they were willing to use mandatory pupil reassignment to remedy demographically caused segregation—segregation that was not demonstrably the result of affirmative government policy. Might such a state curb on busing that is not itself required by the Fourteenth Amendment (inasmuch as the Fourteenth Amendment addresses only state-caused segregation) nonetheless violate that amendment? The key precedent in answering that question is *Hunter v. Erickson.*[114] There the Court struck down an amendment to the city charter of Akron, Ohio, which had been adopted by an initiative procedure. The amendment required that henceforth all ordinances dealing with private discrimination in housing—discrimination by religion or race—had to be approved by a majority of the electorate. Although the law was in a sense facially neutral, the Court had no difficulty in striking it down under the Equal Protection Clause since it was obvious that it would place unique legal obstacles in the path of minorities seeking equal access to housing.

In 1978, Seattle School District No. 1 ordered extensive busing in order to counteract the segregative effects of a neighborhood school policy against the background of race-specific private choices of residence. In response, the electorate of the state of Washington passed Initiative 350, which broadly prohibited the assignment of pupils to other than the closest schools. A number of exceptions allowed pupil reassignment and busing to meet special educational needs and to avert overcrowding, but busing for specifically *racial* purposes was permitted only in the event that it was required by the Fourteenth Amendment pursuant to court order.[115] In what Justice Blackmun characterized as an "extraordinary" move,[116] the Seattle school board went to court and invoked the Fourteenth Amendment to defend its busing program from this state assault.

In *Washington v. Seattle School District No. 1*,[117] a sharply divided Court held that Initiative 350 was unconstitutional.[118] Writing for the Court, Justice Blackmun concluded that the principle of *Hunter v. Erickson* disposed of the case.[119] Just as the charter amendment in *Hunter* selectively removed the power to eliminate de facto housing discrimination from the Akron City Council and placed it in the hands of the city's electorate, Initiative 350 stripped the Seattle School District of the authority to remedy de facto school segregation and gave it to the voters of the entire state of Washington. Although it was neutral on its face, the Court had "little doubt that the initiative was effectively drawn for racial purposes."[120] Since it was riddled with exceptions to allow busing for almost every conceivable purpose other than racial integration, "the initiative expressly require[d] those championing school integration to surmount a considerably higher hurdle than persons seeking comparable legislative action."[121] By singling out a form of government action of particular interest to racial minorities and lifting it to a different and less accessible level of government, the Washington initiative changed the rules of the legal and political game in a way that put minorities at a distinct disadvantage.[122]

The facts in the companion case, *Crawford v. Board of Education of Los Angeles*,[123] seemed similar; the result was not. In the wake of state court decisions holding that the Equal Protection Clause of the California Constitution outlawed de facto as well as de jure segregation, California voters ratified Proposition I, an amendment to the state constitution that denied state courts the power to order busing to remedy school segregation except when a federal court would do so under the Fourteenth Amendment of the Federal Constitution.[124] When asked whether this change constituted an impermissible shift in legal-political structure like those in *Hunter* and *Seattle*, the Supreme Court answered "no" with only a single dissenting vote.[125]

Justice Powell, who wrote the dissent in *Seattle v. Washington* and had lamented the use of busing in *Estes v. Dallas NAACP*,[126] wrote the opinion for the Court in *Crawford*. He concluded that *Hunter v. Erickson* was not relevant since Proposition I was a change not in legal remedies but in substantive legal rights.[127] The voters of California had simply changed the state constitution that the courts enforce, and there is nothing in the Equal Protection Clause that prohibits the states from changing their minds and stepping back to the reduced level of protection guaranteed by the Fourteenth Amendment.[128]

In a concurring opinion, Justice Blackmun,[129] the author of the Court's opinion in *Seattle*, similarly argued that, unlike Initiative 350, California's Proposition I did not work a change in the *structure* of the political process—it "simply repeal[ed] the *right* to invoke a judicial busing remedy."[130] Those who sought busing in California were not ousted from a decision-making, policymaking forum; the substantive law that the state courts were applying had simply been redrawn. Justice Blackmun even invoked the view that courts do not create rights but merely enforce them.[131] Earlier in the same Term, however, Justice Blackmun had responded to Justice O'Connor's assertion that courts were mere oracles by characterizing them as "a co-equal part of the states' decision-making apparatus."[132]

In fact, the change wrought by Proposition I was strikingly analogous to that wrought by Initiative 350, or that wrought by the *Hunter* charter amendment. In *Crawford* the shift in authority was from the courts to the state legislature or the state electorate; in *Seattle*, from the local school board to the legislature or the electorate; and in *Hunter*, from the city council to the city's voters. The majority and concurring opinions in *Crawford* misconstrued the impact of Proposition I because of confusion over just what "right" was at issue. At stake was not some sort of derivative "right to invoke a judicial busing remedy,"[133] but a substantive, state-created "right to be free from racial isolation in the public schools."[134] As the majority repeatedly admitted,[135] Proposition I did *not* remove from the courts[136] the state constitutional obligation to combat such de facto segregation; it merely stripped the courts of the power to use mandatory pupil reassignment as a tool to that end. That change left the right in place but removed the major remedy to a different level of government: "After the adoption of Proposition I, the only method of enforcing against a recalcitrant school board the state constitutional duty to eliminate racial isolation is to petition either the state legislature or the electorate as a whole. Clearly, the rules of the game have been significantly changed."[137]

However one views the role of a state's courts, they are always subservient to the state's constitution. If that constitution is amended as it was in *Crawford*, the important question is whether the resulting change in the law, whether substantive or remedial or both, is *itself* consistent with the Fourteenth Amendment. If a state has a system of open-ended, judicially enforceable civil rights—dealing with everything from speech[138] to educational finance[139]—that are not mere copies of their Fourteenth Amendment counterparts, may the state pick out of this dynamic system the right to end racially isolated public education and relegate *that right alone* to the status of a federal facsimile? The answer to that question must be the same as the answer to the question of whether the state might, in the first place, establish dynamic judicial protection for all state-created rights *except* the right under the state's law to end de facto racial segregation in its schools. California's taking three legal steps forward and then one race-specific legal step back is the same as California's selectively omitting that one step at the outset.

The clearest precedent for saying that a state may do no such thing is, of course, *Shelley v. Kraemer*.[140] In *Shelley*, contracts restraining the alienability of property were not automatically enforceable under Missouri law. On the contrary, racially restrictive convenants were included by Missouri within the special subclass of restraints on alienability which the state's courts would *not* set aside as presumptively contrary to public policy. The Supreme Court's decision to strike down the Missouri court's enforcement of racially restrictive covenants in *Shelley*—despite the fact that other covenants such as those excluding whites (if any such covenants existed) were enforced along with covenants excluding blacks—meant that the Fourteenth Amendment required Missouri to make judicial invalidation of private agreements causing racial isolation just as available as judicial invalidation of *other* disfavored restraints on the free alienability of real property.

Since *Shelley*, like *Crawford*, could not meet the *Washington v. Davis*[141] standard by showing discriminatory intent in the creation of the legal rules at issue, *Shelley* survives *Davis* only if the Missouri law that selectively omitted judicial protection against private racial isolation in housing could be deemed *facially* invalid even without a showing of discriminatory intent. And if *Shelley v. Kraemer* is still correct, then

Crawford seems wrong inasmuch as it upholds a system of laws that selectively omits just such judicial protection against racial isolation— in
schooling rather than in housing.

Given the rising tide of popular as well as judicial dissatisfaction
with busing, *Crawford v. Los Angeles* should probably be understood as
more politically inevitable than legally intelligible and should not be
taken to cast doubt on those cases, such as *Shelley v. Kraemer*, that
have established that state endorsement of or acquiescence in "consensual," "private" ordering has its limits and may sometimes be state
action subject to constitutional restraints.[142] Such precedents remain
problematic because of a psychological and ideological predilection to
perceive the existence of a private sphere—albeit circumscribed by the
state—in which actions are autonomous. To see all social intercourse
as behavior conditioned by and therefore attributable to the state is to
deny the existence of a private realm. Many of us, therefore, cling to
such institutions as freedom of contract and private property, viewing
them as a natural, "given" part of the legal landscape which provides a
background for our private, consensual transactions.

It has, therefore, been an important step for the Court to recognize that, as long as litigation is properly structured, the legal landscape itself becomes challengeable state action. By this recognition,
the Court has opened the possibility of adjudicating on the merits the
allocation of power and privilege under what we have traditionally referred to as "private" law: contracts, torts, and property.[143]

It is helpful to think of the universe of state action as a circle, divided
into four quadrants. The first is implicated when the challenged state
action consists of the invocation of state law to award judicial relief
against a defendant in a private suit brought by a private actor. Thus,
the state of Alabama's award of damages against the *New York Times*
would have been state action, even if the plaintiff in the suit had not
been a government official.[144]

The second quadrant is implicated when the background state law
gives to a private party unusually government-like recourse to public
enforcement machinery, as in *Marsh v. Alabama*,[145] where the Gulf Oil
Company, as owner of Chickasaw, Alabama, was placed in a position
to have the state enforce the rules of a company town against leaflet-
ters.

The third quadrant includes the state action of placing a private
party in such a position that others have no alternative but to deal
with him. Thus, in *Jackson v. Metropolitan Edison Co.*,[146] although the

monopoly position in which the state had placed the power company was not enough to make that company a "state actor," there was no question that "state action" was involved in the selection of that particular power company as the only one from whom citizens could purchase electricity.

A fourth form of state action consists of the invocation of state law to authorize or immunize the offending act of a private party—and to deny those injured by the act any relief. The private party causing the injury, such as the warehouseman in *Flagg Brothers v. Brooks*,[147] remains private, but it is the state that acts to deny judicial relief according to its law.

The actions that fall into the second and third quadrants present litigants with the temptation to argue that the private actor has become a state actor; but, as we have seen above, current Supreme Court doctrine has greatly limited the scope of the symbiosis theory of *Burton v. Wilmington Parking Authority.*[148] Interestingly, the actions which fall into the fourth quadrant are, in essence, the flip side of those which fall into the first: either the state is acting by helping someone bring the force of law down on someone else or it is acting by denying someone judicial relief from private injury. This is not to say, of course, that all cases brought employing this approach to state action will meet with success on the merits. The Constitution often leaves the state free, as a substantive matter, to choose between the first and fourth quadrants. And there remain many other ways of slamming the door on the underlying substantive claim. Thus the Court may defer to economic custom by employing a minimal level of rationality review. For example, the dispossessed would doubtless meet with no success in attacking the constitutionality of private property as an institution. The present Court would presumably deny the existence of an affirmative duty on the part of government to rescue people from their economic plight or even to subsidize their meaningful enjoyment of various fundamental rights.[149]

But, however the Court chooses to rebuff assaults on the legal order's allocations of power, the constitutional validity of those allocations may at least be challenged on the merits in suitably structured litigation. And such litigation, even if ultimately unsuccessful, may help unmask the contingency of—and the state's complicity in—the patterns of social and economic domination that permeate and in part define our society. It is one thing for a court to uphold a problematic rule or system of rules after considering fully the challenges to its justification and tolerability; it is another, far worse, thing for a court to treat the political choices underlying a legal regime as unassailable by refusing even to recognize them as *choices*.

The unanimous decisions to reach the merits in *Prune Yard*,[150] *Martinez*,[151] and *Grendel's Den*[152] mean that litigants have gotten their feet in at least one doorway to the opportunity of challenging the constitutionality of large slices of the legal order; the Court can no longer easily slam that door shut by the use of state action doctrine. This is a development both welcome and overdue. For it would be ironic indeed if, in a nation that purports to have a "government of laws, and not of men,"[153] only individuals—and not the laws themselves—could be brought to the bar of justice and judged by the standards of the Constitution.

EPILOGUE

The Constitution presents all of us with an unending series of choices. We are called upon to choose what "the Constitution" is to *include*: Text? Intentions? (Whose?) Structural inferences? (Which ones?) Political and moral premises? (Of what sort?)

We are called upon also to choose how the Constitution by which we are bound is to be *regarded*: As a repository of past political compromises or a projection of future aspirations? As a device for assuring that nature's occasional distortions by law and government are corrected or as a mechanism for guaranteeing that nature's recurring reflections in law and government are at least subjected to criticism?

We are called upon finally to recognize and acknowledge the more particular choices that are made daily in the Constitution's name—choices of structure and procedure, made in the service of one or another vision of substance; choices of concrete meaning, rarely as constrained by circumstance as those who would escape accountability wish they could pretend; choices about what significance to attach to the actions or inactions of others on the constitutional stage, whether framers or contemporaries.

The pretense that such choices may be avoided by some interpretive or analytic magic—whether functioning as a solvent for the mists that obscure meaning or as a master plan which none of *us*, at least, is free to "choose" or to reject—is pervasive. To abandon that pretense is a beginning of wisdom, if only a small one. To abandon it is to begin the process of replacing arrogant certitudes about our often unshared pasts with a more open search for a shared future. But it is a future we are not free to share only with those who join us in dreaming of it. We are bound to share it with all those whose dreams have been entrusted into our care and all those whose fates we have the power to affect.

It has been said that we can be truly free to pursue our ends only if we act out of obligation, the seeming antithesis of freedom; to follow our everchanging wants wherever they might lead is license, but license is a pale shadow of liberty. To choose without losing the thread of continuity that makes us whole with those who came before, we must be able to reason about what to choose—to choose in terms of constitutive commitments we have made, however tentatively, to bodies of principle by which we feel bound, a constitutional system that endures even as it evolves.

We must make choices but must renounce the equally illusory freedom to choose however we might *wish* to choose. For it is a Constitution—a specific, necessarily imperfect Constitution—in whose terms we are, after all, choosing. And that is the paradox, the mystery, of the struggle we cannot avoid if it is the Constitution, and not solely our own priorities, that we would choose to follow, and to lead, into a better world.

Notes
Index of Cases
General Index

Notes

Preface

1. Recent examples abound. The Fourth Amendment promises that all shall be "secure" against unreasonable searches and seizures; this security is breached whenever judges permit courtroom use of evidence that police obtained in a forbidden search. Similarly, the Fifth Amendment promises that no one shall be tried on the basis of coerced testimony; that promise is broken whenever judges allow into evidence confessions extracted during police custody that is inherently coercive because there have been no warnings about the rights to silence and counsel. Whether the police searched a home in "good faith" reliance on an illegal warrant, or questioned someone coercively solely to preserve "public safety," may be relevant to whether the police should be condemned for what they did, but neither their good faith nor the reasonableness of their concern for the public's protection has any plausible bearing on whether trial judges should be allowed to erode the security guaranteed by the Fourth Amendment or the dignity assured by the Fifth. Yet the Supreme Court found the "benefits" of excluding evidence to be zero when it was obtained illegally but in good faith, see United States v. Leon, 52 U.S.L.W. 5155 (1984), or coercively but to protect the public, see New York v. Quarles, 104 S. Ct. 2626 (1984), simply because the police in such cases acted reasonably and thus should not (see *Quarles*) or could not (see *Leon*) be deterred by the threat of exclusion. Thus, to the Court, *any* tangible "costs" of enforcing these constitutional guarantees would exceed the more nebulous "benefits" of vindicating the Fourth and Fifth Amendments in good faith and public safety cases. In the Court's view, the amendments are unable to "pay [their] way." *Leon*, 52 U.S.L.W. at 5157 n.6. Justice White delivered the opinion of the Court enunciating the "good faith" exception to the exclusionary rule in *Leon*. Justices Brennan, Marshall, and Stevens dissented. Justice Rehnquist wrote the opinion in *Quarles* which created the "public safety" exception to the rule of *Miranda v. Arizona*, 384 U.S. 436 (1966). Justice O'Connor filed an opinion concurring in part in the judgment and dissenting in part; Justices Marshall, Brennan, and Stevens dissented.

   Mesmerized by this cost-benefit language, which Justice Brennan warned in dissent creates an "illusion of technical precision and ineluctability," United States v. Leon, supra at 5163 (Brennan, J., dissenting); cf. Tribe, "Policy Science: Analysis or Ideology?" 2 *Philosophy and Public Affairs* 66, 97 (1972), the Court ignored those purposes of the Fourth and Fifth Amendments that address the judiciary itself rather than simply the police, and that cannot be neatly reduced to conjectures about deterrence.

2. Thus, in a manner suggestive of its cost-benefit approach, the Supreme Court has adopted the tendency of managers and bureaucrats to assume that their own conduct has been exemplary, and to measure their options only at the margin—asking what each option would add to, or subtract from, their latest actions rather than how the option squares with basic principles. For example, in upholding a city's authority to maintain a nativity scene in the center of town (while according no similar honor to any other religion's sacred symbols) in Lynch v. Donnelly, 104 S. Ct. 1355 (1984), the Court favorably compared the resulting aid to Christianity with forms of aid the Court had recently endorsed—such as state-paid legislative chaplains in Marsh v. Chambers, 103 S. Ct. 3336 (1983)—rather than seriously considering whether the challenged practice could be reconciled with government's First Amendment duty of religious neutrality.

Those who justify what they do today by calling it a small step beyond what they did yesterday may soon wander far indeed from their original commitments; what economist Alfred E. Kahn once dubbed the "tyranny of small decisions," 19 KYKLOS: *International Review for Social Sciences* 23 (Fasc. 1, 1966), is being transposed from bureaucratic life to an institution whose reason for being is its supposed commitment to first principles—the independent judiciary.

A correlative tendency of managers and administrators—to present each new grab for power as a trivial variant of power they already enjoy—has likewise been assimilated into the Supreme Court's increasingly sympathetic response to executive claims. Thus, despite the long-standing constitutional principle that a citizen's freedom to travel abroad may not be curtailed without clear authorization from Congress, see Kent v. Dulles, 357 U.S. 116 (1958), discussed in chapter 4, this Term the Court upheld President Reagan's virtual ban on tourist travel to Cuba despite a 1977 Act of Congress that the four dissenting justices read as forbidding such action absent a presidential declaration of national emergency and, if possible, consultation with Congress. Regan v. Wald, 52 U.S.L.W. 4966 (1984). Justice Rehnquist delivered the opinion of the Court; Justices Blackmun, Brennan, Marshall, and Powell dissented. The Court's rationale was that the ban was nothing new; it was but a variation of the preexisting ban on trade with Cuba in cigars and other goods. Cigars, people—a mere shift in commodities: less the perspective of a court dedicated to liberty and respectful of Congress' role than of a ministry of foreign trade carrying out the executive's will.

Nor has the Court's reductive treatment of human beings as little more than objects for efficient executive management stopped with restraints on travel: it has extended to the elimination of all rights of privacy in prison cells, for persons awaiting trial as well as those convicted. Thus the Court upheld, as a minor extension of prior rulings, e.g., Bell v. Wolfish, 441 U.S. 520 (1979), the power of prison authorities to destroy, however maliciously, all of a prisoner's personal papers, from a photograph of a child to a letter from a spouse, see Hudson v. Palmer, 52 U.S.L.W. 5051 (1984), and to forbid all physical contacts with visiting family members, see Block v. Rutherford, 52 U.S.L.W. 5063 (1984). In the words of Justice Stevens, the Court effectively declared "prisoners to be little more than chattels," according them *no* measure of human dignity while incarcerated, in the name of efficient jail administration. Hudson v. Palmer, 52 U.S.L.W. at 5062 (dissenting opinion).

1. The Futile Search for Legitimacy

1. TWA v. Franklin Mint Corp., 52 U.S.L.W. 4445, 4455 (U.S. April 17, 1984) (Stevens, J., dissenting).

2. Id. (footnote omitted); id. at 4455 n.12 (arguing that, although "[j]udges, of course, must perform a lawmaking function, . . . the limits of [judicial] authority and . . . ability to develop the law should always be respected").

3. E.g., J. Ely, *Democracy and Distrust* (1980).

4. E.g., M. Perry, *The Constitution, the Courts, and Human Rights* (1982) [hereinafter cited as Perry].

5. Judicial power to go beyond the specific text as needed to enhance, say, the truly "representative" character of the political process leads readily to judicial authority to protect the autonomy of independent centers of value formation (lest the government "represent" only the views it has itself nudged people into holding) and hence to protect small-group privacy and intimacy and decentralized educational opportunities as aspects of the American ideal of personal development and dignity. Conversely, judicial power to enforce that ideal extratextually leads readily to judicial authority to protect effective political participation and meaningfully representative self-government as the only political structures genuinely compatible with the dignity and self-respect of individuals and groups.

6. See chapter 6.

7. See United States v. Brown, 381 U.S. 437 (1965), discussed in L. Tribe, *American Constitutional Law* §§10–4, 10–5, at 484–93 (1978).

8. New York Times Co. v. Sullivan, 376 U.S. 255 (1964).

9. Thus, I mean to go beyond the notion that legitimacy is the product, rather than the ground or premise, of constitutional practice, see P. Bobbitt, *Constitutional Fate* 3, 181, 237–38 (1982); I regard the very search for "legitimacy," and for the repose it promises, as a pastime to be resisted.

10. Cf. Parker, "The Past of Constitutional Theory—And Its Future," 42 *Ohio St. L.J.* 223 (1981).

11. Roe v. Wade, 410 U.S. 113 (1973).

12. E.g., Ely, "The Wages of Crying Wolf: A Comment on *Roe v. Wade*," 82 *Yale L.J.* 920 (1973).

13. E.g., Perry, supra note 4.

14. Judges might see themselves in this reassuring light when convinced that they are "merely" carrying out the will of the framers; or "simply" removing obstacles to the fair workings of democracy; or "only" detecting, more disinterestedly than those who seek reelection could, the ethos latent in the American experi-

ence; or doing whatever else it is that some legitimating theory sets up as clearly right for unelected judges to do.

15. See R. Nozick, *Philosophical Explanations* 1–24 (1981).

2. The Pointless Flight from Substance

1. The best known statement of this view by the Supreme Court was written by Justice Stone in United States v. Carolene Prods. Co., 304 U.S. 144, 152 n.4 (1938): "It is unnecessary to consider now whether legislation which restricts those political processes which can ordinarily be expected to bring about repeal of undesirable legislation, is to be subjected to more exacting judicial scrutiny under the general prohibition of the Fourteenth Amendment than are most other types of legislation . . . Nor need we enquire whether similar considerations enter into the review of statutes directed at particular religious, . . . or national, . . . or racial minorities . . .; whether prejudice against discrete and insular minorities may be a special condition, which tends seriously to curtail the operation of those political processes ordinarily to be relied upon to protect minorities, and which may call for a correspondingly more searching judicial inquiry."

2. The doctrinal forms in which the Supreme Court expresses its decisions at least sometimes support the view that the Court is attempting to portray itself as working *with*, or at least not *against*, Congress or state legislatures. Judicial review should continue to leave room for legislative action or so, at least, Justice Jackson suggested in defending equal protection analysis. See Railway Express Agency v. New York, 336 U.S. 106, 111–12 (1949) (Jackson, J., concurring) (preferring use of Equal Protection Clause to use of Due Process Clause to invalidate legislation, as former leaves government option of drafting more equitably framed legislation to regulate conduct). Some commentators have thought that a similar idea partly explained the appeal (for a time) of the First Amendment overbreadth doctrine. See, e.g., G. Gunther, *Constitutional Law* 1134 (1975).

3. See, e.g., L. Lusky, *By What Right?* (1975); Ball, "Judicial Protection of Powerless Minorities," 59 *Iowa L. Rev.* 1059 (1974); Black, "The Unfinished Business of the Warren Court," 46 *Wash. L. Rev.* 3, 8–9 (1970); Brest, "The Supreme Court, 1975 Term—Foreword: In Defense of the Antidiscrimination Principle," 90 *Harv. L. Rev.* 1, 6–12 (1976); Fiss, "Groups and the Equal Protection Clause," in *Equality and Preferential Treatment* 85, 130 (M. Cohen, T. Nagel & T. Scanlon eds. 1977); Karst, "The Supreme Court, 1976 Term—Foreword: Equal Citizenship Under the Fourteenth Amendment," 91 *Harv. L. Rev.* 1, 8–10, 24–26 (1977); Tribe, "Structural Due Process," 10 *Harv. C.R.-C.L. L. Rev.* 269 (1975); Note, "Mental Illness: A Suspect Classification?", 83 *Yale L.J.* 1237 (1974). See generally Rostow, "The Democratic Character of Judicial Review," 66 *Harv. L. Rev.* 193 (1952). Sometimes the concern for process is coupled with an effort to ground constitutional law in fundamental values, such as respect for individual dignity. See, e.g., Brest, supra, at 11 (prevention of stigmatic harms to particular individuals supports antidiscrimination principle in equal protection doctrine); Karst, supra, at 8 (participation in community decision-making processes contributes to self-respect).

4. J. Ely, *Democracy and Distrust* 87 (1980) (footnotes omitted) [hereinafter cited as Ely].

5. See B. Bailyn, *The Ideological Origins of the American Revolution* 246–72 (1967).

6. See Note, "The Thirteenth Amendment and Private Affirmative Action," 89 *Yale L.J.* 399, 406 (1979) (framers of amendment intended to guarantee blacks "meaningful freedom" by obliterating all vestiges of slavery). To say that the nation's experience with slavery shows the folly of incorporating substantive matters in the Constitution, see Ely, supra note 4, at 93, 100, 226 n.68, is simply to invert the lessons of our history.

7. Just compensation cases, arising under the Constitution or under statutes that Congress and the state legislatures have adopted in response to constitutional requirements, are a steady and continuing part of the business of the courts. See generally B. Ackerman, *Private Property and the Constitution* (1977).

8. Contracts clause cases, rarer than just compensation cases, are often thought to be less important because the clause itself imposes no significant restriction. The conventional view is that the Supreme Court, in limiting the clause's protection to that against retroactive legislation, see Ogden v. Saunders, 25 U.S. (12 Wheat.) 213, 303 (1827), had long rendered the clause less significant. The traditional learning holds that whatever residual importance the clause retained has all but disappeared. See Home Bldg. & Loan Ass'n v. Blaisdell, 290 U.S. 389 (1934) (reasonable legislation, even if retroactive, disturbs no legitimate expectation interest of contracting parties). The Court, however, has on some one hundred occasions since *Ogden* voided state statutes and municipal ordinances under the clause. Moreover, the Court that decided *Blaisdell* did not act as if that decision vitiated the clause. See, e.g., Wood v. Lovett, 313 U.S. 362 (1941) (state law that removed procedural rights from purchasers at a tax sale violates clause); Indiana ex rel. Anderson v. Brand, 303 U.S. 95 (1938) (state teacher tenure law held to have created a binding obligation under clause). Indeed, the Court has very recently invalidated state legislation under the Contracts Clause. See, e.g., Allied Structural Steel Co. v. Spannaus, 438 U.S. 234 (1978); United States Trust Co. v. New Jersey, 431 U.S. 1 (1977).

9. See, e.g., Coppage v. Kansas, 236 U.S. 1 (1915) (protecting employer's constitutional right under Due Process Clause to choose not to hire union member employees); Lochner v. New York, 198 U.S. 45 (1905) (invalidating maximum-hour work laws as violative of contractual liberties protected by Constitution).

10. See, e.g., Whitney v. California, 274 U.S. 357, 373 (1927) (Brandeis, J., concurring); Ely, supra note 4, at 18 ("[T]here is simply no avoiding the fact that the word that follows 'due' is 'process.'").

11. See, e.g., Hurtado v. California, 110 U.S. 516, 535–36 (1884): "It is not every act, legislative in form, that is law. Law is something more than mere will exerted as an act of power. It must not be a special rule for a particular person or a particular case, . . . thus excluding, as not due process of law, acts of attainder, bills of pains and penalties, acts of confiscation, acts reversing judgments, and acts directly transferring one man's estate to another, legislative judgments and decrees, and other similar special, partial and arbitrary exertions of power under the forms of legislation."

The form that substantive due process analysis took has recently begun to receive scholarly attention. See Kennedy, "The Structure of Blackstone's Commentaries," 28 *Buffalo L. Rev.* 205 (1979); Miller, "The Forest of Due Process of Law: The American Constitutional Tradition," in *Due Process: Nomos XVIII* 3 (J. Pennock & J. Chapman eds. 1977). "Due process *of law*" was elaborated through a theory of legislation founded upon ideals of separation of powers. The theory distinguished legislation from adjudication by assigning to adjudication the task of rearranging vested rights; it distinguished among types of legislation by asking whether the various types infringed vested rights; and it identified vested rights by treating the common law as a mirror of individual expectations, by regarding that which the common law protected—liberty of contract, for example—as something that individuals rightly presupposed and upon which individuals justifiably relied. See T. Cooley, *Constitutional Limitations* 500–75 (7th ed. 1903).

The form of the old substantive due process doctrine is important here for two reasons. That the doctrine *had* form—and a form that drew upon such traditional sources of legal principles as ideas about the common law and separation of powers—suggests that the substantive due process cases were not some mad judicial tear, which we may today safely and gladly forget. See L. Tribe, *American Constitutional Law* §8–2 (1978) [hereinafter cited as Tribe, *ACL*]. Moreover, the fact that the form of the doctrine drew in part upon separation-of-powers concepts illustrates a more general point: the Constitution may *appear* in large part to address the structure and arrangement of government—process writ large and small—but the concerns that *underlie* and *explain* the structures and arrangements ordained by the Constitution are themselves undeniably substantive.

12. See Wood, "Rhetoric and Reality in the American Revolution," 23 *Wm. & Mary Q.* 3 (3d ser. 1966).

13. See, e.g., *The Federalist* no. 10 (J. Madison).

14. For example, witness which responsibilities the framers gave to the federal government—particularly the power to regulate interstate and foreign commerce. See *U.S. Const.*, art. I, §8, cl. 3. Many of the prohibitions of art. I, §10, also have an economic cast: "No state shall . . . coin Money; emit Bills of Credit; make any Thing but gold and silver Coin a Tender in Payment of Debts; pass any . . . Law impairing the Obligation of Contracts . . . No State shall, without the Consent of Congress, lay any Imposts or Duties on Imports or Exports . . . No State shall, without the Consent of Congress, lay any Duty of Tonnage."

15. See *The Federalist* no. 10, at 79 (C. Rossiter ed. 1961) ("But the most common and durable source of factions has been the various and unequal distribution of property. Those who hold, and those who are without property, have ever formed distinct interests in society. Those who are creditors, and those who are debtors, fall under a like discrimination."); G. Wood, *The Creation of the American Republic* 503–04 (1969) (federal bicameralism as means of protecting minority property rights).

It is a mistake to view the concern of the Federalists with property rights in contemporary terms. Property rights in the late eighteenth century partook more of status than of exchange; debtor legislation was perceived as threatening not only because it represented the loss of wealth but also because it portended the triumph of the "licentious," the disruption of an order of virtue and merit in society. See id. at 393–425. Yet, even if the concern with property is recast in eighteenth-century terms, the protection of individual property rights remains intact as an aim of the Constitution. See id. at 609 ("The liberty that was now emphasized was personal or private, the protection of individual rights against all governmental encroachments, particularly by the legislature . . . Government was no longer designed merely to promote the collective happiness of the people, but also . . . 'to protect citizens in their personal liberty and their property.'")

16. See, e.g., *U.S. Const.*, art. I, §§2, 3.

17. See, e.g., id., art. II, §1.

18. See, e.g., Reynolds v. Sims, 377 U.S. 533, 568 (1964) (Equal Protection Clause requires apportionment of state legislative seats by population).

19. See, e.g., Bi-Metallic Inv. Co. v. State Bd. of Equalization, 239 U.S. 441 (1915) (no hearing necessary before assessments of all taxable property uniformly increased); Londoner v. City of Denver, 210 U.S. 373 (1908) (hearing required before costs of local improvements are assessed to property owners on the basis of relative benefit).

20. See, e.g., Cleveland Bd. of Educ. v. LaFleur, 414 U.S. 632, 645 (1974) (mandatory maternity-leave rules that create an irrebuttable presumption violate Due Process Clause in failing to recognize individual differences); Stanley v. Illinois, 405 U.S. 645, 656–57 (1972) (statute containing irrebuttable presumption that all unmarried fathers are incompetent to raise children is unconstitutionally overbroad). For a discussion of these and related cases, see Tribe, *ACL* §16–32.

21. See, e.g., Lockett v. Ohio, 438 U.S. 586, 605 (1978) (Eighth and Fourteenth Amendments require death penalty statutes to permit individualized consideration of mitigating factors for each defendant); Woodson v. North Carolina, 428 U.S. 280, 304 (1976) (opinion of Stewart, Powell, and Stevens, JJ.) (process must treat offenders on individualized basis in capital cases); Gregg v. Georgia, 428 U.S. 153, 197–98 (1976) (death penalty held constitutional when statute is drafted to ensure jury consideration of individual circumstances of crime and offender).

22. 438 U.S. 265, 320 (1978) (Powell, J., announcing judgment of the Court) (relying on "personal rights" theory of Equal Protection Clause to invalidate racial quotas in medical school admission); see chapter 14.

23. See, e.g., City of Eastlake v. Forest City Enterprises, Inc., 426 U.S. 668, 676–77 (1976). But see Tribe, *ACL* §10–5, at 493–95.

24. See Steele v. Louisville & N.R.R., 323 U.S. 192, 202 (1944).

25. See, e.g., Hines v. Anchor Motor Freight, Inc., 424 U.S. 554, 563–64 (1976); Vaca v. Sipes, 386 U.S. 171, 182 (1967).

26. See, e.g., Miranda v. Arizona, 384 U.S. 436, 457–58 (1966) ("incommunicado interrogation" is "destructive of human dignity" and conflicts with privilege

against self-incrimination); Green v. United States, 355 U.S. 184, 187 (1957) ("underlying idea" behind guarantee against double jeopardy "is that the State . . . should not be allowed to make repeated attempts to convict an individual for an alleged offense, thereby subjecting him to embarrassment, expense and ordeal and compelling him to live in a continuing state of anxiety and insecurity").

27. Payton v. New York, 455 U.S. 573, 586–88 (1980) (absent exigent circumstances, Fourth Amendment requires warrant to arrest person in home even with probable cause); Griswold v. Connecticut, 381 U.S. 479, 485 (1965) (Fourth Amendment implies "right to privacy"); Boyd v. United States, 116 U.S. 616, 630 (1886) (Fourth Amendment applies to all government invasions of "the sanctity of a man's home and the privacies of life"). That privacy alone cannot account for the Fourth Amendment (see Ely, supra note 4, at 96, 172) obviously does not show that procedural concerns alone—such as limiting official discretion—can suffice to explain it. But see id. at 97.

28. See generally Packer, "Two Models of the Criminal Process," 113 *U. Pa. L. Rev.* 1, 6–23 (1964) (tension in criminal process between crime control model—seeking efficient, expeditious, and reliable screening and disposition of persons suspected of crimes—and due process model—seeking maintenance of dignity and autonomy of individual).

29. See generally C. Fried, *An Anatomy of Values* 125–32 (1970) (criminal procedure has "expressive aspects" and implicitly evidences societal ends).

30. One difficulty with a positivist theory of entitlements is that, if the Constitution requires government to deliver *only* what it promises, government is likely to respond by promising little. The present confusion in the law of procedural due process is strikingly illustrated by the Supreme Court's failure to require even the government to honor its procedural commitments. See, e.g., United States v. Caceres, 440 U.S. 741 (1979) (evidence obtained by method contrary to agency regulations not excluded under exclusionary rule).

31. See, e.g., Vitek v. Jones, 445 U.S. 480, 489–91 (1980); Carey v. Piphus, 435 U.S. 247, 266 (1978); Arnett v. Kennedy, 416 U.S. 134 (1974).

32. See, e.g., Michelman, "Formal and Associational Aims in Procedural Due Process," in *Due Process: Nomos XVIII* 126, 127 (J. Pennock & J. Chapman eds. 1977) (due process vindicates substantive values of "participation" and "revelation"); Saphire, "Specifying Due Process Values: Toward a More Responsive Approach to Procedural Protection," 127 *U. Pa. L. Rev.* 111, 117–25 (1978) (due process standard should measure whether conduct in question comports with basic notions of fairness and dignity). Values like accuracy do not by themselves justify a constitutional right to procedural due process. "Accuracy" is inevitably an instrumental concept. To give it content, to decide which procedures a concern for accuracy requires, we must look to the entitlement in question. The legislature, in drafting the statute conferring the entitlement, may deliberately define it in ambiguous terms. If the entitlement is not precisely defined, a concern for accuracy presumably would not result in elaborate procedure. Thus, an instrumentalist approach leaves an opening for positivism.

33. What process is due depends on what is at stake in a given case. The interest at stake is pertinent to what procedures, in a given circumstance, are consistent with individual dignity. See, e.g., Cafeteria & Restaurant Workers Local 473 v. McElroy, 367 U.S. 886, 895 (1961) (consideration of what procedures due process may require under any given set of circumstances must begin with determination of private interest affected); Note, "Specifying the Procedures Required by Due Process: Toward Limits on the Use of Interest Balancing," 88 *Harv. L. Rev.* 1510, 1528–30 (1975) (process due depends on interest at stake).

34. See Ely, supra note 4, at 95–96.

35. See *U.S. Const.*, amends. XV, XIX, XXIII, XXVI.

36. See City of Phoenix v. Kolodziejski, 399 U.S. 204 (1970) (franchise cannot be limited to property owners); Kramer v. Union Free School Dist. No. 15, 395 U.S. 621 (1969) (franchise in school board election cannot be limited to property owners and parents); Holt Civic Club v. City of Tuscaloosa, 439 U.S. 60 (1978) (nonresidents can be denied vote even in jurisdiction that taxes and regulates them); Rosberg, "Aliens and Equal Protection: Why Not the Right to Vote?" 75 *Mich. L. Rev.* 1092 (1977).

37. See "Developments in the Law—The Constitution and the Family," 93 *Harv. L. Rev.* 1156, 1201–02, 1221–42, 1350–83 (1980) [hereinafter cited as Developments].

38. Conventionally, it is treated as if it were a matter of procedure. See, e.g., Ely, supra note 4, at 98–99.

39. Consider the question of whether fetuses are persons with rights, a question raised by the right-to-life critique of Roe v. Wade, 410 U.S. 113 (1973). See Tribe, *ACL* §15–10, at 926–29.

40. See Town of Lockport v. Citizens for Community Action at the Local Level, Inc., 430 U.S. 259 (1977) (sustaining constitutionality of electoral procedures requiring concurrent majorities for restructuring constituent political units).

41. See Salyer Land Co. v. Tulare Lake Basin Water Storage Dist., 410 U.S. 719 (1973) (sustaining rule tantamount to "one acre, one vote" in composition of special water districts).

42. See, e.g., Reynolds v. Sims, 377 U.S. 533, 567–68 (1964).

43. See R. Dworkin, *Taking Rights Seriously* 273 (1977).

44. See, e.g., Ely, supra note 4, at 124.

45. Nor can such theorists rest with a view that accepts a purely instrumental role for procedural norms and defends the constitutional plan as an indirect scheme for implementing substantive values that are not authoritatively established by the Constitution itself. For if the realization of such substantive values is the Constitution's aim, then their elaboration is appropriately the task of all who would interpret the Constitution.

46. See McCulloch v. Maryland, 17 U.S. (4 Wheat.) 316, 435–36 (1819) (state has no power to tax federal instrumentality because it would thereby act on national population, not represented in its legislature).

47. United States v. Carolene Prods. Co., 304 U.S. 144, 152 n.4 (1938) (strict judicial review for statutes that are directed against "discrete and insular minorities"); South Carolina State Highway Dep't. v. Barnwell Bros., 303 U.S. 177, 184 n.2 (1938) (Commerce Clause may prohibit legislation burdening political outsiders).

48. See Ely, "The Chief," 88 Harv. L. Rev. 11, 12 (1974) (Warren sought to ensure that machinery of democratic process does not become self-serving organ of privileged class).

49. See, e.g., L. Lusky, supra note 3, at 11–12; Tribe, ACL, passim.

50. See Ely, supra note 4, at 135–79.

51. See id. at 153–70.

52. Fiss, "The Supreme Court, 1978 Term—Foreword: The Forms of Justice," 93 Harv. L. Rev. 1, 8 (1979); see Sugarman v. Dougall, 413 U.S. 634, 657 (1973) (Rehnquist, J., dissenting) (no "extraordinary ingenuity" needed for lawyers to "find 'insular and discrete' minorities at every turn in the road").

53. Immutability by itself is plainly not sufficient. Intelligence, height, and strength are all immutable for a particular individual, but legislation that distinguishes on the basis of these criteria is not generally thought to be constitutionally suspect. Discreteness and insularity are also insufficient: chiropractors may be a discrete and insular minority, but legislation that singles them out would not be subject to strict scrutiny on that basis alone. Even all three factors in combination may not be sufficient. Old age is an immutable characteristic, and the elderly may well be a discrete and insular minority. However, age is not per se a suspect criterion or classification. See Massachusetts Bd. of Retirement v. Murgia, 427 U.S. 307 (1976) (per curiam). For background discussion, see Tribe, ACL §16–29.

54. Alienage is properly treated as a classification at least partially suspect, despite its mutable character. See, e.g., Nyquist v. Mauclet, 432 U.S. 1 (1977) (denying state scholarship aid to resident aliens who choose to remain noncitizens violates equal protection). And even if race or gender became readily mutable by biomedical means, I would suppose that laws burdening those who choose to remain black or female would properly remain constitutionally suspect.

55. This point is neatly illustrated by a passage quoted by Foucault, in which Borges cites a Chinese encyclopedia's assertion that "animals are divided into: (a) belonging to the Emperor, (b) embalmed, (c) tame, (d) sucking pigs, (e) sirens, (f) fabulous, (g) stray dogs, (h) included in the present classification, (i) frenzied, (j) innumerable, (k) drawn with a very fine camelhair brush, (l) et cetera, (m) just having broken the water pitcher, (n) that from a long way off look like flies." M. Foucault, The Order of Things xv (1970).

56. See W. Jordan, White over Black (1968).

57. See C.V. Woodward, The Strange Career of Jim Crow (2d ed. 1966).

58. Individuals who disapprove of the options that society presents them may nevertheless accept their treatment as a differentiated group and accept as natural or inevitable their inferior status. Even individuals with options more favorable than those of most group members may accept the social characterization of the group in order to differentiate themselves from the group. See Castaneda v. Par-

tida, 430 U.S. 482, 503 (1977) (Marshall, J., concurring); cf. G. Weinberg, *Society and the Healthy Homosexual* 74–82 (1972) (homosexual self-loathing, contempt, and prejudice parallel societal attitudes).

59. Thus, some blacks may differentiate themselves as a way of rejecting, or of expressing a critical judgment about, the options with which society at large leaves them.

60. See Fiss, supra note 3, at 124–33; cf. G. Myrdal, *An American Dilemma* 27–30 (1944).

61. See Ely, "The Constitutionality of Reverse Racial Discrimination," 41 *U. Chi. L. Rev.* 723, 732 (1974).

62. See Ely, supra note 4, at 154.

63. See Rivera, "Our Straight-Laced Judges: The Legal Position of Homosexual Persons in the United States," 30 *Hastings L.J.* 799 (1979).

64. See Ely, supra note 4, at 163 ("serious social costs" of encountering prejudice upon admission); C. Reich, *The Sorcerer of Bolinas Reef* 71–73 (1976) (fear of societal opprobrium caused repression of homosexuality). But see L. Humphreys, *Out of the Closets* (1972) (chronicling organizational activism, political action, and violence by homosexuals in response to oppression).

65. See, e.g., Doe v. Commonwealth's Attorney for City of Richmond, 403 F.Supp. 1199, 1203 (E.D. Va. 1975), *aff'd mem.*, 425 U.S. 901 (1976) ("ancestry" of state statute prohibiting sodomy goes back to Judaic and Christian law); Barrett, "Legal Homophobia and the Christian Church," 30 *Hastings L.J.* 1019 (1979) (arguing that Christian morality is responsible for legal homophobia).

66. See Karst, "The Freedom of Intimate Association," 89 *Yale L.J.* 624, 633–35 (1980).

67. See Developments, supra note 37, at 1176 n.119.

68. See, e.g., Craig v. Boren, 429 U.S. 190, 210 n.23 (1976) (dictum) (disapproving earlier decision that upheld occupational exclusions of women); Loving v. Virginia, 388 U.S. 1 (1967) (invalidating ban on racial intermarriage). If, as some suggest (see, e.g., Ely, supra note 4, at 256 n.92), a governmental decision to impose a burden could be defended simply by showing that the decision reflects "a bona fide feeling that [the burdened choice] is immoral," id., then even racial segregation would be sustainable.

69. Even assuming that laws burdening groups such as women are founded on no moral convictions, a process-based analysis is still fatally inadequate. Although legislation discriminating against women need not (at least superficially) reflect hostility toward women, and despite the fact that women are not a minority, there is nonetheless reason (a process theorist might argue) for strict judicial scrutiny of such legislation. Male legislators no doubt frequently regard women as "they" rather than "we." See Ely, supra note 4, at 164. In process terms, however, this is a weak case. Arguably, all that keeps women from full participation is the fact that many women (as well as men) accept a view of society in which women are subject to men or are otherwise inappropriate participants in public life. But that view of society is increasingly controversial. To conclude that women are an "excluded" group is simply to challenge the support of many

women and men for contemporary legislation. Thus, only sexist laws enacted long enough ago may be struck down as mere expressions of prejudicial stereotypes. See id. at 166–67.

Disputes over the place of women, however, are hardly a recent development. See E. Pagels, *The Gnostic Gospels* 59–63 (1979) (tracing Gnostic treatment of women as equals); A. Kelly, *Eleanor of Aquitaine and the Four Kings* 163–64 (1950) (women of late twelfth-century Poitevin court sat in judgment upon points of courtly love). The fact of contemporary dispute is thus not necessarily a sign of progress. But if the idea of equal rights for women is a perpetually contested concept, then the constitutionality of legislation that treats men and women differently cannot turn, as process theorists might argue, on whether such legislation preceded or followed dispute about the status of women.

70. See, e.g., Orr v. Orr, 440 U.S. 268 (1979) (state statutory scheme cannot exempt women from alimony obligations imposed on men).

71. Neither drinking age, see Craig v. Boren, 429 U.S. 190 (1976), nor age of expiration of parental support obligations, see Stanton v. Stanton, 421 U.S. 7 (1975), involve independently fundamental rights; but in both areas the Supreme Court has invalidated gender-based lines that lock the sexes into their traditional roles.

72. See Ely, supra note 4, at 105–34.

73. See A. Meiklejohn, *Free Speech and Its Relation to Self-Government* 27 (1948).

74. See, e.g., Tribe, ACL §12–7; Ely, supra note 4, at 113 n. *; chapter 13.

75. See Yudof, "When Governments Speak: Toward a Theory of Government Expression and the First Amendment," 57 *Tex. L. Rev.* 863 (1979).

76. See Buckley v. Valeo, 424 U.S. 1 (1976); San Antonio Independent School Dist. v. Rodriguez, 411 U.S. 1 (1973). But see Serrano v. Priest, 5 Cal. 3d 584,487 P.2d 1241, 96 *Cal. Rptr.* 601 (1971) (interpreting state constitution as creating a cause of action for violation of equal protection in suit to invalidate local property tax funding of public schools).

77. Compare, e.g., Moore v. City of East Cleveland, 431 U.S. 494 (1977) (protecting extended families) with Village of Belle Terre v. Boraas, 416 U.S. 1 (1974) (households of unrelated individuals not protected); compare NAACP v. Button, 371 U.S. 415 (1963) (group legal services protected) with Garcia v. Texas State Bd. of Medical Examiners, 384 F.Supp. 434 (W.D. Tex. 1974), *aff'd mem.*, 421 U.S. 995 (1975) (group health plans not).

78. Ely notes this phenomenon in connection with his discussion of the idea of progress as an organizing basis for constitutional law: "[T]oday's judicial decision (no matter what its source of judgment) will inevitably have an important influence on the values of tomorrow's majority." Ely, supra note 4, at 70. Cf. id. at 165 (societal stereotypes accepted by the stereotyped). He does not, however, generalize this insight to government action generally.

79. See Linde, " 'Clear and Present Danger' Reexamined: Dissonance in the *Brandenburg* Concerto," 22 *Stan. L. Rev.* 1163 (1970); Linde, "Due Process of Lawmaking," 55 *Neb. L. Rev.* 197 (1976).

80. See H. Pitkin, *The Concept of Representation* (1967).

3. The False Equation of Proceduralism with Passivity

1. See chapter 2.

2. See chapter 1.

3. See also chapters 4, 6, 7, 8 and 9.

4. See Sedler, "The Legitimacy Debate in Constitutional Adjudication: An Assessment and a Different Perspective," 44 *Ohio State L.J.* 93, 123 (1983).

5. 307 U.S. 433 (1939) (Black, J., joined by Roberts, Frankfurter & Douglas, JJ., concurring).

6. Id. at 459.

7. Cf. Marbury v. Madison, 5 U.S. (1 Cranch) 137, 177 (1803) (Marshall, C.J.) (implying that the "law" that courts must apply may itself on occasion dictate complete deference to the political process within boundaries fixed by the judiciary).

8. I say "not exclusively" because I have no doubt of the need for judicial resolution of such "antecedent" issues as whether Article V may ever permit rescissions even with Congress' approval, cf. Goldwater v. Carter, 444 U.S. 966, 1007 (1979) (Brennan, J., dissenting) (arguing that political question doctrine "does not pertain when a court is faced with the *antecedent* question whether a particular branch has been constitutionally designated as the repository of political decisionmaking power"); or whether a congressional resolution proposing an amendment requires the President's signature, see Hollingsworth v. Virginia, 3 U.S. (3 Dall.) 378 (1798); or whether a state legislature's ratification may ever be overridden by a referendum vote of the people of the state, see Hawke v. Smith (Hawke I), 253 U.S. 221 (1920) (holding that a state's ratification may not be submitted to a referendum).

9. Dellinger, "The Legitimacy of Constitutional Change: Rethinking the Amendment Process," 97 *Harv. L. Rev.* 386, 395 (1983). Professor Dellinger proposes a body of rules—including a blanket rule denying effect to all attempts to rescind ratification, see id. at 423-24—that are designed to prevent Congress from making the amendment process more difficult. But an argument that the courts should resolve amendment process issues ought not to be based on the dubious assumption that the courts will resolve those issues according to the proponent's particular set of preferred rules. One can hardly argue for a more active judicial role as though one could control judicial decisions by fiat.

10. See id. at 413. That premise is dubious: not even such garden-variety issues as whether a state may rescind its ratification vote or whether the time for ratification should be extendable by Congress lend themselves to categorical solutions. Consider, for example, the matter of rescissions. The argument for disregarding rescissions in particular cases may be compelling; indeed, in certain circumstances recognizing rescission would seem totally unacceptable even if one rejected the view that rescissions should *never* be given effect. Suppose, for instance, that in proposing an amendment with a five-year deadline for ratification, Congress states in the proposing resolution that rescissions will be disregarded, and suppose that the thirty-eighth state—the last one necessary to meet Article V's requirement of three-quarters—ratifies days before the five years are

up. Suppose further that, one month before the final vote, the legislature of a state that has ratified the proposed amendment resolves by majority vote (and without debate) to rescind, and a resolution introduced the following day to nullify the rescission receives majority support but is defeated—according to the state legislature's rules—because it fails to garner a two-thirds vote. It seems difficult indeed to argue that this rescission must be given decisive weight.

Conversely, however, a flat rule that states can never rescind votes of ratification seems equally unacceptable. Suppose, for example, that Congress proposes an amendment, sets no deadline for its ratification, and expressly states in the proposing resolution that rescissions *will* be given effect. Suppose that thirty-five states ratify within a few months and that a decade then passes with no further action on the proposed amendment. Suppose, finally, that within the next two-year period three other states vote to ratify, but that between the thirty-sixth and thirty-eighth ratification votes lopsided majorities in the legislatures of twenty of the original thirty-five ratifying states vote to rescind. To ignore those votes and insist on accepting the amendment as part of the Constitution would seem absurd.

The weight to be given to votes of rescission seems best left to an ad hoc decision that takes into account not only the conditions under which Congress proposed the amendment, but also the political structure of a particular ratification battle. In any event, just as a determination by Congress "would not definitively resolve these uncertainties for future amendments" inasmuch as "[a] determination by one Congress would not bind another," id. at 395, so too one Court is notoriously incapable of binding its successors on matters of constitutional interpretation, over which even notions of stare decisis exert little influence. Clear and enduring rules are therefore, as a practical matter, unattainable even if one is willing to purchase clarity with truly procrustean rigidity in any given era. Cf. infra note 21 (discussing state consideration of the ERA).

11. 444 U.S. 996 (1979).

12. Id. at 1001 n.2 (Powell, J., concurring in the judgment); accord, Scharpf, "Judicial Review and the Political Question: A Functional Analysis," 75 *Yale L.J.* 517, 587–89 (1966).

13. See Dellinger, supra note 9, at 414–15.

14. See id. at 416.

15. Such dissatisfaction, however, need not portend manipulation by constitutional decision makers. In particular, as long as an amendment is proposed by a two-thirds vote of both houses, there seems little reason to fear that Congress will intentionally sabotage the amendment by rigging the ratification process, at least in the years immediately following the proposal. Decades later Congress may have a change of heart, but even in such circumstances there is no clear reason to trust the courts more than Congress. If, however, an amendment is ever proposed by a constitutional convention reluctantly called by Congress on petition by the states in the face of congressional inaction, there may be special cause to fear legislative sabotage, and the courts should perhaps then be less deferential to procedural determinations thereafter made by Congress. For an argument that such a constitutional convention should be avoided unless com-

pelling circumstances manifestly warrant taking the drastic step of calling one or unless Article V is itself first amended to clarify the process of amendment by convention, see Tribe, "Issues Raised by Requesting Congress to Call a Constitutional Convention to Propose a Balanced Budget Amendment," 10 *Pac. L.J.* 627, 632–40 (1979).

16. Because discourse about what *should* be contained in the Constitution is difficult if not impossible to segregate completely from discourse about what *is* contained in the Constitution, see infra notes 23–47 and accompanying text, the resort to forms of politics beyond law need not always signal a change in rhetoric or reasoning. Indeed, the appeals made by revolutionaries are often similar to those made by jurists. See, e.g., McCulloch v. Maryland, 17 U.S. (4 Wheat.) 316, 428–31 (1819) (applying the principle, articulated almost a half-century earlier at the Boston Tea Party, of no taxation without representation). Nonetheless, the quasi-revolutionary process of constitutional amendment may often allow access to results not attainable by better traveled routes of law reform. Revolution, or the amendment process, may be law by other means, but the means matter.

17. See, e.g., H.R.J. Res. 59, 98th Cong., 1st Sess. (1983) (Proposing the following amendment to the Constitution: "A right to abortion is not secured by this Constitution. The Congress and the several States shall have the concurrent power to restrict and prohibit abortions: *Provided*, That a law of a State which is more restrictive than a law of Congress shall govern.").

18. See chapter 1.

19. See chapter 5.

20. See Dellinger, supra note 9, at 423.

21. Far from rejecting such an approach, I argued, on behalf of the National Organization for Women in litigation growing out of state consideration of the ERA, in favor of congressional authority to treat votes of rescission precisely this way. See Appellant's Jurisdictional Statement at 24 n.25, National Org. for Women, Inc. v. Idaho, 103 S. Ct. 22 (1982) (Nos. 81–1283, 81–1312 & 81–1313).

    The ERA litigation illustrated the inherently political character of the rescission and extension issues, as well as the hazards of judicial oversight of such subjects. When Congress originally proposed the ERA in 1972, it included a seven-year time limit for ratification in the proposing clause of the resolution but not in the amendment's text. See H.R.J. Res. 208, 92d Cong., 2d Sess., 86 Stat. 1523 (1972). In 1978 the President signed a resolution extending the period for ratification until June 30, 1982—a resolution passed by a majority of each house after extensive consideration of its wisdom and constitutionality. See H.R.J. Res. 638, 95th Cong., 2d Sess., 92 Stat. 3799 (1978). The following year the states of Idaho and Arizona, along with certain members of their legislatures, sued for, inter alia, a declaratory judgment that the time extension was unconstitutional and that Idaho had validly rescinded its ratification of the proposed amendment. Idaho's rescission vote had been clouded by the state legislature's failure to adhere to its own rule requiring a two-thirds vote and by several prior opinions of the state's attorney general—and his counterparts in other states—assuring legislators that the only effect of such a vote would be advisory. See Appellant's Jurisdictional Statement at 24 n.25. Nevertheless, the district court granted summary judgment to the Idaho legislators. Idaho v. Freeman, 529 F.Supp. 1107 (D. Idaho 1981), *vacated as moot sub nom.* National Org. for Women, Inc. v. Idaho, 103 S. Ct. 22 (1982). The decision was widely criticized—even by those who had opposed the extension—as judicial usurpation of a properly political task and as an unjust eleventh-hour disruption of state consideration of the ERA. See, e.g., "Equal Rights and Unfair Meddling," *N.Y. Times*, Dec. 30, 1981, at A14, col. 1. After the requisite thirty-eight states had failed to ratify the ERA by the end of the extended period for ratification, the Supreme Court avoided the thorny questions presented by the case by vacating the district court judgment as moot. See National Org. for Women, Inc. v. Idaho, 103 S. Ct. 22 (1982). Because the ERA was aimed in part at overriding some of the Court's own gender discrimination decisions, any attempt by the Court to address the merits of the controversy, particularly in a decision that might have affected the amendment's passage, could well have embroiled the Court deeply and awkwardly in a democratic effort to do through Article V what the Court—in part because of the very pendency of the ERA—had refused to do on its own. See Frontiero v. Richardson, 411 U.S. 677, 692 (1973) (Powell, J., concurring) (arguing that the Court should not treat sex as a suspect classification, because adoption of the ERA, then pending before the states, would make it so).

22. The Court has, however, summarily affirmed the substantive validity of amendments. See Lester v. Garnett, 258 U.S. 130, 136 (1922) (Fifteenth Amendment); National Prohibition Cases, 253 U.S. 350, 385–88 (1920) (Eighteenth Amendment).

23. See Gudridge, "False Peace and Constitutional Tradition," 96 *Harv. L. Rev.* 1969, 1981–90 (1983).

24. See, e.g., Reynolds v. Sims, 377 U.S. 533 (1964); Wesberry v. Sanders, 376 U.S. 1 (1964).

25. See, e.g., National League of Cities v. Usery, 426 U.S. 833 (1976); *The Federalist* no. 9 (A. Hamilton); id. no. 32, at 203 (J. Cooke ed. 1961) (A. Hamilton); id. no. 62, at 416–17 (J. Madison); cf. Powell, "The Compleat Jeffersonian: Justice Rehnquist and Federalism," 91 *Yale L.J.* 1317, 1363–70 (1982) (arguing that Justice Rehnquist has adopted an Anti-Federalist vision rejected by the framers).

26. See, e.g., Immigration & Naturalization Serv. v. Chadha, 103 S. Ct. 2764 (1983); United States v. Nixon, 418 U.S. 683 (1974); Myers v. United States, 272 U.S. 52 (1926); I *Annals of Cong.* 604 (J. Gales ed. 1789) (statement of Rep. James Madison, asserting that the most sacred principle of our Constitution is "that the power of the three great branches of the national government be largely separated from one another").

27. See, e.g., Brown v. Board of Educ., 347 U.S. 483 (1954); M. Walzer, *Spheres of Justice* (1983).

28. See, e.g., Stanley v. Georgia, 394 U.S. 557 (1969); Griswold v. Connecticut, 381 U.S. 479 (1965); Skinner v. Oklahoma, 316 U.S. 535 (1942); Pierce v. Society of Sisters, 268 U.S. 510 (1925); Meyer v. Nebraska, 262 U.S. 390 (1923); Gerety, "Redefining Privacy," 12 *Harv. C.R.-C.L. L. Rev.* 233 (1977); Warren & Brandeis, "The Right to Privacy," 4 *Harv. L. Rev.* 193 (1890).

29. See, e.g., Joint Anti-Fascist Refugee Comm. v. McGrath, 341 U.S. 123 (1951); J. Pennock & J. Chapman, *Due Process* (1977); J. Rawls, *A Theory of Justice* 85–86, 195–201 (1971) (discussing procedural dimensions of justice).

30. In addition to the moral and political guidance provided by the Constitution—guidance that we are in a sense committed to respect—there are more strategic reasons for taking existing constitutional norms into account when assessing the merits of a proposed amendment. First, each amendment will later be construed by courts in ways calculated to reconcile it with the parts of the Constitution that it was not clearly designed to destroy. Further, one can neither favor nor oppose an amendment without at least paying attention to how it either accords or clashes with basic constitutional postulates—postulates that a given amendment might, after all, be construed to displace.

31. See, e.g., West Va. State Bd. of Educ. v. Barnette, 319 U.S. 624, 642 (1943) ("If there is any fixed star in our constitutional constellation, it is that no official, high or petty, can prescribe what shall be orthodox in politics, nationalism, religion, or other matters of opinion or force citizens to confess by word or act their faith therein.").

32. Cf. Torcaso v. Watkins, 367 U.S. 488 (1961) (striking down state constitutional provision requiring declaration of belief in God as condition of becoming a notary public).

33. See, e.g., J. Noonan, *A Private Choice* (1979).

34. See, e.g., *Constitutional Amendments Relating to Abortion: Hearings on S.J. Res. 17, 18, 19 & 110 Before the Subcomm. on the Constitution of the Senate Comm. on the Judiciary*, 97th Cong., 1st Sess. 97–102 (1981) (statement of Laurence Tribe).

35. See L. Tribe, "Constitution as Point of View," 3–4 (Apr. 1981) (unpublished manuscript on file in Harvard Law School Library).

36. See id. at 1–8.

37. See generally Dworkin, "Law as Interpretation," 60 *Tex. L. Rev.* 527, 540–46 (1982) (describing mixture of freedom and constraint inherent in legal interpretation). The overlap between conventional constitutional questions ("What does the Constitution mean?") and metaconstitutional questions ("What should be part of the Constitution and how should it be approached?") has important implications for constitutional theory as a whole. Because the answers to metaconstitutional questions cannot come entirely from "the Constitution," there can be no *entirely* "neutral" or "objective" reading of the Constitution: its readers must take a stand at the outset. It is unclear what those who concede the necessity of such an initial commitment believe they gain by seeking a constitutional theory that minimizes subsequent appeals to values "outside" the Constitution—values the reader brings to the document. See Tribe, supra note 35, at 7.

38. See *U.S. Const.*, amend. XVIII.

39. See, e.g., S.J. Res. 58, 97th Cong., 2d Sess., 128 *Cong. Rec.* S9777–78 (Daily ed. Aug. 4, 1982). A balanced budget amendment would seem particularly inap-

propriate—as would a requirement of deficit financing to assure stated levels of welfare—because, in addition to saddling the Constitution with a specific economic policy and injecting accounting technicalities into constitutional law, such a provision would require the federal courts to carry out detailed budgetary analyses for which they are poorly suited, would facilitate legislative and executive obstructionism, and, unless it were unacceptably inflexible, probably could not deliver the frugality it promised. See *Constitutional Amendments Seeking to Balance the Budget and Limit Federal Spending: Hearings Before the Subcomm. on Monopolies and Commercial Law of the House Comm. on the Judiciary*, 97th Cong., 1st & 2d Sess. 295–316 (1982) (statement of Laurence Tribe) [hereinafter cited as *Balanced Budget Hearings*]; Tribe, supra note 15, at 628–31; Note, "The Balanced Budget Amendment: An Inquiry into Appropriateness," 96 *Harv. L. Rev.* 1600 (1983).

40. See generally *Balanced Budget Hearings*, supra note 39, at 295–316 (statement of Laurence Tribe) (discussing "Ten Commandments of constitutional government"). I do not argue that such provisions should never be included—only that their inclusion always comes at a high price.

41. Elsewhere I have argued that Prohibition could not have been enacted statutorily. See, e.g., Tribe, supra note 15, at 630. Assuming that the Commerce Clause as construed in 1919 would not have authorized Congress to legislate temperance, amending the Constitution to broaden Congress' commerce power in a general way would have been sounder than directly constitutionalizing a controversial regulation of specific primary conduct. Similarly, if the Second Amendment were thought to bar desirable firearms regulations, the proper course would be to change the Second Amendment, not to incorporate gun control as such into the Constitution. Cf. Quilici v. Village of Morton Grove, 695 F.2d 261 (7th Cir. 1982) (upholding local gun control ordinance), *cert. denied*, 104 S. Ct. 194 (1983).

42. Statements of fundamental principle necessarily leave their specific implications open to future debate. See R. Dworkin, *Taking Rights Seriously* 134–36 (1977) (distinguishing between general "concepts" and specific "conceptions"). Just as we should be wary of overly concrete substantive amendments, so should we resist demanding too much specificity in any proposed amendment that is properly general. Such an amendment may, of course, be evaluated in part by considering how it might bear on the disposition of hypothetical cases— a matter likely to be largely uncertain in advance—but any evaluation along these lines should also consider the equally uncertain matter of how the hypotheticals might be resolved under the Constitution *absent* the proposed amendment. Consideration of both halves of this equation compels one to recognize, and indeed to respect, the inherent open-endedness and unpredictability of the evolution of constitutional doctrine with or without the proposed amendment. Had the Bill of Rights or the Fourteenth Amendment, for example, been subjected to the withering, and sometimes nitpicking, one-sided anticipatory dissection to which the ERA has been exposed for over a decade, those earlier amendments would likely never have been added to the Constitution.

43. The cluttered and rapidly changing contents of state constitutions may partially explain why even the most enduring and fundamental provisions of these documents rarely command the respect routinely paid to federal constitutional guarantees. See "Developments in the Law—The Interpretation of State Constitutional Rights," 95 *Harv. L. Rev.* 1324, 1353–56 (1982).

Despite the encyclopedic nature of the United States Code, however, it must be admitted that some statutes, such as 42 U.S.C. §§1981–83 (1976) and the National Labor Relations Act, 29 U.S.C. §§151–169 (1976 & Supp. V 1981), have achieved a status similar to that enjoyed by federal constitutional provisions. But our ability to understand these statutes as laws deserving special allegiance may depend on the availability of a canonical constitution to which they can be analogized. Indeed, such statutes have at times been described as "quasi-constitutional." See, e.g., Levinson, "New Perspectives on the Reconstruction Court," 26 *Stan. L. Rev.* 461, 483 (1974).

44. On the argument that amendments ought to reflect a "contemporaneous consensus," see Dellinger, supra note 9, at 388, 394–96, 422.

45. But see Murphy, "An Ordering of Constitutional Values," 53 *S. Cal. L. Rev.* 703, 755–56 (1980) (arguing that the Court could invalidate an amendment wholly contrary to the Constitution's paramount value of human dignity).

46. I do not mean to suggest that the Constitution expressly entrusts these questions to Congress or to the states, cf. Baker v. Carr, 369 U.S. 186, 217 (1962) (political question may be created by "textually demonstrable constitutional commitment of the issue to a coordinate political department"), but rather that concern for the constitutional order as a whole counsels strongly against judicial involvement in this area, see generally Bickel, "The Supreme Court, 1960 Term—Foreword: The Passive Virtues," 75 *Harv. L. Rev.* 40 (1961) (urging a jurisprudence of selective restraint).

47. What I have termed "true" political questions should be distinguished from matters on which the Constitution is simply neutral—that is, from decisions the Constitution leaves completely to the discretion of Congress or the President. In this latter category of "false" political questions are decisions such as the proper size of the federal budget; whether to terminate a treaty in accordance with its terms, see Goldwater v. Carter, 444 U.S. 996, 1007 (Brennan, J., dissenting) (the power to withdraw recognition from a foreign government is committed exclusively to the President); and how best to fulfill the Constitution's substantive guarantees, see City of Revere v. Massachusetts Gen. Hosp., 103 S. Ct. 2979 (1983) (how state procures medical treatment required by Due Process Clause is not a federal constitutional question). Cf. L. Tribe, *American Constitutional Law* §3–16 (1978) (arguing that the political question doctrine does not preclude judicial interpretation of certain parts of the Constitution, but only requires that federal courts consider whether constitutional provisions lend themselves to judicial enforcement); Henkin, "Is There a 'Political Question' Doctrine?" 85 *Yale L.J.* 597 (1976) (suggesting that all "political questions" identified by the Supreme Court are "false" in the sense described above).

We can best understand the matter by categorizing decisions according to the type of reasoning they seem to call forth and the institution to which they are entrusted. Typically, courts are thought to be assigned responsibility for relatively "principled" decision making, including constitutional interpretation; questions requiring more ad hoc, instrumental approaches are normally deemed to be charged to the political branches. False political questions are examples of the latter unremarkable assignment. But just as some ad hoc, instrumental decisions are properly made by courts—for example, the selection of a remedy for a constitutional wrong, see Bell v. Hood, 327 U.S. 678, 684 (1946); cf. Chayes, "The Role of the Judge in Public Law Litigation," 89 Harv. L. Rev. 1281, 1292–96, 1298–1302 (1976) (discussing ad hoc fashioning of remedy in modern institutional litigation); Eisenberg & Yeazell, "The Ordinary and the Extraordinary in Institutional Litigation," 93 Harv. L. Rev. 465, 478–86, 510–16 (1980) (tracing historical roots of complex remedial orders)—so too the political branches have responsibility for some sorts of principled, constitutional decision making. This last category of issues consists of true political questions and includes the appropriateness of proposed constitutional amendments.

It is difficult to identify other examples of true political questions in this sense, but legislative reapportionment seemed to be such an issue before Baker v. Carr, 369 U.S. 186 (1962). In Colegrove v. Green, 328 U.S. 549 (1946), despite ruling that the Constitution, for institutional reasons, committed responsibility for apportionment decisions exclusively to Congress, the Court had hinted that Congress, in carrying out its responsibility, should itself be guided by constitutional norms of fairness. See id. at 554; see also Baker, 369 U.S. at 270 (Frankfurter, J., dissenting) (arguing that "relief [from malapportionment] must come through an aroused popular conscience that sears the conscience of the people's representatives"); id. at 339 (Harlan, J., dissenting) (suggesting that Court should not be viewed "primarily as the last refuge for the correction of all inequality or injustice, no matter what its nature or source").

48. See supra notes 11–21 and accompanying text. The Supreme Court has recognized that the political question doctrine is rarely if ever an all-or-nothing proposition: the concerns underlying the doctrine have at times been thought to warrant deference on some issues that nonetheless do not qualify as full-fledged political questions and, thus, do not require complete judicial abstention. See, e.g., Mathews v. Diaz, 426 U.S. 67, 81–82 (1976).

49. For example, suppose that the judicial reading of Article V, before an amendment's ratification, rendered purported rescissions ineffectual and that the amendment in question contained a section specifying that it would become null and void immediately upon ratification if the number of ratifying states, subtracting those that had purported to rescind, was less than thirty-eight. If ratified by thirty-eight states of which one had rescinded, the amendment would take effect for only a moment, during which time its impact would be to require that rescissions be counted and thus to render itself void. See Dellinger, supra note 9, at 409.

4. Construing the Sounds of Congressional and Constitutional Silence

1. 91 Cong. Rec. 2627 (Mar. 22, 1945). My colleague Terry Martin deserves credit for bringing this Coolidgism to my attention.

2. R. Dickerson, The Interpretation and Application of Statutes (1975).

3. B. Dauenhauer, *Silence: The Phenomenon and Its Ontological Significance* (1980).

4. Id. at 3.

5. A. Miller, *The Crucible* 97 (1971).

6. Brown v. Louisiana, 383 U.S. 131, 142 (1966).

7. Traditional story reported by former Vermont Representative Will Hunter (D. Weathersfield).

8. H.P. Hood & Sons v. Du Mond, 336 U.S. 525, 535 (1949).

9. This was the notion underlying the divination of supposed "general principles of commercial law" in Swift v. Tyson, 41 U.S. (16 Pet.) 1 (1842), and of supposed contours of "natural rights" of property and contract in the era of Lochner v. New York, 198 U.S. 45 (1905).

10. See L. Tribe, *American Constitutional Law* §17-3, at 1144 (1978); Linde, "Due Process of Lawmaking," 55 *Neb. L. Rev.* 197 (1976). Compare Tribe, "Structural Due Process," 10 *Harv. C.R.-C.L. L. Rev.* 269, 290-91, 300-01 (1975).

11. Logan v. Zimmerman Brush Co., 455 U.S. 422, 433 (1982) (emphasis added); see also Bi-Metallic Inv. Co. v. State Board, 239 U.S. 441, 445-46 (1915).

12. See generally H. Hart & A. Sacks, "The Legal Process" 1410-11 (tent. ed. 1958) (unpublished manuscript in Harvard Law School Library) (a court's function in interpreting a statute is to decide what the *words* of the statute mean so as best to carry out its *purpose—"not . . .* to ascertain the *intent* of the legislature").

13. 341 U.S. 384 (1951) (Jackson, J., concurring).

14. Id. at 395-97 (Jackson, J., concurring).

15. United States v. Public Utilities Comm'n, 345 U.S. 295, 319 (1953) (Jackson, J., concurring) (emphasis added).

16. Id. (Jackson, J., concurring).

17. 329 U.S. 14 (1946) (Rutledge, J., concurring).

18. Id. at 22 n.4. (Rutledge, J., concurring) (emphasis added). Justice Rutledge also noted that "negative inferences" of legislative intent from legislative silence lack the sort of evidentiary basis that supports positive inferences from the enactment of legislation "pursuant to prescribed procedures, including reduction of bills to writing, committee reports, debates, . . . voting records and executive approval." Id. at 22 n.5. (Rutledge, J., concurring).

19. Id. at 22 (Rutledge, J., concurring) (emphasis added). See also, e.g., R. Dickerson, *The Interpretation and Application of Statutes* 181 (1975) ("The first question is whether legislative silence can constitute effective legislative action. It seems obvious that a legislature cannot legislate effectively by not legislating at all.").

20. 309 U.S. 106 (1940).

21. Id. at 121 (emphasis added); see also Scripps-Howard Radio v. FCC, 316 U.S. 4, 11 (1942) ("The search for significance in the silence of Congress is too often the pursuit of a mirage."). The particular sort of legislative silence discussed both by Justice Rutledge in *Cleveland* and by Justice Frankfurter in *Hallock* was Congress' failure to repudiate prior judicial constructions of its acts. Both wrote that this sort of silence could not be read as tantamount to congressional acquiescence in those constructions. Justice Frankfurter distinguished such silence

from Congress' *reenactment* of a statute, from which legislative adoption of settled judicial constructions might fairly be implied. See *Hallock*, 309 U.S. at 120–21 n.7.

Both justices emphasized that the meaning of Congress' failure to repudiate such constructions was ambiguous, for "[v]arious considerations of parliamentary tactics and strategy," id. at 121, or other reasons indicating no approval of what the courts had done—such as the "sheer pressure of other and more important business," *Cleveland*, 329 U.S. at 23 (Rutledge, J., concurring)—might account for Congress' inaction. Professors Hart and Sacks summarize a dozen such possible reasons, suggesting that a court—necessarily uncertain which ones explained a given legislative failure to act—cannot infer from legislative silence "'sanction and approval' of an outstanding decision." Hart & Sacks, supra note 12, at 1155–56. Cf. Sibbach v. Wilson & Co., 312 U.S. 1, 18 (1941) (Frankfurter, J., dissenting) ("Having due regard to the mechanics of legislation and the practical conditions surrounding the business of Congress when the [Federal] Rules [of Civil Procedure] were submitted, to draw any inference of tacit approval from non-action by Congress is to appeal to unreality.").

The upshot of refusal to read approval in this sort of congressional silence is to leave courts free to reconsider and overrule their earlier constructions of the relevant statutes, thus avoiding what Justice Rutledge described as improper buck-passing: "shift[ing] to Congress the responsibility for perpetuating the Court's error," *Cleveland*, 329 U.S. at 22 (Rutledge, J., concurring); see also United States v. South Buffalo Ry., 333 U.S. 771, 792 (1948) (Rutledge, J., dissenting).

22. 87 U.S. (20 Wall.) 590 (1875).
23. Id. at 618.
24. Id. at 619.
25. Id. at 617.
26. Youngstown Sheet & Tube Co. v. Sawyer, 343 U.S. 579 (1952).
27. C. Sawyer, *Concerns of a Conservative Democrat* 257 (1968).
28. Id. at 260.
29. Id. at 267.
30. 343 U.S. 579 (1952).
31. Id. at 586 (emphasis added).
32. Id. at 587.
33. Id. at 601 (Frankfurter, J., concurring).
34. Id. at 700–03 (Vinson, C.J., dissenting).
35. Id. at 603 (Frankfurter, J., concurring).
36. Id. at 657 (Burton, J., dissenting).
37. Id. at 662 (Clark, J., concurring in judgment).
38. Id. at 637 (Jackson, J., concurring) (emphasis added).
39. Explicit rejection of legislation might appear different from mere congressional inaction, such as the omission to repudiate judicial interpretations of statutes

discussed supra note 21, and is in some respects closer to speech than silence. This is a difference that both Justice Frankfurter (*Youngstown*, 343 U.S. at 602 [Frankfurter, J., concurring] [Congress "clearly and emphatically" withheld authority for executive seizures]) and Justice Jackson (id. at 637 [Jackson, J., concurring] [result might have been different had Congress' omission reflected only "inertia, indifference, or quiescence"]) sketched in their *Steel Seizure* concurrences. But under the view that, at least in such cases as this, only the *positive enactments* of Congress may form the touchstone of legislative legitimacy, see infra note 59 and accompanying text, the silence left in the law by a failed proposal is little different from that left by a nonproposal. Contrast the use of failed proposals as part of the context that gives meaning to subsequent enactments, see infra text accompanying notes 81–91.

40. See Monaghan, "The Supreme Court, 1974 Term—Foreword: Constitutional Common Law," 89 *Harv. L. Rev.* 1 (1975).

41. Shenton, "Interstate Commerce During the Silence of Congress," in 3 *Selected Essays on Constitutional Law* 842 (1938).

42. *U.S. Const.*, art. I, §8, cl. 3.

43. 135 U.S. 100 (1890) (striking down Iowa statute prohibiting sale of intoxicating liquor).

44. Id. at 109–10.

45. See The License Cases, 46 U.S. (5 How.) 504 (1847) (upholding authority of states to license and regulate the importation of liquor).

46. 135 U.S. at 160 (Gray, J., dissenting) (joined in dissent by Justices Harlan and Brewer). Accord, Joseph v. Carter & Weekes Stevedoring Co., 330 U.S. 422, 428 (1947) (majority treats Congress' inaction as "acquiescence in [Court's] former rulings").

47. Powell, "The Still Small Voice of the Commerce Clause," in 3 *Selected Essays on Constitutional Law* 931, 932 (1938).

48. The inflexible unitary regime might have followed from the Madisonian view, see *The Federalist* nos. 41, 42 (J. Madison), that power over interstate commerce having been reposed exclusively in Congress, the states are powerless to regulate in that area even when Congress is silent, see, e.g., Gibbons v. Ogden, 22 U.S. (9 Wheat.) 1, 209 (1824) (Marshall, C.J., dictum), while the regime of state autonomy might have followed from the view of Chief Justice Marshall's successor Roger Taney that, so long as Congress did *not* speak affirmatively through federal legislation to preempt them, the states were free to regulate commerce, see, e.g., The License Cases, 46 U.S. (5 How.) 504, 573 (1847) (opinion of Taney, C.J.). The reconciliation of these two poles of early Commerce Clause jurisprudence in Cooley v. Board of Wardens, 53 U.S. (12 How.) 299 (1851) (distinguishing commerce local in character from that national in character and therefore regulable solely by Congress), created the norm around which judicial interpretations of congressional silence vacillated as Professor Powell describes.

49. Towne v. Eisner, 245 U.S. 418, 425 (1918).

50. Bread Political Action Comm. v. Federal Election Comm'n, 455 U.S. 577, 584 (1982). See generally Note, "Intent, Clear Statements, and the Common Law:

Statutory Interpretation in the Supreme Court," 95 *Harv. L. Rev.* 892, 894–95 (1982) (modern touchstone of statutory interpretation is literalist reading of words as surrogates for legislative intent).

51. Such an inversion finds parallels in many other areas of the law: for example, when the "will" theory of contracts prevails over the "objective" theory.

52. For a recent example of the magnetism of the common law mentality, see G. Calabresi, *A Common Law for the Age of Statutes* (1982). The author, in effect, overrides the Constitution's separation of powers, suggesting that if the legislature remains silent toward statutes that the courts perceive as no longer "fitting" the evolving legal landscape, courts should themselves revise or abandon those statutes, even if they are perfectly constitutional. See Mikva, "The Shifting Sands of Legal Topography," 96 *Harv. L. Rev.* 534, 542–43 (1982) (reviewing Calabresi's book) (cautioning that the virtually unlimited legislative updating power that Calabresi proposes for judges could undermine the independence of the judiciary). See, in partial accord with Calabresi, Tribe, "Structural Due Process," 10 *Harv. C.R.-C.L. L. Rev.* 269, 308–12 (1975). This approach avoids attributing responsibility to the silent Congress, but nonetheless disclaims judicial responsibility for reworking the legal landscape by passing off that activity as merely astute, judicially "expert" observation.

53. S. Sontag, "The Aesthetics of Silence," in her *Styles of Radical Will* 810–11 (1969).

54. Cf. L. Wittgenstein, l *Philosophical Investigations* §580 (1958 ed.) ("An 'inner process' stands in need of outward criteria").

55. Cf. S. Cavell, *Must We Mean What We Say?* 16–18 (1976) (defending heavy reliance on context for meaning of language).

56. 343 U.S. 579 (1952).

57. See supra notes 31–39 and accompanying text.

58. *Steel Seizure*, 343 U.S. at 631–32 (Douglas, J., concurring) (emphasis added) (footnotes and citations omitted). Cf. United States v. Hudson, 11 U.S. (7 Cranch) 32 (1812) (no federal common law of crimes).

59. Where constitutional principles require such consent, the *type* of legislative silence—whether or not it follows speech and debate and whether it is omission or rejection—does not matter, for anything short of clearly expressed consent must have similar operative effect. Cf. supra note 39.

60. *U.S. Const.*, art. I, §10, cl. 3.

61. Id. at art. II, §2, cl. 2.

62. See, e.g., Virginia v. West Virginia, 78 U.S. (11 Wallace) 39, 59–60 (1870).

63. See supra notes 42–48 and accompanying text.

64. Note that, at least on those occasions when Congress' silence must be conceded to express neither a "yes" nor a "no," a situation which all must acknowledge sometimes obtains, there is no way for a court to *avoid* deciding what the background constitutional norm—i.e., the rule that governs when Congress is *silently* silent—is to be.

65. Dames & Moore v. Regan, 453 U.S. 654 (1981).

66. Id. at 663–64. Cf. Persian proverb (date unknown) ("Trust in God, but tie your camel").

67. See Exec. Order No. 12, 294, 46 Fed. Reg. 14,111 (1981) (implementing the Hostage Agreement).

68. *Dames*, 453 U.S. at 674, 686.

69. Id. at 673.

70. Id. at 688–89.

71. International Emergency Economic Powers Act, 50 U.S.C. §1702 (1977) (which the Court said authorized nullification of the attachments, but not—although it came close—the suspension of the claims); Hostage Act of 1868, 22 U.S.C. §1732 (1976) (so named only for purposes of this litigation and not directly applicable in any event); International Claims Settlement Act of 1949, 22 U.S.C. §§1621–1627 (1976) (not directly applicable). See *Dames*, 453 U.S. at 669–88.

72. *Dames*, 453 U.S. at 677.

73. 357 U.S. 116 (1958).

74. Id. at 129.

75. Id.

76. Id. at 130 (emphasis added). See also New York Times Co. v. United States, 403 U.S. 713 (1971) (per curiam); id. at 718 (Black, J., concurring); id. at 720 (Douglas, J., concurring); id. at 742 (Marshall, J., concurring).

77. 453 U.S. 280 (1981).

78. Id. at 303–06; see also id. at 315–18 (Brennan, J., dissenting) (protesting only that the Court might have misread Congress' intent).

79. *Kent*, 357 U.S. at 130. See also Regan v. Wald, 52 U.S.L.W. 4966 (1984), in which Justice Rehnquist, writing for himself, Chief Justice Burger, and Justices White, Stevens and O'Connor, purported to find, in a factual situation that was at best ambiguous, clear authorization for the Reagan administration's summary ban on most travel to Cuba. In 1977 Congress enacted the International Emergency Economic Powers Act (IEEPA), imposing procedural restrictions—including requirements of congressional consultation and explicit presidential declaration of national emergency—on various executive powers over international trade and travel. But the Act exempted from the new procedures the exercise of "authorities conferred upon the President . . . which were being exercised with respect to a country on July 1, 1977." Although the Court acknowledged that "most travel-related transactions with Cuba and Cuban nationals were permitted" on that date, it nonetheless found that "the President was [then] exercising his authority over travel-related transactions with Cuba and Cubans by means of a general license which exempted them" from a general prohibition of all transactions involving Cuba, while at the same time "restrictions on commodities purchases" such as cigars remained in effect. Id. at 4969 & n.18. The Court concluded that "the grandfathered authorities of [that prohibition] provide an adequate statutory basis for the 1982 amendment restricting the scope of permissible travel-related transactions with Cuba and Cuban nationals." Id. at 4972. Justices Blackmun, Brennan, Marshall, and Powell

criticized the majority for "claim[ing] that the statutory language is without ambiguity" and argued that, in addition, the legislative history demonstrated no congressional intent to allow the President "to increase the restrictions applicable to a particular country without following the IEEPA procedures." Id. at 4975.

80. Immigration & Naturalization Serv. v. Chadha, 103 S. Ct. 2764 (1983). See chapter 6.

81. See, e.g., Merrill Lynch v. Curran, 456 U.S. 353, 382 (1982) (finding implied private right of action under Commodities Exchange Act, in part because several courts had found such a right under the precursor statute). To say that such silence may be contextually relevant is *not* to say that reenactment is always to be rigidly construed as adoption of existing judicial interpretations or that silence toward such interpretations in the context of reenactment necessarily carries the same legal significance as if those very interpretations had been originally enacted. Those constructions were urged by Chief Justice Stone in his well-known dissent to Girouard v. United States, 328 U.S. 61, 75–76 (1946) (Stone, C.J., dissenting) (in reenacting provisions of the naturalization law that had been subject to controversial judicial interpretation, Congress must be presumed to be "*adopting* and *confirming*" that interpretation). Professors Hart and Sacks persuasively criticize such a flat adoption rule as a disincentive to amendment and codification, inasmuch as it in effect instructs a legislature that it has a duty to review all controversial interpretations of its prior statutes before reenacting them—at the peril of having committed itself to existing interpretations for having failed to do so. See Hart & Sacks, supra note 12, at 1162–64. They do not rule out, however, the possibility that reenactment may *sometimes* justify an inference of legislative approval. See id. at 1164–65.

82. A unanimous Supreme Court found significance in just such a congressional rejection of proposed legislation in Pacific Gas & Elec. Co. v. State Energy Resources Comm'n, 103 S. Ct. 1713 (1983), which involved a preemption challenge to California's moratorium on construction of new nuclear power plants so long as the federal government has not developed viable methods and facilities for the ultimate disposal of nuclear waste. In passing the Nuclear Waste Policy Act of 1982, Pub. L. No. 97–425 (1982), Congress in the end rejected an amendment proposed by Senator McClure, and initially included in the Senate bill, that would have provided that passage of the Act "should be construed in any federal, state, and local administrative or judicial proceeding to satisfy any legal or statutory requirement" for the existence of a federally approved technology for the disposal of nuclear waste or for assurance of the safe storage and disposal of such waste. See 128 *Cong. Rec.* S4310 (daily ed. Apr. 29, 1982).

Notwithstanding Congress' omission of that amendment from the House version of the bill that was ultimately signed into law ten days before oral argument in *Pacific Gas & Elec.*, the utility petitioners and the solicitor general urged the Court in that case to interpret the Act as declaring a federal solution to the nuclear waste disposal problem, thereby effectively preempting the challenged state requirement by decreeing it to have been met as a matter of federal law. See Transcript of Oral Argument in *Pacific Gas & Elec.* at 4–10 (argument of petitioners); id. at 20–21 (argument of the Office of the Solicitor General of the United States as amicus curiae in support of reversal).

As counsel for the respondents in *Pacific Gas & Elec.*, I argued that the deletion of the McClure Amendment from the Act demonstrated, on the contrary, that the Act was not intended to preempt state regulation by declaring the nuclear waste problem solved. See id. at 33. In response to Justice Rehnquist's query whether "bills that Congress didn't pass" should carry weight with the Court, I argued that, while in the ordinary case congressional inaction should not carry such weight, Congress' previous explicit deletion from legislation of the very outcome a litigant seeks from the federal judiciary has clear significance: "the provisions that were specifically deleted in [this bill] at least suggest that what the petitioners asked the federal judiciary to do is something that the industry has repeatedly asked Congress to do and Congress has repeatedly refused to do." Id. at 33–34. In his opinion for the Court, Justice White agreed: "While we are correctly reluctant to draw inferences from the failure of Congress to act, it would, in this case, appear improper for us to give a reading to the Act that Congress considered and rejected." *Pacific Gas & Elec.*, 103 S. Ct. at 1730.

See also, e.g., United States v. Security Indus. Bank, 103 S. Ct. 407, 413 (1982) (construing provision of Bankruptcy Reform Act of 1978 to be nonretroactive, in part because earlier proposed version would have been explicitly retroactive).

83. *Girouard*, 328 U.S. at 69 (1946) (emphasis added) (overruling three prior judicial interpretations of the naturalization statutes despite Congress' intervening reenactment of those statutes without any changes repudiating those interpretations). This opinion has been much praised. See, e.g., R. Dickerson, supra note 2, at 254. But *Girouard*'s rejection of an inference of congressional *intent* from congressional silence should not be equated with a denial that such silence deserves any weight as part of statutory context.

84. See, e.g., *Merrill Lynch*, 456 U.S. at 396–98, 401–02, 408 (Powell, Rehnquist, O'Connor, JJ., & Burger, C.J., dissenting).

85. Cf. R. Nozick, *Philosophical Explanations* 615 (1981) (describing the boundaries "in those intriguing drawings [two profiles and vase, old woman and young woman, duck and rabbit]" and asking, "Are not both patterns equally there?").

86. Kalaris v. Donovan, 697 F.2d 376 (D.C. Cir. 1983).

87. Id. at 390.

88. Id. at 392–93.

89. See, e.g., Consumer Prod. Safety Comm'n v. GTE Sylvania, 447 U.S. 102, 118 n.13 (1980).

90. See, e.g., Bob Jones University v. United States, 103 S. Ct. 2017 (1983) (invoking failure of Congress to act on proposed bills that would have overturned Internal Revenue Service ruling as evidence of congressional ratification of that ruling); Patsy v. Board of Regents, 457 U.S. 496 (1982) (invoking evidence of Congress' perception in 1980 that 1871 Civil Rights Act, 42 U.S.C. §1983, had not required exhaustion of state remedies); Baldridge v. Shapiro, 455 U.S. 345,

358 (1982) (invoking 1977 rejection by Congress of proposals to make census data accessible to local officials as evidence that Congress in 1929 intended data to be confidential); Federal Election Comm'n v. Democratic Senatorial Campaign Comm., 454 U.S. 27, 35–56 & n.12 (1981).

91. See generally C. Black, *Structure and Relationship in Constitutional Law* (1969).

92. See supra text accompanying notes 8, 42.

93. *U.S. Const.*, amend. X.

94. See supra note 22 and accompanying text.

95. For example, the Eleventh Amendment must be read in the context of Chisholm v. Georgia, 2 U.S. (2 Dall.) 419 (1793), which it overruled. Thus it has not been read literally as barring only federal suits by citizens of *other* states or as barring *all* federal suits by a state's (or another state's) citizens but rather—in keeping with the concepts of sovereign immunity which it restored in the wake of *Chisholm*—as barring the federal judiciary from deriving power from Article III to entertain citizen suits for which the defendant state does not waive immunity. See generally Field, "The Eleventh Amendment and Other Sovereign Immunity Doctrines: Part One," 126 *U. Pa. L. Rev.* 515 (1978); Field, "The Eleventh Amendment and Other Sovereign Immunity Doctrines: Congressional Imposition of Suit upon the States," 126 *U. Pa. L. Rev.* 1203 (1978). Likewise, the Fourteenth Amendment must be read in the context of Dred Scott v. Sandford, 60 U.S. (19 How.) 393 (1857), which it implicitly overruled, and the Twenty-first Amendment in the context of the Eighteenth Amendment, which it expressly repealed.

96. 17 U.S. (4 Wheat.) 316 (1819).

97. 418 U.S. 683, 705–06 n.16 (1974) ("the silence of the Constitution on this score is not dispositive").

98. This silence as to executive privilege contrasts, for example, with the express immunity conferred on members of Congress by the Speech and Debate Clause.

99. Specifically, the Court noted "the supremacy of each branch within its own assigned area of consitutional duties" and the separation of powers doctrine. See *Nixon*, 418 U.S. at 705–06.

100. *U.S. Const.*, amend. IX.

101. See generally J. Ely, *Democracy and Distrust* 34–41 (1980).

102. Most recently the Court expressly took up that invitation in Richmond Newspapers v. Virginia, 448 U.S. 555, 579–80 & n.15 (1980) (plurality opinion).

103. See 1 *Annals of Congress* 439 (Gales & Seaton eds. 1834).

104. It is difficult to take literally the Supreme Court's recent assertion that "when we . . . have evidence that a particular law *would have offended the Framers,* we have not hesitated to invalidate it *on that ground alone.*" Minneapolis Star and Tribune Co. v. Minnesota Comm'r of Revenue, 103 S. Ct. 1365, 1371 n.6 (1983) (emphasis added). Cf. T. S. Eliot, *The Four Quartets* (1941) ("we cannot revive old factions / we cannot restore old policies /or follow an antique drum.

/ These men, and those who opposed them / and those whom they opposed / accept the constitution of silence / and are folded into a single party").

105. I am indebted to David Sklansky, J.D., Harvard Law School, 1984, for helping me see the importance of this distinction. Close structural analogies may be found in the distinctions between acts and omissions, and between state action and state inaction. For although there are many things that an individual or the state might *do* about a given matter, the option of failing to do *anything at all* need not itself bespeak a rejection of any *particular* affirmative option. Yet, although we must therefore articulate background norms—notions of affirmative duties—to determine *when* individuals' omissions or the state's failures to act are culpable, such an articulation is potentially determinate, as articulating rules about acts and actions is not. Cf. C. Fried, *Right and Wrong* 19-20 (1978) (on acts versus omissions).

106. See generally D. Hofstadter, *Gödel, Escher, Bach: An Eternal Golden Braid* (1979) (on paradoxes of self-reference).

107. L. Wittgenstein, *Tractatus Logico-Philosophicus* §7 (1921).

5. Silencing the Oracle

1. These proposals purport to limit federal jurisdiction over *abortions or abortion funding*: H.R. 73, H.R. 867, H.R. 900, H.R. 3225; *busing*: H.R. 761, H.R. 869, H.R. 1079, H.R. 1180; *gender discrimination in military service*: H.R. 2365, H.R. 2791; *"voluntary" prayer in public schools*: H.R. 72, H.R. 326, H.R. 408, H.R. 865, H.R. 989, H.R. 1335, H.R. 2397; and *state orders reviewable by the state's highest court*: H.R. 114.

   All references to congressional bills in this essay are to measures that were pending in 1981 before the 97th Congress, 1st Session.

2. United States v. Klein, 80 U.S. (13 Wall.) 128, 145 (1871).

3. "The Congress, whenever two thirds of both Houses shall deem it necessary, shall propose Amendments to this Constitution, or, on the Application of the Legislatures of two thirds of the several States, shall call a Convention for proposing Amendments, which, in either Case, shall be valid to all Intents and Purposes, as part of this Constitution, when ratified by the Legislatures of three fourths of the several States, or by Conventions in three fourths thereof, as the one or the other Mode of Ratification may be proposed by the Congress" (*U.S. Const.*, art. V).

4. I must confess to some doubt, however, as to this sort of consensus criterion. (Would the Civil War Amendments have met it? The proposed Equal Rights Amendment? The First Amendment?).

5. 410 U.S. 113 (1973) (state cannot ban previability abortions).

6. Cf. Runyon v. McCrary, 427 U.S. 160, 190-92 (1976) (Stevens, J., concurring) (stating the case against turning back the pages of a progressive history even if one would have written it differently).

7. J. Dugard, *Human Rights and the South African Legal Order* 35 (1978).

8. Cf. L. Tribe, *American Constitutional Law* §3–6, at 51 (1978) (a majoritarian Congress put federal courts "in a position to exercise . . . antimajoritarian power").

9. See, e.g., C. Black, *Decision According to Law* 18–19, 37–39 (1981). See also M. Perry, *The Constitution, the Courts, and Human Rights* 128–39 (1982).

10. See United States v. Nixon, 418 U.S. 683 (1974).

11. In contrast, in Marbury v. Madison, 5 U.S. (1 Cranch) 137 (1803), the Court was "in the delightful position . . . of rejecting and assuming power in a single breath." R. McCloskey, *The American Supreme Court* 42 (1960).

12. See, e.g., United States v. Nixon, 418 U.S. 683, 703–05 (1974); Cooper v. Aaron, 358 U.S. 1, 18 (1958); Marbury v. Madison, 5 U.S. at 137, 177–78.

13. See, e.g., Hart, "The Power of Congress to Limit the Jurisdiction of Federal Courts: An Exercise in Dialectic," 66 *Harv. L. Rev.* 1362, 1387 (1953).

14. *Marbury*, 5 U.S. at 178.

15. Nevada v. Hall, 440 U.S. 410, 433 (1979) (dissenting opinion). There have been many more recent variations on the themes stated here, but the only original contribution I have read on this topic since the June 1981 testimony reflected in this essay is Professor Lea Brilmayer's article, Brilmayer & Underhill, "Congressional Obligation to Provide a Forum for Constitutional Claims: Discriminatory Jurisdictional Rules and the Conflict of Laws," 69 *Va. L. Rev.* 819 (1983). Brilmayer's central thesis is that congressional statutes excluding from federal courts some or all claims *arising under the Constitution*, while including substantively parallel claims *arising under Acts of Congress*, discriminate against claims arising from a coequal or higher source of law within the federal system in violation of a basic axiom requiring full interjurisdictional cooperation in that system: "[I]t is not clear why all independent sources of law within our federal system whose mandates are insulated from the control of the jurisdiction-determining legislature should not be protected in the same way as federal legislation or the legislation of another state. It is not dispositive that the independent source of rights is a text and not a legislative body because states must afford equal access to federal constitutional claims. Moreover, if a source of 'sovereignty' must be found before constitutional claims are entitled to equal access, one need only allude to the sovereignty of the people of the United States, which predates the sovereignty of Congress and is the foundation of *Marbury* itself" (Id. at 832). One weakness of this intriguing conflict-of-laws approach to the jurisdictional gerrymandering issue is that, unlike the approach taken in this chapter, it would leave Congress free to take such steps as "creat[ing] a federal statutory right to abortion in order [then] to strip federal courts of jurisdiction to hear abortion claims generally" without running afoul of the interjurisdictional-nondiscrimination axiom. Id. at 846 n.133. The answer that Congress would be reluctant to "create a new [statutory] right to abortion enforceable in state courts," as a prelude to excising abortion cases from federal courts, id., erroneously assumes that the hypothesized federal statutory right would not be limited from the outset to enforcement exclusively in federal courts. And the further answer that congressional enactment of federal statutory rights fol-

lowed by jurisdiction-stripping measures would be subject to invalidation as impermissibly motivated, id., seems far too optimistic given the difficulty of establishing forbidden motive as a basis for invalidating congressional legislation. Cf. United States v. O'Brien, 391 U.S. 367 (1968).

16. That Congress could no longer simply abolish the federal district courts is urged in Eisenberg, "Congressional Authority to Restrict Lower Federal Court Jurisdiction," 83 *Yale L.J.* 498 (1973). See infra note 55.

17. This was the holding of Marbury v. Madison, 5 U.S. at 137.

In any event, the Court's original jurisdiction is severely constricted by the Eleventh Amendment's limit on citizen suits against unconsenting states in Article III courts. Though Congress could nonetheless compel states to submit to such suits as part of a plan to enforce Fourteenth Amendment rights, Fitzpatrick v. Bitzer, 427 U.S. 445 (1976), doing so would not seem consistent (to say the least) with the mood of the day.

18. Some have argued, however, that the clause was intended solely to empower Congress to deal with the scope of appellate review of jury findings of fact. See, e.g., R. Berger, *Congress v. The Supreme Court* 285–96 (1969).

19. Hart, supra note 13, at 1365.

20. See generally Cohens v. Virginia, 19 U.S. (6 Wheat.) 264, 416–18 (1821); Martin v. Hunter's Lessee, 14 U.S. (1 Wheat.) 304 (1816); *The Federalist* nos. 22, 81 (A. Hamilton); id. no. 39 (J. Madison); O.W. Holmes, *Collected Legal Papers* 295–96 (1921).

21. H.R. 73 (Ashbrook) and H.R. 114 (Bennett).

22. For example, H.R. 867 (Crane) would take all controversies arising out of state laws relating to abortion out of all federal courts; H.R. 2365 (Evans) would deprive all federal courts of authority to rule on any question as to whether excluding women in military registration or induction is constitutional. In Rostker v. Goldberg, 453 U.S. 57 (1981), the Court recently upheld all-male military registration. H.R. 2365 would purport to extend and freeze that decision.

23. No particularly helpful federal precedent exists either way on the matter. The seminal cases of Ex parte McCardle, 74 U.S. (7 Wall.) 506 (1868), and Ex parte Yerger, 75 U.S. (8 Wall.) 85 (1868), are certainly not to the contrary, since they together establish only that Congress may extinguish *one avenue* to the Supreme Court for appellate review of a constitutional claim (even when appellant is *en route*) if other avenues for bringing that claim to the Court for review remain open.

24. Marbury v. Madison, 5 U.S. at 137, 178.

25. See United States v. Klein, 80 U.S. (13 Wall.) 128, 145–47 (1871) (Congress cannot require jurisdictional dismissal of suit for return of property by compelling Supreme Court to treat possession of pardon without a disclaimer of guilt as conclusive proof of disloyalty).

26. *Marbury*, 5 U.S. at 178.

27. See infra note 78. But see supra note 22.

28. Cf. Ex parte Milligan, 71 U.S. (4 Wall.) 2, 127 (1866) (no inherent executive power to declare martial law when civil courts are open).

29. See United States v. Nixon, 418 U.S. 683, 704–05 (1974).

30. Muskrat v. United States, 219 U.S. 346, 362 (1911).

31. Maryland v. Louisiana, 451 U.S. 725, 735 (1981) (quoting Massachusetts v. Missouri, 308 U.S. 1, 15 (1939)). Glidden Co. v. Zdanok, 370 U.S. 530 (1962), is not to the contrary. The Court's holding that the tribunals there at issue could be Article III courts despite their inability to compel the United States to satisfy their judgments rested on the reasonableness, absent a showing to the contrary, of "rely[ing] on the good faith of . . . public bodies to respond to [the Court's] judgments," id. at 571 (Harlan, J., announcing judgment, joined by Brennan and Stewart, JJ.).

32. While declaratory relief in an Article III court typically entails no "award of process or [of] damages," it must be embodied in a "decree of a conclusive character, as distinguished from an [advisory] opinion." Aetna Life Ins. Co. v. Haworth, 300 U.S. 227, 241 (1937).

33. Cf. Baker v. Carr, 369 U.S. 186, 204 (1962) (litigants must have concrete stake in outcome of decision).

34. The provisions also violate the Fifth Amendment. See infra text accompanying notes 72–77.

35. 410 U.S. 113 (1973). In such circumstances a "litigant is entitled to resort to a federal forum in seeking redress under 42 U.S.C. §1983 for an alleged deprivation of federal rights" without awaiting state prosecution or otherwise submitting to state adjudication. Wooley v. Maynard, 430 U.S. 705, 710, 712 (1977).

36. If I am correct that a prosecution in such a case could not possibly succeed, see infra note 38, then she is entitled not simply to an acquittal but to a prevention or cessation of any such prosecution. See Younger v. Harris, 401 U.S. 37, 48–49 (1971). Cf. Roe v. Wade, 410 U.S. at 125 (pregnancy is an event capable of repetition, yet evading review).

37. See, e.g., H.R. 900, §1 (Hyde).

38. That such an effort would violate the Due Process Clause of the Fifth Amendment if construed either to empower or to require the states to enforce homicide laws against all abortions from conception onward is argued at some length in my testimony of May 21, 1981, on S. 158 and H.R. 900 before the Subcommittee on Separation of Powers, Senate Judiciary Committee. See also infra note 97.

39. H.R. 867 (Crane); H.R. 900 (Hyde); H.R. 3225 (Mazzoli).

40. Schneiderman v. United States, 320 U.S. 118, 168–69 (1943) (Rutledge, J., concurring).

41. The same infirmity brings H.R. 1079 and H.R. 1180 into conflict with Fifth Amendment due process. Cf. North Carolina v. Swann, 402 U.S. 43 (1971) (state cannot ban busing where needed to cure de jure segregation). The dubious constitutionality of congressional restrictions on federal court remedies, even those couched in jurisdictional terms, has often been discussed. See, e.g.,

Note, "The Nixon Busing Bills and Congressional Power," 81 *Yale L.J.* 1542 (1972).

42. Williams v. Rhodes, 393 U.S. 23, 29 (1968) (emphasis added).

43. Gomillion v. Lightfoot, 364 U.S. 339, 345 (1960) (rejecting such a conclusion where the "garb" was the "realignment of political subdivisions").

44. 80 U.S. (13 Wall.) 128, 147–48 (1871).

45. Battaglia v. General Motors Corp., 169 F.2d 254, 257 (2d Cir.), *cert. denied*, 335 U.S. 887 (1948) (footnote omitted) (upholding the Portal-to-Portal Act of 1947, which had wiped out back-pay liability for travel to and from work stations and had withdrawn jurisdiction to adjudicate these back-pay claims in any state or federal court; the court said that if retroactive destruction of such claims had violated the Fifth Amendment, the jurisdictional withdrawals would all be void as well).

46. Cf. Ex parte Garland, 71 U.S. (4 Wall.) 333 (1867) (former Confederate sympathizers may not be refused right to practice in federal courts).

47. See, e.g., Frost & Frost Trucking Co. v. Railroad Comm'n, 271 U.S. 583, 594 (1926) ("inconceivable that guaranties embedded in the Constitution . . . may thus be manipulated out of existence"), quoted with approval, Western & S. Life Ins. Co. v. State Bd. of Equalization, 451 U.S. 648, 664–65 (1981).

48. Thomas v. Review Bd. of Indiana Employment Security Div., 450 U.S. 707, 717 (1981).

49. See Memorial Hospital v. Maricopa County, 415 U.S. 250, 261 (1974) (striking down one-year waiting period before indigent who had exercised right to move into state could receive nonemergency medical care at public expense; diseases, "if untreated for a year, may become all but irreversible paths to pain, disability, and even loss of life"). The Court evidently found insufficient hardship in a one-year wait for reduced state college tuition, Starns v. Malkerson, 401 U.S. 985 (1971), *aff'g without opinion*, 326 F.Supp. 234 (D. Minn. 1970), or for divorce, Sosna v. Iowa, 419 U.S. 393, 410 (1975).

50. Shapiro v. Thompson, 394 U.S. 618, 629–31 (1969); United States v. Jackson, 390 U.S. 570, 581 (1968). See Pike v. Bruch Church, Inc., 397 U.S. 137, 145 (1970).

51. Contrast the intent requirement where a law is facially neutral and only disproportionate burdens by gender or race are shown. See, e.g., Personnel Adm'r of Mass. v. Feeney, 442 U.S. 256 (1979); Washington v. Davis, 426 U.S. 229 (1976).

52. Thomas v. Review Bd. of Indiana Employment Security Div., 450 U.S. 707, 716–718 (1981); Memorial Hospital v. Maricopa County, 415 U.S. 250, 256–69 (1974); Shapiro v. Thompson, 394 U.S. 618, 634 (1969); United States v. Jackson, 390 U.S. 570, 582–83 (1968); Sherbert v. Verner, 374 U.S. 398, 404–07 (1963).

53. On failure to protect one's citizens as a purely political breach, see Ogden v. Saunders, 25 U.S. (12 Wheat.) 213, 350–51 (1827) (Marshall, C.J., joined by Story and Duvall, JJ., dissenting); Ex parte Bollman, 8 U.S. (4 Cranch) 75 (1807) (Marshall, C.J.) (even failure to provide power to issue habeas, see *U.S. Const.*, art. I, §9, treated as purely political failing, not judicially redressable).

304

NOTES TO PAGES 56-57

54. Marbury v. Madison, 5 U.S. at 137, 163. See Boddie v. Connecticut, 401 U.S. 371, 374-75 (1971). Cf. United Transportation Union v. State Bar of Mich., 401 U.S. 576, 585 (1971) ("collective activity undertaken to obtain meaningful access to the courts is a fundamental right within the protection of the First Amendment").

55. See Eisenberg, supra note 16. To strengthen Eisenberg's case, one might well draw upon the Civil War Amendments and their presuppositions regarding the need for federal protection. Whether the argument can in the end be made persuasively enough even as so augmented is a matter on which I reserve judgment.

56. Lindsey v. Normet, 405 U.S. 56, 77 (1972).

57. See Buckley v. Valeo, 424 U.S. 1, 93 (1976) (per curiam); Bolling v. Sharpe, 347 U.S. 497, 499 (1954).

58. See supra note 52.

59. The Supreme Court found neither, for example, in the withdrawal from indigent women of public funding for both elective and therapeutic abortions under programs in which costs of other medical procedures, including childbirth, were covered. Harris v. McRae, 448 U.S. 297, 324-25 (1980); Maher v. Roe, 432 U.S. 464, 474 (1977). But there is no valid comparison between remanding a choice to the private realm (it was, after all, a privacy analysis that the Court employed in Roe v. Wade), and remitting to hostile territory anyone who chooses to exercise a right, leaving any such individual without the usual weapons for self-defense. Access to police protection and its analogues—including judicial remedies—may not be rights, but they have never been equated with mere "subsidies." See, e.g., Roemer v. Board of Pub. Works, 426 U.S. 736, 747 (1976) (no forbidden financial support when public pays for police to protect churches) (dictum).

60. See, e.g., Lynch v. United States, 189 F.2d 476, 479-80 (5th Cir.), cert. denied, 342 U.S. 831 (1951) (police guilty of "culpable official inaction" and held responsible for beating administered to prisoner by mob while police looked on passively). Cf. Reitman v. Mulkey, 387 U.S. 369, 376-80 (1976) (state responsible for private discrimination that state had expressly immunized "from [official] censure or interference"); NAACP v. Alabama ex rel. Patterson, 357 U.S. 449, 462-63 (1958) (state responsible for private injuries likely to be triggered when it withdraws protection of anonymity); Feiner v. New York, 340 U.S. 315, 325-27 (1951) (Black, J., dissenting) (state abridges speech if it fails to give speaker reasonable police protection from hostile audience); Miller v. Schoene, 276 U.S. 272, 279 (1928) (state failure to cut down diseased trees to protect more valuable crop, although an omission, would have been "none the less a choice").

61. Act of April 9, 1866, ch. 31, §2, 14 Stat. 27 (codified at 18 U.S.C. §242 (1976)). See Screws v. United States, 325 U.S. 91, 108 (1945) (opinion of Douglas, J.) ("The fact that [the unlawful action] is also a violation of state law does not make it any the less a federal offense punishable as such"); id. at 114-16, 133-34 (opinion of Rutledge, J.).

62. Act of April 20, 1871, ch. 22, §1, 17 Stat. 13 (codified at 42 U.S.C. §1983 (1976)). See Monroe v. Pape, 365 U.S. 167, 173–74 (1961) (§1983 was enacted to "override certain kinds of state laws," to provide "a remedy where state law was inadequate," and "to provide a federal remedy where the state remedy, though adequate in theory, was not available in practice"); see also id. at 184–85.

63. See Bantam Books, Inc. v. Sullivan, 372 U.S. 58, 68–70 (1963) (state impermissibly abridged speech by blacklisting disfavored books, thereby encouraging private censorship without need to prosecute anyone).

64. United States v. Hall, 26 Fed. Cas. 79, 81 (C.C.S.D. Ala. 1871) (No. 15,282). See generally chapter 16.

65. See, e.g., Parratt v. Taylor, 451 U.S. 527 (1981) (negligent loss of prisoner's property); accord, Phillips v. Comm'r, 283 U.S. 589, 596–97 (1931) (upholding congressional restriction on injunctions against tax collections since subsequent remedy at law wholly adequate).

66. See, e.g., Roe v. Wade, 410 U.S. 113, 125 (1973) (brevity of nine-month gestation period); id. at 153 (permanence of harm if right abridged).

67. Exemplifying such cases are the Norris-LaGuardia Act of 1932, imposing strict rules on the issuance of injunctions by federal courts in labor disputes, upheld in Lauf v. E.G. Shinner & Co., 303 U.S. 323 (1938) (not ruling, however, on the provisions probably of most doubtful constitutionality in the 1930s—those denying employers injunctive enforcement of "yellow dog contracts"); and the Emergency Price Control Act of 1942, channeling federal judicial review of OPA orders through a special Federal Emergency Court of Appeals, upheld in Yakus v. United States, 321 U.S. 414 (1944), and Lockerty v. Phillips, 319 U.S. 182 (1943). The Emergency Court's inability to grant interim relief was upheld with special reference to the exigent circumstances of the war. Yakus, 321 U.S. at 429. In no respect do these precedents resemble focused excisions of identified *rights*, or of *the only effective means of their vindication*, from the reach of federal judicial power.

68. It seems exceedingly unlikely that any overriding governmental purpose unrelated to the suppression of a list of disfavored rights would fit the withdrawal of those rights from one or more aspects of federal protection closely enough to survive strict scrutiny.

69. See United States v. Hudson & Goodwin, 11 U.S. (7 Cranch) 32 (1812) (no federal common law of crimes).

70. In some cases the consequences of such selective repeal may be even worse. Insofar as rights against *federal* officials are removed from the protective reach of federal courts, for example, severe limits on the authority of state judges to grant relevant relief, even if they wish to do so, are built into the Constitution. See, e.g., Tarble's Case, 80 U.S. (13 Wall.) 397 (1871) (no state habeas available against federal jailer); McClung v. Silliman, 19 U.S. (6 Wheat.) 598 (1821) (no state mandamus available against federal officer). Thus, the provisions purporting to insulate military registration and induction laws and the like from federal judicial review, see H.R. 2365 (Evans) and H.R. 2791 (Evans), are particularly infirm because they leave constitutional claims thoroughly unprotected.

71. Screws v. United States, 325 U.S. 91, 124 (1945) (concurring in result).

72. See supra text accompanying notes 34–40.

73. See supra note 37. Although H.R. 900, §1, "declares" only that the fetus "from conception" falls within "the obligation of the States . . . not to deprive persons of life without due process of law," and says nothing of a state's obligation under the Equal Protection Clause as such, it is settled that due process encompasses a notion of impartial governance that is identical in content to that derived from equal protection. See Buckley v. Valeo, 424 U.S. 1, 93 (1976) (per curiam).

74. The Supreme Court in Roe v. Wade evidently assumed that, if nonviable fetuses were deemed "persons" for Fourteenth Amendment purposes, states would have to protect them no less vigorously than they already protect children and adults. See 410 U.S. 113, 156–57 & n.54 (1973). It has been suggested that no such conclusion need follow, inasmuch as "there are compelling justifications for giving . . . less protection" to beings, whether or not considered "persons," whose "destruction can be prevented only at the cost of a vastly greater imposition on other persons (i.e., the women who carry them) than is required for the protection of infants." Tribe, "Foreword: Toward a Model of Roles in the Due Process of Life and Law," 87 *Harv. L. Rev.* 1, 32 n.144 (1973); Thomson, "A Defense of Abortion," 1 *Philosophy & Pub. Aff.* 47 (1971). But any such argument seems precluded for those who would have the law declare the states' Fourteenth Amendment "obligation . . . not to deprive persons of life" to be *independent* of "age, health, defect, *or condition of dependency*," H.R. 900, §1 (emphasis added).

75. United States v. Klein, 80 U.S. (13 Wall.) 128, 147–48 (1871). See supra text accompanying note 44.

76. Battaglia v. General Motors Corp., 169 F.2d 254, 257 (2d Cir.), *cert. denied*, 335 U.S. 887 (1948). See supra text accompanying note 45.

77. A final insult in this group of provisions is the proposal in H.R. 3225 (Mazolli) for expedited Supreme Court review—which is, of course, no more an excuse for irreparably injuring rights here than it was in the *Pentagon Papers* case, New York Times Co. v. United States, 403 U.S. 713 (1971) (per curiam). Worse yet, the expedited review in H.R. 3225 is conspicuously tilted in one direction: *no* expedited review of *state* court decisions and expedited review of lower federal court decisions *only if "contrary to any part of this Act or . . . hold[ing] unconstitutional any part of this Act."* H.R. 3225, §5 (emphasis added).

78. United States v. Klein, 80 U.S. (13 Wall.) 128, 145 (1871). Approximately as transparent as the abortion provisions in this respect are those dealing with the all-male draft: H.R. 2365 (Evans), which purports to instruct federal courts not to trouble themselves over any challenge to the validity of any Act of Congress providing for military registration or induction of males if the challenge is "on the ground that such Act does not also provide for the registration or induction of female persons," id., §2; and H.R. 2791 (Evans), which invokes Congress' Article I, Section 8, power to raise, support, and regulate armies and navies, and then purports to eliminate from all federal courts any case arising out of a statute or regulation concerning different standards for men and women in mili-

tary registration, induction, or duty assignments. I have very little doubt that both these measures would basically rise or fall on the merits of the substantive position they put forth—that men may continue to be the core of the military despite principles of equality under the Fifth Amendment. See, in this connection, Rostker v. Goldberg, 453 U.S. 57 (1981) (upholding constitutionality of male-only military registration).

79. 393 U.S. 385 (1969).

80. Id. at 386.

81. Id. at 390.

82. Id. at 391.

83. Id. (emphasis added).

84. See Washington v. Davis, 426 U.S. at 229.

85. *Hunter*, 393 U.S. at 390-91 ("[the law] disadvantages *those who would benefit from laws* barring racial, religious, or ancestral discrimination as against *those who would bar* other discriminations *or who would otherwise regulate* the real estate market in their favor") (emphasis added). But see the analysis of Crawford v. Los Angeles Bd. of Educ. in chapter 16.

86. See supra text accompanying notes 50-52.

87. H.R. 72 (Ashbrook); H.R. 326 (Holt); H.R. 408 (Quillen); H.R. 865 (Crane); H.R. 989 (McDonald); H.R. 1335 (Nichols); H.R. 2397 (Crane).

88. See supra text accompanying notes 16-23.

89. 374 U.S. 203 (1963) (ten verses of Bible daily).

90. 370 U.S. 421 (1962) (New York Regents' Prayer). H.R. 2397, alone among the seven bills, would exclude such prayers written by state officials from the definition of "voluntary."

91. H.R. 72, H.R. 326, H.R. 989, and H.R. 1335.

92. (Emphasis added). H.R. 761 (McDonald) is a bit like H.R. 869 in that it deprives all federal courts of jurisdiction *"to make any decision*, or issue any order, which would have the *effect* of requiring any individual to attend any particular school." (Emphasis added). I suspect *every* "decision" finding de jure segregation could be shown to have such an "effect" in one way or another.

93. 347 U.S. 483 (1954).

94. For example, some courts might be reluctant to rely on judicial findings of forbidden congressional motive to invalidate jurisdictional restrictions that are neutral on their face and that are too ambiguous in their effects to be struck down on an impact basis alone. See, e.g., United States v. O'Brien, 391 U.S. 367, 383-84 (1968). But see Washington v. Davis, 426 U.S. at 229; Epperson v. Arkansas, 393 U.S. 97 (1968), and cases cited supra note 50.

95. See Oregon v. Hass, 420 U.S. 714, 719 (1975).

96. Measures like those pending before the House in 1981 have regularly been introduced in Congress in reaction to unpopular Supreme Court rulings in recent decades; their fate in Congress has been a uniformly unhappy one.

97. There is little difference, in my view, between telling the federal courts to speak no more on matters like school prayer or abortion so that the (supposed) majority may resume marching to the beat of its own drummer and filtering federal judicial pronouncements on such matters, Orwell-like, through a device that makes them conform to the majority's preferred meanings. The Supreme Court has ruled, for example, that fetuses cannot be regarded as "persons" within the meaning of the Fourteenth Amendment, Roe v. Wade, 410 U.S. 113, 158 (1973); and that the distinct and "difficult question of when life begins," id. at 159, "need not [be] resolve[d]" judicially for the Court to hold that a state may not, "by adopting one theory of life . . . override the rights of the pregnant woman that are at stake" in deciding whether she is to terminate a pregnancy not yet involving another "person." Id. at 162. In the face of this unambiguous if much-criticized holding in Roe v. Wade, it is a wholly transparent evasion for Congress to seize upon the Court's disclaimer on the question of when human life begins by "answering" that "human life exists from conception," H.R. 900, §1, so as to circumvent the Court's constitutional determination that governmental views on this obviously nonempirical matter simply cannot suffice, under the Constitution as currently written, to usurp a pregnant woman's right to choose. See supra note 38. (The Court's disclaimer was, of course, meant to identify a moral rather than a scientific puzzle. Accord, Resolution of the National Academy of Sciences, April 28, 1981, reported in 212 *Science* 760 (1981)). Circumvention by such linguistic sleight-of-hand does not differ in kind from circumvention by the creation of jurisdictional lacunae.

    Note in this regard that Congress certainly enjoys no more license to override a woman's Fifth Amendment due process rights in the name of its power to enforce the Fourteenth Amendment than a state enjoys to override a woman's Fourteenth Amendment due process rights in the name of its reserved powers under the Tenth Amendment.

98. Edwards v. California, 314 U.S. 160, 186 (1941) (Jackson J., concurring).

6. Entrusting Nonlegislative Power to Congress

1. 103 S. Ct. 2764 (1983).
2. 424 U.S. 1, 140 (1976) (per curiam) (holding the Federal Election Commission to be composed in a manner violative of *U.S. Const.*, art. II, §2, cl. 2, and of the separation of powers, insofar as some of the commission's voting members were appointed by the Speaker of the House and by the president pro tempore of the Senate rather than by "the President, . . . the Courts of Law, or . . . the Heads of Departments"). See infra note 68; L. Tribe, *American Constitutional Law* §4-8 (1978) [hereinafter cited as Tribe, *ACL*]. Throughout this chapter, references to *Buckley* deal only with this holding—not with that decision's substantive rulings with respect to campaign finances.
3. 426 U.S. 833, 845 (1976) (holding that Congress violated the rights of the "States as States" when it extended the federal minimum wage and maximum hour provisions to state and municipal employees). See Tribe, *ACL* §5-22.
4. *Buckley*, 424 U.S. at 126.
5. *Chadha*, 103 S. Ct. at 2781, 2785 n.16.

6. See EEOC v. Wyoming, 103 S. Ct. 1054, 1062-64 (1983); FERC v. Mississippi, 456 U.S. 742, 758–59 (1982); United Transp. Union v. Long Island R.R., 455 U.S. 678, 686–90 (1982); Hodel v. Virginia Surface Mining & Reclamation Ass'n, 452 U.S. 264, 293 (1981); Massachusetts v. United States, 435 U.S. 444, 456 n.13 (1978); Fitzpatrick v. Bitzer, 427 U.S. 445, 453 n.9 (1976).

7. See Community Communications Co. v. City of Boulder, 455 U.S. 40 (1982) (holding that a municipality is not entitled to exemption from the Sherman Antitrust Act, 15 U.S.C. §§1–7 [1982], under a home-rule delegation of state power); cf. Parker v. Brown, 317 U.S. 341 (1943) (states are exempted from the Sherman Antitrust Act).

8. See Tribe, *ACL* §4-2, at 163. Indeed, with new appointments to the Court, even *National League of Cities* could still be transformed into an enduring source of law. See generally chapter 9.

9. 103 S. Ct. at 2788.

10. *The Federalist* no. 78, at 490 (B. Wright ed. 1961) (A. Hamilton).

11. See, e.g., F. Frankfurter, *The Public and Its Government* 77-78 (1930) (the separation of powers principle is "what Madison called a 'political maxim,' and not a technical rule of law."); K. Loewenstein, *Political Power and the Governmental Process* 34–37 (1957) (doctrine is "obsolete and devoid of reality"); Miller & Knapp, "The Congressional Veto: Preserving the Constitutional Framework," 52 *Ind. L.J.* 367, 390 (1977) ("It is doubtful that the concept of separation of powers could really have any objective meaning."); Parker, "The Historic Basis of Administrative Law: Separation of Powers and Judicial Supremacy," 12 *Rutgers L. Rev.* 449, 464–65 (1958) (separation of powers doctrine is at best vague and uncertain).

12. See, e.g., Buckley v. Valeo, 424 U.S. 1, 124 (1976) (per curiam); 1 *Annals of Cong.* 604 (J. Gales ed. 1789) (statement of James Madison) ("[I]f there is a principle in our constitution, indeed in any free constitution, more sacred than another, it is that which separates the legislative, executive, and judicial powers.").

13. 103 S. Ct. at 2781.

14. The first legislative veto provision was included in the Legislative Appropriations Act for fiscal 1933. Act of June 30, 1932, ch. 314, §407, 47 Stat. 382, 414 (repealed 1966); see Abourezk, "The Congressional Veto: A Contemporary Response to Executive Encroachments on Legislative Prerogative," 52 *Ind. L.J.*, 323, 324 n.5 (1977), cited in *Chadha*, 103 S. Ct. at 2793 (White, J., dissenting).

15. See 103 S. Ct. at 2792 (White, J., dissenting); Abourezk, supra note 14, at 324.

16. See 103 S. Ct. at 2811–16 app. (White, J., dissenting); 128 *Cong. Rec.* S2575 (daily ed. Mar. 23, 1982) (listing thirty-three laws containing legislative veto provisions enacted by the 96th Congress).

17. See supra note 14.

18. For a useful compilation of conflicting views, see 103 S. Ct. at 2797 n.12 (White, J., dissenting).

19. See, e.g., J. Bolton, *The Legislative Veto: Unseparating the Powers* 8–10 (1977).

20. See, e.g., Javits & Klein, "Congressional Oversight and the Legislative Veto: A Constitutional Analysis," 52 *N.Y.U. L. Rev.* 455, 459-65 (1977).

21. See Act of Oct. 24, 1962, Pub. L. No. 87–885, §4, 76 Stat. 1247, 1248, *amending* Immigration and Nationality Act, ch. 477, §244(c), 66 Stat. 163, 216 (1952) (codified at 8 U.S.C. §1254(c)(2) [1982]).

22. 103 S. Ct. at 2770.

23. 8 U.S.C. §1254(a)(1) (1982).

24. Transcript of Hearing of Deportation Proceedings held Jan. 11, 1974, Joint Appendix to the Briefs at 12–15, 33–46, INS v. Chadha.

25. 103 S. Ct. at 2770.

26. H.R. Res. 926, 94th Cong., 1st Sess., 121 *Cong. Rec.* 40,800 (1975). "So far as the record . . . shows, the House consideration of the resolution was based on Representative Eilberg's statement from the floor that '[i]t was the feeling of the committee, after reviewing 340 cases, that the aliens contained in the resolution [Chadha and five others] did not meet these statutory requirements, particularly as it relates to hardship; and it is the opinion of the committee that their deportation should not be suspended.' " *Chadha,* 103 S. Ct. at 2772 (quoting 121 *Cong. Rec.* 40,800 (1975)).

27. 121 *Cong. Rec.* 40,800 (1975).

28. 103 S. Ct. at 2772. The Court properly rejected the contention that no Article III controversy existed simply because "Chadha and the INS [took] the same position on the constitutionality of the one-House veto." Id. at 2778.

29. Chadha v. INS, 634 F.2d 408 (9th Cir. 1980), *aff'd,* 103 S. Ct. 2764 (1983). The Supreme Court recognized the House and Senate as parties in the case. INS v. Chadha, 103 S. Ct. at 2773 n.5.

30. INS v. Chadha, 103 S. Ct. 2764 (1983).

31. See, e.g., President's Memorandum of Disapproval of the Amendments to the Education Consolidation Improvements Act, 19 *Weekly Comp. Pres. Doc.* 38 (Jan. 12, 1983) (Reagan); President's Memorandum of Disapproval of the Amendments to the Tribally Controlled Community College Assistance Act, 19 *Weekly Comp. Pres. Doc.* 7 (Jan. 3, 1983); President's Message on Regulatory Reform, 15 *Weekly Comp. Pres. Doc.* 491 (Mar. 26, 1979) (Carter); President's Message on Legislative Vetoes, 14 *Weekly Comp. Pres. Doc.* 1146 (June 21, 1978); International Security Assistance Act of 1977: Statement on signing H.R. 6884 into Law, [1977] 2 *Pub. Papers* 1431 (Aug. 5, 1977); Veto of the Atomic Energy Act Amendments, 1974 *Pub. Papers* 294 (Oct. 12, 1974) (Ford); President's Statement upon Signing the Public Buildings Amendment of 1972, 8 *Weekly Comp. Pres. Doc.* 1076 (June 17, 1972) (Nixon); President's Statement upon Signing the Second Supplemental Appropriations Act, 8 *Weekly Comp. Pres. Doc.* 938 (May 28, 1972); Statement by the President upon Signing the Omnibus Rivers and Harbors Bill, [1965] 2 *Pub. Papers* 1082 (Oct. 23, 1965) (Johnson); Memorandum on Informing Congressional Committees of Changes Involving Foreign Economic Assistance Funds, 1963 *Pub. Papers* 6 (Jan. 9, 1963) (Kennedy); Special Message to the Congress upon Signing the Department of Defense

Appropriations Act, 1955 *Pub. Papers* 688 (July 13, 1955) (Eisenhower); Disapproval of House Bill after Sine Die Adjournment, 98 *Cong. Rec.* 9756 (July 19, 1952); Veto of Bill Relating to Land Acquisition and Disposal Actions by the Army, Navy, Air Force, and Federal Civil Defense Administration, 1951 *Pub. Papers* 280 (May 15, 1951) (Truman); F. D. Roosevelt, Memorandum for the Attorney General (Apr. 7, 1941), *reprinted in* Jackson, "A Presidential Legal Opinion," 66 *Harv. L. Rev.* 1353, 1357 (1953) (Roosevelt); Veto Message from the President of the United States—The First Deficiency Bill (H. Doc. No. 529), 76 *Cong. Rec.* 2445 (Jan. 24, 1933) (Hoover); Veto Message—The Budget Bill, 59 *Cong. Rec.* 8609 (June 4, 1920); Legislative, Executive, and Judicial Appropriations Bill—Veto Message, 59 *Cong. Rec.* 7026 (May 13, 1920) (Wilson).

32. Presidents Eisenhower, Johnson, Nixon, Ford, and Carter. See, e.g., Veto of Department of Energy Authorization Bill, [1977] 2 *Pub. Papers* 1972 (Nov. 5, 1977) (Carter); Veto of the Federal Fire Prevention and Control Bill, [1976-1977] 2 *Pub. Papers* 1984 (July 7, 1976); Veto of Atomic Energy Act Amendments, 1974 *Pub. Papers* 294 (Oct. 12, 1974) (Ford); President's Message Vetoing the War Powers Resolution, 9 *Weekly Comp. Pres. Doc.* 1285 (Oct. 24, 1973) (Nixon); Veto of the Military Authorization Bill, [1965] 2 *Pub. Papers* 907 (Aug. 21, 1965) (Johnson); Veto of Bill Providing for the Conveyance of Lands Within Camp Blanding Military Reservation, Florida, 1954 *Pub. Papers* 507 (May 25, 1954) (Eisenhower); see also Dixon, "The Congressional Veto and Separation of Powers: The Executive on a Leash?" 56 *N.C. L. Rev.* 423, 428 & n.21, 429 & n.24, 432 & n.29 (1978). Members of the Ford and Carter administrations testified against legislative vetoes in various legislative hearings. See, e.g., *Improving Congressional Oversight of Federal Regulatory Agencies: Hearings on S. 2258, S. 2716, S. 2812, S. 2878, S. 2903, S. 2925, S. 3318, and S. 3428 Before the Senate Comm. on Governmental Operations,* 94th Cong., 2d Sess. 124 (1976) (statement of Asst. Atty. Gen. Antonin Scalia); Letter from Asst. Atty. Gen. Patricia Wald to Rep. Peter Rodino, Jr. (D-N.J.) (May 5, 1977) (letter prepared in response to congressional request for Justice Dept. opinion), cited in McGowan, "Congress, Court and the Control of Delegated Power," 77 *Colum. L. Rev.* 1119, 1141-42 (1977).

33. The most famous example is that of President Franklin Roosevelt, who signed the Lend-Lease Act of 1941 despite its legislative veto provision but filed a memorandum with his attorney general asserting the President's constitutional objections to the concurrent resolution veto section of the bill. F. D. Roosevelt, Memorandum for the Attorney General (Apr. 7, 1941), supra note 31. Presidents have often restrained their opposition to specific legislative veto provisions where they greatly desired the statutory authority vested in the bills containing such provisions. See J. Bolton, supra note 19, at 10-13.

34. Then Assistant Attorney General Rex Lee, for example, made such an admission to the Court of Claims in Atkins v. United States, 556 F.2d 1028, 1079 (Ct. Cl. 1977) (Skelton, J., concurring in part and dissenting in part), *cert. denied,* 434 U.S. 1009 (1978).

35. 103 S. Ct. 2764 (1983).

36. The Chief Justice's opinion was joined by Justices Brennan, Marshall, Blackmun, Stevens, and O'Connor.

37. 103 S. Ct. at 2785.

38. Id. at 2784; see also id. at 2786.

39. Id. at 2781.

40. *U.S. Const.*, art. I, §§1, 7; see 103 S. Ct. at 2783-84.

41. *U.S. Const.*, art. I, §7, cl. 2; see 103 S. Ct. at 2782-83.

42. 103 S. Ct. at 2781.

43. Id. at 2781, *quoting* Buckley v. Valeo, 424 U.S. 1, 124 (1976) (per curiam).

44. 103 S. Ct. at 2784.

45. Id. at 2787.

46. Id. at 2787-88.

47. Id. at 2786 (emphasis added). The four provisions are *U.S. Const.*, art. I, §2, cl. 6 (House impeachment); *U.S. Const.*, art. I, §3, cl. 5 (Senate trial and conviction in impeachment cases); *U.S. Const.*, art. II, §2, cl. 2 (Senate approval of presidential appointments); *U.S. Const.*, art. II, §2, cl. 2 (Senate treaty ratification).

48. See 103 S. Ct. at 2804 n.21 (White, J., dissenting).

49. 103 S. Ct. at 2784.

50. Id. at 2784-85 (emphasis added).

51. Id. at 2785 (footnote omitted).

52. In another sense, *none* of this is so. For example, as Justice White argues in his dissent, the structure and history of §244(c) make plain that, unless and until Congress ratifies a deportable alien's permanent residence by the silence of both the House and the Senate in the congressional session in which the attorney general reports his suspension order and in the next session, the suspension order merely *defers deportation*. This order alters no legal rights; it merely proposes such an alteration. 103 S. Ct. at 2804-08 (White, J., dissenting). The retort of the *Chadha* majority—that this understanding of the legal sequence would impermissibly allow Congress to legislate by inaction, see 103 S. Ct. at 2787 n.22—is less than convincing. See discussion in chapter 4 of why constitutional objections to lawmaking by inaction are inapposite when Congress itself enacts a statute ascribing operational meaning to its own future silence. See chapter 4, text accompanying note 80; see also 103 S. Ct. at 2796 n.11 (White, J., dissenting).

53. 103 S. Ct. at 2801-04 (White, J., dissenting).

54. Process Gas Consumers Group v. Consumer Energy Council of America, 103 S. Ct. 3556, 3558 (1983) (White, J., dissenting).

55. 103 S. Ct. at 2803 (White, J., dissenting) (citing United States v. Rock Royal Coop., 307 U.S. 533, 577 [1939] [statutory delegation to affected producers of specified commodities]; Currin v. Wallace, 306 U.S. 1 [1939] [statutory delegation to farmers affected by restrictions upon production or marketing of agricultural commodities]).

56. 103 S. Ct. at 2803 (White, J., dissenting).

57. Id. at 2802 (emphasis added). Rather than reflecting generic problems with the very *logic* of self-reference, inhibitions of a "constitutional" character against self-delegation would presumably reflect more particularistic concerns as to the *psychology* of roles and of their behaviofal elaboration. Cf. D. Hofstadter, *Gödel, Escher, Bach: An Eternal Golden Braid* (1979). An analogy between legislators and testators is useful in discussing this point. Rules permitting testators—so long as various formalities are observed—to delegate to independent *others* the discretionary authority to act with less formality than is demanded of the testamentary disposition itself need not entail the existence of rules permitting the same testators, acting with identical formality, to attach decisive consequences to their *own* future informal actions (e.g., "I hereby bequeath to my nephew whichever bonds I happen to leave in my desk the day I die"). Similarly, it might be supposed that rules permitting legislators—as long as they comply with the formalities of bicameral agreement and presentment—to delegate to agencies the discretionary authority to act informally (i.e., without the safeguards of bicamerality and presentment) need not entail the existence of rules permitting the same legislators, acting identically, to attach decisive consequences to their own future nonlawmaking acts. However, the *reasons* for taking this view as to testators—reasons grounded in a fear that ritualized solemnity in the assumption of a role will assure adequately considered choice, while informal, independent action might not do so—seem difficult to extend to the congressional-administrative context.

58. 103 S. Ct. at 2785 n.16.

59. Id.

60. For a relatively rare exception, see 20 U.S.C. §1232(d)(1)(1976 & Supp. IV 1980) (specifying that a regulation by the Secretary of Education may be vetoed by concurrent resolution only if deemed by Congress to be "inconsistent with the Act from which [the regulation] derives its authority").

61. *U.S. Const.*, art. I, §6, cl. 1 ("[F]or any Speech or Debate in either House, [members of Congress] shall not be questioned in any other Place.").

62. It is, perhaps, a theoretical possibility that deciding whether or not to cast such votes might be deemed a task so inherently nonlegislative in character as to fall outside the protection of the Speech or Debate Clause. But the breadth of the protection the clause has been deemed to confer seemingly precludes such a result, see Tribe, *ACL* §5–18, and certainly precludes it for a Court that deems a one-house veto an inherently *legislative* act.

63. 103 S. Ct. at 2787 n.21 (invoking this observation as a reply to Justice Powell's rationale, 103 S. Ct. at 2788–92 [Powell, J., concurring], that the one-house veto in *Chadha* usurped a judicial function); see 103 S. Ct. at 2803, 2810 (White, J., dissenting).

64. See, e.g., Motor Vehicle Mfrs. Ass'n v. State Farm Mut. Auto Ins. Co., 103 S. Ct. 2856 (1983) (holding that the National Highway Traffic Safety Administration acted in disregard of its statutory duties in revoking passive-restraint requirements without adequate substantive basis).

65. 103 S. Ct. at 2785 n.16 (emphasis added).

66. "[The President] shall nominate, and by and with the Advice and Consent of the Senate, shall appoint Ambassadors, other public Ministers and Consuls, Judges of the Supreme Court, and all other Officers of the United States, whose Appointments are not herein otherwise provided for, and which shall be established by Law; but the Congress may by Law vest the Appointment of such inferior Officers, as they think proper, in the President alone, in the Courts of Law, or in the Heads of Departments." *U.S. Const.*, art II, §2, cl. 2, *applied in* Buckley v. Valeo, 424 U.S. 1, 40–41 (1976) (per curiam).

67. *U.S. Const.*, art. I, §6, cl. 2 ("[N]o Person holding any Office under the United States, shall be a Member of either House during his Continuance in Office.").

68. The Court cited Buckley v. Valeo, 424 U.S. 1 (1976) (per curiam), only in passing and only for a less directly relevant proposition. See 103 S. Ct. at 2774, 2781, 2785 n.16.

69. See 103 S. Ct. at 2784–87.

70. 103 S. Ct. at 2810 (White, J., dissenting).

71. See Tribe, *ACL* §4–8.

72. Presumably someone like Chadha—i.e., someone adversely affected by an action taken by a member of Congress in an allegedly "incompatible" role—would have standing to invoke the clause in a lawsuit urging that the action be disregarded. Cf. Schlesinger v. Reservists Comm. to Stop the War, 418 U.S. 208 (1974) (holding that individuals suing only in their capacity as citizens lack standing to invoke the Incompatibility Clause against members of Congress holding commissions in the Armed Forces Reserve). See also Tribe, *ACL* §3–20, at 89–91.

73. Lewis v. BT Inv. Managers, 447 U.S. 27, 44 (1980) (emphasis added). See generally Tribe, *ACL* §6–31. See also chapter 10.

74. 306 U.S. 1 (1939) (marketing restrictions effective only upon approval by majority of affected farmers).

75. 307 U.S. 533 (1939) (marketing orders issued by Secretary of Agriculture subject to veto by certain affected producers).

76. Federal Election Campaign Act of 1971, Pub. L. No. 92–225, 86 Stat. 3, *amended by* Federal Election Campaign Act Amendments of 1974, Pub. L. No. 93–443, 88 Stat. 1263 (codified at 2 U.S.C. §§431–455 (1982)); see Buckley v. Valeo, 424 U.S. 1 (1976) (per curiam). The 1974 amendments to that 1971 Act vested in the eight-member FEC primary responsibility for administering and enforcing the Act by bringing civil actions against violators, making rules for carrying out the Act's provisions, temporarily disqualifying federal candidates for failing to file required reports, and authorizing convention expenditures in excess of the Act's specified limits. Because such powers of enforcement, rule making, and adjudication could not "be regarded as merely in aid of the legislative function of Congress," id. at 138, they could be "exercised only by persons who are 'Officers of the United States,' " id. at 141.

77. See supra note 52.

78. See supra note 69 and accompanying text.

79. See *The Federalist* no. 76 (A. Hamilton). See also J. Story, *Commentaries on the Constitution of the United States* §1523 (1833); cf. Florida Lime & Avocado Growers v. Paul, 373 U.S. 132, 150–51 (1963) (refusing to accord national preemptive effect to federal marketing rules not drafted "by impartial experts in Washington or even in Florida, but rather by the South Florida Avocado Administration Committee," under a delegation of federal regulatory authority).

80. See 103 S. Ct. at 2810 (White, J., dissenting).

81. In fact, without so much as setting the issue for separate briefing or argument, the Court summarily extended *Chadha* to legislative vetoes of entirely generic rule making by administrators or executives less than two weeks later in a set of eight related cases. Process Gas Consumers Group v. Consumer Energy Council of America, 103 S. Ct. 3556 (1983), *aff'g mem.* Consumer Energy Council of America v. FERC, 673 F.2d 425 (D.C. Cir. 1982) (Nos. 81–2008, 81–2020, 81–2152, and 81–2171), *denying cert. to* 673 F.2d 425 (Nos. 82–177 and 82–209), and *rev'g mem.* Consumers Union of United States v. FTC, 691 F.2d 575 (D.C. Cir. 1982) (Nos. 82–935 and 82–1044). *Process Gas* invalidated the one-house legislative veto provision of the Natural Gas Policy Act of 1978, as applied to a FERC regulation shifting part of the burden of higher natural gas prices from residential to industrial users, and invalidated the two-house legislative veto provision of the Federal Trade Commission Improvements Act of 1980, as applied to an FTC Regulation requiring used car dealers to disclose major defects to buyers.

82. See, e.g., FEC v. Democratic Senatorial Campaign Comm., 454 U.S. 27, 39 (1981).

83. 103 S. Ct. at 2789–90 (Powell, J., concurring); see *U.S. Const.*, art. I, §9, cl. 3. See generally Tribe, *ACL* §§10–4 to 10–5.

84. That Congress' action would thereby comply with Article I's formal requirements for legislation certainly would not preclude its invalidation on these Article III grounds. See, e.g., United States v. Klein, 80 U.S. (13 Wall.) 128, 146–47 (1872), discussed in Tribe, *ACL* §3–5, at 39–40, and in chapter 5, above.

85. Cf. Tribe, *ACL* §10–6. Justice Powell seems to recognize as much when he compares "the effect on Chadha's personal rights" with the impact "had he been acquitted of a federal crime and thereafter found by one House of Congress to have been guilty." 103 S. Ct. at 2791 n.8 (Powell, J., concurring). Needless to say, such a legislative "conviction" would fare no better if decreed by both houses with the President's express approval. See id. at 2792 n.9 (Powell, J., concurring). But see id. at 2776 n.8, 2785 & n.17 (purporting to leave this question open).

86. 103 S. Ct. at 2796 (White, J., dissenting).

87. Justice White may have just this in mind. He finds in the majority's holding "a profoundly different conception of the Constitution than that held by the Courts which sanctioned the modern administrative state." Id. at 2810 (White, J., dissenting); see also supra note 64; cf. American Textile Mfrs. Inst. v. Donovan, 452 U.S. 490, 543–48 (1981) (Rehnquist, J., dissenting, joined by Burger, C. J.) (arguing that OSHA was an unconstitutional delegation of legislative power to the executive branch); Industrial Union Dep't., AFL-CIO v. Ameri-

can Petroleum Inst., 448 U.S. 607, 671–88 (1980) (Rehnquist, J., concurring) (same).

88. 103 S. Ct. at 2810-11 (White, J., dissenting).

89. Press, "The Court Vetoes the Veto," *Newsweek*, July 4, 1983, pp. 16, 17 (quoting Stanley Brand, counsel to the House of Representatives).

90. See 28 U.S.C. §2072 (1976) (Rules of Civil Procedure take effect 90 days after reported to Congress); 28 U.S.C. §2076 (1976) (Rules of Evidence take effect 180 days after reported to Congress); see also Sibbach v. Wilson, 312 U.S. 1 (1941), cited with approval in *Chadha*, 103 S. Ct. at 2776 n.9. On July 20, 1983, four senators introduced a bill under which *no* proposed agency rule could go into effect until 30 days had elapsed. During that time, if a congressional committee approved a joint resolution of disapproval, the rule would be delayed for a further 60 days, in which time the House and Senate could pass the resolution and send it to the President for his signature or veto. S. 1650, 98th Cong., 1st Sess. (1983); see *N.Y. Times*, July 21, 1983, at A19, col. 5.

91. Such a provision, sponsored by Representative Eliot Levitas (D-Ga.), was tentatively added to an appropriations bill for the Consumer Product Safety Commission, H.R. 2668, incorporated into S. 861, 98th Cong., 1st Sess. (1983). See 129 *Cong. Rec.* H4773 (daily ed. June 29, 1983) (statement of Rep. Levitas).

92. Arguments such as those of House Counsel Stanley Brand that, once Congress has delegated power, it cannot "involve [itself] in the rule-making process on a return trip," *N.Y. Times*, June 29, 1983, at A19, col. 1, col. 4, greatly overstate *Chadha* by misconstruing its disapproval of one *method* of ex post restraint on the executive as a blanket prohibition of *any* form of after-the-fact legislative oversight.

93. *U.S. Const.*, art. I, §5, cl. 2.

94. For an example of an action that *is* beyond Congress' constitutional power to restrict, see Myers v. United States, 272 U.S. 52 (1926) (holding that Congress may not protect certain executive officials appointed by the President with the approval of the Senate from removal by the President without the Senate's consent).

95. Thus, it seems plain that nothing in *Chadha* casts doubt on the validity of those provisions of the War Powers Resolution that impose *reporting requirements* on the President, War Powers Resolution §4(a), 50 U.S.C. §1543(a) (1976), and set *durational limits* of sixty to ninety days on the presence of United States Armed Forces in "hostilities" abroad "unless the Congress . . . has declared war or has enacted a specific [statutory] authorization for such use of United States Armed Forces," War Powers Resolution §5(b), 50 U.S.C. §1544(b) (1976 & Supp. V 1981). As the Court expressly stated in *Chadha*, "other means of control [by Congress], such as durational limits on authorizations and formal reporting requirements, lie well within Congress' constitutional power." 103 S. Ct. at 2786 n.19. It follows from *Chadha*, however—as well as from the purpose of §5(b) of the War Powers Resolution—that such reporting requirements and durational limits must be triggered by the objective presence of events such as "hostilities"—events whose presence or absence a court can itself ascertain—and *not* by a one-house or even two-house "resolution" that such events have indeed oc-

curred. The contrary reading of §5(b) in Crockett v. Reagan, 558 F.Supp. 893, 899–901 (D.D.C. 1982) (holding that the time limit in §5(b) does not begin to run until Congress "take[s] action to express its view that the [War Powers Resolution] is applicable to the situation"), is thus manifestly untenable after *Chadha.*

96. See, e.g., Dames & Moore v. Regan, 453 U.S. 654 (1981) (upholding President Carter's Iranian hostage settlement), discussed in chapter 4, above, at text accompanying notes 65–73.

97. See, e.g., Youngstown Sheet & Tube Co. v. Sawyer, 343 U.S. 579 (1952) (invalidating President Truman's Steel Seizure), discussed in chapter 4, above, at text accompanying notes 27–38, 56–59, 72.

98. It follows that §5(c) of the War Powers Resolution, 50 U.S.C. §1544(c) (1976 & Supp. V 1981), is invalid under *Chadha* insofar as that section purports to require a removal of United States Armed Forces in specified circumstances "if the Congress so directs by concurrent resolution."

99. 103 S. Ct. at 2786 n.19.

100. 103 S. Ct. at 2795 (White, J., dissenting) (footnote omitted).

101. See supra note 98.

102. Certainly §5(b), see supra note 95, is in no way jeopardized by the invalidity of §5(c).

103. A federal district court in 1983 reached just this conclusion in striking down the Carter Administration's transfer of Equal Pay Act enforcement authority from the Labor Department to the Equal Employment Opportunity Commission. This transfer occurred under a plan adopted pursuant to the Executive Reorganization Act of 1977, 5 U.S.C. §906 (1982), which gave the President authority to restructure the executive branch subject to a one-house veto. Finding such a scheme unconstitutional under *Chadha,* the district court deemed the veto provision inseverable from the act as a whole because Congress would not, in the court's view, have delegated such broad power to the President without reserving a veto. The Court thus held the transfer of authority to EEOC void, although no legislative veto was exercised. EEOC v. Allstate Ins. Co., 98 Lab. Cas. (CCH) ¶ 34,431 (S.D. Miss. Sept. 9, 1983). The approach urged in this essay would require that decision to be reversed.

104. See 103 S. Ct. at 2774–76.

105. 103 S. Ct. at 2816–17 (Rehnquist, J., dissenting).

106. See Tribe, *ACL* §12–27, at 717–18.

107. *Chadha,* 103 S. Ct. at 2775 (quoting Champlin Ref. Co. v. Corporation Comm'n, 286 U.S. 210, 234 (1932)).

108. See supra note 103.

109. See Tribe, *ACL* §§3–23, 3–25 to 3–29.

110. See Tribe, *ACL* §§12–24, 12–29.

111. As David Shapiro has remarked, "No matter what language is used in a judicial opinion, a federal court *cannot* repeal a duly enacted statute of any legislative authority." Shapiro, "State Courts and Federal Declaratory Judgments," 74 *Northwestern U. L. Rev.* 759, 767 (1979) (emphasis added).

112. The *Chadha* majority may be understood to have suggested as much, see 103 S. Ct. at 2787 n.22, but only in response to Justice White's dissenting argument that the *exercise* of a one-house veto should be viewed not as unicameral lawmaking but as a failure to obtain bicameral approval. See 103 S. Ct. at 2808 (White, J., dissenting).

113. See supra note 52.

114. Compare Justice Rehnquist's argument in Arnett v. Kennedy, 416 U.S. 134, 154 (1974) (plurality opinion), that one who relies on an Act of Congress for his underlying substantive entitlement "must take the bitter with the sweet." See Tribe, ACL §10-12.

115. The Speech or Debate Clause, *U.S. Const.*, art. I, §6, cl. 1, would presumably immunize Congress at least to that degree.

116. That is, after all, the theory of Marbury v. Madison, 5 U.S. (1 Cranch) 137, 177–78 (1803).

117. See *Chadha*, 103 S. Ct. at 2816 (Rehnquist, J., dissenting); Carter v. Carter Coal Co., 298 U.S. 238, 312 (1936).

118. To be sure, legislative history and intent may shed light on this issue of meaning just as on other issues of statutory construction. But there is a major, even if subtle, difference, both in principle and as a practical matter, between (a) treating evidence of what Congress would have done, or would have wanted courts to do, in the event of partial invalidation as shaping our understanding of what Congress' law *means*; and (b) treating Congress' unenacted wishes or inclinations as the very *objects* of the Court's search. See, e.g., chapter 4, above, at text accompanying notes 50–55, 81–90, and n.105. In practice, the former perspective—which I regard as the only defensible one—is much less likely than the latter to generate rulings of inseverability. For such rulings follow with considerably greater ease when the question put is whether Congress *might have preferred* no law to a severed law had the choice been unavoidable, than they do when the question put is whether Congress *in fact meant*, and all but expressly *agreed*, to enact a law that would indeed self-destruct rather than survive a certain form of partial invalidation. Whenever the law's language and logic leave the matter in doubt, only the clearest evidence that a majority of both houses of Congress actually *meant to choose self-destruction over severability* should suffice to yield an interpretation of inseverability. And, whenever the law's language and logic compel the contrary interpretation (i.e., one of severability), that should end the matter whatever the evidence of intent.

119. *Chadha*, 103 S. Ct. at 2795 (White, J., dissenting).

7. Entrusting Federal Judicial Power to Hybrid Tribunals

1. Buckley v. Valeo, 424 U.S. 1, 122 (1976) (per curiam).

2. INS v. Chadha, 103 S. Ct. 2764, 2795 (1983) (White, J., dissenting).

3. *The Federalist* no. 78 (A. Hamilton), at 466 (New American Library ed. 1961). Hamilton drew on Montesquieu's belief that " 'there is no liberty if the power of judging be not separated from the legislative and executive powers.' " Id., quoting 1 *Spirit of Laws* 181.

4. *The Federalist* no. 79 (A. Hamilton), at 472 (New American Library ed. 1961). See note 62 infra.

5. 458 U.S. 50 (1982).

6. 103 S. Ct. 2764 (1983), discussed in chapter 6.

7. Pub. L. 95–598, 92 Stat. 2549.

8. In fact, at times it has appeared that the controversy over the status of the bankruptcy courts and judicial officers has been about everything *except* the independence of bankruptcy judges. The Bankruptcy Reform Act of 1978 provision that the judges would serve for fourteen-year terms represented a compromise between competing camps concerned with the effect on the federal bench of the addition of over two hundred more Article III judges. The Bankruptcy Commission had originally recommended that the jurisdiction of the old bankruptcy courts be expanded with the judges appointed for fifteen-year terms. See H. Doc. No. 93–137, Part II, p. 30 (1973). The House Judiciary Committee was basically supportive of this position, but polled a group of constitutional scholars (including Professors Charles Alan Wright, Herbert Wechsler, Terrance Sandalow, David Shapiro, and Paul Mishkin) in 1976 to inquire, among other things, whether these judges would be constitutionally entitled to the structural safeguards of Article III. House Hearings on H.R. 31 and H.R. 32, pp. 2682–2706 (1976). Although the responses to the inquiry were not unanimous, the committee was convinced that the judges should be given life tenure, and the proposal was so amended. H.R. Rep. No. 95–595, p. 39 (1977). The Judicial Conference—and its chairman, Chief Justice Burger—was opposed to "giving Article III tenure to referees in bankruptcy" and conveyed this objection to congressional committees, individual congressmen, and eventually the White House. See *Report of Proceedings of the Judicial Conference of the United States*, pp. 23–24 (March 10–11, 1977); *House Hearings on H.R. 8200*, 95th Cong., 1st Sess., p. 112 (1977); *Wall St. Journal* Oct. 2, 1978, p. 5; *N.Y. Times*, Nov. 12, 1978, p. 29. The House passed a bill giving the bankruptcy judges Article III protection, but the compromise bill eventually signed into law by President Carter gave them fourteen-year terms. 92 Stat. 2549 (1978).

When the Supreme Court in *Marathon* struck down this arrangement as unconstitutional, it stayed its order until Oct. 4, 1982, in order to give Congress a chance to pass remedial legislation. It extended the stay until Dec. 24, but refused the Justice Department's request for a further postponement. For the next two years, final congressional action was stalled by debate over substantive changes in bankruptcy law as well as debate between factions motivated by political concerns about which President would get to appoint more than two hundred lifetime federal judges and what their influence on civil rights litigation would be: "In 1978 Congress created 153 new judgeships, giving President Carter an historic opportunity to shape the federal judiciary. But rather than use the opportunity to make history by appointing the most qualified judges ever, he decided to break other records so that he would become known as the President who appointed the most women, the most blacks, the most Hispanics, and the like. Today fear runs high in some quarters that President Reagan will not challenge those records but will instead return to the traditional notion that merit is of primary importance . . . and that he will try to find more Posners, Borks, and Scalias—quality judges with no apparent bias in favor of special causes. There is a fear that the panscales of justice will appear balanced rather than tilted in someone's favor. The discerning observer will note that such fear is not a fear that bankruptcy judges will decide, for example, civil rights cases . . . , it is a fear that judges who have not been soldiers in the army of the civil rights community will decide civil rights cases. The distrust of judges who have no bias in favor of civil rights causes is one which this House should not honor." "Separate Views of Mr. Hyde" in H. Rep. 98-9, 98th Cong., 1st Sess., pp. 116–118 (Feb. 24, 1983).

In June 1984, after more than two years of deadlock, Congress overwhelmingly approved the Bankruptcy Amendments and Federal Judges Act of 1984, 52 U.S. L.W. 2023 (1984); Keller, "Conferees Adopt Plan to Overhaul Bankruptcy Field," *New York Times*, June 29, 1984 at A1. The legislation restructures the bankruptcy court system by providing for the appointment of 232 bankruptcy judges for 14-year terms with compensation set under the Federal Salary Act. The judges are to be appointed by federal circuit court judges and are to operate as adjuncts of the district courts, with no jurisdiction over the matters at issue in *Marathon*. The legislation also includes a number of substantive changes in the bankruptcy laws, including a section which effectively overrules part of the Court's decision in NLRB v. Bildisco & Bildisco, 104 S. Ct. 1188 (1984), by limiting employers' freedom to escape union contracts by filing for bankruptcy. *Bildisco* permitted debtors in possession to reject collective bargaining agreements without any showing that the business was likely to fail unless the agreement was rejected.

9. See, e.g., Crowell v. Benson, 285 U.S. 22, 88 & 93 (1932) (Brandeis, J., dissenting).

10. Ex parte Bakelite Corp., 279 U.S. 438, 449 (1929).

11. 26 U.S. (1 Pet.) 511, 546 (1828).

12. Id. at 546, referring to art. IV, §3, cl. 2. Chief Justice Marshall's opinion held that the territorial courts "are not Constitutional courts, in which the judicial power conferred by the Constitution on the general government can be deposited." 26 U.S. (1 Pet.) at 546. Nonetheless, it has always been held that the Supreme Court may review decisions of a territorial court, suggesting some of the conceptual problems created by the existence of "legislative courts." See, e.g., Durousseau v. U.S., 10 U.S. (6 Cranch) 307 (1810).

13. 26 U.S. (1 Pet.) at 546.

14. There may be more limits on the power of Congress to channel matters susceptible of judicial determination through non–Article III courts in the District of Columbia than in the territories.

15. The discretion may be not totally unfettered; a grossly unfair arrangement might be struck down as violative of the Due Process Clause.

16. 59 U.S. (18 How.) 272 (1856).

17. Id. at 283.

18. *U.S. Const.*, art. III, §2, cl. 1.

19. 59 U.S. (18 How.) at 284.

20. Id.

21. The Court found that the summary proceeding in question in *Murray's Lessee* did not violate due process of law when "[t]ested by the common and statute law of England prior to the emigration of our ancestors, and by the laws of many of the States at the time of the adoption of [the Fifth] amendment." Cf. Ingraham v. Wright, 430 U.S. 651, 675–76 (1977) (no due process violation when school child is subjected to corporal punishment without a hearing, because child has right under common law since Blackstone to recover damages after the fact if punishment is excessive).

22. 59 U.S. (18 How.) at 284.

23. This rule applies only to federal courts in the states. In the territories, where the Congress exercises plenary power, it may create tribunals which are not subject to the structural safeguards of Article III, but which may hear cases involving these core "private rights." See American Insurance Co. v. Canter, supra note 11.

24. 458 U.S. at 108 (White, J., dissenting). Justice White based his argument on language in *Murray's Lessee* which he read to mean that "the Court will review the legislative record to determine whether there appeared to Congress to be compelling reasons for not establishing an Art. III court." Id. at 108 n.9.

25. 279 U.S. 438 (1929).

26. Id. at 459.

27. Id. at 458.

28. Id. at 453.

29. 285 U.S. 22 (1932).

30. Id. at 51.

31. Id. at 46.

32. Id. at 51.

33. Id. at 54.

34. Id. at 85.

35. See text accompanying notes 84 to 86. To the extent that *Crowell* has been undermined, it is with regard to the limitations on—not the existence of—administrative power. Plumb, "The Tax Recommendations of the Commission on Bankruptcy Laws: Tax Procedures," 88 Harv. L. Rev. 1360, 1468 (1975). But see Currie, "The Federal Courts and the American Law Institute," 36 U. Chi. L. Rev. 1, 13 n.67 (1968) (contending that the decision in Glidden Co. v. Zdanok, 370 U.S. 530 (1972), undercuts the Crowell principle and entitles litigants to a tenured judge).

36. 289 U.S. 553 (1933).

37. H. Hart & H. Wechsler, *The Federal Courts and the Federal System* 258 (P. Bator, P. Mishkin, D. Shapiro, H. Wechsler ed. 1973) [hereinafter cited as Hart & Wechsler].

38. 289 U.S. 516 (1933).

39. 47 Stat. 382.

40. Id. §107.

41. 289 U.S. at 526, 560.

42. 289 U.S. at 545.

43. Id. at 546–47.

44. 289 U.S. at 580. Since Congress can assign settlement of claims against the government to the executive, a court, or itself, "such power, in whatever guise or by whatever agency exercised, is no part of the judicial power vested in the constitutional courts by the third article," and the Court of Claims is therefore not an Article III court. Id. at 580–81.

45. *U.S. Const.*, art. III, §2, cl. 1.

46. *Williams*, 289 U.S. at 577 (emphasis added). See Hart & Wechsler, supra note 37, at 398–99 (discussing the flaws of the *Williams* case and labeling it an "intellectual disaster"); C. A. Wright, *Federal Courts* (3d ed. 1976) at 33, criticizing the reasoning but not the result in *Williams*.

47. 370 U.S. 530 (1962).

48. Justice Harlan was joined by Justices Brennan and Stewart. Chief Justice Warren and Justice Clark concurred in the result. Justices Black and Douglas dissented. Justices Frankfurter and White took no part in the decision.

49. The Court relied on legislation enacted by Congress subsequent to those decisions in which Congress declared these tribunals to be Article III courts, 370 U.S. at 540–43, despite its holding in *Bakelite* that congressional intent is irrelevant. 279 U.S. at 459.

50. 370 U.S. at 547.

51. 411 U.S. 389 (1973).

52. Id. at 407–8 (emphasis added) (upholding the constitutionality of conferring jurisdiction over criminal matters on courts in the District of Columbia unprotected by Article III salary and tenure requirements).

53. 370 U.S. at 552.

54. Northern Pipeline Construction Co. v. Marathon Pipe Line Co., 458 U.S. 50, 113 (1982) (White, J., dissenting).

55. 458 U.S. 50 (1982).

56. Joined by Justices Marshall, Blackmun, and Stevens. Justices Rehnquist and O'Connor concurred in the result.

57. He was joined by the Chief Justice and Justice Powell.

58. Justice Rehnquist so characterized the dissent in his concurring opinion, 458 U.S. at 91.

59. 458 U.S. at 113 (White, J., dissenting).

60. 458 U.S. at 58–59.

61. Id. at 60.

62. It is settled, for example, that Congress may decide, in its unfettered discretion, whether or not to award cost-of-living salary increases to federal judges so as to prevent inflation from working de facto reductions in the salaries of such judges—so long as, having enacted a salary increase, Congress does not then re-

peal any such increase after the date on which it was scheduled to go into effect. See United States v. Will, 449 U.S. 200 (1980) (striking down retroactive repeals but upholding repeals whose effective date fell *prior* to the effective date of the scheduled salary increase). Arguably, the Bill of Attainder Clause, Article I, Section 9, Clause 3, as well as Article III, continue to protect *individual* federal judges even from *prospective* repeals targeted at identifiable judges; but the holding of *Will*, in which the Court's justices were required to rule on the validity of measures affecting their own compensation, leaves Congress free—both by calculated omission and by prospective rescission—to retaliate against the federal judiciary as a whole for a corpus of decisions with which Congress is displeased.

63. 458 U.S. at 59.

64. Id. at 64.

65. See American Insurance Co. v. Canter, 26 U.S. (1 Pet.) 511 (1828).

66. See, e.g., Palmore v. United States, 411 U.S. 389 (1973).

67. 458 U.S. at 64–65.

68. See, e.g., Dynes v. Hoover, 61 U.S. (20 How.) 65 (1858); Burns v. Wilson, 346 U.S. 137 (1953).

69. 458 U.S. at 66.

70. See, e.g., Murray's Lessee v. Hoboken Land & Improvement Co., 59 U.S. (18 How.) 272 (1856); Ex parte Bakelite Corp., 279 U.S. 438 (1929); Crowell v. Benson, 285 U.S. 22 (1932); Atlas Roofing Co. v. Occupational Safety Comm'n., 430 U.S. 442 (1977).

71. 458 U.S. at 70.

72. Id. at 71.

73. *U.S. Const.*, art. I, §8, cl. 4.

74. 458 U.S. at 71.

75. The plurality found it significant that Congress constituted the bankruptcy courts as "adjuncts" to the district courts and not as legislative courts, 458 U.S. at 63 n.13, and chided the dissenters for not appreciating the distinction. Id. at 77 n.29. The plurality concluded that the bankruptcy court was in fact a "non–Art. III adjunct." Id. at 87. It may be ill-advised to take the plurality's taxonomic distinctions too seriously, since it had difficulty in using its own vocabulary precisely; the administrative entity in Crowell v. Benson, 285 U.S. 22 (1932), is variously referred to as a "legislative court," id. at 72, an "administrative agency," id. at 78, and an "adjunct," id. at 77. For an amusing variation on the immortal question, "What's in a name?" see "Federal Jurisdiction Haiku," 32 *Stan. L. Rev.* 229, 230 (1979): "Legislative Courts /Are but agencies in drag; /Glidden is but paint" (K. Karst).

76. 458 U.S. at 105. If one adds the three exceptions together, rather than subtracting them seriatim from Article III, one discovers that the plurality has put its stamp of approval on Article I courts which "operate throughout the country" (administrative agencies), "adjudicate both private and public rights" (courts of the territories and the District of Columbia), and adjudicate matters in "areas in which congressional control is 'extraordinary' " (courts-martial and the D.C.

courts). Id. Justice White found it impossible to distinguish the last category from "the general 'arising under' jurisdiction of Art. III courts." Id.

77. Id. at 70.

78. Id. at 70 n.25. This reliance on history seems ironic in an opinion that goes to such lengths to paper over inconsistencies and reversals in the case law.

79. 458 U.S. at 104.

80. Cf. Pennhurst State School & Hospital v. Halderman, 52 L.W. 4155 (1984). There, Justice Powell, joined by the Chief Justice and Justices White, Rehnquist, and O'Connor, rejected arguments that " 'considerations of judicial economy, convenience, and fairness to litigants' that underlie pendent jurisdiction" should permit maintenance of a federal suit against state officials on the basis of state law in spite of the jurisdictional bar posed by the Eleventh Amendment. "[C]onsiderations of policy cannot override the constitutional limitation on the authority of the federal judiciary to adjudicate suits against a State." Id. at 4164.

81. 458 U.S. at 73 (citation omitted). Article III's "command of an independent Judiciary must be honored . . . where 'laws of national applicability and affairs of national concern are at stake.' " Id. at 76 (citing Palmore v. United States, 411 U.S. 389, 408 (1973)). Statutes enacted under Congress' legislative authority in the bankruptcy field certainly fit that description, and therefore an untenured bankruptcy court judge may assist in the adjudication of issues arising under them only if the "essential attributes" of judicial power are retained by the supervising Article III district court judge. 458 U.S. at 84–85. The *Marathon* plurality distinguished both the administrative scheme upheld in Crowell v. Benson, 285 U.S. 22 (1932), and the Federal Magistrates Act upheld in United States v. Raddatz, 447 U.S. 667 (1980), on this ground. The United States Employees' Compensation Commission in *Crowell* was empowered to decide only a narrow range of factual questions, and its compensation orders could be enforced by a district court judge only if they were found to be in accord with the law and supported by the record. 285 U.S. 44, 54; 485 U.S. at 84–5. Similarly, the Supreme Court approved of the referral of suppression motions to federal magistrates because " '[t]he authority—and the responsibility—to make an informed, final determination . . . remains with the judge.' " 458 U.S. at 81, quoting *Raddatz*, 447 U.S. at 682 (citation omitted). The plurality in *Marathon* also twice distinguished *Raddatz* by quoting Justice Blackmun's concurring observation that, because magistrates are appointed and removed by the district court, the only threat to their independence "comes from within, rather than without the judicial department." 458 U.S. at 79 nn.30, 31, quoting 447 U.S. at 685. Yet the salaries of magistrates are not immune from reduction, see 28 U.S.C. §634(b) (1976 ed., Supp. III), and under the Bankruptcy Reform Act of 1978, bankruptcy judges were appointed for fourteen-year terms and could be removed only by the judicial council of the circuit, 28 U.S.C. §§152, 153(a)(b), so the distinction seems exaggerated.

The Ninth Circuit recently relied on *Marathon* to find §636(c) of the Magistrates Act unconstitutional in Pacemaker Diagnostic Clinic of America, Inc. v. Instromedix, Inc., 712 F.2d 1305, *reh'g en banc granted*, 718 F.2d 971 (1983). Section 636(c), which authorizes a magistrate, on consent of the parties, to conduct trials and enter judgments, was struck down because it delegated judicial powers to magistrates who do not enjoy Article III salary and tenure protections. The court rejected arguments that the waiver by both parties overcame the constitutional obstacles to the delegation, observing that "rather than being exclusively a due process right of the litigants waivable by them, the requirement of an Article III judge is jurisdictional and thus not waivable." Id. at 1312. The Third Circuit has reached a contrary decision on the same question, finding relevant the fact that the reference to a magistrate is consensual; that the district judge has the power to vacate the reference; that the magistrate is appointed by the district judge, is a part of the district court, and is specially designated to try cases; and that the parties have a right of appeal to a district judge or the court of appeals. Wharton-Thomas v. United States, 721 F.2d 922 (3d Cir. 1983).

82. U.S. Const., art. III, §1 (emphasis added).

83. See Marathon, 458 U.S. at 86 n.39 (plurality opinion).

84. 285 U.S. 22, 86-87 (1932).

85. See, e.g., Tribe, ACL §3-5, at 43; Hart & Wechsler at 396.

86. See 28 U.S.C. §1334.

87. See Marathon, 458 U.S. at 82 n.33 (independence of federal judiciary is not "simply [a] question of due process in relation to notice and hearing," but is "rather a question of the appropriate balance of Federal judicial power," quoting Crowell v. Benson, 285 U.S. 22, 56 (1932)); United States v. Raddatz, 447 U.S. 667, 706 n.6 (1980) (Marshall, J., dissenting) (state courts are necessarily independent of the federal government and therefore, unlike federal judges unprotected from congressional reprisal, provide a reliable buffer against congressional excesses).

88. 458 U.S. at 83.

89. Buckley v. Valeo, 424 U.S. 1, 122 (1976).

90. 458 U.S. at 83 (footnote omitted). The Court's partial catalogue of matters falling within the public-rights doctrine in Crowell is equally applicable here: "Familiar illustrations of administrative agencies created for the determination of such matters are found in connection with the exercise of the congressional power as to interstate and foreign commerce, taxation, immigration, the public lands, public health, the facilities of the post office, pensions and payments to veterans," 285 U.S. 22, 51 (1932) (footnote omitted). The Marathon plurality itself quoted this passage from Crowell, 458 U.S. at 69.

91. 259 U.S. 276 (1922), approved in Agosto v. Immigration & Naturalization Serv., 436 U.S. 748, 753 (1978).

92. Id. at 753.

93. Marathon, 458 U.S. at 86 n.39 (quoting Crowell v. Benson, 285 U.S. at 57). See also id. at 84.

94. Id. at 84.

95. Id. (footnote omitted).

96. Id. at 71.

97. *U.S. Const.*, art. I, §8, cl. 4.

98. The plurality implies in its penultimate footnote that the Court's holding may be just this limited, but that the entire Bankruptcy Reform Act of 1978 must be invalidated because the offending provision is inseverable from the rest. 458 U.S. at 87. Indeed, since the concurring opinion of Justice Rehnquist, joined by Justice O'Connor, limits its agreement with the plurality to the issues of severability and jurisdiction over state-law claims and would not accord standing to Marathon to raise any other objections, id. at 91, the only issue decided by a majority of the Court is that Congress may not grant jurisdiction to decide a state law issue to an Article I court. Since the dissenters—Chief Justice Burger, id. at 92, Justice White, joined by the Chief Justice and Justice Powell, id. at 92, 101 n.6—expressly agreed with the concurring justices that no broader issues need be reached, the bizarre result is that the Bankruptcy Reform Act of 1978 was held unconstitutional 6-3, even though the Court held 5-4 that there was no sweeping invalidation of Congress' broad grant of jurisdiction to the bankruptcy courts.

99. Art. I, §8, cl. 4.

100. Crowell v. Benson, 285 U.S. 22, 50 (1932).

101. 430 U.S. 442 (1977).

102. 84 Stat. 1590, 29 U.S.C. §651, et seq.

103. 430 U.S. at 445.

104. 430 U.S. at 450. See also NLRB v. Jones & Laughlin Steel Corp., 301 U.S. 1, 48–49 (1937) (administrative agency may determine whether employer has violated statutory duty of fair practice and impose statutory remedies of reinstatement and payment for lost time); Oceanic Nav. Co. v. Stranahan, 214 U.S. 320, 339 (1909) (executive officers may enforce civil money penalties for violation of congressionally imposed statutory duties in customs and immigration laws). Although all three of these cases dealt with the specific issue of the applicability to administrative proceedings of the Seventh Amendment guarantee of a civil jury, the Court has treated the analysis in these decisions of the public-private rights distinction as interchangeable with that of the Article III cases. See, e.g., *Atlas Roofing*, 430 U.S. at 450–51 (citing *Crowell*, *Murray's Lessee*, and *Bakelite*); *Marathon*, 458 U.S. at 66–70 (citing *Oceanic* and *Atlas Roofing*).

105. *Atlas Roofing*, 430 U.S. at 458. In *Marathon*, the plurality went so far as to indicate that the presence of the federal government as plaintiff is a *necessary* but not a *sufficient* means of distinguishing public from private rights, and that "even with respect to matters that arguably fall within the scope of the 'public rights' doctrine, the presumption is in favor of Art. III courts. See Glidden v. Zdanok, 370 U.S. 530, 548–49 & n.21 (1962) (opinion of Harlan, J.)." 458 U.S. 69–70 n.23.

106. This may answer the plurality's query in *Marathon* as to how we are to distinguish between Congress' Article I powers and those conferred by various amendments to the Constitution. See *Marathon*, 458 U.S. at 74 n.27.

107. 447 U.S. 667, 683 (1980). Amendments to the Magistrates Act allowing magistrates, with consent of the parties, to conduct any or all proceedings in a jury or nonjury civil case and order the entry of judgment have been found unconsti-

tutional by the Ninth Circuit in Pacemaker Diagnostic Clinic of America, Inc. v. Instromedix, Inc., discussed supra note 81.

108. 28 U.S.C. §636(b)(1).

109. 447 U.S. at 674.

110. Id. at 682.

111. 447 U.S. at 686–87 and n.* (Powell, J., concurring in part and dissenting in part).

112. He was joined by Justices White, Blackmun, Rehnquist, and Stevens.

113. 447 U.S. at 681 n.7.

114. See 447 U.S. at 703 (Marshall, J., dissenting).

115. 458 U.S. at 83 n.35.

116. The plurality explicitly declined to specify any further limitations. 458 U.S. at 80–81 n.32.

117. See, e.g., 458 U.S. at 101–2, 113. See also Justice White's dissent in the legislative veto decision, discussed in chapter 6.

118. 285 U.S. 22 (1932). See 458 U.S. at 84–86.

119. 458 U.S. at 101–02 (White, J., dissenting).

120. See, e.g., 5 U.S.C. §557 (general rule under Administrative Procedure Act); 29 U.S.C. §160(c) (National Labor Relations Board); 17 CFR §207.17(g)(2) (1979) (Securities and Exchange Comm'n.).

121. See, e.g., Universal Camera Corp. v. NLRB, 340 U.S. 474 (1951); Morgan v. United States, 298 U.S. 468 (1936). See generally J. Mashaw, *Bureaucratic Justice* (1983).

122. 458 U.S. at 82 n.34. See also 4 K. Davis, *Administrative Law Treatise* §29.08 (1958).

123. 458 U.S. at 102 (White, J., dissenting).

124. 458 U.S. at 80 (plurality opinion).

125. 430 U.S. at 460.

126. St. Joseph Stock Yards Co. v. United States, 298 U.S. 38, 84 (1936) (Brandeis, J., concurring) ("The supremacy of law demands that there shall be an opportunity to have some court decide whether an erroneous rule of law was applied."); see also Tribe, *ACL* §3–5, at 43.

127. 458 U.S. 70 n.23 (citing *Atlas Roofing*).

128. Id. at 69 n.23.

129. See also chapter 6.

8. Choke Holds, Church Subsidies, and Nuclear Meltdowns

1. 5 U.S. (1 Cranch) 137 (1803) (asserting power of judicial review to invalidate Act of Congress purporting to confer jurisdiction that Court deemed itself without authority to exercise under Article III).

2. See L. Tribe, *American Constitutional Law* §§3–17 to 3–29 (1978) [hereinafter cited as Tribe, *ACL*].

3. States may generally grant broader rights of standing in their courts to assert federal claims than Article III and prudential considerations the United States Supreme Court has imposed would grant in federal courts. See Princeton University v. Schmid, 455 U.S. 100, 102 n.* (1982) (per curiam): City of Los Angeles v. Lyons, 103 S. Ct., 1660, 1671 (1983); Tribe, ACL §§3–18. This freedom might arguably be limited where the Supreme Court has rolled standing inquiries into the substantive rights asserted. See Rakas v. Illinois, 439 U.S. 128, 140 (1978) (holding that the question of who may object to the introduction of evidence allegedly seized illegally "belongs more properly under the heading of substantive Fourth Amendment doctrine than under the heading of standing"); City of Revere v. Massachusetts General Hospital, 103 S. Ct. 2979, 2983 n.5 (1983) (finding the questions of a hospital's standing to assert prisoners' alleged rights to publicly funded emergency medical care and the existence of the right itself to be "inextricably intertwined"). As a practical matter, however, state courts' supervisory power over proceedings before them and subordinate officers, state courts' freedom to structure substantive property law, and similar powers allow them to respond to any claims they choose to entertain. States may not limit standing to assert federal claims *more* than the federal courts would if in so doing they offer narrower access to federal claimants than they do to parties with analogous state claims, Testa v. Katt, 330 U.S. 386 (1947), or where in so doing they "impose unnecessary burdens upon" federal rights. Brown v. Western Ry. of Alabama, 338 U.S. 294, 298 (1949).

4. Tribe, ACL, §3–18; see also infra, notes 95–122 and accompanying text.

5. Congress may create a substantive right not to be subjected to the act complained of or a procedural right of judicial redress for the alleged illegality of the act at issue. Statutes providing that certain people's views or interests be taken into account administratively may imply either or both kinds of rights. See Tribe, ACL §3–18 n.5.

6. See Tribe, ACL §§3–18 n.6 and 3–19 n.27.

7. See Tribe, ACL §3–21.

8. Id.

9. See Tribe, ACL §3–22 n.2.

10. Flast v. Cohen, 392 U.S. 83, 102 (1968); ACL §3–22.

11. "Hohfeldian" plaintiffs are conceived to be those with "traditional" "personal and proprietary interests" as opposed to more general "representative and public interests." Flast v. Cohen, 392 U.S. 83, 119 n.5 (1968) (Harlan, J., dissenting). See L. Jaffe, *Judicial Control of Administrative Action* (1965); Tribe, ACL §3–18 n.2.

12. See Tribe, ACL §3–21.

13. See Tribe, ACL §§3–23 to 3–29.

14. See Simon v. Eastern Ky. Welfare Rights Org., 426 U.S. 26 (1976) (indigents lack standing to challenge validity of IRS regulations reducing the amount of free medical care hospitals must provide); Valley Forge Christian College v. Americans United for Separation of Church and State, 454 U.S. 464 (1982), discussed infra notes 54–75 and accompanying text; City of Los Angeles v. Lyons, 103 S.

Ct. 1660 (1983), discussed infra notes 16–53 and accompanying text; Allen v. Wright, 52 U.S.L.W. 5110 (1984), discussed infra notes 86 and 105.

15. See Duke Power Co. v. Carolina Environmental Study Group, 438 U.S. 59 (1978), discussed infra notes 76–94 and accompanying text, which removed a cloud over the nuclear power industry by upholding the Price-Anderson Act's limitation on power companies' liability for nuclear accidents. In a similar vein, see Justice Stevens' dissent in the reargument order in New Jersey v. T.L.O., 52 U.S.L.W. 3935 (1984), in which he criticized the Court's recent "voracious appetite for judicial activism . . . at least when it comes to restricting the [Fourth Amendment] rights of the citizen." In T.L.O., Justice Stevens objected to the Court's order to the parties "to argue a constitutional question that they have no desire to raise [whether the Fourth Amendment was violated by a school administrator's search of a student's purse], in a context in which a ground for decision that the Court currently views as nonconstitutional is available, and on which the State's chief prosecutor believes no guidance from this Court is necessary." Id. at 3936. See also Justice Stevens' concurring opinion in Firefighters Local Union No. 1784 v. Stotts, 104 S. Ct. 2576, 2594 (1984), noting that the Court had embarked on a long and "wholly advisory" discussion of issues under Title VII when all that needed to be decided in the case was a narrow question of the administration of a consent decree. See discussion in chapter 14 below. See also Larson v. Valente, 456 U.S. 228, 255 (1982) (striking down a statute selectively controlling certain religious groups' fundraising as "religious gerrymandering" when evidence suggested the statute was passed because the legislature was "hot to regulate the Moonies"); Clements v. Fashing, 457 U.S. 957 (1982) (attempting by plurality to create a new, more lax standard for equal protection analysis). But see id. at 973 (Stevens, J., concurring in judgment) (rejecting the proposed new theory); id. at 976 (Brennan, J., joined by White, Marshall, and Blackmun, JJ., dissenting) (same). See also the comparison of Regents of the University of California v. Bakke, 438 U.S. 265 (1978), and City of Los Angeles v. Lyons, 103 S. Ct. 1660 (1983), infra, notes 198–220 and accompanying text.

16. City of Los Angeles v. Lyons, 103 S. Ct. 1660, 1671 (Marshall, J., dissenting). This and many other facts are blithely omitted from the Court's one-sentence rendition of the record. Compare id. at 1663 (opinion of the Court by White, J.) with id. at 1671–74 (Marshall, J., dissenting).

17. Lyons, 103 S. Ct. at 1671 n.1 (Marshall, J., dissenting).

18. See Terry v. Ohio, 392 U.S. 1 (1968); Michigan v. Long, 103 S. Ct. 3469 (1983). Searches of this kind, which are conducted without probable cause, take place and are justified to ensure that the person stopped is unarmed and not dangerous to the police. Terry, 292 U.S. at 27, 23–24. They are "performed in public," they tend to be very extensive, and they are "a serious intrusion upon the sanctity of the person, which may inflict great indignity." Id. at 16–17 and n.13. Compare infra note 251.

19. Lyons, 103 S. Ct. at 1672 (Marshall, J., dissenting). No evidence was offered to suggest that Lyons ever menaced or provoked the officers. See also id. at 1667–68 n.7 (opinion of the Court).

20. Id.

21. Id. at 1663 (opinion of the Court).

22. Id. at 1672 (Marshall, J., dissenting). Only 9 percent of Los Angeles' population are black males. Id. at 1672 n.3. Justice Marshall noted that it is undisputed that choke holds pose a high and unpredictable risk of serious injury to the larynx, trachea, or thyroid or of death from cardiac arrest or asphyxiation. "The victim experiences extreme pain. His face turns blue as he is deprived of oxygen, he goes into spasmodic convulsions, his eyes roll back, his body wriggles, his feet kick up and down." Id. at 1673.

23. Id. at 1668.

24. Id. at 1663, 1672–74. The city provided instruction in the use of choke holds that, according to the testimony of city officials, falsely minimized their danger. Id.

25. Id. at 1664. The injunction prohibited use of choke holds "under circumstances which do not threaten death or serious bodily injury." It also ordered improved training, record-keeping, and reporting concerning the choke holds. Meanwhile, Lyons's damages claim had apparently been severed or delayed. Id. at 1667 n.6.

26. The Court held that the moratorium on choke holds was by its nature temporary. Id. at 1664–65.

27. Flast v. Cohen, 392 U.S. 83, 99 (1968) (emphasis added). The Court did cite to this page of *Flast. Lyons*, 103 S. Ct. at 1665.

28. Jenkins v. McKeithen, 395 U.S. 411, 423 (1969) (opinion of Marshall, J., joined by Warren, C. J., and Brennan, J.). The Court did cite to this page of *Jenkins. Lyons*, 103 S. Ct. at 1665.

29. Justice Marshall dissented in an opinion joined by Justices Brennan, Blackmun, and Stevens.

30. Id. at 1667.

31. Id. at 1667, 1669, 1671. Yet the Court on occasion spoke in general terms of a lack of "a case or controversy between these parties" without limiting itself to the injunctive count. Id. at 1667.

32. "Lyons would have had not only to allege that he would have another encounter with the police but also to make the incredible assertion either, (1) that *all* police officers in Los Angeles *always* choke any citizen with whom they happen to have an encounter, whether for purposes of arrest, issuing a citation or for questioning or, (2) that the City ordered or authorized police officers to act in such a manner." Id. (emphasis in original).

33. See, e.g., Duke Power Co. v. Carolina Environmental Study Group, Inc., 438 U.S. 59 (1978), discussed infra notes 76–94 and accompanying text, and Watt v. Energy Action Education Federation, 454 U.S. 151 (1981), discussed infra note 160 and accompanying text. See also Larson v. Valente, 456 U.S. 228 (1982), discussed infra notes 154–57 and accompanying text.

34. *Lyons*, 103 S. Ct. at 1667 & n.7.

35. The Court also did not explain why it was abandoning the usual rule that for evaluating litigants' standing the allegations in the complaint are assumed to be

true. See Havens Realty Corp. v. Coleman, 455 U.S. 363, 377–78 (1982). Indeed, in *Havens* the Court recognized standing on the basis of an allegation it explicitly found "implausible," that a single realtor's alleged racial "steering" had "palpable effects" throughout a 269-square mile metropolitan area of almost 400,000 people. Id. at 377. Perhaps the *Lyons* Court intended only to hold the plaintiff's showing insufficient to support the relief he had already received, not that the complaint must be dismissed without opportunity for further proceedings. The Court noted no formal remand, but the court of appeals judgment it reversed had covered only the preliminary injunction. Since the plaintiff had come to oppose the injunction as well, perhaps the Court thought a remand would serve no obvious purpose. But the Court did suggest that the district court should have dismissed the injunctive count for lack of standing. Id. at 1669–70, 1670 71. On these and many other issues in the case, the Court made little effort to explain itself.

36. *U.S. Const.*, amend. 4, provides in part: "The right of the people to be *secure in their persons*, houses, papers, and effects, against unreasonable searches and seizures, shall not be violated" (emphasis added). Neither the First Amendment nor any other part of the Constitution contains a textual prohibition on "chills" even approaching the clarity of this provision. Cf. Tribe, *ACL* §§12–2 to 12–14, 12–15 to 12–26, 12–28 to 12–30, 13–26, 15–17, 16–25 and 16–28 (discussing various "chill" theories in First Amendment and equal protection contexts).

37. *Lyons*, 103 S. Ct. at 1668 n.8. If Lyons was intimidated from going out onto the streets or engaging in conduct that might invite the unfavorable attention of the police, he would probably be deterred from exercising many public First Amendment and due process rights—including pressing his damage claims. He might also be coerced into leaving Los Angeles, where he is constitutionally entitled to stay. See Edwards v. California, 314 U.S. 160 (1941); Memorial Hospital v. Maricopa County, 415 U.S. 250 (1974).

38. Since the Court had already concluded that Lyons lacked standing sufficient to create a case or controversy, this discussion was dictum. Cf. Tribe, *ACL* §3–41 at 155 n.16.

39. 414 U.S. 488 (1974).

40. 423 U.S. 362 (1976).

41. 413 U.S. 1 (1973). Oddly, the Court never mentioned *Gilligan*.

42. *Lyons*, 103 S. Ct. at 1668–69.

43. Id.

44. Id. at 1665–68, 1670–71. The Court also invoked the "inchoate principles of federalism which underlie" Younger v. Harris, 401 U.S. 37 (1971), despite its "uncertain pedigree," to support avoiding disputes that involve the administration of criminal justice. Tribe, *ACL* §3–41, at 155. Cf. Allen v. Wright, 52 U.S.L.W. 5110, 5117 (1984) (principle of granting government wide discretion in "dispatch of its own internal affairs," which is "grounded . . . in the idea of separation of powers counsels against recognizing standing in a case brought, not to enforce specific legal obligations whose violation works a direct harm, but

to seek restructuring of the apparatus of the Executive Branch to fulfill its legal duties.").

45. It is difficult to see a basis for denying the equitable jurisdiction of a federal judge who happened onto the scene as Lyons was being choked, assuming the judge could be given the proper papers and could conduct any necessary assignment procedure. But see infra notes 48–50 and accompanying text.

46. *Lyons*, 103 S. Ct. at 1669.

47. Id. The Court of Appeals obviously meant that the case did not become moot, did not cease to be a case or controversy, when the officer dumped the unconscious Lyons on the ground. Since the inadequacy of the *past* injury to supply a case or controversy was a necessary precondition to the Court's analysis of the likelihood of a recurrence, see id. at 1667–68 n.7, the Court was implicitly required to find that the former choking had become moot at the time of dumping. It therefore asserted that the Court of Appeals was denying that the city's moratorium—enacted over two years *after* the court of appeals' decision—had mooted the issue. See Lyons v. City of Los Angeles, 615 F.2d 1243, 1248 (9th Cir. 1980). The officer's release of Lyons, like the moratorium, was, of course, a voluntary cessation of conduct that could be resumed at will. The thrust of the Court's argument is plainly predicated on mootness, which it has until recently admitted is fundamentally the same inquiry as standing. See United States Parole Commission v. Geraghty, 445 U.S. 388, 397 (1980). Justice White, the author of *Lyons*, was the only member of the Court in the majority in both cases.

48. *Lyons*, 103 S. Ct. at 1669. See Lyons v. City of Los Angeles, 615 F.2d at 1249.

49. "The City is free to continue the policy indefinitely as long as it is willing to pay for the injuries and deaths that result." *Lyons*, 103 S. Ct. at 1671 (Marshall, J., dissenting). Cf. Ingraham v. Wright, 430 U.S. 651 (1977) (availability of common law tort action for excessive corporal punishment after the fact eliminates need for hearing of any kind before punishment is inflicted).

50. *Lyons*, 103 S. Ct. at 1670. It hardly bears discussion that permanent bodily injury, such as that which Lyons suffered, or death, are among the classic kinds of injuries for which an award of damages is considered an inadequate remedy. See 2 J. Story, *Commentaries on Equity Jurisprudence as Administered in England and America* §926 (1843). Fear of injury, too, see supra notes 36–37, is not adequately compensable by damages. O. Fiss, *The Civil Rights Injunction* 76 (1978).

51. The Court also recast its discussion of the uncertainty of another attack on Lyons as negating the immediacy it found necessary for a showing of "irreparable injury." *Lyons*, 103 S. Ct. at 1670. In so doing, it cited *Younger* for the proposition that enjoining state and local law enforcement officers required a particularly strong showing of the prerequisites for equitable jurisdiction.

52. Id. at 1670.

53. Id., quoting Stefanelli v. Minard, 342 U.S. 117, 120 (1951).

54. Valley Forge Christian College v. Americans United for Separation of Church and State, 454 U.S. 464, 468–69 (1982).

55. Id., quoting App. at 34. There was some indication that the land might also be used for nonreligious teaching by the all-Christian faculty.

56. Id. at 468. The property may have been worth as much as $1,303,730 with buildings. See Americans United v. U.S. Dept. of Health, Education and Welfare, 619 F.2d 252, 253 (3rd Cir. 1980). The federal government spent an estimated $10,374,386 to acquire the property. Id.

57. 392 U.S. 83 (1968), discussed in Tribe, ACL §3–19, at 83–84.

58. Allen v. Wright, 52 U.S.L.W. 5110 (1984) (parents of black public school students in school districts undergoing desegregation have no standing to seek injunction against the IRS for alleged failure to enforce its obligation to deny tax-exempt status to racially discriminatory private schools); Princeton University v. Schmid, 455 U.S. 100 (1982) (per curiam) (property owner lacks standing to challenge reversal of alleged trespasser's conviction); Leeke v. Timmerman, 454 U.S. 83 (1981) (per curiam) (prisoners alleging conspiracy to prevent commencement of criminal proceedings against guards who allegedly beat them lack standing to sue under 42 U.S.C. §1983) (Brennan, Marshall, and Blackmun, JJ., dissenting); Linda R. S. v. Richard D., 410 U.S. 614 (1973) (unwed mother not receiving child support from father of her child has no standing to seek injunction against state officials for their refusal to enforce "child neglect" statute against unwed fathers). See Tribe, ACL §3–19, at 87–89.

59. *Flast*, 392 U.S. at 103–04.

60. *Valley Forge*, 454 U.S. at 480. Article IV, Section 3, Clause 2 provides, in relevant part: "The Congress shall have Power to dispose of and make all needful Rules and Regulations respecting the Territory or other Property belonging to the United States."

61. *Valley Forge*, 454 U.S. at 479. Justice Rehnquist wrote for the Court. Justice Brennan, joined by Justices Marshall, Blackmun, and Stevens, dissented.

62. Choper, "The Establishment Clause: Taxpayer Standing," in J. Choper, Y. Kamisar, and L. Tribe, *The Supreme Court: Trends and Developments 1981–1982*, at 68 (1983).

63. See Tribe, ACL §§5–1, 5–3, 5–8 and 5–12; cf. Heart of Atlanta Motel, Inc. v. United States, 379 U.S. 241 (1964); Katzenbach v. McClung, 379 U.S. 294 (1964).

64. 17 U.S. (4 Wheat.) 316, 421–23 (1819).

65. Under current and long-standing law, both realty and money in the federal treasury clearly are "proceeds" of federal tax dollars. See J. White and R. Summers, *The Uniform Commercial Code* §24–6 at 1011–14 (2nd ed. 1980). At most, the plaintiffs in *Valley Forge* should have alleged that they were taxpayers during the year when the land was purchased (1942) or when the buildings were erected. But since current outflows of government assets, whenever acquired, may affect current and future tax needs, even this claim should be unnecessary.

66. See Tribe, ACL §5–17.

67. *Flast*, 392 U.S. at 85.

68. Id. at 87.

69. Id.

70. Id. at 99.

71. *Valley Forge*, 454 U.S. at 512 n.19.

72. Compare id. at 479 n.15, with *Flast* at 87.

73. *Valley Forge*, 454 U.S. at 479.

74. *Flast*, 392 U.S. at 112–13 (Douglas, J., concurring).

75. Id. at 113 & n.9.

76. Carolina Environmental Study Group v. United States, 510 F.2d 796 (D.C. Cir. 1975).

77. 438 U.S. 59 (1978).

78. Id. at 64.

79. The Chief Justice wrote the majority opinion, joined by Justices Brennan, White, Marshall, Blackmun, and Powell. Justice Stewart concurred in the result only. 438 U.S. at 94. Justices Rehnquist and Stevens also concurred in the result only. Id. at 95. The decision on the merits is discussed in chapter 12 below.

80. 438 U.S. at 84 n.28.

81. Id. at 90–91, 93.

82. Id. at 90–93.

83. See, e.g., Roe v. Wade, 410 U.S. 113, 128–29 (1978) (married couple, alleging that they were forced to choose between sexual abstinence and sexual relations coupled with fear of pregnancy if their contraceptive methods failed, denied standing to challenge restrictive abortion statute). See generally Tribe, *ACL* §§3–8 to 3–13; §§3–13, 3–19.

84. *Duke Power*, 438 U.S. at 73 (citation omitted).

85. Id. at 74.

86. Compare Allen v. Wright, 52 U.S.L.W. 5110 (1984) and Simon v. Eastern Ky. Welfare Rights Org., 426 U.S. 26 (1976). *Allen* held that parents of black children attending recently desegregated public schools have no standing to sue to compel the IRS to enforce the congressionally mandated policy of denying tax exemption to racially discriminatory private schools since "[t]he links in the chain of causation between the challenged Government conduct and the asserted injury [the diminished ability of black children to receive a desegregated public education] are far too weak for the chain as a whole to sustain respondents' standing." *Allen*, 52 U.S.L.W. at 5116. *Simon* held that a class of indigents lacked standing to challenge the validity of IRS regulations reducing the amount of free medical care charitable hospitals must provide since it is "purely speculative whether denials of service specified in the complaint fairly can be traced to [the IRS regulations'] 'encouragement' or instead result from decisions made by hospitals without regard to the tax implications." *Simon*, 426 U.S. at 42–43.

87. *Duke Power*, 438 U.S. at 74–77.

88. Id. at 75 & n.20. The case suggests two different ways of reading Warth v. Seldin, 422 U.S. 490 (1975) (poor residents of nearby communities held not to have standing to challenge an exclusionary zoning ordinance), discussed in Tribe, *ACL* §3–21, at 94–97. Chief Justice Burger's opinion for the majority in

Duke Power generously describes the "but/for" causation requirement, see Tribe, *ACL* §3–21, as demanding "no more than a showing that there is a 'substantial likelihood' that the relief requested will redress the injury claimed." 438 U.S. at 75 n.20. Justices Rehnquist and Stevens would instead deny standing to a plaintiff, apparently on Article III grounds, "[w]here the prospect of effective relief against a defendant depends on the actions of a third party." Id. at 101 (Rehnquist, J., joined by Stevens, J., concurring in the judgment), relying on *Warth*. The concurrence's reading of *Warth* seems dominated by a concern for the remedial authority of the judiciary, limiting standing to cases where the relief follows as a direct result of a court's decree and is enforceable by means of the contempt power. Although *Warth* purports to express Article III–based limits on the powers of the federal courts to decide "cases and controversies," the majority's generous statement of the "but/for" requirement leaves Congress room to expand the range of plaintiffs who may have standing while the concurrence's formulation does not. A pliable principle, couched in the language of "substantial likelihood," leaves room for Congress to find *factually* that certain types of injuries are sufficiently likely to be redressed by specified forms of relief to confer standing. Cf. Tribe, *ACL* §5–14 (discussing Congress' power as a fact-finder). If the view of the concurrence had prevailed, little if any room would have remained for Congress to define a more generous standing requirement, since dependence upon third-party action either is present or is not.

89. Such a result would be avoidable only if the just compensation right were conceived as a deterrent to overcasual plant operation. See Tribe, *ACL* §§8–5 and 9–3, at 444–45, 458.

90. *Duke Power*, 438 U.S. at 79.

91. Id. at 78–79. See infra note 93.

92. Id. at 80–81. To the extent that a nexus requirement is thought to be compelled by Article III rather than reflecting only prudential considerations with respect to third-party rights, such a requirement is now used essentially to avoid suits in which the injury is so general to society as to present only an abstract grievance. Although such cases do not pose third-party problems inasmuch as all individuals or classes in society are injured equally, the Burger Court treats such disputes as properly resolved by political processes, telling the injured to organize an election campaign instead of organizing a lawsuit.

93. See Tribe, *ACL* §§3–26 and 3–27. The "nexus" requirement was from the start misguided, productive of unfortunate results and still less fortunate rationales. The unmistakable trend of the cases had been toward easing standing requirements. See Scott, "Standing in the Supreme Court—A Functional Analysis," 86 *Harv. L. Rev.* 645 (1973). Indeed, the decision in Flast v. Cohen, 392 U.S. 83 (1968), from which the nexus requirement has been derived, represented a *grant* of standing to taxpayers to challenge religious expenditures, albeit a grant limited by the nexus requirement in the sense that the Establishment Clause had an historical "nexus" to taxpayer concerns. If the absolute barrier to the taxpayer standing of Frothingham v. Mellon, 262 U.S. 447 (1923), had been followed, the Court would have refused to hear the case. The nexus test in *Flast* was an expedient limit imposed by a Court wishing to *permit* redress despite the most

dubious sort of injury in fact (no tax bills were reduced by victory in *Flast*) and, thus, understandably reluctant to go any further than it felt it had to. Whatever the wisdom of *Flast* itself, there was never any good reason to add the nexus test in cases where the plaintiffs were actually able to demonstrate an injury in fact that a court could prevent or remedy.

Nor is there much reason to retain the nexus requirement even in taxpayer suits. Indeed, if the objective is to assure the "requisite personal stake" and concrete adversity necessary to satisfy Article III requirements, status as a taxpayer—particularly when no tax liability will be affected by the result—is neither necessary nor sufficient: there is no special connection between the status of *taxpayer* and the stake one has or feels in a *constitutional* issue. All citizens, not just taxpayers, have a stake in living under the Constitution; if that stake is insufficient without taxpayer status, adding such status alone can hardly make a decisive difference.

The only defensible objective of the nexus requirement is protection of third parties not before the Court who may not wish to assert their rights or whose interests are not adequately represented by the parties who are before the Court. But these prudential ends are better served through devices less drastic than denying a day in court unless "there are insurmountable obstacles to identifying the absent but legally relevant interests and securing adequate advocacy of those interests." Tribe, *ACL* §3–29, at 114. See infra note 174.

The advocacy problems which might justify something akin to a nexus requirement are well illustrated by the tension between plaintiffs' arguments on standing and on the merits in *Duke Power*. To obtain standing, plaintiffs must argue that if they win on the merits, the two power plants will not be built or operated. On the merits, the government argues that limitation on liability was a justified way of allowing nuclear power to go ahead. Plaintiffs' standing is jeopardized if they reply, on the merits, that government had lawful and effective alternatives open (such as governmental operation of the plants, or public subsidy above the liability ceiling) to achieve its objective of nuclear power generation. See Tribe, *ACL* §§3–25 to 3–29.

94. *Duke Power*, 438 U.S. at 93.

95. Gladstone, Realtors v. Village of Bellwood, 441 U.S. 91, 99 (1979).

96. Havens Realty Corp. v. Coleman, 455 U.S. 363, 372 (1982).

97. Id. See Tribe, *ACL* §3–18.

98. *Havens*, 455 U.S. at 373, quoting Warth v. Seldin, 422 U.S. 490, 500 (1975).

99. In determining issues of standing, courts must "accept as true all material allegations of the complaint, and . . . construe the complaint in favor of the complaining party." *Gladstone*, 441 U.S. at 109, quoting *Warth*, 422 U.S. at 501.

100. See, e.g., United States v. SCRAP, 412 U.S. 669 (1973) (granting law students who liked unspoiled natural areas and disliked litter standing to challenge railroad rates the ICC had proposed, which they alleged would lead to adverse environmental consequences), discussed in Tribe, *ACL* §3–19.

101. *Gladstone*, 441 U.S. at 100.

102. Although many of the Court's constitutional cases on statutory standing have involved relatively clear congressional grants, the Court has established a test for implying standing to assert rights contained in statutes not explicitly conferring rights on the would-be claimant: "In determining whether a private remedy is implicit in a statute not expressly providing one, several factors are relevant. First, is the plaintiff one of the class for whose especial benefit the statute was enacted—that is, does the statute create a federal right in favor of the plaintiff? Second, is there any indication of legislative intent, explicit or implicit, either to create such a remedy or to deny one? Third, is it consistent with the underlying purposes of the legislative scheme to imply such a remedy for the plaintiff? And finally, is the cause of action one traditionally relegated to state law, in an area basically the concern of the United States, so that it would be inappropriate to infer a cause of action based solely on federal laws?" Cort v. Ash, 422 U.S. 66, 78 (1975) (citations omitted). The Court has emphasized the continued vitality of this test for determining jurisdiction over suits alleging injuries resulting from violations of statutes as recently as Merrill Lynch, Pierce, Fenner & Smith v. Curran, 456 U.S. 353, 377–78, 393–94 (1982). See also Cannon v. University of Chicago, 441 U.S. 677, 688–709 (1979) (holding that victims of sex discrimination in federally assisted educational institutions could litigate alleged violations of Title IX); Davis v. Passman, 442 U.S. 228, 234–44 (1979) (establishing a broad presumption in favor of the right to litigate constitutional injuries). Compare *Cannon*, 441 U.S. at 742–45, 749 (Powell, J., dissenting) (finding the Court's implication of jurisdiction in this way unconstitutionally infringes upon Congress' prerogatives); *Merrill Lynch*, 456 U.S. at 408–09 (Powell, J., joined by Burger, C. J., and Rehnquist and O'Connor, JJ., dissenting) (same). See infra note 145 on the relation between "implied causes of action" and standing.

103. See Tribe, ACL §3-19.

104. Id. at 82.

105. Regan v. Taxation With Representation, 103 S. Ct. 1997, 2001 n.8 (1983) (opinion for unanimous Court by Rehnquist, J.) (assuming successful challenge to veterans' tax preference would extend preference to plaintiff organization). Cf. Tribe, ACL §3-21, at 93–94. However, in Allen v. Wright, 52 U.S.L.W. 5110 (1984), the Court denied standing to parents of black public school students in school districts undergoing desegregation who brought a nationwide class action alleging that the Internal Revenue Service had harmed them by failing to enforce its policy of denying tax-exempt status to racially discriminatory private schools. Writing for the Court, Justice O'Connor argued that the parents had suffered no judicially cognizable injury simply by the failure of the IRS to enforce the law, that their children could claim no stigmatizing injury unless they had applied to and been rejected by the discriminatory private schools, and that claims based on the effect of the existence of the discriminatory private schools on the quality of education their children were receiving in the desegregated public schools were too speculative. In his dissent, Justice Brennan noted the conclusions of "[m]ore than one commentator . . . that the causation com-

ponent of the Court's standing inquiry is no more than a poor disguise for the Court's view of the merits of the underlying claims," and criticized the majority for its "indifference . . . to the detrimental effects that racially segregated schools, supported by tax-exempt status from the federal government, have on the respondents' ability to obtain an education in a racially integrated school system." Id. at 5122 (dissenting opinion). Justices Blackmun and Stevens also dissented. Justice Marshall took no part in the case.

106. *Duke Power*, 438 U.S. 59, 73–74 (1978).

107. Id.; Havens Realty v. Coleman, 455 U.S. 363, 376 (1982).

108. Gladstone, Realtors v. Village of Bellwood, 441 U.S. 91, 109–115 (1979) (opinion for the Court by Powell, J., joined by Burger, C. J., Brennan, White, Marshall, Blackmun, and Stevens, JJ.) (granting standing to challenge realtors' alleged racial steering to municipality fearing loss of stable, integrated neighborhoods and to white residents of the "target area" fearing loss of "the social and professional benefits of living in an integrated society"); Havens Realty Corp. v. Coleman, 455 U.S. 363, 372–79 (1982) (opinion for a unanimous Court by Brennan, J.) (allowing white and black residents of the Richmond, Virginia, metropolitan area and an organization providing "counseling and referral services for low- and moderate-income homeseekers" to challenge one realtor's alleged steering in suburban Richmond because of the individuals' alleged losses of "the important social, professional, business and economic, political and aesthetic benefits of interracial associations that arise from living in integrated communities free from discriminatory housing practices" and the impairment or frustration of the organization's activities). See Tribe, *ACL* §3–19, at 87. Justice Rehnquist, joined by Justice Stewart, dissented in *Gladstone*, rejecting the Court's interpretation of §812 of the 1968 Civil Rights Act as providing broad standing to the limits of Article III.

109. Blum v. Yaretsky, 457 U.S. 991, 1000 (1982), quoting Babbitt v. United Farm Workers National Union, 442 U.S. 289, 298 (1979).

110. *Blum*, 457 U.S. at 1000 (opinion for the Court by Rehnquist, J., joined by Burger, C. J., and Blackmun, Powell, Stevens, and O'Connor, JJ.). Justice White's concurrence and Justice Brennan's dissent, joined by Justice Marshall, assumed standing.

111. Clements v. Fashing, 457 U.S. 957 (1982). Justice Rehnquist's opinion, joined on this issue by Chief Justice Burger and Justices Powell, Stevens, and O'Connor, accepted the standing of Texas officeholders who said they would run for the state legislature but for the flat prohibition applicable to one of them or the penalty of automatic resignation that would be imposed upon the others. Justice Brennan's dissent, joined by Justices Marshall and Blackmun and in part by Justice White, did not differ with the Court on this point.

112. *Babbitt* 442 U.S. at 298 (conduct specifically protected by the First and Fourteenth Amendments.)

113. Id. at 297–303 (opinion for the Court by Justice White, joined on this issue by all justices). The Court held, however, that challenges to limitations on the union's access to employers' property and to binding arbitration procedures in

the case of strikes were not justiciable in that access had not been denied and no strike, let alone a demand for binding arbitration, had yet occurred.

114. City of Los Angeles v. Lyons, 103 S. Ct. 1660 (1983), discussed supra notes 16–53 and accompanying text.

115. *Blum*, 457 U.S. at 1001, quoting O'Shea v. Littleton, 414 U.S. 488, 496 (1974). The extremity of the circumstances in the cases where the Court has refused to adjudicate expected future harm illustrates the liberality of the Court's approach here. Typically, the Court's denial of review has been based on the absence of some complex set of facts necessary to an adjudication. In *Babbitt*, 442 U.S. at 303–04, the Court declined to reach the farmworker's union's claim of a right of access to employers' property to organize workers until access was actually denied. Since the Court's state action and First Amendment decisions in this area turn heavily upon the character of the property at issue, the question could hardly be answered in the abstract. See Tribe, *ACL* §§12–22 and 18–6. In Hodel v. Virginia Surface Mining and Reclamation Assoc., 452 U.S. 264, 294–97, 304 (1981), and Hodel v. Indiana, 452 U.S. 314, 334–36 (1981) (opinions of the Court by Marshall, J., joined by seven justices), the Court declined to consider due process and takings challenges to legislation that had yet to be applied to specific property or owners. Justice Powell, concurring in *Virginia*, supported this view. Id. at 306. Chief Justice Burger, concurring in both cases, and Justice Rehnquist, concurring in the judgment in both cases, did not dispute this holding. In both cases, the possible varieties of governmental treatment of property were virtually endless.

116. Democratic Party of United States v. Wisconsin ex rel. La Follette, 450 U.S. 107, 115 n.13 (1981), quoting Rosario v. Rockefeller, 410 U.S. 752, 756, n.5 (1973).

117. See Tribe, *ACL* §3–14, at 64–66.

118. 103 S. Ct. 2979 (1983). Justice Blackmun delivered the opinion of the Court, joined on jurisdictional issues by seven justices. Justice Rehnquist's concurrence, joined by Justice White, did not dispute the Court's standing analysis. Justice Stevens' concurrence did not dispute the Court's determination of standing, although he objected to the Court's review of the case in its entirety on other grounds.

119. Id. at 2981.

120. The Court ultimately held that, although a prisoner awaiting trial had a due process right to treatment, allocating the burden of paying for treatment once rendered was solely a matter of state law. Had the Court decided that requiring state payment was vital to securing the right—e.g., because failure to do so might induce hospitals to provide inadequate care—prisoners would never be able to vindicate that right unless the Court relaxed its traditional view of standing.

121. 447 U.S. 429 (1980). Justice Blackmun delivered the opinion of the Court, joined by Burger, C. J., and Stewart, Marshall, and Rehnquist, JJ. Justice Powell's dissent, joined by Justices Brennan, White, and Stevens, did not dispute the case's justiciability.

122. Id. at 434 n.5. The Court formally cast its holding in terms of mootness, but the structure of the problem is identical to that treated as an "injury in fact" standing problem in City of Los Angeles v. Lyons, 103 S. Ct. 1660, 1669 (1983), discussed supra notes 16–53 and accompanying text. The *Lyons* Court treated the two doctrines as fungible in this context.

123. See Tribe, ACL §3–18, at 81; Princeton Univ. v. Schmid, 455 U.S. 100, 102 n.* (per curiam) (1982).

124. *Princeton*, 455 U.S. at 103. Princeton had been allowed to intervene in the state trespass prosecution of Schmid, a nonstudent who had sought to engage in political activity on Princeton's campus. Its interest in Schmid's conviction clearly would not have have sufficed to confer federal standing. Linda R. S. v. Richard D., 410 U.S. 614 (1974), discussed in Tribe, ACL §3–19, at 84 and supra note 58. When the New Jersey Supreme Court overturned Schmid's conviction on First Amendment grounds, both New Jersey and Princeton sought review, but only Princeton asked the Court to reinstate the conviction. After holding that New Jersey could not invoke the Court's jurisdiction, the Court considered Princeton's argument that it would be bound by the New Jersey court's holding recognizing outsiders' rights to come onto its property for expressional purposes. The Court seemed to accept that premise, but denied Princeton standing because the New Jersey Court's ruling had been expressly limited to an antisolicitation policy that Princeton had since repealed. Therefore, the Court held, the New Jersey judgment was not res judicata with regard to Princeton's ability to enforce its current policy on outsiders' use of its property.

125. 392 U.S. 83 (1968), discussed in Tribe, ACL §3–19, at 84.

126. Valley Forge Christian College v. Americans United for Separation of Church and State, Inc., 454 U.S. 464, 470 (1982), discussed supra notes 54-75 and accompanying text.

127. Marsh v. Chambers, 103 S. Ct. 3330 (1983). Chief Justice Burger wrote for the six-member majority. Justice Brennan, joined by Justice Marshall and Justice Stevens, dissented on the merits. Although the defendant-petitioners "did not . . . challenge the Court of Appeals' decision as to standing," the Supreme Court was, of course, bound to ascertain that standing to invoke its jurisdiction did, in fact, exist, and it held that "Chambers . . . has standing to assert this claim." Id. at 3332 n.4.

128. See Tribe, ACL §11–3. It was "incorporated" through the Due Process Clause of the Fourteenth Amendment in Everson v. Board of Education, 330 U.S. 1 (1947).

129. See *Valley Forge*, 454 U.S. at 479. In fact, it was the Executive Board of the Legislative Council, not the Nebraska legislature itself, that selected and hired the chaplain. *Marsh*, 103 S. Ct. at 3332.

130. *Valley Forge*, 454 U.S. at 479.

131. Three alternate interpretations are possible. First, the Court could be suggesting that, because the Fourteenth Amendment specifically represented a far more violent distrust of the states than the First Amendment expressed concerning the federal government—and because the Fourteenth Amendment was

passed after Martin v. Hunter's Lessee, 14 U.S. (1 Wheat.) 304 (1816), whereas the First Amendment antedated Marbury v. Madison, 5 U.S. (1 Cranch) 137 (1803)—it must be read as an implied expansion of the federal judicial power. Cf. Fitzpatrick v. Bitzer, 427 U.S. 445, 452 (1976) (holding that the Fourteenth Amendment is an implied limitation on the Eleventh Amendment's restraint on federal jurisdiction). Second, the Court may see the crux of its holding in *Valley Forge* in the cessation of public involvement with religion after the one-time grant. Citizens or taxpayers such as Chambers who are offended by what they perceive as *ongoing* constitutional violations may then have broader standing than someone perceiving a one-time, past "outrage," particularly one that may actually be saving the government—and, through it, the taxpayers—money. See *Valley Forge*, 454 U.S. at 480–81 n.17, 486 n.22. Finally, the Court was able to reverse the judgment of the court of appeals in *Marsh* on the merits, whereas it would have been unable to uphold the gift in *Valley Forge*, which was concededly for religious purposes. Id. at 468–69.

132. City of Revere v. Massachusetts General Hospital, 103 S. Ct. 2979, 2983 (1983).

133. Voiding otherwise valid state judgments on federal standing grounds was criticized in Tribe, *ACL* §3–18, at 81–82.

134. Tribe, *ACL* §3–14, at 64–66.

135. *Geraghty*, 445 U.S. at 397: "mootness [has been defined] as 'the doctrine of standing set in a time frame: The requisite personal interest that must exist at the commencement of the litigation (standing) must continue throughout its existence (mootness),'" quoting Monaghan, "Consitutional Adjudication: The Who and the When," 82 *Yale L.J.* 1363, 1384 (1973). For a discussion of how displacing mootness with standing analysis erects a heightened barrier to the protection of federal rights in *Lyons*-type suits for injunctive relief, see Fallon, "Of Justiciability, Remedies, and Public Law Litigation: Notes on the Jurisprudence of *Lyons*," 59 *N.Y.L.Rev.* 1, 24–26 (1984).

136. Gladstone, Realtors v. Village of Bellwood, 441 U.S. 91, 100 (1979).

137. 438 U.S. 59, 80–81 (1978). See Tribe, *ACL* §3–23. See also Havens Realty Corp. v. Coleman, 455 U.S. 363, 372 (1982); *Gladstone*, 441 U.S. at 99–100, 103 n.9.

138. See, e.g., H. L. v. Matheson, 450 U.S. 398, 405–06 (1981) (minor plaintiff could not challenge restrictions on abortions as applied to mature and emancipated minors where she failed to allege that she or any member of her class were mature or emancipated); Harris v. McRae, 448 U.S. 297, 320–21 (1980) (plaintiffs could not challenge restriction of public funding of abortions as an interference with the free exercise of their religion since none of the poor plaintiffs alleged that they were compelled to have an abortion by the tenets of their religion and none of those finding abortion religiously compelled alleged that they were poor, pregnant, or expecting to become pregnant); Martinez v. Bynum, 103 S. Ct. 1838, 1845 n.15 (1983) (denying sister of child who concededly moved to Texas solely for a free public education standing to challenge a tuition requirement as it might have been applied to him had he moved there with any additional reason in mind); Zablocki v. Redhail, 434 U.S. 374, 380 n.6 (1978) (defendant class representative concededly given notice could not object to ap-

plication of injunction to other county clerks in the defendant class on the grounds that they had not received formal precertification notice); Village of Hoffman Estates v. Flipside, Hoffman Estates, 455 U.S. 489, 496–97 (1982) (operator of "head shop" where paraphenalia was clearly advertised for illegal use with drugs could not raise the commercial speech rights of others who might advertise the items for lawful purposes). In each case, the third parties—if indeed there were any meeting some of these descriptions—appeared just as well able to protect their interests. Furthermore, in some of the cases the absence of those parties, even as witnesses, and the doubts that some of them in fact existed, left seriously incomplete records.

139. Tribe, *ACL* §3–26. See also United States Parole Commission v. Geraghty, 445 U.S. 388, 403–04 (1980), which held that proposed class representatives may appeal denial of class certification even though their personal claims on the merits have become moot. The Court treated representative status as an interest whose denial was sufficient to constitute "injury in fact" and a "personal stake" in the litigation. Justice Blackmun wrote for the Court, joined by Justices Brennan, White, Marshall, and Stevens. Justice Powell wrote the dissenting opinion, joined by Chief Justice Burger and Justices Stewart and Rehnquist, arguing that the Court's analysis contained "significant departures from settled law that rationally cannot be confined" to the issues in the case before the Court. Id. at 409.

140. 442 U.S. 228 (1979).

141. 5 U.S. (1 Cranch) 137, 163 (1803).

142. Of course, many statutory liberty and property rights can be recast in constitutional due process or equal protection terms, not that in the ordinary course of things this distinction has much practical meaning. Cf. *Duke Power*, 438 U.S. at 69–70 n.13 (discussing similarity between state law claim and claim for denial of due process for making state law claim ineffective and finding that the due process characterization does not fail because of its similarity to tort action); Perry v. Sindermann, 408 U.S. 593, 601 (1972) (state law protection of right to continued employment triggers protection of Due Process Clause).

143. *Davis*, 442 U.S. at 242. Justice Brennan wrote for the Court, joined by Justices White, Marshall, Blackmun, and Stevens. Chief Justice Burger and Justices Stewart, Powell, and Rehnquist dissented.

144. See Tribe, *ACL*, §§3–1 to 3–6.

145. This analysis forms a continuum with the Court's decisions on whether to infer private rights of action from statutes. Where a statute is silent as to private standing, the Court pursues the relatively rigorous analysis outlined in Cort v. Ash, 422 U.S. 66, 78 (1975). This analysis includes a "nexus" analysis distinguishing first- and third-party rights: "[f]irst, is the plaintiff one of the class for whose *especial* benefit the statute was enacted—that is, does the statute create a federal right in favor of the plaintiff?" (Emphasis in original; citation omitted.) See Tribe, *ACL* §§3–22 to 3–27. The Court defers to Congress' control over both subsantive rights and the jurisdiction of the federal courts: "[s]econd, is there any indication of legislative intent, explicit or implicit, either to create

such a remedy or to deny one?" See Tribe, *ACL* §§3–5, 3–18, 3–31, and 8–7; *Davis*, 442 U.S. at 241. It undertakes an analysis structurally similar to that applied to determine whether an issue has been committed to the discretion of a coordinate political branch—an analysis of whether judicial intervention would destroy the very values sought to be protected: "[t]hird, is it consistent with the underlying purposes of the legislative scheme to imply such a remedy for the plaintiff?" See Tribe, *ACL* §3–16; Coleman v. Miller, 307 U.S. 433, 459 (1939) (Black, J., concurring, joined by Roberts, Frankfurter, and Douglas, JJ.). Presumably, in most cases the alternative to finding private standing would be holding that the matter had been committed to the discretion of the executive branch. See Linda R. S. v. Richard D., 410 U.S. 614 (1973). And finally, the Court conducts a relaxed "necessity" inquiry, focusing on the presence or absence of adequate alternative state court remedies: "is the cause of action one traditionally relegated to state law, in an area basically the concern of the States, so that it would be inappropriate to infer a cause of action based solely on federal law?" Cf. Tribe, *ACL* §§3–39 to 3–41; Jackson Transit Authority v. Local Division 1285 A.T.U., 457 U.S. 15 (1982) (Blackmun, J., writing for a unanimous Court) (holding that state law remedies for violation of collective bargaining agreements are sufficient to obviate the need for a federal cause of action under a statute requiring local governmental entities to preserve the union rights of existing employees when acquiring private transit companies with federal aid).

Where the plaintiff seeks to assert a constitutional right, the Court will more freely grant standing. It will then replace the *Cort v. Ash* formula with the general presumption of *Davis*, apparently backed by more liberal treatment of nexus, necessity, and commitment-to-coordinate-branches questions. See *Davis*, 442 U.S. at 241–42, 243 (relying in part on an allegation that the plaintiff "has no effective means other than the judiciary to vindicate [her] rights" to permit her to challenge under the Fifth Amendment her discharge by a congressman allegedly because of her sex); cf. chapter 5 (arguing that Congress' choices deserve less deference when they work to deny redress for violations of constitutional rights). Where Congress has expressly conferred a right of action under a statute or the Constitution, that generally resolve the question. See Tribe, *ACL* §3–18; supra notes 96–99; Gladstone, Realtors v. Village of Bellwood, 441 U.S. 90 (1979); Monroe v. Pape, 365 U.S. 167 (1961).

146. See *Davis*, 442 U.S. at 242.

147. 454 U.S. 464 (1982).

148. Id. at 489.

149. See, e.g., Allied Stores of Ohio, Inc. v. Bowers, 358 U.S. 522 (1959); Kahn v. Shevin, 415 U.S. 351 (1974); Califano v. Webster, 430 U.S. 313 (1977); Orr v. Orr, 440 U.S. 268, 272 (1979); Minnesota v. Clover Leaf Creamery Co., 449 U.S. 456 (1981). Similarly, in Regan v. Taxation With Representation, 103 S. Ct. 1997, 2001 n.8 (1983), the Court assumed without discussion that holding a tax preference for veterans unconstitutional could lead to its extension to non-veterans' groups such as the plaintiff. The possibility that a successful challenge

would result in the total elimination of the preference, giving the plaintiff no apparent benefit, was not considered destructive to the plaintiff's standing.

150. "Mr. Orr might gain nothing from his success in this Court . . . [W]e have no way of knowing how the state will in fact respond." Orr v. Orr, 440 U.S. 268, 272 (1980) (holding that Mr. Orr had standing to challenge a statute imposing alimony obligations only on husbands).

151. This is particularly true given the requirement that plaintiffs show an intent by the state to discriminate against them. See Washington v. Davis, 426 U.S. 229 (1976); Village of Arlington Heights v. Metropolitan Housing Development Corp., 429 U.S. 252 (1977). It seems likely that plaintiffs will continue to suffer to the limits of the law in a state hostile to their interests. Although it is true that the state may often prefer to extend a benefit to a hated minority group rather than have the majority do without it altogether, such a response is not by any means guaranteed. The majority may be able to purchase the benefit on the private market and, rather than raise the cost of a government service by sharing it with those who cannot afford it, will simply do without it. See, e.g., Griffin v. Prince Edward County School Board, 377 U.S. 218 (1964) (holding unconstitutional a Virginia County's closing of its public schools to avoid desegregating them). Or the service may be one of those things which some people enjoy only when it is not shared. See, e.g., Palmer v. Thompson, 403 U.S. 217 (1971) (swimming pools).

152. Tribe, ACL §3-21, at 92.

153. *Duke Power,* 438 U.S. at 75 n.20. But see Allen v. Wright, 52 U.S.L.W. 5110 (1984), discussed supra notes 86 and 105.

154. Larson v. Valente, 456 U.S. 228, 239 (1982), quoting *Duke Power,* 438 U.S. at 72, and Village of Arlington Heights v. Metropolitan Housing Development Corp., 429 U.S. 252, 261 (1977).

155. See supra note 124 and accompanying text.

156. E.g., Larson v. Valente, 456 U.S. 228, 242-43 (1982). Justice Brennan wrote for the Court. Chief Justice Burger and Justices White, Rehnquist, and O'Connor dissented on the question of standing, with Justices White and Rehnquist also dissenting on the merits. The Rev. Sun Myung Moon's Unification Church challenged an order to register under Minnesota's Charitable Solicitations Act. The Act exempted from its "registration and reporting requirements that are hardly *de minimis*" (id. at 241) those charitable organizations that are both (1) religious and (2) do not raise 50 percent or more of their total contributions from solicitations of nonmembers. The plaintiffs contended that the "fifty per cent rule" impermissibly favored "well-established churches" over newer and poorer churches or ones that "as a matter of policy, may favor public solicitation over a general reliance on financial support from members." Id. at 247 n.23. The state contended that even without the "fifty per cent rule" the plaintiff organization would have to register since it argued that the Unification Church is not a true religion. The Court found an adequate causal link between the rule and plaintiff's injury in that the state's task of showing that the church had to register would be made "more burdensome" if the rule were struck down. Of course, the

religious exemption in its entirety could then be attacked as violative of the Establishment Clause. The Court may have been thinking along these lines when it repeatedly intertwined Free Exercise and Establishment Clause arguments in striking down the "fifty per cent rule" on the merits. On its face, it would seem that the state's limitation of a small denomination's solicitations, especially if they are conducted for religious reasons, would pose primarily a Free Exercise Clause problem.

157. In *Larson*, the Court emphasized that "[i]t was only in 1978, shortly after the addition of the fifty per cent rule to the religious-organization exemption, that the State first attempted to impose the requirements of the Act upon the Unification Church. And when the State made this attempt, it deliberately chose to do so in express and exclusive reliance upon the newly enacted rule" in its formal notification to the plaintiffs that they must register. Id. at 239. It went on to "reject the [dissenters'] novel suggestion that the contents of such a notification of official enforcement action may be ignored by this Court." Id. at 240 n.12. The Court also held that the state was bound by the contents of the letter even though only a relatively low-ranking official signed it. Id.

158. Regents of the University of California v. Bakke, 438 U.S. 265, 280 n.14 (1978) (opinion of Powell, J., joined in this section by Brennan, White, Marshall, and Blackmun, JJ.).

159. Id. at 281 n.14.

160. For example, in Watt v. Energy Action Education Foundation, 454 U.S. 151 (1981), the State of California claimed that the concededly lawful bidding method the Secretary of the Interior was following in allocating offshore oil leases did not yield the government a full fair market return. Id. at 161. The state, which was entitled to a share of the federal government's receipts as owner of adjoining tracts, id. at 160–61, sought to compel the Secretary to exercise his discretion to experiment with one or more of the other bidding methods approved by Congress. Justice O'Connor, writing for the unanimous Court, noted that, even if it held that experimentation was required, the Secretary might choose to experiment on other parcels instead of those off California; that the results might be unfavorable for the methods California proposed; and that, even if those methods did prove superior, the Secretary retained discretion not to use them. Id. at 161–62. The Court might also have pointed out that, since the state had been denied an injunction against the lease sales California had challenged and those sales presumably had gone ahead as scheduled, there was no assurance that further sales would be held at all or that any would still be taking place by the time the results of any experimentation were available to be implemented. See id. at 159–60. Nonetheless, the Court found that requiring experimentation could ultimately help California and therefore granted standing. Then, as in so many cases where it granted standing in order to reach the merits, the Court rejected the claim of California and reversed the lower court judgment.

161. Id., *Duke Power*, 438 U.S. at 74–78; Bryant v. Yellen, 447 U.S. 352, 366–68 (1980) (White, J., writing for a unanimous Court). In *Bryant*, the Court found

that farm workers and other local residents had standing to seek to enforce acreage limits on farmers allegedly created in connection with a federal irrigation project, although it rejected most of their arguments on the merits. If the statute were interpreted as the plaintiffs argued that it should be, it would compel the farmers to sell off all of their land in excess of a 160-acre per person limit at a price fixed far below the fair market value or lose federal irrigation assistance for that land. Since the plaintiffs were people who would like to buy the land at the lower price and who would probably be unable to find similarly cheap land otherwise, the Court concluded they had standing. In so doing, the Court ignored the possibilities that (1) the farmers might choose to turn the land to other uses, (2) the "fire sale" conditions might lead to such an influx of buyers that none of the plaintiffs would acquire parcels, (3) the defendants might prefer buyers other than those who had forced the sale, (4) other cheap land might come onto the market, or (5) the U.S. Government might elect to relieve the farmers of the sale requirement or set a price higher than the plaintiffs would be willing to pay. The Court also did not inquire into whether the plaintiffs had the resources to buy the land even at the reduced prices. Cf. Warth v. Seldin, 422 U.S. 490, 505–07 (1975).

162. United States v. Hasting, 103 S. Ct. 1974, 1980 (1983) (citations omitted). Chief Justice Burger wrote for the Court. Justice Stevens concurred in the result without reaching the harmless error issue. Justice Brennan, joined by Justice Marshall, and Justice Blackmun, would have vacated and remanded for a more thorough consideration of the harmless error rule by the court of appeals.

163. Id. at 1981.

164. In re Winship, 397 U.S. 358, 364 (1970); Mullaney v. Wilbur, 421 U.S. 684, 704 (1975).

165. Duncan v. Louisiana, 391 U.S. 145, 149 (1968) (holding the Sixth Amendment's guarantee of the right to a jury determination of guilt is equally applicable to the states through the Due Process Clause of the Fourteenth Amendment).

166. E.g., Havens Realty Corp. v. Coleman, 455 U.S. 363, 377–79 (1982).

167. See Hasting, 103 S. Ct. at 1981–82. Incredibly, the Court there alluded to the fact that defendants "tendered no evidence placing any of them at other places at the relevant times" to support its conclusion that "prosecutorial allusion to their failure to rebut the Government's evidence" did not cause their convictions. Id. at 1982, 1986.

168. See De Luna v. United States, 308 F. 2d 140, 155 (5th Cir. 1962). The substituted judgment here, where a court effectively supplants the jury to which the defendant is entitled, should not be confused with situations where the constitutionally appropriate decision maker for some reason attempts to guess how another entity might act where neither party is entitled to a decision by the absent entity. See, e.g., Tribe, ACL §§3–4, 3–31, and 5–1 (discussing nonjudicial constitutional decision makers and the Erie doctrine).

169. Rosales-Lopez v. United States, 451 U.S. 182, 190, 192 (1981) (opinion of White, J., joined by Stewart, Blackmun, and Powell, JJ.). Justice Rehnquist,

joined by Chief Justice Burger, concurred in the result that a trial judge's refusal to question prospective jurors about possible racial prejudice against the Mexican-American they then convicted of helping Mexicans enter this country illegally did not constitute reversible error. Justice Stevens, joined by Justices Brennan and Marshall, dissented. See also Zant v. Stevens, 103 S. Ct. 2733, 2747 (1983) ("there can be no perfect procedure for deciding in which cases governmental authority should be used to impose death" and so "not every imperfection is sufficient, even in a capital case, to set aside a state court judgment"). Justice Stevens wrote for the Court in upholding a death sentence imposed by the jury on the basis of three statutory "aggravating circumstances," one of which had later been held unconstitutionally vague. Justices White and Rehnquist concurred in the result. Justice Marshall, joined by Justice Brennan, dissented.

170. Tribe, ACL §3-21, at 93. This section was noted by Justice Brennan in his dissent in Allen v. Wright, 52 U.S.L.W. 5110, 5122 (1984), along with articles by Professors Chayes, Nichol, and Tushnet, all making the argument that causation serves as merely "a poor disguise for the Court's view of the merits of the underlying claims." Id. at 5122. The fluidity of causation analysis, of course, allows results to come out either way the court applying it chooses. See, e.g., Rose v. Mitchell, 443 U.S. 545, 551-59 (1979) (rejecting an argument that "the conviction of the defendant should be a break in the chain of events that preceded it," thus barring an objection based on racial bias in the selection of the indicting grand jury). Justice Blackmun wrote for the Court, joined by Justices Brennan and Marshall and in this section by Justices White and Stevens. He went on to find that the defendant had failed to prove his claim. Justice Stewart, joined by Justice Rehnquist, concurred in the judgment upholding the defendant's conviction, arguing that the trial had broken the causal chain. Justice Powell, joined by Justice Rehnquist, concurred in judgment on the ground that the connection at least was insufficient to warrant reversal on federal habeas corpus. Justices White and Stevens dissented on the merits while Chief Justice Burger and Justice Rehnquist joined the Court's opinion on the merits.

171. See supra note 93.

172. See Tribe, ACL §§3-23 and 3-26.

173. Duke Power Co. v. Carolina Environmental Study Group, Inc., 438 U.S. 59 (1978).

174. Id. at 80. Duke Power presented not merely a third party problem but also a "fourth party" problem: what would Congress have done if it had known that the Price-Anderson Act would be held unconstitutional? Counsel for Duke Power argued that if Congress, in deciding to promote nuclear power generation, had chosen to build the plants itself instead of through private industry, or if Congress had guaranteed government compensation of any damages exceeding the $560 million limit, plaintiffs could not meaningfully claim that injury from power plant operation was caused by the limit on liability inasmuch as the plants might have operated in any event. The Court properly refused to turn the clock back, finding these possibilities were too speculative. Id. at 77-78. The question being one of standing, the issue was whether plaintiffs had a sufficient

stake in the outcome *now*. The findings of the district court indicated that plaintiffs would obtain relief now, even if such relief might last only until Congress had acted in some way to overcome the effects of a judicial holding that the Price-Anderson Act was unconstitutional.

The nexus requirement is best understood as a part of the older policy against third-party standing, see Tribe, *ACL* §3-23, and is best evaluated in light of the representational problems underlying the third-party rule. See id. §§3-26 to 3-29. In *Duke Power*, the Court acted as though the nexus rule presented a different problem from one of third parties. Indeed it assumed that plaintiffs were championing their own rights. 438 U.S. at 80. But that was not quite true. Plaintiffs might not be around if and when the nuclear plants blow up at some point in the future. Nonetheless, plaintiffs in *Duke Power* may be regarded as adequate representatives of the future victims of a nuclear disaster at either of the two power plants. An accident is statistically just as likely to occur sooner as later, and we simply do not know who the third parties might be. Analyzed from this last perspective, the Court's holding in *Duke Power* reaches further than it might at first seem: any party asserting an injury in fact—e.g., one who would want to engage in a competitive form of energy production—would have had standing to challenge the Price-Anderson Act, since such a party could give the same answer to the representation argument as could the actual plaintiffs in *Duke Power*.

175. See Tribe, *ACL* §3-29; supra note 93.

176. Schweiker v. Gray Panthers, 453 U.S. 34, 40 n.8 (1981); Babbitt v. United Farm Workers National Union, 442 U.S. 289, 299 n.11 (1979). But see Harris v. McRae, 448 U.S. 297, 321 (1980) (group cannot assert members' right to abortions as a free exercise of religion since that right is dependent upon a coercive effect upon an actual individual's personal actions).

177. California Medical Ass'n v. Federal Election Commission, 453 U.S. 182, 187 n.6 (1981) (individual members of medical association have "sufficiently concrete stake" in controversy to establish standing to challenge provision of Federal Election Campaign Act affecting rights of the association and its political action committee).

178. See *Babbitt*, 442 U.S. at 301-03 (union may assert speech rights of future participants in consumer publicity campaigns in support of Union).

179. Tribe, *ACL* §3-19, at 82.

180. Compare Havens Realty Corp. v. Coleman, 455 U.S. 363, 379 (1982), with Sierra Club v. Morton, 405 U.S. 727 (1972).

181. E.g., Schad v. Borough of Mt. Ephraim, 452 U.S. 61 (1981); see Tribe, *ACL* §3-26, at 105. But see Village of Hoffman Estates v. Flipside of Hoffman Estates, Inc., 455 U.S. 489 (1982).

182. Maryland v. Louisiana, 451 U.S. 725, 737 (1981). See Tribe, *ACL* §3-24.

183. United States Parole Commission v. Geraghty, 445 U.S. 388 (1980).

184. See Rakas v. Illinois, 439 U.S. 128 (1978) (establishing a general rule that defendants suffering "injury in fact" in the form of a conviction may not raise third parties' privacy rights under the Fourth Amendment against illegal searches

and seizures); United States v. Salvucci, 448 U.S. 83 (1980) (overruling in part Jones v. United States, 362 U.S. 257 (1960)); Rawlings v. Kentucky, 448 U.S. 98 (1980); United States v. Payner, U.S. 727 (1980) (refusing to allow lower courts to entertain third-party claims even on a prudential basis). Note that many of the major arguments for denying third-party standing are lacking in criminal prosecutions. The third parties cannot generally join the litigation to vindicate their own rights, so one cannot say that their absence indicates that "all those the [constitutional provision] intended to benefit seem satisfied." Tribe, *ACL* §§3-22 and 3-27, at 100, 111-12. See also id. §3-26.

185. See Tribe, *ACL* §§13-18 to 13-21, 16-46 and 16-53.

186. Compare *Lyons,* 103 S. Ct. at 1667: "to establish an actual controversy in this case, Lyons would have had not only to allege that he would have another encounter with the police . . ."

187. Compare id. at 1667-68 & n.7: "it is no more than conjecture to suggest that . . . the police will act unconstitutionally and inflict injury without legal provocation or excuse." "[A]ny future threat to Lyons . . . would be no more real than the possibility that he would again have an encounter with the police and . . . illegally resist arrest or detention."

188. Compare id.

189. 457 U.S. 957 (1982) (officeholders who would be forced by state constitutional provision to resign in order to run for higher office, or prevented by state constitutional provision from running for state legislature before the end of their elected term, have standing to challenge such provisions even though they are not now candidates).

190. Id. at 962. The would-be candidates had only to allege that they would run in the future if impediments were removed. Apparently their eligibility under all unchallenged standards and the state's allegedly unconstitutional retention and enforcement of its system of prohibitions and penalties was assumed. These allegations in *Clements* may be contrasted with the insufficient allegation of the plaintiff in Golden v. Zwickler, 394 U.S. 103 (1969), that he might be a candidate again despite apparently uncontested evidence indicating that it was "most unlikely" that he would. Id. at 109. *Lyons,* which cites *Golden,* but not *Clements,* would seem to bear the same relationship to Ashcroft v. Mattis, 431 U.S. 171 (1977) (per curiam), that *Clements* does to *Golden.* In *Mattis* the plaintiff's father failed to win standing to obtain declaratory relief by only alleging the mere possibility that his second son might be killed by the Missouri police's use of deadly force as his first son had been. But while raising the level of likelihood beyond the merely conceivable was sufficient in *Clements,* even with largely conclusory statements, far more was required in *Lyons.* See Tribe, *ACL* §3-21, at 93 (discussing the fickle, manipulable nature of causation analysis).

191. See Tribe, *ACL* §§13-2 to 13-17, 13-23 to 13-25, 16-44 and 16-56. Arguably, *registration* to vote is an on-going interest, denial of which could institute an "injury in fact." States, localities, and parties could still immunize abusive rules by granting registration and merely refusing to allow persons running afoul of their rules to vote. Although elections typically last several hours whereas

choke holds may last only a few minutes or seconds before the victim is released or killed, neither period is long enough to prosecute an action in its entirety or perhaps even to file one. Similarly, one-person, one-vote claims under the *Lyons* test remain speculative until the vote-counting actually occurs. Litigants could cite policies on vote-counting that lead to inequalities but until they actually vote it cannot be certain that *they* are the specific victims of the schemes—rather than beneficiaries or bystanders. The *Lyons* requirement of certainty of injury would presumably deny standing to nonvoters or voters for candidates who would not have won in any event. Under *Lyons*, they are "no more entitled to an injunction than any other citizen . . . : and a federal court may not entertain a claim by any or all citizens who no more than assert that certain practices . . . are unconstitutional" without showing special, personal injuries. 103 S. Ct. at 1670. Cf. Tribe, *ACL* §§3–19 to 3–20. And once the election, like Lyons' choking, was over, injuries could support standing only for damage actions. But see Karcher v. Daggett, 103 S. Ct. 2653 (1983), and Brown v. Thomson, 103 S. Ct. 2690 (1983), two apportionment cases decided after *Lyons* in which standing was assumed without question under circumstances at least this uncertain.

192. See Tribe, *ACL*, §§13–18 and 13–22.

193. See id. §15–10.

194. The Court explicitly rejected this view in Roe v. Wade, 410 U.S. 113, 125 (1973), and has not been troubled by it since. See Tribe, *ACL* §3–14. See, e.g., H. L. v. Matheson, 450 U.S. 398 (1981); Harris v. McRae, 448 U.S. 297 (1980). Recent cases have proceeded on the far more liberal basis of third-party standing by physicians and clinics performing abortions and counseling centers advocating them. See, e.g., City of Akron v. Akron Center for Reproductive Health, 103 S. Ct. 2481, 2490 (1983); Planned Parenthood Association of Kansas City, Missouri, Inc. v. Ashcroft, 103 S. Ct. 2517, 2519 (1983); Simopoulos v. Virginia, 103 S. Ct. 2532, 2534 (1983). Cf. Tribe, *ACL* §3–26. None of these three cases discusses standing; all were decided after *Lyons*. *Lyons'* applicability to prevent issuance of injunctions vindicating the right to an abortion would seem particularly clear since most antiabortion regulation is done by way of the criminal law. See 103 S. Ct. at 1670: "recognition of the need for a proper balance between state and federal authority counsels restraint in the issuance of injunctions against state officers engaged in the administration of the states' criminal laws in the absence of irreparable injury which is both great and immediate." The defendants in *Akron*, *Ashcroft*, Roe v. Wade 410 U.S. 113 (1973), Doe v. Bolton, 410 U.S. 179 (1973), Planned Parenthood of Central Missouri v. Danforth, 428 U.S. 52 (1976), Colautti v. Franklin, 439 U.S. 379 (1979), and Belotti v. Baird, 443 U.S. 662 (1979), included state law enforcement officials, and in each case they were subjected to some injunction the Court found valid. Cf. Tribe, *ACL* §3–41 (discussing the *Younger* doctrine).

195. The right to abortion could be litigated on a case-by-case basis in criminal proceedings, *Simopoulos*, supra, but no injunction prohibiting enforcement of unconstitutional statutes could issue in federal court. Federal courts presumably could not intervene in the on-going prosecutions, even after the law had once been held unconstitutional. See Younger v. Harris, 401 U.S. 37 (1971).

196. See Tribe, *ACL* §§13–12 to 13–13 and 16–8.

197. *Lyons*, 103 S. Ct. at 1664. Sosna v. Iowa, 419 U.S. 393, 399–402 (1975), responded to this problem by recognizing a named plaintiff's claim to represent a class and the continuing claims of current members of the class throughout the litigation as sufficient to create the requisite "case or controversy." See Tribe, *ACL* §3–14. Since Lyons did not bring a class action, this theory was unavailable to him. A plaintiff class therefore might have had standing to challenge the choke holds. Class actions failed in Gilligan v. Morgan, 413 U.S. 1 (1973), and O'Shea v. Littleton, 414 U.S. 488 (1974), but both were decided before *Sosna*. A class action also failed in Rizzo v. Goode, 423 U.S. 362 (1976), but there the plaintiffs attacked only patterns of police behavior and tacit policies, not a clear, public policy and training program like that in Los Angeles. Nonetheless, the *Lyons* Court hinted strongly that a class action on behalf of all Los Angeles citizens would also fail. 103 S. Ct. at 1670. If so, and if the Court would also reject a class action brought by black males, the group disproportionately subjected to lethal choke holds, id. at 1672 (Marshall, J., dissenting), then the rule of *Lyons* would be that plaintiffs like those in *Sosna* lack standing as well.

198. 438 U.S. 265 (1978), discussed in chapter 14.

199. Princeton University v. Schmid, 455 U.S. 100 (1982) (per curiam); Tribe, *ACL* §3–18, at 81.

200. *Bakke*, 438 U.S. at 276–77 (opinion of Powell, J., joined by Brennan, White, Marshall, and Blackmun, JJ.).

201. Id. at 277–78.

202. Id.

203. Certiorari was granted Feb. 22, 1977. 429 U.S. 1090 (1977). The case was decided June 28, 1978. Medical schools, presumably including Davis, provide four-year courses of study.

204. Earlier admission usually would lead to earlier graduation and an earlier entry into the lucrative medical job market. Bakke might also have claimed many other items of damage. Since Lyons' damage claim had been severed, however, the cases came to the Supreme Court on all fours.

205. Even between the two years in which Bakke applied, the admitted applicants' numerical averages varied substantially. *Bakke*, 438 U.S. 277–78 n.7.

206. Bakke's own interview results and "benchmark" scores varied appreciably between the two years. Id. at 276–77.

207. Some medical schools strongly prefer younger applicants because, on average, they are presumed likely to have more years after graduation to provide medical services. The Court has implied that these preferences would face little scrutiny. See Massachusetts Board of Retirement v. Murgia, 427 U.S. 307 (1976) (per curiam), discussed in Tribe, *ACL* §16–29.

208. See *Lyons*, 103 S. Ct. at 1671–72 (Marshall, J., dissenting) (discussing the Los Angeles Police's propensity fatally to strangle black men, such as Lyons). Applicants to the Davis Medical School in 1973 and 1974 had chances of admission of, respectively, one in twenty-four and one in thirty-seven. Figures for 1978 were unavailable or unpresented. *Bakke*, 438 U.S. at 273 n.2 (opinion of Powell,

J., joined by Brennan, White, Marshall, and Blackmun, JJ.). By contrast, during a five-and-a-half year period, the Los Angeles Police strangled at least 975 people, applying choke holds in "more than three-quarters of the reported altercations" with citizens. "These figures undoubtedly understate the frequency of the use of chokeholds" because of incomplete police reporting. *Lyons*, 103 S. Ct. at 1672 & n.6 (Marshall, J. dissenting). However "speculative" Lyons' claim that he would be choked again might have been, Bakke's contention that he would again be denied admission *because* of the Special Admissions Program would hardly have been less so.

209. Id. at 1667 (emphasis in the original).

210. Id. at 1667 n.7.

211. Id. at 1670. See also id. at 1668 n.8 (discussing Lyons' fear), 1672–74 (Marshall, J., dissenting) (discussing the various irreparable injuries that choke hold victims may suffer). The opinions in *Bakke* give no indication of what efforts Bakke made to obtain a medical education elsewhere, although apparently he had not received any other offers of admission.

212. Id. at 1670. The possibility of a damage action following each alleged wrongful rejection would also mean that the rejections, while "capable of repetition," would not "evade review" under the *Lyons* rule, id. at 1669, 1670.

213. In *Lyons*, as the past injury becomes less susceptible to recompense by damages, the likelihood of a future injury tends to decrease. The sixteen dead victims have no adequate remedy at law, but neither will they be choked again or even left in fear. This macabre symmetry helps accomplish the Court's evident objective of denying all possible plaintiffs standing to challenge choke holds.

214. I.e., he did not have to show that "there [was a] real and immediate threat that the plaintiff will be wronged again." *Lyons*, 103 S. Ct. at 1670.

215. Unlike the *Lyons* Court, which tied standing closely to the remedy sought, the majority in *Bakke* dismissed suggestions that Bakke's failure to make this showing deprived him of standing in a footnote saying "[t]he question of Bakke's admission *vel non* is merely one of relief." *Bakke*, 438 U.S. at 280–81 n.14 (opinion of Powell, J., joined by Brennan, White, Marshall, and Blackmun, JJ.).

216. Cf. Illinois v. Gates, 103 S. Ct. 2317, 2336 (1983) (White, J., concurring in judgment) (arguing for a "reasonable belief" or "good faith" exception to the exclusionary rule under the Fourth Amendment). See also Preface, note 1, at page 271.

217. *Lyons*, 103 S. Ct. at 1663. The additional provisions of the actual injunction, including those providing modest structural relief in the form of improved training, were apparently not the plaintiff's idea. Id. at 1664. Nonetheless, they showed far more comity for the Policy Department's internal functions than did the decree in *Bakke*, which put the Court into the Admissions Offices.

218. See, e.g., Weeks v. United States, 232 U.S. 383 (1914) (searches); Mapp v. Ohio, 367 U.S. 643 (1961) (same); Davis v. Mississippi, 394 U.S. 721 (1969) (arrests); United States v. Wade, 388 U.S. 436 (1966) (lineups).

219. See Tribe, *ACL* §3–16 (discussing problems of judicial competence in highly technical areas as an aspect of the "political question" doctrine).

220. Davis received 2,464 applications for the 100 seats in its 1973 entering class and 3,737 for its 1974 class of the same size. *Bakke*, 438 U.S. at 273 n.2 (opinion of Powell, J., joined by Brennan, White, Marshall, and Blackmun, JJ.).

221. The class of those who *will* suffer the alleged deprivation of rights in the future, even if it is virtually certain that some such people will become subject to treatment in the challenged manner, is apparently insufficiently precise to obtain standing. O'Shea v. Littleton, 414 U.S. 488, 496–97 (1974).

222. *Lyons*, 103 S. Ct. at 1670.

223. E.g., *Lyons*, supra; *O'Shea*, supra, Rizzo v. Goode, 423 U.S. 362 (1976); Gilligan v. Morgan, 413 U.S. 1 (1973).

224. The standard formulation in equal protection law, of course, is that *either* a suspect classification *or* a fundamental right will induce the Court to apply "strict scrutiny." See Tribe, *ACL* §16–6. Compare 42 U.S.C. §1983 (protecting constitutional rights) with 42 U.S.C. §§1985(3) and 1986 (enforcing equal protection of the laws). This burden becomes still more unreasonable and abusive since claimants now must show "discriminatory intent" to establish that a suspect class's rights are at issue. See Tribe, *ACL* §16–18. As the four dissenting justices demonstrate, Lyons could have made a powerful claim of discriminatory application of the choke holds against black men like himself. *Lyons*, 103 S. Ct. at 1671–72 (Marshall, J., dissenting).

225. Cf., Gunther, "The Supreme Court, 1971 Term—Foreword: In Search of Evolving Doctrine on a Changing Court: A Model for a Newer Equal Protection," 86 *Harv. L. Rev.* 1, 8 (1972) (discussing the effect of "strict" equal protection scrutiny).

226. See supra notes 194-95.

227. Individuals claiming standing to seek injunctions against antiabortion statutes must almost always "speculate" about the likelihood that they personally will be prosecuted if they engage in proscribed conduct. In most cases it will be utterly fanciful to believe that *all* persons so doing will be prosecuted. And an indefinite class of those who *will* be prosecuted *in the future* is precisely what *Lyons* and *O'Shea* held insufficient.

228. E.g., the pretrial due process rights of Lyons are subordinate to the reproductive rights of women seeking abortions.

229. "To the extent the Courts of Appeals relied on a view of standing under which the Art. III burdens diminish as the 'importance' of the claim on the merits increases, we reject that notion." Valley Forge Christian College v. Americans United for Separation of Church and State, Inc., 454 U.S. 464, 484 (1982).

230. In *Bakke*, for example, Davis' concession that it could not show that its past rejections of Allan Bakke were not the result of its Special Admissions Program was treated as sufficient to deny it the opportunity to conduct a constitutionally legitimate admissions process to determine whether he merited admission in the future. *Bakke*, 438 U.S. at 280 n.13. Similarly, school desegregation cases long have prescribed expansive structural changes taking many choices away from school authorities found to have discriminated. E.g., Swann v. Charlotte-Mecklenburg Board of Education, 420 U.S. 1 (1971); Columbus Board of Edu-

cation v. Penick, 443 U.S. 449 (1979); Dayton Board of Education v. Brinkman, 443 U.S. 526 (1979). See generally, O. Fiss, *The Civil Rights Injunction* 9–11, 13–14, 22–23, 49–50, 92–93 (1978) (discussing the implications of the structural injunction in school, police, and other contexts).

231. *Lyons*, 103 S. Ct. 1670, quoting O'Shea v. Littleton, 414 U.S. 488, 500 (1974), and other cases.

232. Compare Tribe, *ACL* §3–17, at 79; Flast v. Cohen, 392 U.S. 83, 99 (1968).

233. City of Akron v. Akron Center for Reproductive Health, 103 S. Ct. 2481 (1983), Planned Parenthood, Kansas City, Missouri v. Ashcroft, 103 S. Ct. 2517 (1983), Karcher v. Daggett, 103 S. Ct. 2653 (1983), and Brown v. Thomson, 103 S. Ct. 2690 (1983), all decided after *Lyons*, make no mention of its rules or of standing generally, although *Lyons* seems applicable in part to the plaintiffs' actions in those cases. *Lyons*, in turn failed to mention the prior cases on schools, elections, residency, and abortion. Nor did it mention *Bakke*, even though a majority of the Court signed the section of the opinion in that case holding that Bakke had standing.

234. See Tribe, *ACL* §3–21, at 93.

235. 320 U.S. 81 (1943), discussed in Tribe, *ACL* §16–14.

236. 323 U.S. 214 (1944), discussed in Tribe, *ACL* §16–14.

237. Cf. *Korematsu*, 323 U.S. at 245 (Jackson, J., dissenting): "Even if [the orders incarcerating Japanese-Americans from the West Coast] were permissible military procedures, I deny that it follows that they are constitutional. If, as the Court holds, it does follow, then we might as well say that any military order is constitutional and have done with it." See also Warren, "The Bill of Rights and the Military," in *The Great Rights* 89, 101 (E. Cahn ed. 1963): *Korematsu* and *Hirabayashi* "demonstrate dramatically that there are some circumstances in which the Court will, in effect, conclude that it is simply not in a position to reject descriptions by the Executive of the degree of military necessity." But see id. at 102: "if judicial review is to constitute a meaningful restraint upon unwarranted encroachments upon freedom in the name of military necessity, situations in which the judiciary refrains from examining the merit of the claim of necessity must be kept to an absolute minimum."

238. Both parties urged that the district court's injunction be struck down and that the equitable aspect of the case be terminated. See 103 S. Ct. at 1664. No amici briefed or argued any other viewpoint. The case had begun and been maintained as an individual action, yet Lyons sought and received relief against police abuse of all people the police might meet. Id. at 1663–64. Although Lyons could claim as a party strangled with *no* provocation, no party was before the Court who had suffered a choking for *insufficient* provocation. See id. at 1667–68 n.7. The damages claim had been severed from the injunctive one, fortuitously allowing the Court to treat the prayers for relief as unitary cases and blurring the case-wide character of traditional standing analysis. Cf. *Bakke*, 438 U.S. at 281 n.14. The claim for declaratory relief, which would flow much more readily from the action for damages and involve no possibility of federal contempt powers being invoked against the police, was not in the case that came to

the Court. *Lyons*, 103 S. Ct. at 1664. But cf. Samuels v. Mackell, 401 U.S. 66 (1971) (equating declaratory and injunctive relief for purposes of the *Younger* doctrine), and City of Los Angeles v. Lyons, 449 U.S. 934 (1980) (White, J., joined by Powell and Rehnquist, JJ., dissenting from the denial of certiorari) (criticizing the court of appeals for finding standing to raise both the injunctive and declaratory claims). The injunctive action, which began as a mere claim for preventive relief, had taken on some structural aspects like those in *Rizzo* and *O'Shea*. Apart from the absence of disagreement about the proper disposition of the litigation, none of these problems should have prevented the Court from reaching the merits of the police practices at issue. And the Court did not suggest that any of them was crucial to its holding. These failings do, however, suggest ways future litigation might be better structured.

239. Indeed, the Court's opinion is sprinkled with comments assuming various substantive conclusions. In finding that fear of choking did not constitute an injury in fact, it assumed a definition of the substantive rights that the First, Fourth, Eighth, and Fourteenth Amendments protect. *Lyons*, 103 S. Ct. at 1668 n.8. The Court's repeated equation of legality and constitutionality, and its assumption that the police could only "act unconstitutionally" if they "inflict injury without provocation or legal excuse," implies that the Los Angeles Police Department's policy is coextensive with the applicable constitutional parameters. Id. at 1668.

240. The Court's vision does seem to specify *men* in uniform. See Dothard v. Rawlinson, 433 U.S. 321 (1977) (the possibility of women being raped is legitimate reason for refusing to consider them for 75 percent of the prison guard positions in the state of Alabama); Rostker v. Goldberg, 453 U.S. 57 (1981) (male-only military draft registration does not violate equal protection). Uniforms, on the other hand, may be dispensable where a civilian, such as a prosecutor, is cooperating with the uniformed services. Compare Younger v. Harris, 401 U.S. 37 (1971) (prosecutor acting in concert with police in law enforcement); United States v. Hastings, 103 S. Ct. 1974 (1983) (same); Leeke v. Timmerman, 454 U.S. 83 (1981) (victim-prisoners lack standing to challenge decision not to prosecute allegedly brutal prison guards), with City of Akron v. Akron Center for Reproductive Health, 103 S. Ct. 2481 (1983) (police prosecutor sued as representative of city's political government may be enjoined).

241. E.g., *Hirabayashi*, supra note 235 (military authorities' peculiar expertise legitimates their imposition of a curfew on the West Coast against persons of Japanese ancestry); *Korematsu*, supra note 236 (same for incarceration and dispossession of persons of Japanese ancestry); id. at 242, 248 (Jackson, J., dissenting) (incarceration and dispossession unconstitutional but should not be enjoined since it was ordered by the military); Bell v. Wolfish, 441 U.S. 520, 531–41 (1979) (restrictions on inmate liberty that serve jail administrators' managerial purposes generally do not violate the due process rights of unconvicted persons); Illinois v. Gates, 103 S. Ct. 2317 (1983) (authorizing magistrates to show broad deference to the judgments of police officers in issuing search warrants).

242. Cf. Tribe, *ACL* §3–16, at 71–72 (discussing the flaws of this theory even when applied to the coordinate federal political branches).

243. See Marbury v. Madison, 5 U.S. (1 Cranch) 137 (1803); Tribe, *ACL* §§3–2 to 3–4 and 3–16, at 72–73. Justice White does not appear to believe that actions challenging pretrial police practices are always nonjusticiable. Illinois v. Gates, 103 S. Ct. 2317, 2346 n.19 (1983) (White, J., concurring in judgment). His opinion for the Court in *Lyons*, however, as discussed above, offers few clues as to how such actions could possibly be brought.

244. At the same time the Court in cases like *Lyons* is urging recourse to remedies seeking damages as adequate alternatives to injunctions against state officials, the same Court has radically expanded the scope of official immunities protecting those officials. It has also curtailed suits against governmental entities by rejecting traditional principles of liability for servants' wrongs, see Monell v. New York City Department of Social Services, 436 U.S. 658, 691–94 (1978), by narrowing the scope of activities considered "state action," see Polk County v. Dodson, 454 U.S. 312, 326 (1981), and by implying broad theories of sovereign immunity into the Eleventh Amendment. If the officers who choked Lyons were judgment-proof state troopers, he might well not have a meaningful federal damages action, and the violation of his constitutional rights would not necessarily assure him of a state forum. See Martinez v. California, 444 U.S. 277 (1980).

245. This illustrates the true importance of the "exclusionary rule" and attempts on the contemporary Court to eviscerate it. See Illinois v. Gates, 103 S. Ct. 2317, 2336 (1983) (White, J., concurring in judgment) (arguing for a general exception to the prohibition on introducing illegally obtained evidence in criminal trials where the police acted in "good faith" when violating the Fourth Amendment); United States v. Leon, 52 U.S.L.W. 5155 (1984) (establishing good faith exception to rule that evidence obtained with invalid warrant may not be used at criminal trial); Massachusetts v. Sheppard, 52 U.S.L.W. 5177 (1984) (same). Fourth Amendment violations typically occur before trials or against people never charged or tried, see supra notes 36–37 and infra note 246. As cases like *Lyons* and those limiting damage actions indicate, e.g., Baker v. McCollan, 443 U.S. 137 (1979) (no cause of action under §1983 against police for jailing the wrong man for jumping bail), the Court is generally disposed to allow little direct judicial intervention on behalf of constitutionally protected rights at this stage. The exclusionary rule moves the Fourth Amendment issue out of the pretrial zone of practical police immunity and into the realm of evidentiary rulings at trial, where judges are traditionally permitted to vindicate defendants' rights. Confinement of the exclusionary rule to rare cases of demonstrably heinous police conduct would effectively sever this link between the Fourth Amendment and the trial process, dropping the rights it protects back into the pretrial constitutional jungle the Court seems unwilling to disturb. As Sir Francis Bacon said in a passage from *Of Innovations* quoted by the court of appeals in *Lyons*, "And he that will not apply New Remedies, must expect New Evils: for Time is the greatest Innovator." 615 F.2d 1243, 1250 n.12 (1980).

357

NOTES TO PAGES 118–119

246. The Court threatens to render much of its trial-oriented jurisprudence empty and irrelevant when it denies the justiciability of claims of police abuses outside the walls of a courtroom. See supra notes 3, 162–65, 167–70, 184, and 218. As one criminal justice scholar has written, "[j]ustice without trial, with its own unwritten rules and practices, with the herding of defendants, and the low visibility decisions of the police, will become increasingly characteristic of the American criminal justice system." J. Skolnick, *Justice Without Trial* 272 (2d ed. 1975). Perhaps more importantly, "[n]o reasonable person wants a police force that is flaccid, inefficient, and untrained. At the same time, an increasing reliance on police for social stability constitutes a pretty good indication of the weakness of bonds of social community." Id. at 273. As the Court sets out in these cases to create affirmative entitlements on behalf of the police, it owes the individuals whose rights it is sacrificing a more cogent, reasoned explanation of how and why these entitlements are necessary to effectuate a vision of what this country is about that is fairly traceable to the Constitution.

247. The point of earlier doctrines of federal court restraint, such as those announced in Railroad Commission of Texas v. Pullman Co., 312 U.S. 496 (1941), and Younger v. Harris, 401 U.S. 37 (1971), was clearly to divert litigation from the federal courts to state forums. See Tribe, *ACL* §3–40 and 3–41. Increasingly, however, the Court is intervening in state court litigation to enforce perceived federal norms in support of police power. This suggests that the Court contemplates outright rejection, rather than merely displacement, of many of these claims.

248. *Lyons*, 103 S. Ct. at 1670.

249. Recognition that majoritarian political processes cannot be relied on to protect the basic rights of all citizens is at the core of modern theories of judicial review. See United States v. Carolene Products Co., 304 U.S. 144, 152–53 n.4 (1938); Cooper v. Aaron, 358 U.S. 1 (1958); Tribe, *ACL* §§1–7 and 3–6. Modern group theory also demonstrates great differences in political effectiveness between closed, readily identifiable groups facing known dangers and relatively large, diffuse bodies of people each facing only a probabilistic threat until it is too late for individual action. See, e.g., M. Olson, *The Logic of Collective Action: Public Goods and the Theory of Groups* 53–56, 165–67 (1971): "Large or latent groups have no tendency voluntarily to act to further common interests . . . [T]he unorganized groups, the groups that have no lobbies and exert no pressure, are among the largest groups in the nation, and they have some of the most vital interests." Paradoxically, the groups best able to mount effective political action are the ones whose attempts to invoke judicial review are most favored under the Court's ultra-Hohfeldian standing doctrine; conversely, those least able to mount a sufficient political campaign are turned away without a hearing on the merits even when they manage to scrape up the resources to enter federal court.

250. Many public agencies, including those charged with law enforcement, have become increasingly independent of the political authorities and process so that their expert, professional staff will be better able to influence agency policies. See D. Fox, *The Politics of City and State Bureaucracy* 9–11, 12–13 (1974). Yet the

same day it decided *Lyons*, the Court allowed these expert surrogates for fuller political accountability of law enforcement agencies to be muzzled. In Connick v. Myers, 103 S. Ct. 1684 (1983), the Court rejected a former assistant prosecutor's First Amendment claim after she was fired for circulating a questionnaire implicitly criticizing various aspects of office policy. In so doing, it founded its holding on "the practical realities [of] administration" and the importance of "authority," id. at 1694, the very sort of "code words for an overly permissive attitude towards police practices in derogation of the rights secured" by the Constitution it has relied upon to expand delegations of substantive powers to the police. Illinois v. Gates, 103 S. Ct. 2317, 2359 (1983) (Brennan, J., joined by Marshall, J., dissenting). See chapter 13. See also South Dakota v. Opperman, 428 U.S. 364 (1976) (police routine is an adequate substitute for probable cause in "inventory" searches of impounded automobiles). With neither the federal courts nor the expert subordinate employees of agencies available to fight to prevent constitutional abuses, victims of official lawlessness are left to rely upon the increasingly slender reed of the formal majoritarian political processes. See also Forrester, "The New Constitutional Right to Buy Elections," 69 *A.B.A.J.* 1078 (1983).

251. The various intrusions upon constitutionally significant values that have been accepted in the name of police necessity are becoming increasingly redundant. The officers who strangled Lyons, for example, were secured not only by their numerical superiority but also by (1) a patdown *Terry* search conducted without a requirement of probable cause, (2) their drawn revolvers and authority to use deadly force upon (kill) Lyons, (3) their having compelled him to leave his car, (4) their having compelled him to remain with his hands on his head even after they finished the *Terry* search, (5) the handcuffing of Lyons, and (6) a potentially lethal choke hold applied until Lyons was injured and lost consciousness. See *Lyons*, 103 S. Ct. 1671–72. All these measures were applied to someone who apparently never showed any signs of being armed or violent and was charged with nothing more than driving with a burned-out tail light. Id.

252. For example, Terry v. Ohio, 392 U.S. 1 (1968), created an exception to the Fourth Amendment's requirement of probable cause for searches. As reported in *Lyons*, the police had sixteen times imposed death on people without any of the safeguards required for conviction of even petty offenses, let alone capital punishment. Compare Coker v. Georgia, 433 U.S. 584 (1977); Gregg v. Georgia, 428 U.S. 153 (1976). It is, of course, beyond the scope of this chapter to examine in detail the merits of the choices the Court has made in individual substantive cases protecting civil rights against the criminal justice system's encroachment. For the most recent examples as of this writing, see, e.g., New York v. Quarles, 104 S. Ct. 2626 (1984) (public safety exception to rule that coerced confessions may not be admitted at trial); United States v. Leon, 52 U.S.L.W. 5155 (1984) (good faith exception to rule that evidence obtained with invalid warrant may not be used at criminal trial); Hudson v. Palmer, 52 U.S.L.W. 5051 (1984) ("Fourth Amendment has no applicability to a prison cell" since privacy interests of prisoners are subordinate to institutional needs and objectives of prison management); Block v. Rutherford, 52 U.S.L.W. 5063

(1984) (privacy interests of prisoners are secondary to needs of prison administration).

253. In *Terry*, Chief Justice Warren's opinion for the Court noted the "wholesale harassment by certain members of the police community, of which minority groups, particularly Negroes, frequently complain" and the potential of stops and frisks to exacerbate the situation. The Court promised vigilance against police abuses above and beyond the constraining effects of the exclusionary rule: "Under our decision, courts still retain their traditional responsibility to guard against police conduct which is overbearing or harassing, or which trenches upon personal security without the objective evidentiary justification which the Constitution requires. When such conduct is identified, it must be condemned by the judiciary . . . And, of course, our approval of legitimate and restrained investigative conduct undertaken on the basis of ample factual justification should in no way discourage the employment of other remedies than the exclusionary rule to curtail abuses for which that sanction may prove inappropriate." *Terry*, 392 U.S. at 14–15. The "other remedies" Chief Justice Warren relied on to ensure that stops and frisks were not to become mere pretenses to "roust" unpopular individuals have turned out to be practically unavailable even when still more serious abuses are inflicted. Similarly, the dissenters in *Lyons* noted that Chief Justice Burger "asked in Bivens v. Six Unknown Federal Narcotics Agents, 403 U.S. 388, 419 (1971) (dissenting opinion), 'what would be the judicial response to a police order authorizing "shoot to kill" with respect to every fugitive?' His answer was that it would be 'easy to predict our collective wrath and outrage' cannot be translated into an order to cease the unconstitutional practice, but only an award of damages to those who are victimized by the practice and live to sue and to the survivors of those who are not so fortunate. Under the view expressed by the majority today, if the police adopt a policy of 'shoot to kill,' or a policy of shooting one out of ten suspects, the federal courts will be powerless to enjoin its continuation. The federal judicial power is now limited to levying a toll for such systematic constitutional violation." (Citation omitted.) *Lyons*, 103 S. Ct. at 1683–84. The Court ignored another possible prevention "remedy" that would not involve the courts in the policies of law enforcement agencies when it refused to analyze charges of racial discrimination in police departments' hiring and promotion under an "anti-subjugation" theory. See Washington v. Davis, 426 U.S. 229 (1976), discussed in Tribe, *ACL* §16–18.

254. Cf. Johnson v. Louisiana, 406 U.S. 365, 388 (1972), and Apodaca v. Oregon, 406 U.S. 404 (1972) (Douglas, J., joined by Brennan and Marshall, JJ., dissenting). In condemning the Court's acceptance of nonunanimous jury verdicts in state criminal cases, Justice Douglas observed a "diminution of verdict reliability flow[ing] from the fact that nonunanimous juries need not debate and deliberate as fully as most unanimous juries. As soon as the requisite majority is attained, further consideration is not required." As cases such as *Lyons* indicate, Supreme Court judgments require only a majority of five. See also Securities & Exchange Commission v. Chenery Corp., 332 U.S. 194, 214 (1947) (Jackson, J.,

dissenting): "I give up. Now I realize fully what Mark Twain meant when he said, 'The more you explain it, the more I don't understand it.' "

255. The merits were not before the Court immediately since the district court had dismissed the complaint for want of standing. *Valley Forge*, 454 U.S. at 469. Nonetheless, given the value of the property and the fact that the plaintiffs "are firmly committed to the constitutional principle of separation of church and State," id. at 486, the issue seemed certain to reappear if the Court granted standing. The highly sectarian function and structure of the college, as set out in its application for the land, would have made a principled rejection of the claim on the merits most problematic. But see Lynch v. Donnelly, 104 S. Ct. 1355 (1984) (finding no Establishment Clause violation when city spends public money erecting Christian nativity scene). A majority of the Court is also evidently disinclined to interfere with governmental aid to religious education. 454 U.S. at 513 (Brennan, J., dissenting); Mueller v. Allen, 103 S. Ct. 3062 (1983); Choper, supra note 62, at 67.

256. *Valley Forge*, 454 U.S. at 469, 487.

257. Id. at 486–87. It derided what it characterized as the plaintiffs' attempted arrogation of "a special license to roam the country in search of governmental wrongdoing and to reveal their discoveries in federal court."

258. Although most governmental inefficiencies probably do not raise constitutional questions, many would arguably contravene statutes. Fearing, perhaps, that the party-oriented nature of standing analysis might bring parties with these claims into federal court as well, the Court may have preferred to "slam the courthouse door against" all plaintiffs preemptively. Id. at 513 (Brennan, J., dissenting). It would have done better to consider Justice Douglas' injunction on this very point in *Flast v. Cohen*: "[t]here need be no inundation of the federal courts if taxpayers' suits are allowed . . . [W]ise judicial discretion . . . can distinguish between the frivolous question and the substantial question, between cases ripe for decision and cases that need prior administrative processing, and the like." *Flast*, 392 U.S. at 112 (footnote omitted).

259. At least they may come with more copious legislative history than a hidden amendment to a property disposition statute or congressional inaction in light of a pattern of administrative inactivity.

260. "Almost $1,000,000,000 was appropriated to implement the Elementary and Secondary Education Act in 1965." *Flast*, 392 U.S. at 103 n.23. But the overwhelming bulk of this money presumably went to public, nonsectarian schools. As of 1980, transfers of property to religious institutions under the program at issue in *Valley Forge* totaled more than $25,700,000 in government-estimated fair market value. "The initial cost of acquiring this property was over $64,494,000." Americans United v. U.S. Dept. of Health, Education, and Welfare, 619 F.2d 252, 254 (3rd. Cir. 1980).

261. See Ely, "Legislative and Administrative Motivation in Constitutional Law," 79 *Yale L.J.* 1205 (1970).

262. The Court may also have been concerned about the effects of finding a general public "injury in fact" in the disposition of government property. That finding

could have led to claims of a due process entitlement to fair dispositions of such property. See Tribe, *ACL* §10–9. Should the plaintiffs claim that due process requires giving advance public notice of major property dispositions, so that questionable transfers no longer appear first in news releases, the Court would again have been confronted with a problem similar to that in United States v. Richardson, 418 U.S. 166 (1974), discussed in Tribe, *ACL* §§3–19 and 3–20.

263. As objectionable as was the Court's treatment of taxpayers, it did not totally foreclose standing to challenge this sort of transfer. Rejected competing applicants for the property, or persons with aesthetic or environmental objections to the college's proposed uses of the land, presumably could attack the transfer. See United States v. SCRAP, 412 U.S. 669 (1973), discussed in Tribe, *ACL* §3–19, at 86; Duke Power Co. v. Carolina Environmental Study Group, Inc., 438 U.S. 59 (1978), discussed supra notes 76–94 and accompanying text. See also supra notes 172–183 and accompanying text. Since over half of the government tract was set aside for public schools and parks, prospective users of those facilities could have argued for increased acreage allotments, to the exclusion of the college, without claiming to be prepared to take title to the land themselves. See *Valley Forge*, 454 U.S. at 467–68 n.6. The Court strongly suggested that its conclusion was based in part on the assumption that there were other parties who *would* have standing. Id. at 489. In rejecting a variant of the "standing by necessity" theory advanced by the court of appeals, it is noteworthy that the Court found that the *unwillingness* to sue of the best plaintiffs did not necessarily give others standing, and that any violation of the Establishment Clause may not have done any actual damage to anyone since the property would have been a burden to maintain. Id. at 487–88, 480 n.16. If other plaintiffs were nonexistent or *unable* to sue, or if the deleterious effects of the transfer were clearer, the Court's objections would no longer apply. If the Court denied standing in these situations, or if it refused would-be alternative users or local environmentalists standing, it then would clearly be gutting much of the Establishment Clause's protection.

264. The Court's more relaxed general approach to standing and greater emphasis upon "that concrete adverseness which sharpens the presentation of issues upon which the Court so largely depends for illumination of difficult . . . questions," Baker v. Carr, 369 U.S. 186, 204 (1962), is entirely consistent with its recent flirtation with notions of "virtual representation" in the electoral realm. See Holt Civic Club v. City of Tuscaloosa, 439 U.S. 60 (1978) (allowing city to extend its "police jurisdiction" over surrounding unincorporated areas without extending the franchise to the residents there, in part because the Court apparently felt that the same sorts of interests the disenfranchised people had would be shared by city residents, thus giving the nonresidents "virtual" or surrogate representation). Conversely, the special, rigid rules of standing enunciated in cases like *Valley Forge*, *O'Shea*, and *Lyons* suggest that the Court should take more seriously the distinctly personal nature of the franchise.

265. See Gunther, supra note 225.

266. E.g., Valley Forge Christian College v. Americans United for Separation of Church and State, 454 U.S. 464 (1982) (Establishment Clause); *Lyons* (police use of deadly force); Tribe, *ACL* §3-20.

267. *Valley Forge*, 454 U.S. at 490-91 (Brennan, J., joined by Marshall and Blackmun, JJ., dissenting).

9. The Errant Trajectory of State Sovereignty

1. "The powers not delegated to the United States by the Constitution, nor prohibited by it to the States, are reserved to the States respectively, or to the people."

2. 426 U.S. 833 (1976).

3. Id. at 851.

4. Although the Court in *National League of Cities* was vague as to the source of the state sovereignty limitation, see L. Tribe, *American Constitutional Law* §5-22, at 308-09 n.9 (1978) [hereinafter cited as Tribe, *ACL*] and never actually quoted the language of the Tenth Amendment, its subsequent decisions have explicitly addressed the limitation as a matter of Tenth Amendment doctrine. See Hodel v. Virginia Surface Mining & Reclamation Assn., 452 U.S. 264, 287-89 (1981); United Transportation Union v. Long Island R.R. Co., 455 U.S. 678 (1982); FERC v. Mississippi, 456 U.S. 742 (1982).

5. 452 U.S. 264 (1981).

6. 455 U.S. 678 (1982).

7. 456 U.S. 742 (1982).

8. 455 U.S. 40 (1982).

9. 103 S. Ct. 1054 (1983).

10. 452 U.S. 264 (1981).

11. Justice Marshall delivered the opinion of the Court, in which Chief Justice Burger and Justices Brennan, Stewart, White, Blackmun, Powell, and Stevens joined. The Chief Justice filed a concurring statement. Justice Powell filed a concurring opinion, and Justice Rehnquist, the author of the *National League of Cities* opinion, filed an opinion concurring in the judgment.

12. 91 Stat. 447, 30 U.S.C. §1201 et seq. (1976 ed., Supp. III).

13. Although Justice Marshall spoke of the three requirements as derivations of the Tenth Amendment, 452 U.S. at 286-87, the majority in *National League of Cities* did not cite that amendment in formulating any of its broad states' rights language. See 426 U.S. at 845, 846, 852, 854.

14. 452 U.S. at 287-88.

15. Id. at 288.

16. Id. at 289-90.

17. Id. at 291.

18. In their concurring opinions, the only solace that the Chief Justice and Justice Rehnquist could offer the states was the reminder that congressional power under the Commerce Clause extends only to those matters which have a "sub-

stantial effect" on interstate commerce. 452 U.S. at 305 (Burger, C. J., concurring); id. at 312 (Rehnquist, J., concurring). Justice Rehnquist, the author of the
majority opinion in *National League of Cities*, reacted in a manner reminiscent
of P. G. Wodehouse's remark about the fellow who "wasn't actually disgruntled,
but was far from being gruntled." Clearly wishing to be able to say to the plaintiff, "Yes, Virginia, there *are* limits to the Commerce Clause," Justice Rehnquist
was forced instead to reflect that "one could easily get the sense from this
Court's opinions that the federal system exists only at the sufferance of Congress." 452 U.S. at 308.

19. Justice Rehnquist for the majority gave as examples "fire prevention, police pro-
    tection, sanitation, public health, and parks and recreation." 426 U.S. at 851.
    But he noted that this list was not meant to be exhaustive. Id. n.16.

20. 455 U.S. 678 (1982).

21. 45 U.S.C. §151 *et seq.*

22. 455 U.S. at 682-83.

23. 455 U.S. at 685-86.

24. 426 U.S. at 854 n.18. The exempted cases were Parden v. Terminal R.R. Co.,
    377 U.S. 184 (1964); California v. Taylor, 353 U.S. 553 (1957); United States v.
    California, 297 U.S. 175 (1936).

25. 455 U.S. at 687.

26. 455 U.S. at 687-88.

27. Id. at 687.

28. 435 U.S. 389 (1978).

29. 435 U.S. at 422-24. This, of course, cuts against the experimental spirit of feder-
    alism, which the Court has so often championed. See Tribe, *ACL* §5-22, at
    311.

30. 455 U.S. at 690.

31. An extrapolation of the Court's own reading of history supports this argument.
    At not too distant periods in American history such "traditional" state services
    as education, fire protection, health care, sanitation and even the operation of
    bridges and toll roads were commonly and in some states exclusively provided
    by private enterprises. These functions are now largely immunized under *Na-
    tional League of Cities* because state and local governments started performing
    them before it occurred to the federal government to start regulating them.

32. 456 U.S. 742 (1982).

33. 452 U.S. at 287-88.

34. 455 U.S. at 684.

35. 456 U.S. at 763 n.28.

36. Public Law No. 95-617, 92 Stat. 3117.

37. Mississippi also argued unsuccessfully that the Act was beyond the scope of the
    power delegated to Congress by the Commerce Clause.

38. 456 U.S. at 758 (majority opinion); id. at 775 n.1 (O'Connor, J., dissenting).

39. Under the doctrine of Testa v. Katt, 330 U.S. 386 (1947), a state may not exercise its judicial power so as to discriminate against federal causes of action. 456 U.S. at 759–61 (majority opinion); id. at 775 n.1 (O'Connor, J., dissenting).

40. Justice Blackmun was joined in the majority by Justices Brennan, White, Marshall, and Stevens. Justice Powell concurred in part and dissented in part, as did Justice O'Connor in a separate opinion, which was joined by Justice Rehnquist and the Chief Justice. References to the dissent, unless otherwise noted, refer to Justice O'Connor's opinion.

41. 15 U.S.C. §3203(a) (1976 ed., Supp. IV); 16 U.S.C. §2621(a), 2623(b) (1976 ed., Supp. IV).

42. 452 U.S. 264, 287–88 (1981) (quoting National League of Cities, 426 U.S. at 854, 845, 852).

43. 456 U.S. at 776–77.

44. Id. at 778–81.

45. Id. at 781–82.

46. Id. at 763 n.28. Even if a statute violates all three parts of the test, there may still be instances in which an overwhelming federal interest would outweigh the Tenth Amendment concern and justify state submission. Hodel, 452 U.S. at 288 n.29; Long Island R.R., 455 U.S. at 684 n.9. Yet as Justice O'Connor correctly points out, neither of those cases involved such an exception to the rule of National League of Cities, and the Court has never explored the circumstances that might justify such an exception. 456 U.S. at 778 n.4.

47. 456 U.S. at 761.

48. Id.

49. The majority conceded that this was a case of first impression, 456 U.S. at 759, and that the "Court never has sanctioned explicitly a federal command to the States to promulgate and enforce laws and regulations." Id. at 761–62 (citation omitted).

50. 421 U.S. 542 (1975).

51. 456 U.S. at 762.

52. 426 U.S. at 852.

53. Id. at 853.

54. Id.

55. 456 U.S. at 762 & n.27.

56. 443 U.S. 658 (1979).

57. 456 U.S. at 762 & n.27.

58. 443 U.S. at 695.

59. Id., citing, inter alia, North Carolina Bd. of Educ. v. Swann, 402 U.S. 43 (1971).

60. Id. This is what in fact happened, and the Court never had to confront the question of ordering state governmental entities to do anything but stay out of the way—a simple matter of preemption.

61. 330 U.S. 386 (1947).

62. 456 U.S. at 762–63.

63. Justice Blackmun's retort to this argument was an observation that courts "have always been a co-equal part of the State's sovereign decision-making apparatus and it seems evident that requiring state tribunals to entertain federal claims interferes, at least to a degree, with the State's sovereign prerogatives." 456 U.S. at 762 n.27. Yet just four weeks later Justice Blackmun, concurring in *Crawford v. Bd. of Educ. of Los Angeles*, 458 U.S. 527, 546 (1982), seemingly contradicted himself by describing state courts as mechanical enforcers that have no control over and therefore no interest in which cases they hear, and by denying that the addition or deletion of a certain class of cases from a state court's docket constitutes a structural change in the state's decision-making mechanism. See chapter 16.

64. 456 U.S. at 773 n.4 (Powell, J., concurring in part and dissenting in part). See Note, "Utilization of State Courts to Enforce Federal Penal and Criminal Statutes: Developments in Judicial Federalism," 60 *Harv. L. Rev.* 966, 971 (1947) (nothing in *Testa* upsets "the traditional doctrine that Congress may not interfere with a state's sovereign right to determine and control the jurisdictional requirements of its own courts").

65. 456 U.S. at 764.

66. Id. As in *Hodel*, "[t]here can be no suggestion that the Act commandeers the legislative processes of the States by directly compelling them to enact and enforce a regulatory program." 452 U.S. at 288.

67. Id. (emphasis added).

68. 456 U.S. at 786 (O'Connor, J., dissenting). In his dissent Justice Powell agreed, arguing that since "the Commerce Clause and the Tenth Amendment embody distinct limitations on federal power," the fact "[t]hat Congress has satisfied one demonstrates nothing as to whether Congress has satisfied the other." Id. at 773.

69. 330 U.S. 127, 143 (1947), cited at 456 U.S. at 766.

70. Id., quoting United States v. Darby, 312 U.S. 100, 124 (1941), as quoted in Civil Service Comm'n.

71. 330 U.S. at 143.

72. Cf. Coyle v. Oklahoma, 221 U.S. 559, 565 (1911).

73. *National League of Cities*, 426 U.S. at 851.

74. See Tribe, ACL §5-22, at 315–16. The Court's summary affirmance in *North Carolina v. Califano*, 435 U.S. 962 (1978), affirming 445 F.Supp. 532 (E.D.N.C. 1977), is not contrary to this conclusion. There the Court held that Congress could condition federal health aid on the state's imposition of certain standards on health-care facilities, even if the state's supreme court had found those conditions to be prohibited by the state constitution. The Court apparently found no violation of state sovereignty as articulated in *National League of Cities* in presenting North Carolina with a choice between amending its constitution and foregoing $50 million in federal aid, thereby accepting the principle that when Congress pays the piper it may call the tune. The pivotal fact is that *North Carolina v. Califano* concerned a denial of health funds if health standards were not met. So the holding of that case is that, if Congress pays the piper, it may

call the tune *that particular piper plays*; it does not follow that Congress gets to tell all other state minstrels what to play.

75. 426 U.S. at 852 n.17. See also Fitzpatrick v. Bitzer, 427 U.S. 445, 453 n.9 (1976), and Tribe, *ACL* §5–22, at 315–17. The Court in *National League of Cities* also suggested that Congress may have greater power to intrude upon state sovereignty under its war power than under its commerce power, 426 U.S. at 855 n.18.

76. 456 U.S. at 773. Justice O'Connor, joined by the Chief Justice and Justice Rehnquist, similarly charged that the majority's principle would relegate the states "to mere departments of the National Government." Id. at 795.

77. Elrod v. Burns, 427 U.S. 347, 375 (1976) (dissenting opinion). Recent reversals of the Napoleonic centralist policies under French President François Mitterrand have dated the Chief Justice's comparison.

78. 426 U.S. at 841.

79. 456 U.S. at 769 n.32.

80. Id.

81. 456 U.S. at 764.

82. Id. at 769 nn.31, 33, 34.

83. Id. at 761 (citations omitted).

84. Another way of narrowing *FERC* is to read it as announcing a rule for congressional Commerce Clause power in emergency situations. Justice Blackmun, writing for the Court in *FERC*, characterized PURPA as legislation "designed to combat the nationwide energy crisis." 456 U.S. at 745, and in his concurring opinion in *National League of Cities* he interpreted the majority's approach as a balancing test with special relevance to crises requiring prompt, uniform national action. 426 U.S. at 856. The majority there distinguished the Economic Stabilization Act upheld in Fry v. United States, 421 U.S. 542 (1975) (imposing a temporary wage freeze on state and local employees), noting that the limits on the Commerce Clause as applied to the states "are not so inflexible as to preclude temporary enactments tailored to combat a national emergency." 426 U.S. at 853. The *FERC* majority indicated that a national emergency might justify even greater inroads on state sovereignty than those embodied in PURPA, but that it was not necessary to lay down a definitive rule in order to decide the case at hand. 456 U.S. at 763–64.

85. Id. at 782 n.9.

86. There is a sense in which *Hodel* and *FERC* are consistent both with each other and with *National League of Cities*. The legislation in *Hodel* provided for federal regulation at federal expense in case of state default. 452 U.S. at 288. Similarly, although no provision was made for the federal government to step in should the state refuse to comply with the legislation in *FERC*, PURPA did provide federal funds to cover the added costs of state compliance, 456 U.S. at 751 n.14. Both legislative schemes were upheld by the Court, in contrast to the legislation in *National League of Cities* which imposed substantial financial burdens on the states without providing any federal assistance. The problem with attempting to reconcile the cases in this way is that the Court in *National League*

of Cities carefully avoided resting its decision on any factual conclusions about the actual financial impact of the challenged regulations, see 426 U.S. at 851, and in both *Hodel* and *FERC* it expressly noted that the determinative factor in a Tenth Amendment challenge is "the nature of the federal action, not the ultimate economic impact on the States." 452 U.S. at 292 n.33, quoted in *FERC*, 456 U.S. at 770 n.33.

87. See 456 U.S. at 746–50.

88. The *FERC* majority's use of the term "local" seems ill-advised. The Court clearly means that federalism favors state participation in government, for as it made clear in Community Communications Co., Inc. v. City of Boulder, 455 U.S. 40 (1982), discussed below, federalism has no concern with cities, counties, or other forms of local government as such.

89. See 456 U.S. at 765 n.29, 766.

90. Attorney General Edward H. Levi once remarked that "it is an insidious point to say that there is more federalism by compelling a State instrumentality to work for the Federal Government." Hearings on S.354 before the Senate Committee on Commerce, 94th Cong., lst Sess. 503 (1974), quoted by Justice O'Connor in her dissent, 456 U.S. 786 n.17.

91. Tribe, *ACL* §5–20, at 302, quoted by Justice Powell in his dissent, 456 U.S. 774–75.

92. See Tribe, *ACL* §5–22, at 310.

93. Younger v. Harris, 401 U.S. 37, 44 (1971), quoted by Justice O'Connor in her dissent, 456 U.S. at 796–97. One need have little sympathy for the states' rights view of the *Younger* line of cases, see Tribe, *ACL* §3–41, in which individual rights may be in real jeopardy, in order to lament such decisions as *FERC*, which subordinate the states not to protect the rights of individuals but to exalt the prerogatives of Congress.

94. 456 U.S. at 767 n.30.

95. The Court has not expressly embraced the interpretation of *National League of Cities* proposed in §5–22 of Tribe, *ACL*. However, that reading of the case, as presupposing the existence of individual rights to essential government services with which the federal government may not interfere, is by no means necessarily inconsistent with subsequent developments. Neither *Hodel* nor *Long Island Railroad* involved the provision of basic, essential government services, and *FERC* dealt not with the provision or generation of electricity by the state but with its administrative regulation. The legislation challenged in those cases did not implicate a state's capacity to provide basic services. Furthermore, in Massachusetts v. United States, 435 U.S. 444 (1978), the Court upheld a federal registration tax on civil aircraft as applied to a state police helicopter in part because the tax, amounting to $131.43, created no undue danger of use by the federal government "to control, unduly interfere with, or destroy a state's ability to perform essential services," id. at 467. Still, the absence from these cases of any analysis along the lines suggested in *ACL* indicates that the Court is reading *National League of Cities* as establishing a more general state right against federal encroachment.

96. 455 U.S. 40 (1982).

97. 317 U.S. 341 (1943).

98. *Colo. Const.*, art. XX, §6.

99. Id.

100. 455 U.S. at 45–46.

101. He was joined by Justices Marshall, Blackmun, Powell, and Stevens. Justice Stevens also filed a concurring opinion. Justice Rehnquist, joined by the Chief Justice and Justice O'Connor, dissented. Justice White took no part in the case.

102. 455 U.S. at 53 n.16.

103. Id. at 52 (citations omitted).

104. Id. at 52–56. The majority expressly declined to consider whether the Boulder moratorium also had to satisfy the "active state supervision" test applied in California Retail Liquor Dealers Assn. v. Midcal Aluminum, Inc., 445 U.S. 97, 105 (1980). See 455 U.S. at 51 n.14. Justice Rehnquist considered the majority's avoidance of this issue understandable, since "[i]t would seem rather odd to require municipal ordinances to be enforced by the State rather than the city itself." Id. at 71 n.6 (dissenting opinion).

105. 455 U.S. at 53.

106. Id. at 57 (citation omitted).

107. 207 U.S. 161 (1907).

108. Id. at 178–79; accord, Trenton v. New Jersey, 262 U.S. 182, 186–90 (1923).

109. 455 U.S. at 70, citing City of Burbank v. Lockheed Air Terminal, Inc., 411 U.S. 624 (1973); Huron Portland Cement Co. v. Detroit, 362 U.S. 440 (1960).

110. "As the denomination 'political subdivision' implies, the local governmental units which Congress sought to bring within the [Fair Labor Standards] Act derive their authority and power from their respective States. Interference with integral governmental services provided by such subordinate arms of a state government is therefore beyond the reach of congressional power under the Commerce Clause just as if such services were provided by the State itself." 426 U.S. at 855–56 n.20. Indeed, most of the services which the Court gave as examples of traditional governmental functions—fire prevention, police protection, sanitation, id. at 851, hospital services, and education, id. at 855—are provided by local, not state, governments.

111. *Colo. Const.*, art. III, §6.

112. Not even by Justice Rehnquist in his dissent, even though he was the author of the majority opinion in *National League of Cities.*

113. 456 U.S. 742, 769 n.32 (1982).

114. Justice Brennan wrote for the Court, joined by Justices White, Marshall, Blackmun, and Stevens. Chief Justice Burger, joined by Justices Powell, Rehnquist, and O'Connor, dissented.

115. 103 S. Ct. 1054 (1983).

116. 103 S. Ct. at 1060.

117. 103 S. Ct. at 1061; id. at 1069 (Burger, C. J., dissenting).

118. Since a Tenth Amendment challenge succeeds only if all four prongs of the *Hodel* test are met, the Court had no need to decide this issue. The majority noted that it could discern no guidance in the precedents for determining just what an "undoubted attribute of state sovereignty" would look like. 103 S. Ct. at 1061 n.11.

119. 103 S. Ct. at 1062.

120. Id.

121. Id. (emphasis in original).

122. See id. at 1071–72 (Burger, C. J., dissenting).

123. Id. at 1063 (opinion of Brennan, J.). A "legal" inquiry into practical effects which is not concerned with facts sounds like a strange animal indeed—perhaps some chimerical creature with the body of a lawyer and the head of a systems analyst.

124. Id.

125. See Tribe, ACL §5–22; supra note 95.

126. 103 S. Ct. at 1064.

127. See id. at 1070–71 (Burger, C. J., dissenting).

128. Id. at 1064 n.17. Justice Blackmun's vote swung the balance in *EEOC*, even though the ADEA did not concern the kind of emergency that Justice Blackmun had written of in his *National League of Cities* concurrence, 426 U.S. at 856, or in *FERC*, 456 U.S. 745. It may be that the FLSA's direct interference with wages bothered the justice more than the ADEA's requirement of justifying differential treatment of older employees, because of his general admiration for free enterprise and the ability of the market to set prices. See, e.g., Va. State Bd. of Pharmacy v. Citizens Consumer Council, 425 U.S. 748 (1976), discussed in Tribe, ACL §12–15, and in chapter 13.

129. 456 U.S. at 782 n.9.

130. 455 U.S. at 70 (Rehnquist, J., dissenting).

131. The majority in *FERC* buttressed Justice O'Connor's observation by explicitly denying that it is even undervaluing *National League of Cities*. 456 U.S. at 769 n.32. The absence of such explicit reassurance from Justice Brennan's opinions for the Court in *Boulder* and *EEOC* may be foreboding. Justice Brennan wrote a vigorous dissent in *National League of Cities*, 426 U.S. at 856 et seq., and his plurality opinion in *Massachusetts v. United States*, 435 U.S. 444, 453–463 (1978), was a thinly veiled assault on the Court's position in that case. In all probability, Justice Brennan knows exactly what he is doing.

132. As noted above, the Tenth Amendment was never even quoted by the majority in that case.

133. In his concurring opinion in *EEOC*, Justice Stevens argued that *National League of Cities* should be formally pronounced dead. 103 S. Ct. at 1067.

134. The unanimous reargument order in Donovan v. San Antonio Metropolitan Transit Auth., 52 U.S.L.W. 3937 (1984), requesting briefing and argument on the question "[w]hether or not the principles of the Tenth Amendment as set forth in National League of Cities v. Usery should be reconsidered," may mean

that Justice Blackmun, without whose narrow concurrence there would have been no *National League of Cities* doctrine, is considering abandonment of his position in that case.

10. Congressional Action as Context Rather Than Message

1. 12 U.S.C. §1842(d).
2. See infra notes 13–22 and accompanying text.
3. 1983 Conn. Acts 411 (Reg. Sess.) (codified at 36 Conn. Gen. Stat. (various sections)).
4. 1982 Mass. Acts ch. 155 (codified at Mass. Ann. Laws ch. 167 §§38 and 39, ch. 167A (Supp. 1983)).
5. 1983 R.I. Pub. Laws ch. 201 (codified at R.I. Gen. Laws §§19–30–1, 19–30–2) (effective July 1, 1984).
6. The New England geographical limitation in the Rhode Island statute expires in July 1985. Thereafter, the statute becomes a full reciprocity statute.
7. The situation is, thus, directly analogous to those in which congressional *silence* constitutes an operative fact affecting constitutional analysis, rather than a window into Congress' state of mind. See chapter 4.

   The analysis of this chapter was reinforced by litigation in which I am assisting in the defense of the constitutionality of regional banking plans instituted by Massachusetts and Connecticut in response to this congressional attempt to cede some control of interstate banking to the states. See infra note 26.
8. For a way in which the state's choice might be seen as giving its own banks a competitive edge, see infra, text following note 50.
9. 12 U.S.C. §§1841–49 (1980).
10. Act of May 9, 1956, ch. 240, §3, 70 Stat. 134 (codified at 12 U.S.C. §1842(d) (1) (1980)).
11. The legislative history consists mainly of generalities about the value of local banking. 102 *Cong. Rec.* 6858–60 (1956). There is one potentially revealing statement by Senator Paul Douglas, sponsor of the amendment, who noted in congressional debate that the amendment would allow out-of-state bank holding companies to acquire banks "to the degree that state laws expressly permit them." Id. at 6858.
12. Id.
13. Alaska Stat. §06.05.235. Alaska permits acquisition of established, but not newly formed, banks by out-of-state holding companies.
14. Me. Rev. Stat. Ann. tit. 9–B §§417, 1013, 1020 (1984).
15. New York Banking Law §142–b (McKinney Supp. 1983).
16. Fla. Stat. Ann. §658.29 (West Supp. 1983); Ill. Ann. Stat. ch. 17 & 2510 (Smith-Hurd 1981); Iowa Code Ann. §524.1805 (West Supp. 1982–83).
17. Del. Code Ann. tit. 5, §801 et seq. (Supp. 1982); Md. Fin. Inst. Code Ann. §5–903 (Supp. 1983); 1983 Neb. Laws Nos. 454 and 58; S.D. Statutes §51–16–41 (1983); Va. Code §6.1–392 (1983).

18. 1983 Or. Laws ch. 367; 1983 Wash. Laws ch. 157. The Oregon statute further limits permissible acquirers to holding companies from states contiguous to Oregon.

19. Utah Code Ann. §7-1-102 (1984).

20. Ga. Code Ann. §7-1-620-625 (1984); Ky. Rev. Stat. Ann. §287.900(6)(a) (Baldwin 1984). Legislation similar to that of Georgia and Kentucky has been enacted by the lower houses of the Florida and South Carolina legislatures. *Wall St. Journal*, April 30, 1984, at 4.

21. See supra notes 3–5.

22. See supra notes 3–6.

23. See Sporhase v. Nebraska, 458 U.S. 941, 960 (1982); New England Power Company v. New Hampshire, 455 U.S. 331, 342 (1982); Prudential Insurance Co. v. Benjamin, 328 U.S. 408, 427 (1946).

24. 15 U.S.C. §101.

25. 328 U.S. 408 (1946).

26. Iowa Independent Bankers v. Board of Governors of the Federal Reserve System, 511 F.2d 1288, 1296–97 (D.C. Cir.) (finding in the Douglas Amendment no implicit prohibition against an Iowa statute allowing interstate acquisitions only by the one Minnesota holding company already operating at least two banks within the state), *cert. den.*, 423 U.S. 875 (1975). More recently, in Conference of State Bank Supervisors v. Conover, 715 F.2d 604 (D.C. Cir. 1983), the Court of Appeals noted its "ruling" in *Iowa Bankers* "that the legislative history [of the Douglas Amendment] demonstrated that Congress intended to allow" the states "to discriminate among bank holding companies when deciding which could enter." Id. at 613, 615. More recently, in rejecting a challenge to the regional banking statutes enacted by Massachusetts and Connecticut, supra notes 3 and 4, the Court of Appeals for the Second Circuit held that "Congress authorized Massachusetts and Connecticut to enact the statutes challenged here." Northeast Bank Corp. v. Board of Governors of the Federal Reserve System, nos. 84-4047, slip op. at 11 (2d Cir. Aug. 1, 1984). Because the court found that Congress had authorized the states' action, it did not need to reach the more subtle issues discussed infra at text accompanying notes 29–50.

27. The D.C. Circuit noted in *Iowa Bankers* that "[n]ot once in the entire debate is the discrimination question raised," but went on to conclude that "Senator Douglas seem[ed] to anticipate that states might be selective in allowing bank holding companies to cross state lines." *Iowa Bankers*, 511 F.2d at 1296. There is, however, no clue in the legislative history as to what type of discrimination might be appropriate under the amendment. Facially neutral discriminations, such as the one in *Iowa Bankers*, may not *seem* to raise the constitutional problems that geographically specific prohibitions do, but the Iowa limitation was de facto a discrimination against all holding companies outside Minnesota; that it may have discriminated against some inside Minnesota as well is immaterial. See Dean Milk Co. v. Madison, 340 U.S. 349, 354 n.4 (1951).

28. The Supreme Court has decisively rejected any argument that might be raised to the effect that, since the state could exclude out-of-state holding companies

altogether, there is *no* restriction on the nature of the regulations the state may impose. In Lewis v. BT Investment Managers, Inc., 447 U.S. 27, 44–49 (1980), the Court refused to permit the state of Florida to condition entrance by an out-of-state holding company on the company's acceptance of extraneous state regulation of the company's business once it had been admitted: "The only authority granted to the States [by the Douglas Amendment] is the authority to create exceptions to this general prohibition, that is, to *permit* expansion of banking across state lines where it otherwise would be federally prohibited." Id. at 47 (emphasis in original).

29. For an argument that the Connecticut plan also creates an advantage for Connecticut bank holding companies, see infra, text following note 50.

30. Contrast *Lewis*, supra note 28, where the state of Florida attempted to prohibit the acquisition by an out-of-state bank holding company of a local investment subsidiary. Such an acquisition was perfectly legal under federal law, so the state's attempt constituted an impermissible burden on interstate commerce.

31. Compare Great Atlantic & Pacific Tea Company v. Cottrell, 424 U.S. 366 (1976), where the Supreme Court struck down a Mississippi regulation providing that milk could be imported into the state only from states that accepted Mississippi milk on a reciprocal basis. The Court reasoned that, although voluntary reciprocity agreements might promote mutually beneficial objectives, "Mississippi may not use the threat of economic isolation as a weapon to force sister States to enter into even a desirable reciprocity agreement." Id. at 379.

32. See generally Note, "The Supreme Court, 1982 Term," 97 *Harv. L. Rev.* 70 (1983). However, this exception to certain forms of state action otherwise impermissible under the Commerce Clause does not automatically immunize the action from challenge under other constitutional provisions, e.g., the Privileges and Immunities Clause. United Building and Construction Trades Council v. Camden, 104 S. Ct. 1020 (1984) (municipal ordinance requiring that at least 40 percent of employees of contractors and subcontractors working on city construction projects be city residents is subject to strictures of the Privileges and Immunities Clause). Justice Rehnquist delivered the opinion of the Court, with only Justice Blackmun dissenting.

33. 426 U.S. 794 (1976).

34. 447 U.S. 429 (1980).

35. 103 S. Ct. 1042 (1983).

36. See Note, supra note 32. But see United Building and Construction Trades Council v. Camden, supra note 32, suggesting that municipal local hire ordinances, although immune from Commerce Clause attack because of the status of the municipality as "market participant," may not be immune from challenge under the Privileges and Immunities Clause. Four justices have also recently suggested that the "market participant" exemption does not extend to a state provision that purchasers of state-owned timber partially process the timber before shipping it out of state. South-Central Timber Development v. Wunnicke, 104 S. Ct. 2237 (1984) (plurality opinion). Writing for the Court, Justice White

held that, in the absence of express congressional authorization of state-imposed burdens on interstate commerce, this restriction was impermissible under the Commerce Clause. In a portion of the opinion joined only by Justices Brennan, Blackmun, and Stevens, Justice White concluded that Alaska's situation was not analogous to that in either *Hughes*, *Reeves*, or *White*, since here Alaska had done nothing to create the market in timber; it simply happened to own it because it was there. Justice White noted that language in *Reeves* itself suggested that the state's ownership of the man-made cement plant gave it "market participant" exemption, while ownership of "a natural resource 'like coal, timber, wild game or minerals' " would not. Id. at 2245, quoting Reeves v. Stake, 447 U.S. at 443–44. The Chief Justice and Justice Powell would have remanded on the "market participant" question, while Justices Rehnquist and O'Connor criticized Justice White's view as "unduly formalistic." Id. at 2249 (dissenting opinion).

37. *Hughes*, 426 U.S. at 796–97.

38. *Reeves*, 447 U.S. at 430–33.

39. Id. at 438–39.

40. Id. at 438 (citation omitted).

41. Id. at 441.

42. Id.

43. See Varat, "State 'Citizenship' and Interstate Equality," 48 *U. Chi. L. Rev.* 487, 549–52 (1981); Note, supra note 32, at 73–78.

44. However, in his separate concurrence in *Hughes*, Justice Stevens stressed that the "creation" of commerce is not in itself decisive of the question of Commerce Clause applicability. 426 U.S. at 814.

45. More recently, in United Building & Construction Trades v. Camden, 104 S. Ct. 1020 (1984), the Court reiterated the mechanical market regulator–market participant distinction to explain why the reasoning of the *Hughes* line of cases is not applicable to analysis under Article IV's Privileges and Immunities Clause, which is concerned not with regulation of commerce per se, but with discrimination against out-of-state residents on matters of fundamental concern. Although the Court did not exempt from Privileges and Immunities scrutiny a Camden ordinance requiring that at least 40 percent of the employees of contractors and subcontractors working on city construction projects be Camden residents, the Court expressed concerns similar to those underlying the "market participant" exception. Id. at 1030.

46. Cf. Baldwin v. Seelig, 294 U.S. 511 (1935) (Commerce Clause is no less concerned with trade impediments imposed to offset deterrents to purchase from New York dairies created by New York's own legislature than with trade impediments imposed to offset deterrents to purchase created by natural economic conditions in New York).

47. The Supreme Court has not spoken directly to the issue of state favoritism toward companies based in some outside states over companies based in others. In Exxon Corp. v. Governor of Maryland, 437 U.S. 117 (1978), the Court

found no special Commerce Clause concern triggered by a state regulation that had the effect of shifting business from "one interstate supplier to another," id. at 127, without reducing the net volume of interstate commerce. The state statute in *Exxon*, however, although having a differential impact on some interstate business, did not discriminate on its face or de facto according to firm location. See *Lewis*, 447 U.S. at 40–42. See also American Trust Co. v. South Carolina State Board of Bank Control, 381 F.Supp. 313, 322–23 (D.S.C. 1974) (three-judge panel), which rejected a Commerce Clause challenge to a South Carolina statute that permitted banks located in states not contiguous to South Carolina to serve as testamentary trustees for local decedents while prohibiting banks located in contiguous states from so serving. The court found implicit congressional authorization for the discrimination among states in a federal statute, 12 U.S.C. §92a, that permits national banks to engage in the provision of trust services in a state so long as state banks are not prohibited from doing so in that state. Since South Carolina treated state and national banks alike under its law, the court found that the state statute had been authorized by the federal statute and therefore did not violate the Commerce Clause, even though the federal law mentioned neither discrimination among states nor interstate commerce. The court invalidated another provision of South Carolina banking law, but under an equal protection analysis based on Morey v. Doud, 354 U.S. 457 (1957), which was subsequently overruled in New Orleans v. Dukes, 427 U.S. 297, 306 (1976).

48. Cf. Baldwin v. Seelig, supra note 46.

49. See Southern Pacific Co. v. Arizona, 325 U.S. 761, 767 n.2 (1945); South Carolina State Highway Department v. Barnwell Brothers, Inc., 303 U.S. 177, 185 (1938). Justice Stone's concern with political representation in *Barnwell*, see 303 U.S. at 184–85, presaged his famous "discrete and insular minorities" footnote in United States v. Carolene Products Co., 304 U.S. 144, 152–53 n.4 (1938). See generally J. Ely, *Democracy and Distrust* 83–84 (1980).

50. A contrary argument would have to say that New England states are so homogeneous and tight-knit a group that courts should treat action by any of those states favoring any of the others as equivalent to self-dealing. But if that extreme model were adopted, it would be difficult to argue that Congress, in authorizing each state to prefer its own banks to all outside banks, would have balked at authorizing a regional preference. Either a Connecticut preference for Massachusetts banks is so *similar* to the home-state preference Congress authorized as to fall within the authorization of the Douglas Amendment, or a preference for Massachusetts banks is so *different* from a home-state preference that core Commerce Clause values are not at stake.

At least, absent proof that a state such as New York has been unacceptably isolated by the *cumulative* impact of many such state schemes, no further congressional authorization seems necessary. In the analogous context of nondiscriminatory taxation of multistate business, a business must demonstrate *actual* cumulative burdens created by multistate taxation, not just the theoretical *possibility* of such burdens, in order to establish an exemption from an otherwise valid tax. See L. Tribe, *American Constitutional Law* §6–17, at 360 (1978).

11. Guam's Vanishing Bonds

1. Guam is one of four insular territories of the United States. Located just west of the international date line, it takes some 19 hours to fly there from Washington, D.C. Guam has a population of about 100,000, and although its society is more advanced than that of the surrounding Marianas, it is not self-supporting. More than two-thirds of the work force is employed by the Government of Guam or the Government of the United States, with many of the workers employed at large defense bases. Much of the population receives food stamps. Guam, like the other insular territories and the District of Columbia, has an elected representative to Congress who has floor privileges and a vote in committee, but who is not entitled to vote on the floor of the House of Representatives. 48 U.S.C. §1711 et seq.

2. Lewis, "The Rule of Law (II)," *New York Times*, Jan. 9, 1984, at A17.

3. Courts may, in fact, hold that many serious threats to the spirit of the Constitution are not justiciable. See, e.g., Valley Forge Christian College v. Americans United for the Separation of Church and State, 454 U.S. 464 (1982), discussed in chapter 8.

4. H.R. Rep. No. 413, 91st Cong., 1st Sess., reprinted in 1969 U.S. Code Cong. & Ad. News, 1645, 1826–27.

5. The proceeds from most arbitrage bonds are invested in this way, giving the bondholders the security of federal bonds with the tax-exempt benefit of state instruments. Id. at 1825–28. The proceeds from the Guam Economic Development Bonds would have been invested in their entirety in U.S. Treasury obligations. See Preliminary Official Statement of GEDA, dated Dec. 14, 1983.

6. Tax-exempt bonds in general have long been a target of Treasury policy. See Surrey, "Federal Income Tax Reforms: The Varied Approaches Necessary to Replace Tax Expenditures with Direct Government Assistance," 84 *Harv. L. Rev.*, 352, 371–80 (1970).

7. Tax Reform Act of 1969, Pub. L. No. 91-172, 83 Stat. 656–57 (codified as amended in scattered sections of 26 U.S.C.). The 1969 Tax Reform Act removed the provision in the Internal Revenue Code that had been used to find a tax exemption for all arbitrage bonds. The territories were entitled to continue to issue arbitrage bonds under independent statutory authorization. In the case of Guam, this was 48 U.S.C. §1423a.

8. One of the concerns of Treasury and Congress alike has been that, as the number of tax-exempt bonds in the market has grown, the spread between taxable and tax-exempt rates has shrunk. "While the tax-exempt rate historically has been about 65 to 75 percent of the taxable rate, tax-exempt bonds are now generally yielding about 80 to 85 percent of the taxable rate." S. Rep. No. 494, 97th Cong., 2d Sess. 167 (1982), reprinted in 1982 U.S. Code Cong. & Ad. News 781, 929. As tax-exempt issues proliferate, an ever greater share of the revenue lost by the federal government flows to the investor rather than the borrower; for every dollar saved by the states in interest costs, the federal government loses more than $1.35 in taxes. At the same time, interest rates paid by state and local governments on bonds for traditional public purposes (schools,

roads, etc.) are greatly increased. See generally, *The Tax Exemption on State and Local Bonds* (Washington, D.C.: Congressional Budget Office, 1975).

9. H.R. Rep. No. 413, 91st Cong., lst Sess., reprinted in 1969 U.S. Code Cong. & Ad. News 1645, 1825–28. Although it is possible that a statutory change making the interest on *all* state and local obligations taxable would encounter a constitutional barrier under National League of Cities v. Usery, 426 U.S. 833 (1976), discussed in chapter 9, there could certainly be no constitutional objection to removing the tax provisions that made it profitable for states and localities to play the money market.

10. *1985 Budget of the United States* 9–62 (1984).

11. The Treasury suffers a tax loss of more than $23 billion per year from tax-exempt bonds. *1985 Budget of the United States, Special Analyses* H-12 (1984).

12. H.R. 4170, §725.

13. H.R. Rep. No. 432, 98th Cong., lst Sess., 384–85.

14. See, e.g., *1984 Budget of the United States* 5–144 (1983). General governmental assistance to U.S. territories has been cut from $192 million in FY 82 to zero (requested) for FY 84. The 1985 budget proposes elimination of federal grants to Guam's Economic Development Loan Fund, which received $500,000 in FY 83, and of "construction grants" to the territory, which totaled an estimated $11,350,000 in FY 84. *1985 Budget of the United States* I-M54 (1984). In addition, Reagan cutbacks in the area of food stamps and other social programs have had a disproportionate impact on Guam, where a high percentage of residents are eligible for various forms of federal assistance.

15. Weberman, "Guam Throttles Golden Goose," *Forbes*, Jan. 16, 1984, p. 34. Merrill Lynch Capital Markets, underwriter for the Puerto Rico deal, was credited by Weberman with "pioneering" the territorial arbitrage idea.

16. The bond issue was originally planned for $250 million. However, when the territory received a triple-A rating on the bonds from rating services, the total was increased to $850 million at the suggestion of Kidder, Peabody & Co., the underwriter chosen by the Guam Economic Development Authority for the issue. Id. Treasury officials estimated that the interest rate differential on the $850 million bond issue they contemplated would net Guam $380 million over the thirty-year life of the bonds. The money would be appropriated by the Guam Legislature for various public purposes, including such large capital projects as improving hospitals and schools. Preliminary Official Statement of GEDA, dated Dec. 14, 1983, p. 1; *Wall St. Journal*, Jan. 3, 1984, at 46.

17. Weberman, "Guam Throttles Golden Goose," supra note 15.

18. Because the proceeds from the arbitrage bonds were to be invested in Treasury obligations, the prospect of the bonds may have been particularly irksome to federal officials. Normally, the Treasury recoups part of the interest it pays on its bonds through the federal income taxes paid by bondholders; if the bondholders are, like territories, themselves exempt from paying taxes on their income, the upshot is a tangible and visible revenue loss to the federal government.

19. News Release R-2464, Department of the Treasury (Dec. 20, 1983); "Guam Bond Offer of $850 Million Halted by Kidder," *Wall St. Journal*, Dec. 22, 1983, at 37. Treasury also threatened to ask Congress to cut Guam's appropriation by an amount equivalent to any profit it might earn on the bonds. Because the bond issue was never consummated, that threat has not been carried out. Treasury has said it might ask Congress for a reduction in Puerto Rico's appropriation to compensate the government for the lost revenue associated with the arbitrage profit on its $450 million bond issue. Id. To date, this threat has not been carried out either.

20. I was briefly retained in late December 1983, by Kidder, Peabody for consultation on the constitutional issues posed. Kidder, Peabody and its bond counsel had been researching whether retroactive legislation of the kind proposed by the Treasury would be constitutional; I soon focused on what seemed to me a more salient issue: whether the Treasury's action in making the announcement was itself appropriate under the Constitution's separation of powers.

21. Justice Brennan, writing for a unanimous Court in Pension Benefit Guaranty Corp. v. R.A. Gray & Co., 52 U.S.L.W. 4810 (1984), held that although "retroactive legislation does have to meet a burden not faced by legislation that has only future effects, . . . that burden is met simply by showing that the retroactive application of the legislation is itself justified by a rational legislative purpose . . . As we recently noted when upholding the retroactive application of an income tax statute in *United States v. Darusmont*, 449 U.S. 292, 296–97 (1981) (per curiam), the enactment of retroactive statutes 'confined to short and limited periods required by the practicalities of producing national legislation . . . is a customary congressional practice.'" Id. at 4814.

22. 305 U.S. 134 (1938).

23. Id. at 146–47.

24. 276 U.S. 440 (1928).

25. 275 U.S. 142 (1927).

26. Id. at 147. Cf. Judge Learned Hand's observation that a taxpayer complaining of a change in the rate of taxation on a previously completed transaction is in a different position from "one who, when he takes action, has no reason to suppose that any transactions of the sort will be taxed at all." Cohan v. Commissioner, 39 F.2d 540, 545 (2d Cir. 1930), cited with approval in United States v. Darusmont, 449 U.S. at 298. In *Untermyer*, the Court suggested that the fact that a bill proposing a new tax may be pending in Congress at the time the previously untaxed transactions were made does not make a difference of constitutional dimension. 276 U.S. at 445. See further discussion infra notes 39, 47.

27. Alternatively, if the question were viewed through the lens that Martin Feldstein advocated in his well-known article "Compensation in Tax Reform," 29 *National Tax Journal* 123 (June 1976), while he was still a Harvard academic and before he had become a high-ranking (if highly ignored) White House adviser, the proposed legislation might be deemed a "taking," which would conceivably require compensation under the Fifth Amendment. That is, since the histori-

cally tax-exempt status of the bonds is a distinct part of their value as property, any change in the tax structure that effectively removed that separate element of their value should not be effected without some effort to make the owners whole through financial compensation. Although this is a powerful political argument which might deter Congress from enacting such a change, it is most doubtful that the Supreme Court would strike down such legislation on Fifth Amendment grounds for want of fair compensation. See the discussion of *U.S. Railroad Retirement Board v. Fritz*, 449 U.S. 166 (1980), in chapter 12.

28. See chapter 12.

29. See, e.g., Perry v. United States, 294 U.S. 330 (1935) (invalidating, as violative of the power to borrow money on the credit of the United States, a congressional statute purporting to abrogate a clause in government bonds calling for payment in gold coin), and U.S. Trust Company of New York v. New Jersey, 431 U.S. 1 (1977) (invalidating, as violative of Contract Clause, a retroactive 1974 repeal of a 1962 bi-state statutory covenant that had limited the ability of New York and New Jersey to subsidize rail passenger transportation from revenues and reserves pledged as security for bonds issued by the Port Authority). Writing for a unanimous Supreme Court in Pension Benefit Guaranty Corporation v. R.A. Gray & Company, 52 U.S.L.W. 4810, 4814 (1984), Justice Brennan suggested that the federal government is more free than are the states to impair the obligation of contracts. "It could not be justifiably claimed that the Contract Clause applies, either by its own terms or by convincing historical evidence, to actions of the National Government." Id. at 4814 n.9. Although federal legislation is of course subject to the limitations of due process, "[w]e have never held . . . that the principles embodied in the Fifth Amendment's Due Process Clause are coextensive with prohibitions existing against state impairments of pre-existing contracts." Id. at 4814.

30. 431 U.S. at 26. See discussion in L. Tribe, *American Constitutional Law* §9–7, at 473 (1978) [hereinafter cited as Tribe, *ACL*].

31. In Lichter v. United States, 334 U.S. 742 (1948), the Court upheld provisions of the 1942 War Contracts Renegotiation Act for recovery of excessive profits made on war contracts. Although the Act covered not only subcontracts but also contracts made by manufacturers with the government directly, *Lichter* involved only the subcontracts; there was no "issue as to the recovery of excessive profits on any contract made directly with the Government," and the Court gave no indication of how it would decide such a case. Id. at 788–89.

32. *U.S. Const.*, art. I, §8, cl. 1. ("The Congress shall have the Power to lay and collect Taxes, Duties, Imposts and Excises, to pay the Debts and provide for the common Defense and general Welfare of the United States; but all Duties, Imposts and Excises shall be uniform throughout the United States.")

33. See, e.g., United States v. Ptasynski, 103 S. Ct. 2239 (1983) (rejecting a constitutional challenge based on the Uniformity Clause in the context of a windfall profit tax exemption for certain oil produced in Alaska).

34. During the Senate debate on the Windfall Profits Tax, for example, opponents of the tax argued that the preferential treatment of Alaska oil might make the tax unconstitutional on uniformity grounds. See, e.g., 126 *Cong. Rec.* 6294

(1980) (statement of Sen. Bellmon). The proper forum for venting questions of this kind of uniformity of treatment may well be the Congress.

35. *U.S. Const.*, art. II, §3.

36. See supra note 1.

37. See *1985 Budget of the United States* (Washington, D.C.: Government Printing Office, 1984) at 9–62.

38. See, e.g., "Treasury Bond Sale Brings 11.95% Yield, Highest Since 1981," *Wall St. Journal*, Dec. 30, 1983, p. 17.

39. Of course the same Congress that made municipal bonds tax-exempt might always decide to make them taxable at some point in the future. The risk of that occurrence is one that all investors in the tax-exempt market always take; it is generally perceived to be a minimal one. There are numerous policy objections to making such a radical change in the treatment of income from capital already invested. See, e.g., Feldstein, "Compensation in Tax Reform," supra note 27. In addition, although the Supreme Court has never squarely decided the question, the absence of notice by the government to the investor prior to the making of the investment might well convince a court that such retroactive imposition of tax liability would violate due process. Cf. Pension Guaranty Corp. v. R.A. Gray & Co., 52 U.S.L.W. 4810, 4814 & n.8 (1984); United States v. Darusmont, 449 U.S. 292, 299 (1981) (per curiam). Finally, it seems highly unlikely that a Congress that has repeatedly rejected most invitations to make *prospective* changes in the treatment of tax-exempt bonds is likely to go so far as to make *retroactive* ones of this magnitude.

40. In part because of the recent proliferation of tax-exempt issues, see supra note 8, the "spread" between taxable and tax-exempt interest rates—Guam's margin of profit on the arbitrage deal—was not more than 1 percent. Weberman, "Guam Throttles Golden Goose," supra note 15.

41. Cf. McCulloch v. Maryland, 17 U.S. (4 Wheat.) 316, 327 (1819).

42. For further discussion of this aspect of the facts surrounding the Guam bonds, see infra note 48.

43. The statutory provision is the Hart-Scott-Rodino Pre-merger Notification Act of 1976, 15 U.S.C. §18a(e)(1), 90 Stat. 1390 (1976).

44. See, e.g., New Motor Vehicle Board v. Fox, 439 U.S. 96 (1978). The Supreme Court there held that a state statute that prohibited a motor vehicle franchisor from franchising a new operation until after a public hearing if an existing franchisee in the area at issue objected to the move did not deprive the franchisor (or the new franchisee) of liberty or property without due process of law. The Court reasoned that the underlying state law gave the franchisor the right to open up a new operation without the public hearing only if there was no objection from existing franchisees. Thus, the objection from the existing franchisee did not *alter* the status quo; silence simply made it unnecessary to hold the hearing. By contrast, the underlying law at the time of the Treasury announcement was clear that Guam's bonds would be tax-exempt. Far from *maintaining* the status quo, the Treasury announcement had the effect of changing it altogether—but without legislation of any kind.

45. The 152 substantive provisions of the Tax Reform Act of 1969, 83 Stat. 487 (1969), for example, took effect according to 85 different time schedules which employed more than 40 different specific dates, 20 of which were prior to the enactment date. These preenactment effective dates included the dates of the presidential message, of press releases about specific provisions of the proposal issued during congressional consideration of the bill, and of other milestones along the legislative path. See Note, "Setting Effective Dates for Tax Legislation: A Rule of Prospectivity," 84 *Harv. L. Rev.* 436 (1970).

46. Although this latter value is not spelled out with great specificity in the Constitution itself, evidence of it can be found in such cases as Powell v. McCormack, 395 U.S. 486, 548 (1969) (the "Constitution does not vest in Congress a discretionary power to deny membership by a majority vote"), and Wesberry v. Sanders, 376 U.S. 1, 7–8 (1964) (the "command of Art. I, §2, that Representatives be chosen 'by the People of the several States' means that as nearly as practicable one man's vote in a congressional election is to be worth as much as another's.") See also *Mason's Legislative Manual*, whose rules of parliamentary law govern many state legislatures, at §52—Equality of Members ("the equality of members is presumed") and §519—Delegation of Powers (the power of a legislative body to do any act requiring the use of discretion cannot be delegated to a minority of that body).

47. Indeed, the Supreme Court held in Untermyer v. Anderson, 276 U.S. 440, 445 (1928), that a citizen "cannot foresee and ought not to be required to guess the outcome of pending measures. The future of every bill while before Congress is necessarily uncertain. The will of the lawmakers is not definitely expressed until final action thereon has been taken."

48. The situation is somewhat analogous to the problem of the pocket veto, where the absence of Congress gives the President the power to extinguish a piece of legislation submitted to him with no possibility of override. But the pocket veto power is one the Constitution explicitly gives to the President in Art. I, §7, cl. 2. See the Pocket Veto Case, 279 U.S. 655 (1929) (upholding pocket veto exercised during five-month intersession adjournment); Wright v. United States, 302 U.S. 583 (1938) (invalidating pocket veto exercised during three-day adjournment of single house); Kennedy v. Sampson, 511 F.2d 430 (D.C. Cir. 1974) (invalidating pocket veto exercised during five-day intrasession adjournment). The problem of unilateral executive enactment which occurred here is, in a sense, more serious than any abuse of the pocket veto. For the veto of a piece of legislation by the President's inaction with no possibility of override changes the status quo only subject to the possibility of congressional reenactment after the legislative session resumes; the unilateral executive enactment of de facto "legislation" is more likely to work a change beyond Congress' power to undo.

49. See Tribe, *ACL* §12–4, and review by S. Shiffrin of Yudof, "When Government Speaks," in 96 *Harv. L. Rev.* 1745 (1983).

50. *U.S. Const.*, art I, §6, cl. 1.

51. See chapter 2, and Tribe, *ACL* §3–16 (political questions). Note similarities to, and differences from, Goldwater v. Carter, 444 U.S. 996 (1979) (Senator's suit against President for violation of treaty dismissed): like that case, this is largely

an interbranch dispute; unlike that, this is an issue bearing on individual rights—no taxation without legislation.

52. Immigration and Naturalization Serv. v. Chadha, 103 S. Ct. 2764, 2781 (1983), discussed in chapter 6.

53. Buckley v. Valeo, 424 U.S. 1, 124 (1976) (per curiam).

54. *Chadha*, 103 S. Ct. at 2780–81.

55. Id.

56. See chapter 6.

57. The announcement was, however, made pursuant to an informal "political invention," *Chadha*, 103 S. Ct. at 2745 (White, J., dissenting), developed by the Treasury in cooperation with the staff members of the House Committee on Ways & Means, the Senate Finance Committee, and the Joint Committee on Taxation. These representatives of the executive and legislative branches have developed a method for preventing what they consider flagrant abuses of the tax system. When they become aware of a practice they consider abusive, they confer and devise a plan for corrective legislation. Treasury then announces that it will seek enactment of the legislation with an effective date retroactive to the date of the announcement. The announcement carries with it a high enough probability that the legislation will be enacted as proposed that most informed actors abandon the practice immediately. This procedure was followed in 1982 when the Treasury announced it would seek legislation retroactive to the date of its announcement changing the tax status of Original Issue Discount and Stripped Coupon Bonds. The Tax Equity and Fiscal Responsibility Act of 1982 (TEFRA), 96 Stat. 324, included the proposed changes with a slightly different retroactive effective date. However, the Treasury announcement had the intended effect, immediately drying up the market for the financial instruments in the form to which Treasury objected. From interviews with Bruce Davie, Ways and Means Committee Staff (Feb. 8, 1984) and Bob Woodward, Department of the Treasury (Feb. 16, 1984).

58. Youngstown Sheet and Tube Co. v. Sawyer, 343 U.S. 579 (1952).

59. Id. at 587.

60. Id. at 588–89.

61. Id. at 650, 655. Jackson observed that there was worldly wisdom (if not good law) in Napoleon's maxim that the tools belong to the man who can use them, suggesting that "power to legislate in emergencies belongs in the hands of Congress, but only Congress itself can prevent power from slipping through its fingers." Id. at 654.

62. 343 U.S. at 629.

63. Id., quoting 272 U.S. 52, 193 (1926).

64. 343 U.S. at 630–32.

65. See chapter 4.

66. One of those is the provision in Article I, Section 7, Clause 1, that "All Bills for raising Revenue shall originate in the House of Representatives." Taxpayers

have asserted claims under the origination clause over the years. See Twin City Bank v. Nebeker, 167 U.S. 196 (1897); Miller v. Roberts, 202 U.S. 429 (1906); Flint v. Stone Tracy Co., 220 U.S. 107 (1911). More recently, several members of the House of Representatives have sued the United States for allegedly violating this requirement in the enactment of the mid-1982 tax increase of $98.3 billion. Ron Paul v. United States, No. 82–2352, and W. Henson Moore v. United States, No. 82–1218. The tax bill signed by the President had originated in the House, but as it passed the House, it provided only for tax reductions. The Senate amended the bill in its entirety, and turned it into a revenue *raising* bill. The United States prevailed in the District Court for the District of Columbia, where Judge Joyce Green dismissed the actions under the doctrine of equitable discretion announced in Riegle v. Federal Open Market Committee, 656 F.2d 697 (D.C. Cir. 1981), *cert. denied*, 102 S. Ct. 636 (1982) (court should dismiss actions brought by congressmen where relief is available from fellow legislators through statutory action). The U.S. Court of Appeals for the D.C. Circuit affirmed the lower court's dismissal, holding that although the congressmen had standing to challenge the tax increase under the Origination Clause, the suit was properly dismissed because of prudential concerns about the separation of powers. The same concerns for the separation of powers that should discourage courts from assuming essentially legislative roles might well likewise discourage the executive from making itself a superlegislature.

67. Somewhat analogous is the void-for-vagueness doctrine, which requires that a penal statute define the criminal offense with sufficient definiteness that ordinary people can understand what conduct is prohibited *and* in a manner that does not encourage arbitrary and discriminatory enforcement. As Justice O'Connor made clear in her opinion for the Court in Kolender v. Lawson, 103 S. Ct. 1855 (1983), "the more important aspect of vagueness doctrine 'is not actual notice, but the other principal element of the doctrine—the requirement that a legislature establish minimal guidelines to govern law enforcement.' Where the legislature fails to provide such minimal guidelines, a criminal statute may permit a 'standardless sweep [that] allows policemen, prosecutors, and juries to pursue their personal predilictions.' " Id. at 1858–59, quoting Smith v. Goguen, 415 U.S. 566, 574–75 (1974). The requirement of minimal guidelines thus protects the public against the unfettered exercise of executive discretion. In a footnote, Justice O'Connor quoted United States v. Reese, 92 U.S. 214, 221 (1875), for the proposition that the absence of minimal guidelines in criminal statutes would leave too much to judicial discretion, "substitut[ing] the judicial for the legislative department of government."

68. *Youngstown*, 343 U.S. at 633–34 (1952) (concurring opinion). See also United States v. Bethlehem Steel Corp., 315 U.S. 289, 309 (1942): "It may be that . . . other measures [of protecting government contract rights] must be devised. But if the Executive is in need of additional laws by which to protect the nation against war profiteering, the Constitution has given to Congress, not to this Court, the power to make them."

69. 343 U.S. at 633.

12. Compensation, Contract, and Capital

1. To be sure, these limits prevent some blatantly demoralizing exploitations of some individuals for the benefit of others. See Michelman, "Property, Utility, and Fairness: Comments on the Ethical Foundations of 'Just Compensation' Law," 80 *Harv. L. Rev.* 1165 (1967). But neither the public purpose requirement nor the just compensation requirement could prevent states from occasionally—or even routinely—uprooting relatively powerless people, including minority communities, from the places in which they had made their homes and grounded their spiritual and political lives, paying them a fair market value for the property taken and contracts impaired, and putting what was once theirs to such indisputably public uses as highway construction or job creation.

2. Calder v. Bull, 3 U.S. (3 Dall.) 386, 388 (1798) (seriatim opinion).

3. The State of Hawaii took that ban as a given in defending before the Supreme Court an ambitious state statute authorizing use of the eminent domain power to enable homeowners with long-term land leases to purchase the lots on which they lived. The state argued that such transfer of title between private individuals served several purposes traditionally recognized as public—including loosening restraints on alienation, broadening opportunities for land ownership, decentralizing control of a unique economic resource, and stabilizing the state economy. Deferring to the legislature's assessment of the likely effects of the transfers, the Supreme Court upheld the statute's constitutionality, holding that the scope of the "public use" requirement of the Taking Clause is "coterminous with the scope of a sovereign's police powers." Hawaii Housing Authority v. Midkiff, 104 S. Ct. 2321, 2329 (1984). (I argued the case as counsel for the State of Hawaii.)

   Indeed, when a taking for a public purpose is effected by an Act of Congress, that taking is constitutional so long as Congress does not specifically withdraw "the Tucker Act grant of jurisdiction to the Court of Claims to hear a suit involving the [statute] 'founded . . . upon the Constitution.'" Ruckelshaus v. Monsanto Co., 52 U.S.L.W. 4886, 4894 (1984) (citation omitted). The Tucker Act, 28 U.S.C.§1491, provides a mechanism for persons claiming that the United States had taken their property to seek compensation from the government. *Monsanto* involved a claim that the provisions of the Federal Insecticide, Fungicide, and Rodenticide Act (FIFRA) permitting the Environment Protection Agency (EPA) to disclose to the public, and to use in support of subsequent competing applications, test results—including trade secrets—submitted by license applicants to the EPA as part of the licensing process were unconstitutional because they served only private rather than public purposes and deprived the applicants of property without compensation. Although the Court agreed with Monsanto that part of FIFRA did result in the taking of a property interest by the government, Justice Blackmun's opinion upheld the act as a legitimate exercise of Congress' legislative power. Of course, if the Tucker Act were repealed, or for some other reason the property owners were barred from receiving just compensation in the event of such a taking, FIFRA would not have withstood scrutiny.

Takings of a fungible good like money—once it is held that those takings require compensation—make no sense from a legislative point of view inasmuch
as compensation in such cases would simply reverse the effect of the taking. See,
e.g., Webb's Fabulous Pharmacies, Inc. v. Beckwith, 449 U.S. 155 (1980), discussed infra, text accompanying note 30. Other takings, involving the appropriation of nonfungible goods such as scarce house lots or experimental results
from the testing of new chemicals, may well make legislative sense even though
compensation is required by the Constitution. In a case involving the question
whether, when a municipality lays off some of its workforce, it does so in a way
that protects the seniority rights of long-time white workers or in a way that
preserves minority hiring goals, District Judge H. Lee Sarokin sensibly ordered
that the affirmative action goals be maintained, but that those whose seniority
rights were taken be compensated by the government. Vulcan Pioneers v. New
Jersey Department of Public Service, 588 F.Supp. 717 (D.N.J. 1984), vacated in
light of Firefighters Local Union No. 1784 v. Stotts, 588 F.Supp. 732 (D.N.J.
1984). See below, chapter 14.

4. *U.S. Const.*, art. I. §10: "No State shall . . . pass any. . . Law impairing the Obligation of Contracts." Although the Constitution does not explicitly protect
against similar federal legislation, the Due Process Clause of the Fifth Amendment has much the same effect. See Lynch v. United States, 292 U.S. 571 (1934)
(congressional attempt to cancel government war risk life insurance held invalid). But see note 29 on page 378 supra.

5. The final clause of the Fifth Amendment provides that "private property [shall
not] be taken for public use, without just compensation." The Due Process
Clause of the Fourteenth Amendment imposes a parallel prohibition on the
states. See Chicago, Burlington & Quincy Ry. v. Chicago, 166 U.S. 226, 233,
236–37 (1897).

6. This is especially so given the Supreme Court's ruling that a legislative determination that a taking will serve a public purpose must receive "well-nigh conclusive" deference in federal court. Berman v. Parker, 348 U.S. 26, 32 (1954).

7. Not all disaggregation of economic power is thus prevented, only disaggregation designed solely to transfer wealth directly. The just compensation requirement poses no barrier to takings designed to break up control of unique economic resources.

8. 198 U.S. 45 (1905).

9. See, e.g., West Coast Hotel v. Parrish, 300 U.S. 379 (1937) (sustaining minimum
wage laws).

10. NLRB v Jones & Laughlin Steel Corp., 301 U.S. 1 (1937) (upholding National
Labor Relations Act).

11. *U.S. Const.*, amend. XVI (authorizing federal income tax).

12. Brushaber v. Union Pacific RR Co., 240 U.S. 1, 25 (1916), upholds the progressivity of income taxes under the Sixteenth Amendment, thus indirectly approving a redistributive agenda. The case also establishes that income taxes
must be geographically uniform and based on reasonable classifications—not
"so arbitrary as to constrain to the conclusion that it was not the exertion of

taxation, but a confiscation of property; that is, a taking of the same in violation of the 5th Amendment; or what is equivalent thereto, . . . so wanting in basis for classification as to produce such a gross and patent inequality as to inevitably lead to the same conclusion." Id. at 24–25. See also Knowlton v. Moore, 178 U.S. 41, 109–10 (1900) (upholding the progressivity of a federal inheritance tax).

13. United States v. Ptasynski, 103 S. Ct. 2239 (1983) (reaffirming the importance of the Uniformity Clause, but holding that the clause is not violated by exemption from windfall profits tax of certain oil produced in Alaska).

14. 260 U.S. 393 (1922).

15. Id. at 415.

16. Andrus v. Allard, 444 U.S. 51, 65 (1979) (holding federal wildlife law effects no taking by prohibiting trade in body parts of endangered species while allowing other remunerative uses).

17. 438 U.S. 104 (1978).

18. Id. at 134–35.

19. The New York Landmarks Preservation Law applies to all buildings in thirty-one historical districts and to more than four hundred individual structures. Id. at 134.

20. Id. at 136–37.

21. 447 U.S. 255 (1980).

22. This, of course, might mean the *very* long run which John Meynard Keynes had in mind when he said, "In the long run, we're all dead."

23. 447 U.S. at 262–63. One issue in *Agins* was left unresolved. The California Supreme Court had held that "inverse condemnation"—a claim by the regulated owner that there has been a de facto confiscation for which he or she must be compensated—is inappropriate where only unconstitutional regulation is alleged. Compensation, the court reasoned, is called for only when the state is literally exercising its power of eminent domain, not the police power. See 24 Cal. 3d 266, 272, 598 P. 2d 25, 28 (1979). If a zoning regulation is so intrusive as to deprive someone of property without just compensation, the victim's remedy lies solely in an action for mandamus or declaratory or injunctive relief to invalidate and set aside the regulation. The question whether a state may in this manner avoid the need to compensate for regulatory "takings" could have been resolved in San Diego Gas & Electric Co. v. San Diego, 450 U.S. 621 (1981), but the Court dismissed the appeal in that case for lack of a final judgment: the Court believed that the California court had yet to determine whether there had been a taking. Id. at 633.
    Dissenting in *San Diego Gas & Electric*, Justice Brennan argued persuasively that the California court did not discuss whether there had been a taking because it believed an exercise of the police power could *never* be a compensable taking. 450 U.S. at 639–40. On the merits, Justice Brennan concluded quite reasonably that, although nothing in the Compensation Clause empowers a court to compel the government to exercise its power of eminent domain where

the regulatory "taking" is temporary and reversible and the government would rather end the "taking" than purchase the property, the government must compensate the property owner for whatever taking occurred between the enactment and the repeal of the offending regulation. 450 U.S. at 654, 658.

24. 260 U.S. 393 (1922).

25. Lochner v. New York, 198 U.S. 45 (1905).

26. See, e.g., Board of Regents v. Roth, 408 U.S. 564, 577 (1972) ("Property interests, of course, are not created by the Constitution. Rather they are created and their dimensions are defined by existing rules or understandings that stem from an independent source such as state law—rules or understandings that secure certain benefits and that support claims of entitlement to those benefits.").

27. See B. Ackerman, *Private Property and the Constitution* 88–167 (1977).

28. United States v. Butler, 297 U.S. 1, 62 (1936).

29. Cf. Note, "Justice Rehnquist's Theory of Property," 93 *Yale L.J.* 541 (1984) (arguing that the Court, and particularly Justice Rehnquist, accords "new" property rights only due process protection and treats them as largely state-defined, but is much less tolerant of positivist modifications of "old" property interests, to which the Court applies both the Due Process Clause and the Compensation Clause).

30. 449 U.S. 155 (1980).

31. Id. at 157.

32. Id. at 156 n.1.

33. Id. at 162 (citations omitted).

34. The Court suggested that the result might have been different had the expropriated interest been the only service charge levied by the state, but also pointed out that such a "charge" would give the state a dangerous incentive to retain the interpleader fund for as long as possible. Id. at 162–65. Despite this dictum, it seems doubtful that the mere act of calling the confiscation of interest a service charge would allow a state to oust the traditional notions of property to which the Court in *Webb's* clung so tightly.

35. Id. at 164.

36. Id. at 163.

37. Id. at 161. The Court quoted Board of Regents v. Roth, 408 U.S. 564, 577 (1972), quoted supra note 26.

38. Cf. Arnett v. Kennedy, 416 U.S. 134, 153–54 (1974) (plurality opinion) (where state creates the right, recipient "must take the bitter with the sweet").

39. 449 U.S. at 164.

40. See United States v. Causby, 328 U.S. 256 (1946), cited in *Webb's*, 449 U.S. at 165.

41. 407 U.S. 67 (1972).

42. Id. at 90–91.

43. Id. at 80–84; see also North Georgia Finishing, Inc. v. Di-Chem, Inc., 419 U.S. 601 (1975) (requiring probable cause hearing before garnishment of corporate bank account, despite contract between creditor and garnishee corporation

that, construed in light of preexisting state law, conditioned corporation's property interest on relinquishment of right to such hearing).

44. In dissent, Justice White questioned even the short-run value of the Court's decision to consumers. See *Fuentes*, 407 U.S. at 97.

45. 438 U.S. 59 (1978).

46. See chapter 8.

47. See 438 U.S. at 103 (Stevens, J., concurring).

48. 438 U.S. at 85–86.

49. Id. at 88 n.33.

50. Id. at 64.

51. Id. at 86–87 n.39, 90–91, 93.

52. Id. at 88 n.32. See also Railroad Retirement Bd. v. Fritz, 449 U.S. 166 (1980), discussed infra.

53. 453 U.S. 654 (1981).

54. See Brownstein, "The Takings Clause and the Iranian Claims Settlement," 29 *U.C.L.A.L.Rev.* 984, 991–92 (1982).

55. 453 U.S. at 674 n.6.

56. See Brownstein, supra note 54, at 1069.

57. The majority concluded that, unlike the attachment issue, the question whether the suspension of claims against Iran constituted a taking was not ripe for review, although the Court of Claims would have jurisdiction to consider a suit presenting the question. 453 U.S. at 688–89 n.14. See also chapter 4.

58. 447 U.S. 74 (1980).

59. Id. at 77–78.

60. The California Supreme Court could not rest its decision on the First Amendment to the federal Constitution, for the Supreme Court had construed the First Amendment not to demand free public access to shopping centers for expressive purposes, see Hudgens v. NLRB, 424 U.S. 507 (1976); Lloyd Corp. v. Tanner, 407 U.S. 551 (1972), and had held that state courts may not give the amendment more bite than the Supreme Court would, see Zacchini v. Scripps-Howard Broadcasting Co., 433 U.S. 562 (1977).

61. 447 U.S. at 82.

62. Id. at 83–84.

63. Id. at 84.

64. 449 U.S. 155, 161, 164 (1980), discussed supra, text accompanying note 30.

65. 444 U.S. 164 (1979).

66. Id. at 166–67.

67. Id. at 167–68.

68. Id. at 180.

69. Id. at 176.

70. Id. at 169, 175, 176, 180.

71. Id. at 179–80. See Brownstein, supra note 54, at 1064–66.

72. 458 U.S. 419 (1982).

73. Id. at 423–24.

74. Id. at 423 n.3.

75. Id. at 426–27, 441. The split on the Court crossed over traditional ideological lines: Justice Marshall wrote the majority opinion, and Justice Blackmun wrote a dissent joined by Justices Brennan and White.

76. Id. at 438–39.

77. Id. at 436.

78. Id. at 438 n.16. The majority added that the size of the physical invasion is relevant only to the amount of compensation required, not to the prior question of whether there has been a taking. Id. at 437, 438 n.16.

79. See id. at 435 n.12.

80. Although the expropriation rhetoric in *Teleprompter* seemed unusually harsh given the triviality of the actual injury suffered by the property owner, *Teleprompter* was far from being the first case in which the Supreme Court seemed to give physical invasion a nearly talismanic significance. See cases cited in L. Tribe, *American Constitutional Law* §9–3, at 460 n.2 (1978) [hereinafter cited as Tribe *ACL*].

81. 458 U.S. at 440 n.19.

82. Id.

83. An important premise underlying all three of the foregoing cases—*PruneYard*, *Kaiser Aetna*, and *Teleprompter*—is that uncompensated physical invasions by third parties acting under the authorization of government are just as unconstitutional as are takings in which the government itself is the trespasser. See, e.g., *Teleprompter*, 458 U.S. at 433 n.9 ("A permanent physical occupation authorized by state law is a taking without regard to whether the State, or instead a party authorized by the State, is the occupant."). This premise buttresses the nascent understanding of modern state action law that a private citizen who violates the rights of others pursuant to state authorization may be as much a state actor as is a policeman or an attorney general. See, e.g., Lugar v. Edmondson Oil, 457 U.S. 922, 926–35, 941–42 (1982) (private party who participates with state officials in seizure of disputed property is "state actor" for purposes of Fourteenth Amendment and may act "under color of state law" for purposes of 42 U.S.C. §1983), discussed in chapter 16.

84. See Tribe, *ACL* §9–6; B. Wright, *The Contract Clause and the Constitution* (1938).

85. The Supreme Court has held consistently that "[c]ontract rights are a form of property and as such may be taken for a public purpose provided that just compensation is paid." *United States Trust Co.*, 431 U.S. at 19 n.16; see also El Paso v. Simmons, 379 U. S. 497, 533–34 (1965) (Black, J., dissenting); United States v. General Motors Corp., 323 U.S. 373, 377–78 (1945); Lynch v. United States, 292 U.S. 571, 579 (1934); Contributors to the Pennsylvania Hospital v. City of Philadelphia, 245 U.S. 20, 23–24 (1917).

86. 290 U.S. 398 (1934).

87. 290 U.S. at 435.

88. 25 U.S. (12 Wheat.) 213 (1827).

89. See, e.g., Wood v. Lovett, 313 U.S. 362 (1941) (invalidating 1937 repeal of 1935 state statute protecting buyers at state tax sales from state attempts to rescind for irregularities); Worthen Co. v. Kavanaugh, 295 U.S. 56 (1935) (striking down retroactive change in procedure for enforcing payment of benefit assessments pledged as security for municipal bonds).

90. 260 U.S. 393 (1922).

91. See, e.g., East New York Savings Bank v. Hahn, 326 U.S. 230, 232 (1945); Veix v. Sixth Ward Bldg. & Loan Ass'n., 310 U.S. 32, 38 (1940).

92. Justice Black, dissenting alone from a decision sustaining a state-imposed time limit on reinstatement rights of purchasers who had bought land from the state and then defaulted on interest payments, lamented that the Court had completely "balanced away" the limitation on state action imposed by the contract clause. El Paso v. Simmons, 379 U.S. 497, 517 (1965) (Black J., dissenting).

93. 431 U.S. 1 (1977).

94. Justice Blackmun wrote for the Court. Justice Brennan, joined by Justices Marshall and White, dissented. Justices Stewart and Powell took no part in the case.

95. 431 U.S. at 32.

96. Id. at 18.

97. Id. at 26.

98. 438 U.S. 234 (1978).

99. Id. at 237.

100. Id. at 238 (emphasis added).

101. Again, Justice Brennan dissented, joined by Justices Marshall and White. Justice Blackmun took no part in the case.

102. 438 U.S. at 250.

103. Id. at 247.

104. Id. at 255, 257–58 (Brennan, J., dissenting).

105. See, e.g., id. at 242, 247 (noting that statute had not been shown to be "necessary to meet an important social problem").

106. Id. at 249–50.

107. See id. at 261 n.8 (Brennan, J., dissenting).

108. See id. at 248; id. at 254 (Brennan, J., dissenting).

109. 428 U.S. 1 (1976).

110. Id. at 15–16.

111. Id. at 18–19.

112. 438 U.S. at 261 (Brennan, J., dissenting). Justice Brennan charged that "[t]he only explanation for the Court's decision is that it subjectively values the interests of employers in pension plans more highly than it does the legitimate expectation interests of employees." Id. n.8.

113. 103 S. Ct. 697 (1983).

114. Justice Blackmun wrote a majority opinion joined by five other justices. Justice Powell, joined by Chief Justice Burger and Justice Rehnquist, concurred separately on the ground that the existence *vel non* of a legitimate state purpose for the regulation was irrelevant, because no contract had in fact been impaired.

115. 103 S. Ct. at 702.

116. Id. at 703.

117. Id. at 705 n.13.

118. Id. at 708 n.25.

119. Id. at 705 n.14.

120. Id. at 706 & n.18.

121. Id. at 707–08.

122. 103 S. Ct. 2296 (1983).

123. Id. at 2306–07.

124. 449 U.S. 166 (1980).

125. Id. at 172–73.

126. Justices Brennan and Marshall dissented.

127. 449 U.S. at 186–87 (Brennan J., dissenting).

128. See id. at 176–77.

129. Id. at 180 (Stevens, J., concurring in the judgment).

130. Id. at 182 (Stevens, J., concurring in the judgment). One may be forgiven for wondering what the difference is between this rationale and the merely "plausible" explanations offered by the majority and derided by Justice Stevens.

131. Id. at 189 (Brennan J., dissenting).

132. This notion of a due process right to adequate participation in the enactment of legislation affecting one's economic interests can also be found in Justice Brennan's opinion for the Court in Florida Lime & Avocado Growers, Inc. v. Paul, 373 U.S. 132 (1963). The Court there upheld a California avocado regulation as not preempted by federal law, in part because of concern that the federal regulations had been drafted not "by impartial experts in Washington or even in Florida, but rather by the South Florida Avocado Administrative Committee" and indeed constituted "a 'self-help' program" in the long-standing competition between California and Florida growers". 373 U.S. at 150–51 & n.17.

133. Energy Reserves Group v. Kansas Power & Light Co., 103 S. Ct. 697, 708 n.25 (1983).

134. Id. at 705 n.13; see Allied Structural Steel v. Spannaus, 438 U.S. 234, 247–48 & n.20. (1978).

135. Railroad Retirement Board v. Fritz, 449 U.S. 166, 179 & n.12 (1980).

136. 431 U.S. 1, 61–62 (1977) (Brennan, J., dissenting, joined by Marshall and White, JJ.).

137. Id. at 62 n.18.

138. The Court's decision in Energy Reserves Group v. Kansas Power & Light Co., 103 S. Ct. 697 (1983), suggests that it will sometimes also defer to political processes when legislation has an explicit proconsumer purpose, even if the direct effect of the statute is to benefit one powerful economic interest (such as utility companies) at the expense of another (such as gas producers). See discussion supra, text accompanying notes 113–21.

139. 449 U.S. at 174; cf. Flemming v. Nestor, 363 U.S. 603, 608–11 (1960) (holding that social security benefits, unlike annuities, are not "accrued property rights"). Because receipt of such tranfer payments is not directly related to an individual's withholding contributions, their termination does not necessarily disrupt investment-backed expectations. Neither, however, does the elimination of a government-created property interest, such as a copyright or a patent, that provides the holder with exclusive rights enforceable against third parties—and yet copyrights and patents may not be legislatively revoked without just compensation. Reliance on such rights, unlike reliance on welfare or social security benefits, is apparently not regarded as a mere wager on the government's continued sufferance.

140. Logan v. Zimmerman Brush Co., 455 U.S. 422, 433 (1982) (dictum).

141. After all, in addition to prohibiting the state from "taking private property . . . without just compensation"—whatever all that is read to mean—and from "impairing the Obligation of Contracts"—however that is understood—the Constitution also guarantees all citizens "equal protection of the laws". Even the ban on titles of nobility, found in Article I, Section 9, Clause 8, may be deemed relevant. Cf. Zobel v. Williams, 457 U.S. 55, 69 n.3 (1982) (Brennan, J., concurring) (suggesting that this ban reflects an "American aversion to aristocracy").

13. Speech as Power

1. L. Tribe, *American Constitutional Law* §12–1 at 576 (1978) [hereinafter cited as Tribe, *ACL*].

2. See generally, *The Politics of Law* (D. Kairys ed. 1982).

3. See Karst, "Equality as a Central Principle in the First Amendment," 43 *U. Chi. L. Rev.* 20, 21 (1975).

4. See, e.g., T. Emerson, *The System of Freedom of Expression* 5 (1970) ("Those who warn us not to rely too much on legal forms are entirely correct that excessive emphasis can easily be placed upon the role of law. Yet in the United States today we have come to depend upon legal institutions and legal doctrines as a major technique for maintaining our system of free expression."). My treatise did little to dispel this exaggeration.

5. See, e.g., G. Gunther & N. Dowling, *Cases and Materials on Constitutional Law* 1050 (1970); Rabban, "The First Amendment in Its Forgotten Years," 90 *Yale L.J.* 514, 516 19 (1981).

6. See generally Rabban, supra note 5.

7. 1 Stat. 596 (1798).

8. See generally L. Levy, *Legacy of Suppression: Freedom of Speech and Press in Early American History* 245–46 (1960).

9. See Berns, "Freedom of the Press and the Alien and Sedition Laws: A Reappraisal," 1970 S. Ct. Rev. 109; Koch & Ammon, "The Virginia and Kentucky Resolutions: An Episode in Jefferson's and Madison's Defense of Civil Liberties,"5 Wm. & Mary Q. (3d ser.) 145, 174–76 (1948). The Supreme Court did have occasion to rule on the question of seditious libel when, in United States v. Hudson and Goodwin, 11 U.S. (7 Cranch) 32 (1812), it overturned the convictions of newspaper editors who had been charged with the offense as a common-law crime. The Court did not discuss any First Amendment problem in the convictions but held that there can be no federal common law of crimes—i.e., that only Congress has the power to establish federal criminal offenses.

10. See Rabban, supra note 5, at 522–33.

11. United States v. Press Publishing Co., 219 U.S. 1 (1911).

12. Gompers v. Bucks Stove & Range Co., 221 U.S. 418 (1911).

13. Davis v. Massachusetts, 167 U.S. 43 (1897).

14. Mutual Film Corp. v. Industrial Commission of Ohio, 236 U.S. 230 (1915). The challenge was based on the free speech provision of the Ohio Constitution.

15. In American School of Magnetic Healing v. McAnnulty, 187 U.S. 94 (1902), the Court ruled that the postmaster general could not lawfully refuse to deliver payments to a business dealing in Christian Science healing aids. Many other First Amendment cases of the period are collected and analyzed in Rabban, supra note 5.

16. Popular criticism was directed primarily at the Court's practice of striking down social and economic legislation in the name of protecting property and liberty of contract, see Tribe, ACL §8–6, at 446–49, but criticism of the Court reached other areas as well.

17. David Kairys gives primary credit to the persistence and organization of the left and labor movements. Kairys, "Freedom of Speech" in The Politics of Law 140, 161-62 (D. Kairys ed. 1982). To the extent that Kairys is claiming that these movements mechanically caused the shift, however, his argument is undercut by a number of factors. First, the earliest breakthroughs came between 1925 and 1931, a period when the left and labor movements were at low ebb. Gitlow v. New York, 268 U.S. 652 (1925), extended the First Amendment to the states via the Fourteenth Amendment Due Process Clause; Stromberg v. California, 283 U.S. 359 (1931), and Near v. Minnesota, 283 U.S. 697 (1931), both upheld free speech claims. On the condition of the left and labor movements during that period, see I. Bernstein, The Lean Years (1966). Second, there was a strong minority trend within the legal profession which supported increased First Amendment protection prior to World War I. Rabban, supra note 5, at 559-79. Finally, a number of the most important cases were brought by Jehovah's Witnesses. See, e.g., Lovell v. Griffin, 303 U.S. 444 (1938), and Cantwell v. Connecticut, 310 U.S. 296 (1940). See generally Levinson, "Escaping Liberalism: Easier Said Than Done," 96 Harv. L. Rev. 1466, 1477 n.38 (1983). But Kairys' more general point—that the shift resulted from the changing consciousness of society and of the justices, not from "more legal research or any legal principle," see Kairys, supra, at 161—surely seems a valid one.

18. See De Jonge v. Oregon, 299 U.S. 353 (1937), and Herndon v. Lowry, 301 U.S. 242 (1937) (Communists); Hague v. C.I.O. , 307 U.S. 496 (1939), and Thornhill v. Alabama, 310 U.S. 88 (1940) (labor activists); cases cited supra note 17 (Jehovah's Witnesses).

19. For a relatively dispassionate account, see R. McCloskey, *The Modern Supreme Court* 64–83 (1972).

20. Justice Black commented: "It has been only a few years since there was a practically unanimous feeling throughout the country and in our courts that this could not be done in our free land." Barenblatt v. United States, 360 U.S. 109, 147 (1959) (Black, J., dissenting).

21. Labor Management Relations Act, 29 U.S.C. §§141 et seq. (1976) (establishing unfair labor union practices and requiring anti-Communist affidavits of union officials).

22. 310 U.S. 88. Teamsters v. Vogt, Inc., 354 U.S. 284 (1957), capped the line of cases withdrawing protection. For a useful discussion of the cases, see Note, "Political Boycott Activity and the First Amendment," 91 *Harv. L. Rev.* 631, 659, 663–71 (1978).

23. H. Kalven, *The Negro and the First Amendment* 66 (1965).

24. See Tribe, *ACL* §12–23.

25. NAACP v. Alabama, 357 U.S. 449 (1958).

26. Louisiana v. NAACP, 366 U.S. 293 (1961).

27. Gibson v. Florida Legislative Investigation Committee, 372 U.S. 539 (1963).

28. Cox v. Louisiana, 379 U.S. 536 (1965) (Cox I).

29. See H. Kalven, supra note 23, at 123–72.

30. See H. Kalven, supra note 23. For example, compare Louisiana v. NAACP, 366 U.S. 293 (1961), with American Communications Ass'n v. Douds, 339 U.S. 382 (1950) (anti-Communist affidavit requirement imposed on unions as a condition of utilizing the services of the National Labor Relations Board does not violate First Amendment).

31. The key case, of course, was Brown v. Board of Education, 347 U.S. 483 (1954) (Brown I). See Tribe, *ACL* § 16–15, at 1019–22.

32. See Cover, "The Origins of Judicial Activism in the Protection of Minorities," 91 *Yale L.J.* 1287, 1311–12 (1982) (arguing that the Court made a "dramatic shift in emphasis from protecting the 'minority' blacks, to protecting the political activity and movements of that 'minority'").

33. Citizens Against Rent Control v. City of Berkeley, 454 U.S. 290 (1981); First National Bank of Boston v. Bellotti, 435 U.S. 765 (1978); Buckley v. Valeo, 424 U.S. 1 (1976).

34. First National Bank of Boston v. Bellotti, 435 U.S. 765 (1978).

35. Virginia Pharmacy Board v. Virginia Consumer Council, 425 U.S. 748 (1976).

36. NAACP v. Claiborne Hardware, 102 S. Ct. 3409 (1982).

37. International Longshoremen's Ass'n v. Allied International, 456 U.S. 212 (1982); NLRB v. Retail Store Employees Union (Safeco), 447 U.S. 607 (1980).

38. Bush v. Lucas, 103 S. Ct. 2404 (1983); Connick v. Myers, 103 S. Ct. 1684 (1983); Perry Education Ass'n v. Perry Local Educators' Ass'n, 103 S. Ct. 948 (1983); Minnesota State Bd. for Community Colleges v. Knight, 104 S. Ct. 1058 (1984). But see Givhan v. Western Line Consolidated School District, 439 U.S. 410 (1979) (holding that dismissal of public school teacher because of her allegations that school's policies were racially discriminatory violates First Amendment).

39. Hudgens v. NLRB, 424 U.S. 507 (1976).

40. See generally Blum, Greaney, Hanifin & Sousa, "Cases That Shock the Conscience: Reflections on Criticism of the Burger Court," 15 *Harv. C.R.–C.L. L. Rev.* 713 (1980) (urging more candid treatment of political values and choices in legal analysis).

41. See, e.g., Reynolds v. Sims, 377 U.S. 533 (1964); Baker v. Carr, 369 U.S. 186 (1962).

42. See, e.g., Harper v. Virginia Bd. of Elections, 383 U.S. 663 (1966).

43. See, e.g., Gomillion v. Lightfoot, 364 U.S. 339 (1960).

44. According to much social contract theory, which is often said to shape the political values embodied in our Constitution, government must be founded on the informed consent of the governed. But, it is said, the rational individual will consent to government only if guaranteed an equal voice in its deliberations. See J. Locke, *Two Treatises of Government*. For more modern expositions of this view, see J. Rawls, *A Theory of Justice* 221–34 (1971); J. Ely, *Democracy and Distrust* 73–104 (1980).

45. It should be noted that constitutional protection for voting rights, like judicial enforcement of the First Amendment, is a relatively recent phenomenon. As recently as the early twentieth century, "Jim Crow" codes denied the franchise to southern blacks. See C. Van Woodward, *The Strange Career of Jim Crow* (1974). And, of course, it took a separate constitutional amendment to extend the franchise to women.

46. See, e.g., Budde, "The Practical Role of Corporate PAC's in the Political Process," 22 *Ariz. L. Rev.* 555 (1980); Wertheimer, "The PAC Phenomenon in American Politics," 22 *Ariz. L. Rev.* 603 (1980); Mayton, "Politics, Money, Coercion, and the Problem with Corporate PACs," 29 *Emory L.J.* 375 (1980). For a concise review of the literature, see Wright, "Money and the Pollution of Politics: Is the First Amendment an Obstacle to Political Equality?" 82 *Colum. L. Rev.* 609, 614–25 (1982).

47. 408 U.S. 92 (1972).

48. Id. at 96. The irony of this proclamation in a case forbidding discrimination in *favor* of picketing cannot pass unnoticed. See text at notes 98–105 below.

49. See Kalven, "Upon Rereading Mr. Justice Black on the First Amendment," 14 *U.C.L.A. L. Rev.* 428, 432 (1967).

50. See, e.g., Shuttlesworth v. City of Birmingham, 394 U.S. 147 (1969) (striking down ordinance governing parade permits because it gave police officials too much discretion to determine who could demonstrate).

51. See, e.g., Minneapolis Star & Tribune Co. v. Minnesota Commissioner of Revenue, 103 S. Ct. 1365 (1983) (striking down a tax which applied only to a small number of periodical publishers); Larson v. Valente, 456 U.S. 228 (1982) (invalidating registration requirement imposed only on narrow class of religious organizations).

52. See Metromedia, Inc. v. San Diego, 453 U.S. 490, 563–64 (1981) (Burger, C.J., dissenting).

53. See infra notes 59–67 and accompanying text.

54. See Karst, supra note 3, at 21. Karst argues that equal liberty of expression is essential to the fulfillment of all First Amendment values: self-expression and individual dignity, the search for truth, and self-government. Id. at 23–26.

55. To put it another way, ownership of a car can be useful even if someone else owns two—or a hundred. But the right to cast a vote is diluted if someone else has the right to cast more than one. This point assumes that any value derived from feelings of superiority or inferiority relative to others is less important than the value of the liberty itself. See J. Rawls, supra note 44, at 143.

56. See Westen, "The Empty Idea of Equality," 95 *Harv. L. Rev.* 537 (1982) (arguing, perhaps exaggeratedly, that the concept is wholly devoid of content). But see Tribe, *ACL* §16–1, at 991 (the ideal may be given content by positing substantive ideals to guide collective choice).

57. See Tribe, *ACL* §§8–2 through 8–6.

58. The classic statement came in Coppage v. Kansas, 236 U.S. 1 (1915). At issue was the constitutionality of a Kansas law that prohibited the making of "yellow dog" contracts, individual employment contracts that conditioned employment upon the employee's refraining from joining a union. The Court struck down the law, reasoning that the freedom to contract was "as essential to the laborer as to the capitalist, to the poor as to the rich." Id. at 14.

59. The House committee report on the Federal Election Campaign Act of 1974 stated: "The unchecked rise in campaign expenditures, coupled with the absence of limitations on contributions and expenditures, has increased the dependence of candidates on special interest groups and large contributors. Under the present law the impression persists that a candidate can buy an election by simply spending large sums in a campaign." H.R. Rep. No. 1239, 93d Cong., 2d Sess. 3 (1974). Some commentators have argued that such restrictions are not only constitutionally permissible but should be constitutionally required to preserve democracy. Cf. J. Rawls, supra note 44, at 221–28 (there should be absolute equality of resources in the political sphere); Parker, "The Past of Constitutional Law—And Its Future," 42 *Ohio St. L.J.* 223, 240–46 (1981) (relative equality of wealth is essential to the popular republican vision of the constitution). See also Wright, supra note 46 (criticizing the Supreme Court's approach to regulation of political campaigns).

60. See Buckley v. Valeo, 424 U.S. 1, 48–49 (1976) (per curiam); Citizens Against Rent Control v. Berkeley, 454 U.S. 290, 295–96 (1981).

61. *Viewpoint*: Wooley v. Maynard, 430 U.S. 705 (1977) (striking down requirement that motor vehicles bear license plate embossed with state motto "Live Free or

Die"); Stromberg v. California, 283 U.S. 359, 361 (1931) (striking down statutory ban on display of "red flag . . . as a sign, symbol or emblem of opposition to organized government").

Subject matter: Carey v. Brown, 447 U.S. 455 (1980) (striking down ordinance that exempted labor picketing from general ban on picketing in residential areas); Consolidated Edison Co. v. Public Service Commission, 447 U.S. 530 (1980) (state may not prohibit public utility from inserting commentary on controversial public issues in billing envelopes) ; Metromedia, Inc. v. San Diego, 453 U.S. 490 (1981) (striking down ordinance which imposed greater restrictions on political than on commercial billboards) (plurality opinion).

Speaker identity: First National Bank of Boston v. Bellotti, 435 U.S. 765 (1978) (striking down restrictions on political spending by certain corporations but not by other speakers); Minneapolis Star & Tribune Co. v. Minnesota Commissioner of Revenue, 103 S. Ct. 1365 (1983) (invalidating tax that affected only a small number of periodical publishers); Larson v. Valente, 456 U.S. 228 (1982) (striking down registration requirement imposed on only a narrow class of religious organizations).

62. Tribe, ACL §12–5.

63. See id., §12–20, at 683.

64. *The Federalist* no. 10. (J. Madison) (New American Lib. ed. 1961).

65. See Kovacs v. Cooper, 336 U.S. 77, 102 (1949) (Black, J., dissenting): "Laws which hamper the free use of some instruments of communication thereby favor competing channels. [Such laws] can give an overpowering influence to views of owners of legally favored instruments of communication."

66. See Martin v. Struthers, 319 U.S. 141, 146 (1943): "Door to door distribution of circulars is essential to the poorly financed causes of little people."

67. 454 U.S. 290 (1981).

68. Id. at 296, quoting Buckley v. Valeo, 424 U.S. 1, 48–49 (1976). Justices Brennan, Powell, Rehnquist, and Stevens joined the Chief Justice's opinion for the majority. Justices Marshall, Blackmun, and O'Conner concurred in the judgement; Justice White was the lone dissenter. Neither the dissenting nor the concurring justices challenged the conception of equality advanced by the majority, apparently regarding the issue as settled by *Buckley* .

69. 453 U.S. 114 (1981).

70. Id. at 144 (Marshall, J. dissenting) ("By traveling door to door to hand-deliver their messages to the homes of community members, appellees employ the method of written expression most accessible to those who are not powerful, established, or well financed."). Cf. Heffron v. ISKCON, 452 U.S. 640 (1981) (upholding a state fair regulation that confined leafletting and solicitation of funds to booths). In ISKCON, the plaintiffs were members of a religious organization who sought to conduct these activities while circulating among the crowd. They argued that the restriction invidiously discriminated against their preferred method of communication and against groups which others would be reluctant to seek out. Justice White, writing for the Court, dismissed this argument in a footnote, reasoning—somewhat conclusorily—that the confinement

to booths that would have to be sought out was inherent in the rule. 452 U.S. at 649 n.12. Also cf. City Council of Los Angeles v. Taxpayers for Vincent, 104 S. Ct. 2118 (1984), in which the majority upheld the city's ban on the posting of all signs on public property. Justice Brennan, joined by Justices Marshall and Blackmun, argued in dissent that "signs posted on public property are doubtless 'essential to the poorly financed causes of little people.'" Id. at 2137, quoting Martin v. City of Struthers, 319 U.S. 141, 146 (1943).

71. Somewhat ironically, the pathbreaking opinion in Hague v. C.I.O., 307 U.S. 496 (1939), relied heavily on an allegedly timeless tradition of access to public places for communication and expression: "Wherever the title of streets and parks may rest, they have immemorially been held in trust for the use of the public and, time out of mind, have been used for purposes of assembly, communicating thoughts between citizens, and discussing public questions. Such use of the streets and public places has, from ancient times, been a part of the privileges, immunities, rights, and liberties of citizens." Id. at 515. The irony arises from the fact that, in order to proclaim this "ancient" privilege, the Court was obliged to overrule a direct precedent, Davis v. Massachusetts, 167 U.S. 43 (1897). See also Greer v. Spock, 424 U.S. 828, 838 (1976) (upholding exclusion of political speakers from military base in part because of "the historically unquestioned power of [its] commanding officer summarily to exclude civilians from the area of his command") (citation omitted).

72. 453 U.S. at 120–26.

73. Id. at 119, 127.

74. 454 U.S. at 300.

75. See generally Tribe, ACL §12–21.

76. See, e.g., Buckley v. Valeo, 424 U.S. 1, 19 (1976) ("The electorate's increasing dependence on television, radio, and other mass media for news and information has made these expensive modes of communication indispensable instruments of effective political speech.").

77. See sources supra note 46 (noting increasing use of PACs).

78. See supra notes 16–18 and accompanying text.

79. See generally H. Lynd & R. Lynd, Middletown (1929), and H. Lynd & R. Lynd, Middletown in Transition (1937).

80. See generally I. deSola Pool, Technologies of Freedom (1983).

81. See Amalgamated Food Employees Union v. Logan Valley Plaza, 391 U.S. 308, 324–25 (1968): "The large-scale movement of this country's population from the cities to the suburbs has been accompanied by the advent of the suburban shopping center, typically a cluster of individual retail units on a single large privately owned tract . . . Business enterprises located in downtown areas would be subject to on-the-spot public criticism for their practices, but businesses situated in the suburbs could largely immunize themselves from similar criticisms by creating a cordon sanitaire of parking lots around their stores."

82. See Miami Herald Publishing Co. v. Tornillo, 418 U.S. 241, 249–51 (1974).

83. Near v. Minnesota, 283 U.S. 697, 716 (1931).

84. Haig v. Agee, 453 U.S. 280 (1981).

85. See Ely, "Flag Desecration: A Case Study in the Roles of Categorization and Balancing in First Amendment Analysis," 88 *Harv. L. Rev.* 1482, 1501 (1975).

86. See Rabban, supra note 5, at 531–33.

87. 221 U.S. 418 (1911).

88. Id. at 439.

89. The opinion did show a concern with the potentially coercive impact on the public and on boycotted businesses of speech by unions because of their potentially "vast concentrations of power." Id. But it is hard to see how this concern hinged on the distinction between "verbal acts" and speech.

90. See Tribe, *ACL* §12–7, at 599; see also BeVier, "The First Amendment and Political Speech: An Inquiry into the Substance and Limits of Principle," 30 *Stan. L. Rev.* 299, 319–21 (1978) (questioning whether a principled speech-conduct distinction is possible).

91. On such uses of psuedo-scientific and "objective" forms of reasoning, see Horwitz, "The Doctrine of Objective Causation," in *The Politics of Law* 201 (D. Kairys ed. 1982).

92. See, e.g., Blum, Greaney, Hanifin & Sousa, supra note 40, at 729–31.

93. See Tribe, *ACL* §12–7. The doctrine was revived by Justice Frankfurter as a justification for removing protection from labor picketing. See Note, supra note 22, at 669–70.

94. Tribe, *ACL* §12–7, at 601.

95. See cases cited at id. n.21.

96. See, e.g., Hughes v. Superior Court, 339 U.S. 460 (1950) (upholding injunction against picketers urging consumers to boycott store until it agreed to implement affirmative action plan); Teamsters Union v. Vogt, 354 U.S. 284 (1957) (affirming injunction against peaceful picketing designed to gain union recognition); Cox v. Louisiana, 379 U.S. 559, 562 (1965) (rejecting First Amendment challenge to conviction for parading and demonstrating near courthouse grounds); Adderley v. Florida, 385 U.S. 39 (1966) (demonstration on jailhouse grounds is unprotected conduct).

97. Buckley v. Valeo, 424 U.S. 1, 39 (1976).

98. See, e.g., Teamsters v. Vogt, 354 U.S. 284, 289 (1957); NLRB v. Retail Store Employees Union (Safeco), 447 U.S. 607, 618–19 (1980) (Stevens, J., concurring); International Longshoremen's Ass'n v. Allied International, 456 U.S. 212, 226–27 (1982). See generally Pope, "The Three-Systems Ladder of First Amendment Values: Two Rungs and a (Labor) Black Hole," 11 *Hastings Constit. L.Q.* No. 2 (forthcoming 1984).

99. For the origin of the apellation of "signal" picketing, see Cox, "Strikes, Picketing, and the Constitution," 4 *Vand. L. Rev.* 574, 591–602 (1951).

100. 447 U.S. 607, 619 (1980). In International Longshoremen's Ass'n v. Allied International, 456 U.S. 212, 226 & n.26 (1982), a unanimous Court adopted this

view. The idea harks back to Gompers v. Bucks Stove & Range Co., 221 U.S. 418, 439 (1911) ("verbal acts" have "a force not inhering in the words themselves"). It also recalls Roth v. United States, 354 U.S. 476 (1957), in which Justice Brennan, writing for the Court, justified the removal of protection from obscenity by its alleged total lack of ideological content. Id. at 484–85. This line of reasoning was largely rejected in subsequent obscenity cases. In Kingsley International Pictures Corp. v. Regents, 360 U.S. 684 (1959), for example, the Court recognized that even obscenity could serve as a vehicle for the transmission of ideas. There, the Court struck down a New York statute that banned any film that "portrays acts of sexual immorality . . . or which expressly or impliedly presents such acts as desirable, acceptable or proper patterns of behavior." Id. at 685. The analogy to labor picketing is striking. Picketing, like emotionally upsetting language, may serve as a vehicle for effective advocacy. See also Chaplinsky v. New Hampshire, 315 U.S. 568, 573 (1942), where the Court held that an implied legislative judgment that certain epithets would almost certainly provoke violence was sufficient to justify their prohibiton. This deferential approach to the regulation of "fighting words" was later cut back in such cases as Eaton v. City of Tulsa, 415 U.S. 697 (1974). There, the Court reversed a conviction for contempt based on a witness's use of the words "chicken shit," because there was no evidence that use of the words had posed "an imminent . . . threat to the administration of justice." Id. at 698. See Tribe, ACL §12–10, at 617–18. Note that the signal doctrine goes further even than *Chaplinsky*, effectively removing protection from speech not because of its likelihood of provoking violence or unlawful activity, but because of its lack of affirmative value in the eyes of the court.

101. In *Safeco*, for example, a union picketed a retail store that sold products of the employer with which the union had a dispute. There was no allegation that the picket line coerced would-be shoppers; the only coercion was directed against the store and resulted from the communicative impact of the picket line on consumers. *Safeco*, 447 U.S. at 616 (plurality opinion).

102. This argument was hinted at in the *Gompers* case. See 221 U.S. at 439 and discussion supra notes 86-88 and accompanying text. It was articulated by Felix Frankfurter at a time when the Court had not yet adopted the "signal" appellation formulated by Professor Cox in his article, supra note 99. See Hughes v. Superior Court, 339 U.S. 460, 465 (1950) ("The loyalties and responses evoked and exacted by picket lines are unlike those flowing from appeals by printed word") ; see also T. Emerson, supra note 4, at 444–49.

103. See generally Note, "Labor Picketing and Commercial Speech: Free Enterprise Values in the Doctrine of Free Speech," 91 *Yale L.J.* 938 (1982); Note, "Peaceful Labor Picketing and the First Amendment," 82 *Colum. L. Rev.* 1469 (1982).

104. See Rabban, supra note 5, at 543–49.

105. See Z. Chafee, *Free Speech in the United States* 24 (1941).

106. 458 U.S. 886 (1982). Justice Marshall disqualified himself because of his previous work with the NAACP. Justice Rehnquist concurred in the judgment, without opinion.

107. The complete list of demands is reprinted in the opinion of the Mississippi Supreme Court, NAACP v. Claiborne Hardware, 393 So. 2d 1290, 1295–96 (1981).

108. 458 U.S. at 904–06, 909–10.

109. Id. at 911.

110. Id. at 915–25.

111. Id. at 913–14. See Pope, supra note 98.

112. See International Longshoremen's Ass'n v. Allied International, 456 U.S. 212, 225–26 (1982) ; Connick v. Myers, 103 S. Ct. 1684, 1698-99 (1983) (Brennan, J., joined by Marshall, Blackmun, and Stevens, JJ., dissenting).

113. 456 U.S. 212 (1982).

114. Id. at 226–27. The reasoning consisted of references to the character of labor picketing as "speech plus" and a statement of deference to Congress in matters involving labor.

115. Also see Pope, supra note 98. In this highly illuminating article , Pope argues that the distinctions among political, commercial, and labor speech are highly determinate. The distinctions can be summed up in four rules: "(1) Political speech, defined as speech directed at influencing governmental institutions through formal democratic channels, is entitled to the highest level of protection. (2) Commercial speech, defined as speech, other than political speech, which is directed at influencing market institutions (i.e., the buying and selling of commodities other than labor power) is entitled to an intermediate level of protection. (3) Labor speech, defined as speech other than political speech which is uttered by employers or employees, and directed at influencing employers or employees, is virtually unprotected . . . (4) Speech raising grievances concerning racial treatment is entitled to the highest level of protection regardless of institutional target." Underlying the first three rules are supposedly "neutral process" values. The fourth rule may be viewed either as the antidote to a cross-system malfunction, or as a new and more integrated conception of political and economic life as yet applied only in the civil rights sphere.

116. 458 U.S. at 889 n.3.

117. Id. at 918.

118. Id. at 933–34. See generally Harper, "The Consumer's Emerging Right to Boycott: NAACP v. Claiborne Hardware and Its Implications for American Labor Law," 93 Yale L.J. 409, 422 (1984) (arguing that Claiborne should be thought of as establishing consumers' right to boycott as a "constitutionally protected political act.").

119. See generally Pope, supra note 98.

120. Abood v. Detroit Bd. of Education, 431 U.S. 209 (1977).

121. See Pope, supra note 98 at n.13, discussing Brudney, "Business Corporations and Stockholders' Rights Under the First Amendment," 91 Yale L.J. 235 (1981).

122. See Pope, supra note 98, citing Wright, supra note 46, at 614 n.35.

123. See Weiler, "Promises to Keep: Securing Workers' Rights to Self-Organization Under the NLRA," 96 *Harv. L. Rev.* 1769, 1771 (1983). Although the *ILA* Court expressly deferred to Congress' "careful balancing of interests" on matters concerning labor, the Court has shown no signs of heightened solicitude for the approximately seventy million nonunionized, nonpublic employees who lack congressional protection under the NLRA or civil service regulations. See Note, "Protecting Employees at Will Against Wrongful Discharge: The Public Policy Exception," 96 *Harv. L. Rev.* 1931, 1934 (1983).

124. See Note, "Subjects of Bargaining Under the NLRA and the Limits of Liberal Political Imagination," 97 *Harv. L. Rev.* 475 (1983).

125. See, e.g., Connick v. Myers, 103 S. Ct. 1684 (1983), discussed infra notes 161–70 and accompanying text.

126. United States Postal Service v. Council of Greenburgh Civic Ass'ns, 453 U.S. 114 (1981), discussed infra notes 145–48 and accompanying text.

127. The use of this term is not meant to endorse the idea that government benefits are equivalent to charity. It does, however, accurately sum up one strand of the Court's thinking on the topic. See, e.g., Wyman v. James, 400 U.S. 309, 319 (1971) (holding that conditioning receipt of welfare benefits on sacrifice of Fourth Amendment rights is justified in part because " [o]ne who dispenses purely private charity naturally has an interest in and expects to know how his charitable funds are utilized and put to work. The public, when it is the provider, rightly expects the same.").

128. See also the "market participant" line of cases discussed in chapter 10.

129. See Tribe, *ACL* §10–8, at 509–10.

130. Adler v. Board of Education, 342 U.S. 485, 492 (1952) (upholding restrictions on political organizations to which public school teachers could belong).

131. See e.g., Wyman v. James, 400 U.S. 309 (1971) (government may condition receipt of welfare benefits on recipient's sacrifice of Fourth Amendment right to be free from warrantless search).

132. Davis v. Massachusetts, 167 U.S. 43, 47 (1897) ("For the legislature absolutely or conditionally to forbid public speaking in a highway or public park is no more an infringement of the rights of a member of the public than for the owner of a private house to forbid it in his house.").

133. *Statistical Abstract of the United States—1982–83* 303 (U.S. Dept. of Commerce, Bureau of the Census, 1982).

134. See Tribe, *ACL* §10–8, at 510.

135. 391 U.S. 563 (1968).

136. See id. at 572–73 (holding that a teacher's public criticism of the performance of the school board is an impermissible ground for discharge). See also Elrod v. Burns, 427 U.S. 347 (1976) (holding that nonpolicymaking government employees may not be discharged solely on the basis of their political affiliations).

137. See Tribe, *ACL* §12–21. It is worth noting, however, that the ban on content discrimination in the last category of property did not preclude differential treatment of speech according to subject matter, as opposed to viewpoint. See

id. at 692; see, e.g., Greer v. Spock, 424 U.S. 828 (1976) (upholding ban on political but not other speakers appearing on military base); Lehman v. Shaker Heights, 418 U.S. 298 (1974) (plurality opinion) (upholding ban on political but not commercial advertising on city buses).

138. See supra notes 125–27.

139. United States Postal Service v. Council of Greenburgh Civic Ass'ns, 453 U.S. 114 (1981) (government as property owner); Perry Education Ass'n v. Perry Local Educators' Ass'n, 103 S. Ct. 948 (1983) (government as property owner and employer). Cf. Heffron v. ISKCON, 452 U.S. 640 (1981) (government as property owner).

140. Connick v. Myers, 103 S. Ct. 1684 (1983) (government as employer); Perry Education Ass'n v. Perry Local Educators' Ass'n, 103 S. Ct. 948 (1983); Regan v. Taxation with Representation, 103 S. Ct. 1997 (1983) (government as philanthropist). But see Widmar v. Vincent, 454 U.S. 263 (1981) (state university may not discriminate against religious speech by student groups seeking to use school facilities as forum); Thomas v. Review Board, 425 U.S. 707 (1981) (government may not condition receipt of unemployment benefits upon recipient's willingness to violate his religious beliefs in order to retain employment).

141. For a report of parallel developments in the procedural due process area, see Smolla, "The Reemergence of the Right-Privilege Distinction in Constitutional Law: The Price of Protesting Too Much," 35 *Stan. L. Rev.* 69 (1982).

142. 442 U.S. 289 (1979).

143. As found by the district court. United Farm Workers v. Babbitt, 449 F. Supp. 449, 460 (D. Ariz. 1978), *rev'd*, 442 U.S. 289 (1979).

144. 442 U.S. at 313. *Babbitt* falls somewhere between the classic right-privilege doctrine and the conceptually related principle that legislative reforms may proceed "one step at a time." This doctrine, generally applied in the field of equal protection, operates not on the private side of government power, but on legislation and law enforcement. It holds that, where government is not obligated to regulate at all, its entrance into the field does not immediately bring down the full force of constitutional scrutiny. For the classic statement, see Williamson v. Lee Optical Co., 348 U.S. 483, 489 (1955) ("the reform may take one step at a time, addressing itself to the phase of the problem which seems most acute to the legislative mind.").

145. 453 U.S. 114, 131 n.7 (1981).

146. Id. at 138 (Brennan, J., concurring in judgment).

147. Id. at 135 (quoting Consolidated Edison Co. v. Public Service Comm'n, 447 U.S. 530, 535 (1980)). In a dissenting opinion, Justice Marshall agreed that the mails were a public forum but argued that the standard articulated by Justice Brennan had not been met. In particular, Justice Marshall underscored the district court's finding that "ample alternative channels" were *not* available and that the statute thus constituted a serious burden on appellees' ability to communicate with their constituents. Id. at 145 (Marshall, J., dissenting).

148. See also Heffron v. ISKCON, 452 U.S. 640 (1981) (upholding fairgrounds regulations which, inter alia, confined leafletting activities to booths). The opinion

in *Heffron*, at least rhetorically, applied the standard test for time, place, and manner restrictions, but upheld the restrictions as justified by a speculative possibility of disorder. Id. at 661 (Brennan, J., joined by Marshall and Stevens, JJ., dissenting in part).

149. 103 S. Ct. 948 (1983).

150. Justice White was joined by Chief Justice Burger and Justices Blackmun, O'Connor, and Rehnquist. Justice Brennan wrote a dissenting opinion in which Justices Powell, Marshall, and Stevens joined.

151. 103 S. Ct. at 955.

152. Id.

153. Id.

154. In *Greenburgh*, the Court studiously avoided citing any cases in this category. See also Widmar v. Vincent, 454 U.S. 263 (1981) (state must permit religious group to use college auditorium on same basis as other groups). But see Minnesota State Bd. for Community Colleges v. Knight, 104 S. Ct. 1058 (1984) (holding that statutorily created "meet and confer" sessions for state professional employees do not constitute a "public forum" and therefore exclusion of such employees, who were within the bargaining unit but not members of the employees' union, does not violate the First Amendment).

155. *Perry*, 103 S. Ct. at 956.

156. See supra note 61 and accompanying text.

157. *Perry*, 103 S. Ct. at 966 (Brennan, J., dissenting).

158. 429 U.S. 167, 175–76 (1976) (holding that school board may not prohibit non-union teacher from speaking at public school board meeting where representatives of the union certified as exclusive bargaining agent are permitted to speak).

159. See Tribe, *ACL* §12–21, at 692–93.

160. To say that the restriction is justified because of the state's interest in "preserv-[ing] the property under its control for the use to which it is lawfully dedicated," *Perry*, 103 S. Ct. at 958 (quoting *Greenburgh*, 453 U.S. at 130) is merely to restate the problem, since the determination of whether property is a limited forum hinges precisely on the question of what is the lawful purpose.

161. 103 S. Ct. 1684 (1983).

162. Id. at 1694.

163. Id. at 1687.

164. Id. at 1689, 1694. Although acknowledging that the question regarding political pressure concerned a public issue, the Court found that the survey, viewed as a whole, was "most accurately characterized as an employee grievance." Id. at 1693-94.

165. Id. at 1692. According to the majority, Connick's interest in preventing possible future disruption was sufficient to justify the discharge. Indeed, the Court hinted that the mere fact that the purpose of the questionnaire was to undermine management's authority may have been sufficient, regardless of the likely result. Id. at 1693.

166. Id. at 1690.

167. Id. at 1698–99 (Brennan, J., dissenting, joined by Marshall, Blackmun, and Stevens, JJ.).

168. Givhan v. Western Line Consolidated School District, 439 U.S. 410 (1979). It has been argued that a "racial exception" runs throughout labor speech cases. See Pope, supra note 98.

169. See Pickering v. Board of Education, 391 U.S. 563, 572 (1968) ("Teachers are, as a class, the members of a community most likely to have informed and definite opinions as to how funds allocated to the operation of the schools should be spent. Accordingly, it is essential that they be able to speak out freely on such questions without fear of retaliatory dismissal.").

170. See Connick, 103 S. Ct. at 1720 (Brennan, J., dissenting).

171. 103 S. Ct. 1997, 2002 (1983). The 1976 case of Buckley v. Valeo, 424 U.S. 1, 85–108, had already gone part way. There, the Court permitted Congress to condition receipt of federal funds by political candidates on their participation in primaries and upheld differential subsidies to political candidates based on their success in previous elections. However problematic those distinctions may have been, see Tribe, ACL §13–31, at 810–11, they did not single out a particular interest group for increased influence in the legislature. Outside the First Amendment area, revival of the right-privilege doctrine began some time ago. See also Harris v. McRae, 448 U.S. 297 (1980), and Maher v. Roe, 432 U.S. 464 (1977) (upholding probitions on subsidies for abortions, to which there is a constitutional right, but not for other medical procedures).

172. TWR also raised another line of attack, discussed later in this section.

173. Compare Speiser v. Randall, 357 U.S. 513, 518 (1958) ("It cannot be gainsaid that a discriminatory denial of a tax exemption for engaging in speech is a limitation on free speech."). In Regan, the Court did not discuss Speiser in the equal protection portion of its opinion.

174. Regan, 103 S. Ct. at 2002–03. The concurring justices ignored this point, finding the discrimination constitutional because not based on the content of speech. They did not address the level of scrutiny applied. Id. at 2004 (Blackmun, J., joined by Brennan and Marshall, JJ., concurring).

175. Id. at 2003–04. However, in F.C.C. v. League of Women Voters, 52 U.S.L.W. 5008 (1984), the Court rejected a right-privilege justification for a government prohibition on editorials by public broadcasting stations receiving federal funds, and concluded that the prohibition could not survive strict scrutiny. Writing for the Court, Justice Brennan distinguished the situation from that in Regan on the ground that, although the charitable organizations challenging the restriction in that case had the option of creating affiliates who could lobby but could not receive tax-deductible contributions, such a separation of activities by a public broadcasting station was not possible. Id. at 5017–18. Justice Rehnquist, joined by Chief Justice Burger and Justice White, dissented in an opinion which relied heavily on cases upholding Hatch Act restrictions on partisan political activities of federal employees, a reliance which, in Justice Bren-

nan's words, "only reveals his misunderstanding of what is at issue in *this* case."
Id. at 5018 n.27 (emphasis in original).

176. For example the idea, hinted at by Justice Rehnquist, that the veterans should
be compensated for the political influence they lose while in the service. Id. at
2003 ("Veterans have 'been obliged to drop their own affairs and take up the
burdens of the nation' "). Of course, such an objective might run up against the
Court's prohibition on government restricting the speech of some in order to
enhance that of others. Citizens Against Rent Control v. Berkeley, 454 U.S.
290, 295–96 (1981). That *Regan* involved a subsidy, not a restriction, is a tenous
ground for circumventing this prohibition in the tax context. The imposition
of a selective tax, which has been held to burden constitutional rights even if
not motivated by viewpoint discrimination, Minneapolis Star & Tribune Co.
v. Minnesota Commissioner of Revenue, 103 S. Ct. 1365 (1983), is difficult to
distinguish from the award of a tax exemption that favors a particular interest
group. Certainly the effect is the same. Unless *Minneapolis Star* represents only
the long-awaited surrender of the Court to the notion of a preferred position
for the press, its nondiscrimination principle should have been applied in *Regan*
to trigger strict scrutiny.

177. John Rawls has suggested that equality in the sphere of political participation
and liberty of expresson should be absolute—insulated from any trade-off for
economic benefits. J. Rawls, supra note 44, at 64–65. In this view, a selective
subsidy to political activities such as that upheld in *Regan* violates the principle
of equality. See also Emerson, "The Affirmative Side of the First Amendment,"
15 *Ga. L. Rev.* 795, 802–03 (1981).

178. See, e.g., *Greenburgh*, 453 U.S. at 140 (Brennan, J., dissenting) ("Having determined that a letterbox is not a public forum, the Court inexplicably terminates
its analysis."); *Perry* , 103 S. Ct. at 961 (Brennan, J., dissenting) (criticizing majority's conclusion that since an employee's interschool mailbox is not a public
forum, school board may therefore make distinctions in access on the basis of
subject matter and speaker identity if such distinctions are "reasonable in light
of the purpose which the forum at issue serves.").

179. See, e.g., *Greenburgh*, 453 U.S. at 132–33 ("Congress may, in exercising its authority to develop and operate a national postal system, properly legislate with
the generality of cases in mind, and should not be put to the test of defending in
one township after another the constitutionality of a statute under the traditional 'time, place and matter' analysis."); *Connick*, 103 S. Ct. at 1691 ("To presume that all matters which transpire within a government office are of public
concern would mean that virtually every remark—and certainly every criticism
directed at a public official—would plant the seed of a constitutional case.
While as a matter of good judgment, public officials should be receptive to con-
structive criticism offered by their employees, the First Amendment does not
require a public office to be run as a roundtable for employee complaints over
internal office affairs."). In *Perry* and *Regan*, the Court gave no reason for withdrawing scrutiny other than the right-privilege distinction.

180. *Perry* and *Regan* also introduce a strange perversion of the Court's traditional
approach, under which even a facially neutral restriction on speech must be

subjected to rigorous scrutiny if the government's motivation was to suppress particular viewpoints. *Perry* and *Regan* turn this principle on its head, exempting facially discriminatory restrictions from strict scrutiny in part because the purpose of the government was *not* to suppress particular viewpoints. Thus, in the view of the Court, good intentions can serve as an affirmative defense to an allegation of invidious ideological discrimination.

181. *Regan*, 103 S. Ct. at 2000.

182. Id. at 2004 (Blackmun, J., joined by Brennan and Marshall, JJ., concurring). That was the question posed in F.C.C. v. League of Women Voters, supra note 175, and Justice Brennan's opinion for the Court answered it as the concurring opinion in *Regan* had suggested.

183. 450 U.S. 707 (1981) (holding that government cannot condition receipt of unemployment benefits upon recipient's willingness to violate his religious beliefs to retain employment).

184. 454 U.S. 263 (1981) (holding that government cannot discriminate among speakers in nontraditional public forum opened to the public by designation).

185. See Pope, supra note 98.

186. See Elrod v. Burns, 427 U.S. 347 (1976); Branti v. Finkel, 445 U.S. 507 (1980).

187. Abrams v. United States, 250 U.S. 616, 624, 630 (1919)(Holmes, J., joined by Brandeis, J., dissenting). The notion that truth is best served by "free trade in ideas," id. at 630, has long captivated the legal imagination. When ideas, like products, freely compete in a rough-and-tumble marketplace, consumers will choose among them and only the most worthy will "sell" well enough to keep their vendors—their advocates—"in business." Just as in the economic marketplace some products, such as dangerous drugs, snake-oil remedies, and diseased animals, have no value and may be outlawed, so in the intellectual agora some speech—such as obscenity, see Roth v. United States, 354 U.S. 476 (1957); fighting words, see Chaplinsky v. New Hampshire, 315 U.S. 568 (1942); deceptive advertising, see Virginia Board of Pharmacy v. Virginia Citizens Consumer Council, 425 U.S. 748, 771–72 (1976); and perhaps group libel, see Beauharnais v. Illinois, 343 U.S. 250 (1952)—have no value and may be regulated or suppressed. Beyond that, however, regulation is regarded as interference and is generally suspect.

188. This is how Justice Douglas, who joined the court in *Valentine*, later characterized the opinion. Cammarano v. United States, 358 U.S. 498, 514 (1959) (concurring opinion).

189. 316 U.S. 52 (1942).

190. The *Valentine* leaflet—whose distribution was prohibited by an ordinance banning the distribution of commercial advertising in the streets—had urged visitors to attend for a fee the exhibition of a former Navy submarine. On the reverse of the leaflet, the petitioner had printed a protest against New York City for refusing to allow him to exhibit his submarine at a municipal pier. The Court considered this political message a mere ruse to evade the city ordinance. 316 U.S. at 55.

191. Cammarano v. United States, 358 U.S. 498, 514 (1959) (Douglas, J., concurring).
192. 421 U.S. 809 (1975).
193. Id. at 822.
194. The Court has itself construed *Bigelow* as its first case protecting "purely commercial advertising." See Bolger v. Youngs Drug Products, 103 S. Ct. 2875, 2879 & n.6 (1983).
195. 425 U.S. 748 (1976). Even here, the Court could not fully escape its reflex of attributing significant public interest to freedom of advertising. The Court characterized the citizen's interest in the "free flow of commercial information" as even keener than that in political debate, because it is "a matter of public interest" that consumer choices of pharmacy wares be "well informed." Id. at 763, 765. Thus, the lofty rhetoric of the marketplace of ideas is pertinent even if the commodity in question is a tranquilizer or a prescription laxative.
196. Id. at 771 n.24.
197. Ohralick v. Ohio State Bar Ass'n, 436 U.S. 447, 455–56 (1978).
198. *Virginia Bd. of Pharmacy* , 425 U.S. at 771 n.24. In Friedman v. Rogers, 440 U.S. 1 (1979), the Court held that trade names are unprotected by the First Amendment and that government regulation of them is therefore to be tested merely by the minimum rationality standard applicable to other economic regulations, since trade names convey no inherent meaning and contain an irreducible element of likely deception. Such deference to fanciful state legislative justifications may be inappropriate where those who would benefit by the restriction wield too much influence in the legislature. See, e.g., Ferguson v. Skrupa, 372 U.S. 726 (1963) (upholding law limiting debt-adjustment to licensed attorneys); Williamson v. Lee Optical Co., 348 U.S. 483 (1955) (upholding restrictions on opticians but not on sellers of ready-to-wear eyeglasses).
199. 447 U.S. 530 (1980).
200. 447 U.S. 557 (1980).
201. Justice Blackmun wrote a dissenting opinion, which was joined in part by Justice Rehnquist.
202. 447 U.S. at 532.
203. Id. at 532–33 (citation omitted).
204. Id. at 535.
205. Id. at 533. See also First Nat'l Bank of Boston v. Bellotti, 435 U.S. 765 (1978). The central teaching of *Bellotti*, in which the Court struck down a state ban on corporate advocacy, is that the First Amendment protects certain forms of speech regardless of who the particular speaker is. The Court did *not* decide that corporations have First Amendment rights; it reserved that question. 435 U.S. at 777 & n.1. The Court decided only that otherwise protected speech does not lose its consitutional shield simply because its source is a corporation. See also *Con. Ed.*, 447 U.S. at 533–34.

The Massachusetts statute invalidated in *Bellotti* was a bold attempt to silence corporate opposition to a proposed constitutional amendment authorizing the state legislature to impose a graduated individual income tax. The law forbade certain categories of corporations to expend funds to communicate their views about any referendum subject that did not materially affect the corporate business. See M.G.L. ch. 55 §8. To be sure that the courts would not miss its point, the legislature further specified that a ballot question concerning the taxation of individuals shall not be deemed materially to affect the business of any corporation. Id. Thus, the law identified a particular issue and silenced a particular class of speakers with regard to it. Little could be more problematic than government "dictating the subjects about which persons may speak and the speakers who may address a public issue." 435 U.S. at 785. The Court's approach to the law's invalidation would have been more persuasive if it had stressed more clearly the peculiarly offensive nature of the law at issue.

The Court's analysis instead emphasized that the interests of the potential audience are independent of the identity of the speaker. The rights at stake were those of Massachusetts voters to information that would enable them to evaluate the merits of a referendum issue, and "[t]he inherent worth of the speech in terms of its capacity for informing the public does not depend upon the identity of its source, whether corporation, association, union, or individual." 435 U.S. at 777.

206. 447 U.S. at 537–39. But see Stone, "Restriction on Speech Because of Its Content: The Peculiar Case of Subject-Matter Restrictions," 46 *U. Chi. L. Rev.* 81 (1978) (arguing that subject-based selectivity is unlike content-based selectivity).

207. 395 U.S. 367 (1969).

208. 447 U.S. at 543.

209. See id. at 532.

210. Id. at 543.

211. But see Tribe, *ACL* §12–22.

212. See United States Postal Service v. Council of Greenburgh Civic Ass'ns, 453 U.S. 114 (1981) (discussed supra notes 145–48 and accompanying text).

213. 447 U.S. at 543 n.13.

214. 447 U.S. at 554–55 (Blackmun, J., joined in part by Rehnquist, J., dissenting).

215. 447 U.S. 557 (1980).

216. Id. at 561.

217. Id. at 566.

218. Id. at 571.

219. Id. at 569.

220. Id. at 570.

221. Id. at 591 (Rehnquist, J., dissenting).

222. Id. at 591–92.

223. See id. at 592–94 & n.5 (Rehnquist J., dissenting).

224. Id. at 570–71 & n.13.

225. Id. at 570–71.

226. See Tribe, *ACL*, ch. 8.

227. See id. at §8–4.

228. 447 U.S. 530 (1980).

229. Cf. Lathrop v. Donohue, 367 U.S. 820, 856–57 (1961) (Harlan, J., concurring in the judgment) (no First Amendment violation in use of compulsory bar dues to fund expression with which dissenting lawyer disagrees).

230. 447 U.S. at 543. But see id. at 554–55 (Blackmun, J., dissenting).

231. Id. at 570–71 n.13.

232. Id. at 592–93 (Rehnquist, J., dissenting).

233. Id. at 591–93.

234. Id. at 571–72.

235. Id. at 567.

236. The ultimate futility of trying to draw such a distinction between allocative and distributive concerns is illustrated by Miller v. Schoene, 276 U.S. 272 (1928), discussed in Tribe, *ACL* §8–5, at 445–56, which foreshadowed the collapse of the *Lochner* approach. There, the Commonwealth of Virginia faced a difficult decision: either order the destruction of certain diseased—but not ruined—red cedar trees, thus halting the spread of the fungoid contagion, or permit nearby commercial apple orchards to be devastated. Virginia ordered the cedars felled, and their owners sued, claiming that the state was favoring one private interest over another. The Court upheld the state action, even without compensation, reasoning that the public interest in protecting the apple orchards, a mainstay of the state economy, justified the redistribution from the cedar owners to the apple growers. 276 U.S. at 279–80.

237. 454 U.S. 290 (1981).

238. Id. at 295–96, quoting Buckley v. Valeo, 424 U.S. 1, 18–19 (1976).

239. See First National Bank of Boston v. Bellotti, 435 U.S. 765 (1978); Buckley v. Valeo, 424 U.S. 1 (1976); but see California Medical Ass'n v. Federal Election Commission, 453 U.S. 182 (1981).

240. See Tribe, *ACL* §13–29, at 807.

241. 454 U.S. at 296–99.

242. 453 U.S. 490 (1981).

243. Among the excepted categories were religious symbols, temporary political campaign signs, and commemorative historical plaques as well as all government signs. See id. at 494–95 & n.3.

244. Justice White wrote for a plurality consisting of himself and Justices Stewart, Marshall, and Powell. Justice Brennan, joined by Justice Blackmun, concurred in the judgment. Justice Stevens concurred in part of the plurality opinion but dissented from the judgment. Chief Justice Burger and Justice Rehnquist filed dissenting opinions.

245. See Central Hudson Gas & Electric v. Public Service Comm'n, 447 U.S. 557, 563–66 (1980).

246. 453 U.S. at 507–08 (plurality opinion) (city "may believe" that on-site billboards are somehow less distracting to drivers). See Comment, "The Supreme Court, 1980 Term," 95 *Harv. L. Rev.* 211, 213 & n.21 (1981).

247. 453 U.S. at 511–12 (plurality opinion).

248. 453 U.S. at 503 (plurality opinion).

249. A requirement first applied to commercial speech in Linmark Assocs. v. Willingboro, 431 U.S. 85, 93 (1977).

250. See Jt. Stipulation of Facts, Jurisdictional Statement app. H, para. 28 at 126a ("Many businesses and politicians . . . rely upon outdoor advertising because other forms of advertising are insufficient, inappropriate and prohibitally [sic] expensive.").

251. 453 U.S. at 520–21 (plurality opinion).

252. See 453 U.S. at 567 (Burger, C.J., dissenting).

253. See supra note 250 and accompanying text. A similar discrimination between political candidates who can persuade private property owners to allow them to post signs and their opponents who cannot was implicitly upheld in City Council of Los Angeles v. Taxpayers for Vincent, 104 S. Ct. 2118 (1984), sustaining Los Angeles' municipal ordinance prohibiting the posting of all signs on public property. Justice Stevens wrote for the majority, while Justice Brennan, joined by Justices Marshall and Blackmun, dissented, criticizing the majority for posing the right questions (whether the city's interest is substantial and whether the effect of the ordinance on speech is no greater than necessary to achieve the city's purpose), but then answering them in a cursory way that "reflects a startling insensitivity to the principles embodied in the First Amendment." Id. at 2136 (dissenting opinion).

254. This might be done in exactly the same way that pornographers tailored their wares to meet prevailing standards—e.g., Roth v. United States, 354 U.S. 476, 484 (1957) (excluding from definition of obscenity material that is not "utterly without redeeming social importance").

255. See, e.g., International Longshoremen's Ass'n v. Allied International, 456 U.S. 212 (1982) (longshoremen protesting invasion of Afghanistan by refusing to unload Soviet ship not protected); NLRB v. Retail Store Employees Union (Safeco), 447 U.S. 607 (1980) (Stevens, J., concurring) (labor picketing which constitutes "signalling" not protected).

256. For a theoretical analysis of the use of doctrinal boundaries to reconcile inconsistent cases, see Kennedy, "Toward an Historical Understanding of Legal Consciousness: The Case of Classical Legal Thought in America, 1850–1940," in 3 *Research in Law and Sociology* 3 (S. Spitzer ed. 1980).

257. See, e.g., Southeastern Promotions, Ltd. v. Conrad, 420 U.S. 546, 557 (1975); FCC v. Pacifica Foundation, 438 U.S. 726, 748 (1978); Joseph Burstyn, Inc. v. Wilson, 343 U.S. 495, 503 (1952).

258. 453 U.S. at 501.

259. "[O]nce divided, subsets of commercial speech [become] categories easily conquered." Comment, supra note 246, at 220.

260. See, e.g., Schneider v. State, 308 U.S. 147 (1939) (striking down municipal ordinance that banned distribution of handbills); *Metromedia* , 453 U.S. at 568 n.9 (Burger, C.J., dissenting) (allowing only on-site billboards favors speakers who can afford to own property); Comment, supra note 246, at 221 ("a demand that no one speak unless he does so tastefully and unobtrusively will often amount to a requirement that he speak expensively or not at all"); cf. Murdock v. Pennsylvania, 319 U.S. 105 (1943) (striking down prohibitive fees for distributing religious literature and soliciting donations). For a billboard advertiser to reach the same size audience through other media costs from four (newspaper ad) or five (30-second radio spot) to eleven (30-second TV commercial) or fifteen (full-page magazine ad) times as much. *Metromedia* Jurisdictional Statement at 18 n.*.

261. For a poignant treatment of the dilemma posed for civil libertarians by the *Skokie* case, see generally A. Neier, *Defending My Enemy* (1979). Neier was executive director of the ACLU when that organization agreed to represent the Nazis in their effort to obtain a march permit.

262. Smith v. Collin, 439 U.S. 916, 916 (1978) (Blackmun, J., dissenting from denial of certiorari).

263. Collin v. Smith, 447 F. Supp. 676 (N.D. Ill.), *aff'd* 578 F.2d 1197 (7th Cir.), *cert. denied*, 439 U.S. 916 (1978).

264. 578 F.2d at 1206, quoting Terminiello v. Chicago, 337 U.S. 1 (1949) (reversing conviction for making race-baiting statements under statute banning speech that "stirs public to anger").

265. 578 F.2d at 1206, quoting Street v. New York, 394 U.S. 576, 592 (1969) (holding that statement "We don't need no damn flag," made while burning an American flag, was not so "inherently inflammatory" as to come within the class of "fighting words").

266. The Nazis never marched in Skokie, but they did obtain a permit to rally in Chicago's Marquette Park. For about an hour on a Sunday afternoon, two dozen brown-shirted members of the neo-Nazi group waved their swastikas and advocated "free speech for the white man." More than four hundred police wearing riot gear stood in phalanxes around the barricaded Nazis to protect them from several thousand on-lookers. There were frequent outbursts of scuffling, and over seventy arrests were made. A. Neier, supra note 261, at 169–70.

267. Lathrop v. Donohue, 367 U.S. 820, 849 (1961) (Harlan, J., concurring in the judgment).

268. Or, perhaps, the defense of pornography which degrades and objectifies women. See, e.g., the antipornography ordinance, drafted by Professors Catharine MacKinnon and Andrea Dworkin, which was passed by the Minneapolis City Council but vetoed by the mayor. See *New York Times*, Dec. 31, 1983, at A25; Jan. 6, 1984, at All.

269. See First National Bank of Boston v. Bellotti, 435 U.S. 765 (1978).

270. See, e.g., International Longshoremen's Ass'n v. Allied International, 456 U.S. 212 (1982); NLRB v. Retail Store Employees Union (Safeco), 447 U.S. 607 (1980); Connick v. Myers, 103 S. Ct. 1684 (1983).

271. See, e.g., Buckley v. Valeo, 424 U.S. 1 (1976); Citizens Against Rent Control v. Berkeley, 454 U.S. 290 (1981).

272. See e.g., City Council of Los Angeles v. Taxpayers for Vincent, 104 S. Ct. 2118 (1984) (city ordinance prohibiting posting of signs on public property constitutional even as applied to posting of political campaign signs); United States Postal Service v. Council of Greenburgh Civic Ass'ns, 453 U.S. 114 (1981); Hudgens v. NLRB, 424 U.S. 507 (1976) (First Amendment does not protect right to speak in privately owned shopping centers open to the public); Kovacs v. Cooper, 336 U.S. 77 (1949) (upholding ban on sound trucks).

14. Dismantling the House That Racism Built

1. The elder Justice Harlan would have made it so. Plessy v. Ferguson, 163 U.S. 537, 552, 559 (1896) (Harlan, J., dissenting).

2. See, e.g., North Carolina v. Swann, 402 U.S. 43, 45–46 (1971); L. Tribe, *American Constitutional Law* §16–21, at 1043 & nn.5, 9 (1978) [hereinafter cited as Tribe, *ACL*].

3. 438 U.S. 265 (1978).

4. Id. at 320. For Justice Powell, id. at 315, the relevant racial "reality" was evidently that of racially diverse experience inasmuch as he was willing to uphold a race-conscious admissions process to achieve a "diverse" student body; for Justices Brennan, White, Marshall, and Blackmun, the relevant racial "realities" included the rectification of societal handicaps and discriminations traceable to America's racially divided past and its persistent racism, id. at 326–27 (Brennan, White, Marshall & Blackmun, JJ., concurring in the judgment in part and dissenting in part).

5. See "The Supreme Court, 1977 Term," 92 *Harv. L. Rev.* 57, 131–48 (1978), for a full statement of the facts and the differing opinions expressed in the case.

6. 438 U.S. at 320. Four justices simply found the quota defective on statutory grounds. Id. at 412–21 (Stevens, J., concurring in the judgment in part and dissenting in part, joined by Burger, C.J., & Stewart & Rehnquist, JJ.) (university's special admissions program violates Title VI of the Civil Rights Act of 1964, 42 U.S.C. §§2000d to 2000d-4 (1976)). And each of those justices has at least once voted to approve *some* form of affirmative action. See Califano v. Webster, 430 U.S. 313 (1977) (per curiam) (upholding constitutionality of social security retirement benefits formula providing higher payments to women than to men with equal past earnings); United Jewish Organizations v. Carey, 430 U.S. 144 (1977) (Justices Rehnquist and Stevens joining plurality opinion and Justice Stewart joining concurring opinion upholding constitutionality of race-conscious reapportionment plan enhancing nonwhite minority voting strength); Kahn v. Shevin, 416 U.S. 351 (1974) (Chief Justice Burger and Justices Stewart and Rehnquist joining majority opinion upholding statute allowing property tax exemption for widows but not widowers). See also Ely, "The Supreme Court, 1977 Term—Foreword: On Discovering Fundamental Values," 92 *Harv. L. Rev.* 5, 9 n.33 (1978).

7. 438 U.S. at 287–99.

8. Id. at 358–62 (Brennan, White, Marshall, & Blackmun, JJ., concurring in the judgment in part and dissenting in part).

9. Id. at 387 n.7 (opinion of White, J.).

10. Id. at 387.

11. Id. at 294 n.34 (Powell, J. plurality opinion).

12. See Ely, supra note 6 at 12 n.47.

13. 438 U.S. at 319 n.53.

14. Id. at 318–19.

15. Id. at 318.

16. Id. at 318 n.52.

17. See also Michelman, "Formal and Associational Aims in Procedural Due Process," in *Nomos XVIII: Due Process* 126, 130–31 (J. Pennock & J. Chapman eds. 1977); Subrin & Dykstra, "Notice and the Right to Be Heard: The Significance of Old Friends," 9 *Harv. C.R.–C.L. L. Rev.* 449, 451–58 (1974).

18. 438 U.S. at 318.

19. Id. at 317.

20. Id. at 319.

21. Id. at 318.

22. Id. at 319 n.53.

23. Id. at 303.

24. Id. at 304 n.42.

25. Id. at 294 n.34.

26. Id. (emphasis in original).

27. Id. at 319 n.53 (emphasis added).

28. Id. at 378–79 (Brennan, White, Marshall, & Blackmun, JJ., concurring in the judgment in part and dissenting in part).

29. Id. at 318 (Powell, J.).

30. See id. at 378–79 & n.63 (Brennan, White, Marshall & Blackmun, JJ., concurring in the judgment in part and dissenting in part). See also id. at 406–07 (opinion of Blackmun, J.).

31. Id. at 377 (Brennan, White, Marshall & Blackmun, JJ., concurring in the judgment in part and dissenting in part) (emphasis added).

32. Id. at 378 n.63.

33. Justice Powell did not believe that Justice Brennan and the justices who joined with him had even addressed his objection. Id. at 318 n.52.

34. For a discussion of the distinction between the instrumental and intrinsic values associated with due process, see Tribe, *ACL* §10–7. See also "Developments in the Law—Zoning," 91 *Harv. L. Rev.* 1427, 1505–08 (1978) (differentiating among efficiency, representational, and dignity interests served by procedural due process) [hereinafter cited as "Developments"].

35. 435 U.S. 247 (1978).

36. Justice Marshall concurred in the result; Justice Blackmun took no part in the consideration of the case.

37. 42 U.S.C. §1983 (1976).

38. 435 U.S. at 260.

39. Id. at 263.

40. See id. See also id. at 266.

41. Id. at 266 (footnote omitted).

42. Id. at 262.

43. See Tribe, ACL §10–7; "Developments," supra note 34, at 1508 n.26.

44. Indeed, some cases have gone so far as to suggest—at least by implication—that due process protects only the right to an accurate and efficient decision. See, e.g., Codd v. Velger, 429 U.S. 624, 627–28 (1977) (no hearing required by due process where nontenured employee does not challenge the "substantial truth of the material in question"); Mathews v. Eldridge, 424 U.S. 319, 335 (1976) (testing what process is due basically by the "risk of an erroneous deprivation"); Mitchell v. W.T. Grant Co., 416 U.S. 600, 609–10 (1974) (upholding Louisiana replevin statute allowing ex parte determination of default where the required procedure minimized the risk of wrongful determination). See also Michelman, supra note 17 at 132–38. In other instances, the Court has not clearly differentiated the intrinsic and instrumental values behind due process, but has at least arguably recognized both concerns. See, e.g., Fuentes v. Shevin, 407 U.S. 67, 81 (1972); "Developments," supra note 34, at 1505 n.13. See generally Tribe, ACL §10–7.

45. See Yick Wo v. Hopkins, 118 U.S. 356, 370, 372–73 (1886), for an early recognition of a due process right to nonarbitrary government treatment. Probably the most familiar judicial statement that due process protects against more than inaccurate deprivations of liberty or property is Justice Frankfurter's concurrence in Joint Anti-Fascist Refugee Comm. v. McGrath, 341 U.S. 123, 171 (1951). Justice Frankfurter's statement stops short, however, of embracing the full notion of fair process and individualized government treatment presented in this essay. His concern for "generating the feeling, so important to a popular government, that justice has been done," id. at 172 (footnote omitted), is based at least as much on the utilitarian benefits of having people believe they are being treated fairly as it is on a concern for human dignity as such.

46. See supra note 44. But see Morrissey v. Brewer, 408 U.S. 471, 484 (1972); Goldberg v. Kelly, 397 U.S. 254, 264–65 (1970); Marshall v. Jerrico, Inc., 446 U.S. 238 (1980) (where the Court granted explicit if limited recognition to the intrinsic value of due process).

47. Fuentes v. Shevin, 407 U.S. 67, 97 (1972). See also Codd v. Velger, 429 U.S. 624, 627–28 (1977); Morrissey v. Brewer, 408 U.S. 471, 484 (1972); Mullane v. Central Hanover Bank & Trust Co., 339 U.S. 306, 313 14 (1950).

48. See Tribe, ACL §10–7, at 505; id. §10–12, at 536–38; id. §10–13.

49. As I have developed elsewhere, see id. §§17–1 to 17–3, the relation of structure to the substance of constitutional rights has appeared in a number of constitu-

tional settings and can rightfully be seen to transcend the more traditional rubrics of equal protection and due process.

50. See generally id. §16–32.

51. See 438 U.S. at 406 (opinion of Blackmun, J.).

52. See Tribe, "Structural Due Process," 10 *Harv. C.R.-C.L. L. Rev.* 269 (1975); Tribe *ACL* §§16–32, 17–1 to 17–3. See also Linde, "Due Process of Lawmaking," 55 *Neb. L. Rev.* 197 (1976).

53. Tribe, supra note 52, at 269 (emphasis in original).

54. Professor Sager has recently reiterated and elaborated this view in connection with the Supreme Court's treatment of mandatory referenda. See Sager, "Insular Majorities Unabated: *Warth v. Seldin* and *City of Eastlake v. Forest City Enterprises, Inc.,*" 91 *Harv. L. Rev.* 1373, 1411–23 (1978).

55. 426 U.S. 88 (1976) (Stevens, J.). See also Kent v. Dulles, 357 U.S. 116 (1958) (interpreting a statutory delegation of authority to State Department narrowly, in light of the constitutional doubts any broader interpretation would pose, so as to require an explicit delegation by Congress to restrict passport issuance).

56. 426 U.S. at 105–14.

57. However, Justice Stevens, author of the majority opinion in *Hampton*, did not join in this part of Justice Powell's opinion.

58. See 438 U.S. at 366 n.42 (Brennan, White, Marshall & Blackmun, JJ., concurring in the judgment in part and dissenting in part).

59. Id. at 311–15.

60. Id. at 307–10 (footnotes and citations omitted).

61. Id. at 366 n.42 (Brennan, White, Marshall & Blackmun, JJ., concurring in the judgment in part and dissenting in part).

62. McGautha v. California, 402 U.S. 183, 248–312 (1971) (Brennan, J., dissenting). Justice Brennan's views ultimately prevailed on this point. See Furman v. Georgia, 408 U.S. 238 (1972) (invalidating statutes providing for wholly discretionary infliction of capital punishment); Woodson v. North Carolina, 428 U.S. 280 (1976) (invalidating statutes providing for mandatory infliction of capital punishment).

63. 373 U.S. 132, 150–51 (1963).

64. 432 U.S. 1 (1977).

65. Justices Brennan, White, Marshall, and Stevens joined the opinion; the dissenters, including Justice Powell, thought the purpose a permissible one even for a state. Id. at 16–17 (Powell, J., dissenting, joined by Burger, C.J., & Stewart, J.).

66. 438 U.S. at 379 (Brennan, White, Marshall, & Blackmun, JJ., concurring in the judgment in part and dissenting in part).

67. 45 C.F.R. §80.3(b)(6)(ii) (1977), *cited,* 438 U.S. at 344–45.

68. Hampton v. Mow Sun Wong, 426 U.S. at 102 (footnote omitted).

69. Id. at 103.

70. 438 U.S. at 379.

71. Id. at 400–02 (Marshall, J., dissenting).

72. 438 U.S. at 412.

73. Id. at 379–87 (separate opinion of White, J.).

74. Id. at 283–84 (opinion of Powell, J.); id. at 328 & n.8 (opinion of Brennan, White, Marshall, and Blackmun, J. J.).

75. See, e.g., Tennessee Valley Auth. v. Hill, 437 U.S. 153 (1978) (Endangered Species Act means what it says, even if tiny snail darter prevents completion of billion dollar dam project). But see cases cited in United States v. Culbert, 435 U.S. 371, 374 n.4 (1978).

76. 438 U.S. at 284–87 (opinion of Powell, J.).

77. Id. at 353 n.28 (opinion of Brennan, White, Marshall, and Blackmun, JJ.). Compare chapter 9.

78. 443 U.S. 193 (1979).

79. He was joined by Justices Stewart, White, Marshall, and Blackmun. Justice Rehnquist, joined by the Chief Justice, dissented. Justices Powell and Stevens took no part in the case.

80. 443 U.S. at 201–04.

81. Id. at 204–07. The Court took special note of the fact that Title VI, considered in *Bakke*, supra, contains no provision comparable to §703(j). Id. at 206 n.6. Title VI was an exercise of the spending power, whereas Title VII invoked the commerce power—"to regulate purely private decision-making and was not intended to incorporate and particularize the commands of the 5th and 14th Amendments." Id.

82. See id. at 226–53.

83. 393 U.S. 385 (1969), discussed in Tribe, *ACL*, §16–16 at 1024, and in chapter 16, below.

84. See, e.g., Jones v. Alfred H. Mayer Co., 392 U.S. 409 (1968) (42 U.S.C. §1982 prohibits racial discrimination in the sale of private homes); McDonald v. Santa Fe Trail Transp. Co., 427 U.S. 273 (1976); Johnson v. Railway Express Agency, 421 U.S. 454 (1975) (42 U.S.C. §1981 prohibits racial discrimination by private employers).

85. 334 U.S. 1 (1948). See chapter 16.

86. 448 U.S. 448 (1980).

87. Chief Justice Burger joined the five members of the Court who had voted to uphold affirmative action in *Bakke*: Justices Powell, Brennan, White, Marshall, and Blackmun. Justice Stewart, who had voted with the majority in *Weber*, dissented, joined by Justice Rehnquist. Justice Stevens also filed a dissenting opinion.

88. He was joined by Justices White and Powell. Justice Marshall filed an opinion concurring in the judgment, in which Justices Brennan and Blackmun joined, which treated their joint opinion in *Bakke* as dispositive of what was "not even a close [question]." 448 U.S. at 519 (Marshall, J., concurring in the judgment).

89. 448 U.S. at 475 (opinion of Burger, C.J.) See Calif. Brewers' Ass'n v. Bryant, 444 U.S. 598 (1980).

90. 448 U.S. at 482.

91. Id. at 484.

92. Id at 485.

93. Id. at 489.

94. Id. at 484. The Court had made the same observation in United Steelworkers v. Weber, 443 U.S. 193, 208-09 (1979).

95. 448 U.S. at 485-86.

96. Id. at 481-82, 487-89. The Chief Justice even appended portions of what he took to be the relevant administrative guidelines to his opinion. Id. at 492-95.

97. Id. at 487-88.

98. Id. at 472, 488.

99. See J. Choper, Y. Kamisar and L. Tribe, *Supreme Court Trends & Developments* 67-69 (1979-1980). See 448 U.S. at 492-95 app. (opinion of Burger, C.J.) for the text of the regulations.

100. 448 U.S. at 477-78.

101. Id. at 465-66.

102. Id. at 550 n. 25 (Stevens, J., dissenting).

103. Id. at 458 (opinion of Burger, C.J.).

104. See id. at 549-50 & n.25 (Stevens, J., dissenting).

105. 104 S. Ct. 2576 (1984).

106. The Court was criticized by Justice Stevens, in his opinion concurring in the judgment, for embarking on a "wholly advisory" discussion of Title VII which was not necessary to resolve the case. *Stotts*, 104 S. Ct. at 2594.

107. *Stotts*, 104 S. Ct. at 2585.

108. See Hawaii Housing Authority v. Midkiff, 104 S. Ct. 2321 (1984), discussed in chapter 12; Vulcan Pioneers v. New Jersey Department of Civil Service, 588 F.Supp. 716 (D.N.J. 1984) (requiring layoffs in a way that preserves affirmative action goals, but compensating those whose seniority is sacrificed for their loss), vacated in light of *Stotts*, 588 F.Supp. 732 (1984).

15. Reorienting the Mirror of Justice

1. 450 U.S. 455 (1981).

2. 441 U.S. 347 (1979).

3. Justice Stewart wrote for the Court, joined by Chief Justice Burger and Justices Rehnquist and Stevens. Justice Powell concurred in the judgment.

4. 441 U.S. at 355-56.

5. The Court's willingness to allow discrimination that it perceives to be based on differences between the sexes—more specifically, the divergence of women from the male model—is analyzed in C. A. MacKinnon, *Sexual Harassment of Working Women* 101-41 (1979). Segal, "Sexual Equality, the Equal Protection Clause and the ERA," *33 Buff L. Rev. 1* (1984), criticizes the Court's narrow definition of sexual inequality and the inability of this definition to recognize all but the most blatant forms of sexual discrimination.

6. 417 U.S. 484 (1974).

7. Id. at 496–97 n.20.

8. General Electric Co. v. Gilbert, 429 U.S. 125 (1976).

9. 42 U.S.C. §2000e(k) (Supp. IV). The amendment to Title VII explicitly includes pregnancy classifications within the definition of sex discrimination. *See* Note, "Sexual Equality Under the Pregnancy Discrimination Act," 83 *Col. L. Rev.* 690, 691–99 (1983).

10. The fact that the insurance packages in *Geduldig* and *Gilbert* were not shown to be worth less to *women as a group* than they were worth to *men as a group, Geduldig* at 497 n.21; *Gilbert* at 138, is not relevant to the insurance schemes' validity. As the Court has recognized, statistical tendencies do not justify burdens placed on individuals on the basis of their sex. In Frontiero v. Richardson, 411 U.S. 677 (1973), the Court held unconstitutional categorizations for armed services benefits that declared *all* spouses of male members "dependents" but declared spouses of female members "dependents" only if they were in fact dependent on their wives for over one-half of their support. No less than in *Frontiero,* the insurers in *Geduldig* and *Gilbert* sought to justify discrimination by claims of statistical accuracy and administrative convenience. It is no more true that in the insured groups *each woman* received insurance benefits greater than or equal to those of any man than it is true that *all* wives are dependent on their husbands for support; yet, on the basis of *average* package value, the Court allowed a coverage exclusion affecting only women. The fact that statistics may accurately report *average* costs for certain groups does not tell us whether the state may choose to classify according to those groups. In this sense, an exclusion of pregnancy coverage is no different from exclusion of coverage for a disease affecting only blacks, for example. That the average package value to black insureds may be equal to the average value to nonblack insureds despite the exclusion of the disease is as weak an excuse for discrimination as is the average-package argument in *Geduldig* and *Gilbert. See Arizona Governing Comm'n v. Norris,* 103 S. Ct. 3492 (1983); *Los Angeles Dept. of Water and Power v. Manhart,* 435 U.S. 702 (1978).

11. 450 U.S. 464 (1981).

12. But see infra note 16.

13. Id. at 473. But, as Professor MacKinnon notes, "Not all statutorily underage girls are even 'potentially pregnant' since many have not reached puberty; not all underage girls who have intercourse conceive (the plaintiff in *Michael M.* for example); not all (or even most) unwed mothers are underage; male sterility is not a defense; and not all underage children at risk of intercourse are girls. By contrast, as a matter of rational fit between gender, the characteristic, and its application, all 'persons' at risk of noncoverage for pregnancy disabilities are women and all who would receive benefits would be both pregnant and female." C. A. MacKinnon, "Introduction to Symposium on Sexual Harassment," 10 *Capitol U. L. Rev.* i, v–vi n.21 (1981).

14. 450 U.S. at 473–74 & n.9.

15. Id. at 495–96 (Brennan, J., who was joined by White and Marshall, JJ., dissenting); id. at 500–501 (Stevens, J., dissenting).

16. Indeed, a significant number of underage females are actually arrested for this offense in California. *See* 450 U.S. at 477 & n.5 (Stewart, J., concurring) ("approximately 14% of the juveniles arrested for participation in acts made unlawful by [this statutory rape law] between 1975 and 1979 were females.").

17. 450 U.S. at 476.

18. 433 U.S. 321 (1977).

19. *Michael M.*, 450 U.S. at 469.

20. See generally Rubenstein, "Procedural Due Process and the Limits of the Adversary System," 11 *Harv. C.R.-C.L. L. Rev.* 48 (1976).

21. 436 U.S. 149 (1978).

22. See 436 U.S. at 160, 162 n.12.

23. Chapter 16 explores an approach for nonetheless securing Supreme Court review of the constitutional validity of the state law purporting to render lawful such a unilateral seizure by private creditors.

24. M. Walzer, *Spheres of Justice* (1983).

25. Id. at 11.

26. Recognizing this inequity and the law's role in producing it need not undermine meritocracy. Personal qualities and social goods have their own spheres of operation, which are governed by different principles of distribution: welfare to the needy, health care to the infirm, honors to the deserving, political influence to the persuasive, salvation to the pious, luxuries to those inclined and able to pay for them. *Id.* at 11–12. Injustice results when the distribution principle of one sphere, such as material wealth, is allowed to invade the spheres of other social goods to determine who gets what. The end result is not just an inequitable distribution of social goods, but the subjugation of those people who do not possess that particular item by which other social goods are valued. As Walzer puts it, "Birth and blood, landed wealth, capital, education, divine grace, state power—all these have served at one time or another to enable some people to dominate others. Domination is always mediated by some set of social goods." Id. at xiii.

27. See id. at 11–12.

28. The dangerous inadequacy of a vision that sees racial equality as the "neutral" maintenance of the status quo, when the status quo is itself the culmination of years of oppression, is exemplified by Washington v. Davis, 426 U.S. 229 (1976). In that case, the Court upheld a system that screened out applicants for the District of Columbia police force on the basis of a verbal skills test. Under the Court's vision of discrimination as isolated, arbitrary events, the constitutionality of the facially neutral verbal skills test could be challenged only by asserting a government *intent* to eliminate black police candidates. But the subjugation of blacks and other groups that goes on today is neither isolated nor arbitrary. Indeed, for purely practical reasons no caste system could long endure if it were necessary to visit conscious, personalized discrimination on every member of the victimized group on a daily basis. See Schnapper, "Perpetuation of Past Discrimination," 96 *Harv. L. Rev.* 828, 834 (1983). A requirement of

equality that is satisfied by a supposedly evenhanded reflection of "nature" defends the verbal skills test of Washington v. Davis as simply having sorted out the literate from the less so—it just so happening that more blacks fell into the latter category. Yet, by incorporating the "natural" into a model of equality, this vision incorporates the more blatant discriminations of the past which created the status quo. See also *Personnel Administrator v. Feeney*, 442 U.S. 256 (1979). Thus, if the use of a verbal skills test has the *effect* of subjugating blacks, its constitutionality should be in doubt. To avoid denying blacks social and economic opportunity, and to stop perpetuating the aura of white supremacy by maintaining a predominantly white police force in a predominantly black city, the system must consider changing how it operates and what it looks for. See also the discussion of Firefighters Local Union No. 1784 v. Stotts, 104 S. Ct. 2576 (1984), in chapter 14 at notes 105-09 and accompanying text.

29. 448 U.S. 297 (1980).

30. *Roe v. Wade*, 410 U.S. 113 (1973).

31. Justice Stevens' dissent asserted that the government, "[h]aving decided to alleviate some of the hardships of poverty by providing necessary medical care . . . must use neutral criteria in distributing benefits." 448 U.S. at 356 (Stevens, J., dissenting). This argument, however, appears to beg the question of how the government may define the *context* in which it has decided to provide financial assistance. If the government may describe its decision as one to provide necessary medical care that does not terminate potential human life, then a ban on abortion funding would seem to survive Justice Stevens' "neutral criteria" requirement.

32. There is no assurance, however, that such an altered perspective would result from passage of a constitutional amendment mandating that "equality of rights under the law shall not be abridged" by government "on account of sex." To a mind that perceives no sex-based denial of equal treatment under law in exclusions of women from prison jobs, see *Dothard*, or of pregnancy from state disability programs, see *Geduldig*, it would presumably take more than an Equal Rights Amendment to make abortion restrictions appear as forms of gender discrimination.

33. See, e.g., J. Thompson, "A Defense of Abortion," 47 *Philosophy and Public Affairs* 1 (Fall 1971); D. Regan, "Rewriting Roe v. Wade," 77 *Michigan Law Review* 1569 (1979).

34. For a different perspective, see Griffin v. Illinois, 351 U.S. 12, 23 (1956) (Frankfurter, J., concurring in the judgment) ("To sanction such a ruthless consequence would justify a latter-day Anatole France to add one more item to his ironic comments on the 'majestic equality' of the law . . . '[which] forbids the rich as well as the poor to sleep under bridges, [and] to beg in the streets[.]' ") (citation omitted). Contrast the dismissive treatment by the Court, in Selective Service System v. Minnesota Public Interest Research Group, 52 U.S.L.W. 5140, 5145 n.17 (1984), of the claim that denying federally subsidized loans to students who fail to register for the draft violates equal protection because it discriminates against less wealthy nonregistrants: "That argument is meritless. Section 1113 treats all nonregistrants alike, denying aid to both the poor and

the wealthy." In dissent, Justice Marshall attacked the "superficial, indeed cavalier" attitude of the Court as demonstrative of its " 'callous indifference to the realities of life for the poor,' " pointing out that federal student loans go overwhelmingly to students with limited financial resources. "The wealthy do not require, are not applying for, and do not receive federal financial assistance." Id. at 5150 (dissenting opinion). Whatever one's position might be on the merits of the substantive holding, little could be more revealing of the Court's current attitude toward the burdens imposed by the unequal distribution of wealth than this footnote in the Chief Justice's opinion.

35. Jenness v. Fortson, 403 U.S. 431, 442 (1971) (emphasis added).

36. These concerns with respect to sex discrimination also figure in some of the most interesting work in the newly emerging feminist jurisprudence. See, e.g., MacKinnon, "Feminism, Marxism, Method, and the State: Toward Feminist Jurisprudence," 8 *Signs: Journal of Women in Culture and Society* 1 (Summer 1983); MacKinnon, supra note 5; Freedman, "Sex Equality, Sex Differences, and the Supreme Court," 92 *Yale L.J.* 913 (1983); Olson, "The Family and the Market: A Study of Ideology and Legal Reform," 96 *Harv. L. Rev.* 1497 (1983). Cf. Law, "Rethinking Sex and the Constitution," 132 *U. Pa. L. Rev.* 955 (1984); Segal, supra note 5. I began developing some of these themes in "The Supreme Court in the Mirror of Justice," 4 *Justice Department Watch* 1 (Spring 1981).

16. Refocusing the "State Action" Inquiry

1. That amendment's prohibition of slavery applies to both private and governmental action. See Civil Rights Cases, 109 U.S. 3, 20 (1883). Congress also has broad power under the amendment to regulate private conduct, see Jones v. Alfred Mayer Co., 392 U.S. 409 (1968), discussed in L. Tribe, *American Constitutional Law* §5–13 (1978) [hereinafter cited as Tribe, *ACL*], although the Court has thus far hesitated to define "slavery" broadly. See Memphis v. Greene, 451 U.S. 100 (1981); Palmer v. Thompson, 403 U.S. 217, 226–27 (1971).

2. 109 U.S. 3, 9–10 (1883). Recent historical studies suggest that post bellum thinking about state action may have been far more complex and unsettled than is often assumed. See, e.g., Note, "Federalism and Federal Questions: Protecting Civil Rights Under the Regime of *Swift v. Tyson*," 70 *U. Va. L. Rev.* 267 (1984).

3. Jackson v. Metropolitan Edison Co., 419 U.S. 345, 349 (1974). The civil, 42 U.S.C. § 1983, and criminal, 18 U.S.C. §242, civil rights statutes enacted under §5 of the Fourteenth Amendment apply only to action taken "under color of law." Although the Court long treated the "state action" and "color of law" requirements as identical, United States v. Price, 383 U.S. 787, 794 n.7 (1966); Monroe v. Pape, 365 U.S. 167, 185 (1961), it has on occasion stated that they "denote two separate areas of inquiry." Flagg Bros. v. Brooks, 436 U.S. 149, 155–56 (1978). The official line now seems to be that all Fourteenth Amendment state action is also action under color of law, but that all conduct under color of law is not *necessarily* state action, since §1983 is applicable to other constitutional and statutory provisions which have no state action requirement. Lugar v. Edmondson Oil Co., 457 U.S. 922, 935 n. 18 (1982).

4. The best description remains G. Myrdal, *An American Dilemma* (1944).

5. Cover, "The Origins of Judicial Activism in the Protection of Minorities," 91 *Yale L.J.* 1287, 1303 (1982).

6. Bowers v. DeVito, 686 F.2d 616, 618 (1982) (Posner, J.).

7. Id.

8. See L. Tribe, *ACL* §§18–1 to 18–7; Brest, "State Action and Liberal Theory: A Casenote on *Flagg Brothers v. Brooks*," 130 *U. Pa. L. Rev.* 1296 (1982); Nerkin, "A New Deal for the Protection of 14th Amendment Rights: Challenging the Doctrinal Bases of the Civil Rights Cases and State Action Theory," 12 *Harv. C.R.–C.L. L. Rev.* 297 (1977); Alexander, "Cutting the Gordian Knot: State Action and Self-Help Repossession," 2 *Hastings Const. L.Q.* 893 (1975); Black, " 'State Action,' Equal Protection, and California's Proposition 14," 81 *Harv. L. Rev.* 69 (1967); Van Alstyne, "Mr. Justice Black, Constitutional Review, and the Talisman of State Action," 1965 *Duke L.J.* 219; Horowitz, "The Misleading Search for 'State Action' Under the 14th Amendment," 30 *S. Cal. L. Rev.* 208 (1957). For two recent efforts to explicate this doctrinal realm, see Choper, "Thoughts on State Action: The 'Government Function' and 'Power Theory' Approaches," 1979 *Wash. U. L.Q.* 757 (1979); Rowe, "The Emerging Threshold Approach to State Action Determinations: Trying to Make Sense of *Flagg Brothers, Inc. v. Brooks*," 69 *Geo. L. Rev.* 745 (1981).

9. Burton v. Wilmington Parking Authority, 365 U.S. 715, 722 (1961) (opinion of Clark, J.) (citation omitted).

10. Jacobellis v. Ohio, 378 U.S. 184, 197 (1964) (Stewart, J., concurring).

11. Brest, supra note 8, at 1325.

12. 227 U.S. 278 (1913).

13. Id. at 287.

14. Id. at 286.

15. 325 U.S. 91 (1945).

16. 18 U.S.C. §242.

17. 325 U.S. at 111 (opinion of Douglas, J.). The policemen had in effect executed the decedent without according him his due process right to be tried by a jury and sentenced by a court. 325 U.S. at 117 (opinion of Rutledge, J.).

18. 454 U.S. 312 (1982).

19. Id. at 320.

20. Id. at 319. See also Ferri v. Ackerman, 444 U.S. 193, 204 (1979) (although court-appointed counsel serves pursuant to state authorization and in furtherance of constitutional requirement of Sixth Amendment, his duty is not to the public at large but to his client).

21. United States v. Classic, 313 U.S. 299, 326 (1941), quoted with approval in *Polk County*, 454 U.S. at 317–18.

22. Id. at 323 & n.14 (citing ABA Standards for Criminal Justice).

23. Id. at 325, citing Branti v. Finkel, 445 U.S. 507 (1980) (First Amendment protects assistant public defenders from being hired and fired as patronage employees based on party affiliation).

24. 454 U.S. at 325 & n.19; United States v. Senak, 477 F.2d 304 (7th Cir.), *cert. denied*, 414 U.S. 856 (1973).

25. 454 U.S. at 325; cf. Imbler v. Pachtman, 424 U.S. 409, 430–31 & n.33 (1976) (discussing immunity of prosecutors from §1983 suits for damages).

26. 457 U.S. 922, 941–43 (1982).

27. Id. at 924–25; id. at 944 (Powell, J., dissenting).

28. The private actor also may be liable under §1983 for acting in concert with state officers even when no state law, constitutional or not, is involved. 457 U.S. at 931–32 & n.15, discussing Adickes v. S. H. Kress & Co., 398 U.S. 144, 149–50 (1970).

29. 365 U.S. 715 (1961).

30. Id. at 724–26. The case is discussed more fully in Tribe, *ACL* §18–3 at 1159–60.

31. 452 U.S. 1 (1981). The Court never cited *Burton*, but had no difficulty in finding state action while treating *Streater* as a case of equal access to the courts.

32. Id. at 9.

33. Id.

34. 457 U.S. 991 (1982).

35. 457 U.S. 830 (1982).

36. *Yaretsky*, 457 U.S. at 1011; *Rendell-Baker*, 457 U.S. at 840.

37. *Yaretsky*, 457 U.S. at 1004; *Rendell-Baker*, 457 U.S. at 841.

38. See Friendly, "The Public-Private Distinction—Fourteen Years Later," 130 *U. Pa. L. Rev.* 1289, 1291 (1982). But see Moose Lodge v. Irvis, 407 U.S. 163 (1972).

39. See, e.g., Rendell-Baker v. Kohn, 457 U.S. 830, 840, 841–42 (1982).

40. Justice White concurred in the judgment. Only Justices Brennan and Marshall dissented.

41. 457 U.S. at 1003.

42. Id. at 1008 & n.19. This may be the beginning of a new "medical question" doctrine that even the decision of a doctor on the state payroll may not be state action because of an analogy of the doctor-patient relationship to the attorney-client relationship that was isolated from state involvement in Polk County v. Dodson, 454 U.S. 312, 320–21 (1981), discussed supra. However, Justice Blackmun, the member of the Court with the greatest legal experience in medical matters, took strong exception to the majority's analysis in *Polk County* and its use of certain doctor-patient cases. See id. at 330–31 & no.2 (dissenting opinion).

43. 457 U.S. at 1005. Justice Brennan argued cogently in dissent that the decision to discharge was anything but a "private medical decision," since the doctor merely filled in numerical scores of "medical need" in accord with carefully delineated state criteria on a highly detailed state form. The very notion of different levels of nursing care was a product of state money-saving policies, not

medical practice, which made physicians agents of the state cost-control program. See id. at 1016–27 (Brennan, J., dissenting).

44. Justice White again concurred in the judgment and Justices Marshall and Brennan disssented.

45. 457 U.S. at 823–33 & n.1.

46. Id. at 833, 842–43.

47. Id. at 832.

48. Id. at 840–41.

49. It is quite possible that Rendell-Baker could constitutionally have been fired even if she had been a public employee, since her speech may have concerned office and personnel grievances rather than questions of "public concern." See Connick v. Myers, 103 S. Ct. 1684 (1983), discussed in chapter 13.

50. 457 U.S. at 833, 841; id. at 844 (White, J., concurring).

51. 457 U.S. at 1003.

52. 407 U.S. 163 (1972), discussed in Tribe, ACL §18-7.

53. 407 U.S. at 177; see also Lugar v. Edmondson Oil Co., 457 U.S. 922, 938 (1982) (approving analysis in *Moose Lodge*).

54. 451 U.S. 527 (1981).

55. See Logan v. Zimmerman Brush Co., 455 U.S. 422, 435–36 (1982) (discussing *Parratt*). In *Parratt*, the Court found that the defendants had indeed acted under color of state law, 451 U.S. at 535–36, but that an episodic, negligent loss of property did not amount to a deprivation without due process. Id. at 543. Of course, had the plaintiff in *Parratt* challenged the constitutionality of the prison's entire system of rules and regulations, the Court might well have viewed the question presented as political and hence nonjusticiable. Cf. Gilligan v. Morgan, 413 U.S. 1 (1973) (refusing to review training of Ohio National Guard following the deaths at Kent State), discussed in Tribe, ACL §3-16 at 78–79.

56. See 457 U.S. at 1010–11.

57. See 457 U.S. at 842–43.

58. See Tribe, ACL §18-5, at 1163 & n.3; Brest, "State Action and Liberal Theory: A Casenote on *Flagg Brothers v. Brooks*," 130 U. Pa. L. Rev. 1296, 1329 (1982).

59. See, e.g., Evans v. Newton, 382 U.S. 296 (1966) (private trustees appointed to manage previously public park for whites only); Smith v. Allwright, 321 U.S. 649 (1944) (state delegation of primary selection of political candidates to parties which exclude black voters); Rendell-Baker v. Kohn, 457 U.S. 830, 842 n.7 (1982) (distinguishing instant case from Evans v. Newton); but see Evans v. Abney, 396 U.S. 435 (1970) (Fourteenth Amendment not violated by judicial decision to return park from racially restricted trust to private trustees); In re Girard College Trusteeship, 391 Pa. 434, 138 A.2d 844, *cert. denied*, 357 U.S. 570 (1958) (allowing substitution of private trustees to maintain school for whites in accord with testator's wish), rejected in Pennsylvania v. Brown, 392 F.2d 120 (3d Cir. 1968), cert. denied, 391 U.S. 921 (1968).

60. 457 U.S. 991, 1012 (1982) (Brennan, J., joined by Marshall, J., dissenting).

61. 457 U.S. 991, 1003 (1982).

62. 457 U.S. 830, 841 (1982); id. at 844 (White, J., concurring).

63. See, e.g., Lugar v. Edmondson Oil Co., 457 U.S. 922, 941 (1982) ("the procedural scheme created by the statute [itself] is obviously the product of state action.").

64. See Stevens, J., dissenting in Flagg Bros. v. Brooks, 436 U.S. 149, 169–76 (1978); Brest, supra note 58, at 1302, 1316, 1322; Tribe, ACL §18-7, at 1172–73.

65. 436 U.S. 149 (1978).

66. 407 U.S. 163 (1972).

67. 419 U.S. 345 (1974).

68. See Tribe, ACL §§18-2, 18-5.

69. She could theoretically have refused and sought to replevy her goods at any time, but in order to do so she would have had to present the sheriff with a surety's bond worth twice the value of her goods. It goes without saying that few people evicted from their apartments are in a position to obtain such a bond. In dissent, Justice Marshall chided the Court's fanciful assumption that Ms. Brooks would have been able to obtain a bond as a further demonstration of "an attitude of callous indifference to the realities of life for the poor." 436 U.S. at 166–167.

70. 436 U.S. at 157.

71. 395 U.S. 337 (1969), discussed in Tribe, ACL §16-41.

72. 407 U.S. 67 (1972), discussed in Tribe, ACL §§16-41, 16-51.

73. 395 U.S. at 338–39.

74. 407 U.S. at 70–71. See also No. Georgia Finishing Co. v. Di-Chem, 419 U.S. 601, 607 (1975) (court clerk issued writ of garnishment solely on basis of creditor's affidavit).

75. See 436 U.S. at 174 75 (Stevens, J., joined by White and Marshall, JJ., dissenting).

76. Appellee's Brief at 15.

77. See Tribe, ACL §§18-5, 18-4.

78. Compare Lugar v. Edmonson Oil Co., 457 U.S. 922 (1982), where the mere initiation of a defective state attachment procedure involving similarly trivial clerical involvement by state functionaries was held sufficient to make the *private* party a state actor.

79. See Louisville & Nashville R.R. v. Mottley, 211 U.S. 149 (1908) (no federal jurisdiction of case where only federal issue is a defense based on federal law which might be invoked by defendant).

80. 436 U.S. at 161 n.11.

81. 407 U.S. 163 (1972).

82. It is, of course, possible that the plaintiff would still have lost on the merits, given the difficulty of demonstrating a significant net impact on minority drinking opportunities and, more importantly, given the potential requirement of proving a discriminatory governmental purpose if mere inattention to the adverse

racial consequences of licensing bigots were not sufficient to implicate the government. See Washington v. Davis, 426 U.S. 229 (1976).

83. 419 U.S. 345 (1974).

84. 448 U.S. 297 (1980).

85. See chapter 15.

86. 103 S. Ct. 416 (1982).

87. Id. at 420–21. See also NAACP v. Alabama, 357 U.S. 449 (1958).

88. 103 S. Ct. 505 (1982). I argued on behalf of Grendel's Den in the Supreme Court, having represented it in both federal courts below.

89. The Court voided the law by an 8–1 margin; all 9 justices reached the merits.

90. See *Flagg Bros.* 436 U.S. at 164–65.

91. See Moose Lodge No. 107 v. Irvis, 407 U.S. 163, 177–79 (1972); Lugar v. Edmondson Oil Co., 457 U.S. 922, 938 n.20 (1982) (discussing and approving *Moose Lodge*).

92. Given the lack of an exhaustion requirement in §1983 actions, see Monroe v. Pape, 365 U.S. 167 (1961); Patsy v. Board of Regents, 457 U.S. 496 (1982), it may follow that a plaintiff can successfully go directly into federal court at the trial level if the challenged mandatory state law is *predictably* adverse to the plaintiff's claim.

93. See Jackson v. Metropolitan Edison Co., 419 U.S. 345 (1974).

94. See *Flagg Bros.*, Supra note 90.

95. See *Flagg Bros.*, 436 U.S. at 160 n.10, 164–65. However, in Lugar v. Edmondson Oil Co., 457 U.S. 922 (1982), the victim of the defective prejudgment attachment procedure was the private defendant in a privately initiated state court action for debt. The private defendant then filed a §1983 action against his creditor (the state-court plaintiff) in a federal district court. The state did not compel the creditor to make use of its attachment scheme—in fact, the compulsion went the other way: the court clerk *had* to issue the writ and the sheriff *had* to sequester the disputed property upon the creditor's request. And despite confusion about the actual form of the complaint—confusion which persisted even through oral argument, 457 U.S. at 941—the Court held that a ruling on the merits of the attachment scheme was proper since the law itself—as well as the joint use of it by state officials and private creditors—constituted state action.

96. 365 U.S. 715 (1961).

97. 365 U.S. at 726–27 (Stewart, J., concurring). Although they took exception to his reading of the Delaware Supreme Court's interpretation of the statute, Justices Frankfurter, id. at 727, Harlan and Whittaker, id. at 729–30, all agreed that Justice Stewart's approach to state action was sound.

98. See *Flagg Bros.*, 436 U.S. at 161–62 n.11.

99. 444 U.S. 277 (1980).

100. It seems clear that state courts must entertain §1983 actions in their courts of general jurisdiction. See Testa v. Katt, 330 U.S. 386 (1947).

101. *Martinez* differs from *Flagg Bros.* in that the defendant was a state authority, not a private injurer. In *Burton*, both the state and the private actor were sued. Thus, the approach to litigation suggested here is not a rigid one. A suit against the paroled murderer in *Martinez* would not have called into question the state immunity law and, thus, would have been an unsuitable vehicle to challenge that law.

102. A case that raises a slightly different pattern of litigation is Loretto v. Teleprompter, 458 U.S. 419 (1982). There a landlord sought to challenge the New York law that authorized cable television (CATV) companies to install their equipment on privately owned apartment buildings without the landlord's consent and for only a nominal fee. Plaintiff sued the CATV company in state court, challenging the law and alleging an unconstitutional taking. New York City intervened as a defendant. The state courts upheld the law and the Supreme Court reversed on the merits. Had the plaintiff sued the CATV company in federal court, the way Ms. Brooks sued Flagg Bros., and had New York City not intervened, it is likely that the Supreme Court would have considered the state law merely permissive, not compulsory, and refused to attribute the alleged private act of trespass to New York.

103. 326 U.S. 501 (1946).

104. 376 U.S. 254 (1964), discussed in Tribe, *ACL* §§12–12 to 12–14.

105. 458 U.S. 886 (1982).

106. 334 U.S. 1 (1948).

107. Id. at 20.

108. The definitive critique of *Shelley* remains Wechsler, "Toward Neutral Principles of Constitutional Law," 73 *Harv. L. Rev.* 1, 29–31 (1959).

109. It is possible that this was the reasoning of the *Shelley* Court itself. See 334 U.S. at 20.

110. See, e.g., Kennedy, "The Stages of Decline of the Public/Private Distinction," 130 *U. Pa. L. Rev.* 1349, 1352 (1982) ("If state enforcement of the property and contract groundrules of the market was 'state action' for fourteenth amendment purposes, then the fourteenth amendment required the states to outlaw any 'private' actor who practiced racial discrimination.") The only other equally expansive misreading of *Shelley* I have seen is Justice Rehnquist's language for the Court in Moose Lodge v. Irvis, 407 U.S. 163, 179 (1972): "Shelley v. Kraemer makes it clear that the application of state sanctions to enforce [a discriminatory private rule] would violate the Fourteenth Amendment." (citation omitted).

111. 426 U.S. 229 (1976), discussed in chapter 15.

112. However, official statements of a policy of aggressive enforcement of the trespass laws in order to resegregate "white" lunch counters would provide sufficient evidence of a racially discriminatory purpose. See Lombard v. Louisiana, 373 U.S. 267 (1963).

113. See, e.g., Restatement of Property §406 (1944).

114. 393 U.S. 385 (1969), discussed in *ACL* §16–16 at 1024.

115. Washington v. Seattle School Dist. No. 1, 458 U.S. 457, 462–63 (1982).

116. Id. at 459.

117. 458 U.S. 457 (1982).

118. The vote was 5–4. Justice Powell dissented in an opinion joined by Chief Justice Burger and Justices Rehnquist and O'Connor.

119. 458 U.S. at 470.

120. Id. at 471.

121. Id. at 474.

122. The Court noted that Washington State could have reserved to state officials control over *all* pupil assignments, but once it chose to decentralize school authority it had to do so without reserving race-linked measures alone for centralized decision. Id. at 487.

123. 458 U.S. 527 (1982).

124. Id. at 532.

125. Justice Marshall was the sole dissenter. I argued the case in the Supreme Court on behalf of the losing petitioners.

126. 444 U.S. 437 (1980).

127. 458 U.S. at 540.

128. Id. at 540–41.

129. He was joined by Justice Brennan.

130. 458 U.S. at 546 (emphasis added).

131. But see J. Choper, Y. Kamisar & L. Tribe, *Supreme Court: Trends & Developments* 45–46 (1983). As Dean Choper put it, "if Justice Blackmun thinks California courts do not create constitutional rights, he ought to come to California more often." Id. at 44.

132. FERC v. Mississippi, 456 U.S. 742, 762–63 n.27 (1982), discussed in chapter 9.

133. 458 U.S. at 546 (Blackmun, J., concurring); see id. (opinion of the Court).

134. Id. at 557 (Marshall, J., dissenting).

135. Id. at 535, 541–42.

136. Nor was this duty removed from the local school boards. Id.

137. Id. at 555–56 (Marshall, J., dissenting).

138. See PruneYard Shopping Center v. Robbins, 447 U.S. 74 (1980).

139. See Serrano v. Priest, 18 Cal. 3d 728, 557 P.2d 929 (1976), *cert. denied sub. nom.* Clowes v. Serrano, 432 U.S. 907 (1977).

140. 334 U.S. 1 (1948).

141. 426 U.S. 229 (1976).

142. See, e.g., Bell v. Maryland, 378 U.S. 226 (1964) (Fourteenth Amendment requires state to have system of laws, including trespass, which do not deny blacks status as "equal members of the community"); Reitman v. Mulkey, 387 U.S. 369 (1967) (effectively putting a private right to discriminate on the basis of race in the state constitution is state action in violation of Fourteenth Amendment); Burton v. Wilmington Parking Authority, 365 U.S. 715 (1961) (state law

authorizing racial discrimination by restaurant on public property is state action); Lombard v. Louisiana, 373 U.S. 267 (1963) (state use of trespass laws with intent to maintain apartheid in restaurants is state action); Muir v. Louisville Park Theatrical Ass'n, 347 U.S. 971 (1954) (renting public amphitheater to racist theater group is unconstitutional state action even absent showing of intent); Norwood v. Harrison, 413 U.S. 455 (1973) (state may not lend school books to racist private schools—state must "steer clear of giving aid"); Marsh v. Alabama, 326 U.S. 501 (1946) (enforcing state property laws which allow private landowner of "company town" to restrict First Amendment rights of outsiders seeking entry constitutes forbidden state action).

143. See, e.g., Cohen, "Property and Sovereignty," 13 *Cornell L.Q.* 8 (1927); Hale, "Coercion and Distribution in a Supposedly Non-Coercive State," 38 *Pol. Sci. Q.* 470 (1923); Hale, "Force and the State: A Comparison of 'Political' and 'Economic' Compulsion," 35 *Colum. L. Rev.* 149 (1935).

144. New York Times v. Sullivan, 376 U.S. 254 (1964). See, e.g., Gertz v. Robert Welch, Inc., 418 U.S. 323 (1974).

145. 326 U.S. 501 (1946).

146. 419 U.S. 345 (1974).

147. 436 U.S. 149 (1978).

148. 365 U.S. 715 (1961).

149. See chapter 15.

150. PruneYard Shopping Center v. Robbins, 447 U.S. 74 (1980).

151. Martinez v. California, 444 U.S. 277 (1980).

152. Larkin v. Grendel's Den, 103 S. Ct. 505 (1982).

153. Marbury v. Madison, 5 U.S. (1 Cranch) 137, 163 (1803) (Marshall, C. J.).

INDEX OF CASES

Aaron; Cooper v., 357n249
Abington School Dist. v. Schempp, 61
Abney; Evans v., 424n59
Abood v. Detroit Bd. of Educ.,
  400n120
Abrams v. United States, 406n187
Ackerman; Ferri v., 422n20
Adderley v. Florida, 398n96
Adickes v. S.H. Kress & Co., 423n28
Adler v. Bd. of Educ., 401n130
Aetna Life Ins. Co. v. Haworth,
  302n32
Agee; Haig v., 398n84
Agins v. City of Tiburon, 168
Agosto v. INS, 325n91
Aiello; Geduldig v., 239, 418n10,
  420n32
Akron v. Akron Center for
  Reproductive Health, 350n194,
  354n233, 355n240
Alabama; Marsh v., 258, 264, 429n142
Alabama; NAACP v., 393n25, 426n87
Alabama; Thornhill v., 191, 393n18
Alabama ex rel. Patterson; NAACP v.,
  304n60
Alexandria Scrap Corp.; Hughes v.,
  144
Alfred H. Mayer Co.; Jones v., 416n84,
  421n1
Allard; Andrus v., 385n16
Allen v. Wright, 329n14, 331n44,
  333n58, 334n86, 337n105, 344n153,
  347n170
Allen; Mueller v., 360n255
Allied International; International
  Longshoremen's Asso. v., 201,
  393n37, 398nn98,100, 400n112,
  410n255, 411n270
Allied Stores of Ohio, Inc. v. Bowers,
  345n149
Allied Structural Steel Co. v.
  Spannaus, 181, 183, 275n8, 390n134
Allstate Ins. Co.; EEOC v., 317n103

Allwright; Smith v., 424n59
Amalgamated Food Employees Union
  v. Logan Valley Plaza, 397n81
American Insurance Co. v. Canter, 85,
  321n23, 323n65
American Petroleum Inst.; Industrial
  Union Dept., AFL-CIO v.,
  315n87
American School of Magnetic Healing
  v. McAnnulty, 392n15
Americans United for Separation of
  Church and State v. HEW, 333n56,
  360n260
Americans United for Separation of
  Church and State; Valley Forge
  Christian College v., 103, 110, 112,
  119, 328n14, 332n54,
  333nn60,61,65, 340nn126,129,
  353n229, 360n255, 375n3
American Textile Mfrs. Inst. v.
  Donovan, 315n87
American Trust Co. v. South Carolina
  Bd. of Bank Control, 374n47
Anchor Motor Freight, Inc.; Hines v.,
  277n25
Anderson; Untermyer v., 152, 377n26,
  380n47
Andrus v. Allard, 385n16
Arizona; Miranda v., 271n1, 277n26
Arizona; Southern Pacific Co. v.,
  374n49
Arkansas; Epperson v., 307n94
Arnett v. Kennedy, 278n31, 318n114,
  386n38
Ash; Cort v., 377n102, 345n145
Ashcroft v. Mattis, 349n190
Ashcroft; Planned Parenthood Asso. of
  Kansas City Missouri, Inc. v.,
  350n194, 354n233
Atkins v. United States, 311n34
Atlas Roofing Co. v. Occupational
  Safety Commission, 95, 98, 323n70,
  326nn104,105

431

Brown; Parker v., 132, 309n7
Brown; Pennsylvania v., 424n59
Brown; United States v., 273n7
Bruch Church, Inc.; Pike v., 303n50
Brushaber v. Union Pacific R.R. Co.,
384n12
Bryant v. Yellen, 345n161
Bryant; California Brewers Asso. v.,
416n89
BT Investment Managers, Inc.; Lewis
v., 314n73, 372n28
Buckley v. Valeo, 66, 67, 73, 282n76,
304n57, 306n73, 308n4, 309n12,
312n43, 314nn66,68,76, 318n1,
325n89, 381n53, 395n60, 396n68,
397n76, 404n171, 412n271
Bucks Stove & Range Co.; Gompers
v., 198, 392n12, 399nn100,102
Bull; Calder v., 383n2
Burbank v. Lockheed Air Terminal,
Inc., 368n109
Burns; Elrod v., 401n136, 406n186
Burton v. Wilmington Parking
Authority, 250, 257, 265, 422n9,
428n142
Bush v. Lucas, 394n38
Butler; United States v., 386n28
Button; NAACP v., 282n77
Bynum; Martinez v., 341n138

Caceres; United States v., 278n30
Cafeteria & Restaurant Workers Local
473 v. McElroy, 279n33
Calder v. Bull, 383n2
Califano v. Webster, 345n149, 412n6
Califano; North Carolina v., 365n74
California v. Taylor, 363n24
California; Edwards v., 308n98,
331n37
California; Hurtado v., 275n11
California; Martinez v., 258, 266,
356n244, 429n151
California; McGautha v., 415n62
California; Stromberg v., 392n17,
396n61
California; United States v., 363n24
California; Whitney v., 275n10
California Brewers Asso. v. Bryant,
416n89
California Medical Asso. v. Federal
Election Comm'n, 348n176

California Retail Liquor Dealers Asso.
v. Midcal Aluminum Inc., 368n104
Calvert Distillers Corp.; Schwegmann
Bros. v., 30
Camden; United Building and
Construction Trades Coun. v.,
372n36, 373n45
Cammarano v. United States,
406n188, 407n191
Canter; American Insurance Co. v.,
85, 321n23, 323n65
Cantwell v. Connecticut, 392n17
Carey v. Piphus, 226, 278n31
Carey; United Jewish Organizations v.,
412n6
Carolene Prods. Co.; United States v.,
274n1, 280n47, 357n249, 374n49
Carolina Environmental Study Group,
Inc. v. United States, 334n76
Carolina Environmental Study Group,
Inc.; Duke Power Co. v., 106, 111,
112 et seq., 119, 172, 329n15,
330n33, 342n142, 347nn173,174,
361n263
Carr; Baker v., 289n46, 290n47,
302n33, 361n264, 394n41
Carter v. Carter Coal Co., 318n117
Carter; Goldwater v., 23, 283n8,
380n51
Carter & Weekes Stevedoring Co.;
Joseph v., 293n46
Carter Coal Co.; Carter v., 318n117
Causby; United States v., 386n40
Central Hanover Bank & Trust Co.;
Mullane v., 414n47
Central Hudson Gas & Electric v.
Public Service Commission, 211,
213, 409n245
Chadha; INS v., 66, 67, 158, 286n26,
296n80, 308n5, 310nn29,30, 312n52,
316n95, 317n98, 318nn117,2,
381nn52,57
Chambers; Marsh v., 110, 272n2,
340n127
Champlin Ref. Co. v. Corporation
Commission, 317n107
Chaplinsky v. New Hampshire,
399n100, 406n187
Charlotte-Mecklenburg Board of
Education; Swann v., 353n230
Chenery Corp.; Securities & Exchange
Comm'n v., 359n254

Metropolitan Edison Co.; Jackson v.,
253, 255, 264, 421n3, 426n93
Metropolitan Housing Development
Corp.; Village of Arlington Heights
v., 344nn151,154
Meyer v. Nebraska, 286n28
Miami Herald Publishing Co. v.
Tornillo, 397n82
Michael M. v. Superior Court, 239
Midcal Aluminum Inc.; California
Retail Liquor Dealers Asso. v.,
368n104
Midkiff; Hawaii Housing Auth. v.,
383n3, 417n108
Miller v. Roberts, 382n66
Miller v. Schoene, 304n60
Miller; Coleman v., 22, 345n145
Milligan, Ex parte, 302n28
Minard; Stefanelli v., 332n53
Minneapolis Star & Tribune Co. v.
Minnesota Comr. of Revenue,
298n104, 395n51, 396n61, 405n176
Minnesota v. Clover Leaf Creamery
Co., 345n149
Minnesota; Near v., 392n17, 397n83
Minnesota Comr. of Revenue;
Minneapolis Star and Tribune Co.
v., 298n104, 395n51, 396n61,
405n176
Minnesota Public Interest Research
Group; Selective Service System v.,
420n34
Minnesota State Bd. for Community
Colleges v. Knight, 394n38, 403n154
Miranda v. Arizona, 271n1, 277n26
Mississippi; Davis v., 352n218
Mississippi; FERC v., 122, 125, 137,
309n6, 428n132
Missouri; Massachusetts v., 302n31
Mitchell v. W. T. Grant Co., 414n44
Mitchell; Rose v., 347n170
Monell v. New York City Dept. of
Social Services, 356n244
Monroe v. Pape, 305n62, 345n145,
426n92
Monsanto Co.; Ruckelshaus v., 383n3
Moore v. City of East Cleveland,
282n77
Moore; Knowlton v., 385n12
Moose Lodge No. 107 v. Irvis, 252,
426n91, 427n110

Morey v. Doud, 374n47
Morgan; Gilligan v., 102, 351n197,
353n223, 424n55
Morrissey v. Brewer, 414nn46,47
Morton; Sierra Club v., 348n180
Mosley; City of Chicago v., 193
Motor Vehicle Mfrs. Asso. v. State
Farm Mut. Auto Ins. Co., 313n64
Mottley; Louisville & Nashville R.R.
v., 425n79
Mow Sun Wong; Hampton v., 228,
231, 415n68
Mueller v. Allen, 360n255
Muir v. Louisville Park Theatrical
Asso., 429n142
Mulkey; Reitman v., 304n60
Mullane v. Central Hanover Bank &
Trust Co., 414n47
Mullaney v. Wilbur, 346n164
Murdock v. Memphis, 31
Murdock v. Pennsylvania, 411n260
Murgia; Massachusetts Bd. of
Retirement v., 280n53, 351n207
Murray's Lessee v. Hoboken Land &
Improvement Co., 86, 321n24,
323n70
Muskrat v. United States, 302n30
Mutual Film Corp. v. Industrial
Commission of Ohio, 392n14
Myers v. United States, 159, 316n94
Myers; Connick v., 207, 209, 358n250,
394n38, 401n125, 402n140, 424n49

NAACP v. Alabama ex rel. Patterson,
304n60, 393n25, 426n87
NAACP v. Button, 282n77
NAACP v. Claiborne Hardware Co.,
200, 259, 393n36, 400n107
NAACP; Louisiana v., 393n26
National League of Cities v. Usery, 66,
67, 121, 122, 127 et seq., 134, 286n25,
362nn4,13, 363nn18,31, 364n46,
365n74, 366n75 et seq., 369n128 et
seq.
National Organization for Women,
Inc. v. Idaho, 285n21
National Socialist Party v. Skokie, 219
Near v. Minnesota, 392n17, 397n83
Nebeker; Twin City Bank v., 382n66
Nebraska; Meyer v., 286n28
Nebraska; Sporhase v., 371n23

GENERAL INDEX

Abortion: norms underlying amendment banning, 25–26; restrictions on federal court jurisdiction regarding, 53, 58–60, 301n22; advertisement of referral service, 211; restrictions on, 243–245; withdrawal of public funding of, 243, 304n59; Hyde Amendment, 255–256; criminal law used in antiabortion regulation, 302n38, 350nn194,195; fetus's status as person, 306n74; issue of when life begins, 308n97; injunctions against antiabortion statutes, 350nn194,195, 353n127

Adjudicative authority: legislative veto resembling, 74–75; delegated to non-Article III courts, 85–90; over public and private rights, 95–96

Adjudicative process, 11–14

Administrative agencies, 325n90; actions by, as constitutional concern, 9; litigation of public rights by, 95, 98; judicial review of decisions by, 96–97, 98; taxpayer standing to challenge, 104, 105

Advertising, commercial, 211, 213–214, 216–218

Affirmative action plans: college admission plan, 221–222; equal protection considerations, 222–223; procedural fairness of, 223–228; and structural justice, 228–232; and Civil Rights Act, 232–234; regulating government contractors, 234–236; class bias in jurisprudence, 236–237

Age discrimination, 280n53; state sovereignty in areas of, 135–136

Age Discrimination in Employment Act, 135–136

Aliens, excluded from federal employment, 228–229, 230

Amendments: judicial intervention in procedure, 22–28; as de facto reversal of Court rulings, 47–48; rescission of ratification vote, 283n10; extension of time limit to ratify, 285n21. See also specific amendments

Antitrust laws, and home-rule provisions, 132–134

Appointments Clause, 72, 74

Arbitrage bonds, 149–157

Article I: Section 10, 10; Art. III courts distinguished, 87–98; Section 8, 104; legislative provisions of, 158

Article III: Exceptions and Regulations Clause, 51; creation of Supreme Court in, 51–52; concept of judicial power in, 52–54; and creation of hybrid tribunals, 85–90

Article IV, Section 3, taxpayer standing to challenge property dispositions under, 104

Article V, standards for amending process, 23–24

Article VI, binding upon Congress, 62

Association, right of, 191, 196; restrictions on union's, 204

Balanced budget amendment, 287n39

Balancing test, 199

Bank Holding Company Act of 1956, Douglas Amendment to, 138–148

Banking, state control of regional, 138–148

Bankruptcy Reform Act of 1978: and Article III courts, 90–93, 94–95; independence of judges under, 319n8, 324n81; unconstitutionality of, 326n98

Benefits, 55–56; as accrued property rights, 391n139

Bicameralism: and legislative veto, 72, 80, 82; legislative action violating, 157

Billboards, regulation of, 216–218

Bill of Attainder, 75

Black, Justice H. L.: on congressional inaction, 33; on limits of executive power, 158–159

Blackmun, Justice H. A.: on state sovereignty, 126–127; on state action, 262

Blacks, 16, 17; political inequality of, 192; boycott used by, 200–201; and affirmative action plans, 221; standing to challenge tax exemption for discriminatory private schools, 334n86, 357n105; and Jim Crow codes, 394n45

Bonds, arbitrage, See Arbitrage bonds

Boycott: of racially discriminatory businesses, 200–201; and state action doctrine, 259

Brandeis, Justice L. D.: on Art. III, 92–93

Brennan, Justice W. J., Jr.: on Art. III courts, 90–93; on property interests, 182; on state action doctrine, 253; on contract obligation impairment, 378n29

Brilmayer, L., 300n15

Burger, Chief Justice W. E.: on commercial speech, 216; on affirmative action programs, 235–236

Busing: state curb on, 260–261; to cure de facto segregation, 261–262; to cure de jure segregation, 302n41

Cable television installation, as constituting a taking, 177–178

Calabresi, G., 295n52

Campaign contributions, 194–195, 196, 197, 395n59

Campaign disclosure law, 256

Carter, J., during Iranian hostage crisis, 173

Case or controversy: as limiting review of delegated authority, 72; injury in fact requirement, 99

Causation of injury, 100, 112–114

Choice, 4, 267–268

Choke holds used by police, 101–102, 116, 117

Church: federal subsidy to, 103, 105; power to veto liquor license, 256–257; registration under state charitable solicitations act, 344n156

Civil Rights Act, 232–234

Civil rights movement, 191

Claims, arising under acts of Congress and the Constitution, 300n15

Class: and property redistribution, 165–166; takings law preserving status quo, 166–169; redefining property to effect economic redistribution, 169–171; Contract Clause as preserving status quo, 179, 183–187; and political equality, 193–198; and speech-conduct distinction, 198–203; and protection of commercial speech, 212–218; allocational efficiency and distributional equity 214–216, 409n236; and affirmative action programs, 236–237; and classifications, 242–244

Classifications, 16, 17, 224–225, 280nn53,54. See also Class; Gender; Race

Colleges, and affirmative action admission plan, 221–222

Color of law, 249–253, and official immunity, 257, 258; state action distinguished, 421n3

Commerce Clause: construction of "dormant" Clause, 34–35, 37–38; in state sovereignty issues, 123–125; preemption powers under, 127; analysis of regional banking, 139, 141, 143–148; authorization for burdens on interstate commerce, 141–143; in emergency situations, 366n84. See also Interstate commerce

Commercial speech, 210–218, 400n115

Company town, and state action doctrine, 258

Compensation of federal judges, 322n62, 324n81

Conduct: substantive vision of proper conduct, 17; channel-clearing theory regarding, 18; speech-conduct distinction, 198–203; as noncommunicative impact, 199

Homicide: police committing, in course of official duties, 249; enforcement against abortions, 302n38
Homosexuals, 16, 17
Hospital care for indigents, 334n86
Hostage Settlement Agreement, 38
Housing, racial discrimination in, 233–234, 260
Hyde Amendment, 255–256

Illegitimate children: right to sue for wrongful death of, 236–239; unmarried fathers as competent to raise, 277n20
Immunity, and action under color of law, 257, 258, 356n244
Incompatibility Clause, and delegated authority, 72–73, 74
Independent judiciary, 84; as lending legitimacy to Congress, 48; delegation of authority to non-Article III courts, 85–90; as essential to decisionmaking, 92; separation of powers as rationale for, 93
Indians, hiring preferences for, 224
Indigents, and free hospital care, 334n86
Individual autonomy, 25
Individuality, and affirmative action plans, 224–228
Individuals, participation by, 12
Injunctions, against antiabortion statutes, 350nn194,195, 353n227
Injury in fact, 99, 108–110
Instruction and persuasion, 18–19
Insurance, gender-based differences in coverage, 418n10
Intermediate scrutiny. See Scrutiny
International Emergency Economic Powers Act, 173, 174, 294n79
Interstate commerce: burdens on, 141–143; and regional banking 143–148; legislative silence on, 293n48
Iran Hostage Case, 38–39, 173–174

Jackson, Justice R. H., 30; on emergency executive powers, 159
Jim Crow codes, 394n45
Joint enterprise theory, 251
Judicial activism, 9, 20–22, 76–78
Judicial relief, 56

Judicial review, 4; legitimacy of, 3, 6–7, 24, 49; of amendments, 25, 27–28; of delegated authority, 72; due process required in, 92–93; of agency determinations, 96–98; of police action, 118–119
Jurisdiction, of federal court, 47–48; congressional control of, 49; external limits on restriction of, 50, 54–62; internal limits on restriction of, 50–54; Congress's duty toward, 62–63; federalism and restructuring of, 63–65
Jury verdict, 359n254
Just Compensation Clause, 10; as constraint on economic redistribution, 166–169; regulation constituting a taking, 167–169, 385n23; spot redistribution as taking, 167, 171; effect of property on, 169–171; nontraditional property claims, 171–174; and physical intrusion, 174–179, 388n83; and inverse condemnation, 385n23

Kairys, D., 392n7

Labor unions. See Unions
Law and legislation, 275n11
Legislation: as constitutional concern, 9; history of, 30; definition of, 69–76; and law, 275n11
Legislative Appropriation Act of 1932, 88–89
Legislative inaction. See Silence
Legislative intent: relevance of, 30–31; construing, 35; of restrictions on speech, 194; of Civil Rights Act, 232–233
Legislative veto, 67–76; alternatives to, 76–78; severability of invalid provision, 79–83; Presidential opposition to, 311n33
Libel, 258, 406n187
Lobbying, 208–209

Madison, J., 11
Mailboxes: ban on placement of mailable matter in, 194–197, 205; access to school, 205–207
Marshall, Justice T., on state sovereignty, 127–128